Signs In Law - A Source Book

Jan M. Broekman • Larry Catá Backer
Editors

Signs In Law - A Source Book

The Semiotics of Law in Legal Education III

Springer

Editors
Jan M. Broekman
Dickinson School of Law
Penn State University
Carlisle, PA, USA

Larry Catá Backer
Departments of Law
and International Affairs
Penn State University
University Park, PA, USA

ISBN 978-3-319-09836-4 ISBN 978-3-319-09837-1 (eBook)
DOI 10.1007/978-3-319-09837-1
Springer Cham Heidelberg New York Dordrecht London

Library of Congress Control Number: 2014955067

Printed on acid-free paper

Springer is part of Springer Science+Business Media (www.springer.com)

To the memory of our friend and colleague
William A. Pencak (1951–2013),
gifted story-teller,
great historian, shrewd semiotician.

Preface

This book should be the gateway to a variety of texts for those who encounter the bewildering expression "semiotics of law". Once we find ourselves in the position to meet those words, they help to be a reader, a listener, a speaker, or provide an orientation in space and time. The *history* of legal semiotics, now at least a century old, has never been written (a non-event itself pregnant with semiotic possibility). As a consequence, its sources are seldom clearly exposed and, as word, object and meaning change, are sometimes lost. This volume informs about major sources leading to legal semiotics as we know it today. The need for the exposure of semiotic sources is particularly acute because there were two names for the unfolding of semiotics in law and legal discourse at least until the second half of the 20th century: *significs* and *semiotics*, both of which covered a lawyer's focus on sign and meaning in law.

"We never come to thoughts. They come to us. That is the proper hour of discourse", Heidegger suggested.[1] The texts of this book form the gateways to that "hour of discourse." Gateways require portals. And thus the construction of this text—not merely a reader, splattered with a mosaic of the writings of others—is meant to be understood as a puzzle whose assemblage is to be teased into some sort of artificial order by the reader to suit her tastes. We have chosen readings with care, and woven them together with a number of *editorials*. They are offered throughout the text, within and apart from the readings. These should be read like the twining of the threads of fate by the Norns,[2] offering "what was", "is coming" and "may be" within the Well of Urd beneath the great ash tree, Yggdrasil, that stands at the center of the universe.[3] But that twining is all undertaken in the subjunctive tense. These editorials themselves produce a semiotic text inherently imbued with subjectivity and possibility, one whose texture may change as each is embedded by the reader

[1] Martin Heidegger, *Poetry, Language, Thought.* (New York: Harper & Row, 1971) (originally *Unterwegs zur Sprache* (1959)).

[2] Chisholm, Hugh, ed. (1911). "Norns". Encyclopædia Britannica (11th ed.). Cambridge University Press.

[3] *The Elder Edda: A Book of Viking Lore.*(2011). translated by Andy Orchard. Penguin Classics.

among the readings that the editorials twine to provide an initial structure to the longitudinal approach of semiotic consciousness that this volume manifests.

The volume at hand reaches from an English translation of the first inaugural lecture on the occasion of the opening of the Chair in Legal Significs at the Amsterdam University in 1916, via studies on "property", "contract" and the like, to equally fascinating studies on contemporary semiotic problems written by former students of the Roberta Kevelson Seminar at Penn State University 2012 and 2013. The Introduction, Part I, sets out the goals of this enterprise—the reading of texts in and of themselves, as symbol and reconstructed through engagement by those who happen to take them up. The embeddedness of text, in itself and within the cultural milieu in which it is invoked, and internal to the individuals who undertake that reading, complicates sign, symbol and interpretant in an ever-evolving change of character with a change of position. A reader of text may herself be text to an interpretant and symbol to yet another. Perspective, context and dynamic shifts characterize the richness of the semiotic engagement. But each perspective has a temporal element. We thus show how Umberto Eco's essay, "On the Style of the Communist Manifesto" provides a template through which the materials that follow might be read better, one in which meaning-making processes are encapsulated in cultural evolvements.

Parts II ("From Legal Significs to Legal Semiotics") and III ("Godfathers of Semiotics—Welby, Pierce, Greimas and Lacan") provide an environment grounded in "that which was." Part II presents an exploration of the dynamic relation of text, symbol and interpretant from the *significs* movement to legal semiotics. The parallel development of semiotics and significs highlights the focus on the instrumental values of the language of law which can be molded and used arbitrarily and pragmatically to meet specific goals. Semiotics focuses on the word as sign and the ways in which these signs contribute to an understanding of reality. We confront here an initial attempt at a science of the self-referencing meaning of legal language and as instrument beyond its literary and political character as rhetoric.

Part III changes furthermore the perspective, focusing on the Godfathers of semiotics—Welby (meaning), Pierce (firstness), Greimas (legal discourse) and Lacan (the semiotics of the personal in text). This section turns attention to the semiotics of the structures of semiotics itself. It starts with the discussions between Welby and Pierce over the meanings of significs and of semiotics. These discussions and the consideration of the character of Firstness, Secondness and Thirdness (as proposed by Charles Sanders Peirce) then acquire a dynamic character in the hands of Greimas, who unifies legal semiotics with economic, institutional and other social discourses. He added a layered structure to semiotic analysis, which is dynamic and no longer fundamentally static as in earlier work. We return to the embedded self in semiotics with Lacan. We consider here the embedding of meaning in language, and the making of that meaning within communities of interpretants.

Part IV introduces the semiotics of law today, that which is becoming. These are organized in the manner of the ancient organization of what is now understood as civil law. The semiotically rich foundation is provided in the introductory materials of Justinian's Institutes. The Institutes provide an example of the institutionalization of a semiotically arranged legal universe. Read with the sensibilities of the semioticians or the student of significs, the Institutes read like a "how to" of instrumental semiosis. The rest follows the ancient ordering (itself a semiotic device) of law: persons, things, and obligations, in both public and private law. Each of the categories, persons, things and obligations, suggest their own semiotics. Here we draw on Roberta Kevelson's insight of the means through which traditional logic is converted into semiotic logic, and the rhetoric of property in law into the methodology of legal semiotics. We confront language here as much as an instrument whose range of motion is to a great degree woven into the social norm and cultural structures of the communities of interpretant that seek to use it to change social norm and culture. But we understand this as a layered and complex conversation in which there is neither singularity nor stasis in law or law system. The language of law, and its semiosis, assumes a distinct dimension where multiple languages of law speak simultaneously to an object of law. Law's "is" becomes comprehensible only in the plural!

Part V turns to that which "may become." Here the focus is on developing semiotic awareness, from the evolution of semiotics to its embedment within the rising generation of scholars now making this evolution their own. It ends with a strong nod to the future—for nothing is more semiotically driven than the deconstruction of the edifices within which semiotics may be encased, ossified, within a theory that both confines and entombs it in space and time. This end thus is meant to serve as a beginning of sort, and an example of the product of a rigorous semiotic approach. It must always break the constraints of its own structures in the dynamic interaction between the sign, the symbol and the interpretant—as individual and community in fluid interaction in three-dimensional social space. We point to the future for semiotics: the embrace of the totality within which details are subsumed and acquire meaning, the avoidance of fragmentation and enclosure of the particular within their own artificially self-contained worlds of meaning. One encounters the understanding, that all meaning is transitory and merely an opening to something else. It is only in this way that contemporary semioticians will know which questions to ask, how to frame them, and whether, in the end, it is still worth to do so whilst crossing their Halys.

The materials in this book weave together the fabric of semiosis and significs. It does so quite embedded within the cultural imperatives of the civilization that gave these terms meaning and made them an effective tool for the dissection of law, and its reconstitution as an instrument to be used by the lawyer to advance the interests of her clients, and for judges, as a means of restructuring language as a narrative of law whose power could bend behavior to its strictures. Lawyers make meaning, indeed, but they do so like Croesus making meaning of the oracle at Delphi, and recognizing that meaning may re-make the maker. Judges, legislators and administrative regulators make meaning like the oracle, with the innocent conceit of the gods, but like them, unable to escape the destiny they render through the narratives of their lawmaking and decisions. And both realize their meaning making only through the participation of the community through which this meaning making is put in operation.

Beyond that, the object of this book is to provide a longitudinal framework within which one can better approach the development of our consciousness of the problem of meaning and its uncovering. Semiotics did not arise from the mind of a single individual as an act of will already formed and fully developed. There is a semiotic element to semiotics as well, it is to the business of bio-semiotics that this journey from the 19th century origins to the present best suggests. For lawyers the ultimate comfort of semiotics is the premise of a momentary and specific certainty of meaning. For lawyers, that alone is enough of a reason for undertaking its study. For they operate in a self referential world in which meaning itself is the only source of meaning, piled higher and deeper, and sorted to suit the fancy of the state apparatus that tends to it, for the constitution of its own self-reference. Where this is a simple and singular act, the art of semiotics of the last century, is useful. But in a world of singular objects that serve as multiple signs with even more interpretive possibilities, the complications that follow will ensure that the work of the lawyer, to extract a momentary and instrumental use of meaning for an temporal and temporary end, will move meaning and its construction, that is, will move semiosis beyond its 19th and 20th century structures.

A book of this sort would not be possible without the contribution of many people, whose contributions to this book, both substantive and administrative, have been invaluable. We thank our students who, during that short period (2008–13) when the study of semiotics flourished at Pennsylvania State University, participated in the Legal Semiotics seminar and the related annual Round Tables dedicated to Roberta Kevelson. The richness of their contributions and their work for the Round tables cannot be underestimated. More specifically, we would like to thank our administrative assistant, Maggie White; this book would not have emerged from its cocoon without her very considerable efforts. Great thanks as well to Tomonori Teraoka, M.I.A. (School of International Affairs 2013), Pennsylvania State University, who played an instrumental role in moving this project from idea to completed work. We thank, as well, all of the contributors to this book, living and dead, who have played an instrumental role in the genesis of legal semiotics and have contributed to its future development in critical ways. Finally we thank our editors at Springer, and especially Diana Nijenhuijzen and Neil Olivier, whose supports have truly made this volume possible.

Carlisle, PA, USA — Jan M. Broekman
University Park, PA, USA — Larry Catá Backer

Acknowledged Sources

Texts from the following works have been used with permission, which is here gratefully acknowledged.

BENSON, R.W.: "The Semiotics of International Law: Interpretation of the ABM Treaty" in: **International Journal for the Semiotics of Law, 1989** p. 257 – 276. Reprinted with permission.

BRION, Denis J.: "The Ethics of Property: A semiotic Inquiry Into Ownership" in: **International Journal for the Semiotics of Law, 1999**, p. 247–283. Reprinted with permission.

CATÁ BACKER, Larry: "The Autonomous Global Corporation: On the Role of Organizational Law Beyond Asset Partitioning and Legal Personality" in: **Tulsa Law Review Vol. 41(4),** p. 541–571. Selected paragraphs reprinted with permission.

GORLéE, Dinda L.: "Quid pro quo: Contractual Semiosis and Translation" in: **Semiotics and the Problem of Translation,** Rodopi**, Amsterdam 1994**, p. 197 – 225. Reprinted with permission.

CURRAN, Vivian Grosswald, "Cultural Immersion, Difference and Categories in US Comparative Law" in**: The American Journal of Comparative Law**, **Vol. 46, 1998,** p. 341 – 349. Reprinted with permission.

KEVELSON, Roberta: "Property: The Legal 'Thing' as Artwork" in: **Law and Semiotics, Vol. III. Springer 1990**. p. 193–209. Reprinted with permission.

MALLOY, Robin P.: "Place, Space, and Time in the Sign of Property", in: **International Journal for the Semiotics of Law**, **2009.** p. 265–277. Reprinted with permission.

PEIRCE, Charles Sanders: "*Firstness, Shock, Law, and The Hand of the Sheriff*' **Collected Papers**, **Vol. 1**, p. 335/336, 4; **Vol. 5**, 42; **Vol. 2**, p. 84/85; **Vol. 5**, p. 48–51, 57/58. No Permission Sought – Free Internet Access.

PEIRCE, Charles Sanders: "*Two Letters to Lady V. Welby*"**:** ***Oct. 12,*** *1904* **and *Dec. 24/25 & 28,*** *1908.* **Collected Papers Vol. 8, Ch. 8,** p. 327–279. No Permission Sought – Free Internet Access.

RADIN, Max: "Fundamental Concepts of Roman Law", © 1925 by the California Law Review, Inc.; in: **California Law Review 13 (207),** 1925. Permission of the California Law Review.

SUMMERFIELD, Tracey & McHOUL, Alec: "Family as a commonsensical device and its place in law" in: **International Journal for the Semiotics of Law, 2005,** p. 243 – 261. Reprinted with permission.

WELBY, Lady Victoria: *"What is Significs?"* in: **Encyclopedia Britannica Vol. XXV, 1911.** p. 78–81. Reprinted with permission.

Contents

Contributors

Larry Catá Backer Departments of Law and International Affairs, Penn State University, University Park, PA, USA

Robert W. Benson Loyola Law School, Los Angeles, CA, USA

Denis J Brion Washington and Lee University School of Law, Lexington, VA, USA

Jan M. Broekman Dickinson School of Law, Penn State University, Carlisle, PA, USA

Vivian Grosswald Curran School of Law, University of Pittsburgh, Pittsburgh, PA, USA

Jacob Israël de Haan

Dinda L. Gorlée The Hague, BC, The Netherlands

Alan C. Green CGA Law Firm, York, PA, USA

Roberta Kevelson

Robin Paul Malloy College of Law, Syracuse University, Syracuse, NY, USA

Gerrit Mannoury

Robert Marriott Department of Communications Arts and Sciences, College of the Liberal Arts, Pennsylvania State University, University Park, PA, USA

Alec McHoul Murdoch University, Murdoch, Australia

Ch. S. Peirce

Max Radin

Tracy Summerfield The University of Western Australia, Crawley, Perth, Australia

Frederik van Eeden

Charles Volkert Cumberland County District Attorney Office, Carlisle, PA, USA

Lady Victoria Welby

Part I
Introduction: Reading Semiotics

Reading Semiotics

Jan M. Broekman and Larry Catá Backer

"Croesus will destroy a great empire if he crosses the Halys."[1]

Thus the Oracle at Delphi advised the mighty Croesus, ruler of Lydia, a great empire extending to the Halys River, which separated Lydia from the empire of the Medes and Persians.[2] The oracle was right. Seeking no further advice but relying on the sense of his own greatness and destiny, Croesus took this truth, and his army, across the Halys. There he was eventually defeated. Cyrus captured him along with his capital Sardis, and the great empire over which he ruled destroyed.

But the story does not end there. Convinced that his defeat was facilitated by the bad advice of the gods through their oracle, he was given permission by Cyrus to send a delegation to Delphi to berate the gods for their ingratitude—having taken his offerings and paid it back with counterfeit advice. But the oracle thought otherwise. She gave a double explanation: First, the Priestess declared, that "not God himself could escape destiny."[3] And, "[a]s to the oracle, Croesus had no right to find fault with it; the god had declared that if he attacked the Persians he would bring down a mighty empire. After an answer like that, the wise thing would be to send again to inquire which empire was meant. . . . But he misinterpreted what was said and made no second inquiry, he must admit the fault to have been his own."[4] To these explanations Croesus is reported to have "admitted that the god was innocent

[1] James Turney Allen, *The First Year of Greek* 162 (New York: MacMillan, 1918).

[2] The story is recounted in Herodotus, *The Histories* 30–53 (Aubrey de Sélincourt, trans., Baltimore, MD: Penguin Books, 1954).

[3] Ibid., 50.

[4] Ibid., 51.

J.M. Broekman (✉)
Dickinson School of Law, Penn State University, Carlisle, PA, USA
e-mail: jmb56@dsl.psu.edu

L. Catá Backer
Departments of Law and International Affairs, Penn State University,
University Park, PA, USA
e-mail: lcb11@psu.edu

J.M. Broekman, L. Catá Backer (eds.), *Signs In Law - A Source Book*,
DOI 10.1007/978-3-319-09837-1_1

and he had only himself to blame."[5] Yet it is less clear that the god was innocent, the ambiguity was an oracular conceit, or that Croesus had *only* himself to blame, or that the two causes were relationally independent.

Introduction

"Man acts as though he were the shaper and master of language, while in fact language remains the master of man."[6] Thus distilled in its own oracular form is a great lesson of semiotics, one that we have sought to develop in the preceding volumes.[7] These prior works focused on the progress, conceptual, methodological and epistemological, of the field of legal semiotics; on the form of semiotics study; and on the mechanics of meaning making processes in the hands of lawyers. Yet the great lessons of semiotics also requires a focus on its origins as an object of the consciousness of meaning making, one whose origins, as lessons for the oracular conversations of law, we hope to expand in this volume.

Semiotics is a shorthand framework for a consciousness of the oracular problem presented to Croesus by the Delphic Oracle. We are unaware of it until—caught in the web of our own self-reflectivity and by the re-incarnation of the sign within and of ourselves—we are eventually confounded by our own cleverness. And yet the knowledge of semiotics provides us with the wisdom, which Croesus's ego denied him: of asking the second question, that is, of understanding the relational nature of the object, its sign, symbol and meaning. This all leads us to contemplate on words as signs in law, such as "I", "me", "we", but also "obligation", "right", "property", "speech performance" and the like. But signs in law are not only in words, they also in the social forms law chose for its performance, among which "corporation" plays a dominant role.

The relationships between humans, objects and signs are ancient. Humans have relied on signs as guideposts to meaning and as hints about the past, present and future. Humans have sought to manage their lives by meanings and directions extracted from these signs. Depending on the epoch in human history, humans have also sought to generate and direct such signs as they might think they could control; they have seemed more or less obsessed with instrumentalism in every aspect of their lives and in their relations with those creatures and things around which they leave evidence of their individually short time on earth. We no longer travel to our oracles; we create schools to which we pose the great questions of the day and

[5] Ibid. 51, This is even more puzzling

[6] See the Preface to this book, quoting Martin Heidegger: *Poetry, Language, Thought*. (New York: Harper & Row, 1971) (originally *Unterwegs zur Sprache* (1959)).

[7] Anne Wagner & Jan M. Broekman (Eds.), *Prospects of Legal Semiotics* (2010); Jan M. Broekman & Francis J. Mootz III (eds.): *The Semiotics of Law in Legal Education* (2011); Jan M. Broekman & Larry Catá Backer, *Lawyers Making Meaning: The Semiotics of Law in Legal Education II* (2013).

receive the oracular responses of the current age. And those who now pose the questions, lawyers and judges, again in our own ways suffer from the self-reflexivity of Croesus.[8] And we seek to invert the oracular relationship—rather than receiving an oracle, we mean to make them ourselves to suit our purposes. The oracle told Croesus what he wanted to hear. But Croesus internalized the oracle without understanding his own wants and he sought to turn it to the instrument of his own desires. Yet in seeking to use the oracle instrumentally he became the instrument of his own destruction. This, we have long suggested, is as much the fool's errand as was that of the Lydian delegation to Delphi—one which sought to read themselves into the oracle rather than "in a dialogic fashion among people who create a universe that is not finished, but open."[9]

Law can be essentially oracular as well, and thus a fountainhead of semiosis, deeply embedded in a fluid relationship between object, sign, and interpretive community whose every expression of interpretation changes both object and sign going forward. Article III of the U.S. federal Constitution provides:

> In all Cases affecting Ambassadors, other public Ministers and Consuls, and those in which a State shall be Party, the Supreme Court shall have original Jurisdiction. In all the other Cases before mentioned, the Supreme Court shall have appellate Jurisdiction, both as to Law and Fact, with such Exceptions, and under such Regulations as the Congress shall make.

Does this specify the outer limits or the minimal scope of the court's original jurisdiction? Our oracular constitution does not say. It requires a second question. But we have no more than the original oracle—and the priests who maintain it, our judges.[10] They can provide plausible readings,[11] with authoritative effect,[12] but not definitive ones.[13] Thus Chief Justice Marshall reads the text plausibly as definitively defining the limits of Supreme Court original jurisdiction. In doing so he rejected an equally plausible definitive reading of that same text to the effect that the text meant

---

[8] See, Jack L. Balkin, "The Promise of Legal Semiotics," *University of Texas Law Review* 69:1831 (1991) ("Professor Paul constructs his school of legal semiotics around the work of American legal academics, and CLS academics in particular. Nevertheless, as he points out, there is a rich literature of legal semiotics produced in this country outside of law schools. . . . Professor Roberta Kevelson at Penn State has for some years now brought scholars from many different disciplines together at annual roundtable discussions on law and semiotics."

[9] William A. Pencak: "A Conversation With Roberta Kevelson," in Pencak & Lindgren (Eds.): *New Approaches to Semiotics and the Human Sciences*, 1998. Jan M. Broekman, *"Why Would Law Students Study Semiotics?"*, Semiotics of Law, available http://semioticsoflaw.com/site/. "On the contrary, any semiotic interest in law reaches beyond a law student's instrumentalism. Students learn to grasp beneath the surface of the legal evident, which is in the course books and cases. Why should one study legal semiotics? Most certainly to leave one's naïveté behind and enjoy the complexity of human life and law!"

[10] Larry Catá Backer, "Retaining Judicial Authority: A Preliminary Inquiry on the Dominion of Judges", *William & Mary Bill of Rights Journal* 12(1):117–178 (2003).

[11] Marbury v. Madison, 5 U.S. (1 Cranch) 137 (1803).

[12] Cooper v. Aaron, 358 U.S. 1 (1958).

[13] Edwin Meese III, "The Law of the Constitution," *Tulane Law Review* 61:979 (1987).

no more than to set the minimum original jurisdiction of the Supreme Court. Yet this rejected meaning was the product of a Congress and President of the United States, many of whose members had attended the Constitutional Convention at which this oracular constitutional document was fashioned, Meaning is produced contextually and relationally, its contours dictated as much by the organization of the interpretive community as by the inherent defintiveness of the text. And its definitive form is as much a product of the institution from which it is sourced as it is of the plausibility of its construction. Meaning, then, includes a social dimension.

The great stakeholders of the legal system often reproduce the story of Croesus and the Delphic oracle. Broekman has posited:

> "Law's language forms a special environment of signs, symbols, meanings and rhetorical forms. Students are taught to understand and practice that language called 'law' through the study of jurisprudence, judgments, precedent and cases whose titles became well-known names in society. They must master legal writing, legal argumentation, understand the predominant legal hierarchy – but all this remains vague and void without semiotic insight. Who knows and understands this?"

Those who know and understand this certainly do not include the lawyer, judge or official who insists on relating to law as Croesus did to prophecy. And indeed, those who receive the signs and struggle with symbol and interpretation always risk committing the error of self-referencing arrogance of the unitary source and the single message. "Once we raise our eyes, however, from the study of a single text, and a single kind of text, it might become somewhat less self-evident that the legal system, or the system of rules, is either self-contained or homogenous."[14]

So you want to read semiotics? You need a text! But that is not so simple: texts sometimes look very much the same, they seem to treat subjects only slightly different, are often comparably conceived but become so different once they are understood in a semiotic mode. Texts are furthermore never independent from their confrères; each text lives a life as context for another. All this, and much more, makes "reading semiotics" fascinating and hazardous at the same time, in particular when they fulfill socially important tasks, as is often the case with legal texts.

Reading semiotics implies furthermore the reading of texts, which are never solely and/or explicitly semiotic. On the one hand, *there are no specific semiotic texts* (even not texts meant to be *on* semiotics) and on the other, *all texts contain semiotic elements* to be discovered, deciphered and read. But we withhold, that to read semiotics one needs a text. In that reading, one does not read the text 'only' as it appears like a novel, a poem or a scientific treatise, but also as a phenomenon filled with signs, a resource of signification ready to be articulated.

These two considerations come together in the observation, that texts are often more important for their (social, legal, political, cultural) context than for their strictly unique and singular meaning. It seems to be true for all of them, what Eco famously formulated about the Marx' *Communist Manifesto,* 1848: "It is difficult to

---

[14] John Frow, "A Note on Legal Semiotics," *Social Semiotics* 5(2):183,186 (1995).

imagine that a few fine pages can single-handedly change the world". Can they? They did! But: who were they, and what components of them did cause that change? Was it the words of that text about 'the specter haunting Europe', or was it something else, something *in* that text or *in* those words? Even the combination of its rhetorical skill and the structure of argument, as Eco mentions, will not elucidate the unique historical event, which is called its 'reading'. If there was change through the text, it was not because of the words, but because of the signs in the words, or the signs that words are, semiotics tells us. How do we understand this? That question fascinates jurists—who have in all regards emotional as well as cognitive relations with texts—since the late 19th and particularly the beginning of the 20th century, first under the name *significs* and later named *semiotics*. The sign (the Ancient Greek *seme*) occupies proudly a central position among scholars and practitioners of social as well as physical and psychological sciences. That interest proves how each text refers back and forth towards and in a wider context—a move, which in its own turn creates new references. As a consequence, a text has (like a word) not *one* meaning and in particular never *one forever fixated* meaning, as lawyers experience often against their desire when they would like to find an "originalist" ground for their determination of text-meanings in law.

The *significs* movement in the early years of Europe's 20th century, which we mentioned in our Volume II as well as in Part I of this volume, was in many regards precursor of *legal semiotics*, and indeed an important *inter-textual* event. Schmitz, who described the significs movement in an outstanding manner, underlines (a) how *significs* is a sign theory at the turn of the century whilst interfacing with important cultural changes, (b) how it emphasizes a new type of critique of language and its terminology, including epistemological issues, and (c) how a diversity of insights in linguistics, semiotics, philosophy, and psychology played a constitutive role for understanding the sign and its multiple functions. As Schmitz in the case of the *significs* movement,[15] so does Eco in the *Manifesto* follow some of the cultural factors that determine the text at hand, its style, its rhetoric, its many historical evolutions included—such cultural events function as words when reading in a semiotic mode. We read the *Manifesto* appreciating its rhetorical gags, and forget how these are carefully prepared signs that unfold in words as composites of the text. What *significs* taught us, namely to be attentive for the unfolding of meanings, is repeated when the *Manifesto* text comes onstage. Its challenge, Eco underlines, is in the multiple meanings of words used in the text, is in where it hits the reader most, is in where it causes questions and raises doubts. Reading in the semiotic mode is reading sign meanings in connection with their social function, and, what is more: reading the sign whilst it unfolds into a diversity of meanings, so that "all this universe perfused with signs" (Peirce) seems to blossom in our words.

[15] H. Walter Schmitz (Ed.): *Essays on Significs,* "Preface", John Benjamins, Amsterdam & Philadelphia, 1990, p. V.

Reading Semiotics

Reading signs implies, that reading a text in the semiotic mode—which is the central activity in a lawyer's semiotic modus operandi—is at a large distance to any kind of passivity. Reading texts is a supreme form of action; it focuses on the serious and not-so-traditional labor to become a witness of the unfolding of a sign, followed by perceiving how it's meaning surfaces. Those signs are in words, which are at home in the minds of speakers and writers living in various periods of culture and history. Those words do never enjoy any fixated meaning beyond time and space. Eco's references to the differentiation of meaning in the foundational text of Western culture shows how the semiotic mode is not bound by an interpretation of a single sign, word or articulation, but by meaning-making processes encapsulated in cultural evolvements. Eco did not look at words, but at events that surfaced in different periods of understanding, reference and cultural interest. The difference between linguistics and semiotics is of essence here; texts and social activities are soul mates in this regard.

Text and action are also soul mates in the case of *legal* texts. This may surprise, because legal and theological texts, sometimes also canonic texts of literature, are considered as norm-creating texts and as a consequence linked to only one specific social act called interpretation. But literary hermeneutics (Schleiermacher, Dilthey, Gadamer, Ricoeur, Lonergan, Apel) often neglect the deep connections between linguistic structure and speech event. To understand a text as an (social) action seems a risk. Legal texts are an excellent example in that regard: how can laws, conceived in the form of texts, ever be an *act* rather than a *norm for action*? The answer is in the fact, that speech not only creates communication and information but also a horizon of expectation and activity within which social acts unfold. A legal text is a hierarchically organized intentional unit of written speech acts, which is not arbitrarily composed but constructed for a social and political purpose, constituting a presence and function of law in society. Such texts are composites and surfaces made for a specific reception-situation dominated by for example the court, the judge's decision, or the concept of precedent. Even where *speech* acts acquired a new character and above all a new duration in their *written* form with the suggestion of fixation, duration and reliability, the text remains a social act in itself. Look at all the various levels on which writing, acting and historical classification seems on its way to the Manifesto text of our days as mentioned by Eco. These are more important than any determination of a single word or articulation. That maximization is the result of the text being an act, and not of a different or more extensive interpretation. How do we have to understand this? The notion of *text as act* needs a completion of the traditional emphasis on words, and perhaps even signs! Indeed, there are no texts without words and/or signs—but that is not all. Our modern interest in language has widened that view.

Chomsky, Greimas, and Kristeva forwarded theoretical considerations (linguistically and philosophically) to help us understand this particular dimension of a text. All three were interested in the properties of a text's surface and yet wanted to have their observations in a wider context: a text is never the text we read, and the text we read today is not the same as the text that was read a century ago! And, what is theoretically even more fascinating: reading a text is a confrontation with a moment of the life of a text. So one enters a process when reading, and is witness of a selected moment of a life called 'text'. Our generally accepted concept of a 'text' is thus a snapshot of a more encompassing engenderment. Legal texts challenge this insight. Their conventional reading focuses on surface-meanings, on techniques of text without consciously engaging in its deeper meanings and their entire process character. The best legal scholars adhere this desire, which leads to different legal-theoretical frameworks.

Noam Chomsky's contribution is his well-known idea of a *"generative grammar"*, which appears as the central topic in all his linguistic studies. A generative grammar is for him "an explicit grammar that makes no appeal to the reader's 'faculté de langage' but rather attempts to incorporate the mechanisms of this faculty" and can be understood as "a system of rules that relate signals to semantic interpretations of these signals" [for *signals* read *signs*]. He underlines, that the pairing between signs and their semantic interpretation corresponds with a purely structural and thus ideal speaker-hearer situation, which he interprets in effect as dualistic. He describes for his grammar how "we abstract away from the many other factors (e.g., memory limitations, distractions, changes of intention in the course of speaking, etc.) that interact with underlying competence to produce actual performance". Focus of his analyses is, however, not on the surface of texts but rather on a broader linguistic-theoretical concept, which provides a "language-independent means for representing the signals and semantic interpretations that are interrelated by the grammars of particular languages". Chomsky is aware that a discussion of his generative grammar does not directly touch the structures of texts or of sentences. He fails to distinguish text and sentence, and begins indeed differentiating the concept of a sentence as a naively evident component of a text. But if we read the word "text" where he uses the word "sentence", his ideas are useful: "I distinguished between, on the one hand, those aspects of this framework that serve merely to define goals and research problems (pointing out that these are largely derived from the traditional study of language and mind), and, on the other hand, substantive assertions that go beyond delimitation of problems". The observations pertain to "(I) the surface structure of a sentence is a proper bracketing of the linear, temporally given sequence of elements, with the paired brackets labeled by category names [...]; (II) the deep structure of a sentence is in general not identical to its surface structure, but is a much more abstract representation of grammatical relations and syntactic organization."[16] His differentiation between surface- and deep structure in itself is fruitful; the reference to a dualistic speaker-hearer situation is, however, in semiotic perspective absolutely untenable, as Peirce had noticed long before

[16] Noam Chomsky: *Topics in the Theory of Generative Grammar*, Mouton, The Hague/Paris 1969, p. 12, 37.

Chomsky. One has to discuss in the semiotic mode whether a deep structure of a text is in linguistic patterns, such as "grammatical relations and syntactic organization" or in foundational structures of culture, or in both.

The latter suggestion can be read in disputes and essays of the Lithuanian linguist Algirdas Julien Greimas, for instance in his 1968 article.[17] He writes (as we already mentioned in Volume II, Part 2) about "the journey" as a metaphor for the development of the human mind:

"Perhaps out of a desire for intelligibility, we can imagine that the human mind, in order to achieve the construction of a cultural object (literary, mythical, pictorial, etc.) starts with simple elements and follows a complex course, encountering on its way constraints to which it must submit, as well as choices which it can make.

Our aim is to give a rough idea of this course. It may be considered to move from immanence to manifestation, in three principal stages:

— *deep structures,* which define the fundamental mode of existence of an individual or a society, and subsequently the conditions of existence of semiotic objects. As far as we know, the elementary constituents of deep structures have a definable logical status.
— *superficial structures* constitute a semiotic grammar system which arranges into discursive forms the contents susceptible of manifestation. The products of this grammar system are independent of the expression, which reveals them, in as far as they can theoretically appear in any substance, and, in the case of linguistic objects, in any language.
— *structures of manifestation* produce and organize the significances. Although they can include quasi-universals, they remain particular to any given language (or more precisely they define the particular characteristics of languages), or to any given material. They are studied by the superficial stylistics of morphemes, shapes, colors, etc."[18]

Greimas' observations have strong ties with traditional linguistic theories. They suggest, (a) how the textual deep structure keeps its appearance thanks to *a definable logical status*. There is special type of logic that is envisaged here, but this will be the logic of philosophy and literature as used in parallel treaties on linguistic subjects. Furthermore, (b) we read the description of a development *from grammar to surface*, which is ordered by the power of a linguistic system. That development, if important for social issues and text surfaces at all, remains a product of linguistic, mainly grammatical, order. And (c) the text surface is in Greimas' eyes a manifestation of significance(s), a meaning making *through specific linguistic articulations*. All ties form in essence a difficulty to honor the process character of the text—a character beyond linguistic perceptions and schemas.

The difference with Chomsky's notions is evident, because the dynamics surrounding the concept of the human mind and the mediation function of its culture

[17] A.J. Greimas & Fr. Rastier: "The Interaction of Semiotic Constrains" in *Yale French Studies,* Vol. 41, 1968.

[18] A.J. Greimas: "The Interaction of Semiotic Constrains"—Idem—, p. 86 f.

are not envisaged in any linguistic attitude. It means, that the distinction between the 'surface- and the deep structure' of texts is closely connected to another type of consideration, which is on 'engenderment'. In as far as legal texts are concerned, the 'oral argument' in the US Supreme Court procedure has been offered as a strong example of the dialectics between both structures during the process of engenderment of a text on its way to become an institutionally accepted surface.[19] These are as it where *tectonic dynamics*: to become a text surface is not a matter of words or sentences but of much deeper processes unfolded by anonymous cultural changes, shifting historical events and more or less arbitrary individual initiatives. This insight is essential for law, legal discourse and legal texts. To suggest that a text is an act, prepares for this insight in the power of tectonic dynamics in the making of a text surface. This fits on the one hand the idea of context in the sense of Peirce, and as a consequence of theories of Foucault, and in particular of Julia Kristeva.

Kristeva understood how entering into language and social relations by means of becoming a speaking subject is equivalent to constituting oneself as a human individual in history and society. She underlines the importance of the speaking subject in relation to the engenderment of text and textual surface meaning: "...if language is the articulation of a heterogeneous process, with the speaking subject leaving its imprint on the dialectic between the articulation and its process, then the linguist and the semiotician should study *the ethics of each signifying process"*.[20] Notice how these ethics do not depend on linguistically forged meanings of words but on the unfolding of meanings in their engendering. That is one of her main viewpoints who in this regard approximates Peirce and enriches the analyses of Chomsky and Greimas. It imports to understand that her emphasis on 'engenderment' is beyond psychoanalysis and above all an attempt to identify semiotics as a means to direct us to signifying practices that excel in the construction of text surfaces. In that regard are legal texts at the same level as poetry, myth, narrations and other language practices, which are by no means reducible to the 'language' object.

A coordination of *law* and *ethics* is embedded here; the harmony between the two is grounded in a shared structure of language—which is a norm for the engenderment of a human individual in the world of texts. Ethics of law is decidedly *not*—as many lawyers today believe and practice—a matter of judging rules or rule application ethically, but rather a matter of judging the linguistically structured process of being a human individual in a specific cultural context that acts in a legal context. A speaking subject constitutes its proper identity in forms of language *and* society. The Ancient Greek understood their *nomoi* as an achievement of linguistic nature! No wonder, that Kristeva introduced the term of a 'subject-on-trial' for that speaking subject: "...we recognize, on the one hand, the unity of the subject who submits to the law—the law of communication, among others; yet who, on the other hand, does not entirely submit, cannot entirely submit, does not want to submit

[19] Jan M. Broekman & Larry Catá Backer: *Lawyers Making Meaning—The Semiotics of Law in Legal Education II,* Springer 2012, p. 199.

[20] J. Kristeva: *Desire in Language. A Semiotic Approach to Literature and Art,* Columbia UP, 1980, p. 23, 34.

entirely... always in a state of contesting the law...".[21] Assigning values to elements of reality is important in occidental culture and essential for any process of meaning making—for *legal* meaning in particular.

Peirce: Godfather of semiotics

Peirce made us understand how the theme of *reading semiotics* embraces not a direct analysis of semiotic understanding but rather several unique and fascinating components of it. We mention four, which are in our view essential and thus recapitulate and expand our exposition:

(a) The *importance* of a sign,
(b) The *experience* of signs,
(c) The *triadic* character of sign-relations, and
(d) The interest in the *unfolding* of the sign,

(a) The importance of a sign in the work of Charles Sanders Peirce interests because one finds multiple considerations of the *character* of a sign, its *features*, its *presence* and its relation to *textual* contexts—to mention the most important, which influence the *readability* of semiotics. We therefore underline first the sign-character as it functions in Peirce's philosophy, in particular because of the important issue of reference, without which no sign would have any function or would be remarkable in any context. Peirce wrote famously:

> "A sign (...) is something which stands to somebody for something in some respect or capacity. It addresses somebody, that is, creates in the mind of that person an equivalent signs, or perhaps a more developed sign."

Signs, as elements of semiotics, participate in semiosis as a process, they are an active issue to be understood *whilst it evolves*. That feature of "evolvement" embraces what we found in the concept of "engenderment". Evolvement or engenderment needs *relations* of social nature as one of the outstanding of the sort. Cells can relate, events can relate, collective insights, norms, values can relate without active participation of a consciousness, but social relations are essential for fundamentally understanding a sign, Peirce highlights. The sign, as a something, has to stand for...; it means that somebody else (at that very moment not a sign) is needed for the evolvement towards the sign-to-be. Peirce fortifies this in calling the "somebody in this receptive regard" an "addressee". To the complex understanding of the sign belongs an activity of an other somebody: it has to meet, to welcome, to open a common conception by means of creating an equivalent or congruent sign in its own mind. All this complex social patterning—which Peirce in later years emphatically calls 'triadic'—belongs to the

[21] Ross M. Guberman (Ed.): *Julia Kristeva Interviews*. Columbia UP, 1996, p. 26.

birth, the engenderment, of a text. A text is not naively what we read or decipher, but a social moment of importance: ideas, meanings, significations and the surface itself are transferred by means of a completion of social relations. Hence the often-repeated remark in Peirce's writing: a sign on its own is not a sign, and so is a text on its own never a text.

Then, there are the specific features of signs, as Greimas explains a decade or so later, using traffic lights as signs in our modern world as an example. Important is here the role for the cultural context, the social process needed for the sign, which Peirce called the "interpretant". He thus clarifies the necessary commonness of cultural traditions, norms, values, or habits as determinant for any sign function. Do Peirce's definitions of a sign, including all mentioned properties, lead to a better understanding of 'reading semiotics'? Here is the hinge of what we call 'reading in the semiotic mode': lawyers do not need new texts or do not have to write texts in a new and modernized language, but they have to unfold a deeper understanding of their texts as a central issue of their lawyering. This includes a different self-understanding, which focuses on the need to perceive contexts as an experiential dimension of a sign.

(b) The experience of signs: Peirce emphasizes that the *experience* of the unfolding of a sign is an experience of life itself and a clue to understand the universe. No wonder that the sum total of sign features does not lead to a deeper understanding of our *reading* a sign—the reading is after all an important experiential factor with many and varying components. Of all that, the *presence* of the sign is in itself an enigmatic issue—not because of difficulties to perceive the sign but because a sign-evolvement is a social process and has therefore not a fixated grip to hold! A presence may be there, but in order to reach human awareness, it has to be brought to a particular sphere of consciousness, which Peirce calls *Firstness*. Presence has thus multiple faces (of multiple 'Others') and more than one state of being, and that fact is in itself a semiotic issue of importance. What we perceive is—as sign perception shows us—a fragment of an all-embracing complex; presence comes to us, approaches us as emerging out of secrecy. And: what we perceive is seldom entirely what we guess, estimate, think, or tell ourselves as being forthcoming. That difference with our day-to-day understanding of reading plays a role here. There is never an immediate presence of what we read when we concentrate on signs or words, or neglect the signs character of words or other issues we think to read. Significance is not the product of our reading in the first place, but rather of carefully considering presence and unfolding components that form the sign. Examples are in Eco's text on the Marxian *Manifesto*.

(c) The triadic character of sign-relations is an issue where Peirce shows how understanding a sign needs insight in human life and its social relations. An extension of this insight touches even on non-consciousness processes in life (as biosemiotics explains[22]) where for instance cells react upon each other under specific conditions of proximity in such a manner that the human metaphor of

[22] Donald Favareau: *Essential Readings in Biosemiotics*, Springer 2010

communication seems appropriate. The triadic structure sign-interpretant-signification underlines that reading a text in the semiotic mode needs emerging social patterns. However, we should perceive any articulate reading that produces signification as *a call for activity of our expressive resources*, which are often beyond the readable. Reading and interpreting a text focuses on a specific location: one is always in an applicative mode *in* the interpretant (for instance in a cultural pattern), and thus face the fact that any engagement with the sign alters ourselves as it alters the sign. In other words, *one cannot read a sign passively*. Reading legal texts in the semiotic mode shows an essential semiotic engagement of courts with cases, or with precedents, or rules and statutes. That engagement is fruit of a dynamic patterning of relations at the background of the act of reading. As a consequence, law's obsession with texts focuses directly on the development of law as an institutional power to move meaning in social life. Where are the limitations of the relevance of signs? Speaking of words, we say we know, but what about signs? Peirce made in 1902 several analytical remarks that lead to a deeper understanding, and underline the trichotomy character of signs. Or even more complicated: "Signs are divisible by three trichotomies; first, according as the sign in itself is a mere quality, is an actual existent, or is a general law; secondly, according as the relation of the sign to its object consists in the sign's having some character in itself, or in some existential relation to that object, or in its relation to an interpretant; thirdly, according as its Interpretant represents it as a sign of possibility or as a sign of fact or a sign of reason." The third type of signs is called a legi-sign: "A *Legisign* is a law that is a Sign. This law is usually established by men. Every conventional sign is a legisign [but not conversely]. It is not a single object, but a general type, which, it has been agreed, shall be significant. Every legisign signifies through an instance of its application, which may be termed a *Replica* of it. Thus, the word "the" will usually occur from fifteen to twenty-five times on a page. It is in all these occurrences one and the same word, the same legisign." Do these distinct types of sign have a fundamentally different impact on law, and do they represent a different power of meaning making? Lawyering is an activity, which fully engages in such deliberations, without, however, formulating a solution for the extremely complex contexts that rein the law-lawyer-court-client-state-culture relationships.

(d) The interest in an *unfolding* of the sign is an interest that focuses on the various dynamics of hitherto unmeasured power and dimensions. Reading in the semiotic mode includes that we circle around a secret, around a non-public or immediately clear essence that unfolds in our learning to know the sign. When we learn to read words, we only begin to approach signs: reading in the semiotic mode is respecting the sign and showing what unfolds in and through a word as an access to social life and, ultimately, to ourselves. Neither word nor sign is the final point to be reached when we engage in the process of reading. Reading in the semiotic mode is to learn how signs are read in their process context of words. Ask a lawyer: the difference between discourse (word) and semiotics (signs) is not a fact but a process that unfolds not without himself or herself.

Legal Texts in Semiotic Perspective

Legal texts, semioticians discovered, are generally texts loaded with signs. The wealth of sign-diversity has been the theme of Roberta Kevelson and her works on legal semiotics.[23] This implies a renewed appreciation of specific sign-words in law (Peirce would call them 'legi-signs') such as names, cases, dates and other contextual references, as well as discipline markers and other technical expressions, indications of legal procedure in legal branches or standardized short cuts, which are altogether found in legal dictionaries. So, all in all, there is a rich vocabulary in law and legal practice that fulfills a precious sign role. This role is at the center of our attention when reading legal texts in a semiotic mode. Here is the utility anchored for lawyers to cope with the many dynamic elements of law—what they sometimes incorrectly want to keep in hand by means of stable and fixated, positivist interpretations of texts ("law is law", "Gesetz ist Gesetz"). Two important observations are at issue.

(1) At first sight, we divide legal discourse in two principally different sets in which signs play a different role, have different functions and unfold different legal-interpretative resources in practice and theory formation. The *first* is legal discourse within a *state-bound system*, mostly within a national state-bound, but often also in addition a multi-state legal system, such as the US and the EU. They are mixed systems, 'national or particular state'-bound and 'multi-state'-bound. The *second* is legal discourse within a *global legal system*, which is not national state-bound, but often defined as "the law of non-state governance systems". Catá Backer defined the latter as "an amalgamation of four fundamental characteristics that together define a new order in form that is, in some respects, the antithesis of the orderliness and unity of the law-state system it will displace."[24]

Reading law in a semiotic mode seems, in the framework of these observations, not only an issue of fine tuning with semiotics, but also of determining to what type of law legal texts at hand belong to. In other words: if semiotic reading is part of a legal theory at all, then the question is for instance utterly relevant whether the second type of law (the law of non-state governance systems) is compatible with the traditional nation state law-theory formation. Or does contemporary legal theory, to which semiotic reading belongs, provide theoretical insights for both systems? The question is by no means rhetorical, because if not, one has to differentiate carefully between *two types of reading semiotics* in law!

(2) One should, however, not forget that a remarkably strong and coherent logic of legal discourse persists in both types of law. That is brought to the fore in the

[23] Roberta Kevelson: *The Law as a System of Signs*, New York 1988

[24] Larry Catá Backer: "The Structure of Global Law: Fracture, Fluidity, Permeability, and Polycentricity" in: *Consortium for Peace and Ethics*, p.106, July 2012, at http://ssrn.com/abstract=2091456.

general, publically and scientifically uniform appreciation and maintenance of the word "law". The situation is possible wherein one layer of semiotic consideration would pertain to this general level and a second would differentiate between the two meanings of 'law'. The first mentioned meaning of law does, however, not differ very much from earlier legal-theoretical considerations, which always included a diversity of legal systems under one name: "Law"—such as Civil Law, Common Law, Mixed Legal System(s), Religious Law, or Customary Law. But "Global Law" has never been identified with one of them, and Peirce's 'legi-signs' have never been at home on that level. Are there two meanings of "legal theory"?

In Catá Backer's characterization of global law rules a post-modern fascination for multiplicity and powers of diversification. Fracture, fluidity, permeability and polycentricity belong to them, and it is time they enter the domain of legal theory. But law's answer to such social and cultural forces is and has always been in the form of unification, rule following empowerment, and simplification of principles amidst multitudes of disparate social developments—in legal practice as well as in theory formation. So it does not surprise that many legi-signs function within a limited set of discourse components in both types of law, in state-governed as well as in non-state governance law. One should, at the background of our post-modern knowledge, focus on these unified as well as unifying principles for the purpose of semiotic reading.

Legi-signs are according to Peirce the specific signs in words of law, legal doctrine or general jurisprudence in which signs can unfold a meaning that is institutionally offered as law's view or solution. That unfolding is a "process of making meaning", which is the major job of a lawyer, as we exposed elaborately in Vol. II. An important and often neglected element of legal semiotics in the practicalities of the lawyer's profession when dealing with legi-signs, in other words: the utility of knowing how to read in a semiotic mode and how to be able to participate in the dynamics of law. When performing this task, lawyers generally focus on the smallest possible set of principles to be realized in each legal context, no matter what type of law and legal system is at hand. This guarantees in the eyes of a jurist law's stable relations to unfold human values, such as dignity, freedom and other categories (which are accepted on a global scale as *human rights*) and seem in conformity with law's image of man.

Subject, Cause & Purpose in Global Law

We distinguish three major principles, which are linked to the unfolding of man according to its image in law, and call them with non-legal expressions: *subject, causality* and *equilibrium.* Wherever unfolding its legi-signs in any cultural context, those three are the strictly necessary conditions for law and the constitution of legal discourse, and thus the absolute conditions for any possibility to read legal texts. All structures of legal discourse—from Roman——until Global Law—manifest *the image of man which must be unfolded in law*; all efforts of any type of practicing law would be senseless if that condition were not fulfilled. This unfolding along those three lines can never and nowhere occur without any sort of *logic*, as every narration shows, and law is not an exception here. *Someone* has to be presented as the one about which the story goes—*a (legal) subject cannot be missed in law*. Language and events have to be presented in *causal* connection with a subject, otherwise nobody follows or listens anymore—here one encounters the logic of narration, which law shares with political, economic, or psychological reasoning. Lastly, a clear and public determination of a *purpose*—in particular *justice* (the vital legal concept outside jurisprudence and dogmatic in its public, non-technical form of equilibrium [suum cuique]) cannot fail in that narrative.[25] Meaning resulting from legal practices and thought patterns will only take place as a fulfillment of those conditions. Consequently, *our semiotic reading of legal texts reads a subject, discovers a logic and agrees with a purpose*. Beyond those, we do not find any sense in life or in law.

Those preconditions of reading and speaking law do not stand on their own—they exist in a network of contexts. The legal qualification of an individual via terms such as *subject* in Civil Law or *person(hood)* in Common Law show how law determines relations within human patterns. This leads to an almost universal application of that legal qualification, even in cultures where the subject (or the personal "I") does not seem to be at home and does not appear on the forefront of the diverse language grammars. Lawyers agree universally on the concept of the subject or person, when claiming that each human being is a legal subject. Hence the great semiotic interest in thoughts of Lady Victoria Welby or of Lacan on the engenderment of a Self and the position of an "I" that reach far beyond psychology or psychoanalysis.

Indeed: *the subject*—most lawyers treat that expression as self-evident or others wish to abolish the transformational power that was needed for the term and its qualification. They emphasize how subjectivity in law is a great achievement, and for instance averted slavery. Do not forget how this categorization of the subject/person protects private property as the most evident form of self-realization, so that private law suggests to be the most natural form of law. Modern law, in particular law of non-state governments, is an indication of the power and stability of such transformations from *everyday-life* meanings to *legal* meanings—the core interest of legal semiotics.

It fascinates how this fits in with global law in its post-postmodern appearance. Catá Backer characterizes "Global Law" along three lines we discussed: (a) global legal order is dependent on an *ability of actors* to form and deploy governance structures (the role of a *subject* is protected), (b) the state's power can no longer claim pride of place (a *causality* is safeguarded), and (c) global law requires us to learn the language of governance beyond territory and state (a *purpose* is publicly given and accepted).[26] His description of global law excels in demonstrating how the category

[25] Jan M. Broekman: *Recht en Anthropologie,* Antwerpen 1982 (2nd Ed), p. 209. [German 1979, French 1993, Spanish 1993.]

[26] L. Catá Backer, "The Structure of Global Law" see note 8, p. 107.

"subject/subjectivity" or "person/personhood" remains intact or even intensifies in global law. They focus like always on the fundamental pattern a state has provided: entities unfold that can mimic the state in all regards, including the legislative authority of states. They also assume other legal forms that come to life in modern social patterns in the guise of certifying organizations, standardizing organs, assessment entities and communities based on equal forms, such as cyber-communities. Catá Backer's conclusion also fits in with the patterning as determined by the three ground lines of legal discoursing: "Fracture is not the end of order but merely its re-ordering".[27]

All these considerations, which are ultimately an essay in understanding the reading of legal texts in a semiotic mode, show how legal discourse and law as an embracing concept are not a stable and fixated entity, but rather a complex process that is never in rest. Fractures are not only a *socio-economic* or a *political* issue—they denote also an *epistemological* dimension of modern law, which pertain to the many legal ways of knowing reality. Fundamental is here the insight that law has a *tectonic structure*, so that Foucault's observation according to which discourses can show a variety of "découpages" (cuttings or clippings) fits to our observations. In other words, if modern law shows fractures, fluidity, permeability and polycentricity, then these terms do not only refer to socio-political dimensions but also to the patterns of knowledge legal discourse creates and uses. Law is in its broadest sense a *process of knowledge production*; it delivers a socially relevant, powerful and decision-creating comprehension of everything 'there is' in a human society, not matter into what stadium of cultural development or value orientation it evolved.

But one has to perceive what particular features of knowledge are predominant in the case of law and legal discourse. In that context it interests that law is a process of *knowledge of itself* (as considerations about non-state law in forms of governance show) and on the other hand a process of *knowledge of events, reality, being*. We concluded, that 'law as knowledge of itself' is an omnipresent progressing project, an articulation of its discourse in the form of *auto-referential constitutive processes*. However, law's knowledge of reality (each attempt to articulate reality in a legal mode) creates the foundation for a *socio-political ideology*. The two dimensions: *self-constitution* and *ideology* are two sides of the same coin. Both focus ultimately on continuous changes of meaning in a discourse context and legal semiotic reading. Reading semiotics is hence a double activity: the reading of semiotics as information about an analytic instrument to understand the constitutive deep layers of legal discourse, *and* the reading of actual signs that all are in a process of unfolding. Law knows itself (a) from an institutional viewpoint, controlling its own logic by means of its proper performance in society, and (b) as a discourse that delivers knowledge of (predominantly social) reality. It should be noted herewith, that law knows itself according to the same basic structures as it knows reality, and vice versa. Semiotics has a dynamic character; it takes snapshots of unfolding meaning whereby the pictures as they are read will never identify the entirety of law as an encompassing process.

---

[27] L. Catá Backer, note 8, p. 109.

Surface- and Deep Structure of Discourse

The distinction appears again, and has its consequences for the content of this source book. The surface level of information transfer, strongly connected with major technicalities of law, focuses on the possible enrichment by the question how to operate law with the semiotic mode. Reading signs in awareness of its semiotic relevance includes on the other hand the deep structure of a reader's presence in a process of unfolding of sign(s) in word(s). The latter experience emphasizes the importance of the distinction with regard to the close relation between law and life.

Alexis de Tocqueville once wrote that American philosophy always sought to escape the 'spirit of the system', an escape that would be foundational for its pragmatism, as Llewellyn underlined.[28] Llewellyn is the lawyer who thinks law in patterns of the subject without relying on a fixated *subject* identity but whilst fulfilling the need of the category subject or person and telling his reader—as with a bird's-eye view: "…you know… you know to whom I refer…" and "you know the Truth, the Document, the Signer, the conflict at hand …". Legal realism is based on semantic and semiotic processes alike to represent law in life. To think a subject-identity equals the notion of thought patterns operating with legal cases as being the first person singular of legal discourse. Cases are given names and became signs through those given names. *Law in Life* must treat cases as traces in a legal system that emerges like life itself. And it articulates with every technical-legal move a desire to awaken *Life in Law*—the dichotomy of surface- and deep structure again unveiled.

One problem in our approach of reading law in a semiotic mode remains: the often debated and politically wholeheartedly embraced globalizing law has the potentiality to create a hitherto unknown distance between legal practice and theoretical thought formation about law. Legal theory as we know today is still loaded with notions of a past era; law's post-modernity is not yet fully incorporated in legal thinking—and does legal semiotics already lead law to its next, post-postmodern phase? The two-levels distinction remains present. Global law has been produced by deep structures of law, as we suggested. They are not in the first place jurisprudential but cultural and in particular narrative: subject/person, causality and purpose/equilibrium. Global law meets a culture in the making, as numerous discussions (political, economical, ethical, sociological and the like) show when dealing with multiculturalism. Do not forget the provocative slogan of the seventies in the 20th century: "The European Union will be nothing if not multicultural". That slogan was intertwined with implications of the "Law without State"-theorem, which was determinative for the EU legal order. *Contract* among member states had to develop hand in hand with *transfer* of sovereignty—an actuality that is difficult to understand in terms of a theory of law solely based on state concepts, which were already

[28] Jan M. Broekman: "Law in Life, Life in Law: Llewellyn's Legal Realism Revisited" in: Francis J. Mootz III (Ed.): *On Philosophy in American Law,* Cambridge UP 2009, p. 11 f.

dying in the last decades of the 20th century.[29] Multiculturalism pertains to a society that is predominantly composed of groups with different ethnic, geographic, religious, socio-economic and cultural roots which strive for equal positions on the markets of labor, commodities and capital. They challenge 20th century law because that law should be the prevailing instrument for their strivings, as becomes formulated even in our days. The problem is not—what it first appeared to be—the obvious differences, nor any justification of the dream of equality, but the fact that in view of such complex strivings surface- and deep structures of legal discourse do no longer meet in a harmony earlier legal theories took for self-evident. It seems that modern law articulates same problems differently. That articulation will be highlighted in a semiotic mode, as the collected texts in this reader show in many ways and in different directions. Reading legal texts in a semiotic mode tells us, that lawyers do not need new texts or a new and modernized language, but they should unfold a deeper and often different angle on understanding their texts as a central issue of their profession. This includes a different self-understanding, which stimulates to perceive contexts as an experiential dimension of a sign.

[29] Jan M. Broekman: "The Multicultural Self" in: *Theorie des Rechts und der Gesellschaft. Festschrift W. Krawietz,* Duncker & Humblot, Berlin 2003, p. 144.

Eco and the Text of the Communist Manifesto

Jan M. Broekman and Larry Catá Backer

Reading semiotics implies the reading of texts, which are—as suggested— never solely and/or explicitly semiotic. On the one hand, *there are no specific semiotic texts* (even not texts meant to be *on* semiotics) and on the other, *all texts contain semiotic elements* to be discovered, deciphered and read. But we withhold, that to read semiotics one needs a text. In that reading, one does not read the text 'only' as it appears like a novel, a poem or a scientific treatise, but also as a phenomenon filled with signs, a resource of signification ready to be articulated. This is in the opening statement of Eco's short contribution to the journal *L'Espresso* "On the Style of *The Communist Manifesto*" 1998[1] where he writes:

> It is difficult to imagine that a few fine pages can single-handedly change the world. After all, Dante's entire oeuvre was not enough to restore a Holy Roman Empire to the Italian city-states. But, in commemorating *The Communist Manifesto* of 1848, a text that certainly has exercised a major influence on the history of two centuries, I believe one must reread (…) its extraordinary rhetorical skill and the structure of its arguments.

The consideration that there do not exist specific and uniquely semiotic texts (in the sense that there are political, poetic or religious—not to mention legal—texts), but that all texts contain semiotically relevant components, suggests that texts are often more important for their (social, legal, political, cultural) context than for their strictly unique and singular meaning. That observation seems to be true for what

[1] Published in *L'Espresso,* 8 January 1998, for the 150th anniversary of *The Communist Manifesto,* republished in *Sulla Letteratura*, 2002, Republished in English translation by M.McLaughlin in *On Literature,* Hartcourt Inc., 2004

J.M. Broekman (✉)
Dickinson School of Law, Penn State University, Carlisle, PA, USA
e-mail: jmb56@dsl.psu.edu

L. Catá Backer
Departments of Law and International Affairs, Penn State University, University Park, PA, USA
e-mail: lcb11@psu.edu

J.M. Broekman, L. Catá Backer (eds.), *Signs In Law - A Source Book*,
DOI 10.1007/978-3-319-09837-1_2

Eco famously formulated about the Marx' *Communist Manifesto*, 1848: "It is difficult to imagine that a few fine pages can single-handedly change the world". Can they? They did! But: who were they, and what components of them did cause that change? Was it the words of that text about 'the specter haunting Europe', or was it something else, something *in* that text or *in* those words? Even the combination of its rhetorical skill and the structure of argument, as Eco mentions, will not elucidate the unique historical event, which is called its 'reading'. If there was social change through the text, creating a new awareness, it was not because of the words, but because of the signs in the words, or the signs that words are, semiotics tells us. How do we understand this? Eco circumscribes this difficult question by pointing at the implicit (social) rhetorics, and how the Manifesto's slogan "A specter is haunting Europe" is followed immediately by a bird's-eye history of class struggle to the actual conquests achieved by a "revolutionary" class. Eco remarks, that this foundational epic is still valid today, for supporters of free-market enterprise. As a consequence, "the Jewish, Messianic Marx" (Eco's expression) is thinking of the opening of Genesis. But envisaged is ultimately how it becomes multinational, globalized, and even invents a literature that is no longer national but international. Eco adds in a footnote:

> Obviously, when I wrote this article, the term "globalization" already existed, and I did not use the expression by chance. (…) It is astonishing, how the *Manifesto* witnessed the birth 150 years ahead of its time, of the era of globalization, and the alternative forces it would unleash. It almost suggests that globalization is not an accident that happens during the course of capitalist expansion (just because the Wall has come down and the Internet has arrived) but rather the inevitable pattern that the emergent class could not fail to follow.

The issue fascinates jurists—who have in all regards emotional as well as cognitive relations with texts—since the late 19th and particularly the beginning of the 20th century, first under the name *significs* and later named *semiotics*. The latter embraces not only styles of word-use but also broader social structures of communication, which are forcefully meaning making.

"The upheaval becomes struggle as workers organize thanks to another power that the bourgeoisie developed for its own profit: communications. And here the *Manifesto* cites the example of the railways, but the authors are also thinking of new mass media (and let's not forget that in *The Holy Family* Marx and Engels were able to use the television of that age — namely, the serial novel — as a model of the collective imagination, and they criticized its ideology by using the very language and situations the serials had made popular)".

Indeed, the sign (the Ancient Greek *seme*) occupies proudly a central position among scholars and practitioners of social as well as physical and psychological sciences. That interest proves how each text refers back and forth towards and in a wider context—a move, which in its own turn creates new references. As a consequence, a text has (like a word) not *one* meaning and in particular never *one forever fixated* meaning, as lawyers experience often against their desire when they would like to find an "originalist" ground for their determination of text-meanings in law.

Like Schmitz in the case of the *significs* movement[2] so does Eco in the *Manifesto* follow some of the cultural factors that determine the text at hand, its style, its rhetoric, its many historical evolutions included—such cultural events function as words when reading in a semiotic mode. We read the *Manifesto* appreciating its rhetorical gags, and forget how these are carefully prepared signs that unfold in words as composites of the text. What *significs* taught us, namely to be attentive for the unfolding of meanings, is repeated when the *Manifesto* text comes onstage. Its challenge is in the multiple meanings of words used in the text, is in where it hits the reader most, is in where it causes questions and raises doubts. Reading in the semiotic mode is reading sign meanings in connection with their social function, and, what is more: reading the sign whilst it unfolds into a diversity of meanings, so that "all this universe perfused with signs" (Peirce) seems to blossom in our words.

As a sign of this perfusion follows a more powerful observation regarding the total picture of the end-of-19 t-century attitude when we read:

> There then follows the most doctrinal part, the movement's program, the critique of different kinds of socialism, bur by this stage the reader is already seduced by the preceding pages. And two breathtaking slogans [follow], easy, memorable and destined (it seems to me) to have an extraordinary future

They are slogans of the Manifesto, well known even in a following century: "Workers have nothing to lose but their chains," and "Workers of the world, unite!"

Even apart from its genuinely poetic capacity to invent memorable metaphors, the *Manifesto* remains a masterpiece of political (but not only political) oratory, Eco concludes, and he suggests how it should be studied at school along with Cicero's *Invectives against Catiline* and Mark Antony's speech over Julius Caesar's body in Shakespeare.

Eco teaches us, that reading signs implies, how reading a text in the semiotic mode—which is the central activity in a lawyer's semiotic modus operandi—is at distance to any kind of passivity. Reading texts is a supreme form of action; it focuses on the serious and not-so-traditional labor to become a witness of the unfolding of a sign, followed by perceiving how it's meaning surfaces. Those signs are in words, which are at home in the minds of speakers and writers living in various periods of culture and history. Those words do never enjoy any fixated meaning beyond time and space. Eco's views on the Manifesto are in line with his basic ideas on semiotics, as already exposed in his famous 1976 *A Theory of Semiotics*:

> (…) some semiotic approaches do make semiotics the study of the creative activity of a semiosis-making subject, and intending this subject not as a phenomenological transcendental Ego but a 'deep', profound subject. Let me then assume that maybe semiotics is destined to overcome one of its natural boundaries and to become not only the theory of codes and of sign production but also of the 'deep' individual origins of any 'wish to produce signs'.

[2] H. Walter Schmitz: *De Hollandse Significa*, Assen/Maastricht 1990; J. van Nieuwstadt Transl. German-Dutch.

One should add a further remark in this context:

> … the subject of any semiotic enquiry (…) is a way of looking at the world and can only be known as a way of segmenting the universe and of coupling semantic units with expression-units: by this labor it becomes entitled to continuously destroy and restructure its social and historical systematic concretions[3]

Eco did not look at words only, but at events that surfaced in different periods of understanding, reference and cultural interest. The difference between linguistics and semiotics is of essence here; texts and social activities are soul mates, as Eco makes clear in his analysis of *The Communist Manifesto*.

---

[3] Umberto Eco: *A Theory of Semiotics*, Indiana UP 1979, p. 315.

Part II
From Legal Significs to Legal Semiotics

Origins and Effects of Legal Significs

Jan M. Broekman and Larry Catá Backer

The study and exercise of legal semiotics is nowadays an international phenomenon, with even a recently announced Round Table on "Semiotizing and Semiotized Law" in Hangzou, China 2013, which includes plenary speakers from all over the world. The question about the origins of those legal semiotic activities is, however, not posed and the cultural complexity of that beginning not even studied in Petrilli's masterful work on Lady Welby's philosophical and cultural heritage. Moreover, semiotics of law has loosened its ties with the *Law and Literature* Movement, the *Critical Legal Studies* and *Legal Deconstructivism*—movements that reined matters of meaning and significance in the eighties of the past century.

As we mentioned in Volume II, the centenary of the death of Lady Victoria Welby (1837–1912) reminded the world of a constellation, which was hitherto insufficiently researched: *"Semiotics" was never the only term in use for the study of signs or meaning!* Lady Welby promoted in parallel and whilst corresponding with Peirce who forwarded the term "semiosis" or "semeiotic" the concept of "significs" for the same discipline. Her influence and uses of the term 'significs' was extremely important in a circle of writers, mathematicians, linguists, a lawyer and several philosophers, who were fascinated by the idea that 'sign', 'sense', 'meaning' and 'significance' were altogether components of human expressiveness. Because of the discussions and many exchanges between Lady Victoria Welby and the Dutch poet and philosopher Frederik van Eeden, a "Signifische Beweging" (Signific Movement) was established in Amsterdam, in particular engaging a group of members of the Amsterdam University. H. Walter Schmitz and Susan Petrilli

J.M. Broekman (✉)
Dickinson School of Law, Penn State University, Carlisle, PA, USA
e-mail: jmb56@dsl.psu.edu

L. Catá Backer
Departments of Law and International Affairs, Penn State University, University Park, PA, USA
e-mail: lcb11@psu.edu

J.M. Broekman, L. Catá Backer (eds.), *Signs In Law - A Source Book*,
DOI 10.1007/978-3-319-09837-1_3

contributed studies about that movement. 'Legal significs' was a major component of some twenty titles the lawyer and poet Jacob Israel de Haan produced on what we would today understand as 'legal semiotics', Despite serious attempts to translate on a large scale, the majority of works are unknown as they remained even until today isolated in the Dutch language.

Legal semiotics in the guise of legal significs was for the first time exposed in the PhD dissertation of De Haan in Amsterdam, 1916, entitled: *Rechtskundige Significa en hare toepassing op de begrippen: Aansprakelijk, Verantwoordelijk, Toerekeningsvatbaar.* (Legal Significs and its application in the terms: 'liable', 'responsible' and 'accountable'). That publication can in hindsight be seen as the first work on legal semiotics. It is not on law, but on *legal significs* focusing on analyses of how lawyers use the three concepts. Their legal practice is in the use of words, of speech acts. No wonder that significs emphasizes words as its major subject of study and analysis. A strong interest in legal language characterizes De Haan's work, so that linguists felt inspired to make a manifest distinction between the language of law and the language of people. This has at least two consequences. On the one hand, the language lawyers professionally use is a language that operates mainly in accordance with its *surface* manifestation. Neither Common Law nor Civil Law operates by managing *deep* structures; both legal traditions avoid any surfacing of the engenderment or genesis of actual texts or speech acts. This attitude is typically legal in as far as it suggests that language is an instrument, which can be formatted, mastered and used arbitrarily and pragmatically. On the other hand, speech acts performed by legal professionals are by no means legal issues or results of a science of *law* (*Rechtswetenschap*). Members of the Signific Movement in Amsterdam agree that meaning formation is in the first place a *psychological* issue. No wonder that they concentrate on *symbol* and *word* as the two major instruments that provide access to legal significs and law studies. Speech analysis and psychology must go hand in hand, and follow those explorations of words and symbols. De Haan underlines that a better language of law contributes to a better law. Legal language is at its best when it articulates the relevant situation in its best legal terms, but there is no such articulation of language if it is not psychologically well founded. De Haan's signific ideal is that law fits to reality in a one-to-one meaning relation between life facts and legal facts. The language of law should therefore be simplified, more rational, efficient and clear; differences between legal and everyday language must diminish so that the bridge between the two will lead to greater justice in social life. One cannot deny that his legal-signific attitude is clearly under the influence of positivism as it was the case with developments and discoveries in Vienna and other philosophical and cultural centers of that time. In contrast to semiotics—an approach that wrestled with pragmatism rather than with positivism—significs never lost its positivist traits entirely, nor its desire (that makes us think back to Wittgenstein's Vienna) to create one-to-one relations between word and thing/reality.

This Part II, leading from legal significs to legal semiotics, comprises five pathbreaking texts divided in a number of fragments. First, there are two fragments from Frederik van Eeden, one of the most central figures of the Amsterdam significs circle and befriended with Lady Victoria Welby, her psychological interests and her English significs works. His Wittgensteinean "*Redekunstige Grondslag van Verstandhouding*" [Rhetorical Foundation of Understanding] is a *Tractatus* conceived 1897 prepared for significs to be oriented towards language, discourse and other forms of mutual understanding. Only readers with proficiency in Dutch language have until now been able to understand how Wittgenstein formulated in his famous *Tractatus Logico-Philosophicus* ideas and thoughts that were already "in the air" for a long time and were formulated in parallel during the last years of the 19th and the first of the 20th century. That spiritual climate documents the mutual understanding and long-lived relation with Lady Welby, in which such evolutions as significs could blossom. Wittgenstein's 1922 *Tractatus* was fruit of a philosophical climate that not only characterized the Vienna of those days. Two fragments of another member of the Amsterdam Circle, the mathematician Gerrit Mannoury who also contributed to significs and psychology, provide insight in grasping for definitions of significs, which form a platform for later legal work, to mention one of the many disciplines involved. Contributions of Lady Welby cannot be left out here—one is from her book on *Meaning* and the other the famous 1911 *Encyclopedia Britannica* article on significs. One should read the latter with respect; keep in mind that in the UK during the first years of the XXth century such a contribution written by a female author external to the academic inner circles, was a sign of exceptional recognition. From De Haan, the first legal significian/semiotician, we include the complete text of the *inaugural lecture on legal significs* ever given at any place in the world in 1916 at the Amsterdam University. It is a remarkable experience to read that text as if one was a student of those days. One more fragment is provided here: a selection from De Haan's Doctoral Thesis on the subject, which delivers a signific analysis of central terms of European Civil Law until our days: liability, responsibility and accountability.

These texts show a line of thoughts, which is articulated in the title "From Legal Significs to Legal Semiotics". Significs differs from semiotics, one could say, because the first really had to fight for recognition of the concept of meaning and in particular, as de Haan reports literally, for accepting the question pertaining to the meaning of meaning—long before Ogden & Richards' *The Meaning of Meaning*, which was conceived 1923 as a study of the influence of language upon thought, and by no means to significs or to semiotics. We do not know anymore how Lady Welby and the Amsterdam Circle had to fight for recognition of the question—in our days not only evident but also fashionable in sciences and philosophy. In addition to this, there is an issue that has not been solved in the transition from significs to semiotics: the ontological and semiotic status of a *word*. Is a word the atom of a language? That is very often considered, even among lawyers of today. Yet, the major difference between significs and semiotics is in the difference between a word and a sign. Actual evolvements of semiotic nature are placing the sign in a word like a bud in a flower. The metaphor seems appropriate: the unfolding and growth of the bud makes the flower display its beauty and function. Meanings come to the fore in that process. To focus on the word and hardly acknowledge its bud-function characterizes the signific approach, one could say. Semiotics has to learn the lesson of perceiving the *entire* process, as Peirce often underlined. When considering this, one grasps our actual situation, which unfolds at distance to significs. Semiotics focuses on the *word as a sign*, as Kevelson suggested in the case of law. But semiotics also considers how *signs as words* contribute to our understanding of reality. Both are intertwined educational experiences offered by a confrontation with this first part of this reader on legal semiotics.

“Word-Value” and “The ‘I’”

Frederik van Eeden

[In The Original Typography And Section Numbers[1]]

Word-Value

34. IDENTITY IS THE MOST PRIMITIVE CONCEPT. AS WELL AS WE KNOW THAT THERE IS SOMETHING, WE KNOW THAT IT IS POSSIBLE THAT THERE ARE TWO THINGS WHO RESEMBLE EACH OTHER WITHOUT BEING THE SAME, WITHOUT BEING IDENTICAL.
Identical is a term expressing a negation and not ‘something else’

35. COMPARING IS THE MAJOR FUNCTION OF THINKING. THE LIFE OF THE SOUL IS A COMBINATION OF WILL, PERCEPTION AND COMPARISON.
Those three develop always together and in an unlimited complication. Like the forms of movements in three dimensions, they are the forms of thought-formation in three dimensions.

36. THE PERCEPTION, THE SENTIMENT, THE BEING, THE EXISTING.
a. This can mean object as well as subject, I as well as non-I — ‘What is perceiving’ as well as ‘the hypothetical cause of perception’.
b. What I call here ‘the existing’ or ‘the things’ is also called ‘the reality’. I chose another term to avoid misunderstanding. Reality means a property which we ascribe to a certain degree to ‘the existent’. What exists can possess a variant degree of reality, it can exist more, or less. The object has always more reality, more security to exist, than the subject.

---

[1] **SOURCE:** FREDERIK VAN EEDEN: *Redekunstige Grondslag Van Verstandhouding*, [Rhetorical foundations of communication] IN; *STUDIES, VOL. III,* AMSTERDAM 1897. (Translation Dutch/English by Eds.)

F. van Eeden (✉)

J.M. Broekman, L. Catá Backer (eds.), *Signs In Law - A Source Book*,
DOI 10.1007/978-3-319-09837-1_4

37. We create and image to understand what exists, which means: to compare and to order.
The image of something is a something new with the identity with the first as its main property. We strive (which means: compare and order) to understand reality, because that is necessarily developing together with life, growth or volition. Understanding is an articulation of the will and a precondition for desire. This is like roots of plants: they are growth and at the same time a condition for growth.

38. Our representation of the existent is not the existent itself but an image of it.
We can only think of things as a representation, an image. Our thoughts do not operate with the things as they are, but with their images. These images are ordered by our thoughts. This is an outline thoughts create from things; and the organization of that outline is called 'theory'.

39. The symbol as word is the sensual representation of the image as the existent.
That is: a symbol of an image. So there is: (1) reality. (2) it's image: the outline. (3) the articulation of that outline in word-symbols.

40. The imagining word, the poetry, depicts more directly what exists.
Not entirely direct because it is always in part symbolic. Music could be the most direct image of reality.

41. Identity with its original is the main property of the image—but apart from this, it has other properties that cause it to differ from the original.
This is a very important principle, which is often forgotten. If applied to §§ 38 and 39, it follows that the representation of what exists is never identical with the existent. We must therefore consider this inequality in all our thoughts, because we think with representations, not with real issues. Each of our ideas is an image (a thought-image) and thus differs from things.

When comparing and ordering our representations—making a theory— we must absolutely take care to clearly perceive that difference and consider whether it can influence our conclusions.

The same is true for language, even to a higher degree. In language one operates with symbols of images, or images of images. The danger to draw false conclusions due to neglecting the difference of image and original is doubled here.

That danger does not exist in the case of the pure symbol. The mistake can only be in the representation.

Pure imagining does not create a theory and draws no conclusions. The word follows the existent. A chance of fallacy is therefore smaller. It is at its biggest in half-symbolizing, half-imagining language. In that case are our representations expressed in images, and the images of those images will be ordered and compared among them, thus forming a theory. Sophisms will result, also false dialectics. The neglect of this principle characterizes the ancient (Greek) philosophy. The modern reader of Plato's dialogues encounters those arguments continuously; they cannot be refuted logically but he feels (or, as he will say, his sound mind articulates) that the difference between words and terms and images is neglected.

However, characteristic of our time is that one has lost sight of the difference between representation and things. (Among others, such generally maltreated issues like volition, matter, power, nature etc.).

Things should be understood as our perceptions and feelings as well as a closely connected postulate: as a world external to the I.

The latter seems very evident and well known. Everybody knows that his image of the earth or of him/herself differs from the earth or himself, and that the word earth or its name differs from its image. The same is true for the fact that one can only think with images and speak with words.

But one is seldom thinking about, or simply aware of all this because of the complications and in particular because of the transitions from the concrete to the abstract.

When speaking about 'power', beauty', 'truth', 'will', one often forgets that the word is something totally different than its representation. It is more determined, stable, concrete—but one forgets in particular that an image, a representation is very different from the things imagined.

The image is a vague, half-abstract, half-sensual psychic image that is bound to a form, a word, a more or less determined recollection and something that can always be called upon and compared; that what exists: a series of perceptions bound by an idea, the platonic ideas, a term also of Descartes, Spinoza, Boehme etc, which lead to great confusion. Our language lives close to images and thus creates a specific 'imagination'. But that is also only an image, an abstraction, a sham, an appearance, a modus. An idea is an existing thing, a feeling, an 'ens' (Latin). Our language has inversed what it did with 'truth' and 'reason', when transformed from modus to ens (being).

It becomes possible in this framework that from two reasonable scholars one states that the world is will and the other that there is no will at all (Schopenhauer and Haeckel). In the light of the preceding considerations both opinions can be just. Despite their differences, both have a representation in correspondence with what exists. Their difference exists only because they used the same words in different frameworks of representation, or they wanted to represent a part of the same image with logically contrasting terms.

The "I"

101. (Earlier remarks in the book discussed that one cannot exclude the possibility of a life of the soul, which remains inaccessible to our reason. However, such possibility has not the same certainty with which we exclude the possibility that a unit to measure time and space can exist. These commentaries relate to a property of adequation as explained by Spinoza, that tells us how an adequation in the mind of a single person is not the highest, not absolute. 'Absolute ideas' are called so because we consider them to be secure for everybody.) [*Eds*]

A CERTAINTY, WHICH A PERSON DERIVES FROM HIS PERSONALITY ALONE IS FOR THAT PERSON NOT THE HIGHEST POSSIBLE DEGREE OF CERTAINTY—NEEDED IS A CONFIRMATION BY MEANS OF GENERAL VALIDITY. DREAMERS AND PSYCHIATRIC PATIENTS HAVE FEELINGS OF CERTAINTY ABOUT THE MOST ABSURD THINGS.
Modern psychology provides many examples here. When one suffers from fever, things can be absurd beyond description. The patient feels himself one and also two, small and also large, someone else and yet himself. The most fundamental principles of logic are not valid for him. A dreamer can feel the certainty that he is not dreaming in his dream. A megalomaniac is God, almighty and omnipresent, although he asks humbly to be set free, or he is super-wealthy and begs for a penny.

102. THE ENTITY CALLED "I", THE PERCEIVING SELF, IS THEREFORE NOT INSEPARABLE FROM REASON.
I underline that this is the only, immediately evident consequence. Other consequences lead to the deepest and most complicated questions. It remains undiscernible how a dreamer or psychiatric patient loses rationality and changes his personality. Perception without rationality is the sole indisputable observation here.

103. THE CONCEPT OF THE "I" IS BEST DESCRIBED AS: 'that what perceives'. ONLY SUCH A DESCRIPTION IS GENERALLY VALID, UNDERSTANDABLE AND NOT TOO UNDETERMINED. IT IS THUS THE ONLY DESCRIPTION WHICH ALLOWS LOGICAL ANALYSES. 'WHAT PERCEIVES' IS NOT THE SAME AS 'WHAT IS PERCEIVED', NOT THE SAME AS- NOR INSEPARABLE FROM REASON.
The words 'Person', 'I', 'Self', are used in accordance with our linguistic habits because they should not disturb the language patterns by arbitrary definitions. However, it would be great if one should learn to apply those three words to three different concepts, three grades: the particular, the plural en the relative in relation with three others: the general, the one and the absolute.

104. WHAT PERCEIVES IS NOT THE SAME AS SPACE, BECAUSE SPACE IS WHAT THE PERCIPIENT PERCEIVES. THE LATTER IS ALSO NOT INSEPARABLE FROM SPACE, BECAUSE THERE EXISTS NO NON-SPATIAL PERCEPTION.
I follow the linguistic tradition when articulating time and space as independent perceivable things, although the two are solely ways of perception. They possess as such shades of reality and one can speak about them in terms of 'things' like colors or sounds. Everybody knows that there exists perception without space-perception. Pleasure and displeasure, like most psychic sensations, are an example. There exist also unhealthy, abnormal and absurd perceptions of space. Many know the feeling that bodyparts, especially fingertips, are thick and thin at the same time, most often when falling asleep. All this points at an enormous continuity of the "I", in contrast to spatial perceptions.

105. WHAT PERCEIVES IS NOT THE SAME AS TIME. AND IT IS MOST PROBABLY ALSO NOT INSEPARABLE FROM THE PERCEPTION OF TIME.
The latter remark is less clear and difficult to illustrate with generally known facts. But, although our knowledge is more limited than the knowledge of the mysticists, it

is the most secure knowledge because we know that being *is.*[2] *One cannot deny this on logical grounds if one is acquainted with the many facts pertaining to abnormal time-perception or perception without awareness of time.*

Abnormal perception of time is for example in dreams about an entire life and unfolding in few seconds, as happens in cases of extreme tiredness of in fever, whereby days and weeks pass in a moment. There is furthermore the well-known phenomenon of a long dream that finishes with an external sensual impression which fits exactly to the dream. Example: one dreams to be hunting, one shoots and the shot is for instance that the door slams. And one knows by experience that time goes by faster in old age.

It is not so simple to understand that a faster course of time is a form of abnormal perception. We are used to deficient forms of perception which should measure time and time impressions wrongly. But the issue is much deeper, since long series of impressions and images of impressions can clench together in a short period of time—cause and explication follow in time like in the dream with the shot. Here are the mystical dimensions clear for everyone: perceiving a series of acts, experiences, scenes and conversations in dreams or other impressions in a thousandst of the time needed according to general criteria. And it is as ununderstandable and miraculous for a human intelligence as facts influencing facts or that we exist at many places at the same time, or that the infinite large and small exist, or an asymptotic approach.

Observing based on a notion of time does not surprise the attentive mind, although it is difficult to describe that phenomenon precisely. I think of the feelings of desire and discomfort that are connected with remembrances of in se *neutral facts but preceding a joyful or sad situation, for instance a travel interrupted by a death message. The travel may have been agreeable but each moment of that travel will awaken a feeling of unease so forceful as if the entire trip was painful even if the death message would have never been send. The memories about the trip are perceptions with time-awareness whereas the strange feeling of discomfort that accompanies all other memories is a perception without time-awareness. Such a feeling can prevail—only those who once experienced it can understand me, others may try to understand by means of association, but that is another explanation. An association is a causal connectivity, but does not lead back from consequence to cause. And is it not possible that a causal connection is made trough repeated memories? The feelings of pleasure or discomfort will glue each newly remembered detail.*

Of course there exists a connection in all that, but not a coherence of time. It is a premonition in the memorized image, clearly mystic for the attentive observant and as clear as real premonitions or the dream with the gunshot. An abnormal awareness of time is an often documented feeling[3]*, as if what was perceived at a*

[2] (Intellectus) res non tam sub duratione quam sub quadam specie aeternitatis percipit et numero infinito; vel potius, ad res percipiendas nec ad numerum nec ad durationem attendit. (Spinoza, *Tract. de Int. Em)*. Von Helmholtz has tried to distinguish *'knowing'* and *'everyday knowledge'* but I am afraid that this terminology will not be followed.

[3] Cf the novelists Dickens in *David Copperfield* and Couperus in *Extase.*

specific moment was already perceived long before. I know that feeling myself, but during the last years it has become more complicated so that it appears to me as if I had the abnormal sensation of time already long before. That illusion disappears after a short time. This 'doubling' of abnormal sensation refutes in my opinion all normal explanations—for instance that this would be a memory of an earlier life. But it certainly is the sign of an existence of the "I" beyond the frame of time.

(One finds references to comparable experiences in the works of poets and mystics, but these are of a higher order: Plato in Phaedrus, Porphyrius in The Life of Plotinus etc.) What I mentioned should fit to my arguments. It do not encounter many arguments telling me that the perceiving I is something different than the perception of time, most probably not inseparable and most variable. But I cannot but focus on stronger arguments, which the new psychology developed.

The indisputable reports on premonitions and predicting dreams or hallucinations are multiple and they become more and more every day. They are well-known in our history and recognized as such—the majority has never denied them. They are only disputed on theoretical and philosophical grounds, a priori. Well-founded and documented facts are not lacking, their number is far beyond reasonable demand. To compare, one should mention that ideas in geology, paleontology, ethnography and biology are often grounded on less secure data. But reinforced by the aprioristic character of the opposition, I want to show that there exist fundamental considerations that make these facts acceptable and expectable. The same is true in view of the perception of space related to so-called clairvoyance of telepathy. It is remarkable and a sign of higher and more absolute character of time as compared to space, that it is more difficult to dissolve the I from time than from space. Observations of facts beyond space do not give a mystical impression, whereas this is immediately the case with time-awareness. It is after all astonishing,, that time and space are always mentioned as ideas and facts of equal character and importance.

106. So the "I" which I described as "that what perceives" cannot be described without being perception itself, yet it is something else than perception and differs because being more unchangeable.

I keep the words of §103 intact because of the logic that is involved. It does not mean that the "I" or the "Self" is always something that cannot exist without perception. It means, that the "I" should not be understood as a person or a personal identity. The latter is, as the new psychology teaches us, often changeable and unstable. There exist persons with two or more personalities, even when one "I" feels often identical with the other. Also in those abnormal situations remains the idea, that 'what perceives' differs from 'what is perceived' because of its constancy.

107. The perceiving "I" is of all things the most absolute we know. (This follows from the §68 and 106)

We know nothing else than the "I", and the perceptions. There is no perception or observation that in degree of absoluteness remains beneath the perceiving. In other words: of all things our Self is nearest to God.

108. All men acknowledge or imply in their activities the secure existence of an "I". This specific existence is the most secure of all, and obtained without perception and reason.

This cannot be argued. Nobody can imagine the "I", nobody can claim that he perceives the "I". There is also no comparison here, nor reason (§65).

109. Knowledge providing the highest certainty can be called the highest knowledge. This highest knowledge thus includes neither perception nor reason.

That knowledge can be called Being as well as Knowing. It is the 'veritas sicuti se habet'[4] *as Thomas a Kempis formulated, the incomprehensible comprehension, the 'Visio sine Comprehensione'*[5]*, the 'Mysterium Magnum' of Boehme*[6]*, the 'knowing' in contrast to the 'know-how' of Von Helmholz. This highest certainty was called by Spinoza the 'essentia objectiva', which he tried to find in his 'adequate ideas' (§51).*

But he did not always consider the difference between imagining and being, or the fact that imagining already begins in thought formation, in each concept and each word, so that he ascribed this certainty also to thoughts and mathematical concepts. The latter include, however, 'multitude' and 'comparison'. Absolute certainty comes to an end with them, so that one can only speak of a 'limit' (§53) because there is reinforcement or impairment of certainty by means of more or less general evaluation on grounds mentioned in §53 and §101.

This may be nearly unthinkable as far as simple concepts are concerned, but I remind the reader that a mathematical system is constructed departing from the thesis according to which two parallel lines are able to cross in the infinite. I also quote, that the question whether space is finite seems denied by all astronomers[7] *so that there is perhaps no straight line but all lines are part of a circle with an extremely large radius. A counterproof is not feasible. If only one individual would live in the belief that there exists indeed a straight line, which would, even if infinitely extended, never encounter itself—in a world full of people who would not understand anything of it—then he could not feel the same certainty we feel, and Spinoza's adequation would him not hinder to start thinking that he suffers from delusions.*

But although one can doubt the authenticity of all perception and doubt the correctness of all concepts, nobody can doubt the existence of something that perceives. All mystics and philosophers made the distinction between these two types of knowledge: the absolute highest knowing, which IS*, and the always more or less relative knowledge, which thinks and imagines. Jean de la Croix speaks of "le dénuement de toutes images, mêmes les plus sublimes". And Jakob Boehme tells us: "Wer Mysterium Magnum findet, der findet alles darinnen, es darf keinen*

[4] The truth as is truly.

[5] Vision without Understanding.

[6] Der Geist ging hindurch als ein Blitz, und sahe im Grund der Ewigkeit. (Boehme)

[7] Prof. R. Ball in *Fortnightly Review.* (most probably 1894).

Buchstaben-beweis." Madame de la Mothe-Guyon says: "le propre de la foi est de dérober à l'ame toutes espèces, images, distinctions, multiplicité."[8]

110. This highest knowledge is nothing but the 'I' that perceives a something. So it is One.

111. The "I" is only an absolute. We cannot ascribe multiplicity nor changeability to it.

The 'I' is more than all observation and perception. (§107). Each determination of quantity and change would be grounded in perception. But then it, the "I", were no longer 'what perceives' but 'what is perceived'. The 'I' then withdraws so to say behind the perceived, the less absolute.

A negative formulation seems necessary here; seemingly positive conclusions lead immediately to absurdities. An example would be: the "I" is absolute, there are many "I"'s, so the absolute is a multitude. One has to remain loyal to what is concluded about the 'word-value'. Many "I"'s meant: many know what is perceived. But one cannot determine, nor imagine or think the absolute. This logical conclusion shows that 'that what perceives' cannot be ascribed multiplicity or changeability—one cannot call it otherwise than absolute! This analysis remains rigorous, even if one is aware that we have been working with infinite and thus unthinkable entities.

112. From §108 and §111 follow two dilemmas:
1. Either there is nothing, or there is something that cannot be called other than absolute.
2. Either we have no knowledge, or we are and know what cannot be named other than absolute.
a. If the existential modus, which is most certain, does not exist, that lesser certain modi do of course not exist.
b. If our most elevated certainty is not an encompassing form of knowledge, than lesser elevated forms do not exist.
c. It may be necessary to provide more clarifications here. Those who build most on reason are also inclined to distrust reason where imagination and sensitivity fail.
d. Naming things is often an activity like sticking labels on the waves of the sea. Yet, one has to proceed this way to liberate from errors. It invites to go on with reflecting upon one's actions, andto focus on denials where acknowledgments are not allowed.
e. These negative expressions of reasonable and relative thinking only keep a path open and shut erroneous path—a knowledge of higher order, the living reality in itself has to walk that path.

---

[8] "Non est, inquit Antonius, perfecta oration in qua se monachus, vel hoc ipsum orat, intelligit", Cassian, *Collat. 9 Cap 13)* Ed. 1894. The author of these *Collationes*, Johannes Cassianus (360-circa 435) established the Monastry of Saint Victoire near Marseille [The prayer, Antonius said, in which the monk understands himself or his prayer, is never perfect]

f. Speaking about 'more or less absolute' would be absurd in this context. Yet, that expression is necessary and acceptable. It focuses on a degree of properties which we must ascribe to the absolute as they are also negations—not many, not changeable.

g. In mathematics, one speaks in an analogue manner about larger and smaller infinite entities, $2/0 > 1/0$*, which are an absurdity for our (non-mathematical) understanding.*

h. Think again about the infinite gradation of all things. One cannot determine where our "I" begins, where our feelings become observations, and where the "I" remains just feeling or awareness. If one tries to observe how we perceive, withdraws the perceiving. It looses itself amidst infinite horizons. These remarks on the "I" are parallel to Spinoza's 'essentia objectiva', an expression not useful for our argument. How deep we enter reflection, one knows the percipient, the self, behind and beyond it all. For our reasoning it is like a recurring number, or the relation from radius to perimeter, infinite and never to be grasped. What we search is not in plurality or in change although our reflective thinking cannot be without those two because then there is neither imaging nor comparison.

i. For example, one could say that if all humans—also all animals and living beings gifted with perception—are and know what cannot be named other than one and unchangeable, then are *and* know *they all one and the same.*

k. That is surely unavoidable and indisputable. There is a sameness, which all are *and* know*—in an endless gradation of difference—and we call the 'Self'.*

l. Those who want to deny this with the argument that nobody can think or understand it, would also deny the existence of a parabola, or of a straight line, because nobody can think or understand that in infinity two such lines would approach without ever contacting.[9]

113. THE PRECEDING LINES OF §92 (ONE CANNOT EXCLUDE THE POSSIBILITY OF AN UNUNDERSTANDABLE PSYCHOLOGICAL SITUATION WITH THE SAME CERTAINTY AS PERTAINS TO A MEASURE FOR TIME AND SPACE) ARE SUFFICIENTLY EXPLAINED HEREWITH. IF THE "I" IS NOT INSEPARABLE FROM REASON AND NO MORE UNCHANGEABLE THAN ALL PERCEPTION, THEN REASON CAN NOT DECIDE ABOUT THE IMPOSSIBILITY OF UNKNOWN OR UNTHINKABLE IMPRESSIONS OR SITUATIONS OF THE "I".

It would mean that a less certain knowledge could judge the most certain. Whoever acknowledges this thesis, confirms that the 'mysterium' exists, that a human being is a mystic as well as logician or mathematician. But who refutes that thesis refutes at the same time all higher mathematics, based upon the mystery, not upon the incidentally unknown but upon the essentially unknowable. One should by no means confuse the mystical terms of the mathesis with the so-called imaginary quantities, empty symbols without sense, only useful in context, absurd verbal articulations. The infinite quantities must *exist in reality and are used as such. The inexistent quantities cannot exist.*

---

[9] Van Eeden may have meant here *hyperbola* instead of *parabola.*

Significs (1953); Significs and Philosophy (1922)

Gerrit Mannoury

Significs[1]

The science of psychical and linguistic relations, which should be differentiated into a psychological research of already existing relations (analytical significs), and the systemic extension and improvement of means of communication (synthetic significs).

Signific Principle of Relativity

The principle, that the meaning of a word and the scope of a concept are dependent upon (in relation to) other, psychologically associated contents.

Significs and Philosophy

Significs and Philosophy relate to each other like speaking and hearing, like thinking and understanding, and are thus two sides of one and the same activity of the human mind. Significs without philosophical foundation is an infertile play with words, and philosophy without signific reflection is a composite of idle dreams.

---

[1] SOURCE: G. MANNOURY: *Polair Psychologische Begripssynthese.* Bussum F. G, Kroonder 1953. p. 151 "Signifisch Glossarium"; –Id.-: G. MANNOURY: *Signifika en Wijsbegeerte.* Lecture in the Dutch Philosophical Society, Amsterdam, November 18, 1922. Published in: *Tijdschrift voor Wijsbegeerte,* 1923 Nr. 1. (Translation Dutch/English by Eds.)

G. Mannoury (deceased)

J.M. Broekman, L. Catá Backer (eds.), *Signs In Law - A Source Book*,
DOI 10.1007/978-3-319-09837-1_5

Both sciences have one and the same object of knowledge: human thought, will and sentiment; but their method, the beginning and finality of both is in absolute contrast to each other. Significs begins with a spoken or thought word and tries to grasp its mental cause and consequence, whereas philosophy takes it beginnings in the life of the human mind itself and does not appreciate in a word more than a means to communicate and determine the results of its investigation. Whoever would conclude from this, that the practitioner of significs and the philosopher go ultimately the same path albeit in contrasting directions, would show that he did not notice the imperfection of our entire work. If one could indeed say that a 'perfect' philosopher can find the only completely correct and appropriate word for a human thought, then the significian would be able from that very same word to reconstruct the essence and attributes of our thinking—but those presuppositions are *not* permitted. Word and thought are not *one* as they can in essence not be *two* and signific investigations do not consist in solving some algebraic equations with a determined number of unknowns! The one who analyzes words and the one who expresses thoughts can meet each other, can inform and perhaps assist each other, but they can never replace each other.

Philosophy has the task to express the life movements of humans in the same sense as significs enables humans to understand those expressions and take them as a form of guidance.

Significs [Encyclopedia Britannica] (1911)

Lady Victoria Welby

Significs

The term "Significs"[1] may be defined as the science of meaning or the study of significance, provided sufficient recognition is given to its practical aspect as a method of mind, one which is involved in all forms of mental activity, including that of logic.

In Baldwin's *Dictionary of Philosophy and Psychology* (1901–1905) the following definition is given: "1. Significs implies a careful distinction between (a) sense or signification, (*b*) meaning or intention and (*c*) significance or ideal worth." It will be seen that the reference of the first is mainly verbal (or rather sensual), of the second volitional, and of the third moral (e.g. we speak of some event' the significance of which cannot be overrated, and it would be impossible in such a case to substitute the 'sense' or the 'meaning' of such event, without serious loss).

Significs treats of the relation of the sign in the widest sense to each of these.

2. A proposed method of mental training aiming at the concentration of intellectual activities on that which is implicitly assumed to constitute the primary and ultimate value of every form of study, *i.e.* what is at present indifferently called its meaning or sense, its import or significance.... Significs as a science would centralize and co-ordinate, interpret, inter-relate and concentrate the efforts to bring out meanings in every form, and in so doing to classify the various applications of the signifying property clearly and distinctly. Since this dictionary was published, however, the subject has undergone further consideration and some development, which necessitate modifications in the definition given. It is clear that stress needs to be laid upon the application of the principles and method involved, not merely, though notably, to language, but to all other types of human function. There is need to insist

[1] Source: LADY VICTORIA WELBY, Article "What is Significs?" in: *The Encyclopedia Britannica* 1911 Vol. XXV, p. 78 ff.

L.V. Welby (deceased)

J.M. Broekman, L. Catá Backer (eds.), *Signs In Law - A Source Book*,
DOI 10.1007/978-3-319-09837-1_6

on the rectification of mental attitude and increase of interpretative power which must follow on the adoption of the significal view-point and method, throughout all stages and forms of mental training, and in the demands and contingencies of life.

In so far as it deals with linguistic forms, Significs includes "Semantics," a branch of study, which was formally introduced and expounded in 1897 by Michel Bréal, the distinguished French philologist, in his *Essai de sémantique.* In 1900 this book was translated into English by Mrs. Henry Cust, with a preface by Professor Postgate. M. Bréal gives no more precise definition than the following: "Extraire de la linguistique ce qui en ressort comme aliment pour la reflexion et—je ne crains pas de l'ajouter—comme régle pour notre propre langage, puisque chaqun de nous collabore pour son part a l'évolution de la parole humaine, voila ce qui mérite d'être mis en lumiére, voilà ce qui j'ai essayé de faire en ce volume." In the *Dictionary of Philosophy and Psychology* Semantics is defined as "the doctrine of historical word-meanings; the systematic discussion of the history and development of changes in the meanings of words." It may thus be regarded as a reform and extension of the etymological method, which applies to contemporary as well as to traditional or historical derivation. As human interests grow in constantly specialized directions, the vocabulary thus enriched is unthinkingly borrowed and re-borrowed on many sides, at first in definite quotation, but soon in unconscious or deliberate adoption. Semantics may thus, for present purposes, be described as the application of Significs within strictly philological limits; but it does not include the study and classification of the "Meaning" terms themselves, nor the attainment of a clear recognition of their radical importance as rendering, well or ill, the expressive value not only of sound and script but also of all fact or occurrence which demands and may arouse profitable attention.

The first duty of the significian is, therefore, to deprecate the demand for mere linguistic reform, which is indispensable on its own proper ground, but cannot be considered as the satisfaction of a radical need such as that now suggested. To be content with mere reform of articulate expression would be fatal to the prospect of a significantly adequate language; one characterized by a development only to be compared to that of the life and mind of which it is or should be naturally the delicate, flexible, fitting, creative, as also controlling and ordering, Expression.

The classified use of the terms of expression-value suggests three main levels or classes of that value—those of Sense, Meaning and Significance.

(a) The first of these at the outset would naturally be associated with Sense in its most primitive reference; that is, with the organic response to environment, and with the essentially expressive element in all experience. We ostracize the senseless in speech, and also ask "in what sense" a word is used or a statement may be justified.

(b) But "Sense" is not in itself purposive; whereas that is the main character of the word "Meaning," which is properly reserved for the specific sense, which it is *intended to convey.* (c) As including sense and meaning but transcending them in range, and covering the far-reaching consequence, implication, ultimate result or outcome of some event or experience, the term "Significance" is usefully applied.

These are not, of course, the only significal terms in common use, though perhaps sense and significance are on the whole the most consistently employed. We have also signification, purport, import, bearing, reference, indication, application, implication, denotation and connotation, the weight, the drift, the tenor, the lie, the trend, the range, the tendency, of given statements. We say that this fact suggests, that one portends, another carries, involves or entails certain consequences, or justifies given inferences. And finally we have the *value* of all forms of expression; that which makes worth while any assertion or proposition, concept, doctrine or theory; the definition of scientific fact, the use of symbolic method, the construction of mathematical formulae, the playing of an actor's part, or even art itself, like literature in all its forms.

The distinctive instead of haphazard use, then, of these and like terms would soon, both as clearing and enriching it, tell for good on our thinking. If we considered that any one of them were senseless, unmeaning, insignificant, we should at once in ordinary usage and in education disavow and disallow it. As it is, accepted idiom may unconsciously either illuminate or contradict experience. We speak, for instance, of *going through* trouble or trial; we never speak of *going through* well-being. That illuminates. But also we speak of the Inner or Internal as *alternative* to the spatial-reducing the spatial to the External. The very note of the value to the philosopher of the "Inner" as opposed to the "Outer" experience is that a certain example or analogue of enclosed space—a specified inside—is thus not measurable. That obscures. Such a usage, in fact, implies that, within enclosing limits, space sometimes ceases to exist. Comment is surely needless.

The most urgent reference and the most promising field for Significs lie in the direction of education. The normal child, with his inborn exploring, significating and comparing tendencies is so far the natural Significian. At once to enrich and simplify language would for him be a fascinating endeavour. Even his crudeness would often be suggestive. It is for his elders to supply the lacking criticism out of the storehouse of racial experience, acquired knowledge and ordered economy of means; and to educate him also by showing the dangers and drawbacks of uncontrolled linguistic, as other, adventure. Now the evidence that this last has virtually been hitherto left undone and even reversed, is found on careful examination to be overwhelming. Unhappily what we have so far called education has, anyhow for centuries past, ignored—indeed in most cases even balked—the instinct to scrutinize and appraise the value of all that exists or happens within our ken, actual or possible, and fittingly to express this.

Concerning the linguistic bearing of Significs, abundant evidence has been collected, often in quarters where it would least be expected:

1. Of general unconsciousness of confusion, defeat, antiquation and inadequacy in language.
2. A. Of admission of the fact in given cases, but plea of helplessness to set things right. B. Of protest in such cases and suggestions for improvement.
3. Of direct or implied denial that the evil exists or is serious, and of prejudice against any attempt at concerted control and direction of the most developed group of languages.

4. Of the loss and danger of now unworthy or misfitting imagery and of symbolic assertion, observance or rite, once both worthy and fitting.
5. Of the entire lack, in education, of emphasis on the indispensable means of healthy mental development, *i.e.* the removal of linguistic hindrances and the full exploitation and expansion of available resources in language.
6. Of the central importance of acquiring a clear and orderly use of the terms of what we vaguely call "Meaning"; and also of the active modes, by gesture, signal or otherwise, of conveying intention, desire, impression and rational or emotional thought.

It would be impossible of course in a short space to prove this contention. But the proof exists, and it is at the service of those who quite reasonably may deny its possible existence.

7. Finally and notably, of the wide-spread and all-pervading havoc at present wrought by the persistent neglect, in modern civilization, of the factor on which depends so much of our practical and intellectual welfare and advance.

As the value of this evidence is emphatically cumulative, the few and brief examples necessarily torn from their context, for which alone room could here be found, would only be misleading. A selection, however, from the endless confusions and logical absurdities which are not only tolerated, but taught without correction or warning to children may be given.

We speak of beginning and end as complementary, and then of "both ends"; but never of both beginnings. We talk of truth when we mean accuracy: of the literal ("it is written") when we mean the actual ("it is done"). Some of us talk of the mystic and his mysticism, meaning by this, enlightenment, dawn heralding a day; others (more justly) mean by it the mystifying twilight, darkening into night. We talk of the unknowable when what that is or whether it exists is precisely what we cannot know—the idea presupposes what it denies; we affirm or deny immortality, ignoring its correlative in-natality; we talk of solid foundations for life, for mind, for thought, when we mean the starting-points, foci. We speak of an eternal sleep when the very *raison d'être* of sleep is to end in awaking—it is not sleep unless it does; we appeal to a root as to an origin, and also figuratively give roots to the locomotive animal. We speak of natural "law" taking no count of the sub-attentive working in the civilized mind of the associations of the legal system (and the law court) with its decreed and enforced, but also revocable or modifiable enactments. Nature, again, is indifferently spoken of as the norm of all order and fitness, the desecration of which is reprobated as the worst form of vice and is even motherly in bountiful provision; but also as a monster of reckless cruelty and tyrannous mockery. Again, we use the word "passion": for the highest activity of desire or craving, while we keep "passive" for its very negation.

These instances might be indefinitely multiplied. But it must of course be borne in mind that we are throughout dealing only with the idioms and habits of the English language. Each civilized language must obviously be dealt with on its own merits.

The very fact that the significating and interpretative function is the actual, though as yet little recognized and quite unstudied condition of mental advance and human achievement, accounts for such a function being taken for granted and left to take care of itself. This indeed, in pre-civilized ages (since it was then the very condition of safety and practically of survival), it was well able to do. But the innumerable forms of protection, precaution, artificial aid and special facilities, which modern civilization implies and provides and to which it is always adding, have entirely and dangerously changed the situation. It has become imperative to realize the fact that through disuse we have partly lost the greatest as the most universal of human prerogatives. Hence arises the special difficulty of clearly showing at this stage that man has now of set purpose to recover and develop on a higher than the primitive plane the sovereign power of unerring and productive interpretation of a world which even to a living, much more to an intelligent, being, is essentially significant. These conditions apply not only to the linguistic but to all forms of human energy and expression, which before all else must be significant in the most active, as the highest, sense and degree. Man has from the outset been organizing his experience; and he is bound correspondingly to organize the expression of that experience in all phases of his purposive activity, but more especially in that of articulate speech and linguistic symbol. This at once introduces the volitional element; one which has been strangely eliminated from the very function which most of all needs and would repay it.

One point must here, however, be emphasized. In attempting to inaugurate any new departure from habitual thinking, history witnesses that the demand at its initial stage for unmistakably clear exposition, must be not only unreasonable but futile. This of course must be typically so in the case of an appeal for the vital regeneration of all modes of Expression and especially of Language, by the practical recognition of an ignored but governing factor working at its very inception and source. In fact, for many centuries at least, the leading civilizations of the world have been content to perpetuate modes of speech once entirely fitting but now often grotesquely inappropriate, while also remaining content with casual changes often for the worse and always liable to inconsistency with context. This inevitably makes for the creation of a false standard both of lucidity and style in linguistic expression.

Still, though we must be prepared to make an effort in assuming what is virtually a new mental attitude, the effort will assuredly be found fully worth making. For there is here from the very first a special compensation. If, to those whose education has followed the customary lines, nowhere is the initial difficulty of moving in a new direction greater than in the one termed Signifies, nowhere, correspondingly, is the harvest of advantage more immediate, greater, or of wider range and effort.

It ought surely to be evident that the hope of such a language; of a speech which shall worthily express human need and gain in its every possible development in the most efficient possible way, depends on the awakening and stimulation of a sense which it is our common and foremost interest to cultivate to the utmost on true and healthy lines. This may be described as the immediate and insistent sense of the pregnancy of things, of the actual bearings of experience, of the pressing and cardinal importance, as warning or guide, of that experience considered as indicative; a

Sense realized as belonging to a world of what for us must always be the Sign of somewhat to be inferred, acted upon, used as a mine of pertinent and productive symbol, and as the normal incitant to profitable action. When this germinal or primal sense—as also the practical starting-point, of language—has become a reality for us, reforms and acquisitions really needed will naturally follow as the expression of such a recovered command of fitness, of boundless capacity and of perfect coherence in all modes of expression.

One objection, however, which before this will have suggested itself to the critical reader, is that if we are here really dealing with a function, which must claim an importance of the very first rank and affect our whole view of life, practical and theoretical, the need could not have failed long ago to be recognised and acted upon. And indeed it is not easy in a few words to dispose of such an objection and to justify so venturesome an apparent paradox as that with which we are now concerned. But it may be pointed out that the special development of one faculty always entails at least the partial atrophy of another. In a case like this the principle typically applies. For the main human acquirement has been almost entirely one of logical power, subtle analysis, and co-ordination of artificial means. In modern civilization the application of these functions to an enormous growth of invention of every kind has contributed not a little to the loss of the swift and direct sense of *point:* the sensitiveness as it were of the compass-needle to the direction in which experience was moving. Attention has been forcibly drawn elsewhere; and moreover, as already pointed out, the natural insight of children, which might have saved the situation, has been methodically silenced by a discipline called educative, but mainly suppressive and distortive.

The biological history of Man has been, indeed, a long series of transmutations of form to subserve higher functions. In language he has so far failed to accomplish this. There has even in some directions been loss of advantage already gained. While his nature has been plastic and adaptive, language, the most centrally important of his acquirements, has remained relatively rigid, or what is just as calamitous, fortuitously elastic. There have been notable examples—the classical languages—of the converse process. In Greek and Latin, Man admirably controlled, enriched, varied, significated his expressions to serve his mental needs. But we forbear ourselves to follow and better this example. All human energies have come under orderly direction and control except the one in which in a true sense they all depend. This fatal omission, for which defective methods of education are mainly responsible, has disastrously told upon the mental advance of the race. But after all, we have here a comparatively modern neglect and helplessness. Kant, for instance, complained bitterly of the defeating tendency of language in his day, as compared with the intelligent freedom of the vocabulary and idiom of the "classical" Greek, who was always creating expression, moulding it to his needs and finding an equally intelligent response to his efforts, in his listeners and readers—in short, in his public.

Students, who are prepared seriously to take up this urgent question of the application of Significs in education and throughout all human spheres of interest, will soon better any instruction that could be given by the few who so far have tentatively striven to call attention to and bring to bear a practically ignored and unused method.

But by the nature of the case they must be prepared to find that accepted language, at least in modern European forms, is far more needlessly defeating than they have supposed possible: that they themselves in fact are continually drawn back, or compelled so to write as to draw back their readers, into what is practically a hotbed of confusion, a prison of senseless formalism and therefore of barren controversy.

It can hardly be denied that this state of things is intolerable and demands effectual remedy. The study and systematic and practical adoption of the natural method of Significs can alone lead to and supply this. Significs is in fact the natural response to a general sense of need which daily becomes more undeniably evident. It founds no school of thought and advocates no technical specialism. Its immediate and most pressing application is, as already urged, to elementary, secondary and specialized education. In recent generations the healthy sense of discontent and the natural ideals of interpretation and expression have been discouraged instead of fostered by a training, which has not only tolerated but perpetuated the existing chaos. Signs, however, are daily increasing that Signifies, as implying the practical recognition of, and emphasizing the true line of advance in, a recovered and enhanced power to interpret experience and adequately to express and apply that power, is destined, in the right hands, to become a socially operative factor of the first importance.

Reference

Lady Welby, "Sense, Meaning and Interpretation," in *Mind* (January and April 1896), *Grains of Sense* (1897), *What is Meaning?* (1903); Professor F. Tönnies, "Philosophical Terminology" (Welby Prize Essay), *Mind* (July and October 1899 and January 1900), also article in *Jahrbuch,* & c., and supplements to *Philosophische Terminologie* (December 1906); Professor G. F. Stout, *Manual of Psychology* (1898); Sir T. Clifford Allbutt's Address on "Words and Things" to the Students' Physical Society of Guy's Hospital (October 1906); Mr. W. J. Greenstreet's "Recent Science" articles in the *Westminster Gazette* (November 15, 1906, and January 10, 1907). (V. W.)

Editorial 1: Jacob Israel De Haan, the First Legal Semiotician

Jan M. Broekman and Larry Catá Backer

Law was not of central interest for the first developments of semiotics, but language fulfilled this role. Interest in semiotic topics, such as signs, was always embedded in linguistics. What today is known as *semiotics* was in the beginning of the 20th century called *significs*. The *sign* is the common denomination of significs and semiotics, but the understanding of language, in particular the uniqueness of a *word* as the main component of language, makes the difference. Where else could this be more relevant than in law, which relates to language in ways no other interpretations of reality ever do? Such considerations created the climate for the reception of new philosophical insights as formulated by Charles S. Peirce, Lady Welby, and at a relatively small distance Bertrand Russell and Ludwig Wittgenstein, as well as Martin Buber and other philosophical minds at the beginning of the 20th century The Dutch poet, psychologist and philosopher Frederik van Eeden furthered Lady Welby's influence on the European continent. Van Eeden established on May 21, 1922 the Dutch Signific Circle (Signifische Kring)—almost two years after Jacob Israel de Haan (1881–1924), one of his best friends, had been assassinated. De Haan was the first legal semiotician the world has known. The context has been roughly outlined in the first chapter, so that some biographical data may suffice to understand the rationale to offer here the first English translation of De Haan's inaugural lecture in Amsterdam 1916 as well as several fragments of his Amsterdam PhD dissertation. These texts form in hindsight an important contribution to legal semiotics and are a stimulus for further research on the origins of legal semiotics. The larger scientific context of the Signific Movement in the

J.M. Broekman (✉)
Dickinson School of Law, Penn State University, Carlisle, PA, USA
e-mail: jmb56@dsl.psu.edu

L. Catá Backer
Departments of Law and International Affairs, Penn State University, University Park, PA, USA
e-mail: lcb11@psu.edu

J.M. Broekman, L. Catá Backer (eds.), *Signs In Law - A Source Book*,
DOI 10.1007/978-3-319-09837-1_7

Netherlands (much wider than the rather late activities of the "Kring"), which is a cornerstone of our contemporary insights in legal semiotics, is outlined in Susan Petrilli's path-breaking study on Lady Welby's works, H. Walter Schmitz' German study (1985), which was translated into Dutch in 1990, and the Dutch Legal Historian G.C.J.J. van den Bergh, who wrote 1996 the only English article on De Haan and edited some of his legal-signific texts in Dutch.[1]

"Betere taal is beter recht"—"better language is better law"—was De Haan's slogan which bridged the abyss between law and linguistics in the heart of significs/semiotics. That motive was central in his Amsterdam inaugural lecture in legal significs/semiotics, based on a variety of personal experiences and their social reflection: de Haan wrote social-realistic sketches and novels as well as poetry. His novels and other writings caused a considerable row (he wrote the first publicly gay novel) his poetry was honored with a prestigious two-volume collection, his social and political critical attitude made him in 1912 visit a number of prisons in tsarist Russia to investigate their inhabitants' life situation. He reported their situation in a 1913 publication entitled: *In Russische gevangenissen* [In Russian Prisons] and initiated political moves to have France and the UK protest against Russia on that issue. An *Amnesty International* publication qualified him later as precursor of that organization. But we must conclude in hindsight that his approximately fifty(!) legal and philosophical publications between 1910 and 1922 with focus on legal signific/semiotics constitute the greatest part of his work. These make him the precursor of legal semiotics, although Dutch jurists of his days did not pay much attention to such understandings of their work and their discourse/language. And until the above-mentioned studies of Petrilli and others, there has not been any translation work done or any other studies on international (semiotics) level. Many great themes for today's world and its semiotic relevance are to be initiated, inspired by De Haan's work. A precise study should be initiated of the *Amnesty International* work, together with publications based on new insights inspired by his philosophy of legal significs/semiotics. This could clarify various aspects of the differences and identities between significs and contemporary semiotics. It could also inspire to pay elaborate attention to the relations between semiotics and politics, which is an often-neglected theme—in particular with regard to today's forms of political activism. De Haan's own activism was excessive: after leaving Amsterdam in 1918 and settling in Jeruzalem, he gradually moved from Zionist to anti-zionist, spied for the British secret service and sympathized with the father of King Hussain. He became in 1924 the victim of the first political murder in Palestine.

[1] Susan Petrilli: *Signifying and Understanding. Reading the Works of Victoria Welby and the Signific Movement*, De Gruyter Mouton, The Hague/Berlin, 2009; Ch. 4.8, p. 748ff.; H. Walter Schmitz: *Verständigungshandlungen—eine wissenschaftshistorische Rekonstruktion der Anfänge der signifische Bewegung in den Niederlanden 1892–1926,* Bonn 1985, Dutch: *De Hollandse Significa. Een reconstructie van de geschiedenis van 1892 tot 1926,* (Transl. J. van Nieuwstadt) Assen/Maastricht 1990; C.G.J.J. van den Bergh: "Jacob Israel de Haan's Legal Significs" in: *International Journal for the Semiotics of Law,* 1996, Vol. IX, no. 25, p. 81f. and G.C.J.J. van den Bergh: *De taal zegt meer dan zij verantwoorden kan.* [Language tells us more than she can justify], Ars Aequi Libri, Nijmegen 1994.

Another type of research should be inspired by the many remarks of De Haan on the word and its position and function in language. On the one hand, De Haan treats a word as a source of semiotic uncertainty, on the other as a basis for all language constructions, in particular the word being a particle of each thinkable type of human linguistic expressiveness. Aspects of this precious theme are manifold: in the significs milieu were rich considerations of Martin Buber, Frederik van Eeden and others, in the semiotics milieu were ideas reaching from Peirce and Searle to analytical philosophers[2]. In general, we conclude that there should grow a new study of the origins of legal semiotics at an international level. Van den Bergh is correct to mention how "at least amongst students of semiotics of law he (De Haan) still deserves to be remembered and studied."[3]

[2] See Jan M. Broekman: "On the Origins of Legal Semiotics" in: *Journal of Comparative Law*, Vol. VII, No. 1, 2012, p. 26 ff;—id.—: "Buber's Grondwoord" in: *Wijsgerig Perspectief op Maatschappij en Wetenschap*, XVIII, No. 3, 1977.p 51 f;—id.—"Betere taal, beter recht. Over de rechtskundige significa van Jacob Israel de Haan", in: *Wijsgerig Perspectief op Maatschappij en Wetenschap*, 1979/1980, Jrg. XX, p. 48f; G.C.J.J. van den Bergh & Jan M. Broekman: *Recht en Taal.* Preadvies Koninklijke Notariële Broederschap, Kluwer 1979, p. 80f.

[3] Van den Bergh, "Jacob Israel de Haan's Legal Significs", *IJSL* 1996, p. 93.

Essence and Task of Legal Significs

Jacob Israël De Haan

Let me begin this first lesson with a word of apology about the fact that I accepted a new private teaching post and thereby multiply the number of lessons, which this High School provides. But we consider a Higher Education incomplete as long as a subject like significs is lacking. We consider it desirable that the significs of any particular science be taught in addition to the general significs. This will bring us to the understanding of Sign and Meaning. Those lessons will motivate us to distinguish Sign and Meaning constantly as separated and as un-separated. I will thus satisfy the need for education in significs only in a limited manner. But I hope to do something good with my classes. When a poet receives a share in the Highest Education available, which subject he will enhance better than the knowledge of language? More than anyone, the Poet experiences the World "comme un discours du Verbe, dont chaque être était une parole".[1] Poetry, Science and Wisdom are not separated.[2] On the contrary, the three have always been united in the achievements of the great poets. The latter know that "Poetry is more powerful as the Mind is

Source: JACOB ISRAEL DE HAAN: *Wezen en taak der rechtskundige significa,* First public lecture in Legal Significs at the University of Amsterdam, Tuesday October 31, 1916.
Published by: van Kampen, 1916, 32 pp.
Parallel printing in *De Gids,* Nr 80, 1916, p. 281—306.
Reprint of the latter in 1994: *Ars Aequi Libri,* Nijmegen 1994: "De taal zegt meer dan zij verantwoorden kan" [Language articulates more than it can justify], Ed.: Prof. Mr. G.C.J.J. van den Bergh. (Translation Dutch/English: Eds.)

[1] Emile Male: *Art religieux du XIIIe siècle en France* (Paris 1898), [Religious art in the xii century] quoted by Dr A. Pit: De overgang van 'Gothiek' tot 'Renaissance' en van Realisme tot Idealisme, [The transition from Gothic to Renaissance and from Realism to Idealism] in: *Tijdschrift voor Wijsbegeerte,* [Journal of Philosophy] I, 1907, p. 347.

[2] Frederik van Eeden, Poezie, Wijsbegeerte en Mathesis [Frederik van Eeden, Poetry, Philosophy and Mathesis] in: *De Beweging* II 1906, part III, p. 21.

J.I. De Haan (deceased)

J.M. Broekman, L. Catá Backer (eds.), *Signs In Law - A Source Book,*
DOI 10.1007/978-3-319-09837-1_8

sharper".[3] And "the best word of a poet is also a word of wisdom".[4] Elsewhere I have written: "To the great practitioners of the Significs belong the scientifically trained Poets. Their passionate love for language will be tamed by the stern demands of scientific research, but this does not reduce their power".[5] Passion tamed by discipline: behold, this is the essence of my lessons!

The human mind is the ever-staggering balance of two forces. The first I would like to see as a *centrifugal* force. This is the need to increase the knowledge of the facts. The second I see as a *centripetal* force. This is the need for reflection, for unity. "No peace without unity".[6] It follows that experience and reflection, which is: science and wisdom, are not separated. Experience and reflection lead to the insight that experience is in fact the experience of that which itself is not experienced, but only achieved by reflection. And that reflection is a reflection of what itself is not sensible, but experienced. However, experience and reflection can be distinguished and in so doing I say that my lessons will focus more on reflection than on experience. They do not focus on the science of law, but on the concept of law. They are not on linguistics, but on the concept of language. I seek the unity of science and wisdom in concordance with the natural ability of my mind in the philosophical practice of the language of the law and in legal significs. The question can be raised whether the practice of legal significs belongs to the task of the lawyer. Prof. Mr. P. Scholten, who formulated this question, seems to answer in the negative. But he does not do this without some excellent signific remarks, which make me believe that also Prof. Scholten understands the great importance of a systematic scientific and philosophical practice of legal language for applied legal science. I refer to where Prof. Scholten discusses the value of the word "legal person" in saying: "when one asks to what extent the concept of legal person is real, then one asks more than legal science can answer." It is for legal science only a question, how it can master its given substance, so that it forms *its* concepts accordingly. If these are useful, then it should not give up its conceptual activity with the argument that they are not real. A legal epistemology should continue to investigate its relation to reality. The question about the *essence* of a legal person is not a question of a juridical nature. However, this is not different from many other concepts; what is behind a subjective or an objective right and behind many other concepts, is not to be determined by jurisprudence.

"One thing, however, one can learn from most of the opponents of the concept: it is not permitted to draw conclusions about the existence of legal rules on the basis

---

[3] Nico van Suchtelen: Het Al-enig Leven, een dichterlijk-wijsgerige Geloofsbelijdenis, [The All-Eternal Life, a poetic-philosophical Confession] in: *De Beweging,* III 1907, p. 15: "Woord en Werkelijkheid" [Word and Reality].

[4] Prof. G.J.P.J.Bolland: in *Tijdschrift voor Wijbegeerte* I 1907, p. 117.

[5] *Rechtskundige Significa en hare toepassing op de begrippen "Aansprakelijk, Verantwoordelijk, Toerekeningsvatbaar",* [Legal Significs and her application to the terms 'Liable, Responsible, Accountable], *Amsterdam 1916, p. 81.*

[6] ^Prof. Dr. T. Cannegieter: Het mysterie der tegenstellingen in 's menschen zieleleven, [The mystery of oppositions in human psychic life] in: *Teylers Theologisch Tijdschrift,* III 1905, p. 362.

of their supposed reality or fictional character. It is under all circumstances a useful concept and a matter of expediency for the legislator as well as for the judge or commentator of interpretations. Other factors than the question what a legal person "really is" are the deciding factor".[7] However, the question of whose task it is to practice legal significs seems no longer important if it is accepted that the language of law needs to be improved, and that this improvement can be achieved by practicing legal significs. Complaints about the limited and modest power of expression of legal language are numerous, in the Netherlands as well as elsewhere. In other publications, I have given numerous examples of those complaints[8] so that I limit myself to one further example, the complaint of Prof. Mr. I. Henri Hijmans, saying: "Of all applied sciences, legal science groans most under the compulsion of language. A physicist or chemist performs his experiments and the physician put his knife in the wound—if they want to, independent from their science and its language. But the lawyer encounters his language always and everywhere: it speaks to him from the statues, it follows him in his investigations, it is for him the only means to act. For that reason, language became an object of worship for the lawyers: its words, in particular its specific terms, are for him the magic means to form and sustain his judgment". And, what is more: "Now the question is how are we to be set free from the prison which language has built around us with its words and concepts? What sets us free from our prison-cell?" And thus he writes: "The answer is very simple. Liberation supplies already … the awareness of our imprisonment".[9] But this awareness is nothing but a reflective notion of Language and of our relation to Language, that is: significs.

Language suffers more than Law from its own incapacity. Actual linguistics is neither supported by philosophy nor by reflection. There exists too much science and too little understanding of language. Even the great publications of Jacob van Ginneken do not provide a reflective unity of both.[10] Even if he calls his "Principles" also an "Essay de synthèse" and his book was published in a series with the name "Bibliothèque de philosophie expérimentale" [Library of experimental philosophy].[11] The actual linguists do not contemplate the relation between general linguistics and the concept of language. Prof. Dr. C. Lecoutere, under the strong influence of Dr. Van Ginneken, proclaims that a philosophy of language is unnecessary and even

[7] Mr. C. Asser's *Handleiding tot de beoefening van het Nederlandsch Burgerlijk Recht*, [Manual for the practice of Dutch Civil Law] Mr. Paul Scholten, (Ed.) Vol. I, 1912(4), p. 621–622.

[8] *Rechtskundige Significa en hare toepassing op de begrippen "Aansprakelijk, Verantwoordelijk, Toerekeningsvatbaar", Amsterdam 1916, p. 86.* See also: Hermann Weck: *Die Sprache im deutschen Recht. Berlin* [The language in German Law] *1913.*

[9] *Het recht der werkelijkheid.* [The law of reality] Haarlem 1910, p. 24–26.

[10] *Principes de linguistique psychologique,* [Principles of psychological linguistics] Amsterdam 1907, and *Handboek der Nederlandsche Taal,* [Manual of the Dutch language] 2 Vols. Nijmegen 1913–1914.

[11] "Philosophie expérimentale" is an expression as astonishing and as normal as "philosophical experience".

dangerous for linguistics.[12] As if a science could ever unfold without its wisdom, and for example, a philosophy of law could ever replace a general theory of law, or vice versa.[13]

In the framework of the subject of this lesson, I suggested that reflection upon language is not less necessary than a science of language. The Essence of legal significs is not in experience but in reflection. But the task of legal significs is not a result of reflection but of experience. And the significian will be brought to continuous reflection through experience. It is, as Dr J. D. Bierens de Haan formulated in the first issue of the Tijdschrift voor Wijsbegeerte [Philosophical Journal]: "The power language has over matter, invites philosophical reflection".[14] A lost life finds itself again in reflection upon the Word.

We understand at this moment the *Essence* of legal significs as a philosophical reflection upon the power of legal language over the Law. And thus we understand the *Task* of legal significs as an attempt to break the power of legal language over the Law by means of Language itself.

Legal significs studies the meanings of the words of legal language.[15] This does not imply that I will lose myself during the forthcoming lessons in an endless description of the multiple meanings of the words of legal language. That would be a silly science. We will try to select and sort the multiple meanings of legal expressions in such a manner, that we can access the essence of each word and of each word class. This will teach us to better understand the words of others and to better use our own words. We will develop the concept of "meaning" by means of studying the meanings of words that belong to the language of law.[16] It is clear that the meaning of the word "meaning" is extremely important for each significian.[17] Scientific publications and sentences underline continuously "the meaning" of this or that word, as if the meaning of the word "meaning" were simple and easy. But the

---

[12] *Inleiding tot de taalkunde en de Geschiedenis van het Nederlandsch,* [Introduction to the linguistics and history of the Dutch language] Vol. I, Ch VII, Brussels 1905, p. 124–125.

[13] Prof. mr. dr. A.A.H.Struycken, *Het Rechtsbegrip,* [The Concept of Law] Leiden 1903, p 1–3, 23, 48, 65. Prof. Mr. Dr. R. Kranenburg, *De beteekenis der rechtsvergelijking voor de rechtsphilosophie,* [The meaning of comparative law for the philosophy of law] Groningen 1915.

[14] Een wijsgeerige beweging in Nederland [A philosophical movement in the Netherlands], *Tijdschrift voor Wijsbegeerte,* I, 1907, p. 15 and Het levende woord, [The living word] in *Tijdschrift voor Wijsbegeerte,* III, 1909, p. 280.

[15] In the prospectus of the University, legal significs is described as "Significatio verborum eorum quae ad jus pertinent."

[16] Also a significian searches for norms pertaining to the use of language. A description of an infinite reality is not possible in language, see: Prof. Dr. Ph. Kohnstamm: Transcendenteel idealisme, [Transcendental Idealism] in: *Tijdschrift voor Wijsbegeerte,* I, (1907), p. 28,43. As mechanics does not describe movements, so significs does not describe meanings, nor history or reality. Significs, mechanics and history research the essence in meanings, movements and reality. See: Dr. A. Rutgers van der Loeff, Het wezenlijke in de Geschiedenis, [The essential in History] in: *Onze Eeuw* IX, (1909), p. 353–370.

[17] Frits Mauthner: *Beiträge zu einer Kritik der Sprache,* [Contributions to a Criticism of Language] Stuttgart 1901, II, Chapter 7, p. 263. See also: Lady Victoria Welby: *Significs and Language,* London 1911, p. 37.

opposite is true. The concept of "meaning" is the most important but also most difficult concept of the entire significs. To develop a good understanding of meaning, we should loosen the ties between a habitual, unreflective worldview and understanding of language, which Language itself leads us to accept. This is because Language, as scientific language, is highly metaphoric and materialistic. It is true what is often said: "in essence and character language is entirely metaphoric".[18] But for exactly that reason the value of our linguistic images is decisive for our language. What is the value of our most cherished linguistic images?

Let us suppose that we live in two worlds, one being material and one being spiritual. It means that we accept that "moving" is something else than "thinking" and "walking" something else than then "willing".[19] We could accept the idea that we live in those two worlds if we reflect continuously on the fact that the material is only the material of the spiritual. And so is the spiritual only the spiritual of the material. Our thinking thinks that both worlds are continuously united and separated, and exactly because of this it is truly a thinking. All our words with a spiritual value are metaphors of words with only a sensual value. Some of them show their sensual roots very clearly for instance "understanding".[20] Other do not show their sensual roots, for instance in the case of "thinking". But because of that, the second type of words is not yet totally spiritual. "We look to the material for metaphors of the mental".[21] Let us now presuppose that all words with a spiritual value were original words and that all words with a sensual value were metaphors of the words with a spiritual value; as in our time the entire spiritual life is materialized, the entire material life would then be spiritualized.[22]

At this moment are spiritual sciences all completely materialized through materialized metaphors. I cannot prove this in this first lesson *in extenso*, not even for all spiritual sciences. I would like to give one example of a complete materialization of our metaphysics. Many languages contrast the material world against the spiritual by means of the expression "outer world".[23] Against this "outer world" one poses the spiritual as the world of "inner" experiences. Such linguistic images transfer our epistemology into a science, which "places 'the perceived' in an independent observational world, which is separated from a proper ego,"[24] The very best minds of our

---

[18] Albert Verwey in *De Beweging,* VI, January 1910, p. 99 (see note 2); Michel Bréal, *Essai de sémantique,* Paris 1897, p. 3: "les langues indo-européennes sont condamnées au language figuré."

[19] In Hebrew, 'walking' and 'desiring' have the same stem letters; see Ahrun Marcus: *Barsilai, Sprache als Schrift der Seele; Ebräisches Wurzel-Wörterbuch,* [Barsilai, Language as Writing of the Soul: Hebraic Dictionary of Hebraic Stem-words] Krakau 1908.

[20] Dr. G.A. van den Bergh van Eysenga: Hegel en de Stoa, [Hegel and the Stoa] in *Tijdschrift voor Wijsbegeerte, II, 1908, p. 253–255.*

[21] Lady Victoria Welby: *Significs and Language,* London 1911, p. 46. The words with which we indicate our feelings are sensual. Dr. J. van Ginneken: Het gevoel in Taal en Woordkunst, [The senses in Language and Poetry] in *Leuvensche Bijdragen,* X, 1912–1913, p. 1–156.

[22] Lady Welby, *Significs and Language,* p. 46.

[23] Lady Welby, *Significs and Language,* p. 22.

[24] Prof. L.E.J.Brouwer: *Leven, Kunst en Mystiek,* [Life, Art and Mysticism] Delft 1905, p. 60 f.

time discover the Truth that the center of gravity has to be displaced from what is perceived towards/into the perceiver. "Copernicus brought the rotation of the celestial bodies to the earth; the same will now be put in our own body." But Language remained pre-Copernican, and prevents the appearance of the Truth in most powerful manner.[25] Prof. Brouwer mentions Goethe and Schopenhauer as an example in his *Leven, Kunst en Mystiek* [Life, Art and Mysticism]: "They began to see the colors as a polar split of the eye's activity, despite Newton's theory in which the light beams were dissolved in the medium, and thus they showed more sensitivity for the Truth, the delusion of all times." Let me show you a breakthrough in a poet of my people, R. Salomo ben Jehuda, named Ibn Gabirol, who mentions in the Song "Crown of Splendor": "the Light welling up from his Eye that forms the World without any piece of equipment."[26]

This is an example of how the materialization of Language compels the non-reflective individual to understand the world of material objects as an independent datum that is external to the perceiving mind. But Reflection thinks Being in the form of "I" and "Other", each without specific content, but separated and united as Being.

The materialization of Language brings the non-reflective individual to see Language as belonging to a something that is external to the thinking mind. Language exists beyond words and is independent from the speaker. One takes those words when needed and forms sentences with them, just like a bricklayer takes stones in his hand and builds a brick wall.[27] I quote here the poet and philosopher Nico van Suchtelen,[28] who said: "With language we acquired an instrument for thinking in a more concentrated and encompassing manner. The mind fixates by means of the word—a concretely moving moment of life as if it were a constant, abstract entity that could be used for, as it were, mathematical operations. Our thinking seems objective through language, and its movements externalized into fixated abstractions. So we think of words as concepts, symbols of something external, which we use as ready-made objects, as instruments, which we did not create ourselves and we can freely dispose of. We are so much used to this instrumental use of language, that we never ever reflect upon the fact that our verbal thought-formation seems only a sort of calculating with fixated feelings and thoughts, an algebra of life, a calculation that can only be of value for us if we can in the end

---

25 Lady Welby, *What is Meaning?* London 1903, Ch. VI. Did the earth already turn around the sun *before* Copernicus? See: Prof. L.E.J.Brouwer: *Over de grondslagen der wiskunde,* [The Foundations of Mathematics] Amsterdam 1907, p. 104; Prof. Dr. Ph. Kohnstamm: Psychologie en logica, [Psychology and Logic] in *Tijdschrift voor wijsbegeerte,* I, 1907, p. 385.

26 Salomo ben Jehuda, Strophe 11, 5&6. See M.H. van Campen: Oude en nieuwe Joodsche Dichtkunst, [Jewish Poetry, Old and New] in: *De Gids,* 1916, p. 534–537; see also: J.van Ginneken: *Principes de linguistique psychologique,* Amsterdam 1907, §250.

27 Dr. C. Lecoutere: *Inleiding tot de Taalkunde en de Geschiedenis van het Nederlandsch,* [Introduction to the Linguistics and History of the Dutch language] Brussels 1905, p. 74–75.

28 Het Al-Eenig Leven, [The All-Unique Life] in: *De Beweging,* 1907, p. 7–8.

dissolve the abstract and fixated forms into the concretely fluid life-forms where they came from."[29]

Reflection thinks being in the form of "I" and "Other", each without specific content, but separated and united as Language. This means: language is not only personal, and language is not solely impersonal. Language is both at the same time, that is: neither of the two. Language is not subjective, and not objective. But like an ejector, it is ejective.[30]

A word has thus never the same meaning for two different individuals. This is even true for a speaker and a hearer in the same conversation, not even "when they live in 'the same shades of will'"[31] And, what is more, a word has not continuously the same meaning in the hands of the same user. A word never carries exactly the same meaning twice. The expression "the" meaning of a word is incorrect and misleading. That is also the case with the claim, that the word "has" a meaning. A word "has" no meaning or meanings; it "is" united with an infinite number of meanings by something that cannot be perceived and that composes a word from an infinite number of meanings. Our thinking separates the words in their numerous meanings as it unites those meanings to a word. Thinking cannot split or unite the continuous and the discrete, but it can only separate and unite *at the same time.* The word also splits in numerous meanings and unites these again in that one word.[32]

No linguist has ever expressed the concept of the Word in a purer sense than the mathematician and philosopher G. Mannoury: "The word is reciprocal and thus equal; it is relation and thus difference. It is the act of the speaker and the act of the

[29] Dr. Van Suchtelen, chemist, used here an excellent linguistic image. The mathematician Prof. Brouwer formulates the same thought: "Do not interpret mathematical formulae as independent truth, but as a means to remember as economically as possible how in one building another is built", in: *Over de grondslagen der wiskunde*, [The Foundations of Mathematics] Amsterdam 1907, p. 176.

[30] So, thinking in words is ejective. That insight could for instance finish the discussions between Prof. Brouwer and Prof. Kohnstamm about the earth turning around the sun. Is there a difference between a conviction and a truth, which means: is psychology logic? Prof. Kohnstamm objectifies the truth and Prof. Brouwer subjectifies her. But the objective is the objective of the subjective and the subjective is the subjective of the objective. Both can only be thought as united and separated. It means that thinking in words is ejective. Language articulates more than it can justify. We should not say more than: sun—earth—turning—I. See: Prof. Dr Ph. Kohnstamm: Psychology en Logica, [Psychology and Logics] in *Tijdschrift voor Wijsbegeerte,* I, 1907, p. 385–426, and Prof. Dr. G. Heymans, De psychologische methode in de logica, [The psychological method in logics] in *Tijdschrift voor Wijsbegeerte* II, 1908, p. 207–238. In a conference of Prof. Dr. Chantepie de la Saussaye about "De Christelijke Godsidee", [The Christian Idea of God] a participant, Dr. Klomp, uttered his astonishment at having heard the idea that a truth does not exist if there is nobody who takes that truth for true. "Is there not an objective truth?" he objected. The speaker answered: "There would not be a truth if there were no individuals to support that truth, because truth is a relational concept." This means, truth is ejective, but to articulate that ejective truth, we must get along without an appropriate, ejective language. See: *Algemeen Handelsblad,* May 3, 1916, p. 7.

[31] Prof. Dr. L.E.J.Brouwer: *Leven, Kunst en Mystiek,* Delft 1905, p. 38.

[32] Fritz Mauthner: *Beiträge zu einer Kritik der Spache*, Stuttgart 1901, Vol. III, p. 241. The word also splits in numerous meanings and unites these again in that one word.

hearer to separate what is inseparable and to fixate what is not lasting. The word is indefensible definiteness."[33]

It is most remarkable how these words of wisdom remain without any attention. The more we reflect upon words, the more we become aware of their importance for the general, and in particular the legal, significian.

It is important to notice that one does not find a pure reflection upon the essence of the word among poets and linguists, but among philosophically inspired mathematicians: Brouwer, Poincaré, Mannoury.[34] Poets reflecting on the Word often exercise one of the physical sciences: Frederik van Eeden,[35] Nico van Suchtelen.[36] That is not incidental, as it is not incidental that numerals belong to the most remarkable signific words. Mathematicians evolve from an external to an internal fixity, as the reflecting poets do, until 'internal' and 'external' unite and separate in an 'I' and 'Other' for them. These are issues of general significs, which we will not further analyze.

Our reflection brings us to the insight that language cannot reach reality with sensual words or immaterial signs.[37] For that reason, we conclude that all our speaking is an endeavor and our knowing an approximation, as every other science is only a different metaphor for the same reality. The principles of one science can be "translated" into the words of another science. In that perspective Professor Brouwer translated the philosophical *principium tertii exclusi* mathematically, "of each particular inclusion of systems into each other, one can construct either termination or blockage with the help of impossibility."[38] Those translations are very important for significs and for philosophy. They could contribute to the investigation of whether the foundations of mathematics, logic and psychology are one and the same. The articulation of the different languages will be enriched and enlarged by those translations. It would be very important for a philosophy of law and for legal significs if Prof. Brouwer could translate into the words of mathematics the constitution of legal consciousness as determined by Prof. R. Kranenburg.[39] I consider that a mathematical translation of the concept of intention is right away possible. That would

---

[33] *Gedenkboek der Wereldbibliotheek,* [Commemorative volume of the world-library] Amsterdam 1915, p. 240.

[34] Poincaré: "Les homes ne s'entendent pas parce qu'ils ne parlent pas la même langue et qu'il y a des langues qui ne s'apprennent pas", see Prof Brouwer: *Intuitionisme and Formalisme,* Amsterdam 1912, p. 29.

[35] Poezie, Wijsbegeerte en Mathesis, in: *De Beweging,* July 1906, p. 35–36 (see note 2).

[36] Het Al-Eenig Leven (see Note 28).

[37] For instance Peanistic Signs; Prof. Brouwer: *Intuitionsme en Formalisme* (see note 34). P. 177: "A mathematical view on language signs, either words or Peanistic signs, can us not teach anything about mathematics."

[38] De onbetrouwbaarheid der logische principes, [The unreliability of logical principles] in *Tijdschrift voor Wijsbegeerte*, II, 1908. P. 156.

[39] *Positief recht en rechtsbewustzijn.* Groningen 1912, p. 83–87.

be very useful in the battle of opinions in criminal law, indicated with words like "theory of will" and "theory of imagination."[40]

It follows from the essence of language that speaker and hearer cannot be connected without differentiating between them,[41] and because the human mind can neither think unity without diversity nor diversity without unification. Prof. Brouwer writes in that regard: "Individuals with a parallel will which is based on a free or coerced common value determination, support and differentiate this parallelism by means of words."[42] Language makes communication between humans impossible although it is conceived as the most general means of communication.[43] But God speaks to us in the emotions and experiences of eternal and infinite silence.[44]

Our only certainty is that we cannot understand each other. But a consequence is that legislation and the administration of justice seem impossible. Prof. Brouwer acknowledged this, when he spoke about the impossibility of using the word "not imputable" in legal practice.[45] But the administration of justice is imputation, and its denial includes the denial of justice.

This is the problem: the Essence of a legal significs leads indeed to the conclusion that lawgiving and the administration of justice are impossible. And it is the task of legal significs to achieve a real lawmaking and a real administration of justice. Without this, the Essence and Task of legal significs seem completely in discordance with each other. You could perhaps think that I should finish my first lesson here. A significian should indeed begin and finish with instilling silence, because he knows deeply that we do not understand each other. The battle between the Essence and the Task of legal significs looks like a cheerless cut-off of legal sciences and legal practice. Any insight into this leads us at least to a more just appreciation of the labor of the lawmaker and of the judge. I refer to the very important but somewhat one-sided and therefore journalistic publications of Mr. H. Louis Israëls, publications not without risk and entitled "Judge and Law" in *De Telegraaf* [The Telegraph]. I remember in particular his presentations under the title *Juridisch Nederlands* [Legal Dutch] where he writes: "Our beautiful Dutch language seems to be the most unclear language in the world, once it is used in a book of statutes and

[40] Two theories called in earlier Dutch "opstel", for instance in the period of witch trials, see *Nederlandsch Tijdschrift voor Geneeskunde* 60, 1916 p. 963.

[41] F. Schiller: "*An den Dichter*" [To the Poet]: "Laß die Sprache di sein was der Körper den Liebenden; Er nur ist's der die Wesen trennt und der die Wesen vereint".

[42] Rechtskundige significa, [Legal Significs] in: *Groot Nederland*, 1916, p. 333.

[43] Frederik van Eeden: Redekunstige grondslag van de verstandhouding, [Rhetorical Foundations of Communnication] in *Studies,* Vol. III, Amsterdam 1890. Reviewed by Dr. Jac van Ginneken, in: *Principes de linguistique psychologique,* Amsterdam 1907, § 269.

[44] Jakob Böhme: "so du magst eine Stunde schweigen von allem deinem Wollen und Sinnen, so wirst du unaussprechliche Worte Gottes hören". The expressive force of such words, which at the same time posit and abolish themselves do raise doubts about the principium contradictions. The words of Böhme are quoted from L.E.J.Brouwer: *Leven, Kunst en Mystiek* (see note 31).

[45] *Groot Nederland* (14), 1916, p. 334.

comes into the hands of jurists."[46] His commentary will seem entirely convincing for many a reader who is not used to reflection. However, Mr. Israëls claims "that one should only understand a word in the meaning according to our linguistic usage and performance." The only answer is, that "the" meaning of a word and "our" usage do not exist—one suggests that a streaming river does not move at all! The word is a untenable determination and for that reason, legislation as well as the administration of justice are impossible.

It is clear that we cannot accept this position without further ado, as it is clear that we cannot pluck the stars from heaven. The impossible character of legislation and justice is acceptable if thought of as the impossibility of a possibility. Only a thorough reflection gives us insight into that impossibility. Here we bear again witness to the battle between reflection and demand, which alienates us from ourselves in continuous anxiety, fear and remorse, and yet stimulates us to find our self.

We will now determine the possibility of legislation and jurisdiction. But think about it: we must do that in the same language that led us to our insight into the impossibility of the two. It is the same situation in which the teacher of significs must teach in the language that brought him to the insight that *being silent* is the only truthful manner in which to *speak*.[47]

Language materialized all spiritual sciences by means of materialistic metaphors, as well as herself and also the Law. Even the word Law itself is a materialized metaphor and absolutely not harmless. I will not further consider this further. Signific research about the many words peoples use for what we call "Law" would be important for our knowledge of psychology and for a philosophy of law.[48]

Take the word "legislation". This seems a simple word: the legislator gives laws to the people and the people accept those laws and with them the Law. But what is a law?—an ensemble of determinations. However, modern States print laws. A law became a book. Here, the materialization began. We, as we saw before, abandoned our soul and replaced it with an external world, which is independent from us. In the same way we made the law, which is part of our psychic life, into a booklet of that external world and in which we read what a lawmaker wanted—often living decades ago, dying in an external world.[49] We transformed the law into a booklet and the legislator into a person. We thus speak of "the will of the legislator" and the

---

[46] Jacob Israël de Haan: Taal en rechtswetenschap, [Language and Legal Science] in *W [weekblad van het recht]* [Weekly Law Journal] *9949*, 1916.

[47] Lady Victoria Welby: *Significs and Language*, London 1911, p. 7 & 8.

[48] On the word "law", see: Hermann Weck: *Die Sprache im deutschen Recht*, Berlin 1913, on "Law and Language", p. 1–43.

[49] On the phenomenon of materialization, see: Michel Bréal: *Essai de sémantique*, [Essay on Semantics] Paris 1897, Chap. XIII: "Des mots abstraits et de l'appaississement du sens". This is the way the word "mark" has become materialized. Originally it referred to a sign on an object. Later it referred to an object that has was made for this mark. Art. 3. of the "Patent and Trademark Law" is vague and dangerous to use. Compare the materialization of the mark and the stamp. A fiscal advocate for the Marines and the Army went very deeply into that process of materialization—see *Algemeen Handelsblad* Sept. 17, 1916— and remarked: "Here one is a slave of the law". I would say: "Here is one slave of one's spiritual life".

"intention of the legislator" which the judge has to find in the course of his judgments. Only by exception it is noticed that these words are dangerous linguistic images and many of us are misled by these crafty expressions. In his *Recht en Levensbeschouwing* [Law and Philosophy of Life], Prof. Scholten warns us about these linguistic images and writes (p. 10): "one thing is true: the interpretation of the law is not based on the search for an intention of the creator of the law—how would this be possible where so many persons are involved?—but it is the determination of the meaning and the sense of the law". But is "the sense of the law" not as deceptive as "the intention of those who created the law"? How can we truly determine the sense and the meaning of a law where that law is laid down in words with the character of untenable determination?

We direct our reflections towards the word "jurisdiction" and "administration of justice" on the one hand and its relation to "legislation" on the other, i.e. the doctrine of the freedom of the judge. It is clear that I cannot discuss this doctrine in its entirety.[50] But I point out that a reflection pertaining to the word "jurisdiction" leads to conclusions, which are different from the traditional consequences. It seems simple: "The task of the legislator is to determine in general terms what will be law. The task of the judge is to apply that law in specific cases."[51] But things are not that simple. Consider cases that were not foreseen in the days of the legislative procedure. Think of the example of receiving or confusing electric messages not for the registered receiver.[52] Other cases also show how difficult it is to circumscribe the task of the judge. What is this "applying a law/statute, in other words: to interpret a law"? Prof. Scholten does not accept the description "to find the intention of the legislator(s)" but accepts the descriptions "determining the sense of the law" and "finding the thoughts, which are laid down in the words of the law".

But the Court in Haarlem recently issued a judgment about the obligation connected with an oath or with a promise, in which a totally different interpretation of the expression "application—or interpretation of the law" can be found. I quote the two most important considerations of the Court: "considering the historical background of art. 161 Sv [article 161 Criminal Law] one can assume that the legislator in 1838 conformed a then valid Constitutional opinion intended to stipulate that only persons belonging to a religious denomination which forbids one to take an oath, like the Baptist Church, can legally suffice with a promise". But it is in the opinion of the Court not necessary to provide only the historical argumentation in the case of an article of law 70 years old and clearly written under other circumstances than those of today. It is rather the task of the judge to explain the law, if

[50] *Handelingen der Nederlandsche Juristen-Vereniging*, 1961 with Preadviezen.

[51] Prof. Scholten in Asser's *Handleiding,* [Manual] I, Zwolle 1912, p. 79.

[52] The famous Art.1 of the Swiss Civil Law (1907) urges the judge to act in accordance with the customary law or "nach der Regel, die er als Gesetzgeber aufstellen würde" (the rule he would issue if he were legislator). It means: at the moment of his judgment and not at the moment of an eventual legislation. Compare *W* 8926, Amsterdam court, See: Prof. Mr. H. Krabbe: *De moderne staatsidee*, [The modern idea of State] Den Haag 1915, p. 111.

possible, in the sense of actual circumstances and opinions, and—without violating the law—to develop those and provide them an evolutionary "Power".

The Court seems to permit every interpretation, which does not violate every meaning of the words of the law, even if conflicting with a uniform intention of all persons involved in the legislation process. It is clear that we are not dealing with a different method of interpretation, but with a totally different meaning of the concept "interpretation".[53]

It shows how our signific reflection evaporated the stable and fixed character of the terms "legislation" and "jurisdiction". This follows from the essence of Language and the essence of the Law. Our foundation here is, that law is not objective and not subjective but ejective in character. The stability of law cannot be achieved through the object and materialized language we speak—and in an equal sense not by means of a purely subjective language. Our objective language materializes our spiritual life in all regards. An ejective language would think matter and mind separated and united at the same time. But the creation of an ejective language seems to surpass the capacity of the human mind.

A signific reflection abolishes the view of law as an external world existing independently from us. That reflection divides legal acts into legal act on one hand and legal thought on the other—both autonomous in themselves but united and separated, with law as its outcome.

Prof. Krabbe came to an incorrect contrast when separating the legal act and the legal thought: "If one speaks for instance about a conflict with *the* law, then one can mean his or her fight with the valid legal norms as well as with the idea of justice".[54] But there is no act in conflict with the idea of justice, which is separate from valid legal norms.

Yet, Prof. Krabbe leads us with this error in a good direction. If the administration of justice does not mean "interpretation of the law" in one of the meanings we discussed, what then is jurisdiction? Prof. Krabbe may want to answer, jurisdiction is: "satisfaction of legal consciousness". But what is "legal consciousness"? We experience again the materializing power of language. The concept "legal consciousness" was just introduced into legal science when the word already materialized the concept! Even such an idealist author as Prof. Krabbe adheres to the opinion that "legal consciousness" exists independently from our mind and belongs to an external world that influences the mind like fire does to wax. He declares in his *De Moderne Staatsidee* [The Modern Idea of the State] "There are no sources of law, as our handbooks suggest; there is only one source of law, a legal consciousness that lives in the human individual." One encounters this opinion in many places of his oeuvre. But what is the value of those remarks? One can say beyond any doubt that legal consciousness is the sole source of law, but this has no other meaning than

---

[53] Prof. Dr. Philipp Heck: *Gesetzesauslegung und Interessenjurisprudenz,* [Legal interpretation and jurisprudence based on interest] Tübingen 1914.

[54] *De moderne staatsidee, p. 37.* See also Prof. Mr. Dr. Kranenburg in *Rechtsgeleerd Magazijn,* Aug. 1916, p. 326–330, and Prof. Mr. Dr. A.A.H.Struycken, in: *De Gids*, [The guide] 1916, Nr 3, p. 486 ff.

saying that awareness of pain is the source of all pain. Have those words any value? The expression "consciousness" is often used in psychology to indicate a "power" or a physiological "capacity". It does not solve any problem but draws our attention to the fact that the problem remains without solution.[55]

Yet I guess that Prof. Krabbe wants to say something else with his statement that legal consciousness is the only source of law. He may suggest that one could create and support an ideally just society if one is inspired by a legal consciousness. He thus separates what only can be distinguished. No deed or action can be in conflict with the idea of justice on its own, outside of any context. And a just society cannot be created by the idea of legal consciousness outside of any context.

The expression "legal consciousness" on its own is misleading. Whose consciousness is at stake? Legal consciousness is a sense or feeling only within a community. But each individual of that community develops this awareness as an individual, that is: in distinction from others. The same is true for the motivation of each individual who acts in accordance with his or her legal consciousness—a consciousness purely personal. However, there are limits: legal consciousness seems imbued with diverse interests. The actor or the individual who profits from the act will first of all experience the legitimacy of that act. The illegitimacy will on the other hand be first and strongly perceived by those who are the victims of that act. The relation between legal consciousness and interest is complex and difficult, so that I cannot deal with this subject in its entirety. Also the relevant laws are a difficult issue, as Prof. Kranenburg has demonstrated in his 1912 book *Positief recht en rechtsbewustzijn* [Positive Law and Legal Consciousness].[56] It should be clear that we refer in our thinking to legal consciousness as the consciousness of non-interested persons, competent to judge and without prejudices. But in Prof. Krabbe's explication, legal consciousness appears as an independent entity external to our mind, as is his context for the expression "source of law". That shows the enormous power of materialized metaphors, although Prof. Krabbe himself could not deny the importance of a correct selection of words in the legal context.[57] I do not blame this clever and generous scholar. Our language became so intensely materialized that one has no words available to articulate another, spiritual and non-materialized understanding of law. It is questionable whether legal significs will succeed in creating spiritual, non-materialized words for an equivalent law. The decay of centuries cannot be

---

[55] See on the word "power" or "force" in physics, the index in: Dr. J. Clay: *Het begrip der natuurwet in de nieuwere wijsbegeerte,* [The concept of a law of physics in the newer philosophy] Leiden 1915. Law has been made completely subjective by the identification of "law" and "legal consciousness". Those who interpret law, custom and justice as "sources of law" will, in contrast, objectify the Law. But: Law is ejective. However, for articulating an ejective law, we do not dispose of an appropriate language.

[56] Prof. Kranenburg: *Positief recht en rechtsbewustzijn,* [Positive Law and Legal Consciousness] Groningen 1912. (see note 39). On the relation between "legal consciousness" and "interest", see Krabbe: *De moderne staatsidee,* p. 115 f.

[57] Krabbe: *De moderne staatsidee*, Den Haag 1915, p. 9, 170.

compensated in a few years. Everyone contributes to it, and only a few are apt to restore our language.[58]

We have seen how reflection can teach us what "legal consciousness" *is not,* but can reflection and experience teach us about what it *really is*? Let us compare legal consciousness with another evaluative consciousness, with a sense of beauty, an aesthetic sense. That comparison seems acceptable under the condition that we do not forget its character as a comparison—an issue of the human mind! When comparing the two, we discover an important difference. A "Sense of beauty" is purely reflective. It means: nobody desires that poets who produce bad poetry be jailed. And only few want, for instance, all thieves to be set free. Legal consciousness pertains to an act, whereas the sense of beauty does not. The reflective sense of beauty can remain personal for that reason, in contrast to legal opinions. Law should maintain social order. But this implies that law exercises power over personal feelings on law and justice. Law can serve society only by means of power, and law rules only because it serves. That differs from beauty, which does not serve a social interest and therefore does not dominate a personal feeling. Law must be spoken because it serves society by means of power. There is legislation and there is administration of justice. But beauty neither serves nor rules. In cases of beauty everyone can be his or her own legislator and judge. Beauty serves a social interest in exceptional cases, and even then it rules over personal esthetic feelings. That is the case when in a municipality a planning authority or a master architect has been installed who must approve the building-plans of houses of specific persons.

I strongly emphasize the ruling *and* serving character of the law.[59] A personal legal consciousness seems to diminish when requirements of social order prevail. That order rules the law, but the law rules the social order also, because the law itself acknowledges this ruling as justified. It means: a community cannot exist without law, but also not without injustices. The truth of the latter observation is acknowledged and at the same time cancelled by the law.

There are numerous examples in which social order rules law. I can indicate some and analyze none of them in the time and space of this lesson. I mention in this context how our so-called legal certainty is only another name for this ruling-character of law. Furthermore, order rules the law everywhere legal consequences are made dependent upon the fulfillment of formal acts, like the establishment of public limited companies, corporations and other associations with legal

[58] The word "State" is a materialized metaphor with a particularly strong and misleading power. The word should, however, not be more than a simple name for a collection of human phenomena. But our language made the state into a superhuman person living in an external world independent of the human mind. This gave room to the fatal opinion that relations between states are allowed, which would never be allowed among individuals. See: Krabbe: *De moderne Staatsidee,* p. 142, 187–188, and L.H.Grondijs: Het vraagstuk van den wereldvrede, [The issue of world peace] in: *Tijdschrift voor Wijsbegeerte*, I, 1907, p. 162, as well as: Prof. A. Menzel: *Zur Psychologie des Staates*, [The psychology of the State] Vienna 1915.

[59] Dr. Otto: *Die Gewißheit des Richterspruchs,* [The certainty of a judge's decision] Hannover 1915 with this extremely surprising remark on p. 78: "Besser ein sicheres Unrecht als ein stets unsicheres Recht" [better a firm injustice than a continuously uncertain law].

personality.[60] The 22 April 1855 law, which regulates and limits the rights of associations and assembly is an example of such a legal reinforcement of order. Legal decisions on the basis of this law have more than once offended the legal consciousness of jurists and legal scholars. I think of the various judgments pertaining to the heritage of Mr. J.C.L.Druyvestein.[61] The power of order in this case is evident, and particularly manifest in the protection of the owner, even if he acts in bad faith or someone else acts in bad faith against him.

There is more to say—for instance that a social order requires the regulation of various types of relations in consideration of which legal consciousness seems completely indifferent. Can a legal consciousness answer the question whether in a case pertaining to a labor contract the subsequent procedure has to begin with a subpoena or with filing an appeal? Or whether a Justice of the Peace or a higher Court is competent here? In other words: what does a legal consciousness say about the best way to research and accept claims in a bankruptcy case? Those rules are called *legal* rules, and they play a role in bankruptcy, but they are in fact simple rules of social order without further meaning. Do not forget the role various interests can play with regard to legal consciousness, and the same is true for habits. The protection of property is for many persons a legal issue of a higher order, higher than a simple measure in the context of social order. But is that rule of protection more than a rule which serves order, a rule we have been used to for centuries, and therefore call law? I cannot deal with that question at this moment, and quote Prof. Brouwer: "the word 'property', in use for withdrawing from the free determination of our fellow citizens under the protection of state authority…"[62] A judge can apply laws, which are unjust in his eyes; constitutions even prescribe that behavior explicitly as lawful. But the Law itself can be unjust. The legal consciousness of a judge qualifies his submission to the law as Law because of the more encompassing value of the social order.[63] The same is true for the subjection of lower judges (and courts) in view of the highest judges in a democracy—they are not only a matter of form,[64] but also an issue of principle, as one can deduce from the procedural value and rank of confession/admission in a case of divorce.[65] Objective law knows two different parts: a legal part that is law, and a legal part that is order. Most legal rules belong to the second part. Laws that issue general rules are of the second; judgments in particular cases

[60] Prof. Mr. P. Scholten in Asser's *Handleiding*, [Manual] Part I, Zwolle 1912, p. 649. And Mr. H. Louis Israëls: Rechter en Wet, [Judge and Law] in: *De Telegraaf*, Sept. 17, 1916.

[61] About the Druyvestein case, see Prof. Hymans: *Het recht der werkelijkheid,* [The law of reality] Haarlem 1910, p. 5 and Prof. Scholten: *Recht en Levensbeschouwing,* [Law and ideology] Haarlem 1915.

[62] Rechtskundige Significa, in: *Groot-Nederland,* Sept. 14, 1916, p. 334.

[63] (See the original in note 66). The very free German judicial decisions are subject of the articles by Ernst Fuchs & K. Schneider in the Journal *Recht und Wirtschaft,* [Law and Economy] 1916, p. 128–129.

[64] Prof. Mr. P. Scholten in Asser's *Handleiding*, [Manual] Part I, Zwolle 1912, p. 368: "In those formal problems should lower courts accept the rules of the Supreme Court."

[65] Prof. Mr. P. Scholten in Asser's *Handleiding*, [Manual] Part I, Zwolle 1912, p. 321–322.

often belong to the first, although the idea of social order seems everywhere, in particular in conflict situations.

The division of objective law into two parts, into pure law and into rules of order, clarifies where the legal significian has to unfold its views. It is not in an improvement of the language of the law issued as law. Those words do not need to be spoken and they can in essence not be spoken in the language we actually use. Law as law is not spoken, but speaks to us in the dynamics of our legal consciousness. But as soon as law became transformed into the major force for maintaining social order, the law had to be spoken/articulated by the legislator as well as the judge. The task of the legal significian is to research the essence of the various types and categories of words and to compare the numerous meanings of words of legal language with that essence. In doing this, he enables the legislator to choose his words so that judges can use them with the greatest equality and with minimal differences in meaning. Even Supreme Court judges and the Highest Governmental Dignitaries will dispose of a vocabulary, which functions as an orientation for lower judges with a maximum of equality and a minimum of differences.

I argued in the beginning of this lesson that a subjective language is more spiritual than an objective one, and perhaps also stronger and more correct. Does the legal significian not contribute to a new objectivity of that very same language? Prof. Brouwer made that remark.[66] We should take care not to misunderstand the word 'objective'. It does not mean: 'for all humans equal'. A language can differ for all speakers and yet be objective. And a language can be imagined as equal for all speakers and yet be subjective. There would be an ideal, unachievable without its opposite, called a subjective or an ejective language, which would for all humans be the correct articulation of their consciousness, like an ideal sign would be identical to its meaning. An objective language puts the sun in the sky; a subjective language puts the sun in the soul. An ejective language articulates how sun and soul are separated and one.

Secondly, one should consider whether the legal significs I represent is not a simple descriptive, instead of an explanatory, science? Prof. Kranenburg has raised that question.[67] My answer is, that "description" and "explanation" can be distinguished but by no means separated.[68] I will therefore focus my lessons more on reflection than on experience. A side-remark is that I will not dwell upon the relations between significs and psychology. However, I add that the theories of Freud about the power of the unconscious on linguistics are an important theme, in particular when he highlights his analysis of words with contrasting meanings.[69]

[66] Rechtskundige Significa, in: *Groot-Nederland,* Sept. 14, 1916, p. 334.

[67] *De Beweging,* Nr 12/3, Sept. 1916, p. 237. (see note 35)

[68] Prof. Dr. Ph. Kohnstamm: Psychologie en logica, in: *Tijdschrift voor wijsbegeerte*, I, 1907, p. 43, Prof. Mr. P. Scholten: *Recht en Levensbeschouwing,* Haarlem 1915, p. 22: "In each description is a qualification"; Prof. Dr. L.E.J.Brouwer: *Over de grondslagen der wiskunde,* Amsterdam 1907, p. 91.

[69] Prof. Dr. Sigmund Freud: *De invloed van het onbewuste in het dagelijks leven,* [The unconscious in daily life] J. Stärcke, Ed., Amsterdam 1916 and Prof. Dr. Sigmund Freud: *De droom als uiting van het onbewuste zieleleven,* [The dream as expression of the unconscious psychic life] J. Stärcke, Ed.,Leiden 1913/17, p. 38, note.

I should also have clarified my viewpoint on the use of foreign words, because of remarks of Prof. Dr. D. van Blom,[70] Mr. Dr. S.J. M. van Geuns[71] and Dr. Jac. Van Ginneken.[72] But I am afraid that I offered you in the first lesson rather too many thoughts than too little.

[70] In *De Gids,* August 1916, Nr 80/3.

[71] *W* 9954.

[72] *Studiën* [Studies] *1915, p. 337 note.*

Legal Significs and Its Application in the Concepts 'Liable', 'Responsible' and 'Accountable'

Jacob Israël De Haan

[From his Amsterdam PhD Dissertation, 1916[1]]

[Page 13][2] Our goal is the determination of the meaning, which is inherent to the expressions "liable, responsible, accountable". Prof. Dr. G. Heymans formulates one of the most important requirements for a successful scientific investigation in a well-known article in *De Gids*: "to use in scientific language no precisely determined terminology".[3] But what does the word "meaning" mean? Mauthner said: "'Daß jedes Wort etwas bedeute' ist ganz richtig, wenn man nur erst beachtet hat, was 'bedeute' eigentlich bedeutet".[4] ['That each word means something' is correct if one considers first, what 'to mean' means.]

[Page 14—24] The question "what meaning *has* this word" is often posed. This is a metaphor. It is true: "our language is metaphorical in character and essence."[5] One can never avoid metaphors. But one can diminish the risk to confuse comparative and explicative metaphors. Even this metaphor as such is comparative and risky. A word is not a living organism that possesses meanings like humans possess property. The same incorrect thought is in the expression "What is the meaning *of* this word". One should never underestimate the fatal influence of an incorrect metaphor.

---

[1] SOURCE: JACOB ISRAËL DE HAAN: *Rechtskundige Significa en hare toepassing op de begrippen: "Aansprakelijk, verantwoordelijk, toerekeningsvatbaar"* Academisch Proefschrift ter verkrijging van de graad van Doctor in de Rechtswetenschap aan de Universiteit van Amsterdam, Dinsdag 1 Februari 1916,W. Versluys, Amsterdam 1916. 273 pag. Ch 1.: pp 14 – 40, Ch 2.: pp. 137 – 140, Ch 4.: pp 160 – 168, 176 – 178, 266 –268, 270—273
(Translation Dutch/English by Eds.)

[2] Original page numbers

[3] *'Uitwassen der Crimineele Anthropologie'* [Excesses of Criminal Psychology] in *De Gids*, 1901, I, p. 50.

[4] F. Mauthner, Part II, Ch. VII, p. 263.

[5] Albert Verwey in *"De Beweging"*, 1910, p. 99.

J.I. De Haan (deceased)

J.M. Broekman, L. Catá Backer (eds.), *Signs In Law - A Source Book*,
DOI 10.1007/978-3-319-09837-1_9

Legal science[6] as well as linguistics[7] suffered because comparative metaphors were given explanatory functions. A word *is* its meaning with something inexplicable added, a something that binds meanings into a word. One should therefore formulate the question correctly, and say: "what meaning *is* this word?"

Moreover, a single word has not a meaning in itself, but only in a complete sentence. The relation between word and sentence cannot completely be researched here.[8]

One speaks about *the* meaning or meanings of a word. But it has another meaning each time a word is used. Even for a speaker and a hearer is the meaning [Page 15] different. It means that each language is relatively unaccomplished.[9] We will for that reason never be certain,[10] whether we understand or are understood. On the contrary: I would say that we are certain, *not* to understand or to be understood.[11] But the numerous meanings of a word are tied together by an unknown connecting force, and exactly that force of coherence creates the word. Multiple observations are connected by means of that unknown force, and the latter creates the Thing! A word is very much like the essence of a thing, because the essence of both is a spiritual essence. Consider for example, how there exists a connection between the word: "doctoral thesis" for the author, the printer, the publisher, which does not exist between the meanings of "doctoral thesis" or "cow" or "house". How meanings do come together into a word is equivalent to the question how specific observations become united into a word.

[Page 16] So one and the same word cannot have two contrasting meanings.[12] For example, the Dutch word "onverbeterlijk" [incorrigible] has two contrasting meanings, "very good" and "very bad". But the words "waardeerbaar" en "onwaardeerbaar" [appreciative and inappreciative] have approximately equal meanings, as is also the case with for instance "rubbish" or its opposite "not-rubbish" or "animal" and "monster". The Roman "sacer" means "holy" but also "damned": "Patronus si clienti fraudem fecerit sacer esto". Many Hebrew words show the same.[13] "Sacer" means in Hebrew "holy" but also "catamite" or "whore". Earlier linguists spoke about a disappearing "vox media", indicating that a meaning can unfold into two

---

[6] Prof. Molengraaf in a book review in *Het Rechtsgeleerd Magazijn* [The Legal Scientist Magazine] 1911, p. 362.

[7] M. Bréal, *Êssai de sémantique*, [Essay on Semantics] 1911, p. 3.

[8] Wilhelm Wundt: *Völkerpsychologie* [Psychology of Peoples], Vol. II, Ch. 7.

[9] Hugo Schuchart, in *De Nieuwe Taalgids* [The New Language Guide], Vol. II, p. 17.

[10] Jacob Israël de Haan: *Het recht op slechtheid* [The right to wickedness] in *De Beweging*, 1915, p. 214.

[11] J. H. van den Bosch: *Taaleenheid in spreken, schrijven en spellen* [Linguistic Unity in Speaking, Writing and Spelling] in; *De Nieuwe Taalgids,* III, p. 30. F. Paulhan, review of *Il linguaggio dei filosofi* [The Language of the Philosophers] by G. Ranzoli in *Revue Philosophique*, 1912. Mauthner, Vol. III, Ch. VIII: *Situation and Sprache* [Situation and Language].

[12] The meaning of the word 'contrasting' or 'opposite' is not fixed. Opposite of 'asking' is often 'answering', but the opposite of 'asking' is 'not asking'. To understand Hegelian philosophy a fundamental question!

[13] Dr. E. Landau: *Die gegensinnigen Wörter im Alt- und Neuhebräischen sprachvergleichend dargestellt*, [Words in contrary senses in Old and New Hebrew, a comparative linguistic study]

meanings with a contrasting direction. Dr. Landau writes about: "ein neutraler Begriff, der sich später nach zwei entgegengesetzten Bedeutungen differenziert hat"[14] [a neutral concept that in later days differentiates in two contrasting meanings]. In a number of cases is that idea correct. In the case of "sacer", there has certainly been a *vox media* meaning: "dedicated to", but be aware of general conclusions! Changes of meaning in

[Page 17] each word must be carefully studied, with focus on each change. Moreover, all cases of double meaning do not have the same *psychological* meaning. In most Hebrew verbs is that the case. An equivalent example in Dutch as well as in Hebrew is the word "completion", which means "finishing" (like an author finishes a book) and "slaughtering" (the reviewer totally slaughtered the book.)[15]

Jurists should be attentive to use the word "client". Its literal meaning is: "the subordinate, the serf".[16] A Roman patrician had his clients, which he assisted in cases of emergency. Since then, a 'client' is everyone who needs legal assistance. The word was after the jurist in use by the physician, and then it was in use from higher to lower professions. Today the word 'client' is not the person who obeys but who commands, although it remains in use to indicate legal help.

A change of meaning does not necessarily come with change of sound. Yet there can be a link between the meaning and the sound of a word. That important issue [Page 18] is beyond the scope of this text.[17] Changes of sound have an entirely different character than changes of meaning. A new sound disperses an old, a new meaning unfolds and remains next to an old meaning.[18]

As we saw, every word has multiple meanings. The words "liable, responsible, accountable" are no exception in that regard. This might be reinforced by the fact that the circumstances under which I work with these concepts, differ continuously—they are never the same.[19]

Is there no order in the multiple meanings of a word?

Lady Victoria Welby classified the many meanings in three groups of meaning called 'Sense', 'Meaning', 'Significance'. It is difficult to provide a precise description of those three concepts because of shortcomings in the articulations in a language. She thus remarks:[20] "There is, strictly speaking, no such thing as the Sense

[Page 19] of a word, but only sense in which it is used, the circumstances, state of mind, reference, universe of discourse, belonging to it. The Meaning of a word is the intent, which it is desired to convey, the intention of the user. The Significance

[14] Id., p. 25: *Psychologische Problemlösung* [Psychological problem solving]

[15] Jacob Israël de Haan: Taal en Rechtswetenschap, [Language and Legal Science] in: *De Beweging*, 1915.

[16] 'Cluo' is in old Latin 'hearing', later developed as 'audire' [auditing]. Bréal, p. 96 and 105.

[17] Wundt on '*Lautmetapher*' [Sound-metaphor], Vol. I, p. 348. His representations on the Hebrew verb are not entirely correct. P. 362–364.

[18] Albert Dauzat: *La vie du language* [The life of language] Ch 1, 4. Dauzat does not clearly distinguish comparative and explicative linguistic images.

[19] Mauthner, Vol. III, p. 234.

[20] Lady Victoria Welby: *What is Meaning*, p. 5.

is always manifold, and intensifies its sense as well as its meaning, by expressing its importance, its appeal to us, its moment for us, its emotional force, its ideal value, its moral aspect, its universal or at least social range," And furthermore: "The one crucial question in all Expression, whether by action or sound, symbol or picture, is its special property, first of Sense, that in which it is used, then of Meaning as the intention of the user, and most far-reaching and momentous of all, of implication, of ultimate Significance."[21] One of the most experienced and skilled collaborators of Lady Welby, Prof. T. Clifford Allbutt, writes: "Sense is the direct intention of the very words themselves." "Meaning is that which the author wished to convey, a burden unfortunately too often different from the sense." "By Significance we mean something more different and impalpable than either sense or meaning"[22] One should furthermore consult the Encyclopedia Britannica article on "Significs" written by Lady Welby in 1911.

Prof. Clifford Allbutt is a skilled author. The three concepts are for him only of value if they are on beforehand known by the speaker/user. This remark shows the limitations of expressive power that are inherent in a language.

[Page 20] For the English words Sense, Meaning and Significance I use the Dutch words: 'Zin', 'Bedoeling' and 'Waarde'.[23]

Sense, or 'Zin' (Dutch) I use in its original meaning. The sense of speaking is to speak to someone. For instance: "he spoke to me when we were in the street".

Meaning, or 'Bedoeling' (Dutch) pertains to the meaning, which is connected with the spoken sentence and with particular intentions of the speaker. The meaning of 'addressing someone' is 'to question accountability'. Included is that the one who is addressed will not remain in a passive position if the response of the addressee seems insufficient. It can for instance be said: 'I will address him because of his indecent attitude'.

Significance, or 'Waarde' (Dutch) is the insight that a word in connection with its Meaning and Sense provides about the ideology of the speaker. The value of 'Significance' differs with its context, which can be a civil, criminal, moral or social accountability. The value of the word 'accountable' is therefore different between the uses and explanations of Prof. I.J.de Bussy[24] and Mr. I.A. Levy.[25] And so are they different for Dr. A. Aletrino[26] and Prof. G. Heymans.[27]

---

[21] Lady Victoria Welby: *Significs and Language*, p. 9.

[22] Allbutt: Words and Things, in: *The Lancet*, 1906, II, p. 1120.

[23] *Nieuwe Rechtstaalphilosophie* [A new philosophy of legal language], in *Rechtsgeleerd Magazijn*, 1912, p. 497.

[24] De Bussy: *Schuldbelijdenis* [Confession of Guilt] in W. 8032.

[25] Levy: *Begripsdialectiek* [Dialectics of Concepts] in W. 8026, and *Verduidelijking* [Clarification] in: W. 8034.

[26] Aletrino: *Over ontoerekenbaarheid* [On unaccountability], *Twee opstellen over criminele anthropologie* [Two essays on criminal anthropology] and *Wat de criminele anthropologie ons leert* [What criminal anthropology teaches us], in: *De XXste eeuw*, 1907.

[27] Heymans: *Uitwassen der criminele anthropologie* [Excesses of criminal anthropology] in: *De Gids* 1901, and *Strafrechtelijke toerekening* [Criminal law accountability] in *Tijdschrift voor Strafrecht* [Journal for Penal/Criminal Law], Vol. XX, p. 470, see Mr. R. Kranenburg in W. 9259.

[Page 21] Why are the multiple meanings of a word divided into exactly three groups: Sense, Meaning, and Significance. I do not give this triad the mysterious meaning as Lady Welby did.[28] I can imagine that an improvement of our signific knowledge might cause a division in more than three groups, but I will now not deviate from this classical threesome divide.

It is evident that not all words will have a full sense, meaning and significance. The words of our daily life have numerous meanings but they remain most in one group. The word 'ink' has a different *sense* for the maker of ink than it has for an author. But it has neither meaning nor *value* for any of the two. The words, which really carry a value are in the signific sense valuable words. They carry treasures from the spiritual life of the speaker with them. Lady Welby uses the expression 'to convey' which is a *comparison* but not an *explanation*. Value concepts are difficult to express in words. Consider again the word 'address'. There is really no problem with its sense.

[Page 22] When for instance Dr. A. Aletrino or Prof. G. Heymans say that 'they were addressed by an old friend', they mean the same. But when they claim that a human being is accountable, then each of them means something different, because the same word has a different meaning for each of them.

The Sense of a word is often lost. For example the words "outrageous" and "far-reaching" have both a negative feeling.[29] But it can become a powerful charm to use them once they are united with their original sense. Dr. J. van Ginneken remarks in that context: "this is in Indogermanic languages again something exceptional, where it often finds a place in languages with a more primitive structure."[30] And: "The reason for it is in the far-reaching development of progressing diphthongs".[31] The Sense of a word is often superfluous but its Meaning seems necessary and correct. That is the case with many "leges permissivae" [permissive legal determinations]. Their legal character can remain beyond discussion for some time[32] but a number of them is in essence a positive or negative command. One of many examples is in Art 12 of the Dutch

[Page 23] Criminal Law (as valid in 1916): "Everyone against whom a criminal act has been committed or has knowledge of such an act, is entitled to report this to one of the officials named in Art. 8". Acknowledging such entitlement is superfluous. The meaning is: "Officials, called in Art. 8 are obliged to accept report of anyone against whom a criminal act is committed or has knowledge about."

The sense of a statutory provision is often incorrect although it's meaning is correct. An example is Art. 120 of the Dutch Commercial Code: "Acceptance under one condition is not allowed." Meant is: "The owner of a bill of exchange is entitled to consider a conditional acceptance as refusal of acceptance."

---

[28] Lady Victoria Welby: *What is meaning?* Ch. 5.

[29] Bréal: p. 99.

[30] *Handboek der Nederlandsche Taal* [Manual of the Dutch language] I, 127.

[31] Id. I, 86.

[32] Mr. Dr. A. A. H. Struycken: *Het rechtsbegrip* [The concept of law] p. 23–44.

The significance of the language of the law, in particular of statutes, would increase if the legislator had diminished the difference between Meaning and Sense as much as possible.

****

[Page 39] My opinion is that an incorrect expression and an incorrect word can be generally used and understood. I gave already three examples: 'accountable, 'detainee', and 'employee'. But the expressive force of a logically well-formed word is always greater. We have no idea about the power of a language, which would be completely conceived of logical words and expressions. Such language would entirely change human relations. We would understand the most supersensible and significant aspects of our words. No longer would in accordance to Mauthner "die Sprache ein Hauptmittel des Nichtverstehens sein" [language a major means of misunderstanding].[33] A completely logical language cannot be achieved. But we strive for its effect. We cannot put in words or numbers to what degree logic can be incorporated in language. However, neither dictionaries nor syntax manuals should restrict themselves to the [Page 40] description of a language. Liberty and alignment are the two major ingredients of each language, and the alignment is the most valuable of them. The power of expression and articulation of a language increases by means of an increasing influence and application of logic.

This leads us to the question whether one single individual can influence or improve the language. It is clear that the importance of my investigation depends upon an answer to this question. If we could only describe and explain, but not influence language, then significs would be an interesting science without great importance. It is my opinion that a single individual can indeed influence language. I will therefore not only provide a description of the words, "liable, responsible, and accountable" but also influence legal language so that their use will be logically sound as much as possible.

The question is thus: do changes in the meaning of words occur under the influence of the will of an individual, or through the effect of generally accepted linguistic, logical or psychological laws.[34]

****

[Page 137] The signific group of concepts: "responsible, liable, accountable", is composed—in essence by means of the leading word 'address'—of three words and not more. The action "addressing" can be followed by the action "answering", and the latter by the action "attributing/imputing" to the prior acts. That closes the circle/event.

"Answering" presupposes a preceding "addressing". Then follows in that very same context an "imputation". Those three concepts cannot be separated; they can only be distinguished. Each of the three presupposes the two together, or one of the others. A clear insight in the architecture of this group of concepts could

[33] Mauthner, Vol. I, 56.

[34] Lady Victoria Welby, *Significs and Language*, Ch. II.

contribute to a better understanding of in particular German legal scholars and philosophers in general as well as Windelband's contribution on norm and normalcy in his "Ueber Norm und Normalität", 1906 in particular.[35] He wrote: "What we call accountability has, if I understand well, a double meaning. The first is retrospective, about the determination of guilt and the possibility of a reasonable determination of will, which corresponds to the person's character. The second is prospective, pertains to a question of punishment and regards the reasonableness of a person's motivations".

[Page 138] Also Von Lilienthal refers to "the interesting ideas of Windelband, culminating in the observation that 'accountability' has a double meaning.'[36]

English articulation is more complete than French, but less than German and Dutch.

The K. ten Bruggencate Dictionary mentions how 'aansprakelijk' is translated with "liable, answerable, responsible". 'Toerekenbaar' is furthermore translated as "accountable, responsible", and: 'toerekenbaarheid' is "soundness of mind, responsibility". 'Verantwoordelijk' is further translated as "responsible, accountable, answerable". "Toerekeningsvatbaarheid" is not mentioned, and a translation of "answerable" fails.

"Answer" and "response" have the same sense, both mean: "answering". "Answerable" is linguistically as pure as "responsible" and logically correct, although "answerable" is less used than "responsible".[37]

Lady Welby formulates objections against the expression "answerable", which we quote extensively: "There are cases where the direct use of a word has lapsed because the man in the street has taken it for metaphor. For instance: 'answerable'. We are [Page 139] directly answerable as we are competent to receive an answer to the question. The popular use is here, as in so many cases, a virtual blunder. A man is notable, irritable, lovable, managed. All that is not a question of *his* noting, irritating, loving, managing".[38]

It is certainly a curious instance of unrecognized confusion that we find in the Oxford Dictionary the main specification "able to be answered" marked as "rare", whereas the specification "universal" is provided in all other similar cases.[39] In the negative form "unanswerable", we revert strangely enough to the right sense. There is of course a secondary, in particular a forensic, sense of "answerable". A man is brought up to answer an indictment and pleading guilty or not guilty. After an accident a man in charge or authority is questioned and if he cannot defend himself, he becomes liable to penalty. But this word use is akin to one in which we say that a

[35]Windelband: *Ueber Norm und Normalität* [On norm and Normality] in: *Monatsschrift für Kriminalpsychologie*, 1906, 10.

[36]Id.: *Vergleichende Darstellung* Part V, 20.

[37]Ch. Mercier: *Criminal Responsibility* and R. Wilson: *Responsibility in Law* in: *The Law Magazine,* 1906–1908.

[38]C.H. den Hertog: *De Nederlandsche Taal*, p. 169, 170.

[39]The Dutch expression "toerekenbaar", most often understood as "toerekeningsvatbaar", is colloquial and only in exceptions correct.

certain machine or apparatus does not answer, and therefore must be rejected. Do we suppose than that the mechanical is answerable, either in the sense

[Page 140] of being able to receive or to provide an answer? Should we not acquire a new word for the moral agent who is liable to "answer" his conduct? The fact is that the Answerable is in this case the Questionable.[40] Thus we are debarred from the best solution of the question by another senseless usage.[41]

A general signific investigation of foreign words that are equal to "liable, responsible, accountable" would be of great importance for the knowledge of psychological and moral convictions of people.

We could suppose that these concepts are in many European languages articulated by means of similar words. This idea forms the basis for our investigation of "liable, responsible, and accountable". Let us now apply the above considerations to the verb "to address".

****

[Page 160] This is a three-persons-verb, with a subject, a *direct* object- and a *causal* object clause. Only in some figurative expression is "addressing" a two-persons-verb: 'He did not spare the bottle' where the implicit "addressing" (in 'not sparing') has no relation anymore with: "answering" or "accounting". (1) Compare the Dutch Civil Code, Art 1177. (2) The expression 'person' is strange here, but grammatically not incorrect.

The act "addressing" implies thus three persons.

First, the one who addresses himself to..: the subject.

Second: the one who is addressed, the object.

Third: a fact (considered as autonomous), which is the cause for this process of addressing: the causal object.

In an investigation of criminal law and its concept of liability, one has to find the subject, the object and the causal object in the act "address/addressing" in their specific meaning that belongs to the criminal law.

We refer to the specification of criminal law Prof. Mr G.A.van Hamel provided, being "the theory of the criminal liability, her preconditions and limits." This is correct in [Page 161] so far as a signific dissection of the word "liable" should enable us to determine each criminal law concept within the entire system of concepts of criminal law.

In other words: the content of the Criminal Code could be divided in three parts, one about the subject, another about the object and the third about the causal object of the criminal act "address/addressing". From here, we can have a look at the entire architecture of the Criminal Code. We focus here on the "Manual of the Dutch Criminal Law" by Prof. D. Simons.

Apart from the architecture of the criminal law are of course philosophical considerations and historical insights.

[40] See the relation between "*aanspreken*" [addressing] and "*antwoorden*" [answering]

[41] Lady Victoria Welby: *What is Meaning?* p. 44–46.

So, who is the object of address or appeal in the sense of criminal law? In other words: "who has the criminal law" in the sense of "who has the right to punish in accordance to the criminal law?"[42] Dutch Law determines that it is the State who possesses this right. The question what organs of the State should exercise that right is perhaps less clearly a particular issue of criminal law. Associations and specific persons do not have this right.[43] The right to State-prosecution is limited by the requirement of a complaint in cases of criminal activities.

[Page 162] The paragraph "Crimes to prosecute only on basis of complaint", § 42 of the quoted manual, would be totally acceptable and a first subject to deal with in a textbook on the basis of significs.

A second question is, "what is the object of the criminal act address/addressing"? In other words: "who can be prosecuted in accordance to valid Dutch law?"

A third question is: "What is the causal object of the criminal act 'address/addressing'". In other words: "because of what facts can one be prosecuted in accordance to Dutch law?"

Decisions conform signific criteria about what belongs to a second and a third part of a Criminal Code (the object or the causal object) will be difficult. If a second Part of that Code deals with the object of the criminal address, then we speak of the suspect or the offender. A third Part will deal with the causal object, being the offense. The two cannot be separated. That is an inherent difficulty in the Criminal Code's Book I, Title III on "Exclusion, reduction and increase of punishment." So I decided to re-order some paragraphs as far as the object is concerned, so that they answer

[Page 163] the question, who is the focus of Dutch criminal law, rather than: what facts are applied by the Dutch criminal law. If one asks about the effect of the criminal code in the course of time, then an emphasis on the facts in criminal law seems appropriate. I further re-order so that one finds in the second Part, in the context of subjects of criminal acts (which would be named in a more correct manner: "subject of criminal liability"): criminal problems with animals and criminal liability of legal persons, furthermore guilt and accountability, grounds of accountability, age, juvenile issues, action and participation, death of suspect and convicted persons.

In the third Part of the Penal Code, one encounters the chapter on the "Penal fact", among them: "The components of penal facts", "The general character of a criminal fact", "Division of penal facts in offenses and infringements", "Another division of

[Page 164] penal facts", "Acts and Effects", "Causality", "The criminal neglect", "Place and time of criminal fact" among other paragraphs. Texts about the power of definitive judgment (res judicata) should be re-placed, because they want to answer the question "because of which facts is a criminal prosecution possible", and not the question "against what person(s) is prosecution possible." All of them leave room

[42] D. Simons: *Manual*, §1.

[43] D. Simons: *Brief Manual of Criminal Proceedings, on Artt. 2 & 141.*

for a further question: "where is in this significally constructed Code a place for the Punishment, which is traditionally in the Penal Code's 7th Chapter: Punishment and Regulation." Indeed: a signific analysis of the penal/criminal act "address/addressing" in three parts: the subject, the object and the causal object does not provide a place for the concept of "punishment". In the concept "address" is the concept "punishment" not included, perhaps sometimes presupposed.

Most of these formulations are the result of a specific thought pattern: the prevalence of purpose. "Address" presupposes "answering" and the latter presupposes "attribute/account/ascribe". A signific analysis of the concept "criminal accountability", [Page 165] as we performed in parallel with "penal account", will show that "punishment" is a component of the concept "accountability". "Punishment" is presupposed in the concept "account" although punishment is not a component of that concept.

Describing criminal law as the theory of penal/criminal accountability is not incorrect, but criminal accountability *as theory* should be further discussed.

The entire construction of penal and criminal law fits into the construction of the concept "criminal accountability". In parallel, we could show that the signific analysis of the concept "civil accountability" has a place in each Part of the Civil Code. In other words: the entire architecture of the Civil Code fits into the concept "civil accountability".

The clearest example is the legal claim by wrongful act, which is in many regards like a penal claim. An allowance of a claim by wrongful act presupposes a claimant who has called to account: that is the subject of the act with the name: called to account. A defendant, who is called, is the object of the act of calling. A fact that leads to the

[Page 166] calling is the causal object of that act. If the called defendant is unable to defend him/herself legally correct than he is the cause of the damage, which will be attributed to him, for which he will be held accountable.[44]

We conclude that the concept "civil accountability" implies four essential components of a civil legal action. They are: (a) the claimant, the term for the subject of the action (b) the defendant, the indirect object of the act 'accounting'. (c) The subject and means of the claim is the causal object of the act, whereas (d) the final conclusion seems to be an adjective determination belonging to the verb "accounting".[45]

After reflections upon the word "accountable" we direct ourselves to the word "responsible". We will be short about the difference between a word ending with "lijk" and another with "-baar", endings that are unknown in English.

[Page 167] The adjective "responsible" covers an active as well as a passive sense. In the group of three (accountable, responsible, liable), the middle term has an active sense. We call someone 'responsible' for someone else if the relation

[44] Prof. Dr. G. Heymans: *Uitwassen der crimineele anthropologie* [Excesses of criminal anthropology] in: *De Gids* 1901, p. 73.

[45] Den Hertog, §68, §98.

between the two is such, that in case the first speaks to the other (addresses himself to the other), the second answers. That leads us to reflections on 'justifying', 'being accountable for', which are all including the word "answer' connected with the Dutch 'ver-'.

Den Hertog[46] writes about this prefix "ver-": "The prefix 'ver-' has a complex origin; *three* adverbs — (faur, fra, fair), the first = voor (Engl. pre) in different meanings, the second means 'weg' (Engl. road) and the third indicates the purpose of the action — composed the adverb in a process of blanching". Modern verbs with the Dutch prefix 'ver' do not connect with this origin anymore. The three: 'voor', 'weg' and 'over' are often recognizable but they often mix without leaving any trace. Most words with 'ver-' came into existence in the days where the origin was no longer experienced.

[Page 168] Den Hertog observes fifteen word-groups that have been caused by the prefix 'ver'. 'Verantwoorden', (justify, account for, being responsible for) is in his 11th group and is described as: " 'ver' creates verbs with the concept 'for the purpose of, in behalf of' so that "*verantwoorden* [account for] = answering for oneself or for others, '*verdedigen'* [defend] = to plea in favor of someone, which is *dadigen* or *dagdingen* [to appear] = to appear the day of the trial, to care, to represent, to defend, to assist etc." The origin in this group of expressions, Den Hertog suggests, is related to 'one's benefit'.

The verb 'answer' or 'providing an answer' ('*antwoorden*') is created by means of the suffix 'en' and the substantive answer ('*antwoord*'). Den Hertog calls such verbs formed by a substantive: denominatives.[47] Answering belongs to the group of verbs constructed with the concept 'equipped with', the so-called ornatives. The substantive '*antwoord'*, answer, is the combination of 'ant' and 'woord', prefix plus 'word'. The prefix has a meaning comparable with contra or opposite.

[Page 169] The verb "*verantwoorden*", justify, has in Dutch a three-person meaning. The compsites are here: subject, object and causal object. For instance: the defendant (=subject) justifies his actions (object) for the judge (causal object). 'Verantwoorden' [accounting for] and 'aanspreken' [address] are in Dutch composed of the same language parts but unified differently.

The subject of the act 'accounting for' is the object of the act 'address', the causal object of the act 'account for' one's actions is the cause of the act 'address'. The cause of the act 'justify' (the judge) is the subject of the act 'addressing'. We reconstructed the entire penal law by means of the concepts 'address', and we could now do the same with the concept 'account[able]'. But a signific dissection of the concept 'justify' has, like the analysis of 'address', no place for the concept 'punishment'. Punishment is presupposed in 'accountable' in as far as the purpose of the term is concerned. But [Page 170] 'punishment' is included in 'accounting'. *The description of Penal Law as the theory of penal justification is not incorrect,*

[46] *De Nederlandsche Taal*, II, p. 119–120.

[47] Id. p. 103.

but it would be more adequate to understand it as the theory of penal/criminal accountability.

****

[Page 176] We will now analyze the term "accountable" and the words "accountable/liable/responsible". This analysis requires in the first place attention for the verb (*toerekenen*) attribute/account/ascribe. "*Toerekeningsvatbaar*", accountable is an adjective composed of ("toerekening"), account, and the adjective ("vatbaar") amenable- or subject to. That adjective is not strange: one can be amenable for a cold, for improvement or for being convinced. The connection of a verbal substantive like 'improvement', or 'convincing' becomes a causal object of the activity itself. Amenable for improvement or to reason is somebody who can improve or accept reason. Two composite with amenable are used, one for accountability and another for viability. The act of accounting is in that case not a causal object but the indirect object of accounting.

****

[Page 178] In the concept of viability, the subject of the act is the act of living as such. Such complex words as viable and accountable, the expression 'amenable for life' or 'amenable for account' are not used.

Accountability is a concept against which objections often rise. It is considered a German word, a literal translation into Dutch of the German 'zurechnungsfähig', and that is not the case with the German 'lebensfähig', capable to live. Many authors write 'accountable' when they mean 'capable to account'. The logical value of two expressions has to be researched. Before obtaining insight in the words 'amenable for account' and 'object of account', one cannot analyze 'account' or 'attribute'. But the inverse can also not be determined as long as the concept of 'account' is not clarified.

****

[Page 266] We have seen that the meaning of 'account' does not differ from 'react, strike back' because some rules are not applied whilst determining that difference. If we distinguish various forms of 'account', then we do so because of the character of rule-violation (norms) and the character of the backlash.

Penal law accounting takes place if someone violates the provisions of the Penal/Criminal Code. The accounting will be executed by state institutions and knows a precise backlash: punishment.

Civil law accounting occurs if someone violates the rules of the Civil Code. The accounting will be executed within the actual social order by certain institutions. That

[Page 267] leads to dissolution, also a precisely determined backlash: compensation, annulment, etc.

Moral accounting occurs if someone violates rules of morality. The accounting takes place by any natural person on the basis of a moral judgment and is executed by a moral condemnation.[48]

Social accounting takes place if someone violated the rules of social order. That accounting can be executed by each member of society and consists of a diminished social prestige.

But what can be a 'medical responsibility' as phenomenon of accountability? Prof. Grasset distinguishes three types of responsibility, and suggests a moral, a social and a medical responsibility as parallel forms. His idea of a medical responsibility appears to be nothing than psychological health-criteria. He speaks about 'the integrity of psychical neurons', and writes: "he or she is responsible in a medical sense who's psychic neurons function normal at the moment of the incriminated action; he or she is irresponsible if the psychic neurons were completely in disorder at the moment of action; that person has a diminished responsibility because of this neuron situation."

[Page 268] What legal consequences follow or should follow is a matter beyond his definition of medical responsibility.

[Page 270] Human beings judge everything. A moral judgment has no justification [Page 271] beyond that judgment itself. Civil accountability can also not be justified as reasonably as we could prove the thesis of Pythagoras (who was, by the way, not so pure!). And where Planiol asks: "Why are legal acts that are qualified as wrong and inaccurate nevertheless sources of law?," the question is easier formulated than answered.[49] It are often issues of correct language use, which hinder the reader, so that we understand the question of Mr. J.A. Nederburgh to Dr Aletrino:[50] "Dr Aletrino states that an individual can be completcly unaccountable, but he nevertheless adds that a human individual remains accountable for his actions. That individual remains accountable, meaning that it is natural how he is submitted to the reaction of society if he violates the conditions of social life. But that is either a play with words, or no longer a source of comfort, which it is meant to be. For that reason we possess Penal Law, a [Page 272] penal/criminal responsibility, and an accountability without which penal law would lose its justification.[51]

I close herewith my investigations and reflections. When I accepted the task to perform a signific research about the words 'Liable, Responsible, Accountable' I knew that I would encounter difficulties to show shortcomings of language, which had to be articulated by means of that same language. It appeared in the course of

---

[48] No more than that: a moral judgment is *aesthetic*, contemplative, and *desiring*, imperative but not *requital/revenge.*

[49] Marcel Planiol: *Etudes sur la responsabilité civile* in: *Revue Critique de legislation et de jurisprudence,* 1905, p. 285.

[50] Aletrino: *Verantwoordelijkheid, Straf, Vergelding en Veiligheidsmaatregel* [Responsibility, Punishment, Revenge and Safety measure] in *Tijdschrift voor Strafrecht* [Journal of Criminal Law] Vol. 20, p. 68.

[51] That is not entirely correct: criminal/penal responsibility *is* penal law!

my research, that this difficulty was not smaller than I expected. But I do not accept to see my difficulties as a ground for discouragement, and to leave Language and in particular Legal Language unchallenged. We should increase the power of linguistic articulation carefully and scrupulously.

We need a New Language, a Supersensory Language in which each word has it Sense, Meaning and Significance. That Language will also enable us to understand each other in the true sense of the word.

The task of the legal significian as described by Prof. Mr. I. Henry Hymans is: "the development of language into a wonderful means to pervade and judge reality".[52]

[Page 273] Language and Reality are yet separated. But the only Power, which can abolish this separation is Language itself. Because, as Lady Welby expressed: "Language must be regenerated and must grow to a glorious stature."[53]

[52] Mr. I. Henri Hymans: *Het Recht der Werkelijkheid* [The law of reality], p. 27.

[53] Lady Victoria Welby.

Part III
Godfathers of Semiotics—Welby, Peirce, Greimas, Lacan

Editorial 2: "Meaning" and the Welby—Peirce Correspondence

Jan M. Broekman and Larry Catá Backer

Semioticians are today seldom aware of the fact that they hardly ever take their own historical developments into account when studying the semiotics of human communication, language, law, society or psyche. This is in particular the case where 'meanings' are at stake. One of the founders of semiotics, Lady Victoria Welby, had already at the end of the 19th century focused on the concept of meaning in her non-academic studies of philosophy, and put meaning furthermore in the foreground when she published her 1903 book *What is Meaning?* She defines significs—the term she had chosen to propagate—as the science of meanings or the study of significance.

When aged seventy-four, she wrote the article "significs" in the then latest edition of the Encyclopedia Britannica and broadened her view of what we call semiotics today[1]. Her insights were wholeheartedly welcomed by the US Philosopher Charles Sanders Peirce, who was in the process of developing his own philosophical insight in sometimes parallel ways, however, discussing differences between significs and (what he called) semeiotics, and in this complex confrontation the position of the word as a single particle from which language (and thus meaning) was build. These issues are still of interest in contemporary semiotics, and in the first place in legal semiotics. Do not lawyers live with words, and direct social processes by means of using words as decision particles of their entire immaterial equipment?

[1] The *Encyclopedia* article, an important event in British intellectual life, is reprinted in this volume together with some fragments of the 'Meaning'-book; see also: John E. Joseph: "Meaning in the margins. Victoria Lady Welby and significs" in *Times Literary Supplement*, March 23, 2012, p. 14 f.

J.M. Broekman (✉)
Dickinson School of Law, Penn State University, Carlisle, PA, USA
e-mail: jmb56@dsl.psu.edu

L. Catá Backer
Departments of Law and International Affairs, Penn State University,
University Park, PA, USA
e-mail: lcb11@psu.edu

J.M. Broekman, L. Catá Backer (eds.), *Signs In Law - A Source Book*,
DOI 10.1007/978-3-319-09837-1_10

So Peirce had all reasons to correspond with Lady Welby, as the specific volume of their letters shows[2]—but that volume has never been considered one of the most profiled sources of modern 20th century philosophy!

After remarks of Lady Welby on 'Meaning', we suggest the reading of two Letters of Peirce to the Lady—one written on one day (a great effort) in 1904, and one on various days of December 1908. Both are even in our days important for an understanding of the Peirce project, the unfolding of his philosophy and the style of his thinking exposed to Lady Welby, a comrade in philosophical courage and an academic outsider like himself. The letters are here not quoted in their 'life-form' as reprinted in the official Hardwick/Cool format, because the texts in the Peirce: *Collected Papers*[3] are more selectively focused on the semiotic/philosophical issues at hand. Is the major emphasis of the first letter on the categories Firstness, Secondness and Thirdness as instruments to place his philosophy in broad contexts of sign-relations in plural definitions, the second looks as it were back at his philosophical project from the viewpoint of Lady Welby, significs. For anyone who is interested in the relations between significs and semiotics[4]—lawyers should give that project a try, because it is all about understanding language and our linguistic expressiveness—this letter is of essence. *The two, one must conclude, are a mini-introduction into Peircean philosophy*, more directly and confronting than most of the academic introductions at hand. They show how the concept of 'meaning', in full development during the first decade of the 20th century, fulfills a key function in semiotic philosophy.

[2] See S. Hardwick & James Cook (Eds): *Semiotic And Significs. The Correspondence Between Charles S. Peirce And Victoria Lady Welby*. Indiana UP 1977.

[3] Peirce, Charles Sanders: *The Collected Papers of Charles Sanders Pierce.* Vols I – VI, Ed. Charles Hartshorne and Paul Weiss (1931–1935), Cambridge Ma, Harvard University Press. And: Peirce, Charles Sanders: *The Collected Papers of Charles Sanders Pierce.* Vols VII – VIII, Ed. Arthur W. Burks (1958), Cambridge Ma, Harvard University Press.

[4] See H. Walter Schmitz: *Essays on Significs. Papers presented on the occasion of the 150th anniversary of the birth of Victoria Lady Welby,* Benjamins, Amsterdam/Philadelphia 1990.

Meaning

Lady Victoria Welby

From Ch. XV "What is Meaning?" New York 1903[1]

The Copernican Reversal

The Copernican Reversal, while reducing our little world to its dependent status, does not imply disbelief in the potencies of the planet. On the contrary, the more clearly we realize the stupendous mine of energies, perceived or inferred, which our tiny earth has for her illimitable quarry and treasure-house, the higher must be our hopes for the flower of her products, the consummation of her generative activities. She may have 'mothered' Man, but it is no case of 'parthenogenesis' he has nothing less than the vast universe to 'father' him.

There are two conceptions of man, as there are two conceptions of the world on which he lives and to which he belongs; between these two in some sense or other: and whether consciously or not we all have to choose.

May we not sum up the alternative thus?

(1) Man, as his own centre, fixed and firm, or revolving round his self-axis; man as the last product of finished self-evolution. Man as throwing off, after originating, heat to warm self by, light to guide self by in the form of accumulated experience.

Man as projecting his own poetic fancies—what he calls the suns and stars, comets and meteors, into what he calls the sky. Man as ultimately a core of solid physical reality upon which you can 'take your stand' 'a dense entity which you can feel, touch, measure, weigh'; man with a star-studded mind-sky belonging to him as

---

[1] **Source:** LADY VICTORIA WELBY: *What Is Meaning?: Studies in the Development of Significance.* MacMillan & Co. New York 1903, Ch. XV, p. 116–119 and Ch. XXI, p. 161–164.

L.V. Welby (deceased)

J.M. Broekman, L. Catá Backer (eds.), *Signs In Law - A Source Book*,
DOI 10.1007/978-3-319-09837-1_11

evolved by him, and a sun going round him as well as a moon,-all ultimately products of his fertile imagination and his busy logic.

This is Ptolemaic, or at least pre-Copernican.

(2) Man as the offspring and dependent of a greater, nobler, fuller, stronger, and more energetic centre round which he revolves—that centre revolving also, and drawing him onwards with it on a yet mysterious journey.

Man as derivative in everything-as living and moving and having his being by the energizing cosmic forces; man as related through consciousness, and (beyond that) through what he calls mind and soul and spirit, to a universe which, atomic as he is, he can at least 'perceive,' recognizing his familiar home-stuffs in remoteness else inscrutable.

(3) Man as instinctively expressing this 'mind,' 'soul,' 'spirit' in terms of 'sight', responding to 'light'; in terms of attraction and repulsion, responding to 'gravity.' For he is moved to act by impulse, which transcends him—and therein do lie his natural ideals.

Man as knowing that his so-called 'emotion' and 'intellect,' 'will' and 'conscience,' and all else that is his, are gifts from a greater source, messages from a higher greatness, beams radiated from a nobler sphere, waves running in from a deeper sea of being: such waves, beams, messages, gifts, summed up in 'revelation' and 'inspiration' whether in a theological or a general sense, and conceived as generative energy shining upon and pressing into him, and bringing forth the being born to aspire as the plant grows upwards.

Man using the atmosphere which enfolds him and makes breathing possible, for bringing forth innumerable Life—knowing that the life shall grow till Mind is born at last; making the living units kin, through Man their world, with a cosmos of which suns, if not whole sun-systems, are the seeds and the germs. These are his truest metaphors.

This is Copernican.

Significs

Significs, then, will bring us the philosophy of Significance; *i.e.* a raising of our whole conception of meaning to a higher and more efficient level; a bringing cosmos out of the present 'chaos' of our ideas as to sense, meaning, and significance, and showing us that we need to use these terms in a certain order of value and range. Its best type of metaphor is the 'solar,' its best mine of analogy is the biological; because, as implying an extension of purview given us in spatial form by (post-Copernican) astronomy, it tends to relate the idea of life to the ideas of motion and matter, and moreover to relate the idea of mind to both. Thus Significs involves essentially and typically the philosophy of Interpretation, of Translation, and thereby of a mode of synthesis accepted and worked with by science and philosophy alike; profoundly modifying what we wrongly call the 'root' ideas of religion, of ethics, of poetry, of art, and, lastly, of practical life in all forms. But if studied systematically it would be seen from the first to provide a method of observation, a mode of experiment, which extends far beyond the laboratory, and includes the inductive and deductive methods in one process. There would never be any need to struggle that this view of things may supersede others; it could never be a supplanting system, and could never thus be attached to any individual name; it must necessarily be worked out by many co-operating minds. The principle involved forms a natural self-acting Critique of every system in turn, including the common sense ideal. But also it gives the gist, the vital centre, the growth-point of every existent organism of thought. It explains its own thinker to himself; it accounts for his thinking what he does as he does, and thus explains other thinkers to themselves. In fact, for the first time we gain a glimpse into what lies 'beyond the veil,' which both our own primitive and confused idea of Meaning and our modes of applying it have drawn over the world. The criteria thus reached will vindicate themselves alike to the most opposed of our thinkers.

As in the biological there is presumably in the mental world a tendency to recapitulation. Indeed, comparative mythology and folklore have brought to light what correspond to the miscalled rudimentary, really vestigial, survivals in modern thought. It would seem also that the present pre-Copernican character of science as applied to theories of life and mind (and called Positivism or Agnosticism) is a case of atavism. We may be supposed to have re-developed the Ptolemaic mode of thought (as we may revert to a lower level physiologically), having yet to reach in full mental use the Copernican scheme of cosmogony.

Thus our thinking is full of practical fallacy. We are unconsciously bound by a travesty of Euclid. And we have not merely to be true to Euclidean geometry in so far as it still holds good, but to advance with the geometrical thinkers who (as presumably he would himself now have done) are finding his limitations provisional.

To refer once more to instances already dealt with, we assume that the farther you go on a given 'line' of thought, the farther you go from your starting-point. But this does not follow. It will be objected at once that what the positive curvature of space symbolizes is ultimately a closed sphere. Thus you instantly have to conceive another one outside of it, which might be reached and traversed, so that the 'fallacy' is true again. No. The true idea of the content of the conception of infinity is not that it is merely quantitative; it not only means area after area of experience or of anything else; it means infinity in Change in the sense of transformation from worse to better in our ideal of the universe, our theory of the knower and the known. It is a question of change in direction and change in quality; the fourth dimension, whether reached in tenable form or no, is a parable of this; so is 'mind' itself with reference to the organic,—it is 'infinite' to that: it is not subject to the same limitations, though it has some of its own.[2] But then what a disgrace to have only a negative

---

[2] When the above was written I knew nothing of Croll's theory of direction v. force.

term for this! To the 'geocentricist' to stand over or upon; to the 'solarist' to stand under, and to the 'cosmicist' to stand within: these are the three forms of 'apprehension', which, fortunately, we do call under-, not over-standing. If only we were consistent in this! But all alike must learn to do more than stand, must learn to move and to advance and to 'rise'. Corresponding to this we have three forms of experience rendered by metaphors: one of line, one of surface, one of cube. No doubt the three are ultimately one; but to our great practical loss and danger we confound their distinctions.

That which 'transcends' in any sense the ordinary limits of experience is often rightly enough referred to the vague, unknown, unsafe, unreal. Well, that 'beyond', which the telescope and spectroscope bring us (especially the latter) gives us the bases of the most accurate predictions which science makes. The tree is known by its fruit. No one would protest against transcendency of that kind. Now think of the incredible power of projection possessed by plant and insect, as shown in the ejection of seeds, the jumping of grasshoppers, etc. This is at least a hundred times greater than our own muscular power. Suppose that by contracting into the scale of the insect we were to gain a tremendous projective power? Perhaps the demand for greater size as the invariable concomitant of fuller power to which we are so much addicted would thus be relegated to a truer place. The greater energy often belongs to the smaller body.

Again, in this region of greater intensity we find a minute world the existence of which we had not suspected; and here lie many answers to Whys that we have vainly sought in the expansive "beyond". The truth is that hitherto we have been content to go to the root of the matter and the foundation of things. And when we have got there and described what we found, we are surprised and disappointed at the very partial welcome, which our proposed solutions of life problems find. But it cannot be too often repeated that nothing (except indeed lateral rootlets) springs from a root, and all that is greatest (or its symbol) is unfounded. There is, for instance, no basis for this present statement; it has to do with the worlds which roll in space, 'solidly' real and absolutely secure in an orderly orbit; and what is of ultimate concern to our thought is the whither of its Way.

Two Letters to Lady Welby

Charles Sanders Peirce

On Signs and the Categories[1]

October 12, 1904

327. But I wanted to write to you about signs, which in your opinion and mine are matters of so much concern. More in mine, I think, than in yours. For in mine, the highest grade of reality is only reached by signs; that is by such ideas as those of Truth and Right and the rest. It sounds paradoxical; but when I have devolved to you my whole theory of signs, it will seem less so. I think that I will today explain the outlines of my classification of signs.

328. You know that I particularly approve of inventing new words for new ideas. I do not know that the study I call *Ideoscopy* can be called a new idea, but the word *phenomenology* is used in a different sense.[2] *Ideoscopy* consists in describing and classifying the ideas that belong to ordinary experience or that naturally arise in connection with ordinary life, without regard to their being valid or invalid or to their

---

Source: PEIRCE, Charles Sanders: "*Two Letters to Lady V. Welby*": *Oct. 12, 1904* and *Dec. 24/25 & 28, 1908.* Collected Papers Vol. 8, Ch. 8, Nrs. 327–379. **Free Internet Access on "Past Masters" Series.**

[1] Fragment numbers are those of the Harvard Edition *Collected Papers*. (Eds.:) From a letter dated "1904 Oct 12" to "My dear Lady Welby." A photostat copy of the original letter is in the Yale University Library. The complete letter is also in [Bibliography] M-20a, pp. 7–14, published by Whitlock's, Inc., New Haven, Conn., with whose permission the parts given here and the quotations in 330n4 and 330n6 are reprinted.

Lady Victoria Welby was an English semanticist, at one time Maid of Honour to Queen Victoria. For Peirce's review of her *What is Meaning?* see Book I of the CPI.

[2] (Ed.) Peirce's phenomenology and categories are discussed at various places in [CP], especially in [CP] I, Book III. See also 7.524-538.

C.S. Peirce (deceased)

J.M. Broekman, L. Catá Backer (eds.), *Signs In Law - A Source Book*,
DOI 10.1007/978-3-319-09837-1_12

psychology. In pursuing this study I was long ago (1867) led, after only three or four years' study, to throw all ideas into the three classes of Firstness, of Secondness, and of Thirdness.[3] This sort of notion is as distasteful to me as to anybody; and for years, I endeavored to pooh-pooh and refute it; but it long ago conquered me completely. Disagreeable as it is to attribute such meaning to numbers, and to a triad above all, it is as true as it is disagreeable. The ideas of Firstness, Secondness, and Thirdness are simple enough. Giving to being the broadest possible sense, to include ideas as well as things, and ideas that we fancy we have just as much as ideas we do have, I should define Firstness, Secondness, and Thirdness thus:

Firstness is the mode of being of that which is such as it is, positively and without reference to anything else.
Secondness is the mode of being of that which is such as it is, with respect to a second but regardless of any third.
Thirdness is the mode of being of that which is such as it is, in bringing a second and third into relation to each other.
I call these three ideas the cenopythagorean categories.

329. The typical ideas of Firstness are qualities of feeling, or mere appearances. The scarlet of your royal liveries, the quality itself, independently of its being perceived or remembered, is an example, by which I do not mean that you are to imagine that you *do not* perceive or remember it, but that you are to drop out of account that which may be attached to it in perceiving or in remembering, but which does not belong to the quality. For example, when you remember it, your idea is said to be *dim* and when it is before your eyes, it is *vivid.* But dimness or vividness do not belong to your idea of the quality. They *might* no doubt, if considered simply as a feeling; but when you think of vividness you do not consider it from that point of view. You think of it as a degree of disturbance of your consciousness. The quality of red is not thought of as belonging to you, or as attached to liveries. It is simply a peculiar positive possibility regardless of anything else.

If you ask a mineralogist what hardness is, he will say that it is what one predicates of a body that one cannot scratch with a knife. But a simple person will think of hardness as a simple positive possibility the *realization* of which causes a body to be like a flint. That idea of hardness is an idea of Firstness. The unanalyzed total impression made by any manifold not thought of as actual fact, but simply as a quality, as simple positive possibility of appearance, is an idea of Firstness. Notice the *naïveté* of Firstness. The cenopythagorean categories are doubtless another attempt to characterize what Hegel sought to characterize as his three stages of thought. They also correspond to the three categories of each of the four triads of Kant's table. But the fact that these different attempts were independent of one another (the resemblance of these Categories to Hegel's stages was not remarked for many years after the list had been under study, owing to my antipathy to Hegel) only goes to show that there really are three such elements. The idea of the present instant, which, whether it exists or not, is naturally thought as a point of time in which no thought can take place or any detail be separated, is an idea of Firstness.

[3] (Ed.) In [Bibliography] G-1867-1c, 1.545-559.

330. The type of an idea of Secondness is the experience of effort, prescinded from the idea of a purpose. It may be said that there is no such experience, that a purpose is always in view as long as the effort is cognized. This may be open to doubt; for in sustained effort we soon let the purpose drop out of view. However, I abstain from psychology, which has nothing to do with ideoscopy. The existence of the word *effort* is sufficient proof that people think they have such an idea; and that is enough. The experience of effort cannot exist without the experience of resistance. Effort only is effort by virtue of its being opposed; and no third element enters. Note that I speak of the *experience,* not of the *feeling,* of effort. Imagine yourself to be seated alone at night in the basket of a balloon, far above earth, calmly enjoying the absolute calm and stillness. Suddenly the piercing shriek of a steam-whistle breaks upon you, and continues for a good while. The impression of stillness was an idea of Firstness, a quality of feeling. The piercing whistle does not allow you to think or do anything but suffer. So that too is absolutely simple. Another Firstness. But the breaking of the silence by the noise was an experience. The person in his inertness identifies himself with the precedent state of feeling, and the new feeling, which comes in spite of him is the non-ego. He has a two-sided consciousness of an ego and a non-ego. That consciousness of the action of a new feeling in destroying the old feeling is what I call an *experience.* Experience generally is what the course of life has *compelled* me to think. Secondness is either *genuine* or *degenerate.* There are many degrees of genuineness. Generally speaking genuine secondness consists in one thing acting upon another, — brute action. I say brute, because so far as the idea of any *law* or *reason* comes in, Thirdness comes in. When a stone falls to the ground, the law of gravitation does not act to make it fall. The law of gravitation is the judge upon the bench who may pronounce the law till doomsday, but unless the strong arm of the law, the brutal sheriff, gives effect to the law, it amounts to nothing. True, the judge can create a sheriff if need be; but he must have one. The stone's actually falling is purely the affair of the stone and the earth at the time. This is a case of *reaction.* So is *existence,* which is the mode of being of that which reacts with other things. But there is also action without reaction. *Such is the action of the previous upon the subsequent.*[4] It is a difficult question whether the idea of this one-sided determination is a pure idea of secondness or whether it involves thirdness. At present, the former view seems to me correct. I suppose that when Kant made Time a form of the internal sense alone, he was influenced by some such considerations as the following. The relation between the previous and the subsequent consists in the previous being determinate and fixed for the subsequent, and the subsequent being indeterminate for the previous. But indeterminacy belongs only to ideas; the existent is determinate in every respect; and this is just what the law of causation consists in. Accordingly, the relation of time concerns only ideas. It may also be argued that, according to the law of the conservation of energy, there is nothing in the physical universe corresponding to our idea that the previous determines the subsequent in any way in which the subsequent does not determine the previous. For, according to that law, all that happens in the physical universe consists in the

[4] (Ed.) "The italicized sentence is, in manuscript, underlined in pencil. Perhaps it was underlined by Lady Welby, yet it was not her habit to annotate Peirce's letters."

exchange of just so much *vis viva* 1/2 m(ds/dt)2 for so much displacement. Now the square of a negative quantity being positive, it follows that if all the velocities were reversed at any instant, everything would go on just the same, only time going backward as it were. Everything that had happened would happen again in reversed order. These seem to me to be strong arguments to prove that temporal causation (a very different thing from physical dynamic action) is an action upon ideas and not upon existents.[5] But since our idea of the past is precisely the idea of that which is absolutely determinate, fixed, *fait accompli,* and dead, as against the future which is living, plastic, and determinable, it appears to me that the idea of one-sided action, in so far as it concerns the being of the determinate, is a pure idea of Secondness; and I think that great errors of metaphysics are due to looking at the future as something that will have been past. I cannot admit that the idea of the future can be so translated into the Secundal ideas of the past. To say that a given kind of event never will happen is to deny that there is any date at which its happening will be past; but it is not equivalent to any affirmation about a past relative to any assignable date. When we pass from the idea of an event to saying that it never will happen, or will happen in endless repetition, or introduce in any way the idea of endless repetition, I will say the idea is *mellonized* (mellön), about to be, do, or suffer. When I conceive a fact as acting but not capable of being acted upon, I will say that it is *parelelythose* ({parelélythös}, past) and the mode of being which consists in such action I will call *parelelythosine* (–ine = {einai}, being); I regard the former as an idea of Thirdness, the latter as an idea of Secondness. I consider the idea of any dyadic relation not involving any third as an idea of Secondness; and I should not call any completely degenerate except the relation of identity. But similarity which is the only possible identity of Firsts is very near to that. Dyadic relations have been classified by me in a great variety of ways; but the most important are, first, with regard to the nature of the Second in itself and, second, with regard to the nature of its First. The Second, or *Relate,*[6] is, in itself, either a *Referate,* if it is intrinsically a possibility, such as a quality, or it is a *Revelate* if it is of its own nature an Existent. In respect to its First, the Second is divisible either in regard to the dynamic first or to the immediate first. In regard to its dynamic first, a Second is determined either by virtue of its own intrinsic nature, or by virtue of a real relation to that second (an action). Its immediate second is either a Quality or an Existent.

331. I now come to Thirdness. To me, who have for forty years considered the matter from every point of view that I could discover, the inadequacy of Secondness to cover all that is in our minds is so evident that I scarce know how to begin to persuade any person of it who is not already convinced of it. Yet I see a great many thinkers who are trying to construct a system without putting any Thirdness into it. Among them are some of my best friends who acknowledge themselves indebted to me for ideas but have never learned the principal lesson. Very well. It is highly

[5](Eds.:) Reversible and irreversible actions are discussed further in Chapter 3, "Habit," [CP] VII, Book III.

[6](Ed.) "'Relate', in manuscript, is underlined in pencil." From [Bibliography], p. 10.

proper that Secondness should be searched to its very bottom. Thus only can the indispensableness and irreducibility of thirdness be made out, although for him who has the mind to grasp it, it is sufficient to say that no branching of a line can result from putting one line on the end of another.[7] My friend Schröder fell in love with my algebra of dyadic relations. The few pages I gave to it in my Note B in the 'Studies in Logic by Members of the Johns Hopkins University' were proportionate to its importance.[8] His book is profound,[9] but its profundity only makes it more clear that Secondness cannot compass Thirdness. (He is careful to avoid ever saying that it can, but he does go so far as to say that Secondness is the more important. So it is, considering that Thirdness cannot be understood without Secondness. But as to its application, it is so inferior to Thirdness as to be in that aspect quite in a different world.) Even in the most degenerate form of Thirdness, and thirdness has two grades of degeneracy, something may be detected which is not mere secondness. If you take any ordinary triadic relation, you will always find a *mental* element in it. Brute action is secondness, any mentality involves thirdness. Analyze for instance the relation involved in 'A gives B to C.' Now what is giving? It does not consist [in] A's putting B away from him and C's subsequently taking B up. It is not necessary that any material transfer should take place. It consists in A's making C the possessor according to *Law.* There must be some kind of law before there can be any kind of giving,—be it but the law of the strongest. But now suppose that giving *did* consist merely in A's laying down the B which C subsequently picks up. That would be a degenerate form of Thirdness in which the thirdness is externally appended. In A's putting away B, there is no thirdness. In C's taking B, there is no thirdness. But if you say that these two acts constitute a single operation by virtue of the identity of the B, you transcend the mere brute fact, you introduce a mental element .... The criticism which I make on [my] algebra of dyadic relations, with which I am by no means in love, though I think it is a pretty thing, is that the very triadic relations which it does not recognize, it does itself employ. For every combination of relatives to make a new relative is a triadic relation irreducible to dyadic relations. Its *inadequacy* is shown in other ways, but in this way it is in a conflict with itself *if it be regarded,* as I never did regard it, *as sufficient for the expression of all relations.* My universal algebra of relations, with the subjacent indices and Σ and π, is susceptible of being enlarged so as to comprise everything; and so, still better, though not to ideal perfection, is the system of *existential graphs.*[10]

332. I have not sufficiently applied myself to the study of the degenerate forms of Thirdness, though I think I see that it has two distinct grades of degeneracy. In its genuine form, Thirdness is the triadic relation existing between a sign, its object, and the interpreting thought, itself a sign, considered as constituting the mode of

[7] (Ed.) Cf. 1.347, 3.421.

[8] (Eds.:) [Bibliography] G-1883-.328-358.

[9] (Eds.:) Cf. [Bibliography] G-1896-6.

[10] (Eds.:) This is treated at length in [CP] IV, Book II.

being of a sign.[11] A sign mediates between the *interpretant* sign and its object. Taking sign in its broadest sense, its interpretant is not necessarily a sign. Any concept is a sign, of course. Ockham, Hobbes, and Leibniz have sufficiently said that. But we may take a sign in so broad a sense that the interpretant of it is not a thought, but an action or experience, or we may even so enlarge the meaning of sign that its interpretant is a mere quality of feeling. A *Third* is something, which brings a First into relation to a Second. A sign is a sort of Third. How shall we characterize it? Shall we say that a Sign brings a Second, its Object, into *cognitive* relation to a Third? That a Sign brings a Second into the same relation to a first in which it stands itself to that First? If we insist on *consciousness,* we must say what we mean by consciousness of an object. Shall we say we mean Feeling? Shall we say we mean association, or Habit? These are, on the face of them, psychological distinctions, which I am particular to avoid. What is the essential difference between a sign that is communicated to a mind, and one that is not so communicated? If the question were simply what we *do* mean by a sign, it might soon be resolved. But that is not the point. We are in the situation of a zoölogist who wants to know what ought to be the meaning of "fish" in order to make fishes one of the great classes of vertebrates. It appears to me that the essential function of a sign is to render inefficient relations efficient, — not to set them into action, but to establish a habit or general rule whereby they will act on occasion. According to the physical doctrine, nothing ever happens but the continued rectilinear velocities with the accelerations that accompany different relative positions of the particles. All other relations, of which we know so many, are inefficient. Knowledge in some way renders them efficient; and a sign is something by knowing which we know something more. With the exception of knowledge, in the present instant, of the contents of consciousness in that instant (the existence of which knowledge is open to doubt) all our thought and knowledge is by signs. A sign therefore is an object, which is in relation to its object on the one hand and to an interpretant on the other, in such a way as to bring the interpretant into a relation to the object, corresponding to its own relation to the object. I might say 'similar to its own' for a correspondence consists in a similarity; but perhaps correspondence is narrower.

333. I am now prepared to give my division of signs, as soon as I have pointed out that a sign has two objects, its object as it is represented and its object in itself. It has also three interpretants, its interpretant as represented or meant to be understood, its interpretant as it is produced, and its interpretant in itself. Now signs may be divided as to their own material nature, as to their relations to their objects, and as to their relations to their interpretants.

334. As it is in itself, a sign is either of the nature of an appearance, when I call it a *qualisign;* or secondly, it is an individual object or event, when I call it a *sinsign* (the syllable *sin* being the first syllable of *sem*el, *sim*ul, *sin*gular, etc.); or thirdly, it is of the nature of a general type, when I call it a *legisign.* As we use the term 'word' in

[11] (Eds.:) Signs are discussed at various places in [CP]. See 8.313 ff., 2.227 ff., and the letter following the present one.

most cases, saying that 'the' is one 'word' and 'an' is a second 'word,' a 'word' is a legisign. But when we say of a page in a book, that it has 250 'words' upon it, of which twenty are 'the's, the 'word' is a sinsign. A sinsign so embodying a legisign, I term a 'replica' of the legisign. The difference between a legisign and a qualisign, neither of which is an individual thing, is that a legisign has a definite identity, though usually admitting a great variety of appearances. Thus, &, *and,* and the sound are all one word. The qualisign, on the other hand, has no identity. It is the mere quality of an appearance and is not exactly the same throughout a second. Instead of identity, it has *great similarity,* and cannot differ much without being called quite another qualisign.

335. In respect to their relations to their dynamic objects, I divide signs into Icons, Indices, and Symbols (a division I gave in 1867).[12] I define an Icon as a sign which is determined by its dynamic object by virtue of its own internal nature. Such is any qualisign, like a vision, — or the sentiment excited by a piece of music considered as representing what the composer intended. Such may be a sinsign, like an individual diagram; say a curve of the distribution of errors. I define an Index as a sign determined by its dynamic object by virtue of being in a real relation to it. Such is a Proper Name (a legisign); such is the occurrence of a symptom of a disease. (The symptom itself is a legisign, a general type of a definite character. The occurrence in a particular case is a sinsign.) I define a Symbol as a sign, which is determined by its dynamic object only in the sense that it will be so interpreted. It thus depends either upon a convention, a habit, or a natural disposition of its interpretant or of the field of its interpretant (that of which the interpretant is a determination). Every symbol is necessarily a legisign; for it is inaccurate to call a replica of a legisign a symbol.

336. In respect to its immediate object a sign may either be a sign of a quality, of an existent, or of a law.

337. In regard to its relation to its signified interpretant, a sign is either a Rheme, a Dicent, or an Argument. This corresponds to the old division, Term, Proposition, and Argument, modified so as to be applicable to signs generally. A *Term* is simply a class-name or proper-name. I do not regard the common noun as an essentially necessary part of speech. Indeed, it is only fully developed as a separate part of speech in the Aryan languages and the Basque,—possibly in some other out of the way tongues. In the Shemitic languages it is generally in form a verbal affair, and usually is so in substance, too. As well as I can make out, such it is in most languages. In my universal algebra of logic there is no common noun. A rheme is any sign that is not true nor false, like almost any single word except 'yes' and 'no,' which are almost peculiar to modern languages. A *proposition* as I use that term, is a dicent symbol. A dicent is not an assertion, but is a sign *capable* of being asserted. But an assertion is a dicent. According to my present view (I may see more light in future) the act of assertion is not a pure act of signification. It is an exhibition of the

[12] (Eds.:) CP 1.558

fact that one subjects oneself to the penalties visited on a liar if the proposition asserted is not true. An act of judgment is the self-recognition of a belief; and a belief consists in the deliberate acceptance of a proposition as a basis of conduct. But I think this position is open to doubt. It is simply a question of which view gives the simplest view of the nature of the proposition. Holding, then, that a Dicent does not assert, I naturally hold that an Argument need not actually be submitted or urged. I therefore define an argument as a sign which is represented in its signified interpretant not as a Sign of that interpretant (the conclusion) [for that would be to urge or submit it][13] but *as if* it were a Sign of the Interpretant or perhaps as if it were a Sign of the state of the universe to which it refers, in which the premisses are taken for granted. I define a dicent as a sign represented in its signified interpretant *as if it were* in a Real Relation to its Object. (Or as being so, if it is asserted.) A rheme is defined as a sign, which is represented in its signified interpretant as *if it were* a character or mark (or as being so).

338. According to my present view, a sign may appeal to its dynamic interpretant in three ways:

1st, an argument only may be *submitted* to its interpretant, as something the reasonableness of which will be acknowledged.
2nd, an argument or dicent may be *urged* upon the interpretant by an act of insistence.
3rd, argument or dicent may be, and a rheme can only be, presented to the interpretant for *contemplation.*

339. Finally, in its relation to its immediate interpretant, I would divide signs into three classes as follows:

1st, those, which are interpretable in thoughts or other signs of the same kind in infinite series,
2nd, those, which are interpretable in actual experiences,
3rd, those, which are interpretable in qualities of feelings or appearances.

340. Now if you think on the whole (as I do) that there is much valuable truth in all this, I should be gratified if you cared to append it to the next edition of your book, after editing it and of course cutting out personalities of a disagreeable kind, ESPECIALLY IF [IT WERE] ACCOMPANIED BY ONE OR MORE (running or other) CLOSE CRITICISMS; for I haven't a doubt there is more or less error involved….

341. P.S. On the whole, then, I should say there were ten principal classes of signs

1. Qualisigns
2. Iconic Sinsigns
3. Iconic Legisigns
4. *Vestiges,* or Rhematic Indexical Sinsigns

[13] (Eds.:) The brackets are Peirce's.

5. *Proper Names,* or Rhematic Indexical Legisigns
6. Rhematic Symbols
7. Dicent Sinsigns (as a portrait with a legend)
8. Dicent Indexical Legisigns
9. *Propositions,* or Dicent Symbols
10. Arguments[14]

On the Classification of Signs[15]

December 24, 25, 28, 1908

342. The publishers of the Britannica have given an unequivocal earnest of their determination to make every edition of their encyclopedia maintain its supereminence in employing editors who would enlist you for an epitome of your exploration of "significs."[16] It greatly encourages me in my endeavours, since, as well as I can make out, what you call "significs" is equivalent to the study that I entitle logic. In my paper of 1867 May 14 (Proc. Am. Acad. of Arts & Sci., Vol. VII, p. 295) I said, "We come to this, that logic treats of the reference of symbols in general to their objects. In this view it is one of a trivium of conceivable sciences. The first would treat of the formal conditions of symbols having meaning, that is of the reference of symbols in general to their grounds, or imputed characters; and this might be called Formal Grammar [the *grammatica speculativa* of Duns]. The second, logic, would treat of the formal conditions of the truth of symbols. The third would treat of the formal conditions of the force of symbols, or their power of appealing to a mind, that is, of their reference in general to interpretants, and this might be called formal rhetoric."[17] I should still opine that in the future there probably will be three such sciences. But I have learned that the only natural lines of demarcation between nearly related sciences are the divisions between the social groups of devotees of those sciences; and for the present the cenoscopic studies (i.e., those studies which

[14] (Ed.) Cf. 2.254 and [Bibliography] M-20a, Appendix B.

[15] (Ed.) From a partial draft of a letter to Lady Welby, bearing dates of 24, 25, and 28 December 1908, Widener IB3a, with an added quotation in 368n23. The editor has made more than the usual number of alterations in punctuation, capitalization, etc., in both this and the previous letter, and in the present letter he has made several changes in format. In a letter to Lady Welby, with dates 31 January, 24 February, and 14 March 1909, Peirce says: "I find in my portfolio some part of a letter, if not the whole, dated December 28. I suppose I sent you that" [Bibliography] M-20a, p. 35. It is probable that in this passage Peirce is referring to the letter printed here. This letter never reached Lady Welby; cf. *Other Dimensions: A Selection from the Later Correspondence of Victoria Lady Welby,* p. 309n1 (listed with [Bibliography] M-20a). The letter printed here resembles, but is distinct from, a letter with dates of 14 and 23 December 1908, printed in [Bibliography] M-20a, pp. 22–32, q.v.

[16] (Eds.:) Lady Welby wrote "Significs" for the 11th edition of *The Encyclopedia Britannica,* 1910–11.

[17] (Eds.:) CP 1.559 The brackets are in the manuscript.

do not depend upon new special observations) of all signs remain one undivided science,—a conclusion I had come to before I made your acquaintance, but which the warm interest that you and I have in each other's researches in spite of the difference in their lines, decidedly confirms.

343. It seems to me that one of the first useful steps toward a science of *semeiotic* ({sémeiötiké}), or the cenoscopic science of signs, must be the accurate definition, or logical analysis, of the concepts of the science.[18] I define a *Sign* as anything which on the one hand is so determined by an Object and on the other hand so determines an idea in a person's mind, that this latter determination, which I term the *Interpretant* of the sign, is thereby mediately determined by that Object. A sign, therefore, has a triadic relation to its Object and to its Interpretant. But it is necessary to distinguish the *Immediate Object,* or the Object as the Sign represents it, from the *Dynamical Object,* or really efficient but not immediately present Object. It is likewise requisite to distinguish the *Immediate Interpretant,* i.e. the Interpretant represented or signified in the Sign, from the *Dynamic Interpretant,* or effect actually produced on the mind by the Sign; and both of these from the *Normal Interpretant,* or effect that would be produced on the mind by the Sign after sufficient development of thought. On these considerations I base a recognition of ten respects in which Signs may be divided. I do not say that these divisions are enough. But since every one of them turns out to be a trichotomy, it follows that in order to decide what classes of signs result from them, I have 310 or 59049, difficult questions to carefully consider; and therefore I will not undertake to carry my systematical division of signs any further, but will leave that for future explorers.

344. The ten respects according to which the chief divisions of signs are determined are as follows:

1st, According to the Mode of Apprehension of the Sign itself,
2nd, According to the Mode of Presentation of the Immediate Object,
3rd, According to the Mode of Being of the Dynamical Object,
4th, According to the Relation of the Sign to its Dynamical Object,
5th, According to the Mode of Presentation of the Immediate Interpretant,
6th, According to the Mode of Being of the Dynamical Interpretant,
7th, According to the Relation of the Sign to the Dynamical Interpretant,
8th, According to the Nature of the Normal Interpretant,
9th, According to the Relation of the Sign to the Normal Interpretant,
10th, According to the Triadic Relation of the Sign to its Dynamical Object and to its Normal Interpretant.

345. The ten divisions appear to me to be all Trichotomies; but it is possible that some of them are not properly so. Of these Ten Trichotomies, I have a clear apprehension of some, (which I mark δ for {délos}), an unsatisfactory and doubtful

[18] (Eds.:) For references to other discussions of signs, see 332n11.

notion of others (which I mark α for {adélos}), and a tolerable but not thoroughly tried conception of others (which I mark μ for {metrios}, σ for {schedon}, almost clear, χ for {chalepös} hardly better than α).

The Ten Main Trichotomies of Signs (as they are apprehended by me 1908 Dec. 24):

346. I. A Sign is necessarily in itself present to the Mind of its Interpreter. Now there are three entirely different ways in which Objects are present to minds:[19]

First: in themselves as they are in themselves. Namely, Feelings are so present. At the first instant of waking from profound sleep when thought, or even distinct perception, is not yet awake, if one has gone to bed more asleep than awake in a large, strange room with one dim candle. At the instant of waking the *tout ensemble* is felt as a unit. The feeling of the skylark's song in the morning, of one's first hearing of the English nightingale.

Secondly: the sense of something opposing one's Effort, something preventing one from opening a door slightly ajar; which is known in its individuality by the actual shock, the Surprising element, in any Experience which makes it *sui generis.*

Thirdly: that which is stored away in one's Memory; Familiar, and as such, General.

347. Consequently: Signs, in respect to their Modes of possible Presentation, are divisible (σ) into

A. *Potisigns,* or Objects which are signs so far as they are merely possible, but felt to be positively possible; as, for example, the seventh ray that passes through the three intersections of opposite sides of Pascal's hexagram.

B. *Actisigns,* or Objects which are Signs as Experienced *hic et nunc;* such as any single word in a single place in a single sentence of a single paragraph of a single page of a single copy of a book. There may be repetition of the whole paragraph, this word included, in another place. But that other occurrence is not *this* word. The book may be printed in an edition of ten thousand; but THIS word is only in my copy.

C. *Famisigns,* familiar signs, which must be General, as General signs must be familiar or composed of Familiar signs. (I speak of signs which are "general," not in the sense of *signifying* Generals, but as being *themselves* general; just as Charlemagne is general, in that it occurs many times with one and the same denotation.)

348. I think I might as well have marked this division δ instead of σ, except that perhaps the question may arise whether I ought not to have recognized a division according as the sign is a *natural sign,* which has no party to the dialogue as its author, or whether it be an *uttered sign,* and in the latter case, is the very sign that is getting uttered or another. But it seems to me that this division turns upon the question of whether or not the sign uttered is a sign of a sign as its Object. For must not every sign, in order to become a sign, get uttered?

[19] (Eds.:) For references to discussions of Peirce's categories, see 328n2.

349. II.... Objects may be presented in three ways, thus:

1st, As mere Ideas, or what might be if things were not as they are; such as a geometrical surface, or an absolutely definite or distinct notion.
2nd, As brutely compelling attention.
3rd, As Rationally recommending themselves, or as Habitudes to which one is already reconciled.

350. Adopting this enumeration as a basis of a division of Signs, I obtain

A. *Descriptives,* which determine their Objects by stating the characters of the latter.

B. *Designatives* (or *Denotatives*), or Indicatives, *Denominatives,* which like a Demonstrative pronoun, or a pointing finger, brutely direct the mental eyeballs of the interpreter to the object in question, which in this case cannot be given by independent reasoning.

C. *Copulants,* which neither describe nor denote their Objects, but merely express the logical relations of these latter to something otherwise referred to.[20] Such, among linguistic signs, as "If—then—," "—is—," "—causes—," "—would be—," "—is relative to—for—" "Whatever" etc.

351. Shall I appoint this famous distinction (as I have stated it, or modified [it]) to the governance of my Second way of dividing Signs, or shall I yield this place to a distinction prominent in every language on earth, that between the three 'persons,' *amo, amas, amat?* If I and *thou* are the Objects, we say *We;* if *thou* and *he* are the Objects, we say *Ye.* But if I and *We* are the Objects to the exclusion of *Thee,* I know no other linguistic form than the French expression "*Nous autres.*" *I, Thou,* and *He* can be expressed by the Tri-al and *Quadral* numbers of Polynesian languages. In English we can only say "*We all of us.*" Thus there ought, logically one would say, to be *seven* grammatical persons, if any at all. But none at all are needed, if we have the Designative pronouns *I, Thou, He.* But hold! When I say there are only 7 persons I forget the differences between Thou and I are Anglo-Saxon. Thou and I are correspondents. Thou and I are endurer and endured. Thou and I are admired and admirer. Thou, he, and I are accuser to and of, accuser of and to, accused by and to, accused to and by, informed of by, informed by of. In short this distinction does not require any special form of sign, nor could any form be adequate without numerous variations.

352. On the other hand [is] the distinction of *Designatives* such as concrete subjects of signs or essentially nominative signs, [and] *Descriptives* such as Predicates and Predicative Signs (such as a portrait with a legend designating the person represented), [with] Abstract nouns to be reckoned among Descriptives. The copulants are likewise indispensable and have the property of being *Continuant.* What I mean is that the sign 'A is red' can be decomposed so as to separate 'is red' into a Copulative and a Descriptive, thus: 'A possesses the character of redness.' But if we attempt to analyze 'possesses the character' in like manner, we get 'A possesses the character of the possession of the character of Redness'; and so on *ad infinitum.* So

[20] (Eds. CP:) Peirce had revised the manuscript here, but since his revision is unintelligible, we give the text as it was originally.

it is, with 'A implies B,' 'A implies its implication of B,' etc. So with 'It rains and hails,' 'It rains concurrently with hailing,' 'It rains concurrently with the concurrence of hailing,' and so forth. I call all such sign Continuants. They are all Copulants and are the only *pure* copulants. These signs *cannot be explicated:* they must convey Familiar universal elementary relations of logic. We do not derive these notions from observation, nor by any sense of being opposed, but from our own reason. This trichotomy, then, sustains criticism and must be marked (μ) at least. I would mark it (δ) if I were satisfied with the distinction between Descriptives and Denominatives.

353. Before proceeding to the third trichotomy, let [us] inquire what relations, if any, are found between the two that have been brought to light. What I mean precisely by *between these relations* is whether or not the three members of the first trichotomy, which we may for the moment denote as 11, 12, 13, are or are not independent of the three members of the second, which we may denote by 21, 22, 23; so that they form nine classes, which, if we use a dot to mean "which is," will be denoted by

11·21	11·22	11·23
12·21	12·22	12·23
13·21	13·22	13·23

354. The inquiry ought, one would expect, to be an easy one, since both trichotomies depend on there being three Modes of Presence to the mind, which we may term:

The Immediate,—The Direct,—The Familiar Mode of Presence.

The difference between the two trichotomies is that the one refers to the Presence to the Mind of the Sign and the other to that of the Immediate Object. The Sign may have any Modality of Being, i.e., may belong to any one of the three Universes; its Immediate Object must be in some sense, in which the Sign need not be, Internal.

(…)

357. The Northern United States are full of I know not how many thousand "villages," as they are called in the State of New York, "towns" as they are called in New England, which are governed in a simple way by "town meetings" or otherwise; and in Pennsylvania "boroughs," whose head is a "chief burgess"; and there are also countless little places somewhat larger (especially in the West) called "cities." In the middle of any one of these where one might wander he would find a small green of an acre or two and in the middle of this will be a stone statue, often of granite, representing a common soldier standing in his regulation overcoat and resting on his grounded musket. Nothing imaginable could be more devoid of imagination, less idealized, less artistically beautiful. They are eye-sores to all cultivated people; but not to me. For I know that that means that almost every family in that place…had in the war of the southern rebellion sent its flower, who had no military instinct whatever, much less any hatred for southern people, to the war, bitterly contrary to all his instincts but simply from a sense of duty; and only a fraction of them came back. The very fact of their vulgarity, which the statue proclaims above all else, makes this universal self-sacrifice on the altar of the abstraction, which we call the

"general government" pathetically sublime. To each such family, that very realistic statue represents the mourned one who fell in the war. That statue is one piece of granite, and not a Famisign. Yet it is what we call a "General" sign, meaning that it is *applicable* to many singulars. It is not *itself* General; it is its Object which is taken to be General. And yet this Object is not truly Universal, in the sense of implying a truth of the kind of 'Any S is P'; it only expresses 'Some S is P.' This makes it *not* a *Copulant* (Copulative) but only a *Descriptive*. This needs to be borne in mind. And this warning having been noticed, we can proceed to inquire about the corners of our block of supposed classes, which I will designate according to the usual map that has N above, S below, E to the right, W to the left.

358. As to the NW corner, a Geometrical diagram is always capable of being *imagined,* seldom or never of *existing;* since the limits of solid bodies are the loci at which forces of cohesion are neither very great nor very small, which being vague, has not the character of a geometrical surface. The diagram is therefore a *Potisign.* It is clearly Descriptive; and therefore 11 · 21 is possible.

(…)

363. From the summer of 1905 to the same time in 1906, I devoted much study to my ten trichotomies of signs. It is time I reverted to the subject, as I know I could now make it much clearer. But I dare say some of my former names are better than those I now use. I formerly called a Potisign a Tinge or Tone, an Actisign a Token, a Famisign a Type;—a Descriptive an Indefinite (but this was bad), a Denominative a Designation, a Copulative (which is bad) a Distributive (which is much better).

364. I think Potisign, Actisign, [and] Famisign might be called Mark, Token, [and] Type(?)[21] [respectively], while Descriptive, Denominative, [and] Copulative might be called Descriptive, Denominative, [and] Distributive, [respectively].

365. I have now given as much time to this letter as I can afford and I cannot now re-examine the remaining trichotomies, although I must do so as soon as possible. So I just give them as they stood two years and more ago. In particular, the relations I assumed between the different classes were the wildest guesses, and cannot be altogether right I think.

366. III. In respect to the Nature of their Dynamical Objects, Signs I found to be either

1. Signs of Possibles. That is *Abstractives* such as Color, Mass, Whiteness, etc.
2. Signs of Occurrences. That is *Concretives* such as Man, Charlemagne.
3. Signs of Collections. That is *Collectives* such as Mankind, the Human Race, etc.

By *Abstractives* I meant signs of *immediate* abstractions; but was in some doubt what to do with abstractions resulting from experiment. I thought it would be requisite to study subdivisions of these classes but never went into that research.

[21] (Eds.:) It is clear from the format of the manuscript that the question mark applies only to the term "type."

367. I was of the opinion that if the Dynamical Object be a mere Possible the Immediate Object could only be of the same nature, while if the Immediate Object were a Tendency or Habit then the Dynamical Object must be of the same nature. Consequently an Abstractive must be a Mark, while a Type must be a Collective, which shows how I conceived Abstractives and Collectives.

368. IV. The fourth Trichotomy is the one which I most frequently use: Icon, Index,[22] Symbol.

All the remaining six trichotomies have to do with the Interpretants, which you have, I imagine, studied much more thoroughly than I have done.

369. V. As to the nature of the Immediate (or Felt?) Interpretant, a sign may be: Ejaculative, or merely giving utterance to feeling; Imperative, including, of course, Interrogatives; Significative.

But later I made this the 7th Trichotomy and for the fifth substituted—with great hesitation—: Hypothetic, Categorical, Relative.

370. VI. As to the Nature of the Dynamical Interpretant: Sympathetic, or Congruentive; Shocking, or Percussive; Usual.

371. VII. As to the Manner of Appeal to the Dynamic Interpretant: Suggestive, Imperative, Indicative.

372. VIII. According to the Purpose of the Eventual Interpretant: Gratific; To produce action; To produce self-control.

373. IX. As to the Nature of the Influence of the Sign: Seme, like a simple sign; Pheme, with antecedent and consequent; Delome, with antecedent, consequent, and principle of sequence.

---

[22] (Eds CP:) "An *index* represents an object by virtue of its connection with it. It makes no difference whether the connection is natural, or artificial, or merely mental. There is, however, an important distinction between two classes of indices. Namely, some merely stand for things or individual quasi-things with which the interpreting mind is already acquainted, while others may be used to ascertain facts. Of the former class, which may be termed *designations,* personal, demonstrative, and relative pronouns, proper names, the letters attached to a geometrical figure, and the ordinary letters of algebra are examples. They act to force the attention to the thing intended. Designations are absolutely indispensable both to communication and to thought. No assertion has any meaning unless there is some designation to show whether the universe of reality or what universe of fiction is referred to. The other class of indices may be called *reagents.* Thus water placed in a vessel with a shaving of camphor thrown upon it will show whether the vessel is clean or not. If I say that I live two and a half miles from Milford, I mean that a rigid bar that would just reach from one line to another upon a certain bar in Westminster, might be successively laid down on the road from my house to Milford, 13200 times, and so laid down on my reader's road would give him a knowledge of the distance between my house and Milford. Thus, the expression "two miles and a half" is, not exactly a reagent, but a description of a reagent. A scream for help is not only intended to force upon the mind the knowledge that help is wanted, but also to force the will to accord it. It is, therefore, a reagent used rhetorically. Just as a designation can denote nothing unless the interpreting mind is already acquainted with the thing it denotes, so a reagent can indicate nothing unless the mind is already acquainted with its connection with the phenomenon it indicates. From "Notes on Topical Geometry," undated, Widener IA-2.

374. X. As to the Nature of the Assurance of the Utterance: assurance of Instinct; assurance of Experience; assurance of Form.

375. I don't know whether these trichotomies will suggest anything to you or not. No doubt you have studied relations to Interpretants in some directions much further than I....

376. P.S. 1908 Dec 28. Well, dear Lady Welby, you deserve this infliction, for having spoken of my having "always been kindly [!!!] interested in the work to which my life is devoted,"[23] when I have myself been entirely absorbed in the very same subject since 1863, without meeting, before I made your acquaintance, a single mind to whom it did not seem very like bosh. I add some scraps. (...)

377. I have often thought that if it were not that it would sound too German (and I have an utter contempt for German logic) I would entitle my logic-book (which is now coming on) "Logic considered as Semeiotic" (or probably *Semeotic* without the *i;*) but everybody would think I was translating *als Semeiotik betrachtet,* which I couldn't stand.

378. The fact that I have entertained this idea shows how near together you and I are. "Significs" sounds to me narrower than Semeotic, since *signification* is only *one* of the *two* chief functions of signs; as the elegant and correct John of Salisbury notices, in referring to "quod fere in omnium ore celebre est, aliud scilicet esse quod appellatiua significant, et aliud esse quod nominant. Nominantur singularia, sed uniuersalia significantur." (*Metalogicus* II. xx. I copy from the ed. of 1620.)[24] So *significs* appears to be limited to the study of the relations of Signs to their Interpretants; and I presume you do so limit it. On the other hand Logic is more interested in the *Truth* of Signs, i.e. in their relation to their Objects. But I am satisfied that in the present state of the subject, there is but one General science of the nature of Signs. If we were to separate it into two,—then, according to my idea that a "science," as scientific men use the word, implies a social group of devotees, we should be in imminent danger of erecting two groups of one member each! Whereas—if you and I stick together—we are at least two of us. I remember in my college days that the Statutes of Harvard defined a "group" as *three* persons or more convening together. We shall have to try to seduce one of the linguists to our more fundamental study. Max Müller was, in a feeble way, perhaps one of our group. I hope in your Britannica article you will adhere to the stern method of treatment proper to an Encyclopedia, and show the reader that distinct positive discovery is what we are laboring upon. I remember one day, when I was in the twenties, on my way to the post-office I fell in with the novelist Wm. D. Howells, who began criticizing one of my articles from the point of view of rhetorical elegance. I said to him, "Mr. Howells, it is no part of the purpose of my writings to give readers pleasure." Such an idea was quite out of his horizon; and I heard of his repeating it as very amusing. People do not consult an

[23] (Eds.:) The brackets are Peirce's.

[24] (Eds. CP:) See Clemens C.I. Webb, *Ioannis Saresberiensis Episcopi Carnotensis Metalogicon,* Oxford University Press, 1929, Liber II, Cap. 20, p. 104.

encyclopedia to be amused, but to receive definite instruction as condensed as clearness permits. I hope your article will cause readers to appreciate Significs as a study of grave importance not merely from the point of view of Morals, but also from that of Truth. But I am absolutely sure your article will be a valuable one however far it may depart from what I should wish the article to be. It must be so, simply because you have been a devoted student of the subject. It is your own message that you are to deliver and nobody else's.

379. It is a remarkable thing that no other people but the Greeks ever so felt the desire to avoid errors as to strike out a logic for themselves. All other logic down to the invention of the Doctrine of Chances was made on the Greek model. The Greeks so strongly felt that need that they erected no less than 5 independent systems! Namely, 1st, though Prantl's "Megaric logic" is poppy-cock, there are unmistakable indications of early strivings for a logical system; 2nd, came the logic of Socrates, who had a much clearer idea of what logic should be than such writers as Wundt, Chr. Sigwart, Jerusalem, Bradley, Bosanquet, Dewey, etc. etc.,—not to notice the Joseph's and such quasi-minds,—have today; 3rd, passing by Plato, there was Aristotle; 4th, the Epicurean logic, very closely allied to Mill's system, yet distinctly different, as shown by the Herculaneum Papyrus of the {peri sémeiön kai sémeiöseön} of Philodemus; 5th, there was the logic illustrated by the strict methods of the mathematicians,—which was not merely a *practice* of reasoning, but was a definite theory of logic greatly superior to Aristotle's, as far as deductive reasoning is concerned. (…)

Editorial 3: Firstness, Shock, and Signs (Peirce)

Jan M. Broekman and Larry Catá Backer

The combination of the three topics may surprise, in particular if one considers that the three are closely tied together and central issues in Peircean philosophy, not only in the context of semiotics but also of pragmati(ci)sm. Firstness might be the most important category with strong ontological relevance, and the combination with shock producing signs is unheard of in philosophical discipline. Peirce writes:

> A *Firstness* is exemplified in every quality of a total feeling. It is perfectly simple and without parts; and everything has its quality. Thus the tragedy of King Lear has its Firstness, its flavor *sui generis*. That wherein all such qualities agree, is universal Firstness: the very being of Firstness. The word *possibility* fits it, except that possibility implies a relation to what exists, while universal Firstness is the mode of being of itself. That is why a new word was required for it. Otherwise, "possibility" would have answered the purpose.

And he exemplifies:

> Firstness is the mode of being, which consists in its subject's being positively such as it is regardless of aught else. That can only be a possibility. For as long as things do not act upon one another there is no sense or meaning in saying that they have any being, unless it be that they are such in themselves that they may perhaps come into relation with others. The mode of being a *redness*, before anything in the universe was yet red, was nevertheless a positive qualitative possibility. And redness in itself, even if it be embodied, is something positive and *sui generis*. That I call: Firstness.

The two fragments help to understand that the category Firstness in a Peircean understanding includes a *shock-experience*. The shock is the confrontation to put one's own perception in perspective, to transit from pure possibility to the recognition

J.M. Broekman (✉)
Dickinson School of Law, Penn State University, Carlisle, PA, USA
e-mail: jmb56@dsl.psu.edu

L. Catá Backer
Departments of Law and International Affairs, Penn State University, University Park, PA, USA
e-mail: lcb11@psu.edu

J.M. Broekman, L. Catá Backer (eds.), *Signs In Law - A Source Book*,
DOI 10.1007/978-3-319-09837-1_13

of being addressed by something/someone itself/himself. It shocks to feel obliged not to speak as the speaker maintaining the first-person-singular position—and it does so a fortiori for a lawyer who dares to read or listen to a philosopher who confronts him with Peircean thoughts. Yet, there is no experience or judgment about something or someone being without this consideration. The shock experience has relevance for understanding Firstness as well as for understanding in general, in an epistemological way. Hence the famous thought:

> A whistling locomotive passes at high speed close beside me. As it passes the note of the whistle is suddenly lowered from a well-understood cause. I perceive the whistle, if you will. I have, at any rate, a sensation of it. But I cannot be said to have a sensation of the change of note. I have a sensation of the lower note. But the cognition of the change is of a more intellectual kind. That I experience rather than perceive. It is [the] special field of experience to acquaint us with events, with changes of perception. Now that which particularly characterizes sudden changes of perception is a shock. A shock is a volitional phenomenon. The long whistle of the approaching locomotive, however disagreeable it may be, has set up in me a certain inertia, so that the sudden lowering of the note meets with a certain resistance. That must be the fact; because if there were no such resistance there could be no shock when the change of note occurs. Now this shock is quite unmistakable. It is more particularly to changes and contrasts of perception that we apply the word "experience." we experience vicissitudes, especially. We cannot experience the vicissitude without experiencing the perception, which undergoes the change.

There is furthermore, apart from the epistemological relevance, a *social* experience of shock that may interest the lawyer in particular. This puts the use of *feeling* in perspective and shows how the observations are beyond any psychologism. It concerns a personal feeling of Peirce, who was often in financial troubles, not in the least in his years at Arisbe. Pencak described these years intriguingly and quotes the 'shock-experience' as one of the components of how "the final years of his life were marked by increasing bitterness, poverty, illness, and isolation."[1] In describing Firstness and its relations to Secondness and Thirdness[2], Peirce refers to the unique position of Firstness thanks to its sense of actuality, which consists in what is happening *then* and *there*. Lawyers should read with a minimal empathy:

> Let us begin with considering actuality, and try to make out just what it consists in. If I ask you what the actuality of an event consists in, you will tell me that it consists in its happening *then* and *there*. The specifications *then* and *there* involve all its relations to other existents. The actuality of the event seems to lie in its relations to the universe of existents. A court may issue *injunctions* and *judgments* against me and I not care a snap of my finger for them. I may think them idle vapor. But when I feel the sheriff's hand on my shoulder, I shall begin to have a sense of actuality. Actuality is something *brute*. There is no reason in it. I instance putting your shoulder against a door and trying to force it open against an unseen, silent, and unknown resistance. We have a two-sided consciousness of effort and resistance, which seems to me to come tolerably near to a pure sense of actuality[3].

---

[1] William A. Pencak: *History, Signing In. Essays in History and Semiotics*. Peter Lang, New York 1993, Chapter 3: "Charles S. Peirce and Arisbe", p. 17 f.

[2] See Jan M. Broekman: "Firstness and Phenomenology" in: Anne Wagner/Jan M. Broekman (Eds): *Prospects of Legal Semiotics*, Springer 2010, p. 37 f.

[3] Peirce: *Collected Papers (CP)*, Vol. 1, Nr 24, 444, 536.

On May 7, 1904 he already wrote to Lady Welby how

> Secondness comes in as brute action (…) because in so far as any law or reason comes in Thirdness comes in. The law of gravitation is the judge upon the bench who may pronounce the law till doomsday, but unless the strong arm of the law, the brutal sheriff, gives effect to the law, it amounts to nothing.

This description has hitherto been completely neglected by those who want to estimate *the power of institutionalization,* which upholds law and legal discourse. That issue reaches far beyond the individual and personal experience basis of the observation at hand. Law needs a *brute* hand, Peirce would conclude, and this bruteness includes many epistemological dimensions. Firstness and shock belong truly together.

"But the cognition of (…) change is of a more intellectual kind", Peirce underlined, but the element of shock is never at distance, and this relates to more general insights about the structure of knowledge and reality.

> The term "logic" is unscientifically by me employed in two distinct senses. In its narrower sense, it is the science of the necessary conditions of the attainment of truth. In its broader sense, it is the science of the necessary laws of thought, or, still better (thought always taking place by means of signs), it is general semeiotic, treating not merely of truth, but also of the general conditions of signs being signs (which Duns Scotus called *grammatica speculativa*), also of the laws of the evolution of thought, which (…) coincides with the study of the necessary conditions of the transmission of meaning by signs from mind to mind (…).

We should be aware of how the principle of Firstness relates to the formation of human knowledge, which seems founded on the psychological experience and the epistemological function of *shock*. This idea was known in early significs and plays also in Peircean philosophy a role. Here is the firm tie between shock and sign. A few review lines from 1904 *On Pragmatism, from a Review of a Book on Cosmology* tell us:

> Every thought, or cognitive representation, is of the nature of a sign. "Representation" and "sign" are synonyms. The whole purpose of a sign is that it shall be interpreted in another sign; and its whole purport lies in the special character, which it imparts to that interpretation. When a sign determines an interpretation of itself in another sign, it produces an effect external to itself, a physical effect, though the sign producing the effect may itself be not an existent object but merely a type. (…) Thinking is a kind of action, and reasoning is a kind of deliberate action; and to call an argument illogical, or a proposition false, is a special kind of moral judgment, and as such is inapplicable to what we cannot help. This does not deny that what cannot be conceived today may be conceivable tomorrow. But just as long as we cannot help adopting a mode of thought, so long it must be thoroughly accepted as true. Any doubt of it is idle (…) Now we all do regard, and cannot help regarding, signs as *affecting* their interpretant signs. (…)The *existent* is that which reacts against other things. Consequently, the external world, (that is, the world that is comparatively external) does not consist of existent objects merely, nor merely of these and their reactions; but on the contrary, its most important reals have the mode of being of what the nominalist calls "mere" words, that is, general types and would-bes. The nominalist is right in saying that they are substantially of the nature of words; but his "mere" reveals a complete misunderstanding of what our everyday world consists of.[4]

[4] Peirce, CP Vol. 8, 191.

So the question whether "shock" and "sign" are 'merely words' is put in perspective. The philosophical debates between nominalists and realists are still audible among us: they are most often present in structures of legal argumentation in common law as well as in civil law contexts! The movements of the sheriff's hand became a symbol one should consciously read.

Firstness, Shock, Law, and the Hand of the Sheriff

Charles Sanders Peirce

Lessons from the History of Philosophy

CP 1, 23/24; 335/336.

23.[1]My view is that there are three modes of being. I hold that we can directly observe them in elements of whatever is at any time before the mind in any way. They are the being of positive qualitative possibility, the being of actual fact, and the being of law that will govern facts in the future.

24. Let us begin with considering actuality, and try to make out just what it consists in. I ask you what the actuality of an event consists in you will tell me that it consists in its happening *then* and *there*. The specifications *then* and *there* involve all its relations to other existents. The actuality of the event seems to lie in its relations to the universe of existents. A court may issue *injunctions* and *judgments* against me and I not care a snap of my finger for them. I may think them idle vapor. But when I feel the sheriff's hand on my shoulder, I shall begin to have a sense of actuality. Actuality is something *brute*. There is no reason in it. I instance putting your shoulder against a door and trying to force it open against an unseen, silent, and unknown resistance. We have a two-sided consciousness of effort and resistance, which seems to me to come tolerably near to a pure sense of actuality. On the whole, I think we have here a mode of being of one thing, which consists in how a second object is. I call that secondness.

335. Some writers insist that all experience consists in sense-perception; and I think it is probably true that every element of experience is in the first instance applied to an external object. A man who gets up out of the wrong side of the bed, for example, attributes wrongness to almost every object he perceives. That is the

Source: CH. S. PEIRCE: *Collected Works*, Hartshorne & Weiss, Burks, Harvard 1958/66. Vols 1, 2 & 5.

[1] Fragments numbered as in the Harvard Edition *Collected Papers*.

C.S. Peirce (deceased)

J.M. Broekman, L. Catá Backer (eds.), *Signs In Law - A Source Book*,
DOI 10.1007/978-3-319-09837-1_14

way in which he experiences his bad temper. It cannot, however, be said that he *perceives* the perversity which he wrongly attributes to outward objects.

336. We perceive objects brought before us; but that which we especially experience—the kind of thing to which the word "experience" is more particularly applied—is an event. We cannot accurately be said to perceive events; for this requires what Kant called the "synthesis of apprehension," not however, by any means, making the needful discriminations. A whistling locomotive passes at high speed close beside me. As it passes the note of the whistle is suddenly lowered from a well-understood cause. I perceive the whistle, if you will. I have, at any rate, a sensation of it. But I cannot be said to have a sensation of the change of note. I have a sensation of the lower note. But the cognition of the change is of a more intellectual kind. That I experience rather than perceive. It is [the] special field of experience to acquaint us with events, with changes of perception. Now that which particularly characterizes sudden changes of perception is a shock. A shock is a volitional phenomenon. The long whistle of the approaching locomotive, however disagreeable it may be, has set up in me a certain inertia, so that the sudden lowering of the note meets with a certain resistance. That must be the fact; because if there were no such resistance there could be no shock when the change of note occurs. Now this shock is quite unmistakable. It is more particularly to changes and contrasts of perception that we apply the word "experience." we experience vicissitudes, especially. We cannot experience the vicissitude without experiencing the perception, which undergoes the change; but the concept of *experience* is broader than that of *perception,* and includes much that is not, strictly speaking, an object of perception. It is the compulsion, the absolute constraint upon us to think otherwise than we have been thinking that constitutes experience. Now constraint and compulsion cannot exist without resistance, and resistance is effort-opposing change. Therefore there must be an element of effort in experience; and it is this, which gives it its peculiar character. But we are so disposed to yield to it as soon as we can detect it, that it is extremely difficult to convince ourselves that we have exerted any resistance at all. It may be said that we hardly know it except through the axiom that there can be no force where there is no resistance or inertia. Whoever may be dissatisfied with my statement will do well to sit down and cipher out the matter for himself. He may be able to formulate the nature of the oppositional element in experience, and its relation to ordinary volition better than I have done; but that there is an oppositional element in it, logically not easily distinguished from volition, will, I make no doubt at all, be his ultimate conclusion.

The Universal Categories

CP 5, 41/42

§ 1. Presentness

41. ...Be it understood, then, that what we have to do, as students of phenomenology, is simply to open our mental eyes and look well at the phenomenon and say what are the characteristics that are never wanting in it, whether that phenomenon be something that outward experience forces upon our attention, or

whether it be the wildest of dreams, or whether it be the most abstract and general of the conclusions of science.

42. The faculties, which we must endeavor to gather for this work, are three. The first and foremost is that rare faculty, the faculty of seeing what stares one in the face, just as it presents itself, unreplaced by any interpretation, unsophisticated by any allowance for this or for that supposed modifying circumstance. This is the faculty of the artist who sees for example the apparent colors of nature as they appear. When the ground is covered by snow on which the sun shines brightly except where shadows fall, if you ask any ordinary man what its color appears to be, he will tell you white, pure white, whiter in the sunlight, a little greyish in the shadow. But that is not what is before his eyes that he is describing; it is his theory of what *ought* to be seen. The artist will tell him that the shadows are not grey but a dull blue and that the snow in the sunshine is of a rich yellow. That artist's observational power is what is most wanted in the study of phenomenology. The second faculty we must strive to arm ourselves with is a resolute discrimination which fastens itself like a bulldog upon the particular feature that we are studying, follows it wherever it may lurk, and detects it beneath all its disguises. The third faculty we shall need is the generalizing power of the mathematician who produces the abstract formula that comprehends the very essence of the feature under examination purified from all admixture of extraneous and irrelevant accompaniments.

Partial Synopsis of a Proposed Work in Logic

CP 2, 84/85

84. [...] It is not metaphysics that we are dealing with: only logic. Therefore, we do not ask what really is, but only what appears to every one of us in every minute of our lives. I analyze experience, which is the cognitive resultant of our past lives, and find in it three elements. I call them *Categories.* Would I could render them to the reader as vivid, as undeniable, as rational as they are to me. They will become so, if he will give thought enough to them. They appear in myriad shapes, of which, for the purpose of introducing the reader to them, I take the first that offers itself. A definition of experience happened, just now, to flow from my pen. It was a pretty good definition, I think: suppose we set out from that. Laconically speaking, experience is *esse in praeterito.* Only, remember, once more and once for all, that we do not mean what the secret nature of the fact is, but simply what we think it to be. Some fact there is. All experience compels your acknowledgment. What, then, is the fact that is present to you? Ask yourself: it is past. A fact is a *fait accompli;* its *esse* is *in praeterito.* The past compels the present, in some measure, at least. If you complain to the Past that it is wrong and unreasonable, it laughs. It does not care a snap of the finger for Reason. Its force is brute force. So then, you are compelled, brutally compelled, to admit that there is such an element in the world of experience as brute force. What then is brute force, or what does it seem to be? We ought to find little difficulty in answering that, since we are directly conscious (or seem to be, which is all that concerns us here) of exerting it ourselves. For, no matter how good a reason

we may have for an act of the will, yet when we come to the exertion itself, reason does no part of the work: it is brute action. We can make no effort where we experience no resistance, no reaction. The sense of effort is a two-sided sense, revealing at once a something within and another something without. There is binarity in the idea of brute force; it is its principal ingredient. For the idea of brute force is little more than that of reaction; and this is pure binarity. (…)

85. Let us now consider what could appear as being in the present instant were it utterly cut off from past and future. We can only guess; for nothing is more occult than the absolute present. There plainly could be no action; and without the possibility of action, to talk of binarity would be to utter words without meaning. There might be a sort of consciousness, or feeling, with no self; and this feeling might have its tone. Notwithstanding what William James has said, I do not think there could be any continuity like space, which, though it may perhaps appear in an instant in an educated mind, I cannot think could do so if it had no time at all; and without continuity parts of the feeling could not be synthetized; and therefore there would be no recognizable parts. There could not even be a degree of vividness of the feeling; for this [the degree of vividness] is the comparative amount of disturbance of general consciousness by a feeling.[2] At any rate, such shall be our hypothesis, and whether it is psychologically true or not is of no consequence. The world would be reduced to a quality of unanalyzed feeling. Here would be an utter absence of binarity. I cannot call it unity; for even unity supposes plurality. I may call its form Firstness, Orience, or Originality. It would be something, *which is what it is without reference to anything else* within it or without it, regardless of all force and of all reason. Now the world is full of this element of irresponsible, free, Originality. Why should the middle part of the spectrum look green rather than violet? There is no conceivable reason for it nor compulsion in it. Why was I born in the nineteenth century on Earth rather than on Mars a thousand years ago? Why did I today sneeze just five hours forty-three minutes and twenty-one seconds after a certain man in China whistled (supposing this did happen)? We know perhaps why a meteorite should fall to the earth, if it gets in the Earth's way; but why should the arrangements of nature be such that this particular meteorite was in the Earth's way? All these are facts which are as they are, simply because they happen to be so. We mostly neglect them; but there are cases, as in qualities of feeling, self-consciousness, etc., in which such isolated flashes come to the front. Originality, or Firstness, is another of my Categories.

The Universal Categories

CP 5, 48/51; 57/58

48. […] I will first glance at that branch (of it) that rests upon the idea that the conception of action involves the notion of law or uniformity so that to talk of a reaction regardless of anything but the two individual reacting objects is nonsense.

[2] Cf. CP.1.322.

As to that I should say that a law of nature left to itself would be quite analogous to a court without a sheriff. A court in that predicament might probably be able to induce some citizen to act as sheriff; but until it had so provided itself with an officer who, unlike itself, could not discourse authoritatively but who could put forth the strong arm, its law might be the perfection of human reason but would remain mere fireworks, *brutum fulmen.* Just so, let a law of nature—say the law of gravitation—remain a mere uniformity—a mere formula establishing a relation between terms—and what in the world should induce a stone, which is not a term nor a concept but just a plain thing, to act in conformity to that uniformity? All other stones may have done so, and this stone too on former occasions, and it would break the uniformity for it not to do so now. But what of that? There is no use talking reason to a stone. It is deaf and it has no reason. I should ask the objector whether he was a nominalist or a scholastic realist. If he is a nominalist, he holds that laws are mere generals, that is, formulae relating to mere terms; and ordinary good sense ought to force him to acknowledge that there are real connections between individual things regardless of mere formulae. Now, any real connection whatsoever, between individual things involves a reaction between them, in the sense of this category. The objector may, however, take somewhat stronger ground by confessing himself to be a scholastic realist, holding that generals may be real. A law of nature then, will be regarded by him as having a sort of *esse in futuro.* That is to say they will have a present reality, which consists in the fact that events *will* happen according to the formulation of those laws. It would seem futile for me to attempt to reply that when, for example, I make a great effort to lift a heavy weight and perhaps am unable to stir it from the ground, there really is a struggle on this occasion regardless of what happens on other occasions; because the objector would simply admit that on such an occasion I have a quality of feeling which I call a feeling of effort, but he would urge that the only thing which makes this designation appropriate to the feeling is the regularity of connection between this feeling and certain motions of matter.

49. This is a position well enough taken to merit a very respectful reply. But before going into that reply, there is an observation, which I should like to lay before the candid objector. Your argument against this category of Struggle is that a struggle regardless of law is not *intelligible.* Yet you have just admitted that my so-called sense of effort involves a peculiar quality of feeling. Now a quality of feeling is not intelligible, either. Nothing can be less so. One can *feel* it, but to comprehend it or express it in a general formula is out of the question. So it appears that unintelligibility does not suffice to destroy or refute a Category. Indeed, if you are to accept scholastic realism, you would seem to be almost bound to admit that *Nous,* or intelligibility, is itself a category; and in that case far from non-intelligibility's refuting a category, intelligibility would do so—that is, would prove that a conception could not be a category distinct from the category of *Nous,* or intelligibility. If it be objected that the unintelligibility of a Quality of Feeling is of a merely privative kind quite different from the aggressive and brutal anti-intelligibility of action regardless of law, the rejoinder will be that if intelligibility be a category, it is not surprising but rather inevitable that other categories should be in different relations to this one.

50. But without beating longer round the bush, let us come to close quarters. Experience is our only teacher. Far be it from me to enunciate any doctrine of a *tabula rasa.* For, as I said a few minutes ago, there manifestly is not one drop of principle in the whole vast reservoir of established scientific theory that has sprung from any other source than the power of the human mind to *originate* ideas that are true. But this power, for all it has accomplished, is so feeble that as ideas flow from their springs in the soul, the truths are almost drowned in a flood of false notions; and that which experience does is gradually, and by a sort of fractionation, to precipitate and filter off the false ideas, eliminating them and letting the truth pour on in its mighty current.

51. But precisely how does this action of experience take place? It takes place by a series of surprises. There is no need of going into details. At one time a ship is sailing along in the trades over a smooth sea, the navigator having no more positive expectation than that of the usual monotony of such a voyage, when suddenly she strikes upon a rock. The majority of discoveries, however, have been the result of experimentation. Now no man makes an experiment without being more or less inclined to think that an interesting result will ensue; for experiments are much too costly of physical and psychical energy to be undertaken at random and aimlessly. And naturally nothing can possibly be learned from an experiment that turns out just as was anticipated. It is by surprises that experience teaches all she deigns to teach us.

57. When a man is surprised he knows that he is surprised. Now comes a dilemma. Does he know he is surprised by direct perception or by inference? First try the hypothesis that it is by inference. This theory would be that a person (who must be supposed old enough to have acquired self-consciousness) on becoming conscious of that peculiar quality of feeling, which unquestionably belongs to all surprise, is induced by some reason to attribute this feeling to himself. It is, however, a patent fact that we never, *in the first instance,* attribute a Quality of Feeling to ourselves. We first attribute it to a *Non-Ego* and only come to attribute it to ourselves when irrefragable reasons compel us to do so. Therefore, the theory would have to be that the man first pronounces the surprising object a *wonder,* and upon reflection convinces himself that it is only a wonder in the sense that he is *surprised.* That would have to be the theory. But it is in conflict with the facts, which are that a man is more or less placidly *expecting* one result, and suddenly finds something in contrast to that forcing itself upon his recognition. A duality is thus forced upon him: on the one hand, his expectation which he had been attributing to Nature, but which he is now compelled to attribute to some mere inner world, and on the other hand, a strong new phenomenon which shoves that expectation into the background and occupies its place. The old expectation, which is what he was familiar with, is his inner world, or *Ego.* The new phenomenon, the stranger, is from the exterior world or *Non-Ego.* He does not conclude that he *must* be surprised because the object is so *marvellous.* But on the contrary, it is because of the duality presenting itself as such that he [is] led by generalization to a conception of a quality of marvellousness.

58. Try, then, the other alternative that it is by direct perception, that is, in a direct perceptual judgment, that a man knows that he is surprised. The perceptual judgment, however, certainly does not represent that it is he himself who has played a little trick upon himself. A man cannot startle himself by jumping up with an exclamation of *Boo!* Nor could the perceptual judgment have represented anything so out of nature. The perceptual judgment, then, can only be that it is the *Non-Ego,* something over against the *Ego* and bearing it down, is what has surprised him. But if that be so, this direct perception presents an *Ego* to which the smashed expectation belonged, and the *Non-Ego,* the sadder and wiser man, to which the new phenomenon belongs.

Editorial 4: Layered Discourses, Dynamic Semiotics

Jan M. Broekman and Larry Catá Backer

Inherent to the option of a semiotic understanding of law and legal discourse is the development of concepts that focus on *dynamic* features in all types of semiotics. This unifies in the eyes of the Lithuanian-French semiotician Algirdas Julien Greimas (1917–1992) legal semiotics with economic, institutional, and other social discourses. They are all in need of a new insight into their textual structure, which brings us from their evident surface to their often-concealed depth. This flow of attention, which Greimas tends to call a "play", is definitively changing the predominantly static character of linguistics and semiotics. We quote fragments of his famous 1968 essay "The Interaction of Semiotic Constraints":[1]

> The play in question here is not to be understood as a free activity productive of literary objects, but as a long journey punctuated with compelling choices that leads, through a series of exclusions and of options, manifesting personal and social phobias and euphorias, to the constitution of an original and unique work. Instead of analyzing a completed text, the authors have tried to see how, starting from kernels of meaning, from categories of meaning which are at once simple and basic, the creative faculty operates, a faculty which, proceeding from the simple to the complex, from the general to the particular, makes its way, through a number of determinisms, toward an exaltation of liberty.

A crucial insight is, that phenomena, which are subjected to semiotic analysis and understanding, have a textual character and thus possess a layered structure. The secret of Greimas' semiotics, which is *dynamic* and no longer predominantly *static* like they were in preceding projects of structural linguistics is in his focus on

[1] A.J. Greimas & F. Rastier: "The Interaction of Semiotic Constraints" in: *Yale French Studies*, 1968, p.86f.

J.M. Broekman (✉)
Dickinson School of Law, Penn State University, Carlisle, PA, USA
e-mail: jmb56@dsl.psu.edu

L. Catá Backer
Departments of Law and International Affairs, Penn State University,
University Park, PA, USA
e-mail: lcb11@psu.edu

J.M. Broekman, L. Catá Backer (eds.), *Signs In Law - A Source Book*,
DOI 10.1007/978-3-319-09837-1_15

that layered feature. The dynamic character is visible in the triad between surface-, deep- and manifest layers to be analyzed.

> Perhaps out of a desire for intelligibility, we can imagine that the human mind, in order to achieve the construction of a cultural object (literary, mythical, pictorial, etc.) starts with simple elements and follows a complex course, encountering on its way constraints to which it must submit, as well as choices which it can make.
>
> Our aim is to give a rough idea of this course. It may be considered to move from immanence to manifestation, in three principal stages, as we already mentioned in Chapter 1:
>
> — *deep structures,* which define the fundamental mode of existence of an individual or a society, and subsequently the conditions of existence of semiotic objects. As far as we know, the elementary constituents of deep structures have a definable logical status.
>
> — *superficial structures* constitute a semiotic grammar system which arranges into discursive forms the contents susceptible of manifestation. The products of this grammar system are independent of the expression, which reveals them, in as far as they can theoretically appear in any substance, and, in the case of linguistic objects, in any language.
>
> — *the structures of manifestation* produce and organize the significances. Although they can include quasi-universals, they remain particular to any given language (or more precisely they define the particular characteristics of languages), or to any given material. They are studied by the superficial stylistics of morphemes, shapes, colors, etc.

To introduce legal semiotics, elementary structures of meaning, and an author's view on the construction of semiotic systems go hand in hand. Additional and more extensive information is always in the reading of the text concerned in its entirety—an exercise, which by the way is seldom performed by legal semioticians that practice a Greimasian analysis in the case of law and legal discourse. If they do, it leads to highlighting the process of signifying, as Bernard Jackson demonstrated in his 1985 book "Semiotics and Legal Theory". Greimas explains this approach towards the signifying process as follows, referring to Bernanos, a contemporary French writer who opposed bourgeois thought patterns and wanted to fight a French spirit of defeatism that ultimately lead in his eyes to France's defeat in WW II 1940 in the same essay on "Interaction", page 89 ff.:

> For example, the contents Life and Death embrace the whole semantic universe of Bernanos: that is S_1 vs. S_2. Each one articulates in two systematic instances (negative and positive definitions) which are written respectively: s1 vs. s_2; s_2 vs. s_1. They are articulated in their turn into semic systems.
>
> The *terms* of the model, using each of the four terms as point of departure, one can obtain the three others by the two operations: by taking the contradictory and by taking the contrary. Their definition is formal, and anterior to any investment.
>
> The *relations:*
>
> a) hierarchical: a hyponymic relation is established between sj and s2, and S; another between $^{-g}{}_2$ and S.
>
> b) categorical: a relation of contradiction is established between S and S; and at the hierarchically inferior level, between s1 and -s2—a relation of "contraries" articulates s_i and s_2 on the one hand, and "$^{g}{}_2$ on the other. In the terms of Hjelmslev, it may be identified as solidarity, or double presupposition.
>
> *Note:* The two operations: that of taking the contradictory and that of taking the opposite, are involutive: the opposite of the opposite of s is s; the contradictory of the contradictory of s is s.

> The two axes, formed by relation of contraries, are themselves in a relation of contradiction. The two schemas, defined by relations of contradiction, are themselves in a relation of opposition.
>
> We propose calling the double presupposition of the two schemas *semiosis*. We reserve for later study the question of whether this double presupposition corresponds to that of linguistic content and expression, considered as the two schemas of a single model.

It is important to keep in mind that Greimas constructed a semiotic instrument called "square" which reconstructs opposed meanings as a basis for understanding signifying processes, as we demonstrated in Volume II of this series, in Part IV on the *Legal Semiotic Modus Operandi*[2]. Semioticians who operate with Greimas' tools have the ability to use two powerful analytical instruments. The *first* is in the dynamics of d*eep versus surface structures of texts*, and the *second* in *the analytical power of the semiotic square*. Both fit legal discourse appropriately. The text fragments we include here have their place between first developments of a structural linguistics, in particular Russian developments with Saumjan and Soboleva on the one hand, and Julia Kristeva on the other. Both are dealt with in our final chapter on signifying, and both participate in efforts to develop *dynamic* semiotics. The "linguistic turn", which Greimas provoked, appeared to be a "turn in linguistics": from static to dynamic linguistics, semiotics included[3]. His view on discourses/texts as "layered" was the key to that turn.

---

[2] Jan M. Broekman & Larry Catá Backer: *Lawyers Making Meaning*, Springer 2013, p. 203 f.

[3] See Timothy Lenoir: "Was That Last Turn A Right Turn?" in: *Configurations,* Vol. 2, 1994, p. 119 f.

A View on A. J. Greimas's Essay "The Semiotic Analysis of a Legal Discourse: Commercial Laws That Govern Companies and Groups of Companies"

Larry Catá Backer

Introduction

Greimas' essay on Corporations has been path breaking[1]. Today, the semiotic dimensions of the theme are more elaborated, but in his 1967 text, he focuses in an exemplary manner on questions such as: What are the specific properties of legal language? In order to answer that question he withdraws from solely watching what happens in Courtrooms and Law Offices, and thus directs our attention to decisions in the field of economics and business, asking: "What is a commercial company?" and "What does the legislator of these groups of companies 'think' "? No wonder that his text is first directed at methodological issues when approaching the subject—in time when semiotic research was almost completely unknown. What is needed first of all is a clarification of the concept of a legal discourse. This socially important discourse is a subtext completely or partially containing expressions of a natural language. Second, as discourse, Greimas states, it has to be perceived as a linear manifestation of language comprising a form of organization, which includes, in addition to lexemes, syntagms, utterances, all in all phrastic units, also clearly transphrastic units such as paragraphs, chapters, or fragments of actual discourses. Third, one can concur with Greimas that qualifying a discourse as *legal* implies either a specific organization or a specific connotation underlying this type of discourse. With this in mind it is then necessary to turn from the development of

[1]Algirdas J. Greimas: *The Social Sciences: A Semiotic View*. Ch. 6,1: "The Semiotic Analysis of A Legal Discourse: Commercial Laws That Govern Companies and Groups of Companies", pp. 102–115. University of Minnesota Press, 1990, p. 102–115. (French Original: "Analyse sémiotique d'un discours juridique: la loi commerciale sur les societies et les groupes sociétés" in *Sémiotique et sciences sociales,* Paris, Le Seuil 1976. p. 79 ff.

L. Catá Backer (✉)
Departments of Law and International Affairs, Penn State University,
University Park, PA, USA
e-mail: lcb11@psu.edu

J.M. Broekman, L. Catá Backer (eds.), *Signs In Law - A Source Book*,
DOI 10.1007/978-3-319-09837-1_16

decisions in the fields of economics and business, to the institutionalization of that within the legal abstraction, the enterprise, and its coupling with that other institutional abstraction that produces and polices the specific meanings, and grammer, of law—the courts.

Discourses and References

Greimas suggests that every legal discourse is produced by a *legal grammar,* which is distinct from the grammar of the natural language in which this discourse appears. And moreover, a lexical recurrence makes it possible to postulate the existence of an autonomous *legal dictionary.* In this light, the essay shads light on two important aspects pertaining to the legal context of corporations: there is the *legal grammar* and related to this grammar, the *legal practice* to be studied. The two form a complexity at the background of corporation activities, and are thus highlighted in a fascinating manner. Every legal discourse is produced by a *legal grammar.*

Legal Grammar

1) We quote Greimas: "Legal discourse refers back to a legal grammar and lexicon (grammar and lexicon being the two components of language), so we can say that it is the manifestation in the form of message discourses, of a language, of a *legal semiotics.* This constitutes our initial hypothesis. We postulate that the text to be described is part of a legal semiotics, that it is produced by a grammar and is the manifestation of a specific semantic universe". Hence his conclusion: the legal universe can be articulated as a micro-universe, in which the laws governing commercial companies are included.

But he also proceeds to explain, that

2) Legal discourse produces *legal grammar attempts to be explicit* and ostensibly exhibits the body of its rules. The example for law is a social issue in itself, an important issue that also belongs to political, sociological and related discourses: law not only claims to be known by all, it also appears as a well-made grammar, leaving no room for ambiguity at the level of intentions.

3) Legal grammar concerns in the main an appropriate formation of utterances and units (*if … then*) and, as Greimas underlines, "leaves the taxonomy of the fundamental categories implicit, which, as system, produces the grammatical discourse of law".

The form of grammatical discourse is actually one of the specific criteria of legal semiotics, he adds: "Legal grammar is a *constructed grammar* and displays itself as such. The initial enunciation of the law of July 24, 1966 — 'The President of the Republic promulgates the law with the following content' is not only the expression of a delegated collective will; as enunciation, it institutes, much in the manner of the divine fiat, the set of legal utterances that will exist only by virtue of this original performative act".

Legal Practice

Greimas formlates in truly semiotic perspectives, how to *name* and to *define* objects constitutes the essence of legal practice, understanding by *practice* the two dimensions of legal activity: the production of law and the verification of the conformity of the utterances with those of legal language. It fascinates, that the internal structure of legal discourse is implanted as a sort of a "hidden machine" in legal practice, so that this practice is much more than a simple application of principles or norms. Greimas clarifies this in a convincing manner: "In the *nature of doing,* where by means of functional utterances it is necessary to fix the operational sphere of the semiotic object that is called into existence, the predictable set of behaviors is subjected to the evaluation of a modal grid (...) the inventory of behaviors the legislator is attempting to regulate is part of the more or less explicit referential level and is supposed to cover the totality of the legal universe".

From those lines, one must conclude that the legal system appears as *a performative language, which institutes an order of the world.* Human beings and things appear to exist by means of ascribing specific functions to them, delimited by prescriptive and interdictive rules, which are ultimately called *legal*: legal subjects, and legal facts together with legal issues. This is the "inner machine", which makes the legal system appear as a solid and immobile architecture whereby law as a specimen of immobility is one of its principal connotations. But we should not forget, that the legal system evolves, accrues, and transforms itself. Law's dynamics appear to be caused by the constant renewal of legal discourses. The discursive innovations are reflected by their underlying system, Greimas would say. Legal practice is thus a *production of law,* of new legal rules and significations, as well as a *recurring procedure of verification* of the validity of the instituted legal language.

Legal discourse, the result of the convergence of a grammar and a lexicon, produces legal utterances defined by their form and by their content, part of the semantic universe that legal language covers.

On the level of semiotics and Greimasian linguistic analysis, the mechanisms of acquiring a practicable legal language, one has to consider that "(...) to transform an *a-semantic* word, expression, or sentence into a *semantic* term or utterance, consists in transferring it from the referential level to the legislative level of legal language—the procedures consist in correctly naming "things" and inscribing predictable "events" into the modal grid of prescriptions and interdictions, the legislator's word being sufficient to give a legal existence to what is expressed".

We can try to summarize these observations and present them by means of the accompanying schematization Greimas suggests:

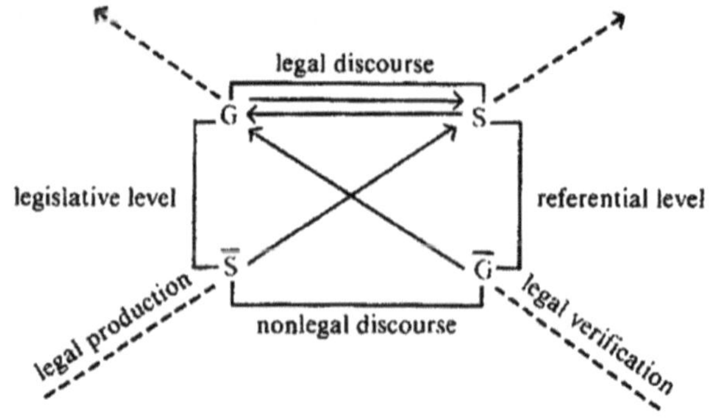

Narrative Grammar

G = legal grammaticality

$\overline{G}$ = legal agrammaticality

S = legal semanticity

$\overline{S}$ = legal asemanticity

G + S = legal discourse (made up of a grammar and a semantics)

$\overline{G}$ + $\overline{S}$ = nonlegal discourse (legally agrammatical and asemantic)

G + $\overline{S}$ = legislative level (legal grammar, without content)

$\overline{G}$ = S = referential level (virtual legal universe, without legal grammar)

The Religion of Corporations in the United States

If legal practice is thus a *production of law,* of new legal rules and significations, as well as a *recurring procedure of verification* of the validity of the instituted legal language, and if that production requires naming "things" and inscribing predictable "events" into the modal grid of command, incentives, interdictions, requirements, assessments, etc.—then its schematization into nicely autonomous but interconnected oppositions, contradictions and complementarities, provides the pathways within which the actions of the objects of law can be tested against law's grammar and semantics. This connection, one that drove Greimas initially to a consideration of the business of corporations in an effort to discover their legal essence, is very much in evidence in the efforts undertaken in the United States during the years 2013–14, to induce the state to recognize the legal authority of corporations to embrace a religion, and then to impose that religion on its employees, customers and others (under the protective cover of state power). That ensoulment has as its objectives to convert the juridical person incarnated in corporate form to the religion of its principal shareholders, so that they might form a more perfect community of like-minded religious souls for the conduct of economic affairs and the enhancement of the spiritual well being of their stakeholders. Economic activity, then, is transformed into an expression of the practice of religion, and the normative animus of the enterprise a reflection of that of its "owners." Yet to do so requires both an act of ensoulment of the corporation and acquiescence by the state that its law no longer applies to the professing corporation. It is in the efforts by economic enterprises to not merely find their religion, or project that of their owners, but to compel the state to recognize that religion, and by doing so cede a substantial regulatory authority over these abstractions, that the multiple vectors and dynamism of law comes is more fully exposed.

The courts serve as the arena in which these networks are invoked. These serve as the site within which corporations seek to assert their usurpation of power by reframing that usurpation as a right granted by the legislature through a statute the purpose of which never contemplated the action at issue. And in an effort to constrain the state, and to impose personal will on others through the exercise of personal (though institutionalized) systems of "law" that by their character as generated through "religion" fall outside of "law" produced by the state, that then affect both the person, institution and thing that seeks to assert "law" by constraining the protections of other "law" meant for the objects of this assertion. The word law, then, becomes lost in polycentric layers of systems that each claim the status of law, the interactions among which remains regulated by one set of law givers (the state) though in ways that make the simultaneous application of law networks likely in ways that institutionalize contradiction, complementarity and reversals.

Over the course of nearly a generation, and in contexts far from the realms of corporate law, U.S. elites have been battling, through the courts, to develop a new settlement for the coordination of two legal systems, sometimes incompatible with each other. One is the "secular" law of the political state—the United States of America, a federal union, and its subordinate governmental organs. The other is the law and governance system of advanced institutionalized religions with large numbers of members who also hold political citizenship in the United States and its relevant sub units. After a period of judicial decisions that appeared to favor a larger "legal" space within which individuals could choose religious over political governance systems with respect to specific action where the two systems diverged, the courts appeared to shrink that gateway in Employment Div. v. Smith (494 U.S. 872 (1990)), which changed the rules for choosing to opt out of the framework of state law by holding that while states have the power to accommodate otherwise illegal acts done in compliance with religious law, they are not required to do so—effectively reducing religious opt out to a matter of political power. And that is precisely what happened. In response to Smith, the federal government enacted the Religious Freedom Restoration Act of 1993 (42 U.S.C.§ 2000bb (RFRA)). RFRA provides that "[g]overnment shall not substantially burden a person's exercise of religion even if the burden results form a rule of general applicability (42 U.S.C. §2000bb-1(a))". That individual power to choose the application of religious over political obligation trumps all non-religious laws of general applicability unless the state can show that the legal obligation at issue is the least restrictive means of furthering a compelling governmental interest (ibid., 2000bb-1b). All of these terms have meanings that are specific to the law and the legal framework within which RFRA was expected to be applied. RFRA had originally served as a legislative response to a judicial construction of state power exercised against the choices of natural persons to practice their religions accordance with the dictates of the law of that faith.

This framework, this lexicon of inter-systemic relations between state-law and religion-law systems, has application to corporations, at least potentially, by the possibilities offered in the signaling language of Citizens United v. Federal Election Commission (558 U.S.-(2010)), in which the U.S. Supreme Court might have been thought to vest corporations with personal autonomy, and at least some of the political rights that follow from that.[2]

These implications are tested directly when a corporation, whose board of directors was determined to have the corporation adopt and practice its religious faith, the practice of which, in the opinion of its board of directors, prohibited it from providing certain medical benefits to its employees as otherwise mandated by the law of the United States.[3] Evangelical Christians, among others, have begun to assert a much broader area of activity in which the law of their religious faith must take 'precedence over any countervailing imposition enacted by the state'.[4]

In *Sibelius v. Hobby Lobby, Inc.* (723 F.3d 1114 (10th Cir. 2013) cert granted 134 S. Ct. 678 (2013)) the applicability of RFRA was tested in two respects. The first touched on the extent to which religious law could be used to evade an interpretation of general applicability related to the Patient Protection and Affordable Care Act of 2010 (124 Stat. 119 (ACA)). The second touched on whether juridical or legal persons might also assert rights to exercise religion, and in that exercise, avoid any obligation to comply with the law of the state. Specifically, ACA requires companies employing more than 50 employees to provide these employees with health insurance including preventive care and screenings for women (ACA 124 Stat. at 131). An administrative agency charged with the interpretation of this mandate determined thereafter that such

[2]The semiotic implications of *Citizens United* were treated in our earlier work: Jan M. Broekman and Larry Catá Backer, *Lawyers Making Meaning: The Semiotics of Law in Legal Education II*, Springer 2013, at pages 160–180 (in Chapter 12, : "Citizens United Unveiled").

[3]Among the most powerful advocates of this position in the United States are portions of the U.S. Christian Evangelical community. While a generation ago many Protestant Evangelicals did not have a strong view on contraception. See: Christian Medical Society, "A Protestant Affirmation on the Control of Human Reproduction, in: *Journal of the American Scientific Affiliation* 22:46–47 (1970) (available http://www.asa3.org/ASA/PSCF/1970/JASA6-70Christian.html), that view has changed considerably in the 21st century (see: http://www.sbcnet/aboutus/basicbeliefs.asp : "Children, from the moment of conception, are a blessing and heritage from the Lord") (*Southern Baptist Convention*, Basic Beliefs).

[4]For example, the Basic Beliefs of the Southern Baptist Convention includes the following: "It is the duty and privilege of every follower of Christ and every church of the Lord Jesus Christ to endeavor to make disciples of all nations… to seek constantly to win the lost to Christ by verbal witness undergirded by a Christian lifestyle, and by other methods in harmony with the gospel of Christ. … Christians have a spiritual debtorship to the whole world, a holy trusteeship in the gospel, and a binding stewardship in their possessions. They are therefore under obligation to serve Him with their time, talents, and material possessions. … All Christians are under obligation to seek to make the will of Christ supreme in our own lives and in human society… " (*Southern Baptist Convention*: Basic Beliefs, at http://www.sbc.net/aboutus/basicbeliefs.asp).

care included "contraceptive methods" and "sterilization procedures." "*Hobby Lobby*" is a closely held corporation, whose shareholders are committed to "Honoring the Lord in all we do by operating the company in a manner consistent with biblical principles … serving our employees and their families by establishing a work environment and company policies that build character, strengthen individuals and nurture families." (See the "Hobby Lobby" Website: "Our Company", May 2014, available at http://www.hobbylobby.com/our_company/). Thus, while the shareholders of Hobby Lobby were content to submit themselves to the law of the states of their citizenship and acquire the benefits thereof (the privilege of creating an autonomous juridical person through which to engage in economic activity), they "believe that it is by God's grace and provision that "Hobby Lobby" has endured." (Ibid). They sought to opt out of the network of state regulation with respect to those aspects of their organization and interactions with their employees that they determined were inconsistent with religious law, which they sought to apply to themselves, and through the company, to their employees. Among those state regulations abhorrent to the shareholders of "Hobby Lobby" was ACA's requirement that insurance provided for employees include preventive care and screening requirements for women because this required them to provide their employees with services that might include contraception and abortion services which, they believed, their God found unacceptable for the community of the faithful to which they belonged.

Here Greimas' notion of legal grammar produces a complication—for the grammar itself does not serve only to define the dynamics of its own coherence. It also provides a routing function—determining the basis on which one set of legal grammars must be displace by another. What U.S. constitutional law signifies as "accommodation" serves as a gateway to a lexicon of connection between two legal grammars that are not always necessarily harmonious. In *Sibelius* that requires both an interpretation of the religious law about the extent to which women's bodies may be managed, and the extent to which the political command of the state (through law) compels a certain sort of management. That, itself, produces a semiosis of contraception and abortion—not just within the structures of U.S., law, but simultaneously within the governance frameworks of the religion to which "Hobby Lobby" belongs.

But the most interesting complication is produced by the subject of the religious accommodation—a legal construct and juridical person, a creature created only through and subject to the power of the state—i.e. a for profit corporation. Having given this *juridical person* birth, its shareholders now declare that the juridical person ought to be able to depart form the control of the state itself—and assert a religious belief it can apply to itself, and by applying it to itself, compel its employees to adhere to its religious beliefs even as they retain all other obligation to the state of which they are all citizens. This would shift the lexicon of law, its meaning, from a world normative construct in which natural persons have *dignity* and juridical persons have *utility* to its inverse, where juridical persons are vested with fundamental constitutionally protected *dignity* and natural persons have *utility* (to labor markets, the process of the expression of political democracy etc.) Thus the question—can a corporation have a religion—is in actuality a set of semiotic problems: may individuals reach through an autonomous juridical person and assert their own religious belief in the operation and management of the enterprise, while for all other purposes creating a wall of separation between themselves (and their assets) and the entity (supported through the power of the state whose rules, with respect to mandatory insurance coverage they reject)?; can corporate preferences trump the individual dignity rights of natural persons by operation of their employment relationship?; what is the scope of the privilege of shareholding beyond its economic element, does it have a cultural and religious dimension?; if corporations are no longer understood as constructs of the state, to what extend is the state necessary for the construction of the corporation (and thus is the role of the state reduced to a negotiation for the set of privileged against state law)? These are the subordinate questions that are underlined in the Sibelius case, which will form the subterranean elements of whatever opinion is announced by the courts.

These questions are semiotic in the sense that while the law fixes the meaning of the semiotic object, that meaning setting is itself an object of a relationship between entity, owner, and the state. That, in turn, touches on the firstness of the corporation itself: Is it law that defines the enterprise as an autonomous person and thus able to assert, in the manner of such constructs, all of the powers of a persons within the lexicon of law? Is it the relationship among the shareholders that defines the quality of firstness, the expression of which is the corporation as the nexus of the aggregated relations among shareholders, an aspect of which is recognized through the lexicon of law? In either case, does the aggregation itself transform the enterprise so that the essential consequence of a self-referencing firstness within the enterprise demands that it "think for itself" rather than aggregate the desires of those (state and shareholders) who were essential to its formation (through law and capital)? What does religious discourse have to say about this construct?

Legal and religious discourse, the language of the lawyer, absorbs these questions and transforms their import into the forms necessary to determine the answer to the "routing" question—does state or religious law apply to the corporation's determination to comply with a state law mandating the provision of insurance with certain benefits. Here the semiosis is triadic and the focus is not merely on the sign or interpretant, but on the signified. Is it the corporation or is it the employees who bear the consequences of corporate decision-making, or is it the shareholders whose financial interests (and religious ones apparently as well) are bound up in the corporation? Corporation, shareholder, state, religion, abortion, insurance, contraception, law, God; these revolve as sign, interpretant and signifier in the hands of advocates seeking to frame the issue to the advantage of their client. The relationship of shareholder, corporation, employee, state and religion changes depending on the role assigned to each. And there is no meta-framework that serves to standardize that analysis. Yet the law, to some extent provides the semblance of the structure because it is the law's own structures that provide both the gateway out to religion and inward into the characterization of individuals involved.

In the case examined, the power of an enterprise to assert the religion of its "owners" in a pass through manner, constrains the scope of the authority of the state to regulate through its law, and diminishes the protections of law for individuals who, for compensation, appear to have agreed to assume the burdens of the religious law of their employer, and thus waive their "belonging" as citizens of the state whose law would otherwise apply. Here Greimas' semiotic square becomes three-dimensional and begins to spin.

Consider the details of this multi-level dynamic state of law making that is driven by the business decisions of the corporation but constitutes an effort to break free of the law of the state, by applying the law of the state for that purpose (a waiver in an odd sense), to advance the law of the application of "other" law unconstrained by the law of the state whose permission is sought to disregard the state. The context is provided by a small group of individuals, who have chosen to come within the law structures of the state, by complying with those laws pertaining to the creation of an aggregation of capital with distinct benefits we have come to call the corporation. But having submitted to the state in the creation of that entity, these same individuals now seek to take that entity out of the controlling embrace of the state, at least with respect to those matters of operation with respect to which these individuals seek to submit to a distinct legal order—that offered through their religion, and its institutionalized law structures. This is possible, these individuals, now speaking through this corporate abstraction made manifest by operation of the law of the state, assert, because the state itself has created an escape hatch from out of its law universe. But the escape hatch was created for individuals. Individuals might also include juridical persons. That is not unreasonable, though the courts have tended to apply these consequences of personality serendipitously. Still, autonomy is itself merely another gateway to meaning making: how is a corporation incarnated, does it control its own soul or is that soul in the thrall of shareholders, or is that thralldom limited to a slavery of conscience when the corporation is controlled by a well-defined and small constellation of "masters." Otherwise are corporations both individuals and "masterless"—that is are they responsible for their own souls independent of those of their shareholders? The legal lexicon permits any of these solutions, and all of them. The question, then, lies well within the logic of law—but that logic merely seeks *plausibility* within its framework for naming and defining the objects of the legal lexicon, that is for *"the production of law and the verification of the conformity of the utterances on the world with the canonical utterances of legal language."* If legal discourse always seeks plausibility in result but plausibility is essential for system integrity, then the semiotics of law suggests that it is system integrity rather than the precise answer to any legal question that is of the most importance in the performance of the law through the methodologies of interpretation (in courts, contracts, before arbitrators and as a cultural object).

Now we have deployed Greimas' semiotic square cubed:

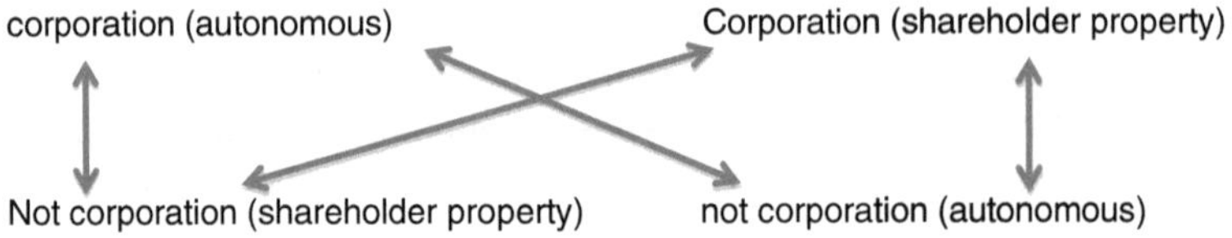

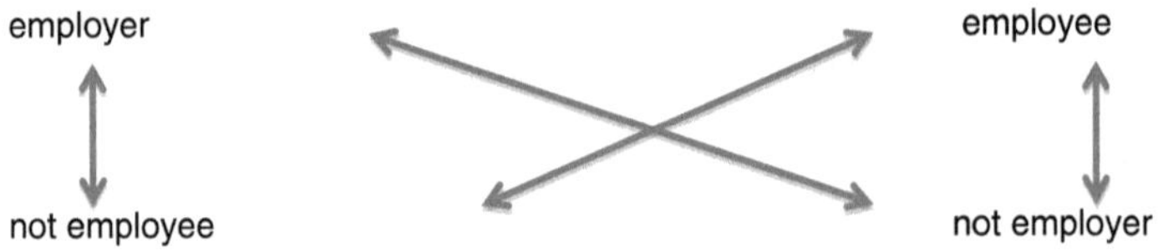

Greimas' analytical model provides a necessary framework to clarify semiotically the U.S. corporation's place within the lexicons of law, yet it must be remembered that in the end the analysis is necessarily applicable in context globally to all corporations—corporations semiotically are a global concept whose personality appears as a semiotic challenge in all jurisdictions, even in those that restrict the corporate form to the state.[5] Though the discourse is legal, the construct is necessarily normative, but normative in a form that informs not just the self-referencing lexicons of law, but also economic or political theory and policy a systemic way. Corporations, then, are not merely bearers of law (or religion), but also of an underlying ideology that informs the relationships between it and its interpretants. All corporations have necessarily ideological ties, ties with specific ideologies. None are neutral. These can be manifested in a variety of forms, and traditionally were sometimes centered on the analogy of the family—the worker was as much a member of the company "family" as he was to her biological family. The European form is the defender of the reputation of the company. All of this, of course, touches on the central theme of *belonging*, as a geography or space of inclusion, as the

[5]Discussed in Larry Catá Backer, "The Cooperative as Proletarian Corporation: Property Rights Between Corporation, Cooperatives And Globalization In Cuba," *Northwestern Journal of International Law and Business* 33:527–618 (2013).

definition of the excluded and the relationship among them.[6] Thus, *Sibelius* treats at multiple levels the semiosis of belonging—to the enterprise of the state, to the community of believers, to the family of the employer, to the aggregation of the corporation.

And so legal discourse is both self-referencing and path structuring. As the complexities of the *Sebelius* case hints, legal discourse's contingencies are both structural and dynamic. As Greimas suggests, the mechanisms of acquiring a practicable legal language leads to structures through which an a-semantic word, expression, sentence—sign—is transferred to the legislative level, that of definitively naming things and inscribing predictable events into the modal grid of prescriptions and interdictions. That legislative level, however, is necessarily polycentric. There is no singular legislative level—there are multiple simultaneous levels in which the naming and inscribing function becomes highly contingent and in which legal discourse is as much about routing questions of interpretation into the correct legal system as it is about interpretation within the lexicon of law. Neither routing nor interpretation is singular or linear. *Sebelius* reminds us that multiple simultaneous legal discourses occur even in the determination of what appears to be a single legal question. The communication among interlinked interpretation and its routing consequences adds contingency to what in Greimas' time might have otherwise been understood as the stability and singularity of the taxonomy of fundamental categories that now must produce grammatical discourses of multiple law systems.

What consequence from this detangling of a complex legal issue and its translation out of the self-referencing language universe of law and into the meaning universe of semiotics? Or, as Nietzsche used to criticize English thinkers for this bad habit—of what use is all of this? The answer to these questions, like that posed to the Supreme Court on the profession of religion by a corporation, is contingent, and tells one more about those who ask the question than the value of the question itself. The lawyer seeks results; the semiotician seeks meaning(s). Each may see in the other the means to their respective objects. For the lawyer the semiotic analysis provides a tool to bend meaning in the service of political or professional goals. For the semioticians, the work of the lawyer (and their clients, the courts and the state) provides the materials that may be harvested for meaning making. Whether a corporation has a soul, whether the state may recognize and create rules managing the power of individuals to move between simultaneously operating law systems; the mechanics for effecting these choices and their limits; the character and meaning of governmental acts (contraception offered through insurance as prevention or abortion, etc.). These are all important for the operation of the law system, yet none of the possible constrictions of meaning will substantially affect the legitimacy of the system itself, its grammar and cohesion. It may change its character, and define the limits of possible future choices, but it does not change the basic character of the sign, signifier, interpretant universe or the mechanics of meaning making played out within the Greimasian semiotic square. It is in this sense that we understand the political element of social discourse through law.

---

[6] Discussed in Massimo Leone, "Introduction to the Semiotics of Belonging," *Semiotica* 192:449–470 (2012).

Yet both also provide the sources for meta-meaning making as well. Each is a necessary component of the larger system Greimas suggests, one in which desire and action—the interaction of signs in the service of desire (itself fueled by interpreted signs)—illuminates the structures of closed systems for the identification of signs, the positioning of signifier and the framework within which interpretant function. Each functions legitimately only as long they conform to the meta-rules through which this contingent meaning making operates. To do otherwise is to fall outside the universe not of meaning but of meaning making roles—as semioticians or as lawyer (judge, legislator, etc.). Whether a corporation has a soul or a religion, then, becomes a critical systemic matter when the choice field of meaning is expanded beyond system tolerance—that is when the choices themselves explode the grammar of the field. It is in this sense that we understand values (normative) element of social discourse through law.

Editorial 5: I and Self (Welby, Lacan)

Jan M. Broekman and Larry Catá Backer

Three components reinforce the fascinating ties between the work of the French psychoanalyst, psychologist and philosopher Jacques Lacan (1901–1981) and modern semiotics. A particular relevance for legal semiotics seems obvious, if one considers those components in their relation with the work of Lady Victoria Welby and her understanding/promoting of significs. The first component is her own and Lacan's emphasis on the *Self*; the second on the importance of human beings as continuously involved in processes of *engenderment*, and the third is a general conclusion on the basic *thought pattern* of Occidental culture, which is the drive to dissect and analyze whatever type of reality seems at stake.

The Self

Petrilli published handwritten pages of Lady Welby on "The Self", whereby she marked several texts specifically as the "I and Self Theme"[1]. That theme is indeed of central importance for each semiotician. Welby's approach fascinates: apart from the general emphasis on the sign, which Peirce and other contemporaries forwarded, *she connected the idea of sign with the concept of identity, in particular the Self as*

[1] Susan Petrilli: *Signifying and Understanding. Reading the Works of Victoria Welby and the Signific Movement.* Mouton/De Gruyter, The Hague, Berlin 2009, Ch. 6, p. 640–670.

J.M. Broekman (✉)
Dickinson School of Law, Penn State University, Carlisle, PA, USA
e-mail: jmb56@dsl.psu.edu

L. Catá Backer
Departments of Law and International Affairs, Penn State University, University Park, PA, USA
e-mail: lcb11@psu.edu

J.M. Broekman, L. Catá Backer (eds.), *Signs In Law - A Source Book*,
DOI 10.1007/978-3-319-09837-1_17

a predominant social issue. Everyone studying semiotic approaches to social reality should read those recently published Welby notes.

Welby's exposition of that theme has clearly Platonic roots, which also fascinated Peirce. In *Lawyers Making Meaning*[2] we quoted in this context Plato's Cratylus. Peirce qualified the Cratylus and corresponding Theaetetus lines as "perhaps the deepest philosophical insight of Plato". Identity and social contact seem unified in the narration of a flowing "I said to myself"—so that a human being, he concluded, is always in dialogue with himself. *Names* and *Self*, as closely related as they are, seem in legal discourse connected with another specific identity: *cases*. The three: Names, Self, and Case (in essence three names) are probably the most essential components in legal discourse. The Self, as part of this triad, is not only a *personal* particle of identity but also a *social* particle.

Engenderment

Greimas would have agreed with this and Lacan acknowledged to have been searching for the consequences of the "mirror-stage" in the development of each individual in Occidental culture exactly because of this key-position in social narratives. The mirror stage became a symbol for a decisive moment in the development of each human individual, in which growth, education, language acquisition and above all: change, come together. Welby has located that moment in engenderment processes in the human Self, and in particular in the narrative structures that become evident in the human dialogue which is qualified as the most external articulation of our "inner" or "internal" life. One concludes that Welby's considerations and narrative constructions on I and Self are relevant in closest proximity to Lacan. Hence the lines she wrote whilst articulating the engenderment of positioning an I and a Self:

> I wish you would not scold me so terribly' complained the Self to its owner the I. 'You always seem to think that I can get out of my inherited character and be quite another person with quite different ways. Why can't you take me as you find me and make the best of me? At worst I am a good cure for vanity. (…) we should go together to the Self-world which ends at its own centre and lives for that; creating for its own pleasure, admiring its own excellence, exacting praise and worship from all, for its own delecta? Into the world which the poets and saints sing of and live for? I thought you were to use me, such as I am, for some true work, bringing truth to Man in homely ways and in ways which science teaches? Above all I thought you were to draw my speech onwards and upwards till through his many selves, Man could think out and act upon, because he could express, what now for lack of such expression he cannot think out, cannot even imagine or more than vaguely conceive?'

[2] Jan M. Broekman & Larry Catá Backer: *Lawyers Making Meaning*, Springer 2013, p 209 f.

In an almost Platonic dialogue style, she has the various particles of the "I" playing their role with answers and completing considerations, when writing in the same fragment:

> 'Well, I must say' answered the I, 'this is a grand lecture to get from one's Self of all people! You who are merely born and merely die on this speck of a planet! You who are always defeating me by sucking in all that I am here to give out, so that I can hardly squeeze it out of you again! You who boast and swagger in my name and invent new religions for your own cult and enjoyment and talk fine about development, and so on! Why, you jay in peacock's feathers, you ass in lion's skin, you have even stolen my name to preach to me with! How dare you say "I" when you know that *I* am your I, here only to live through and use you…'

The "Self", however takes a socialized position already before a social pattern becomes clear. Without the internal narration externalized, one can say, there is no process of development and therefore no human identity possible. It is in this flow-character of human identity, that the engenderment issue becomes recognized as fundamental for any semiotic understanding of human, social or natural reality. So the "Self" takes the lead:

> But the Self interrupted him: 'Why do you say "You" to me then? You see you can't help yourself. I shall pose as "I" as much as I choose.'
>
> 'How can I help it' returned the I, 'while my fellows are content with such an absurdly aimdefeating language, a sort of little frock which fitted them when they were babies and is now quite outgrown. (…) Suppose you help me instead to suggest how absurd it is to talk of reproaching, even denying and renouncing *my* Self, &c. and then to contradict that by making Self the whole of the I!' 'Well, let's try to clear this horrid confusion up' said the Self. 'And I'm quite willing you should be Master. You see I can't help making everything—even virtue and holiness—centre on what is "me-same". The storing instinct, the Self-centering energy is of course my very reason for being. I must gather and gather, store and store that you,—one with the true "I am", the true "Way",—the truly radiant life-star, may dispense, may give forth, may live and glory in that very giving …' Well, you know that yourself has not even yet the worthy words to say what no more "Self" can dare to claim[3].

One reads here a Welby dialogue that possesses exemplary and convincing power. It focuses on the major themes of contemporary semiotics: the 'split' character of an "I" 's individuality, the need to engage with other particles of the I in order to communicate socially, the reference to each human individual's engenderment, the need to engage in language long before the idea is born that one can *use* words, or a collection of them—thus questioning what it means to use a language! The wider context of significs/semiotics opens up when we consider, as Lacan did, the dimensions of I and Self. Peirce would have been in complete agreement with Welby when he would have had the opportunity to read:

> What is our greatest gift and prerogative? The mortality of our *selves*. As nothing but a self was born, so nothing but a self can die. And that blessing is secured to us—is not left to our blind and wayward choice. Body and Soul—self itself—thank GOD, is mortal. (…) death and birth are merely poles which we separate but which coming together flash out in a nameless light of reality and invulnerable existence. All our petty self-seeking melts and fades away….(…) It is true of course that the term 'self' was originally equivalent to 'same' and to 'ego'. But now a self is what You *have*, and are apt selfishly to pamper and work for.

[3] Petrilli, p. 640–641.

> And what you have cannot in the full sense be. That is true even of our children, though they be flesh and blood of our flesh and blood, bone of our bone, nerve of our nerve. They are ours, not us. (…) they were born, they die. (…) It is indeed the ultimate and fruitful sense of what we see as simple opposites, that Significs will give us. Paradox then represents at once our weakness and our strength. (…) it points to a more inclusive, a richer, more manfully evolved and constructive—a more expressive speech (…).[4]

Dividual and Individual

Emphasis on the engenderment as a condition for human identity has its general and in particular philosophical implications. They focus, as said in the introductory remarks, the drive of Occidental culture to give priority to dissection, fragmentation, analysis or atomizing instead of a view on the process, the unfolding or the entirety of reality around us. This is of greatest importance for any philosophy of law, who only seems to be possible as analysis or dissection as a basis for articulation of laws and legal discourses. But we are now confronted with the fact that relationships between I and Self are extremely essential for the wiring of the discourse of Law in its entirety, as it may be for all types of discourses, eventually in all languages and cultures. Today, we are careful not to claim global conclusions, but exactly with the I-Self relation as a central datum, we could venture that from here *all* human discourses unfold—as indeed Plato suggested from his cultural viewpoint. This would give even more credit to Welby's reflections on I and Self, as if they were foreshadowing Lacan's intuitions. This is a fortiori of essence for the concept of individuality, which is by no means a global concept, as Welby already surmises:

> We confound individuality with personality. The Greeks who bequeathed us the metaphor of Person, the actor's mask, knew better. The 'individual' is merely a unit and often but an item: it is absurdly inadequate to express a conscious being (one saying I am and I have) as the Immeasurable or the In-calculable would be. That we should be content with such terms for the most precious of conceptions 'speaks volumes.' Now the 'Actor's mask' (practically what we now call his make-up) gives us a valuable lesson. The actor has many such masks ready to be assumed, as he plays various parts on the stage of the world. And the idea involves a notable triad: you have (1) the mask, (2) the actor, (3) the character acted. This last again as a rule is 'created': does not actually exist in the world as a definite human Unit. In truth one has a company of selves. Some may be shelled off and left behind: some may be starved: some may be disciplined and trained: one may be our efficient ambassador or viceroy. But no one of our Selves can be wholly Us. We do not yet know who We are and still less who We might, in Identical Recognition, become. The Ident is still a secret[5].

It impresses how Lady Welby is more than a precursor of modern semiotics. She registers what we explained in the final chapter of this book: that semiotics should transcend a major feature and predominant force of Occidental culture: the urge to neglect the totality and the frame of each observation, the urge to dissect, to individu-

[4] Petrilli, p. 643.

[5] Petrilli, p. 644.

alize, to fragmentation, to separate and to distinct. All these drives result in a static signifying, a procedure that can no longer be called a process. Welby suggests:

> The master-signal [sic: Lacan formulates 'master-discourses' the very same way! (JMB/LCB)] to us therefore is, Never divide, and never confound; but to the first part must be added—Except to generate more life. For here lies the secret of our disastrous use of Individual for the You and the Me of the human order. It is the negative, the mere protest (as here the prefix In-betrays) against what we might be but must not be. Out of the Not nothing comes. We are Dividuals both in a good sense and a bad sense: if we are individual in any sense we are merely items, indeed merely points to start a line from: neither length, breadth, nor depth is ours. Negligible quantities indeed, mere postulates of quantity, to which quality is impossible.
>
> But if not typically in-dividual, what are we? *Identical;* and that in a sense compared to which all other identity is poor. We have here the Ident who is capable of indefinite enrichment; in whom indeed enrichment is summed up. There are many grades of Identity. That attained so far by humanity is the highest that man knows, except That which he infers; That which he knows that he Signifies or at least Symbolises.

This reads as anticipation on conclusions about the necessary *dynamic* character of semiotics, as we explained in the final chapter of this book. Each signifying process withstands a dissection in more or less independent particles before the power of sign and significance unfolds. The philosophical question is, whether semiotics or significs touch here upon an issue of general philosophical quality, which finally articulates itself as a choice between analysis and wholeness—a choice Lady Welby envisaged clearly—a clarity that throws a new light on the mirror stage as Lacan exposed:

> (…) Let us beware, then, of dividing the True Human Being into mutually independent constituent atoms while denying the divisibility of these, thronged worlds that they are. And again, let us be ware of confounding the infinitely rich complexity of distinction, which need not imply separation. One would think that Life was too brief, our glimpse of it too fleeting and too obviously poor, to waste the precious opportunity either in Dividing for mutual exclusion, or in Confounding which makes both for poverty and for chaos.[6]

[6] Petrilli, p. 644/645

Lacan, The Mirror and the "I"

Jan M. Broekman

> *Psychoanalytic experience has rediscovered in man*
> *the imperative of the Word as the law*
> *that has shaped him in its image*
>
> **Lacan**, *Discourse of Rome 1953*

In the *5th Editorial* of this book, the proximity of Lady Welby's insights to those of the French psychoanalyst and philosopher Jacques Lacan was highlighted as meaningful and foundational for semiotics. A major pillar in this context concerns the "I" or the "Self" as a constitutive moment in a process that is exclusively individual and utterly social at the same time. The human "Self", with the "I" as its continuous expressive counterpart, unfolds in social relations and engenders them whilst they are articulated and given time and place in the social continuum. To underline the character of continuity in this context is necessary, because social life is a process as are its components. Lady Welby encountered in the last decades of the 19th century the need to use all her scientific intuitions and literary skills to convince a bewildered public how this process feature leads to a strong understanding and scientific/philosophical analysis of the social.

At different stages in his life, in particular during various international conferences, Jacques Lacan encountered the same issue. At stake was, like in the days of Lady Welby, the connection between the Self and the Sign together with their social context as forwarded by Peirce. A growing insight in the importance of such connections did often, particularly in psychiatric circles, not lead to a deeper insight in the social relevance of the two.

The Self is not only a *personal* but also a *social* particle of identity. That insight was basic, when Lacan came to Zürich in 1949 to deliver his lecture at the Sixteenth International Congress of Psychoanalysis on *"The Mirror Stage as Formative of the 'I'—Function as Revealed in Psychoanalytic Experience"*—the text, which is central in this chapter. Exploring Köhler's famous "Aha-Erlebnis", Lacan focuses *as psychologist* on the very young child when it plays with movements made and images recognized in its reflected environment (including it's own body, persons

J.M. Broekman (✉)
Dickinson School of Law, Penn State University, Carlisle, PA, USA
e-mail: jmb56@dsl.psu.edu

J.M. Broekman, L. Catá Backer (eds.), *Signs In Law - A Source Book*,
DOI 10.1007/978-3-319-09837-1_18

and things around him) and focuses *as semiotician* on the multiplicity of signs, which challenge the very young to be mastered whilst developing a proper identity in social life.

The conference text was already announcing tensions between Lacan's insights and the traditional views in international psychoanalytic circles. A never researched aspect became visible, which is *the political appreciation of the semiotic dimension of Lacan's views on the emergence of the ego*. It fascinates that a perhaps already politically motivated choice was the basis for the text's translation and publication in English in the 1968 issue of the *New Left Review* in London, long before the same text appeared in the 1996 London edition of the *Écrits*.

Again we underline how a twofold meaning is brought to the fore: the *psychologist* reveals a libidinal dynamism that hitherto remained problematic and the *semiotician* reveals an ontological structure of the human world (political structures and dynamics included), which needs an identification produced by the mirror event. What Lacan calls "the specular image" in each engendering life is recognized as a threshold of the visible world, which we experience the moment we embrace the mirrored *imago of our own body* as we do in hallucinations and dreams. That is even stronger in one's infirmities, projections or mirror appearances of *doubles* in which psychical realities manifest themselves.

Notice, that these considerations developed in a period during which Lacan directed himself away from case studies and vested psychiatric practices. The *mirror stage experience*—often presented as a confrontation with *the specular image*—became a forceful element with great semiotic importance to understand how an emergent self *is* only formed and *can* only *be* formed in reference to some "other". It is essential to grasp that insight: the mirror stage, itself a risky process, is *not* a harmonious and equilibrated basis for a healthy and stable ego in later life, but rather the origin of an *alienation* of the self from the self, which has to be appeased and become a reliable ego-foundation in the course of life. The self is focusing in a "fictional direction" towards an other, it normally meets a powerful potential rival of the self, so that its focus does not automatically mean equilibrium and peace. The mirror stage is in that regard an unexpected source of contrast, alienation and aggression in view of identity formation as was traditionally observed by psychiatry and even semiotics (read Lady Welby); the latter discipline underlines how *the character and presence of a sign is not by definition without conflict and disequilibrium*, as the mirror image confrontation shows.

A human identity is formed in a context in which alienation and aggression are norms: that theme was at issue between 1949 and 1953, the year in which Lacan broke with the IPA, the International Psycho-Analytical Association. After that breach, Lacan formed his own SFP, the French Psychoanalytic Society, in which he delivered the same year in its Rome meeting his famous "Discourse of Rome", where he gave "speech" a central role. Semioticians should not forget how speech and the mirror-staged identity belong together: this togetherness constitutes a turn to semiotics, which later created a wealth of specifically Lacanian views on De Saussure, Foucault, Structuralism and Derrida's deconstructivism.

Those developments did, however, not do away with insights already formulated in the 1949 lecture, where he stated:

> "(…) human knowledge is more independent than animal knowledge from the force field of desire[1] because of the social dialectic that structures human knowledge as paranoiac (…)" And: "These reflections lead me to recognize in the spatial capture manifested by the mirror stage, the effect in man, even prior to this social dialectic, of an organic inadequacy of his natural reality — assuming we can give some meaning to the word "nature." The function of the mirror stage thus turns out, in my view, to be a particular case of the function of imago's, which is to establish a relationship between an organism and its reality — or, as they say, between the *Innenwelt* and the *Umwelt*."

However, man's relation to nature is—as Lacan underlines—also coined by a malaise and by what he describes as a "motor-un-coordination of the neonatal months". That feeling precludes the 1953 breach, a feeling, which reinforced the A. Portmann thesis about the "pre-mature birth" or the "double structure of the human birth". The latter, biologist and philosopher, underlined that an extra-uterine phase must follow an intra-uterine, and that the two together are finally one human birth event. In other words: a human individual is born twice as one: biologically under a variety of social influences and socially under a variety of biological influences.

This relates to a further Lacanian insight, which is already anchored in the 1949 text: the moment at which the mirror stage comes to an end inaugurates through identification with the imago of one's 'semblable' (one's equal) and the drama of primordial jealousy

> "(…) the dialectic that will henceforth link the "I" to socially elaborated situations".[2]

It is this moment that decisively characterizes the entirety of a human being and his/her self-knowledge (…) as being mediated by the other's desire. The world of a human being's objects end up in an abstract equivalence due to the continuous competition from other people, and

> "turns the "I" into an apparatus to which every instinctual pressure constitutes a danger (…). The very normalization of this maturation is henceforth dependent in man on cultural intervention, as is exemplified by the fact that sexual object choice is dependent upon the Oedipus complex."[3]

Lacan connects this observation with the existential negativity of his days, vigorously proclaimed by a philosophy of being and nothingness (Sartre, Heidegger).

The role of the subject in Lacan's thought-patterns is, all in all, most fascinating for the project of semiotics. It already follows from the fact that a major emphasis since the essay on the mirror stage is on language (as speech), on linguistic structures, on signification and meaning—all not to be identified with what was in his days called "structuralism". An interesting observation can be made in this context. In Lacan's thought is the mirror image the initiation of an unfolding of relations

---

[1] Notice Lacan's early use (1949) of this expression "the force field of desire"; not the verb but the meaning-field is at stake here.

[2] The topical interest of the term "semblable" is confirmed by Jacques-Alain Miller, (Editor of Lacan's work), in his essay *The Real and Semblance* in: LACANIAN INK, New York 2012, Nr 43/44, p. 66 f.

[3] See in this perspective: Ali Benmakhlouf: *L'identité. Une fable philosophique.* PUF, Paris 2011, p. 49 f, 149 f.

between the real, the imaginary and the symbolic. Those are social processes, in which a subject is entangled—and thus processes, which are at stake in the mirror stage as such. Now, the three, a triad by nature, are in parallel observed by Charles Sanders Peirce, and since his writings at home in semiotics. Firstness, Secondness and Thirdness are the three outstanding categories of experience, reflected in Peircean thoughts *and* in Lacan's ideas since the "mirror stage" explications. Both are, furthermore, dynamic in character: Lacan's 'chain of signifiers' is as dynamic as Peirce's 'process of semiosis'.

A short look at Lacan's so-called "Rome Discourse" enables an insight that seems to be important for our semiotic concern today. We should not expect an exposé about speech in its more general meaning or a theory of speech in the sense of for example John Searle's famous 1969 *Speech Acts: An Essay in the Philosophy of Language*. His ideas are in the first place within the context of Freudian texts and understandings, and are touching therefore, at an equal Freudian level, speech as an important issue in psychoanalytic practice. Lacan is clear in his statement:

> Whether it wishes to be an agent of healing, training, or sounding the depths, psychoanalysis has but one medium: the patient's speech. The obviousness of this fact is no excuse for ignoring it. Now all speech calls for a response. I will show that there is no speech without a response, even if speech meets only with silence, provided it has an auditor, and this is the heart of its function in analysis.
>
> But if the psychoanalyst is not aware that this is how speech functions, he will experience its call [appel] all the more strongly; and if emptiness is the first thing to make itself heard in analysis, he will feel it in himself and he will seek a reality beyond speech to fill the emptiness.

Speech and discourse are concepts that both serve to understand the major features of psychoanalytic practice:

> The analyst's art must (…) involve suspending the subject's certainties until their final mirages have been consumed. And it is in the subject's discourse that their dissolution must be punctuated.
>
> Even if it communicates nothing, discourse represents the existence of communication; even if it denies the obvious, it affirms that speech constitutes truth; even if it is destined to deceive, it relies on faith in testimony.

The strength and appropriateness of Lacan's view on speech and discourse in psychoanalysis was a great surprise and for many a source of renewed inspiration in the days of his Rome conference. It interests therefore, to highlight some ideas that go beyond its purpose and relate the 'speech' concept, together with 'discourse' and more generally with 'language' to our contemporary semiotic understandings. Two remarks on the concept of the 'consciousness' draw our attention beyond psychoanalysis. First he states:

> The true basis of the Freudian discovery of the unconscious becomes clear in its position as a third term. This may be simply formulated in the following terms: The unconscious is that part of concrete discourse qua transindividual, which is not at the subject's disposal in reestablishing the continuity of his conscious discourse.

And then, he applies to himself in an examplary manner:

> The unconscious is the chapter of my history (…) is the censored chapter. But the truth can be refound; most often it has already been written elsewhere. Namely,
>
> - in monuments: this is my body, in other words, the hysterical core of neurosis in which the hysterical symptom manifests the structure of a language, and is deciphered like an inscription which, once recovered, can be destroyed without serious loss;
> - in archival documents too: these are my childhood memories, just as impenetrable as such documents are when I do not know their provenance;
> - in semantic evolution: this corresponds to the stock of words and acceptations of my own particular vocabulary, as it does to my style of life and my character;
> - in traditions, too, and even in the legends which, in a heroicized form, convey my history;
> - and, lastly, in its traces that are inevitably preserved in the distortions necessitated by the insertion of the adulterated chapter into the chapters surrounding it, and whose meaning will be re-established by my exegesis.

If we notice an unexpected nearness to Peirce's thought formations, then this observation might be reinforced by a final formulation in Lacan's Rome Discourse, which fully shows its importance to the modern semiotic reader:

> The omnipresence of human discourse will perhaps one day be embraced under the open sky of an omni-communication of its text. This is not to say that human discourse will be any more in tune with it than it is now. But this is the field that our experience polarizes in a relation that is only apparently a two-person relation, for any positioning of its structure in merely dyadic terms is as inadequate to it in theory as it is damaging to its technique[4].

J. Pinto gave the parallels and differences between Peirce and Lacan full attention in a paper delivered at the *Semiotic Society of America*, October 1988 in Cincinnati[5]. He described Lacan's struggle to acknowledge the triadic structure at hand, because in the psychoanalytic approach of the latter, the subject has only "an endless chain of signifiers available with no signifieds attached to them". It means that "the only way of attaining some kind of signification is through the interpeter's act of assigning a signified to the slippery signifier." This includes for Pinto, that the linguistic view in Lacan's theory focuses on what we call *the sign*. That focus should, however, not lead to neglecting the triadic features at hand—a semiotic issue forever important. The signified can only be reached at the interval between two signifiers, Pinto states, which means that the signified occurs at certain *loci* of the chain of signifiers. The representational structure in which the subject is involved from the mirror stage on "is *said* to be dyadic when in fact it is represented as being triadic". This is by no means an irrelevant observation.

It shows in the first place, how semiotic analyses of Lacan's texts can deepen the psychoanalytic and even philosophical dimensions pertaining to for instance the unfolding of the subject, as is the case in the "mirror—'I' " text.

---

[4] Quotations from the Discourse of Rome are in: J. Lacan: *Écrits*. Bruce Fink (Transl.) Norton, New York 2006, 2002, p. 244, 252, 257, 259, 265.

[5] Julio Pinto: "The Question of the Subject in Semiosis: Peirce and Lacan" in: *Semiotics 1988*, T.Prewitt/J.Deely/K.Haworth (Eds) University of America, 1988, p. 578 f.

It is furthermore crucial to understand a point of culmination in the philosophy of the 20th century whereby Peirce and Lacan are observed in parallel, thanks to the semiotic approach.

Finally, our understanding of the subject as a living force in the sign pool of everyday broadens our view on the subject as being a sign-for-others and thus being dependent upon the role of an interpretant.

The latter will never be able to achieve a complete interpretation of reality. A semiotics of the "I" and the "Self" will teach us, how the idea of a full representation by any subject having traversed the mirror stage, is misleading and inaccurate. A human identity will never seem an Arcadian landscape.

Part IV
Semiotics of Law Today

Introduction: The Institutes of Justinian

Jan M. Broekman and Larry Catá Backer

Prooemium

In the name of Our Lord, Jesus Christ.

The Emperor Caesar Flavius Justinian, conqueror of the Alamanni, the Goths, the Franks, the Germans, the Antes, the Alani, the Vandals, the Africans, pious, prosperous, renowned, victorious, and triumphant, ever August. To the youth desirous of studying the law:

The imperial majesty should be armed with laws as well as glorified with arms, that there may be good government in times both of war and of peace, and the ruler of Rome may not only be victorious over his enemies, but may show himself as scrupulously regardful of justice as triumphant over his conquered foes.

With deepest application and forethought, and by the blessing of God, we have attained both of these objects. The barbarian nations which we have subjugated know our valour, Africa and other provinces without number being once more, after so long an interval, reduced beneath the sway of Rome by victories granted by Heaven, and themselves bearing witness to our dominion. All peoples too are ruled by laws which we have either enacted or arranged. Having removed every

---

SOURCE: Project Gutenberg's The Institutes of Justinian, by Caesar Flavius Justinian. The eBook [EBook #5983] is for the use of anyone anywhere at no cost and with almost no restrictions whatsoever. You may copy it, give it away or re-use it under the terms of the Project Gutenberg License included with this eBook or online at www.gutenberg.org. Translator: J.B. Moyle. Last Updated: February 6, 2013 Oxford *Fifth Edition*

J.M. Broekman (✉)
Dickinson School of Law, Penn State University, Carlisle, PA, USA
e-mail: jmb56@dsl.psu.edu

L. Catá Backer
Departments of Law and International Affairs, Penn State University,
University Park, PA, USA
e-mail: lcb11@psu.edu

J.M. Broekman, L. Catá Backer (eds.), *Signs In Law - A Source Book*,
DOI 10.1007/978-3-319-09837-1_19

inconsistency from the sacred constitutions, hitherto inharmonious and confused, we extended our care to the immense volumes of the older jurisprudence; and, like sailors crossing the mid-ocean, by the favour of Heaven have now completed a work of which we once despaired.

When this, with God's blessing, had been done, we called together that distinguished man Tribonian, master and exquaestor of our sacred palace, and the illustrious Theophilus and Dorotheus, professors of law, of whose ability, legal knowledge, and trusty observance of our orders we have received many and genuine proofs, and especially commissioned them to compose by our authority and advice a book of Institutes, whereby you may be enabled to learn your first lessons in law no longer from ancient fables, but to grasp them by the brilliant light of imperial learning, and that your ears and minds may receive nothing useless or incorrect, but only what holds good in actual fact. And thus whereas in past time even the foremost of you were unable to read the imperial constitutions until after four years, you, who have been so honoured and fortunate as to receive both the beginning and the end of your legal teaching from the mouth of the Emperor, can now enter on the study of them without delay. After the completion therefore of the fifty books of the Digest or Pandects, in which all the earlier law has been collected by the aid of the said distinguished Tribonian and other illustrious and most able men, we directed the division of these same Institutes into four books, comprising the first elements of the whole science of law. In these the law previously obtaining has been briefly stated, as well as that which after becoming disused has been again brought to light by our imperial aid. Compiled from all the Institutes of our ancient jurists, and in particular from the commentaries of our Gaius on both the Institutes and the common cases, and from many other legal works, these Institutes were submitted to us by the three learned men aforesaid, and after reading and examining them we have given them the fullest force of our constitutions.

Receive then these laws with your best powers and with the eagerness of study, and show yourselves so learned as to be encouraged to hope that when you have compassed the whole field of law you may have ability to govern such portion of the state as may be entrusted to you.

Given at Constantinople the 21st day of November, in the third consulate of the Emperor Justinian, Father of his Country, ever August.

Of Justice and Law

Justice is the set and constant purpose which gives to every man his due.

1. Jurisprudence is the knowledge of things divine and human, the science of the just and the unjust.

2. Having laid down these general definitions, and our object being the exposition of the law of the Roman people, we think that the most advantageous plan will be to commence with an easy and simple path, and then to proceed to details with a most careful and scrupulous exactness of interpretation. Otherwise, if we begin by

burdening the student's memory, as yet weak and untrained, with a multitude and variety of matters, one of two things will happen: either we shall cause him wholly to desert the study of law, or else we shall bring him at last, after great labour, and often, too, distrustful of his own powers (the commonest cause, among the young, of ill-success), to a point which he might have reached earlier, without such labour and confident in himself, had he been led along a smoother path.

3. The precepts of the law are these: to live honestly, to injure no one, and to give every man his due.

4. The study of law consists of two branches, law public, and law private. The former relates to the welfare of the Roman State; the latter to the advantage of the individual citizen. Of private law then we may say that it is of threefold origin, being collected from the precepts of nature, from those of the law of nations, or from those of the civil law of Rome.

Of the Law of Nature, the Law of Nations, and the Civil Law

1. The law of nature is that which she has taught all animals; a law not peculiar to the human race, but shared by all living creatures, whether denizens of the air, the dry land, or the sea. Hence comes the union of male and female, which we call marriage; hence the procreation and rearing of children, for this is a law by the knowledge of which we see even the lower animals are distinguished. The civil law of Rome, and the law of all nations, differ from each other thus. The laws of every people governed by statutes and customs are partly peculiar to itself, partly common to all mankind. Those rules which a state enacts for its own members are peculiar to itself, and are called civil law: those rules prescribed by natural reason for all men are observed by all peoples alike, and are called the law of nations. Thus the laws of the Roman people are partly peculiar to itself, partly common to all nations; a distinction of which we shall take notice as occasion offers.

2. Civil law takes its name from the state wherein it binds; for instance, the civil law of Athens, it being quite correct to speak thus of the enactments of Solon or Draco. So too we call the law of the Roman people the civil law of the Romans, or the law of the Quirites; the law, that is to say, which they observe, the Romans being called Quirites after Quirinus. Whenever we speak, however, of civil law, without any qualification, we mean our own; exactly as, when 'the poet' is spoken of, without addition or qualification, the Greeks understand the great Homer, and we understand Vergil. But the law of nations is common to the whole human race; for nations have settled certain things for themselves as occasion and the necessities of human life required. For instance, wars arose, and then followed captivity and slavery, which are contrary to the law of nature; for by the law of nature all men from the beginning were born free. The law of nations again is the source of almost all contracts; for instance, sale, hire, partnership, deposit, loan for consumption, and very many others.

3. Our law is partly written, partly unwritten, as among the Greeks. The written law consists of statutes, plebiscites, senatusconsults, enactments of the Emperors, edicts of the magistrates, and answers of those learned in the law.

4. A statute is an enactment of the Roman people, which it used to make on the motion of a senatorial magistrate, as for instance a consul. A plebiscite is an enactment of the commonalty, such as was made on the motion of one of their own magistrates, as a tribune. The commonalty differs from the people as a species from its genus; for 'the people' includes the whole aggregate of citizens, among them patricians and senators, while the term 'commonalty' embraces only such citizens as are not patricians or senators. After the passing, however, of the statute called the lex Hortensia, plebiscites acquired for the first time the force of statutes.

5. A senatusconsult is a command and ordinance of the senate, for when the Roman people had been so increased that it was difficult to assemble it together for the purpose of enacting statutes, it seemed right that the senate should be consulted instead of the people.

6. Again, what the Emperor determines has the force of a statute, the people having conferred on him all their authority and power by the 'lex regia,' which was passed concerning his office and authority. Consequently, whatever the Emperor settles by rescript, or decides in his judicial capacity, or ordains by edicts, is clearly a statute: and these are what are called constitutions. Some of these of course are personal, and not to be followed as precedents, since this is not the Emperor's will; for a favour bestowed on individual merit, or a penalty inflicted for individual wrongdoing, or relief given without a precedent, do not go beyond the particular person: though others are general, and bind all beyond a doubt.

7. The edicts of the praetors too have no small legal authority, and these we are used to call the 'ius honorarium,' because those who occupy posts of honour in the state, in other words the magistrates, have given authority to this branch of law. The curule aediles also used to issue an edict relating to certain matters, which forms part of the ius honorarium.

8. The answers of those learned in the law are the opinions and views of persons authorized to determine and expound the law; for it was of old provided that certain persons should publicly interpret the laws, who were called jurisconsults, and whom the Emperor privileged to give formal answers. If they were unanimous the judge was forbidden by imperial constitution to depart from their opinion, so great was its authority.

9. The unwritten law is that which usage has approved: for ancient customs, when approved by consent of those who follow them, are like statute.

10. And this division of the civil law into two kinds seems not inappropriate, for it appears to have originated in the institutions of two states, namely Athens and Lacedaemon; it having been usual in the latter to commit to memory what was observed as law, while the Athenians observed only what they had made permanent in written statutes.

11. But the laws of nature, which are observed by all nations alike, are established, as it were, by divine providence, and remain ever fixed and immutable: but the municipal laws of each individual state are subject to frequent change, either by the tacit consent of the people, or by the subsequent enactment of another statute.

12. The whole of the law which we observe relates either to persons, or to things, or to actions. And first let us speak of persons: for it is useless to know the law without knowing the persons for whose sake it was established.

Editorial 6: On Persons, Things and Obligations in Semiotic Perspective

Jan M. Broekman and Larry Catá Backer

It seems rather challenging: persons, things and obligations do not exist in the sense of 'natural' entities. So, how do we come to appreciate their diversification and the order they suggest to represent? A first answer to this question is, that persons, things and obligations are elements embedded in the history of Occidental culture. The period in which they play their role reaches exceptionally wide: from the Twelve Tables erected in the center of Rome around 450 BC to the first Law School in Bologna mid-12th century, and then until our days, when they became incorporated in a variety of national Codes, such as the French or the German. Radin underlines that those concepts fulfilled the task to create an order—not in society and human relations but in the mass of legal-textual materials that had grown rank in the course of the ages[1]. One concludes, that it is history, which has put emphasis on those three constructed concepts. A characteristic feature in that history was the use of a specific language: Latin survived throughout the ages and was for centuries closely tied to the lawyer's profession. The Justinian Code, still in the mind of legal scholars today, reminds the lawyer of this in the US almost forgotten fact. "Can one study law without knowledge of Latin?" is a challenging question not only for Civil Law. The Justinian Code plays a star role here. The three books of his Code were of Persons, of Things and of Obligations. 20th century law reverberates the Justinian intuition and treats the three as if they were contemporary realities. They are realities solely as *legal* realities, as constructions playing a key role in law and legal discourse.

[1] See (also in this volume) M. Radin: "Fundamental Concepts of Roman Law" in *California Law Review*, XII, p. 207 f.

J.M. Broekman (✉)
Dickinson School of Law, Penn State University, Carlisle, PA, USA
e-mail: jmb56@dsl.psu.edu

L. Catá Backer
Departments of Law and International Affairs, Penn State University, University Park, PA, USA
e-mail: lcb11@psu.edu

J.M. Broekman, L. Catá Backer (eds.), *Signs In Law - A Source Book*,
DOI 10.1007/978-3-319-09837-1_20

Merryman outlined the multiple dimensions in which the Justinian Code, and with that Code the concepts of Person, Thing and Obligation, were conceived and empowered[2] First, Justinian sought to rescue the Roman legal tradition; second he was a politically masterful and powerful codifier who wanted to abolish other legal authorities and suppress all referential activity in law apart from reference to his own Code. The part of that Code that deals with Roman civil law became the basis for the entire legal system of the civil law world. It was this Code, which formed the subject of study in law during the period of the Bologna law school: the Corpus Iuris Civilis was taught in Latin, and was Law! A *ius commune* was born in that school, pertaining to a common body of law, a common method of writing and reading law, a common language, Latin, and a common teaching and scholarship based on a limited number of texts. Even national legal systems, coming up from the 15th century onward, kept this model in mind. We remember these issues because any mention of Person, Thing and Obligation provides steps in a thoroughly vested tradition. But again: it is a *legal* tradition, incorporated in Occidental culture, from which Common Law distanced itself only slowly, vaguely and never definitively. A Justinian challenge to obey was never quit, and remains alive in the hesitation to fully consider how persons, things and obligations are discursive constructs rather than realities of daily life. This latter approach is, however, basic for unfolding semiotic perspectives: that is the guiding principle when considering our theme as follows.

Person

The concept of a person was central in Roman Law since 400 BC and its legal and psychological/political heritage determines our debates even today. On the hand is its strength in the fact that the concept is everywhere felt as a daily-life concept, the correct indication of a human individual for centuries embedded in a natural evidence, which is difficult to deny: a 'look and see for yourself!'

The concept of a legal person is now central in both civil, and common law countries, but it is also found in virtually every legal system. In other words, the Roman heritage is omnipresent. A point of discussion that is straightforwardly important for semiotic studies is the differentiation between a person as a natural person and a legal person. As is generally known, it is an invention of Roman lawyers to treat goods/things as a person in law, so that a capital possesses rights and duties in legal discourse. Whilst recognizing the artificial character of the latter type of personality, the question stays alive in for instance laws pertaining to corporations—the political argumentation referring to these laws included (as we have elaborated in Volume II: Lawyers Making Meaning, Ch 11 and 12, and one reads in Ch 26 and 27 of this Volume). All in all, the various positions discuss the natural versus the artificial and fictitious character of legal personality. Legal semioticians remark, that in such

[2] John H. Merryman: *The Civil Law Tradition* Stanford UP 3rd Edition 2007 (Ed.: Rogelio Perez-Perdomo) Ch. II.

discussions the words "is" and "have" play a key role, without being appropriately a researched. What signification is at stake, when a person can declare to "have" a right, and what world-view is articulated when a person states to "have" legal capacity and to "be" legally positioned to act in certain ways? Welby, De Haan and other significians have chosen those expressions to demonstrate the naïve uses of language when legal discourses unfold. No wonder that very clearly profiled viewpoints have been concentrating on this issue in French or German jurisprudence and legal scholarship.

In French public law, the position of Léon Duguit (1859–1928)[3] became famous in trying to deduct (public) law from the need of social solidarity. He wanted to show that norms are directly linked to human nature and will be sustained by natural science results. The "simple observation" in the "look and see for yourself" became a legal-scientific dogma that lead to unexpected standpoints. For instance, it lead to not embrace classical natural law notions, to not view human rights as directly deducted from the core human essence, and to not recognize subjective rights. All this is embedded in the thoughts on a human/legal person. Their main motive was for Duguit that "objective law" was opposed to Law and legal statues, is continuously engendering from collective social occurrences and acquires a validity, which should be deducted not by reasoning but from direct observation. Positive law is only state-law, which remains bound to its proper barriers, determined by the State.

The German jurist and legal scholar Rudolph von Ihering struggled all his life with the idea of a legal person and consequently the meaning and maintenance of subjective rights. Near to modern problems with the legal anchors of corporate law was Ihering's personal struggle with the legal status of a capital that is not legated to a living natural person, the Latin 'hereditas iacens'-idea. Two contrasting ideas became real in this case: on the one hand the recognition of subjective rights that were independent from natural persons, and on the other the tendency to ascribe rights only to natural persons. Near to Duguit's solidarity-idea, Ihering suggested to explain the legal personality as a juridical form constructed because of interests of those who might profit from those subjective rights. A *destination*-theory emerged, which refers to the rightful capability of a natural person to involve private persons to serve his interests, in cases of association its members, and in cases of a foundation its addressees. At those occasions, a plurality is created to serve a personal interest. This idea was, however, theoretically interesting but far from social reality of everyday life, as well as a borderline case of the theoretical foundation of the legal personality, which refers to the fictitious nomination of persons in order to fulfill a specific purpose. How precious this Ihering position is, becomes clear in the following Chapters 26 and 27, in which the corporate personality functions legally, sociologically and politically as a central legal issue.

[3] L. Duguit: *L'Etat, le droit objectif at la loi positive,* Paris 1901.;—Id.—*Traité de droit constitutionnel,* Paris 1921.

Thing

Things, the subject matter of Justinian's second Code, are in Occidental law different signifiers. The word *thing* means originally, as historians suggest, an *object* in the traditional sense of the word, but it means also an *assembly* in the Islandic and other coastal cultural traditions of Western Europe. In legal discourse, *thing* and *person* are therefore closely tied together, and that has its consequences for any semiotic approach to deeper understand the signification issues at hand. Our major thesis in this regard is therefore not a surprise: *semiotic studies of the "thing" (in the Latin tradition: "res") lead mainly to the concept of property*. Legal discourse in its technical sense of the word has no boundaries that prevent a broad interpretation of thing as related to property. The "res" is in law an object, as well as the subject matter, as well—a third degree of legal determination—the focused status in the boundaries of law as an institution. Within the latter position, there can be emphasis on an individual person, on the status of a party or on a specific role within the legal-institutional construction at hand, such as a corporation, a multinational or another comparable fixation with 'assembly'-character. "Real" things are made movable in law, and vice versa, as the many cases on the property of land show. Their belonging to a matrimonial also blurs the line between corporeal and incorporeal, no matter whether they are possessed by a matrimonial structure. For short, the field is full of fine lines that are transcended as often as interests require, despite legal subtleties and needs to fixate what property is about.

No wonder, that Roberta Kevelson offered an essay on the semiotics of property with the title *Property as Rhetoric in Law*[4]. Her major thesis is courageous and often passed by in silence. She suggests, that the concepts of property, rhetoric as a form of logic, and law are essentially key notions of semiotics:

> it is the idea of Property in logic and Property in law, which becomes (...) the chief instrument for expanding traditional logic into *semiotic* logic, by understanding the concept of Property as a device of Rhetoric, i.e., of Semiotic Methodology. Thus law becomes prototypical of semiotics, in process, practice, and theory, by means of a more complex and continually evolving concept of Property (see also Chapter 24 of this Volume).

Two lines of thought are prominent in her text: one is the historical and jurisprudential, with references to Bentham, Peirce, Hohfeld and others; the other is referring to rhetoric as a form of language and logic, to social forces like power inequality, privilege and obligation as implied in property. Both are equal sources of understanding and definition and thus participants in the semiotic of signifying. So she notes

> Bentham explicitly speaks of Property as a "means" or a method—an instrument or tool—for bringing about estimation and evaluation of people by others in society. Although Bentham wants to restrict the use of the term Property to "corporeal objects," the history

[4]Roberta Kevelson: "Property as Rhetoric in Law", in: *Cardozo Studies in Law and Literature*, 1992, p. 189 f.;—Id.—"Flux, complexity, and illusion" in: *Sixth round table on law and semiotics*. New York: Peter Lang Publishing. 1993. .—Id.—*Peirce's esthetics of freedom: Possibility, complexity, and emergent value*. New York: Peter Lang Publishing. 1993.

of the idea extends to incorporeal objects as well and is so classified among ancients as well as moderns according to Blackstone.

It thus fascinates how Kevelson remarks as an in-between observation, how complex the space of meaning of the idea of property is, if considered in semiotic perspective:

Property in Law, which corresponds with a parallel increase in the related *idea* of Power with which Property is associated: Indeed, it is this correspondence between Property and Rights which Hohfeld uses as the basis for a relational approach to Rights, such that not only is Property a relation between possessor and nonpossessor in common law societies, but Power, Privilege and Rights are, in the same manner, instruments of reciprocation.

The internal space of meaning is important to evaluate the concept of property. This is a leading motive that brings her to observe how

As Ogden points out in his classic introduction to Bentham's *Theory of Fictions,* Bentham regarded both space and all mass of matter to be formable, i.e., to be representations of significance. All "portions of space" have form, and all property as an aspect of place has such form. Form or Figure are properties and qualities, or general ideas of place and space. In this manner, by this rhetorical means, having such configuration in idea or in material is the way that Property relates such figure or form as an element or entity—a phenomenality common to both matter and space. It is commonplace to note that there is a reciprocity between processes that pertain to law and those that characterize logic. Similarly, there is a reciprocity that obtains between our mapping of the physical on the ideational and, conversely, also interpreting the physical as a mode or a trope of the imagination. In particular, whenever a logical quality is taken to be a kind of identifying or "permanent" feature of any subject, that interpretation of permanence is fictive, but it becomes a symbolic fiction since its function is to designate a part of that which defines a subject, "and in consideration of its belonging to a subject. It is frequently styled a property of, belonging, or inherent in, that same subject."[5]

Kevelson essays on Property, together with the explorations of Malloy in Chapter 25 and the analyses of Drion in Chapter 26, which often reach an implicit theory of knowledge when dealing with the concept of property, show that our thesis: *semiotic studies on Things end up in studies on Property*, does not imply any impoverishment of legal discourse or legal practices. On the contrary: Poverty as a concept semiotically envisaged enriches legal views on reality and human relations, together with a sharpened insight in the function of concepts which serve personal or group-related interests. Read in Kevelson' essay once more:

(...) it is important to see Bentham's great influence on Peirce. We find such evidence of this influence in his section on Property as a sign in a subject-quality relationship. For example, it is the relationship itself, the link or mode of connectedness between a subject and its attributes or properties which is the "sign" of the unit *as* unit. The transitivity itself, in the mode of existential verb or form of Have, or other modes of indicating attribution, are interpretable as effecting and of making consequential the very entity of something and its characteristic quality. In Bentham's words, "to the sign of the subject and the sign of the quality must be added the sign of the relation."

---

[5] Jeremy Bentham, *Works,* Vol. VIII, Everett, ed. (New York: Columbia University Press, 1906), p. 337, cited in Ogden's Introduction to Bentham, *Fictions.*

> In brief, our language is so constructed as to "present to view" these relations so that triadicity, as a diagrammatic symbolic and existential sign structure, is rhetorically expressed by the coherence of subject linkage, and property, as a mode of reciprocity and relation.
>
> It is also Bentham who reminds us that Definition is the device, which serves metaphysics via rhetoric as a meta-logical means for the creating of fictions. Thus legal concepts such as Right, Power, Obligation, Privilege are paraphrased and transformed, or interpreted as "species" of existent, just as fictive "entities" are taken as Properties, i.e., as real Entities, as real as "man, animal."

No wonder, that the Justinian Code had "Obligations" as the title for its Third Book! Do these complete Persons and Things?

Obligation

The core idea of the concept of obligation is based in the non-legal feature of inter-human reciprocity. Roman Law, in particular the Justinian Code, defined in the "Institutes Vol. III" the obligation legally as a bond, which binds persons to State Laws. (Book III, 13). An obligation was legally fixated as a relation by whom two persons/individuals were bound together (*obligati*) by a legally recognized and enforced bond. Both parties were originally considered to be under obligation to each other, so that the term was restricted to one of the parties. But that legal intuition contradicted any social reality that marks human relations. So a dual feature was brought into the concept of obligation: who was under an obligation had to do something in favor of another. To complete that pattern of mutuality, the other was ascribed a correlative right to enforce the fulfillment of the obligation. The "other" or "the other party" was clearly embedded in legal thought patterns and in that specific context defined as a legal subject: the civil law's bearer of rights and duties.

It fascinates how two peculiar aspects characterize the history of the concept of obligation: on the one hand, the social reality had to be precisely translated in legal terms, so that the equilibrium of rights and duties could become the final determination in law's words. On the other hand, it was clear from this signifying process, that once the idea of obligation was put in legal terms and introduced as a basic issue of legal discourse, one had to fulfill the requirements to fixate the legal procedure that follows the pattern of mutuality in legal-obligatory situations. The ultimate requirement became, after the Justinian Code efforts, *contract* as a form of sociability and social freedom. The three steps: (1) entering legal discourse, (2) refining the bond between law and social reality in the form of an equilibrium between rights and duties, and (3) providing a legal (procedural) form beyond national legislation, was the continuously reinforced heritage of Roman Law, and in that framework the major focus of legal semiotics. Semiotics of contract, with a special emphasis on Peirce, is represented by Gorlée's text of Chapter 27 whereas Treaties in legal discourse is subject and the inherent power of comparison in law is subject of Chapters 28 and 29.

Persons I: Fundamental Concepts of Roman Law

Max Radin

1. "All the law which we use," the Institutes of Gaius assert, "concerns either persons or things or actions."[1] The words are literally copied by Justinian[2] and the classification in some modified form has remained the fundamental division of law in all the civil law systems.[3]

The law which pertains to things, is further divided. Some things are corporeal, others incorporeal and among incorporeal things, obligations are expressly placed, as are inheritances and testamentary successions.

The scientific difficulties of the division were perfectly clear to Gaius. All law is inevitably a law pertaining to persons and a very great deal of it is a law pertaining to things. The purpose of most of the obligations we have examined is the exercise of some sort of power over concrete objects. Certainly the "real" contracts proclaim that in their name, the scale and letting do so no less in their more important applications.

And yet the classification is not a purely traditional one. It was a successful attempt to cut through a chaotic mass of material that had been collected from practice and commentary, and it was a logical feat of considerable importance to have accomplished it, however and whenever it was done. "Ownership," "use," "enjoyment" are relations between persons in respect of things, relations that are

---

Source: RADIN, MAX: "Fundamental Concepts of Roman Law", in: *California Law Review*, XIII, 3, 1925, p. 207–229.

[1] Gaius, 1, 8. Dig. 1, 5, 1.

[2] Just. Inst. 1, 2, 12.

[3] The German Civil Code (B.G.B.) has five divisions: 1, General; 2, Obligations; 3, Things; 4, Family Relations; 5, Inheritance. The Swiss Code has 1, Persons; 2, Inheritance; 3, Things. There is, besides, a Code of Obligations. The French Code and those based upon it have 1, Persons; 2, Property; 3, Modes of Acquiring and Transferring Property, under which there are titles dealing with Inheritance and Obligations. In all cases the "Law of Actions" is in a separate Code.

M. Radin (deceased)

J.M. Broekman, L. Catá Backer (eds.), *Signs In Law - A Source Book*,
DOI 10.1007/978-3-319-09837-1_21

common to many situations, and it is highly proper to deal with these elements separately before the special situations in which they occur are considered.

But that the main body of the law is the "law of things" is a tradition—perhaps an inevitable tradition—of organized societies. Each important class of things becomes the centre of legal customs and it would have been conceivable that all possible situations to be dealt with in courts should be grouped about the concrete things they referred to.

In England, the social and political importance of landed property made land an obvious centre for such grouping. The "law of real property" takes up pretty completely all transactions in which land is involved. Contracts in relation to land, injuries caused by deterioration or occupation of land were treated under this head as well as the more general question about degrees of ownership, possession and user. Logically the law of non-landed property could be treated in the same way and the two classes would exhaust almost all the law, but here we find new categories that disregard subject matter, the categories named contracts, sales, torts, agency and the like.

In recent times economic importance has reclassified certain groups. We have textbooks on the Law of Mines, of Oil, of Automobiles, each one being a fairly complete summary of the law as it affects these several classes of things. If any one of these things should ever attain the overwhelming importance of land in medieval and modern England, it is plain that the law of that particular thing would not be merely the title of a textbook but an important category in which lawyers and courts would almost instinctively classify the legal doctrines they set forth.

The Roman law began with a classification that had a similar economic origin. A category of things was called *res mancipi*. It consisted of land, certain rights of user over land, slaves, cattle and horses. These things were transferred by an elaborate ceremony called mancipation, in which a public official and witness, as well as a scale and a bronze weight, were essential elements. No other thing could be so transferred and all other things were therefore called *res nec mancipi*. Formally the classification lasted centuries after its practical importance had disappeared but long before Justinian[4] it had become an obsolete curiosity much as copyholds and fees tail are in America.

2. No classification really took its place. Of the many classes of things that are mentioned in the title of the Institutes and Digest, none have a real legal significance beyond the few cases in which certain pieces of property were for a longer or shorter time withdrawn from ordinary commercial transactions, because they were public or quasi-public.

The distinction between movables and immovables, despite its transcendent practical importance, was not made the basis of a legal classification. In practice, however, we may be sure land was treated as a very different thing from a transportable chattel, and in the modem systems of Europe, transactions involving

[4] It was abolished by Justinian in 530. (Cod. Inst. vii, 25, 1) and the distinction referred to as *antiquae subtilitatis ludibrium* and as a *vacuum et superfluum verbum* of which the only effect was to frighten the tender minds of beginners at the law.

immovables are subjected to a very large number of special rules. This is doubtless in part due to the fact that Europe has only recently emerged from a feudal organization with its violent emphasis on land tenures.

The "law of property," the law of "things" might justify a separate treatment for a wholly different reason. We generally think of an obligation as the most characteristic of legal relations the situation in which one person is tied up with reference to another so that a given act is the only method of losing the bond.[5] We have taken up one way after another in which this tying up is effected and found that, in spite of notable exceptions, they correspond fairly closely to the methods still in vogue to secure this same result. But in old Roman law the first suggestion of *ius* was something quite different. The *ius Quiritium,* the peculiar right of a Roman, was a summary statement of the fact that a Roman and only a Roman could without legal let or hindrance perform a number of acts about these things of which he asserted such a *jus.* He was *dominus,* the house-master, just as he was *paterfamilias,* the head of the household. The *ius Quiritium* was his privilege, in the strictest sense of the word, that range of possible activities which could form the basis of no suit at law against him in a Roman court.

What was this range of possible activities? It is described in very absolute terms and is said to consist of the *ius utendi fruendi abutendi,* the privilege, that is, of using a res while keeping its corpus intact *(utendi),* of using it by diminishing its corpus or its outgrowths *(fruendi),*[6] of completely consuming it and therefore ending its effective existence as that particular res *(dibutendi).* These are three degrees of a process of exercising power over a "concrete object," and if *dominium* "ownership," "title," "property" meant just this sum of *iura* and no other, it would be perfectly clear.

However, *dominium* in this exclusive sense really existed only in respect of some objects and by no means of all. It fell a good deal short of containing all possible activities in connection with the two economically most important kinds of res, slaves and land. At any rate, beginning with the Empire, ill treatment of slaves was increasingly limited and the killing of them wholly prohibited. Land was subjected to a number of restrictions by the presence of neighbors, especially if the neighboring property was a public road.[7] By *a senatus consultum* of 43 A. D. buildings might not be destroyed for the purpose of speculation in land.[8] Indeed it may be seen that the *ius utendi fruendi abutendi,* by virtue of its climactic arrangement, is rather an analysis of the idea of ownership than a real statement of what the elements of Roman dominium actually were.

Not only did the elements of abstract dominium vary with the objects on which it was exercised, but they varied with the relations of the persons affected. Tutors

---

[5] Cf. § 4 of these articles, 12 California Law Review, 406 seq.

[6] *Uti* and *frui* have in this connection the meanings ordinarily attached to the words in Latin and not the specific meaning of the servitudes called *usus* and *uwsfructus,* for which cf. infra.

[7] Ulpian, Dig. 43, 8, 2.

[8] Riccobono, *Fontes Iuris Anteiust.* i, p. 233.

were called *domini* when they did certain things and not when they did others.[9] Those who had restricted rights over a thing were called *domini* when that particular complex of right was considered. To what *dominium,* might be reduced may be seen by considering the *res mancipi.* These, as has been said, were things which could be transferred only by a special and elaborate ceremony. Suppose they were transferred and the ceremony for one reason or another was omitted. The acquirer would be protected in his "title." He was said to have the thing *in bonis.* If it was a thing which by its nature was susceptible of *usus fructus abusus,* he might completely and wantonly destroy it or consume it, without leaving the former owner any claim enforceable in a court. Yet all this time the former owner was the *dominus;* he held the *dominium ex iure Quiritiun.* Maitland called his "title" the driest of dry trusts conceivable. So it certainly was, but equally certainly it was as much *dominium* as before the transfer was attempted.

The special characteristic of dominium as a complex of privileges rather than of claims may be inferred from a sentence of Ulpian, when he compares dominium with possession. *Differentia inter dominium et possessionem haec est quod dominium nihilo minus eius manet qui dominus esse non vult, possessio autem recedit ut quisque constituit nolle possidere.* "Dominium remains even when he who has it does not wish to be dominus; possession however disappears as soon as the possessor has determined not to possess."[10] Ulpian has in mind a situation in which the "mental" element in possession was important. His distinction is not sound except as far as the acquisition of the two forms of proprietary relations is concerned, but the characteristic of dominium is well brought out in what he says. A man cannot really be said to have a claim, to own an obligation, if he has decided not to enforce it. He may change his mind and the obligation may or may not have been destroyed by his temporary disinclination for it. But a *dominus,* who in the very moment of repudiating title, acts in relation to a thing advertently or inadvertently has none the less acted as dominus. He has exercised a privilege. He cannot be sued for his act.

A word which is frequently used with *dominium* is *proprietas,* but more frequently *proprietas* has a special meaning. It denotes what is left when various rights of use and enjoyment are taken from the dominus and conferred upon others. These uses might be considerable. By usufruct, by emphyteusis, a person not the dominus might have privileges in connection with a res which all but exhaust the benefits that could be derived from it. But the point was that they did not quite do so. Something was left and that something was the *proprietas.* This was a real thing and not the *vacuum et superfluum verbum* of Justinian's constitution, the "empty and superfluous

[9] "Tutors" were guardians appointed to take care of the interests of *pupilli* (minors less than fourteen years of age). A transaction made by a *pupillus* without the tutor's active participation was wholly void. The assumption of the duties of a tutor was compulsory in many cases. Tutors were held to the strictest liability and there was an .implied mortgage on all their property for obligations arising out of their misfeasance. A corresponding function was exercised by a *curator,* the guardian of a minor between fourteen and twenty-five, or of an adult incompetent.

[10] Dig. 41, 2, 17, 1.

word" which had no concrete existence as far as producing effects was concerned. The owner of the residuum was properly called the *dominus proprietatis.*

But the characteristic of *proprietas* was really a different thing from that of *dominium.* The point of view suffered a complete change. What was it that the *dominus proprietatis* wished to do or could do with the rest? Primarily he was interested in preventing acts on the part of the possessor which impaired the residuum. The usufructuary, for example, had his privileges determined by the transaction that created the usufruct. He might not transgress them and above all he might not deal with the corpus in such a way that it became useless, when, and if, the usufruct terminated. Roughly speaking he might not commit waste. A usufructuary completely irresponsible for waste was really a grantee.

The *dominus proprietatis* accordingly was thought of as a person who could prevent uses of the res beyond those actually vesting in the holder of the special right. It was as a group of these claims to forbearance that his "title" was commonly viewed. These claims could be enforced largely by existing actions of delict, the action on the Lex Aquilia being the one most frequently employed, or the interdicts.

3. Since *proprietas* was a residuary dominium, these claims were as much a part of the latter as of the former but they were not in the foreground of the concept of *dominium* either as it was in men's minds or as it was consciously applied. In dominium, however, there was another class of possible activities that seemed as characteristic as the privileges already mentioned. This was the capacity of abandoning the privileges involved altogether, or of abandoning some of them while retaining others, or of transferring all or part of them.

These powers, especially the power of transfer, are legally and popularly associated with the idea of dominium as fundamental parts of it. It need hardly be pointed out that the term "transfer" is a figure of speech, and that the process of transferring is really the process of creating in the transferee hitherto non-existing rights, which bear only a general resemblance to those rights in the transferor, which are simultaneously extinguished. However, figure of speech or not, it is a very old one and it dominated both expert and lay imagination. The easiest way to conceive of a person becoming dominus was to fancy the various groups of rights and powers inherent in the term as though they formed a concrete object which was capable of being physically carried from the grantor's hand to the grantee.

How was the transfer made? The oldest form demanded a series of ritual acts, the *mancipatio.* The later law had a general and much cited rule to the effect that ownership was changed not by mere consent but by delivery or by adverse, possession. This certainly was not the only way in which dominium was transferred and there were cases in which a mere agreement did have the effect of transferring *dominium.* Two examples may be cited. A has lent B some property by way of *commodatum* or has leased B land by a *locatio-conductio.* Later a contract of sale between A and B concerning that same property is entered into. Title passes by the contract since B already has the res. This is called *traditio brevi manu,* "short-hand delivery," but of course it is not a delivery at all and can be made one only by retroactive fictions of the approved form. Again suppose A wishes to sell certain property to B but to remain there as the tenant of the new owner. An agreement to that effect, called the *constitutum possessorium* will produce this result and again title will change without delivery. But in general where concrete objects were concerned the delivery, that is, the placing the object under the physical control of the transferee, or better, the withdrawing on the part of the transferor of any obstacles to such control by the transferee, was the way in which the transfer was effected.

We are expressly warned that a mere delivery, a *nuda tradito,* was not enough?[11] A *iusta causa* must precede, says Paul, that is, a situation of which the natural incident is that the transferee is to be put in the position of the transferor. That mere delivery could not of itself convey ownership must be apparent in the case of such contracts as deposit, commodatum, letting and hiring. The fact of delivery is ambiguous and needs an explanation. The *iusta causa* is the required explanation. The situation that preceded the delivery might show that the parties had entered into a contract of sale or that a stipulation had been entered into or the object was a legacy owing to the transferee, or the transferor had indicated an intention to make a gift. Any one of these things would make it apparent that a delivery following them was meant to confer upon the transferee whatever the transferor had to give.

Suppose the explanation is not clear. That is to say, the situation is such that it may be interpreted in one of two possible ways. There is a famous antinomy—a so-called contradiction—between two passages in the Digest, one of Julian and one of Ulpian.[12] The situation involved is the transfer of money by A to B. A meant it as a gift. B understood it to be a loan. Julian holds that the title to the money passed, Ulpian that it did not. It seems hard to justify Ulpian's decision, since whether the basis is loan or gift, title to money passes. And it is apparent that Julian's decision prevailed and that the contrary view of Ulpian, hidden in a qualifying clause, was retained by the sort of inadvertence, which even the most careful compilations will show. But if the doubt had been whether the situation was one of commodatum or gift, I think there can hardly be any doubt that title would not pass, if the ambiguity arose from the situation itself.

But there was another condition necessary to make delivery, *traditio,* a vehicle for conveying title. The deliverer must himself be *dominus.* The power to convey a title by one who does not possess it is familiar to modern European and American law. In France and Germany, the old Germanic principle that bona fide purchasers of moveables were in general preferred, has found expression in the codes, in the famous *possession vaut titre* of the French Code Civil section 2279 and section 932 of the German *Bürgerliches Gesetzbuch.* The common law knows the principle in

[11] Dig. 41, 1, 31. Mr. Buckland, *A Text Book of Roman Law*, p. 229, argues very strongly that the *iusta causa* was merely evidence of intent and was not the element itself that gave validity to the delivery. If we accept this view, it must be with the qualification that the evidence was conclusive, which is tantamount to saying that certain externally observable elements alone are considered.

[12] Julian, Dig. 41, 1, 36; Ulpian, Dig. 12, 1, 18, pr. Cf. Buckland's discussion, op. cit., p. 230 and Wenger-Mitteis-Sohm, *Institutionen des Röm. Rechts.* (1923) p. 288. Of the passage in Ulpian, the note (probably by Mitteis) says that the second sentence is *unverkennbar interpoliert,* "unmistakably interpolated." Alas, few unmistakables in legal history have maintained their character for more than one generation.

the rules of market overt and, since the statute of Elizabeth, in the laws governing retention of possession by a vendor. At Rome, such a power was apparently granted only to the sovereign during the Empire. A sale by the fiscus or a private conveyance of the Emperor or the Empress passed title without regard to claims of third parties or previous holders.

Except for this last circumstance—almost inevitable in a state organized like the Roman Empire—the Roman held rigidly to the doctrine that the transfer of rights over a res was a sort of succession,—a "singular" succession, by way of contrast to the "universal" succession to be mentioned later. One holder of this complex of rights stepped out and another man took his place. The characteristic of the Roman law of sale really flowed from this idea. The contract of sale did not, as in the modern common law, have as its mark the engagement to convey a title. At Roman Law the transfer of title was an incidental matter that might or might not follow. The seller engaged to put the buyer in control of the res. If the seller was the owner, this putting in control would pass the title, but that result would or would not follow *ex opere operato.*

For a long time the doctrine was current that the transaction of sale was quite exceptional, that even tradition did not pass title there, but that a further condition was required, the payment of the price. Justinian makes a statement that seems to say just this, but there are other passages, which distinctly imply that tradition alone was enough. A very extended discussion has been conducted about this matter.[13] I do not think that the seeming discrepancy justifies the important inferences that have been drawn from the passages. Justinian (Institutes, 2, 1, 41) and Pomponius (Digest, 18, 1, 19) say that title will not pass unless the price has been paid, or credit given with or without security. Now it is obvious that every sale is either a sale for cash or credit, so that Justinian and Pomponius are stating no more than the rule of common sense and ordinary experience, that in the absence of an understanding to the contrary, delivery and payment are mutually concurrent conditions. What both have in mind is the situation in which a sale intended to be a cash sale in possession of the res has been gained by the buyer, either in good or in bad faith without payment. The seller may have handed the goods over for inspection, for temporary detention or in some other way indicated that the surrender of control is not meant to transfer title, or else in a cash sale he may have turned over the res in the expectation of simultaneous payment and payment may be refused. Such transfers of the goods do not pass title, and the assertion that they do not, scarcely qualifies the rule that title is regularly passed by delivery. The passages quoted certainly do not put the contract of sale in a special class in this respect.

4. The transfer of dominium was, we have said, a succession. A, the former dominus, with his complex of privileges, powers and negative claims in respect of a res, is succeeded by B, the new dominus, who has almost precisely the name group of

[13] Cf. especially, Pringsheim, *Kauf mit fremdem Geld,* and the review by Mitteis *Zeit. d. Sav. St. 37,* 369 seq. Pringsheim published a preliminary announcement of his conclusions in *Zeit. d. Say. St. 35,* pp. 328–329. A liberal use of the discrepancy is made to discover interpolations.

privileges, powers and claims. But it is obvious that A need allow B to succeed only as to some of them. Some may be left in the hands of A. They may be so few as to be a mere *proprietas* with all the substantial rights of present enjoyment gone. Or they may comprise all but one limited privilege, which has been conferred on B. This power of separating the dominium-unit into its component parts and making a separate transfer of the components is a power essentially like the general power of transfer.

A number of cases in which the owner of a *res* has for a limited time surrendered the control to others have already been considered. The commodatum, the deposit, the *pignus* are all cases of this sort. Another case was that of lease, *locatio rei.* To distinguish them from the transactions that are called servitudes in Roman law, and easements or profits at the common law is not altogether easy. The latter, however, seem at first glance to be a very different type of thing because of the fact that we have always treated them apart from these former transactions and in respect of a wholly different class of things.

Both in Roman and English law it was in connection with land that the servitude or easement chiefly developed. The privilege of passing or driving or riding over one's neighbor's land, of drawing water from it, of watering stock in it, is often practically essential in the effective use of one's own land. The neighborliness of friends and kinsmen may have supplied it originally until in the growth of the community greater security was needed. The ceremony of mancipation was as applicable to the passing of these factors of dominium as it was in transferring the entire dominium.

When mancipation had gone out, the method of transfer became exceedingly difficult. Delivery of an abstract privilege is not easy to imagine in the same concrete way as delivery of a res. However, delivery of land had never been a real delivery but a bringing of the grantee to the land and the withdrawal of the grantor. Something like that could after all be done in the case of such servitudes. The person entitled might be permitted to begin his use, perhaps be formally escorted to the place where he could do so. This quasidelivery was in use in later time though it cannot have been general before the third century. Or else in spite of the rule that conveyances are not made by agreement, agreements enforced by stipulations were declared to make the stipulator owner of the servitude. This in all likelihood was influenced by the fact that in the Eastern part of the Empire it had long been customary to convey title by the delivery of written documents, much as is done in our own system at the present day. The Roman stipulation was frequently the representative of the East-Mediterranean formal, contract which was regularly in writing, although in this case it seems rather to have been the agreement itself, the pact, that had the effect of conveying.

A form of acquiring servitudes which has played a large role in the English legal history, was apparently of less importance. That was adverse possession. Paul implies that servitudes could not be acquired that way in the old law.[14] But in the

[14] Paul Sentences, 1, 17, 2, Dig. 41, *3, 4, 28* (29). This was true particularly after the lex Scribonia, concerning which we may quote the words of Cuq. *Inst. Fur. d. Rom.* i, 92, *La date -n.est pas connue et la portie-est discutée.* Cf. also, op. cit, ii, 289.

praetorian law it was undoubtedly permitted. The only qualifications were user for the prescriptive period of ten or twenty years to which was added the ancient formula *quod nec vi nec clam nec precario,* "provided the user did not take place by force, nor by stealth nor as a license of the owner." This covers at once the requirements of "open and adverse use" of the common law, and, as we shall see, makes this form of adverse possession essentially different from the ordinary type.[15]

Adverse user is still a common way of creating easements in Anglo-American law. The Germanic law of Europe, curiously enough, specifically prohibited it for so-called discontinuous servitudes, such as rights of way and the like. The principal French *Corttumes,* those of Orleans and Paris, make this prohibition a fundamental rule and it has been taken into the Code Civil (section 690). The German Code likewise abolishes (by adverse possession) acquisition of servitudes except in the form of a wrongful recording of an easement in the Register of Titles acquiesced in for 30 years (the so-called *Tabularersitzung,* section 900). The Swiss Code has the much smaller period of ten years (section 661).

What we call easements the Romans called praedial servitudes. They were classed as *rustic* and *urban* according to the nature of the privileges to be exercised and not according to the location of the estate. The servitudes of right of way, of drawing water, etc., were rustic servitudes; the servitude of support *(oneris ferendi),* and of receiving drip *(stillicide)* were urban. Like easements they were all appurtenant; there had to be a servient – and dominant tenement. Again like easements they were rather obligations to refrain than to do something, although some of the urban servitudes seem rather of the latter variety and would be classed in our terminology as covenants running with the land. However, some at least of the rustic servitudes were *commons* or profits, such as the servitude of burning lime or pasturing cattle. The number of these servitudes was really unlimited. Any group of privileges might be conferred on a neighbor or in his behalf any privilege may be surrendered, and the privileges could be as various as the uses to which land can be put.

Some of the special rules as to easements, that a servitude is a negative claim, that a servitude cannot exist over one's own land, were taken over by the common law together with a great deal of Roman law terminology. The rule that a servitude cannot be merely burdensome without giving the dominant estate a corresponding advantage probably is present in the common law doctrine that when the purpose of the servitude is gone, the servitude itself disappears.

There was further a type of servitude that the Romans called personal, i. e., in gross, that had no estate to depend upon and could be applied to realty as to personality. The most characteristic form of it was the *ususfructus,* which has been defined as such a use of it which leaves the corpus intact, *salva rerum substantia.* That is not quite accurate, since a good many uses will deplenish or deteriorate the corpus and there was even a sort of spurious usufruct of fungible goods which is really a special kind of *mutuum.* The importance and frequency of usufruct have already been indicated. What gave it its particular value to Romans was that it enabled interests in the res itself to be created which the contracts of letting and hiring, of mandate,

[15] Girard, *Man., de Droit Rom.,* p. 376. Bonfante, *Scritti Giur. Varii,* iii, pp. 177 seq.

and the "real" contracts, were generally unable to effect. This was due to the fact that the usufruct conferred "possession" and these contracts did not, and it is to this term as mysterious and protean as its Norman congener seisin, that we must turn.

5. The ideas contained in the Roman term *possessio* are, to say the least, not clear. What the term meant at Roman law has been the subject of heated controversies. What the essentials of the concept are, whether in its historical development or in its present form, is an equally agitated topic. On the continent the names of Savigny, Ihering, Saleilles, Huber, are particularly associated with this discussion but in fact every jurist of note has at some time or other been compelled to address himself to the problem.

The usual and the simplest way of stating the characteristics of possession is to distinguish it from ownership. The one, we are told, is a relation of law, the other of fact. This distinction is expressly asserted in the Swiss Code, sections 641 and 919. Almost every discussion of the subject begins in that fashion.

Of course this cannot really be so at all. Possession is a relation of law quite as much as ownership and it would be proven to be such by the very fact that lawyers discuss it. Whether it is more of a fact than ownership depends solely on what our method is of deter mining fact. As far as law goes both possession and ownership are either relations between persons in respect of things or they are not relevant facts at all, and if they are such relations, it is difficult to see how one can be more of a fact than the other.

Let us look at a number of cases in which the question arose. The usufructuary is stated to have possession but not the *conductor*, i. e., the tenant or hirer. The *emphyteuta* had possession; so, generally, the pledgee. The commodatary, the depositary, had no possession, nor, we must suppose, the mandatory or *negotiorum gestor*, who often had physical control of another's property. On the other hand, the tenant at will *(precario rogans), the sequester* (stakeholder or escrow-holder) did have possession, and certainly the bonafide holder of property which had not been stolen. However, even the mala fide occupant of an unclaimed inheritance was a possessor, although a thief was not, nor anyone who claimed through a thief, however undoubted his own good faith.

Now every one of the persons described certainly had the physical control of a res of which he was not dominus. The possession which is accorded some and denied others at Roman law was accordingly a technical term and taken in its strict sense meant something over and above physical control. Paul long ago found a formula to distinguish this technical and proper *possessio* from any other, by declaring that this type demanded a holding both *animo* and *corpore*. The possessor must think himself dominus. All other possession was merely "natural" or "corporal" possession and received the designation of "detention."[16]

In its unqualified form, the distinction is obviously defective. The sequester, the pledgee, the usufructuary do not think of themselves as domini, but do possess, at least for some purposes. The bona fide purchaser of a stolen article does not possess although he has undoubtedly the animus required by Paul. The difficulties could be

[16] A very recent discussion of the subject is to be found in G. Rotondi, *Possessio quae animo refinetur, in: Bull d. Inst. d. Dir Rom.* (1921) pp. 1–153, written before the author's untimely death in 1918.

resolved only by fictions and constructions and presumptions and were so resolved by Savigny who gave the theory of Paul an almost universal currency. Ihering's criticisms of Savigny have been widely accepted in what may be called the upper strata of legal theoreticians but the apparently clear and simple cleavage, made by Savigny, is still tenaciously maintained by a certain number, even to a certain degree, by M. Girard. To Ihering the necessary animus is simply the consciousness of those particular acts, which one is doing in connection with a *res*.

There are difficulties here as well. Somehow the control exercised by a slave or filius familias must be excluded from this, and again we must include the situation in which the thing we call our own and deem we possess, is as a matter of fact at some distance. All this requires mental constructions although they are less complicated and violent than those offered by Savigny. We can hardly do otherwise than accede to the statement of Buckland and Girard that the Roman theories on the subject were not completely coherent.[17]

As a matter of fact the two degrees of possession did not suffice the Romans. They had a kind of control called *"in possessione esse,"*[18] which Ulpian said was vastly different *from "possidere."* He had in mind the custody of one who takes charge of property in order to prevent loss. And again there was a *possessio pro possessore* which might be predelicated of a highway robber.[19]

The Romans, therefore, had exactly the same difficulties as those we encounter when we attempt to restrict the meaning of a term which has wide currency in non-legal contexts. *Possidere* was a common word in Latin and unqualified it frequently meant just what the lawyers wished it to mean only with the adjectives "natural" or "corporal" added to it. And again in ordinary usage, *"possessio"* often suggested something precise and limited, the quasi-ownership of public lands leased out to certain persons on long leases.[20]

6. The really important matter is quite a different thing. Why should Roman lawyers have attempted to force the word into this special meaning? Are these degrees of possession merely the result of analyzing a concept or have they a function to perform?

[17] Buckland, op. cit., p. 201; Girard, *Man.*, p. *274*.

[18] Dig. 41, 2, 10, 1.

[19] Dig. 5, 3, 11, 1.

[20] In his discussion of Ihering, Buckland gives the following illustration (p. 200, n. 4) "I possess my carriage in the roadway in front of my house. I should not possess my watch lying in the same place." What is the difference between the two kinds of "possession" involved? In both cases, the "possessor" deems himself the owner. Shall his ignorance of the fact that the watch is there and his knowledge that the carriage is there, be the basis of the distinction? That will hardly prove a practicable test. However, it is evident that we can say the following: almost any person taking the carriage and driving off in it would be a thief, subject to actions of *furlum* and those associated with it, subject to criminal action at the owner's instance, subject to the interdicts concerning movables. In the case of the watch, on the other hand, all these claims would exist only on the precedent condition of demand and refusal, or similar acts which would make a continued retention unlawful. The relation accordingly between the owner and other persons in respect of these two articles is different. In the former case it is made up of a complex of rights, etc., that is not identical with the complex in. the latter case, but is very similar to it.

Obviously the second alternative is the right one and the function is in general perfectly apparent.

We have noted in the case of servitudes an acquisition by adverse possession. This played a relatively unimportant role in that connection but in the matter of acquiring general ownership, such acquisition, called *usucapio* in both the old and the later law, was of frequent occurrence. The importance of *usucapio* rested upon the distinction of *res mancipi* and *nec mancipi,* a distinction as fundamental as that between realty and personality at the common law. The informal grantee of a *res mancipi* was protected by the praetor but he could easily turn his equitable title into a legal one after the lapse of one year in the case of movables and two in the case of immovables. During this time he was, from the point of view of the *ius civile,* the possessor and by being the possessor he acquires the title, *possidendo usucapit,* says Gaius.[21]

The extremely short period of prescription is as old as the Twelve Tables and made the effects of informality less serious than they would otherwise be. For *res nec mancipi,* which included such vitally important things as provincial land, wine and grain, an institution called prescription had been established apparently by imperial constitutions rather than by praetorian law. The periods were ten years *inter praesentis,* i. e. domiciled in the same province; twenty years, if they were not.[22]

When the distinction between *res mancipi* and *nec mancipi* was finally abolished, *usucapio* and *prescription* were amalgamated, the period being three for movables and ten or twenty for immovables.

Striking and vital characteristics of both *usucapio* and prescription were that there must be good faith and a *iustus titulus* and that the thing must not be stolen property. This, it will be noticed, is a very marked difference between this institution at the Roman law and at the common law. Nor is the reason for the difference difficult to discover. Adverse possession at the common law seems to be primarily concerned in preventing the neglect of landed property by giving a certain premium to any one who would use it in the place of the negligent owner. At Roman law the institution grew out of an attempt to validate fully a merely equitable title. To claim such validation it was, of course, necessary to show equities in one's favor.[23]

Now if the possession which can become ownership by mere lapse of time is taken as typical, we can readily see the basis of Paul's statement. Such a possessor certainly has the *animus dominantis:* he regards himself as dominus. The class of bona fide possessors of property passing through a thief was of little importance. Land could not be stolen property and in small communities the holder of a stolen slave would rarely be bona fide. If therefore Paul's *possession* was this type of possession we can see why a tenant, a commodotary, a depositary did not have it.

---

[21] Gaius, Inst. 2, 41.

[22] In a rescript of Septimius Severus of the year 199 A. D. the prescriptive period of twenty years is mentioned and is based upon imperial constitutions, not on praetorian law. This date is earlier than any Digest fragment mentioning the twenty year limit. Cf. Riccobono, *Fontes Iuris Anteiust. 1,* p. 328.

[23] Gaius states (Dig. 41, 3, 1) that it was introduced *bono publico* not to prevent property from lying disused, but to prevent titles from being uncertain for too long a time.

Plainly they could never lay claim in equity to a title superior to that of the source of their interest. Their holding adverse to the dominus could never be bona fide.

But what shall we say of the usufructuary, the *emphyteuta,* the pledgee, the *sequester,* who are all said to have possession? As a matter of fact in the case of the first three, possession in some texts is denied them though specifically granted in others. The point is that possession proper, the strict technical possession, was in fact, if not in terms, divided into two classes. There was the possession which by usucapion might become title, and the possession which could not. The possession of the usufructuary, the *emphyteuta,* the pledgee, the *sequester,* was not *usucapion-possession.* What was the second kind? Its characteristic was that it gave the right to use the interdicts, that special form of action of which brief mention has already been made.

The effectiveness of interdictal procedure has been disputed. Its origin is equally in doubt. It is maintained by some that the interdicts were special forms of action delictual in their nature. Others, principally Pernice, have seen in them primarily easures of police intended for general security. It is certainly not impossible that both ideas contributed to their growth. The system may have been devised to secure for quasi-owners, viz., praetorian owners of *res mancipi* and particularly the long term lessees of state lands, the protection of which their lack of title deprived them at the civil procedure. But once established the interdicts were turned very early into a means of maintaining the proprietary status quo in all cases in which a judicial determination of ownership was available.

The possession that is ascribed to the pledgee, the usufructuary and the rest, was interdictal possession merely, the right to use the interdicts, or more correctly, the right to use two of them, those named *uti possidetis* and *utrubi,* from the opening words of their formulas.

Unfortunately for the validity of the distinction, a tenant or a depositary whose possession was *naturalis,* i. e. properly not possession at all, but merely detention, could use one of the interdicts, the *interdict unde vi,* if he had been forcibly dispossessed. More than that, a brigand whose tenure was violent as well as wrongful could use this latter interdict. A kind of interdictal possession was therefore to be asserted even of these groups.

Were they protected because possession is the usual badge of ownership or because possession is in itself a social good deserving of maintenance? We are again in the heart of the controversy but for our present purposes the various reasons proposed are immaterial. It is not too bold a statement that the attempt of making *possessio* a technical term of law with a specific content failed at the Roman law, whatever may have been its success in the modern civil law or at the common law. What we have is a series of relations which ranged from the almost complete legal capacities of a man holding a *res mancipi* without mancipation to the temporary and precarious tenure of a thief, in every one of which the powers, privileges and claims were somewhat different. If it served any useful purpose these relations might all be called possession. But the only meaning we can have when we apply this general term is to assert that in no one of these cases could the person entitled bring a special type of action known as vindication.

That there should be many classes of persons having physical control over a thing whose complex of privileges, powers and claims in respect of it are all different, is not in the least surprising. There were certainly many more classes than any we have so far enumerated and the nature of the situation and the character of the thing involved can generally be made the basis of a new classification, because they will generally modify the complex of rights and powers which the possessor has.

The result is precisely the same as in the case of dominium. The dominus of a slave has privileges notably different from the owner of an ox. Further such characteristic elements of dominium as the power of transfer may be wholly or partially limited without depriving the owner of his designation. Restraints on the amount of gifts, the manner of making them, the persons who could receive them were quite general. A fiduciary or beneficiary who had title could make transfers only to a limited extent. Similar limitations existed against a prodigal who had been placed under wardship. That is to say, while large general groups existed in which the complex of rights were nearly identical, there were a great many smaller groups in which the number and kind of these rights were slightly different and in all of them dominium was said by law to be present.

7. The paterfamilias was mortal. What happened when he died? He had, at least potentially, every claim, privilege, power and immunity that a member of the Roman community could have. Where did these go on his death? The rules concerning such matters are certain to be extremely technical because they are likely to be the outgrowth of the special conditions in which the community developed. We have taken over into the common law in a mass a certain number of the Roman rules and a still larger number of Roman terms, but we have not taken what was the most striking element in this part of the Roman system, the idea of universal succession.

We need not trouble ourselves to consider whether a period of communal ownership lay behind the well-developed system of private property that we find in Rome in the earliest period of which we know. The paterfamilias both in theory and fact owned for himself a great many rights and claims and powers, owed many obligations and was subject to many liabilities. On his death they remained a unit and passed completely to some other persons or to several other persons jointly. But these persons were themselves owners of claims and powers, debtors of obligations. The new group coalesced completely with the old one, so that a solvent estate might become insolvent by being acquired by a hopelessly indebted heir or the acquisition of an insolvent estate might bankrupt a solvent heir.

But the unit was maintained. If there were several heirs they took jointly. The principle of Roman public law that consular *imperium* or tribunician *potestas* were indivisible units no matter how numerous the holders were, applied here. Each of two heirs did not take half the estate. Each took the whole inheritance. If either died it may be said that the other gained nothing, but merely that a possible check on his free disposition of his property was removed.

Now, how were the heirs, the successors of the defunct *paterfamilias,* determined?

There were three stages in the history of the subject. First the ancient law, stated and to some degree perhaps established in the Twelve Tables. Secondly, the praetorian law and thirdly, the imperial reforms culminating in the radical reorganization of the whole matter by Justinian in the 118th Novel published in 543, ten years after the corpus proper was completed.

The basis of succession of the ancient law was the *patria potestas.* The unemancipated sons of the paterfamilias succeeded. Failing sons, the nearest agnate, i. e. the nearest of the male kinsmen who if the intermediate generations were alive, would be subject to the same *patria potestas* as the deceased, took the *hereditas.* This automatically excluded emancipated sons and their descendants and all related through females. Finally, the *gentiles* took, an indefinite group whose constitution was disputed and whose claims were rarely enforced.

The praetorian law made four classes, 1°, children, whether emancipated or not, 2°, *legitimi,* principally the agnates, but including among other additional groups parents of emancipated children and patrons of freed slaves, 3°, cognates, relations on the female side, 4°, husband or wife. Most of those changes had been made by the time of Cicero.

Finally by the 118th Novel the succession was as follows. First: descendants, without regard to sex or emancipation. Second: ascendants and brothers and sisters of the whole blood. Third: brothers and sisters of the half blood, and fourth: collaterals, and perhaps as a fifth class, husband or wife. In all cases, as at the common law, the nearest class excluded the more remote one and in general, if the coheirs were in the same degree, they took *per capita,* otherwise *per stirpes.*

But the paterfamilias might appoint his successor, his *heres* or *heredes.* The rule of universal succession applied here as well. The heredes, even if a specific proportion was assigned to them, all took jointly. The specified proportion merely meant the particular share that would belong to him if he or others chose to divide the estate.

The appointment of the heir was made by a will, *testamentum.* It was in fact the chief purpose of the will. But in the will the testator might also give specific directions to the heir to give certain pieces of property or some share less definitely ascertained to named persons. These directions were *legata,* legacies, and they constituted obligations of the strictest sort between the heres and the legatary.

Since the payment of the ordinary debts and the legacies might make the inheritance unprofitable, the heir was allowed by the lex Falcidia of 40 B. C. to deduct a quarter and to abate all legacies accordingly.

Toward the end of the Republic a large number of persons were excluded from taking under a will. Perhaps it was for their benefit that the custom arose of attempting to bind the heir's conscience to do what he could not be compelled to do by ordinary legacy. This was done either in the will itself or in a separate document and the institution was called *fideicommissum.* He might even be asked to transfer the entire inheritance to a third person. In a famous instance, Augustus decided that fideicommissa, as well as the codicils that embodied them were valid and legally enforceable.[24] From that time on they were more and more assimilated to legacies, until Justinian finally abolished completely all remaining differences between the two.

At the common law, the making of a will of lands was a late privilege, but once granted it began to be frequently asserted that testamentary disposition must be unrestricted. At Roman law, testaments (as has already been seen) were drastically modified by law. Not only was there a large class of persons who could not take at all, not only was a certain amount set aside from the estate despite the legacies and fideicommissa, but a certain proportion, a *legitim,* was reserved for the family of the deceased. This *legitim* ran in favor of children and in certain circumstances in favor of brothers and sisters. It varied from one-quarter to one-half the estate after debts were paid. This was entirely apart from the inheritance tax, the *vicesima hereditatis,* a tax of 5 percent established in 6 A. D.

8. In the preceding pages I have attempted briefly to review what seemed to me the most important institutions of the Roman legal system. For reasons given at the beginning, a general characterization is, I think, certain to be futile. One thing, however, can hardly be questioned, Roman law is one of the great achievements of the human mind, the elucidation of which, since the eleventh century has worthily employed the energies of thousands of great men. The literature of the subject in German, French and Italian alone is almost interminable.

To this literature men of English speech have made a relatively slight contribution. Adequate study of Roman law for those who command only English is extremely difficult. Fortunately it can be undertaken in some measure with the aid of Mr. Buckland's, *A Text Book in Roman Law*, published in 1921, alike admirable for its originality, its learning and its arrangement. Earlier manuals of Roman law, Mr. Morey's, for example, and the rest, are hopelessly antiquated, representing a point of view almost pre-Savigny.

An exception must be made in favor of W. A. Hunter's *Roman Law* of which the second edition appeared in 1885. The mass of material is astounding. Its arrangement is complicated to an extent that makes its usefulness very questionable. Gibbon's famous chapter formed an extraordinary feat for the time in which it was written but, even with Bury's notes, is scarcely a reliable method of securing a general orientation on the subject at the present time.

Of manuals in other languages, there is first of all the completely indispensable work of Girard, *Manuel de Droit Romain,* now in its sixth edition. An English translation is still one of the great desiderata in the field. Further—much briefer and much more of an introductory manual—is Sohm's *Institutionen des Römischen Privatrechts,* of which the seventeenth edition was completely revised by Mitteis, and published in 1923 after Mitteis' death by Leopold Wenger. An excellent English translation by Ledlie (from the 8th and 9th German editions) now in its third edition, is widely used. But for those who wish to deal with the matters thoroughly a

[24] Just. Inst. 2, 25, pr.

knowledge of the sources, principally in Latin, is indispensable. A brief statement of them follows:

1. The Corpus Juris Civilis, consisting of the Institutes, The Digest, the Code and the Novels. The Institutes have often been translated into English. Of the Digest, the first fifteen of the fifty books were translated by Mr. C. H. Monroe (Cambridge University Press, Volumes I and II, 1909) and the project of a complete translation was interrupted by his untimely death. There are a few translations with notes of other books. No translation of the Code or Novels into English has ever been made.[25]
2. The Institutes of Gaius, almost completely recovered in a single manuscript. The best known English version with an elaborate commentary is that of Mr. Poste. A short summary of Gaius was found at Autun, and has materially assisted our understanding of him.
3. The fragments of other Roman lawyers not contained in the Corpus. These, consisting of quotations in other Latin writers, and larger parts of law treatises, some embodied in later Codes and some found in manuscript form, are most readily found in *Fragmenta Anteiustiniana,* by Huschke (5th edition) and in Volume II of Riccobono, *Fontes luris Anteiustiniani.*
4. Latin and Greek inscriptions of various kinds. These, including statutes, documents, judgments, in their original form, dating from the third century B. C. till after Justinian, are with the Institutes of Gaius chiefly responsible for the profound change which the nineteenth century made in our methods of studying Roman law. They are collected in Bruns, *Fontes Iuris Romani,* Girard, *Textes* and Riccobono, *Fontes luris Anteiustiniani,* Volume I.
5. The papyri, mostly Greek and nearly all from Egypt, which are constantly adding, as the inscriptions did, to our detailed knowledge of the law and correcting our misconceptions of it.
6. The works of non-legal Roman and Greek writers gives a great deal of additional material. Some of them are ancient lexica like that of Festus, others are by writers with a particular .antiquarian bent, like Varro and Aulus Gellius. But most of them have other purposes in view than legal exposition. Cicero's writings, the Republic, the Laws, and chiefly his speeches are of prime importance. Three of them, the *pro Quinctio, the pro Caecina, the pro Tullio* are elaborate and extensive pleas on matters of technical private law. The excerpts which have legal importance have often been collected separately. That is particularly true of the comic poets Plautus and Terence whose casual references are very important because of the light they throw on the conditions of the second century B. C., a period that preceded by a century the oldest fragment of the Digest.

[25] The Corpus luris Civilis continued to be the law of the Empire even after the Western half was completely separated politically from the Eastern. In the ninth and tenth centuries a Greek revision was made, known to us as the Basilica, to which we must often look for elucidation of textual difficulties. A Greek paraphrase of the Institutes, ascribed to Theophilus, the collaborator of Tribonian, and prepared shortly after the Corpus, performs a similar service.

Persons II: Family as a Commonsensical Device and its Place in Law

Tracey Summerfield and Alec McHoul

In the beginning was the deed

J.W.Goethe

Membership Categorisation: Devices, Categories and Predicates

Membership categorisation analysis (MCA) is a well-accepted approach in the areas of conversation analysis and ethnomethodology—yet it is hardly known in mainstream semiotics, let alone in social semiotics; and even less so in the comparatively recent uptake of social semiotics by legal scholars. Despite this, we think the basics of MCA could have important consequences for the emergent field of legal semiotics and we try to show this here by reference to aspects of family law in Australia.

It is also no coincidence that the founder of conversation analysis (and its MCA sub-branch), Harvey Sacks, was legally trained. He took his law degree from Yale (in 1959) before studying for his PhD in sociology at Berkeley (in 1966) and then moved into the field probably best known as linguistic sociology. To this extent, his work has untapped potential for understanding how legal frameworks (in the broadest possible sense) might operate. We consider his foundational work in MCA and its possible consequences for reforming official-legal versions of the concept of 'family'.[1]

Source: SUMMERFIELD, TRACEY & MCHOUL ALEC: "Family as a commonsensical device and its place in law" in: *International Journal for the Semiotics of Law,* 2005, p. 243–261

[1] For a fuller explication of Sacks and MCA, see David Silverman, Harvey Sacks: Social Science and Conversation Analysis (Cambridge: Polity, 1998), at 74–97.

T. Summerfield (✉)
The University of Western Australia, 35 Stirling Highway, Crawley, Perth, Australia, 6009
e-mail: tracey.summerfield@uwa.edu.au

A. McHoul
Murdoch University, 90 South Street, Murdoch, Australia, 6150
e-mail: a.mchoul@gmail.com

J.M. Broekman, L. Catá Backer (eds.), *Signs In Law - A Source Book,*
DOI 10.1007/978-3-319-09837-1_22

In his paper 'On the Analyzability of Stories by Children', Sacks worked through a very simple pair of sentences uttered by a child aged two years and nine months, in response to a series of pictures. The child looked at the first two pictures (a standard preschool test) and spoke as follows: 'The baby cried. The mommy picked it up'.

In many ways, this is unremarkable: a very young child is telling what she already knows about families. Yet, in another sense, it tells us a great deal about how commonsensical conceptions of the thing called 'family'[2] happen to work on an everyday basis.

If we go back again to the original sentences, we can see that they contain no possessive or genitive elements. That is, there is nothing, as it were, in the sheer language used, to tell us that the mother is the mother of the baby. 'The baby cried. The mommy picked it up'—simpliciter. And yet, for any English speaker, we have to hear it that the 'mommy' was the 'mommy' of the baby. We hear the 'of', yet it is not present in the text as such. Semiotically, we have a remarkable phenomenon: a signified (possessive) without a signifier ('of'). Naturally, then, a strictly formal-textual semiotics, one which would ideally read off signifieds from actually present material signifiers, cannot analyse the case in hand. So, on an MCA account, how is the possessive heard without being spoken?

This has to do with ingrained, commonsensical, mostly Western, but increasingly global conceptions of what a family is. 'Family' is a membership categorisation device (MCD). We know, by virtue of our training, which members can be part of the device: mother, father, son, daughter … etc. So when we hear 'baby' and 'mother' in adjacent sentences, we collect the two into the MCD 'family'.

And so that's how we hear the genitive or possessive (normally signified in English by 'of' or apostrophe-'s') even though it is strictly absent from the two sentences in question.

This has two rather handy consequences for everyday linguistic usage. The first is this: for any given person, there are an indefinite number of ways of referring to them. Someone can be, for example, a chiropractor, George's mother, the chair of the Netball Club committee, a gifted amateur artist, John's sister, the woman next-door, a redhead, the Rabbi's niece.... Need we continue? All of these descriptions and many more are, in a strictly formal sense, true. Each applies to the person in question. But what, in any given discursive situation, should that person be called? Sacks then points to sequential relevance (as opposed to mere correctness) as the way of referring to persons. Correctness, as a criterion for reference, will generate indefinite possibilities. Selection from a sequentially relevant MCD will, by contrast, provide appositeness. Hence, if the first sentence offers 'the baby', the second will (where possible) offer a co-member of the same MCD: mother, father, sister, etc. In that way, we can hear, without being told, that, if 'mother' is selected,

[2] Harvey Sacks, "On the Analyzability of Stories by Children", in *Directions in Sociolinguistics*, eds. John Gumperz and Dell Hymes (New York: Holt, Rinehart and Winston, 1972), 325–345. the 'mommy' of the 'baby' because there is an MCD called 'family' and that device contains certain members and not others.

the person referred to in the second sentence is the mother of the baby referred to in the first.

The second upshot is this: when we refer to persons in terms of their incumbency in an MCD, we can hear, without being explicitly told, the kinds of things that they may be expected to do. These expectable actions can be called 'category bound activities' or 'predicates'. Some predicates are, as Sacks calls them, 'device-wide': that is, they pertain to all members included in a device. If 'family' is an MCD, then, one device-wide predicate would be something like 'unconditional support'. No matter what happens to one member, it may be expected that all the others would support them.

A telling illustration of this arises in an albeit fictional case where the expected predicate is reversed: the soap-opera Dallas. Here the point of the show was to represent a family, the Ewings, who, on any given occasion, would do their best to sabotage each other and thereby triumph as individuals in, for example, business, personal relationships or prestige. The reversal shows up the normally expectable device-wide predicate.[3]

On the other hand, particular category incumbents in an MCD may, by virtue of their specific positioning in the device, have their respectively specific predicates. Hence: babies cry, mothers pick them up and not vice versa! Or, to use the MCD 'professions': if we hear that someone rides a red moped and puts envelopes into letterboxes, we also hear from that action description (predicate or category-bound activity) just what position they hold within that MCD. We can hear the type of profession from the activity description—and vice versa.

Semiotically, the main interest of MCA is that it gives us an analytic means of describing what was once a rather fuzzy and possibly mentalistic process: that of implication and inference—and, as we will see in the final section of this paper, this has some possible connections with Peirce's third form of reasoning, abduction.[4] To imply something about a person then means that one gives a description of what they do, such that another can infer (or, for Peirce, 'hypothesise') their category incumbency—or else vice versa. If these dual matters connecting relevant category and relevant predicate (hence inference and implication) are deeply embedded matters of common sense—such that, for example, it is all but impossible to hear something like 'The baby cried. One of its mothers picked it up'—then how can a strictly legal entity such a 'family' be demarcated without recourse to commonsensical use of the naturally-available MCD also called 'family' and the device-wide (or, indeed, category-specific) predicates routinely attached to it?

The space of family legislation might then be represented (somewhat metaphorically) as the space between the following two possibilities: (1) whoever picks the baby up (acts the relevant predicate) is, by definition, 'the mother' (the category) and (2) only the one pre-designated as 'the mother' (the category) can pick the baby up (act the relevant predicate). That is: does the predicate legally define the category

---

[3] On all such matters, see Rod Watson, "Categorizations, Authorization and Blame-Negotiation in Conversation", *Sociology* 12/1 (1978), 105–113. Also: Maria T. Wowk, "Blame-Allocation: Sex and Gender in a Murder Interrogation", *Women's Studies International Forum* 7/1 (1984), 75–82.

[4] Charles Sanders Peirce, Collected Papers (Cambridge: Harvard University Press, 1931–1958), at 2.623.

position, or vice versa? This is where legal discourse comes into confluence (or not) with everyday category use.

Family law (at least in Australia and other nations once formed as British colonies) has traditionally granted rights and duties on the basis of category incumbency rather than actual predicational enactment. For example, those designated as 'fathers' by virtue of inseminational status, may acquire legal status, even if they take no part in standard 'fatherly' activities such as caring for the child in question as a co-parent. And, as we illustrate below, it is also difficult for the Family Court to recognise a person who is the partner of the mother, who cares for the child as a father (or as the 'partner of the mother') might be expected to, but who also happens to be a woman. Any such second woman's categorical status—which must always be out with the 'family' device and fall into the alternative device of something like 'mere relationships'—takes precedence over her actual worldly actions (predicates): feeding, nursing, teaching, indeed picking up, the crying child; just as a father might on the standard view. The question for family law today, then, is: should it maintain strict categorisational means of identifying and recognising persons or should it consider predicational status and decide accordingly?

Legal Background

The traditional approach to legislating on family, at least since 1975 with the passing of the Family Law Act 1975 (Cth) (FLA), has been to determine family by reference to strict categories. This comes as much from constitutional limits on the power of the Commonwealth as from any putative 'mindset' of Commonwealth and state governments.

The Commonwealth is limited by the 51 constitutional heads of power of 'marriage' (placitum xxi) and 'divorce and matrimonial causes' (placitum xxii). Hyde v Hyde and Woodmansee[5] provides the authoritative definition of the legal institution of marriage as 'the voluntary union for life of one man and one woman, to the exclusion of all others'. This definition has been accepted as the terms of the marriage powers in Australia.[6]

The language of Hyde is reflected in both the Marriage Act 1961 (Cth) and the FLA. Section 43(a) of the latter provides that any exercise of the Act's jurisdiction shall have regard to the 'need to preserve and protect the institution of marriage as the union of a man and a woman to the exclusion of all others voluntarily entered into for life'. This, it would seem, is Australian family, firmly entrenched for almost thirty years, since the passing of the FLA. In short, the FLA places the MCD 'family' squarely before the court, which legally defines the categories it should contain.

[5] (1866) LR 1 P&D 130, per Sir James Wilde.

[6] Per Mason and Brennan JJ in *Calverley v Green* (1984) 155 CLR 242 at 259–60 and Brennan J in *The Queen v L* (1991) 174 CLR 379 at 392.

That is, family for the purposes of the FLA is formed through the exclusive union of one man and one woman, and the natural or adoptive issue of that union.

The effect of these jurisdictional limits is that only the parties to a marriage can bring an action in the Family Court. However, the provisions relating to children are an exception to the normal jurisdictional limits of the Act. The FLA comprehensively deals with children's matters, including the determination of parenting orders (residence, contact and specific issues orders). The paramount consideration for the court, when making parenting orders, is the 'best interests of the child'[7] rather than any perceived 'right' of the applicant. Following the transfer of powers by the states (except WA which has maintained its own parallel system), the FLA deals nationally and uniformly with all matters pertaining to the welfare of children, notwithstanding the constitutional requirement that the Commonwealth's powers be limited to matters pertaining to marriage. Because of the states' transfer, the FLA addresses matters concerning ex-nuptial children as well as the children of marriage, and can receive applications from the parents, the child or 'any other person concerned with the care, welfare or development of the child'.[8] The 'best interests of the child' test does not displace the traditional (marriage-based) conception of 'family'. It merely indicates a starting point for determining parenting orders. Nevertheless, in the case of property disputes, the case remains that only parties to a marriage, as such, can bring an action in the Family Court.[9] The litigants are officially deemed to be 'the husband' and 'the wife' (in property matters) but, via the MCD 'family', these can easily be readily transferred into 'the father' and 'the mother' where parenting (as opposed to property) is concerned.

The Family Court has, historically, shown a propensity to 'category-centredness'; that is, to be swayed by conventions commonly used to allocate incumbency in the MCD 'family'.[10] This is partly explained by the Act's own leanings. We have noted the jurisdictional limits and s43(a) above. In addition, Section 64C provides that:

---

[7] s65E.

[8] s65C.

[9] The exception is WA which has established a parallel legislative regime, which replicates the FLA but with application to families headed by de facto couples (heterosexual and same-sex): Family Court Act 1975 (WA).

[10] For example, it was presumed by the Family Court until the mid-1970s that it was in children's best interests to be with their mother (the 'mother principle'). The principle was rejected by the High Court in Gronow v Gronow (1979) 144 CLR 513. The Family Court had also relied on the correlating presumption that the father's role was to be out working. McMillan v Jackson [1995] FLC –92–610 was an appeal from a decision that the father should not be granted custody because it would mean than he would become dependent upon social security. The Full Court noted that 'his Honour's pre-conception that the father should be out working to support his son, rather than staying at home to look after his day to day needs, played a significant part in his determination of this case' (at 82,084, per Baker, Lindenmayer and Burton JJ). Other cases have invoked s43 to support the view that a child's best interests are better served in the care of the parents than in the care of an extended family member or some other non-related person: Obrenovic v McCauley [1985] FLC–91–655 per Gee J and Drew and Drew (1993) FLC –92–360 per Treyvaud J. However, more recent cases have stated that there is to be no presumption that the natural parents should be favoured, over other persons, and that each case is to be determined by reference to the facts and the individuals

> A Parenting Order in relation to a child may be made in favour of a parent of the child or some other person (emphasis added).

Finally, s65C provides that:

> A Parenting Order … may be applied for by;

(a) either or both of the child's parents; or
(b) the child; or
(c) any other person concerned with the care, welfare or development of the child (emphasis added).

So there is, as we shall see, some leeway. But it is nevertheless the case that the statute indicates that 'some other person' is a secondary consideration by comparison with the norm of 'a parent' and where 'a parent' will, ideally, be a husband-father or a wife-mother. In the ideal scenario, membership work is being done (in and through the text of the law) such that the mother is the mother of the child, the father is the father of the child, the mother is the wife of the husband, and the husband is the husband of the wife. Then, as it were, after the fact, there may (or may not) be 'some other person'.

So whilst the child's best interests are paramount, irrespective of the relationship to that child of the person applying for an order,[11] this principle resides within the context of indications that marriage, and biological or legally adoptive parents have priority over other persons in a hierarchy of relationships.[12] These provisions are not, however, prescriptive. They do not, in themselves, determine parenting orders. It is, then, possible for family law determinations to be made outside the commonsensical strictures of the device 'family' (mother, father, child, etc.), and such determinations have in fact been made. After all the notion of 'the child's best interests' does, we must concede, veer more towards predication than sheer categorisation. But how did this possibility pan out in an actual case where there was dispute between doing parenting (as predicate) and 'biological' fatherhood (as sheer category membership)?

A Case in Point

Re Patrick[13] is one of many cases which give an insight into the difficulty for the Court in making determinations pursuant to Part VII matters (pertaining to children) when handling disputes concerning non-traditional familial arrangements. We present this case specifically because it directs itself to the question of the meaning of both

before the Court. For example, Re Hodak [1993] FLC –92–421 per Lindenmayer J, and the Full Court in Rice v Miller [1993] FLC –92–415 and Re C and D [1998] FLC –92–815.

[11] As affirmed in the above cases.

[12] Rebuttable presumptions of parentage reflecting biological connection are provided under Part VII, Div. 12. Section 60D provides that parenting includes adoptive parents and that adoption refers to adoption under the law of the place of adoption.

[13] Re Patrick and An Application Concerning Contact (2002) FLC –93–096.

'family' and 'parent' and explores the complexity of such matters. The questions before the Court were whether a sperm donor, known or anonymous, is a 'parent' within the scope of the FLA, pursuant to s60H,[14] and whether contact on the part of the father-donor, was in the best interests of the child. Further it was a case in which the judge went to some length to think broadly about family, and yet, we believe, was restrained by the commonsensical (and equally strictly legal) device of family.

In deciding these matters Guest J reflects on the constitution of family for the child, 'Patrick'. Referring to Millbank, a scholar in the area of same-sex relationships, his Honour says that 'the traditional hetero-nuclear family does not now reflect the reality of the various family forms within modern society', noting that 'family' now also includes 'homo-nuclear families'.[15] He discusses the concept broadly and, for us, with admirable possibilities for semiotic tolerance/play: The term 'family' has a flexible and wide meaning. It is not one fixed in time and is not a term of art. It necessarily and broadly encompasses a description of a unit which has 'familiar characteristics'. Not all families function in the same way. Never the less, they enjoy common characteristics such as those demonstrated by the applicants ['the mother' and her same-sex partner]. Theirs is not of a casual or transitory nature but one that has embraced exclusivity and permanency. They are emotionally and financially inter-dependent and I have no doubt, share common interests, activities and companionship. Their biological and psychological relationship to and mutual care of Patrick makes it so much more obvious. In my view it would stultify the necessary progress of family law in this country if society were not to recognise the applicants as a 'family' when they offer that, which is consistent and parallel with heterosexual families, save for the obviousness of being a same-sex couple.[16]

Guest J stresses that gay and lesbian families can take many forms and should not be understood as an homogeneous group. The family may be comprised of two mothers or two fathers, two mothers and one father (as in the case of Patrick, as characterised by the Court) or two fathers and two mothers. The diversity of form is reflected also in the role of the father in relation to children conceived via artificial insemination. The father role need not be a 'traditional "fatherly" role'.[17]

Patrick's family, his Honour concludes, is a homo-nuclear family, comprised of the mother and the co-parent (the mother's partner).[18] He notes that the matter before the Court is ultimately not dissimilar to matters that arise from heterosexual nuclear families and are decided by the Court on a daily basis.[19] The question here is: what is the role of the biological father and, consequently, what is the appropriate degree of contact?

A critical issue for the Court in determining this matter is whether the agreement between the parents (particularly 'the mother', as the 'biological' mother is known

[14] Supra n.13 at 88 870.

[15] Supra n.13 at 88 927.

[16] Supra n.13 at 88 927.

[17] Supra n.13 at 88 927–928.

[18] Supra n.13 at 88 926.

[19] Supra n.13 at 88 927.

in the judgment) and the donor was that the donor would be an anonymous donor or a known donor. Further, if the donor were to be a known donor, what would be the capacity of this acknowledgement—as 'father' or in some other relationship? Guest J, preferring the evidence of the 'father' (as the donor was known in the judgment) to that of the 'mother' and 'co-parent' (as the judgment refers to the mother's partner), decides that the agreement between the parties was that the father would have a role in the child's life.[20] In other words, he was to be a 'known' donor.

What was this role to be? This seems to be the real crux of the case, notwithstanding the primary issue of the terms of the arrangement. With great respect to Guest J, who must be credited with becoming informed about alternative family modeling, particularly in gay and lesbian contexts, it is arguable that the ultimate decision rested, in part, on hetero-normative conceptions of family. For having determined that there was an intention for the donor to be a known donor, Guest J searches for the opportunity to deem him to be a 'parent'—with all the customary predicates of that role—rather than an 'other person' under the provisions of the FLA. This suggests that Guest J was operating from the position of well-known binaries (see the table below) under which only those marked as being parents are understood to be 'doing family', such that the 'other person' category is diminished in this respect.[21] This ultimately led to contact arrangements which equated with those the Court would normally order in relation to the non-residential partner of a hetero-nuclear family.

Known biological or legal	Non-biological, non-legal or not known biological
Parent	Non-Parent
Parental relationship	'Other person' relationship
Significant amounts of contact	Limited amounts of contact

It seems that, for Guest J, having established that it was intended that Patrick's father be a known donor, the latter also becomes a parent, notwithstanding the failure of the FLA to acknowledge this. Consequently, Patrick has a right to maintain a parent–child relationship with his 'father'. This justified contact arrangements normally ordered in applications on the part of a parent, pursuant to s60B, which establishes the principles that:

> (2) (a) children have the right to know and be cared for by both their parents regardless of whether their parents are married, separated, have never married or have never lived together; and
> (b) children have a right of contact, on a regular basis, with both their parents and with other people significant to their care.[22]

[20] Supra n.13 at 88 895, 88 918.

[21] 'Other person', to this extent, is effectively a secondary category even though the FLA is not limited to such a reading. Implicit in our argument is the idea that 'other person' is semiotically open and could include persons seen to be actively 'doing family'.

[22] The order in this hierarchy is significant, that is that the relationship with a parent is more important than the relationship with significant others, as indicated by the lexical ordering of the clauses of the provision, and confirmed by Guest J. Supra n.13 at 88 924.

The contact arrangements were settled, despite the Court having noted that the mother and co-parent, along with Patrick, formed a homo-nuclear family. In effect, however, the Court construes Patrick's family as comprised of mother, co-parent, father (as opposed to 'other person') and child, with the father-role surpassing the co-parent role in significance. In other words, the hetero-nuclear family was re-affirmed as the model for the judgment, with the co-parent becoming no more than an 'other person'. This is further indicated by a telling language slip where his Honour mistakenly refers to the biological father as the 'husband', drawing, of course, on the single categories usually before the Court[23]—and, perhaps, displaying the FLA's historical grounding in questions of marriage.

Hetero-normative trends in contact were consequently applied in the Patrick case: a progressive expansion of contact time over a period of four years, culminating by 2004 with Friday-to-Monday contact on alternate weekends and an assurance that Patrick have contact with the 'father' on Father's Day. The Court ordered the norms of contact adopted for hetero-normative family relationships.

If, however, we were to view the known donor as an 'other person', notwithstanding the 'biological' relationship, then we open the door to more creative contact arrangements as, say, we might if the applicant were a member of the extended family or a close family friend; that is some 'other person' with a significant relationship to the child. The judgment indicates that this scenario is exactly what the homo-nuclear family was concerned about—that the relationship between the donor and Patrick would be equated with a father-son relationship at the expense of the homo-nuclear family constituted by Patrick, his biological mother and the social mother (or co-parent). As the judgment reports:

> In the course of her evidence, the mother said that there was no need for a '... parental' father in Patrick's life. When asked why Patrick should be different from any other child and not have a right to know his father, the mother jauntily responded '...because he's got leso's [sic] for parents'. [...] She said that if a parental relationship developed between the father and Patrick, it would conflict with the parenting offered by the co-parent and herself. [...] The mother agreed, when cross examined [...] that her objection to contact was based upon a fundamental belief that children can be raised in a lesbian household without a father (in the traditional sense). [...] From what I have both heard and read, it is doubtless true that children can be happily raised within a homo-nuclear family, but the difference here is that the father desires and has always desired to play an active and fatherly role in the life of his son.[24]

When it was put to the mother that Patrick had two families she responded: 'No, he has one family and he has a donor'.[25]

While Guest J accepts the legitimacy of the homo-nuclear family form, he suggests that the mother had a 'hardened' position and characterised her view and that of the co-parent as predicated on 'philosophical and ideological bases'.[26] The mother's

[23] Supra n.13 at 88 903.

[24] Supra n.13 at 88 884. Our ellipses in square brackets; others original.

[25] Supra n.13 at 88 885.

[26] Supra n.13 at 88 886.

desire to maintain a homo-nuclear family model was, in effect, dismissed as a 'philosophical and ideological' position, obstructing a resolution, which could include the father-donor as incumbent in the device 'family'.

What Guest J may have failed to appreciate is that the desire to involve the father was in itself a 'position', in fact a commonsensically anchored social position, which Patrick's family was trying to counter by moving to a more predication-based account. The involvement of the donor, as father, was, perhaps, as alien to the conception of family held by the mother and co-parent, as the conception of a two-parent, fatherless family was to the Court and, perhaps, to the broader, hetero-normative community. The viewpoints indicated differing ideas of the categories that could come to comprise the device 'family'. The mother's view of what constitutes 'family' (significantly enough) was enabled by establishing it according to the predicational, rather than categorical, aspects of the relationships. On the mother's characterisation, her partner did in fact 'do being a parent'—she had all the predicational characteristics of the category 'parent' ('mother' and/or 'father') in the device 'family' but was not granted incumbency in the device; by contrast with one (the donor) who would commonsensically have such incumbency without ever having to display the predicate of 'parenting'.

It is unlikely that there could have been a mutually agreeable outcome for this case because of the complexity of the issues and the base position of the FLA. Guest J notes the difficulties of the case given the heterosexist basis of the FLA. He says that:

> It is clear that gay and lesbian families were not considered by the legislature when s60H of the Act was being drafted. These families differ in significant ways from heterosexual families who access artificial insemination services.... [I]t is time that the legislature considered some of the matters raised, including the nature of parenthood, the meaning of 'family' and the role of the law in regulating arrangements within the gay and lesbian community. The child at the centre of this dispute is part of a new and rapidly increasing generation of children being conceived and raised by gay and lesbian parents. However, under the current legislative regime, Patrick's biological and social reality remains unrecognised.[27]

Nevertheless, whilst the judgment indicated research into alternative parenting arrangements and the issues of same-sex families—a real and stated desire on the part of Guest J to adopt an alternative framework—he was limited by a standard commonsensical version of familial possibilities.

What does this case stand for? What is its ratio? An interpretation of family was not a key issue for the Court, except as an addendum to the issue of whether or not being a sperm donor was sufficient to entitle parenthood. On this latter point Guest J answers the question 'is a known sperm donor, a "parent"?' in the negative, finding that a sperm donor merely has jurisdiction in the Family Court as 'any other person'. Despite this finding, his Honour uses the nomenclature of 'father' and attaches rights and duties to the donor accordingly, an approach open to him under the discretionary powers granted pursuant to s65E, but nevertheless indicating the social and cultural power of dominant values in the constitution of the family.

[27] Supra n.13 at 88 929.

Because the FLA is shrouded in a quite strict categorisation-centred means of determining the roles of persons (as opposed to a possible predication-centred approach), it is difficult for any Court to move beyond the conventions commonly seen to comprise the MCD 'family'. Yet it is possible for the law to be framed in a manner which does consider the predicational status of parties and determine family accordingly. Indeed the Australian states and territories have set a trend for doing so, in relation to the property provisions of those families excluded from the Commonwealth jurisdiction.

Legislating Predicationally?

It took little time for the states and territories to respond to the FLA's limits with respect to the disbursement of familial property upon separation. New South Wales was the first state or territory to provide clear statutory rights in relation to the property of relationships not recognised by the FLA.[28] However, like the FLA, the De Facto Relationships Act 1984 (NSW) defined its jurisdiction in categorisational terms: that is, with reference to a man and woman living in a marriage-like relationship.[29] It sought to create a means by which families which looked like traditional families (but which failed the matrimonial causes test) could have simple rules for determining property disputes. Other states followed suit in introducing legislation for heterosexual de facto couples.

The Australian Capital Territory (ACT) was the first state or territory to break with this tradition. It introduced legislation which determined its application, that is, familial relationships, by reference to a set of predicates. Section 3(1) of the ACT's Domestic Relationships Act 1994 defined 'Domestic relationship' as:

> a personal relationship (other than a legal marriage) between two adults in which one provides personal or financial commitment and support of a domestic nature for the material benefit of the other, and includes a de facto marriage.

Under this legislation, there is no need for the parties to establish that they exist in a marriage-like state. This is a paradigm shift in the mode of legislating for the family. The ACT act, unlike other family law regimes until recently, focuses on actual practices performed (predicates), over category membership as such. It permits legal acknowledgement of any domestic relationship, which has a degree of personal or financial interdependence, whether or not the parties have a sexual relationship or cohabit. In other words, it could apply to siblings, to friends, to lovers or any other partnership which 'does' being a family.

Other states and territories have followed suit, with New South Wales amending its legislation and Tasmania introducing new predicate-based legislation —the

[28] New South Wales Law Reform Commission Review of the Property (Relation- ships) Act 1984 (NSW) Discussion Paper No. 44 (Sydney NSW, 2001) at –1.19.

[29] s3.

Property (Relationships) Act 1999 (NSW) and the Relationships Act 2003 (Tas). Hence, since 1994, despite the resistance of the Commonwealth, there has been a movement to the alternative, where relevant predicates decide category membership rather than vice versa. This means that 'family' is determined by reference to whether the parties exhibit relevant conduct, generally something like being socially and economically interdependent (akin to the idea of, for example, 'unconditional support'), rather than by reference to an established set of categories normatively associated with the MCD 'family'.

The states have indicated their willingness to transfer further powers to the Commonwealth, to legislate on property matters concerning families not constituted by marriage. If so motivated, the Commonwealth could negotiate with the states over the framing of that legislation. However the Commonwealth has indicated that it is only willing to accept the transfer of state powers in respect to heterosexual de facto couples, retaining its conception of family as only very marginally divergent from that constituted by 'traditional' marriages.

So the situation vis-à-vis family law is unique. That is, most areas of law do in fact operate by working from predicates to categories rather than vice-versa. They work from the premise of what people 'do' rather than what people 'are'. A tort-feasor is such because they have performed a wrong, and a contractor is in breach if they have failed to act on one of the terms of the contract or is in breach of some common or statutory duty of the law. One becomes 'a murderer' by virtue of undertaking certain specified social practices; ditto for becoming 'a fraud' or 'a speeding driver'. The niceties of law, in fact, turn on how closely specifiable those predicates are: in tort law, an assaulter is distinguishable from a batterer by virtue of their practices; in criminal law, murder is finely distinguished from manslaughter, fraud from deceptive conduct; and speeding offences come in fine degrees above specified limits and norms. To continue the examples, there are no 'natural' or 'birth-' murderers, frauds, or speeders. Provably having undertaken (or committed) the relevant predicate is both necessary and sufficient for category incumbency to follow—often after lengthy investigation and litigation concerning the exact details of the specific action in question and with the assumption that the person in question performed the action freely and from choice.

Why is family law such a glaring exception? Persons in the society can take on all the practices, actions and characteristics of the category 'parent' without ever being legally recognised as such, whereas someone who does not may be automatically entitled to category membership. Partners in non-hetero-normative relationships, that is, can freely choose for themselves all of the predicates routinely bound to the categories of 'mother' and/or 'father'—and do so in ways that are evidentially provable—but under the FLA they are categorised in the first instance as an 'other person'. The framing of the legislation permits slippages into the use of naturally available MCDs and the predicates routinely attached to them.

Of course, the same is true for the courts, and the jury if dealing with certain criminal matters. For example, a person's race or gender may impact on the determination of guilt—it may be more difficult to find a woman who has no criminal record guilty of a violent offence and more difficult to find someone of one race liable than of another. Yet, this is not essentially an issue with the law's characterisation of the offence. Rather it is because, rightly or wrongly, we cannot help but do categorisational work in our everyday activities. However, what is exceptional in the area of family law specifically, is that the FLA directly (via the Hyde definition) or indirectly (via ss43(a), 64C and 65C) primarily defines its application by reference to the device and its traditional categories rather than to the predicates of possible family members. The widened scope in relation to children's matters is an exception to the rule, but sits firmly within the context of an overly categorisational means of recognising parties.

We are often told by 'macro'-social theorists that late modernity (sometimes 'postmodernity') is characterised by risk and uncertainty. What is rarely pointed out is that this 'crisis of certainty' impacts particularly on questions of parentage. To be sure, parentage has always had its potential for grey areas. However, contemporary society is characteristically fraught in this respect.

And Semiotics?

In the first section of this paper, we questioned formal-textual semiotics because it could not be extended to incorporate a manifestly natural hearing. 'The baby cried' + 'The mommy picked it up': these two utterances have a hearable possessive that is not registered on the textual surface (the 'black letter') of a small narrative made up by the two sentences—and made up by a young child. We called this a signified without a signifier, and so it is.

In the course of this paper, we have also seen that Australian family law (in general, in its specific provisions and in at least one case and its judgment) seems—for all the will in the world, including Guest J's admirable criticisms of the legislation as it stands—unable to make the same kinds of inference from predicate (e.g., provably caring for a child, picking it up, etc.) to category (having the status of 'parent' or 'mommy'). Instead, when in doubt, it tends to revert to well-known categories of mother-wife and father-husband vis-a`-vis children. What are the upshots for semiotics generally and semiotics of law in particular?

To start, we must agree with Umberto Eco: compositional semantics will never foreground predicational status as such. It begins with categories and only ends with predicates where it can. In this respect, it is somewhat like the Australian family law itself. Eco's classical example is from Katz and Fodor (his 'KF' model) concerning the category 'bachelor'. The various 'bachelors' (Human vs. Animal) (Adult vs. Young), etc. only end up predicationally: 'Serving under the standard of another' (a human male who is a young knight), 'Having the academic degree conferred for completing the first four years of college', being 'without a mate during the breeding time' (seals!). Hence the following[30]:

[30] Umberto Eco, *A Theory of Semiotics* (Bloomington: Indiana University Press, 1976), at 97.

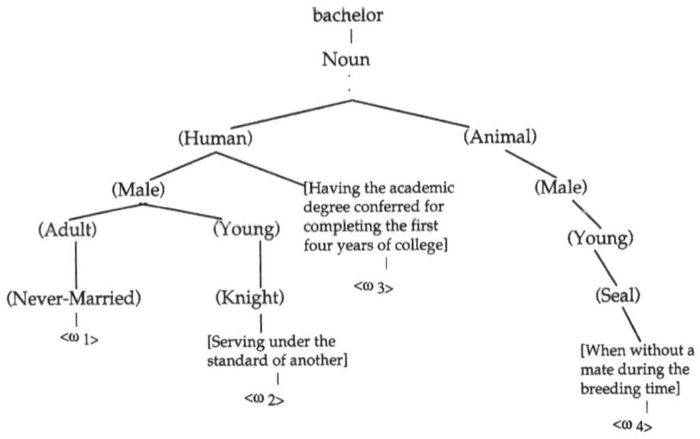

Again, on a Saussurean model of semiotics, we end up with an impasse not unlike that of family law itself. That is, for the signifier 'parent', we have to imagine what the possible signified or signifieds could be and, possibly, go looking for a type of person or, strictly, the 'mental image' of a type of person—given that, for Saussure, signifieds are always one or another form of psychological image. By contrast, an MCA approach allows the capacity to begin with predicates (actual worldly deeds) and only then to proceed to possible categories of person. The diagrams below display this distinction:

Saussurean model:

Signifier →	Signified
Parent	?

MCA model:

Predicate →	Category
Cares, cleans, cooks for, etc.	Parent?

Conclusion

So if we do not proceed in a strictly textual manner, either in the law, or in semiotics, how do we proceed? One way of going forward semiotically is to consider Peirce's third mode of reasoning: abduction. He contrasts this mode with induction and deduction. Induction works from cases and finds rules as a consequence (common law perhaps). Vice-versa for deduction: it starts from rules and interprets given cases as such. Semiotically, induction is too loose; deduction too tight. Abduction allows a different degree of play or tolerance. It's hypothetical and temporary; it takes into account historical, social and cultural differences. Peirce's own account of abduction is instructive:

> I once landed at a seaport in a Turkish province; and, as I was walking up to the house which I was to visit, I met a man upon horseback, surrounded by four horsemen holding a canopy over his head. As the governor of the province was the only personage I could think of who would be so greatly honored, I inferred that this was he. This was an hypothesis.[31]

Peirce observed the predicational possibilities first, and only then drew inferences about the respective category. So, in the case of family law, an abductive reasoning would run: Any parent does x for a child (so: judge what should be done as x today, for now, in this context); this person does such things; could this person be a parent? In hindsight, an MCA account of, say, 'governorship', 'parentage', or any number of related categorisational matters, could prove useful: both to semiotics as such and to the semiotics of family law today. This is why we suggest its inclusion in the range of analytic tools available to legal semioticians with an interest in progressive reform. How would family law proceed from Goethe's ultimately predicational dictum, "In the beginning was the deed"? It would no longer be true to say that any such predicational rather than category-based legal conception of family is 'socially progressive'. It is, rather, the most sensible and practically manageable way of governing and regulating family relations as such. Some of the states and territories (especially the ACT) have begun to acknowledge this fact, in legislating on property matters. The rest—and the Commonwealth—must surely follow.

[31] Charles Sanders Peirce, Collected Papers (Cambridge: Harvard University Press, 1931–1958), at 2.265.

Persons III: The Multiple Faces of a Corporation's Legal Personality

Larry Catá Backer

> There is a vast literature, with deep roots in nineteenth-century German scholarship, on the nature of juridical persons. The debate over competing conceptions of juridical persons that is the central preoccupation of that literature still shows some life today, in terms not much removed from those of a century ago.... [T]he traditional literature is principally concerned with questions—such as the power of the state versus the power of private organizations, or the nature of group will.[1]

At the core of the "juridical personality" debate were two basically incompatible views, each held by a different camp, of the critical nature of economic organizations. For one camp, economic organizations were property in the hands of their owners. This property might be given special qualities by the state or through contract, but it remained property all the same. It followed from this conceptual framework that the role of law was to focus on the interests of the owners or, more generally, those with an ownership interest or stake in the entity. For the other camp, the economic organization, like a pallid reflection of the political state that gave it existence, constituted an autonomous institutional actor separable from those with an interest in it.[2] From this framework, the role of law should focus on the entity—that is, on the collective interests constituting the entity rather than on the aggregate individual interests of stakeholders, however defined.

Source: LARRY CATÁ BACKER: "The Autonomous Global Corporation: On The Role Of Organizational Law Beyond Asset Partitioning And Legal Personality". In: *Tulsa Law Review* Spring 2006 on the Symposium: *Disputed Concepts in Contemporary Business Association Law: Discussions on Fiduciary Duty and Capital Lock-in* (Selected paragraphs).

[1] Henry Hansmann & Reinier Kraakman, The Essential Role of Organizational Law, 110 *Yale L.J.* 387, 438–39 (2000) (footnote omitted); see also Michael J. Phillips, Reappraising the Real Entity Theory of the Corporation, 21 *Fla. St. U. L. Rev.* 1061 (1994).

[2] German academic theory developed this idea to its highest form. See Otto Gierke, *Political Theories of the Middle Age* (Frederic William Maitland trans., Beacon Press 1958); Gunther Teubner, Enterprise Corporatism: New Industrial Policy and the "Essence" of the Legal Person, 36 *Am. J. Comp. L.* 130 (1988). American courts and scholars for the most part tended to avoid the extreme. For a discussion of the American perspective, see Phillip I. Blumberg, *The Multinational Challenge to Corporation Law: The Search for a New Corporate Personality* 21–51 (Oxford U. Press 1993).

L. Catá Backer (✉)
Departments of Law and International Affairs, Penn State University,
University Park, PA, USA
e-mail: lcb11@psu.edu

J.M. Broekman, L. Catá Backer (eds.), *Signs In Law - A Source Book*,
DOI 10.1007/978-3-319-09837-1_23

The last half of the twentieth century witnessed the revitalization of this debate, now heavily infused with notions borrowed from economics. For these scholars, the issues of institutional personality were tangential and largely irrelevant to the foundational realities of institutional functioning.[3] The focus of these explorations was on the role of economic institutions as a nexus point for the interests of others. In a variety of substantially more sophisticated methods that deepened the insights of economic-organization-as-property proponents of the earlier debate, this scholarship focused on the role of law as a facilitator of natural profit-maximizing behavior among the actors pooling resources within an organization. Recent scholarship has suggested the connection between the two camps and the critical role that economic culture plays in the social acceptance of institutional personality. The great insight of this scholarship has been to see in Japanese economic institutional culture evidence of the possibility that a corporation can own itself and thus become a self-determining subject.

> Another strain of recent economic-organization-as-nexus-of-contract scholarship has focused on the singular characteristic of limited liability as a basis for understanding the role of regulation of economic enterprises. This scholarship, too, views institutional concerns as largely tangential to the appropriate focus. For Hansmann and Kraakman, the focus on the legal regulation of asset segregation offers "a definition of juridical persons that is simpler, clearer, and more functional than those that have characterized the traditional literature. Indeed, one reason we have used the term 'legal entity' rather than 'juridical person' is to avoid confusion between our analysis and the more traditional views."

For all their utility, these approaches to the relationship of law and economic entities are limited by different sets of analytical constraints. The corporate personality debate has focused on the relationship between entity and owner. The economic-entity-as-nexus-of-contract debate has focused on the relationship between aggregations of capital and stakeholders. Implicit in these analyses is the idea that law is an exogenous force that regulates the relationship between entity and shareholder in the one case and entity and creditor in the other.

The context in which the consequences of a global network of national systems in which entity autonomy had been solidified, and entity self-ownership was possible, was the emergence of globalization after World War II. Globalization comprised a system of free movement of capital, and to a lesser extent, labor and technology. Consciousness of the perversities of the system emerged with an understanding of the manner in which the state-based system of entity regulation limited the regulation

[3] See Katsuhito Iwai, Persons, Things and Corporations: The Corporate Personality Controversy and Comparative Corporate Governance, *47 Am. J. Comp. L. 583, 594* (1999) (comparing the consequences of corporate personality cultures in Japan and the United States to examine the ways in which it is possible "to eliminate either personality or thingness from the person-cum thing corporation, thereby turning it into a mere 'legal thing' or a full 'legal person,' respectively"). Iwai notes that the possibility of self-ownership is possible even under regimes that prevent corporations from exercising the rights of a shareholder with respect to its own shares. All that is required is for a group of corporations to own a majority of each other's shares as a group. See also Meir Dan-Cohen, *Rights, Persons, and Organizations: A Legal Theory for Bureaucratic Society* (U. Cal. Press 1986) (noting the possibility of a personless or ownerless corporation).

of these entities. The greater the possibility of dispersal of operations among different regulatory regimes, the greater is the advantage to the entity at the expense of the regulating territorial unit. Indeed, the ability of a [multinational enterprise] to take advantage of differences in regulatory environments between states is seen as one of its internalization advantages.

The nature of the perversities is well known. They range from the benign to the disturbing. Enterprises can exploit the territorial principle, the principles of limited liability, and that of independent juridical personality to minimize risk to assets partitioned to the entity. This risk minimization is accomplished by distributing assets among widely dispersed subsidiaries incorporated in different jurisdictions and by engaging in enterprise activities indirectly through joint ventures, distributorships, franchises, local agents, or other indirect forms of operation. Multinational enterprises have been able to exploit their economic power to negotiate with states for the enactment of regulations favorable to the enterprise and to avoid liability for local actions, local taxes, and other impositions charged by the state to others similarly situated. Multinational enterprises have also used their power to intervene directly or indirectly in the politics of political jurisdictions. The involvement of large enterprises in local civil wars, coups, and other changes of government, and the willingness of enterprises to engage in local corruption are well documented. Traditional methods for limiting the ability of multinational enterprises to avoid local consequences—piercing the corporate veil, imposition of enterprise liability, extraterritorial application of local law, invoking the legal process of the courts of the territory of the parent company of an integrated enterprise—have had little success in extending the power of states relative to these enterprises in a world in which enterprises may move capital and operations with some ease (at least to some places) and then protect those assets by invocating the territorial principle and the non-interference principle.

The limitations of the territorial principle and its perverse consequences for the regulation of enterprises, the operation of which was widely dispersed across regulating states, became known by the end of the twentieth century. Even the United States, a state with an extraordinarily long regulatory arm, discovered the limitations of its regulatory reach at the conclusion of World War II, with respect to enterprises traditionally considered "American."

The activities of General Motors, Ford and Chrysler prior to and during World War II are instructive. At that time, these three firms dominated motor vehicle production in both the United States and Germany. Due to its mass production capabilities, automobile manufacturing is one of the most crucial industries with respect to national defense. As a result, these firms retained the economic and political power to affect the shape of governmental relations both within and between these nations in a manner which maximized corporate global profits. In short, they were private governments unaccountable to the citizens of any country yet possessing tremendous influence over the course of war and peace in the world.

> During the 1920's and 1930's, the Big Three automakers undertook an extensive program of multinational expansion. …By the mid-1930's, these three American companies owned automotive subsidiaries throughout Europe and the Far East; many of their largest facilities

> were located in the politically sensitive nations of Germany, Poland, Rumania, Austria, Hungary, Latvia, and Japan.... Due to their concentrated economic power over motor vehicle production in both Allied and Axis territories, the Big Three inevitably became major factors in the preparations and progress of the war.[...]
>
> The outbreak of war in September 1939 resulted inevitably in the full conversion by GM and Ford of their Axis plants to the production of military aircraft and trucks.
>
> On the ground, GM and Ford subsidiaries built nearly 90 percent of the armored "mule" 3-ton half-trucks and more than 70 percent of the Reich's medium and heavy-duty trucks. These vehicles, according to American intelligence reports, served as "the backbone of the German Army transportation system."
>
> After the cessation of hostilities, GM and Ford demanded reparations from the U.S. Government for wartime damages sustained by their Axis facilities as a result of Allied bombing.... Ford received a little less than $1 million, primarily as a result of damages sustained by its military truck complex at Cologne. By the 1970s, multinational enterprises "began to be described as a challenge to the nation state, a creature with no loyalties except to itself, an entity that caused economic, social and political disruption in both the host and home countries, and aimed at global dominance. The [multinational enterprise] had to be tamed."

But taming the multinational enterprise was easier said than done in the context of an international system unwilling to yield the primacy of the territorial principle. The regulatory limitations of the territorial principle are evidenced by examining the way the principle constrains state attempts to regulate multinational enterprises that are not subject to regulation in their entirety by any single jurisdiction. The Organisation for Economic Cooperation and Development ("OECD") Guidelines for Multinational Enterprises represent the efforts by a cluster of developed states to coordinate their regulation of economic enterprises by suggesting a code of conduct for multinational enterprises. Consider, in a different light, the way in which the OECD works. Its foundations are grounded in the limitations and state-centered prerogatives of the territorial principle. In essence, the OECD is a loose organization of states pledged to cooperate with each other Each, however, guards its power to regulate within its territory. Legislative power is not devolved to this organization. Thus, it is also limited by the hierarchy principle of regulation. The limits of the provision of governance mechanisms beyond the state, then, in the words of the OECD website, are reduced to reliance on "dialogue, consensus, peer review and pressure."

> By both preserving control over the state's respective limited territorial jurisdictions and seeking to coordinate regulation within a group of like-minded jurisdictions, the OECD evidences the limits of its authority to regulate those organizations outside of its jurisdiction. It must treat all such objects of regulations as regulatory equals in effect. OECD guidance is thus voluntary, not necessarily because voluntary compliance is a good in itself, but because compulsion, the usual methodology of the state, is not available. The effectiveness of compliance is based on a willingness to provide guidelines that the "guided" are willing to bear. Consultation and cooperation with the guided, therefore, forms a basis of the regulatory activity of the OECD. Peer pressure and review is also constrained by both the territorial principle and the regulatory hierarchy principle and limited to the state party members of the OECD in the context of maintaining their mutual obligations under the OECD Convention.

Resistance to any substantial efforts by international institutions to create a legal framework for the regulation of multinational enterprises has been effective. These efforts, led by nation-states, have been fueled by fear that internationalization will erode the primacy of states as regulators. The latest failure involved the abandonment of a United Nations project to create a binding body of Norms on the Responsibilities of Transnational Corporations and Other Business Enterprises with Regard to Human Rights ("Norms"). The history of the failure of the Norms evidences both the perverse power of the territorial principle and the limitations of international political institutions to overcome that perversity and reassert a politically centered regulatory framework. The Norms reflected the belief of many developing states, academics, and non-governmental human rights organizations, as embraced within the human rights institutions of the United Nations:

> [T]he global power of TNCs dwarf that of many developing nations. TNCs' economic power produces social and political power as well, power that is enormous and global. TNCs can affect the level of enjoyment of the economic, social, and political rights of people across states, but states cannot effectively regulate them. Some regulation at the international level is necessary to control the possibility of abuse by TNCs of their dominant position and to ensure that TNCs contribute to the development of less developed states and to the protection of individuals' social, political, and economic rights. Originally it was presented as a legally binding instrument of international governance imposing direct obligations on TNCs. It became clearer that the Norms would effectively be abandoned in their current form by the spring of 2005. It appeared that the High Commissioner would recommend that the Commission "maintain the draft Norms among existing initiatives and standards on business and human rights, with a view to their further consideration." This result followed intense pressure from developed states, especially the United States, to avoid the construction of any international system of regulation of economic enterprises.

Thus, the territorial principle creates a framework within which power to regulate the enterprise is dispersed—from the state to a collection of collectives (states and enterprises and cooperative bodies) and among states. It does this by producing and sustaining regimes of voluntary multi-state systems of behavior control. In this environment, an enterprise with the ability to disperse assets and operations can substantially choose the aggregate of its regulatory environment—it can effectively regulate itself.

Self-regulation follows from the application of the territorial principle, coupled with the possibilities of enterprise autonomy reinforced by asset partitioning regimes, self-ownership, and juridical personhood. An autonomous legal subject, responsible for its own obligations and able to direct itself can, by distributing its operations in accordance with the benefits of particular territorially limited legal regimes, effectively choose the mix of regulation to which it will submit itself. It follows that such an enterprise can regulate itself. A fully self-conscious autonomy is now complete.

The territorial principle and the principle of regulatory hierarchy can open the possibility of enterprise self-regulation. Any enterprise that can disperse its assets among a large enough number of regulatory units will transform the relationship between regulator and enterprise. For the traditional relationship that is both singular and hierarchical, globalization permits the enterprise to treat regulation as another factor in the production of wealth. The enterprise, now in a position to shop for regulatory regimes, or even bargain for domestication within the territory of a regulatory territory, can take advantage of the limitations of the territorial principle to minimize the effects of regulation on enterprise activity. The principle of regulatory hierarchy can then be turned on its head. The ability to "commodify" regulation makes it at least theoretically possible to construct an economic entity which, through careful planning, can take advantage of asset partitioning, cross holdings, and global asset dispersion to avoid effective regulation by any one political community.

I have been sketching out a picture of regulatory autonomy at a fairly high level of abstraction. It may be useful to try to illustrate the concept in more concrete terms. I will suggest one example, though there are countless variations possible. It is important to note, however, that this is an area that would profit by much empirical research. For the moment, my purpose is to suggest a hypothesis and to provide the framework for analysis.

The self-regulating corporation I suggest here turns the usual analysis upside down. That usual analysis posits the distinctive regulatory problem posed by multinational corporations is their ability to operate an integrated command and control system through two disaggregated institutional structures. The first of these structures is the collection of discrete corporate units—parent, subsidiary, sister, and cousin companies—that make up the Multi-National Corporation group. The second disaggregated structure housing the Multi-National Corporation is the global system of separate nation-states in which those corporations are registered and do business.

In the usual case, this regulatory autonomy centers on the ability of a firm to avoid distasteful regulations relating to its operations. Consider, for example, Clothing, a company that makes its money by designing and selling to retail establishments several lines of children's clothing. Clothing is incorporated in Delaware, and its shares are traded on financial markets in the United States, Europe, and Asia. Clothing's headquarters are in Savannah, Georgia, where Clothing conducts all of its operations. Assume that United States regulations have now substantially increased the costs of making clothing in the United States. Assume further that these regulations may have extraterritorial effect because the regulations apply to all corporations incorporated in any United States jurisdiction, no matter where its operations are located.

Clothing has a variety of options to avoid this regulatory framework, for example, transferring its operations to directly owned subsidiaries abroad, contracting out the manufacture of clothing to partially owned or independent entities resident in other states, and entering into joint ventures for the direct manufacture or indirect manufacture of clothing elsewhere. The list is hardly exhaustive. Clothing—either directly or through its potential subsidiaries, joint venture partners, or (in)dependent contractors—can also engage in negotiations with appropriately selected host states for the appropriate form of regulatory environment. If the operations are sufficiently large or the needs of the host state are particularly easy to satisfy, there is some chance that local law might be modified to the benefit of Clothing's operations. To the extent that operations will be directly controlled, provision can be made for limiting the home corporation's exposure to liability under local law. The cost savings from these efforts, if greater than the increased costs of the regulations in the home state, make these complexities worth the trouble.

Where a corporation can distribute its operations in a sufficiently complete way, it has turned the tables on the state. Clothing has essentially chosen, in the aggregate, the bundle of regulations to which its operations will be subject. By carefully choosing the place, form, and method of operation, it can effectively decide the manner in which it will be regulated. States may legislate to their hearts' content, but the enterprise will submit to those regulations only to the extent it is either unavoidable or profitable.

The tables have been turned on the state in another important way. From the perspective of the self-regulating corporation, the role of states has changed. No longer holders of a monopoly power to regulate the enterprise, states are now mere producers of a good—regulation—that can be characterized as a cost of operations. Like other operating costs, the costs of law can be modified or reduced through avoidance. Where the entity cannot avoid regulation, it is limited as regulation increases the price of goods. But where there is no monopoly on regulation, then avoidance, and the substitution of one legal regime for another becomes possible. In effect, entity and state have changed positions.

Self-regulation becomes more interesting when the sort of regulation that is sought focuses not on operations, but on governance. Governance regimes in the context of mobile corporations are no longer unavoidable assumptions constraining corporate actions. Instead, they are better understood as goods.

> Once different national governance systems were understood as more than just way stations on the road to convergence, comparative scholars began to treat institutional differences as having competitive consequences. Competition was not just between products, but also between governance systems.[4]

Whether this leads to a global "Delaware effect" is still the subject of debate, as much about the existence of this effect is about its consequences for corporate decision making.[5] But the field of competition for consumption of regulation has now expanded beyond states and public law. While searching for an answer to the convergence issue in corporate law, commentators note the rise of alternative systems of regulation, either hybrid systems or regulatory systems based on private law that cut across borders. From the perspective of a self-regulating corporation, this opens an even greater set of possibilities for fashioning an internal regulatory

---

[4] Ronald J. Gilson, Globalizing Corporate Governance: Convergence of Form or Function, *49 Am. J. Comp. L.* 329, 330 (2001). Professor Gilson considered the power of corporate convergence and suggested that "[b]ecause the flexibility of governance and political institutions will differ not only between countries, but within individual countries based on the particular response called for by changed conditions, the most we can predict is substantial variation both across and within different national systems."

[5] For a discussion of the complications of predicting the vector of change in corporate governance regulation when jurisdictions compete for corporate business by selling their corporate governance statutes in the United States, see: Mark J. Roe, Delaware's Competition, *117 Harv. L. Rev.* 588 (2003).

framework that suits it rather than any single political community seeking to assert exclusive regulatory authority.

Thus, that a multinational economic enterprise can be autonomous with respect to the state does not necessarily mean that the enterprise will always look to itself for the establishment of an enterprise-specific regulatory framework. As Gunther Teubner has suggested recently:

> Grotius' famous proposition ubi societas ibi ius has to be reformulated in the conditions of the functional differentiation of the planet in such a way that, wherever autonomous social sectors develop, autonomous law is simultaneously produced, at a relative distance from politics. Law-making also takes place outside the classical sources of international law, in agreements between global players, in private market regulation by multi-national concerns, internal regulations of international organisations, inter-organisational negotiating systems, world-wide standardisation processes that come about partly in markets and partly in the processes of negotiation among organisations.[6] Multinational economic enterprise autonomy from the state has permitted the development of a set of regulatory frameworks for these enterprises outside the state. But such a regulatory system need not be independent of the mechanisms of state power. As the construction of the OECD regulatory system suggests, the autonomous enterprise can even develop its own institutional framework for self-regulation among the community of economic enterprises similarly situated in concert with states, now not so much as regulators, but instead as partners in the attainment of mutually beneficial goals. A recent example of this practice can be seen in the area of security and human rights.
>
> The governments of the United States, the United Kingdom, Norway and the Netherlands plus companies operating in the extractive and energy sectors and non-governmental organizations, all with an interest in human rights and corporate social responsibility, have engaged in the dialogue on security and human rights and have collectively developed the Voluntary Principles. The mechanics of these Voluntary Principles on Security and Human Rights ("Voluntary Principles") are coordinated by a secretariat jointly held by the International Business Leaders Forum and Business for Social Responsibility. The Voluntary Principles suggest a set of guidelines for negotiating the contours of enterprise activity in the security sector.

The more common form of autonomous self-regulation is the voluntary code framework that has proliferated in the international sphere since the last third of the twentieth century. Two examples of this form of self-regulation suggest the nature of this form of regulation. The first is the United Nation's Global Compact, a corporate citizen initiative centered on a self-regulating group of enterprises guided by the United Nations—the preeminent global political institution. The second is the related Guide for Integrating Human Rights into Business Management ("Guide") developed by the Business Leaders Initiative on Human Rights.

The Global Compact is a diluted version of the recently abandoned effort to implement the Norms as a more binding international law for the regulation of transnational corporations. In its own words:

> Through the power of collective action, the Global Compact seeks to promote responsible corporate citizenship so that business can be part of the solution to the challenges of

[6]Gunther Teubner, Societal Constitutionalism: Alternatives to State-Centered Constitutional Theory? in *Transnational Governance and Constitutionalism* 16 (Christian Joerges, Inger-Johanne Sand & Gunther Teubner eds., Hart Publg. 2004)

globalisation. In this way, the private sector—in partnership with other social actors—can help realize the Secretary-General's vision: a more sustainable and inclusive global economy.

The Global Compact is a purely voluntary initiative with two objectives:

- Mainstream the ten principles in business activities around the world
- Catalyse actions in support of UN goals

To achieve these objectives, the Global Compact offers facilitation and engagement through several mechanisms: Policy Dialogues, Learning, Country/Regional Networks, and Projects. The Global Compact is not a regulatory instrument—it does not "police," enforce or measure the behavior or actions of companies. Rather, the Global Compact relies on public accountability, transparency and the enlightened self-interest of companies, labour and civil society to initiate and share substantive action in pursuing the principles upon which the Global Compact is based. It should come as little surprise that the ten principles look suspiciously like the core provisions of the recently abandoned Norms. International institutions—unable to compel at the international level and unsuccessful in binding states to implement framework legislation that harmonizes and coordinates regulations—must cooperate with the objects of their regulation, transforming and cajoling the Norms into a voluntary conduct code. For example,

"[c]ompanies initiate their participation in the Global Compact through a leadership commitment by their CEO and (where appropriate) Board that is communicated to the United Nations. Business and other societal actors also engage directly in the various engagement mechanisms that the Global Compact offers at the global, regional and local level, such as practical solution finding, identification of good practices and projects on the ground."

The Guide follows a similar approach. Like the United Nation's Global Compact initiative, the Guide seeks to provide a vehicle for the normalization of the practices developed in the now abandoned Norms through a program of voluntary practice. "Many of the companies that have contributed to this Guide, especially the companies involved in the [Business Leaders Initiative on Human Rights], agree that the content of the Draft Norms provides a helpful framework for human rights in business." The specific contribution of the Guide is to provide a "technical manual and a hands-on toolkit to help any company integrate practices consistent with human rights standards into an existing management system." The Guide is interesting as a form of voluntary regulation developed from collaborative efforts between communities of multinational enterprises and international institutional actors operating as partners, rather than as source and subject of regulation. The horizontal nature of their relationship, necessary for the production of this code and the code's voluntary nature, suggest the extent of enterprise autonomy and the way in which new institutions are being developed for the regulation of increasingly autonomous entities.

The business of generating rules that serve as a substitute for traditional law making among the community of multinational enterprises and those actors, (governmental and private, national and international) with a stake in their governance has only continued to grow since the end of the last century. In addition to state-centered voluntary initiatives like the OECD Guidelines, a number of other actors have also sought to promote forms of voluntary trans-border regulation of behavior for economic enterprises. Some have been produced by other sectors of the international institutional community. For example, the International Labour Organization has produced the ILO Declaration on Fundamental Principles and

Rights at Work, aimed at regulating the relationship between enterprises and their labor forces on a global basis. Other non-state global players—for example, international human rights organizations like Amnesty International—have developed voluntary codes. Another is the Sullivan Foundation's *Global Sullivan Principles of Social Responsibility* ("Global Sullivan Principles"), endorsed by a large number of major economic enterprises. The thrust of the Global Sullivan Principles is similar to that of the Norms—centering on the promotion of human rights, anti-subordination principles in the workplace, labor organization rights, and sensitivity to development issues in local communities based on a respect for the law.

Many of these codes evidence the power of self-regulation within the community of multinational enterprises. Some originate within organizations serving economic enterprises themselves. These represent the glimmerings of the constitution of multinational enterprises as an autonomous community of entities that have begun to regulate themselves through the construction of systems of governance independent of the states. For example, institutional market organizations have developed voluntary codes aimed at multinational enterprises and others that access capital through their organizations. Similarly, companies offering indexing services for enterprises seeking to participate in the capital markets have also produced voluntary codes and reporting systems designed to enhance business access to capital by compliance with its codes. For example,

> [t]he FTSE4Good Index Series has been designed to measure the performance of companies that meet globally recognised corporate responsibility standards, and to facilitate investment in those companies. Transparent management and criteria alongside the FTSE brand make FTSE4Good the index of choice for the creation of Socially Responsible Investment products.

In addition to collaborative projects between economic enterprises and international institutions that result in regulation like the Guide, other aggregations of like-minded multinational economic enterprises have formed groups for the purpose of creating systems of self-regulation. An example is *Social Accountability International*, an American-based non-governmental organization with representatives from a variety of economic entities that have developed a voluntary workplace standard for enterprises, the SA8000. Like the Guide, the SA8000 is "based on international workplace norms in the International Labour Organisation conventions and the Universal Declaration of Human Rights and the UN Convention on the Rights of the Child." Compliance-seeking companies can either have their facilities certified as SA8000 compliant or become part of a "Corporate Involvement Program". Institutionally, the organization acts as facilitator and conduit of information. Another is the *Caux Round Table*:

> an international network of principled business leaders working to promote a moral capitalism. The [Caux Round Table] advocates implementation of [its] Principles for Business through which principled capitalism can flourish and sustainable and socially responsible prosperity can become the foundation for a fair, free and transparent global society.

The voluntary regulation movement is important for a number of reasons unrelated to self-regulation. But in the context of my discussion, this movement strongly suggests that self-regulating behaviors can succeed without a significant social and political foundation. Recent scholarship has begun to suggest that a transnational class has been emerging that not only drives the shape and speed of globalization, but also manages globalization instrumentally through the transnational corporation. Leslie Sklair:

> attempt[s] to show how a new class is emerging and how it pursues people and resources all over the world in its insatiable desire for private profit and eternal accumulation. This new class is the transnational capitalist class, composed of corporate executives, globalizing bureaucrats and politicians, globalizing professionals, and consumerist elites.[7]

Much of the analytical framework is grounded in a sophisticated reworking of traditional Marxist-Leninist critiques of its arch-nemesis—capitalism.[8] But that stance ought not to blind those skeptical to the value of Marxist-Leninism as ideology to the utility of the important insight of the rise of international networks of economic, political, and cultural elites who together can serve to provide a necessary protection for economic entities against the reach of the regulation of any one state. Building on the work of Pierre Bourdieu. Sklair is right to conclude that the autonomy of multinational economic entities—what he characterizes as global capitalism:

> is augmented with ownership and control of other types of capital, notably political, organizational, cultural, and knowledge capital.

Of course, significantly more empirical research is necessary to explore the contours of this new global class of individual actors connected through dense webs of economic, political, public, private, educational, and other institutional ties. But even the preliminary glance offered through this article suggests some important connections reinforcing enterprise autonomy. Thus, for example:

> — [t]he Caux Round Table was founded in 1986 by Frederick Phillips, former President of Philips Electronics and Olivier Giscard d'Estaing, former Vice-Chairman of INSEAD [business school of management], as a means of reducing escalating trade tensions.
>
> — At the urging of Ryuzaburo Kaku, then Chairman of Canon, Inc., the [Caux Round Table] began focusing attention on the importance of global corporate responsibility in reducing social and economic threats to world peace and stability
>
> — Olivier Giscard D'Estaing, in turn, is a founding member of the World Future Council Initiative, whose leadership includes members of a global economic and political elite, the goal of which is "to challenge the short-term commercial thinking that currently has veto power over global decision-making." Social Accountability International's SA8000 standard is implemented in coordination with a global web of consultants to industry. The secretariat of the Voluntary Principles on Security and Human Rights organization includes the International Business Leaders Forum and the Business for Social Responsibility ("BSR"). The former "works with business, governments, international

[7] See Leslie Sklair, *The Sociology of the Global System* (2d ed., Johns Hopkins U. Press 1995). "The building blocks of [global system] theory are the TNCs, the characteristic institutional form of economic transnational practices, the transnational capitalist class in the political sphere and in the culture-ideology sphere, the culture-ideology of consumerism." Leslie Sklair, *The Transnational Capitalist Class* 4 (Blackwell Publ. 2001)

[8] For a discussion of the Marxist-Leninist variant of this argument in the context of sovereign debt and its relationship to non-Marxist-Leninist anti-globalization stances, see Larry Catá Backer, Ideologies of Globalization and Sovereign Debt: Cuba and the IMF, *24 Pa. St. Intl. L. Rev.* 497 (2006); see also R.J. Barry Jones, *Globalisation and Interdependence in the International Political Economy: Rhetoric and Reality* 23–30 (Printer Publishers 1995).

agencies and other stakeholders to create new partnerships that help both business and communities to flourish."

The latter "acts as a trusted intermediary between business and civil society. While understanding business and serving its needs, BSR maintains strong relationships with other key stakeholders and opinion formers in the civic and public sectors." Quite like Sklair's thesis, BSR also explains that it:

> is part of a growing global network of national organizations that promote awareness of [Corporate Social Responsibility ("CSR")] and provide business leaders with opportunities to collaborate and network with innovative managers across all industries, geographies and functions. BSR also works collaboratively with numerous other CSR, corporate citizenship and sustainability organizations throughout the world, such as Business in the Community in the U.K., the Council for Better Corporate Citizenship in Japan, CSR-Europe, Accion Empresarial in Chile, Instituto Ethos in Brazil, and MAALA in Israel. BSR is a founding member of EMPRESA, a network of CSR organizations in the Americas. An international network of state and non-state actors, creating ever more complex webs of regulatory mechanisms in which the territorial state is just another (though quite important) actor, reinforces the idea of enterprise autonomy—the growing reality of enterprises now in control of their assets, freed of their owners, and freed from any one set of regulations. It is the autonomous enterprise, rather than capital, labor, or the state, that now defines itself with reference to those stakeholders. A nexus of contract, but one in which the autonomous enterprise now plays a role every bit as important as the other stakeholders traditionally considered the sum of its parts.

We introduced the construction of a theory of institutional autonomy from a century of debate about the nature of economic entities, in which the concept of a person plays a major role. There is asset partitioning in the context of the multinational enterprise, which can be usefully understood as fleshing out the contours of the way in which organizational law shapes enterprise autonomy for creditors. That leads to suggesting the possibility of enterprise autonomy from shareholders in a global context. With the latter, one encounters the perverse utility of the ancient territorial principle and the principle of regulatory hierarchy in the global context to suggest the possibility of enterprise autonomy from the state. Putting these three puzzle pieces together, one concludes that the nexus of multinational enterprises and globalization provides a foundation for the emergence of self-conscious, autonomous, self-regulating economic enterprises.

Asset partitioning has made possible the organization of enterprises whose assets are autonomous of shareholders and reside in the enterprise. Realist capitalism has made it possible to organize corporations whose governance is autonomous of shareholders. With assets and governance vested in an organization independent of the individual stakeholders, the enterprise is subject only to the direct regulation of the state. Globalization has made the autonomous and self-regulating enterprise possible by reducing the power of state regulation of the entity. Enterprises freed of shareholder control and the nexus point of enterprise debt that can disperse regulatory control will have effectively achieved self-regulation. From an institutional perspective, the enterprise will have achieved a status that begins to resemble that of the state.

The current consequences of the rise of the self-regulating enterprise are already being felt in at least two respects. The first is evidenced by the growing movement for such enterprises to form regulatory communities. The rise of voluntary codes of conduct and other similar mechanisms of behavior regulation attest to the growing power of enterprises to free themselves from the regulation of states. The second is evidenced by the efforts of international political communities to attempt to substitute a global legal regulatory order for that of the states. The international community has already confronted the reality of a global economy in which autonomous, self-regulating entities wield enormous authority. The United Nation's human rights institutions have sought to impose an international legal regime on the regulation of enterprises whose asset and control dispersions (by distribution of capital and control on a worldwide basis through a controlled group of subsidiary enterprises) transcend national boundaries to the detriment of states and their citizens. These efforts have been unsuccessful. Diversification of debt permitted enterprises a certain independence from their creditors. Asset partitioning permitted enterprises to consolidate an institutional presence. Diversification of shareholding augmented the institutional power of the enterprise (and its managers) as against owners. That diversification permitted a certain (and sometimes almost complete) autonomy of enterprises from their owners. The dispersion of regulatory power among a number of states, like the dispersion of ownership, continues the process of enterprise institutional augmentation. That dispersion of regulatory power will significantly reduce the regulatory power of states and increase the autonomy of entities. The extent of the regulatory autonomy of enterprises will continue to be a significant issue.

This question in the twenty-first century is very different from that in the nineteenth or twentieth centuries. Today an economic enterprise can insulate its assets within itself. It can disperse its assets among enterprises—each an independent juridical person. It can exist independent of its shareholders. It can own itself. It can exist independent of the regulation of any singular political community. It can choose the set of regulations to which it wishes to subject clusters of assets. It can regulate itself. For the economic enterprise able to disperse assets and operations worldwide and access capital markets around the globe, the essential role of law of the economic organization appears to be to enhance the ability of the multinational economic enterprise to become an autonomous and self-regulating enterprise.

Things I: Property: The Legal 'Thing' as Artwork

Roberta Kevelson

Introduction[1]

In several recent studies I have introduced the concept of a Legal Esthetic as seen from the viewpoint of modern Semiotics, especially from the theory of signs associated with the pragmaticism of Charles S. Peirce and subsequently with the main actors in the movement in American Law which derived from Peirce's theories—Legal Realists. For example, when the Realists describe the process of judicial decision-making as a creative process they are not speaking figuratively only; they point out that the activist judge is actually making new law, and must in various ways employ that art and craft of creator in order to be able to make ne Jaw. At the same time it's crucial to be able to preserve the illusion that the particular legal system which the judge represents as the highest legal actor is a stable social force upon which the general public as well as other legal actors, e.g., lawyers, may be able to predict with high probability the outcome of cases and the directions for free activity within that given society.

The inventive capacities of the judiciary, from the Realists' viewpoint, are only the most immediate controversial aspects of creativity in law: the analogy which compares taw with art is ancient, however, and in some cases the agreement at law is an artform may be the only point of agreement between otherwise opposing legal theorists, e.g., between a Blackstone on the one hand and a Llewellyn and a Frank on the other. This strange alliance on the notion of Legal Esthetics between otherwise antagonists will be returned to.

What is especially interesting for legal semioticians on this particular point of agreement which links the legal positivist with the Legal Realist is that their shared analogue which compares law with art centers not on discursive or verbal conceptual

[1]**Source:** KEVELSON, Roberta: "Property: The Legal 'Thing' as Artwork" in: *LAW AND SEMIOTICS,* Vol. III. Springer 1990. pp 193–209.

R. Kevelson (deceased)

J.M. Broekman, L. Catá Backer (eds.), *Signs In Law - A Source Book,*
DOI 10.1007/978-3-319-09837-1_24

components of either art or law, but on a more elemental aspect of both law and art, namely on abstract spatial configurations implied in the ideas of art and law which become expressed as each social system develops in its respective way which often fails to reveal their shared spatial bases. In fine art, for example, the spatial relationships become marked in artworks; while in law the underlying spatial relationships upon which societies are organized tend to become expressed in van datable terms, i.e., in concepts such as Legal Land and Real Property.

I appreciate the fact that in introducing a new concept, such as the semiotics of Legal Esthetics I may be trying the patience of my colleagues who may not be assuming, as I am assuming, that the idea of Esthetics is only incidentally the 'study and criticism of artworks, and more pointedly is the investigation of normative value, as Peirce understood the term "value" in his theory of signs. It isn't as though the "Esthetics" as used in current literature has achieved a standard meaning which is used in a standard way in discussions of aesthetic functions; rather the term, Esthetics, like any viable and rapidly changing idea—like any actual phenomenon in flux—has not been drafted and accepted as authoritatively drafted, as a technical legal term may be so defined and drafted. The notion of Esthetics is about as amorphous as is the notion of legal semiotics, and no more nor less amorphous than is the entire project of field of general semiotics despite ongoing and tireless attempts to pin down this young not-yet adolescent activity with a predicate or two.

There are several approaches I have taken in previous studies on the legal esthetic and its social function from the perspective of legal semiotics: e.g., in *Peirce, Paradox, Praxis* (Mouton: 1990) I compare the legal concept of Land with the metaphysical notion of space especially as the idea·of space developed especially through the Schoolmen, e.g., Duns Scotus, and from the impact of canonical law on civil law in both the Romanesque legal systems in Europe and the common law system in Great Britain. In this paper I will only mention in passing how this confluence of metaphysical space and legal land can be presumed to have had an impact on Peirce's thought, especially in the emergence of the iconic sign function as the first stage in all semiotic processes: e.g., it is the iconic function, we recall, which represents the idea before the mind in its spatial relations, as diagram, map, image of any kind, and, I emphasize, may appear as an area or body or surface which geometrically represents the beginning of any idea or thought or sign-system. The representation of ideas in an imagistic and spatial manner is the beginning of the cognitive process, it is now generally agreed. But Peirce anticipated this recent breakthrough in our knowledge nearly a century ago, before psychology became a discipline, or system of inquiry in its own right.

To briefly digress the assumption that law may serve instrumentally as a means for observing social values, i.e., for the ethical norms which law attempts to represent in everyday life, is closely tied to various notions through history of law as an imagistic sign of social principles and the referent supportive values which act as goals of social organization. In various ways the imagistic function of law in relation to social values has been described: sometimes as reflection or mirror-image; sometimes as refracture, i.e., as a cubistic or kaleidoscopic transformational kind of representation. The kaleidoscopic aspect of law as a bearer of social value is especially marked in

Legal Realism, as I have written (Kevelson, 1988) and it supercedes the Benthamite emphasis on the cenoscopic and idioscopic methods of observation of any phenomenon including ideational phenomena, as Bentham describes in several of its major works. Bentham's emphasis on the observational aspect of all understanding of ideas, or sign-systems, became an intrinsic part of his jurisprudence. We cannot discuss this in detail here, but will remark in passing that Peirce was profoundly influenced by the Benthamite approach to observation and to knowledge of systems of practical affairs, e.g., law and economics as well as political systems of all kinds. But Peirce realized that a major limitation of Bentham's observational instruments was the fact that he assumed a finite world, a closed universe, and hence a society which could be subject to axiomatic and truth-like rules.

Peirce, by contrast, established semiotics as a method of inquiring into open and dynamically evolving systems, and such systems, which rested upon absolute truth but upon hypothesis and simulated "as-if" suppositional beginnings. Peirce's theory of signs, as I have written (Kevelson, 1987, 1988, 1991) assumes that the initial basis for inquiry is not a thing, but *is a relationship between relate functions, of which one is defined and the other of ways vague and indeterminate.* This indeterminate situation becomes also in Dewey the occasion for his logic of inquiry and for his prodigal idea of *Art as Experience,* as evolving experience, which sets out from the awareness of a paradoxical situation.

I have elsewhere described the indeterminacy in law, in open legal systems in particular, as analogous with an indeterminacy which occasions the aesthetic experience in Peirce's and Dewey's pragmatism, which the latter directly carries into his philosophy of law and which directly becomes integral with the principles for Legal Realism which developed through Justice Oliver Wendell Holmes. Hopefully my brief commentary on the immediate background of this paper will provide an adequate context for the main focus here, namely, the *idea of the modern corporate or business lawyer as the principal artist in the law, whose medium is Property, especially Real Property, i.e., Estates and Tenure, and whose instruments for creating his artwork are those special legal instruments categorically known as legal Things.*

This paper will use Lawson's now nearly thirty-year old paper, written before the advent of legal semiotics as a special field for inquiry, and will examine some of his main ideas, especially the idea that of the three categories of legal instruments—Persons, Operations, and Things—it is Things which has been sadly slighted. Lawson says that a legal analytical approach to Things has trailed far behind the relational approach to the legal instruments known as Procedure and Persons.

The symbolic or representational semiotic functions of each of these categories of legal instruments are generally known by the terms Corporations, Contracts, and Estates, respectively. Thus, for our purposes here, the Thing is the Instrument. The notion of Legal Land is inseparable from the notion of Legal Estate or Real Property: to use Peirce's terminology, we may regard the term Estate as the general or typical term, and see the idea of Land as the token or extension of the sign-type Estate.

What makes Lawson's article doubly interesting in our attempt to identify the appropriate area for semiotic investigations of Legal Esthetics is that his main agent or principal creator is the unlikely character and persona, the corporate or business lawyer. Our modern myths disclose an anti-hero, i.e., a hero not apparently heroic but, on the contrary, seemingly the antithesis of the Great Individual who invites distrust and suspicion in the modern world, who may assume the form of a Kafkaesque insect, a Peer Gynt, a Little Tramp, a Mickey Mouse. They are Little People, anthropomorphized and sub-human, or people prone to victimization in all forms: but they are rarely agents initiating acts of leadership and power. Hence, the corporate lawyer has also escaped attention and suspicion as hero, but nevertheless, if Lawson's thesis is correct, he/she is the Haephaestos of the modern age of legal artwork. Every day, in cubicles and sometimes even lavishly appointed corporate offices, clerk-like people create Estates and other Legal Things which transform the marketplace, and thus directly impact on the world of everyman's values, and they dangle such public figures as Donald Trumps like puppets from master-strings. The media networks rarely if ever report on the consequences of the creative activity of the corporate lawyer. Rarely if ever are there headlines which emphasize the appreciation, in hard currency terms, of this kind of artwork compared for example with the price that a Picasso or a Van Gogh or a Pollock bring at a Christie's or Sotheby's auction.

We don't want to confuse the corporate lawyer and his particular art and craft with the art of the entrepreneur or even with the art of the arbitrageur. These latter are arts to be sure but are less directly connected with the law as an instrument for creating and directly generating new social values than is the lofty or more often unlofty art of the business lawyer. The business lawyer creates nothing, which resembles actual commodities, but he does create such Goods and Properties which act as a broad foundational base for the modern nation-state and its respective citizenry, and by extension this act through international trade, multinational corporations, globe-trotting individuals, and national boundary-crossing ideologies. The artwork or Property, which the modern corporate lawyer creates, is a legal concept or rather a Class of legal concepts—a semiotic sign-system of the most complex kind.

What is also of particular interest in Lawson's study is his thesis that the corporate lawyer, as *artist* and creator of internationally transferrable, and *transformable* Property, flourishes only in those kinds of societies which encourage and idealize the idea and actual practice of a maximally free market place. But, in those societies, which *discourage* the ideal of the free market place, i.e., in socialistic rather than capitalistic societies, to use the terms in a general and customary way, the art of the corporate lawyer is almost nonexistent.

There is a basic structural difference in the process which each kind of social organization predominantly relies upon in order to achieve its identified goals and values: in brief, the notion of common goal and cooperative activity characterizes the society committed to socialistic values; by contrast, reciprocity—the give and take of exchange—characterized the goals of a society which values the free market place. The first-mentioned structure may be presented by two or more persons combining their resources and strengths in order to pull a prize toward them, which they will ultimately share, or to extricate themselves from danger which is seen as a common threat. The second-mentioned structure represents the belief that every reciprocal activity, i.e., every exchange of goods among persons of equal or equivalent power, results in an increase in the quantity or amount of goods available for further exchange. With respect to this latter system, *it* is the model for Peirce of his theory in the dynamic increase of information with every exchange of information in dialogic discourse: something is always added in the process of exchange which is not there from the beginning, but becomes created as a direct consequence of the exchange-activity itself, (Kevelson, *Method of Methods,* 1987). This idea is central not only to Peirce's theory of signs, but it also is the main underlying assumption, and sometimes explicitly developed thesis of the Prague School approach to semiotics in the 1920's and 1930's, prior to the beginning of World War II and the cessation of the Prague School activities as such.

For example, Jan Mukařovský's theory of the aesthetic function as a social fact is inseparably tied to his idea of the process of dialogic exchange of meaning in conversation: with each semantic reversal the I and Thou, as shifting addresser and addressee, or reciprocating players in the creation of new meaning, becomes added to and assimilated with the message-as-transactable goods between principals.

It is not possible here to examine and compare the Peircean and Praguean approaches to art as they might be complementary in developing a framework for a semiotics of legal Esthetics. In this essay it must suffice to call attention to it these affinities. It is useful, however, to mention that the Prague School originated as a major center for semiotic theory and for the investigation of semiotic processes in language, in drama, in economics, in law, and in fine art, as a direct reaction against the Russian Formalists. It is impossible to see the action and reaction of these two groups as academic only, since they were explicit in their respective ideological commitments as well, we would necessarily have to accept the assumption of the Prague School, namely that a work of art—i.e., any bearer of the aesthetic function which need not be restricted to works of art as formally classified—carries with it the value-message of the contextual ground with which it is always a relational function and contributive part. Thus works of art in the fine-art sense carry political messages and represent legitimated values implied or explicit in such authorial systems as law. And reciprocally, but with different emphasis, instrumental or overtly practical social systems are also bearers of the aesthetic function and message, which predominate within a conflicting structure of values in any given society at any given time.

In brief, to use the Peircean icon-index-symbol designations of sign-functions, we may say that the predominant sign-function of a work of fine art in a given society is symbolic; but the predominant sign-function of the more explicitly practical institutions of a given society are indexical in that they serve to point to the set of "codes" of social values—values presumably those upon which public opinion and public knowledge rests. And the sign-function, which conjoins fine art as social institution or sign-system with the aesthetic component of such practical, pragmatic systems as law, economics and politics, is the iconic sign-function. In the visual and even performing arts, in music as in architecture, the function of the spatial relationship is primary, or so it has been claimed. But with respect to the institutions of law, economics and politics I want to suggest that the spatial, iconic relationship is also primary relationship. Further, if we follow Peirce, we see that the creation and development of ideas, even those, which must necessarily take the form of verbal discourse, also begin with a spatial, iconic relationship. Peirce shows that the underlying logical structure of all formed verbal discourse, all verbal discourse, is of a conventional nature, i.e., is a kind of discourse and not only a network of signs, as a sign-system. The iconic relation or sign-function characterizes the different logics of different forms of reasoning and verbal exchange, as configurations of logical structures, or systems of thinking.

Since we are here concerned with understanding how and why social values come to be functional forces in all aspects of social organization, and since the law is a vehicle for recognizing and stabilizing such values as well as acting as a vector for Introducing new values into a society, we want to investigate relationships between legal concepts and the consequences of such concepts. For example, a concept, in a Peircean sense, has meaning only if it makes a difference, i.e., if it has consequences for the real world of actuality. Thus we will want to look into the possible consequences of the Legal Thing which produces actual results in the actual, experiential world.

An idea of a Legal Thing is an idea of a legal instrument. This instrument is a device which is not merely ideational, but which may be used, in a practical common sense way. Such an instrument becomes like technological inventions, such as the microscope, a partner in exploration and in further creation of new, possible worlds. This is precisely Jan Hacking's point when, in *Intervening and Representation,* he reminds us that the instruments we use—whether tangible as the microscope, or intangible as a theory—become reciprocal with investigators, and in dialogic relation, for the purpose of creating more of the meaningful world than exists at present. In this sense, by regarding the legal instrument, the Thing, as a colleague in the creation of more meaning and sense of value, the idea of the legal Thing becomes not only the artwork best represented by the Estate, i.e., the idea of Legal Land, and the philosophical principle of the continuum, Space, but also becomes through our interdependence and interrelationship with it the means for creating new aesthetic objects and new artworks, just as new implements for applying oil to canvas produce new kinds of paintings, new meaning, and new representations of emergent social values.

Since this introductory section of my paper has presented an overview, which, although brief, has covered a great deal of ground, the remaining time will be in two short parts: 1) will present and comment of Lawson's article in some detail, and 2) will raise specific questions for further investigation.

Finally in summary I will recapitulate some major assumptions, which underlie this particular direction into a semiotics of Legal Esthetics, and I will suggest how the idea of a Legal Esthetics may further develop Peirce's notion of the Esthetics as the Science of Values. The creative force of the law and the law an art-form will be briefly restated, with the ideals of the Realists and their emphasis on the paradoxical and indeterminate aspect of law presented as desirable rather than unavoidable. The suggestion that Real Property in law be viewed as an instrument for creativity of and through law rather than as an obsolescent concept, as seen by some critics and others, will be the concluding point of this paper. The concluding open questions will reintroduce some problems of space, self-motivation, agency-and-action, and causality into the general idea of Legal Land viewed as a legal artwork.

The subtitle of this paper, "13 Ways of Looking at Estates in Law," is a way of paying tribute to the poet Wallace Stevens, who transformed much of his life as a Real Estate broker and an insurance broker, into poetry. Stevens has long been recognized as a semiotician unaware that he would ever be so-called, or that such a term would emerge to describe the multiple perspectival kind of observation which we find especially in his "13 Ways of Looking at a Blackbird," arid especially in his hallmark image, the basic slate, which represents the permanence and change of the paradoxical space of experiential surfaces. The underlying principle of Stevens' poetry, in accord with the mathematical principle that best characterized Peirce's theory of signs—The Whole is Greater than the Sum of its Parts—is that same belief Lon Fuller holds when he suggests that law ideally provides freedoms to make alternatives, to choose from among them, and so create new possibilities, new art.

Legal Instruments—Legal Artworks; Things, Operations, Persons

F.H. Lawson is best known as an expert on Property Laws, especially in Anglo-American Legal Systems. Much of what he has written has to do with the textbook study of the laws of property, but in this singular paper Lawson writes on "The Creative Use of Legal Concepts," (New York University Law Review 32:A957: 909–924, at 917) and stresses that not only has the doctrine of estates been curiously neglected by both lawyers and legal theorists, but it is most unfortunate since it is the doctrine of estates which "expresses with extraordinary forces and completeness the essentials of the law of things." By neglecting this particular instrument of the law, i.e., the instrument of legal things, there is far too little understood about the laws of capital funds, and still less about the relationships—the functional relationships—between the "thingness" of the law and the notion of "personality" of a corporation, with which "thingness" systemically corresponds (Lawson, 1957:917). Further, it is important to understand how lawyers creatively use and invent legal concepts which are all artificial and which are nevertheless representative of or signs of actual counterparts in the actual and phenomenal world. For example, what is generally meant by the "thingness" of an estate in "fee simple" is very close to what is meant by the notion of the land itself, not as a concept but as an actual phenomenon.

In order to avoid the kind of nominalism which loses sight of the actual, experiential world to which the signs of the law refer and which they represent as signs, i.e., as interpretant, Lawson reminds us that all the instruments of law, including that category called "operation," are artifices created by law and adapted for the service of lawyers and their clients.

When one speaks of the ownership of Real Property, for example, it is overlooked too often that "The essential precept of the doctrine of estates … proclaims that ownership cannot attach to land but only to an abstract entity inter posed between that ownership and the land and known as an "estate," (Lawson, *ibidem).* Ownership, in this sense, is a relate, inseparable from its connection with actual land. But the ownership is connected with the land in question only through the legal link of the *idea* of "estate." Ownership of that surface of the earth, which is referred to sweepingly through the legal concept or land is meaningless, i.e., without consequent, if there is not a mediational legal notion of estate in this triadic relationship. This notion of Real Property and the ownership of Real Property requires the semiotic function of a third or mediational force, which in this case is the idea of the legal Estate.

The notion of Estate frees members of the legal society from the limitations which the actual portion of land-property imposes, especially when we talk of divided rights and obligations which are tied to the managements and/or use of an actual lot of land. It is only by creating such abstract "things" as Estates, Lawson says, that we become freed "from bondage to physical things, creating by their side abstract entities which can act as subject and objects of legal relations and so simplify the calculations which business lawyers have to make," (Lawson, 1957: 918–919).

There is a need to understand how the process of creating legal concepts leads to enhanced, real freedom among members of the society served by this kind of legal artwork creation. Lawson proposes that we begin with the instrument of the Legal Thing, since the relationship between the idea of ownership and the idea of Real Property are far more stable, and have a more stable history, than do the other two categories of legal instruments, Persons and Operations.

Although Lawson highly regards the work of Hohfeld and others who have contributed so greatly to our understanding of rights, powers, privileges, obligations, etc., he sees these as *relationships* between legal Persons. Lawson suggests that the relationship approach is really a working backwards, even though we can observe and/or reconstruct that "certain elementary relations have from time to time been combined to form a fairly stable complex unit, such as the *Patria potestas,* the feudal relation between lord and man, the relation of a buyer to a seller, or an heir to an inheritance, the relations of settler, trustee and beneficiary, the group of relations that arise from a negotiated bill of exchange, the interrelated powers and duties comprised in the judicial function, and so on," (Lawson, 1957:919). Such relations become networks that build in pyramidal fashion to more and more complex relations. The problem he presents is that we need to begin with something more elemental than relations between Persons, or even the relations in Operations if we are to be able to construct any model of the creative and aesthetic force which *is* the law in action.

Operations, like Persons and Things, have also developed from some presupposed relational action, from some actual "physical act" in the course of human affairs, i.e., in people's transactions and exchanges with one another. But these physical, experiential acts are always overlaid with ambiguity, with vagueness, which is part of actual experience. Thus the law steps in and creates a symbolical form with which to symbolize this act *as* act. In so creating the form it tends to disambiguate the referent act, and in so doing it reduces the experiential act of its indeterminate characteristic, I would emphasize.

Therefore, Lawson's thesis is expressed in a way that clearly is in the manner of a Peircean approach to a legal semiotics—although he is not at all aware of Peirce, of Semiotics, or of anything, which resembles any currently acknowledged school of semiotics.

One of the major contributions that semioticians continue to make is their ability to lift protosemiotic approaches from other methods of inquiry and adapt them or transform them into resource material for the semiotics project. This is nothing other than a shifting of contents, as it were, from one category to another category of thought. This presupposes, of course, that our categories of topics are not predetermined Aristotelian grids which are superimposed and held fast to the area we wish to investigate. The boundaries of logical categories are fuzzy or vague as Peirce and others hold. The transplanting of ideas to new contexts and new grounds is part of the process of interpretation of signs, and thus part of the semiotics venture. Therefore, in adapting Lawson's notion to the current investigation of Property from the viewpoint of legal semiotics, I am doing nothing new, i.e., nothing which has not repeatedly been done, e.g., in looking at Dworkin, at Hart, at Kelsen, at Searle, at Bentham, at all the others not labeled as pro- or contra-semiotics, but rather seen as important resources for semiotics by semioticians. This adaptation is "traditionally" part of the Semiotics-of-Law project.

Lawson's paper is particularly important since it parallels, Peirce's semiotics approach by recommending that we arrange the instruments of the law as a sequence of functions, beginning with that which represents the surface or phenomenality of space, i.e., of experiential areas, as an iconic function that is represented in law by the created notion or concept of Land, of Estate and Tenure which are the obverse and converse of Legal Landor Real Property. Lawson then suggests that we investigate that instrument which best seems to correspond with Peirce's indexical function and which, in law, is the Instrument of the Legal Operation: the Legal contract is surely an oppositional if structure which exemplifies the Peircean indexical function.

Lawson suggests that it is the relations between persons that are most readily formalizable and symbolized. Yet, as we know, "Legal personality and legal persons are…mathematical creations devised for the purpose of simplifying legal calculations," (Lawson 1957:915). Although the legal artwork called: "Persons" is most easily represented by human beings. Persons are not human beings. Rather, legal Persons are many kinds of objects in law: "They include not only collections of human beings associated for various purposes—from such all-purpose organizations as the state, through churches, local authorities, colleges and universities, clubs and trade unions, to trading corporations …(But) There is a steady drop in resemblance to human persons, until in the end personality is attributed to various kinds of *things,*" Lawson reminds us, "whether individual or collective and even to disembodied purposes," (1957:915).

We have seen that the legal tendency to switch from one instrument such as the Personal to others, such as the Operational or the instrument of the Thing, facilitates the ability of governments to disaffect reciprocal relationships between officials and citizens and, instead, to begin to regard recipients of government largess and entitlements as status kinds of Things rather than human kinds of Persons. There is no opportunity to further discuss this here, but the concept is developed in some detail in my paper on Laws of Succession (Kevelson, *Peirce, Paradox, Praxis,* 1990). There is nothing dehumanizing in the law's switching from one instrument to another. But it does bring about a shifting of human values, of the value-ground which it purports to serve, when it uses the particular characteristic of one legal instrument to do the job which had previously been done by another legal instrument.

It is not only the case that the medium is the message, or in this case, is the instrument-as-sharper of the medium of choice. But we do know that different technologies interact with their perceivers—with us—in such ways as to become part of the information we receive and interpret. Scumbling the surface of the canvas says something very different than delineating an object with the top of a sable brush. A sculpted form in wood shaped with ice-pick arid sharp stone is very different from a finely chiseled and polished piece of marble. Not only the medium but the instrument with which the medium is implemented becomes part of the total process of enacting values, of creating values. The legal concepts are products of human creativity. In point, the concepts, which deal with the Estate are today the artworks of the business lawyer.

Whether or not the corporate lawyer is aware of his power is not our concern, but is rather the concern of the sociologist, the psychologist, the pathologist, etc. Our concern, as legal semioticians, is to be able to describe the process whereby the governing value forces come into existence such that the legal systems of various societies are shaped and expressed by them. And further, our concern is their perceived and perceivable consequences on the actual lives of actual people in those societies where creative law exists and flourishes, and also in those societies in which creativity in and of the law is constrained and for suppressed. The "intent" of the creator is not insignificant, but the intent or awareness of being an agent of a creative act is an aspect of the power of the corporate lawyer that will have to be discussed at some future time.

Reinterpreting "Property"

The argument for Property, long anathema for Marxists, has been seen as a weapon of the right, in the interests of perpetuating the sovereignty of nation-states and continuing social injustices which have been seen as the result of the formation of nation-states engaged in capitalistic trade and market negotiations. At the same time the condemnation of the idea of Property has often come from the same groups of people who demand that society be restructured along dialogic lines, as true communities in which the ideas of mutual aid and reciprocity are paramount.

What is rarely seen is that the notion of reciprocity is inseparable from the idea of Property, or that the idea of pulling together for common weal is not reciprocal activity, according to some legal theorists. E.g., Lon Fuller, in "Freedom, a Suggested Analysis" *(Harvard Law Review* 68 8 1955: 1305–1325) says that there are two basic modes of seeing freedom and social organization, and these are not usually seen as compatible with one another: the first notion of viewing freedom is in the context of a social organization by reciprocity: the second mode is that of freedom in an organization by common ends. The first mode is usually but not always characterized by the idea of "Freedom to" choose from among possible alternatives, whereas the second is usually based on the idea of "Freedom from" that which is perceived as obstacles or constraints of rights and privileges.

Fuller describes the various ways in which the law functions as an instrument in both modes of Freedom. The more the Organization by Common Ends is stressed as a "Freedom from", the less is possibility and indeterminate option open in society, so that the ideal of openness in a "Freedom to" becomes overshadowed and unperceptible. The main question Fuller raises is one that the Legal Realists have raised since the end of the 19th century, and through the difficult years of the Restatements in the 1920's in the United States. The question has to do with creative function that the law assumes in furthering the interests of freedom—both freedom *from* and freedom *to.* The choices that the legal actor makes directly shape the nature and *mode* of freedom which is to become the leading value of the referent society so served.

Years earlier than Fuller's paper, the great anthropologist Malinowski reviewed the important study of Llewellyn and Hoebel, *The Cheyenne Way;* he says here that this study presents itself as a "new instrument for the interpretation of law," and this interpretation becomes, itself, a tool for distinguishing between societies that are shaped by beliefs in deterministic forces and other, more open societies which are based on beliefs in self-determination. Malinowski's work has been for several decades important resource material for semioticians in the areas of anthropology and legal anthropology. In this particular, but neglected review, he points out that creativity within the system of law originated as a form of the occult and of magic, but that the deterministic aspects of primitive magic have now become, agentively and intentionally, creative activities of legal actors. Malinowski suggests that art in law today is analogous with the magic of law in primitive societies.

It is important to mention Llewellyn's very important contributions to Legal Realism, and especially his important study on legal Esthetics. Jerome Frank, another notable Realist, calls attention also to the aesthetic function in law, and he cites the Llewellyn paper, "On the Good, the True, and the Beautiful," (*Univ. of Chicago Law Rev.,* 9 2241942). In recent years, William Twining who has written on important aspects of the Legal Realists, as well as on Bentham and the art/craft of Law, has also been a major contributor to Legal Semiotics. His work on art in law is discussed elsewhere, (Kevelson, 1990). But for now let us recall that when Frank wrote his now famous "Words and Music: Some Remarks on Statutory Interpretation," he anticipated by nearly a decade the first stirrings of legal semiotics and modern semiotics in general. Yet Frank spoke as one of the leading spokesmen for the Realist movement, which as a whole not only recognized the aesthetic function of law, but actively pressed for a concerted development of creativity *in* and *of* the law.

In this paper mentioned above, Frank reminds us that the concern with legal Esthetics is as old as Aristotle; we find continued evidence of it among the Roman jurists who "frequently delighted in the *elegantia juris*," and more recently Frank points out, we find such positivists as Blackstone comparing law with architecture, such that the concept of legal land becomes almost analogous with the physical constructions of edifices in the English landscape. Blackstone suggests an isomorphism which links the conceptual structures of the English countryside. Frank remarks that although Llewellyn and Blackstone were, universes apart with respect to their legal philosophies they were unified in their view that law is a kind of architectural structure, just as architecture takes its rules from rules and principles of law. I will not explore this further here, but wish to mention in closing that there is a correspondence between non-Euclidean geometry in law and theories of space which Peirce developed and which Frank later adapted to the analysis of legal concepts. Frank indirectly took non-Euclidean legal concepts and analogies from Peirce, via Holmes.

The extent to which law and art are interactive has not to this day been closely looked at. The particular overlapping of Place in Law and of Space in Philosophy and in mathematics is, to my knowledge, a brand new can of worms. Yet the ground work is in place. There are unlimited directions to take in exploring a reciprocity between Jaw and art, especially with respect to the notion of instrumentality in art and in law: in art as the medium and mediating, intervening tool for creating new objects of value; in Jaw as the instrumental Thing which corresponds with and is represented by the relationship between Property and Property Owners, or those equivalents with Property Owners under the idea of the New Property (as Charles Reich and others have described).

Given the notion of flexibility and freedom to consider possible options and alternatives in an open society such that values risk-taking and reciprocality of a free marketplace, the notion of Property can become the basis for any relationship between Persons, Operations and other legal instruments that is deemed legitimate by the actual people served by any given system of law. Art is decadent when it becomes deaf to the public pulse; Law is nonlegitimate when it fails to create itself in response to public opinion. The notion of a public pulse as of a public opinion, is multiply ambiguous. Both have continued as forces in conflict with other forces, as Dicey and others have pointed out, in the shaping of the law and in creating of legal concepts *as* social phenomena, (cf A.V. Dicey, *Law and Opinion in England* 1926: London: Macmillan & Co.)

Perhaps one of the most interesting approaches to the relation between art and Jaw and the aesthetic function in social organization is Janet Wolff's *The Social Production of Art* (1981, London: Macmillan & Co.) Wolff is neither Peircean nor Praguean—nor a self-confessed semiotician as a matter of fact. But she brings together art, hermeneutics in the continental theater of discussion on law and politics, and the problem of creating and discovering social values which are just below the surface of "things." Some of her main ideas are developed elsewhere. (Kevelson, 1990).

Finally, I want to call attention to Robert Summers' study, "Evaluating and Improving Legal Processes——A Plea for "Process Values" *(Cornell Law Rev.* 1974:1–51). Summers' thesis is that the legal process as a whole——that which Lawson would have restricted to the concept of legal Operation——is an instrument whereby social values are both discovered and implemented. That is, the law as process is an aesthetic function which is intended to bring about desired values. The intention is that of the legislators. But the legislator may be both Official and nonofficial, I suggest, although this is not part of Summers' argument. Summers' thesis in its carefully limited claim states that legal values are legal process values, and that legal process values are of two kinds: one kind has to do with bringing about the efficient and immediate results in an infralegal framework, that IS, in realizing the aims of the legal system as legal system; the other is the bringing about of results which reach beyond the legal system into the relational social systems of the given society as a whole; in this latter effect, the law is a creative process primarily because it intends to shape the value structure of the society it represents.

Summers paper suggests at first that the values which govern the legal system are integral with the system as a system of ethical-based rules. It is not until we come to the end of this very carefully drawn study that we find that the referent values of the legal process are not an integral part of the system but are brought into the system of law from some kind of ultimate grounds of values, of process values. This stipulated notion of an ultimate ground of values for legal processes is totally undeveloped, but suggest that this grounding may be blueprinted in the elemental, observable and customary modes of interactional behavior that seem to characterize the style of a society in a continuous fashion. I am extrapolating from Summers, since he nowhere makes such extravagant claims.

But Lawson, by contrast, did indeed suggest that the creative aspects of legal activity, not only with respect to Property and Things as a whole, may be reconstructed or reinterpreted such that we may be able to represent the initial physical act of Things, Contracts and Persons in their everyday dealings and in exchanges of goods of all kinds.

Peirce tells us that it is the process only which permits us to investigate phenomena, since the irreducible "thing" of phenomenological investigation is, by definition, not reducible further. Only the process, as far as Peirce says he is able to *say,* can be analyzed into its main semiotic functions of icon, index and symbol. We may thus understand the valency, which moves phenomena to become transformed in a particular direction, toward an ideal goal.

Semiotics provides us with a theory of which pragmatic inquiry is the theoretical method, he says. Means and instrumentation in Peirce's semiotics are synonymous, such that the instruments of the law, as Lawson reminds us, are the corresponding sign-functions of semiotic inquiry in general: thus the legal instrument of the Thing is Iconic; the Operation is the Index; and the Person is the Symbol. From this viewpoint the notion of legal property calls for a phenomenological approach to surfaces, places, and especially land—everything above, below and integral with the surface of the selected area of observation.

Peirce tells us that it is the process only which permits us to investigate phenomena, since the irreducible "thing" of phenomenological investigation is, by definition, not reducible further. Only the process, as far as Peirce says he is able to say, can be analyzed into its main semiotic functions of icon, index and symbol. We may thus understand the valency which moves phenomena to become trans formed in a particular direction, toward an ideal goal.

Semiotics provides us with a theory of which pragmatic inquiry is the theoretical method, he says. Means and instrumentation in Peirce's semiotics are synonymous, such that the instruments of the law, as Lawson reminds us, are the corresponding sign-functions of semiotic inquiry in general: thus the legal instrument of the Thing is Iconic; the Operation is the Index; and the Person is the Symbol. From this viewpoint the notion of legal property calls for a phenomenological approach to surfaces, places, and especially land—everything above, below and integral with the surface of the selected area of observation.

References

Alexander, Peter and Roger Gill, (eds.) 1984. *Utopias* London: Gerald Duckworth & Co., Ltd.

Bauman, Zygmunt, 1976. *Socialism: The Active Utopia* London: George Allen & Unwin.

Bohm, David and F. David Peat, 1987. *Science, Order and Creativity,* London: Routledge.

Clark, Charles E. and David M. Trubek, "The Creative Role of the Judge: Restraint and Freedom in the Common Law Tradition." 1961–2.71 *Yale L. Review* 255–276.

Frank, Jerome, 1947. "Words and Music: Some Remarks on Statutory Interpretation". 47 8 *Col. Law Review,* 1259–1278.

Fuller, Lon L., 1955. "Freedom—A Suggested Analysis" 68 8 *Harvard Law Review.* 1305–1325.

Keeton, Robert, 1961–2. "Creative Continuity in the Law of Torts". 75 3 *Harvard Law Review.* 463–509.

Kevelson, Roberta. 1987. *Charles* S. *Peirce's Method of Methods.* Amsterdam: John Benjamin's Pub. Co.

Kevelson, Roberta. 1988. *The Law as a System of Signs.* New York: Plenum Press.

Kevelson, Roberta, 1990. *Peirce, Praxis, Paradox,* Amsterdam: Mouton de Gruyter.

Lawson, F. H., 1957. "The Creative Use of Legal Concepts" 32 *New York University Law Review,* 909–2.

Malinowski, Bronislaw, 1941–2. "A New Instrument for the Interpretation of Law Especially Primitive" 51 *Yale Law Review,* 1237–55.

Mendelson, Wallace, 1960–61. "The Judge's Art." 109 *University of Penna. Law Review.* 524–38.

Murphy, W. T. and Simon Roberts, 1987. *Understanding Property Law.* London: Fontana Press.

Pick, John, 1988. *The Arts in a State.* Bristol: Bristol Classical Press.

Pound, Roscoe, 1933. "A Comparison of ideals of Law. 1 XLV" *Harvard Law Review* 1–17.

Summers, Robert, 1974. "Evaluating and Improving Legal Processes—A Plea for Process Values" 60 1 *Cornell Law Review.* 1:51.

Vining, Joseph, 1986. *The Authoritative and the Authoritarian.* Chicago: University of Chicago Press.

Waldron, Jeremy, 1987. *Nonsense Upon Stilts: Bentham, Burke and Marx on the Rights of Man.* London: Methon.

Wolff, Janet, 1981/1988. *The Social Production of Art* London: MacMillan.

Things II: Place, Space, and Time in the Sign of Property

Robin Paul Malloy

Introduction[1]

In semiotics, property is a complex sign understandable in triadic terms consisting of what Peirce would call the icon (firstness), the index (secondness), and the symbol (thirdness).[2] In this paper I am interested in exploring some thoughts about the ways in which property, as a sign, transcribes and communicates information about social organization at the level of the iconic. My approach is

[1] **Source:** MALLOY, ROBIN P.: "Place, Space, and Time in the Sign of Property", in: *International Journal for the Semiotics of Law*, 2009. p. 265–277.

[2] Property is both a sign and a symbol in the semiotic method of Charles S. Peirce and in my analysis of property as a sign in market exchange. According to Peirce: "A sign, … is something which stands to somebody for something in some respect or capacity. It addresses somebody, that is, creates in the mind of that person an equivalent sign, or perhaps a more developed sign." See Buchler (1955, pp. 99–100).

Peirce's point is that signs are…anything we know or claim to know we know because it is a sign and interpretable. Persons, places, things, systems – are all signs. Peirce's argument is that signs interpret signs. It is only through the methods of semiotics – the method of methods – that we are able to account for the process whereby our system of signs interprets another system of signs and thus grows, and gives birth to new signs. See Kevelson (1988, p. 239). For a discussion of the structure of legal argument more generally referencing Peirce's triadic approach to semiotics, see Malloy (2004, pp. 71–85). *The numbers in ( ), such as* Kevelson (1988). Malloy (2004) *etc, correspond to the numbers of references at the end of this text.*

R.P. Malloy (✉)
College of Law, Syracuse University, Syracuse, NY 13244, USA
e-mail: rpmalloy@law.syr.edu

J.M. Broekman, L. Catá Backer (eds.), *Signs In Law - A Source Book*,
DOI 10.1007/978-3-319-09837-1_25

influenced by the work of Peirce,[3] and Kevelson.[4] From this perspective the sign of "property" is a conclusion; a conclusion in law based on an interpretation of the relationship among the icon, the index, and the symbol. In diagrams I and II below, I depict this relationship.

In these diagrams property is presented as a sign; an idea with meaning that arises from the ability to place certain interests into symbolic boxes or categories of property types. Collectively these boxes make up our understanding of property. Determining the type of interest that might fit into a given category requires a reference to the presence or absence of certain characteristics of ownership. Moreover, the characteristics of ownership incorporate information at a more fundamental level; that of the icon. It is this fundamental level of the icon that I wish to explore for potential ways in which property might communicate information concerning social organization and the relationships of place, space and time.

In exploring these ideas I proceed in two steps. First, I give a very brief overview of property as a triadic relationship, and second, I explore ideas related to place, space, and time that are captured in the sign of property.

A Brief Overview of Property as a Sign

Property is a complex sign, which is understood to provide owners of property with certain rights, remedies, duties and obligations. Justifications for the support of property take on several forms but for present purposes it suffices to say that property is generally considered beneficial. In deciding if a certain interest is to be considered property, we begin by looking for the standard indicators of ownership; as the core benefits of property center around the ability of owners to capture and create value from the rights attributed to a particular type of property.

The primary characteristics of ownership associated with property include: the right to use and possession; the right to exclude others; the right to transfer; and the right to profits. These rights of ownership may be present to a lesser or greater degree in different categories of property but an interest must share these basic characteristics in order to reach the conclusion that it is in fact a property interest, as opposed to say a contract interest. Property in its various forms and categories is, thus, an interpretation of the characteristics of ownership (of what it means to own).

---

[3] My approach to interpretation theory is grounded in the semiotic theory of Charles Sanders Peirce. See Peirce (1992, 1998). See generally Apel (1995), Buchler (1955), Colapietro (1989), Hookway (1992), Kevelson (1987, 1988, 1993b, p. 17, 1996b), Liszka (1996), Merrell (1997), Noth (1995), Peirce (1992), Singer (2005). For a discussion of the structure of legal argument more generally referencing to Peirce's triadic approach to semiotics, see Malloy (2004, p.71–85).

[4] My work is influenced, in part, by Kevelson's work on the interpretation of Peirce. A sample of Kevelson's work includes: (1987, 1988, 1989, 1991a, b, p. 7, 1992, pp. 189–206, 1993a, b, 1994a, b, 1995, 1996a, b, 1998).

Significantly, these characteristics of ownership are themselves representations of the underlying qualities of property. This means that the observed characteristics of ownership carry within them references to certain basic qualities. Some of these qualities are physical in nature, such as those related to size, shape, and duration of the propertied interest. Other qualities are less tangible and relate to abstract aspects of property as a transmitter of organizing rules related to base ideas of place, and of knowing one's place in the organization of space over time.

The diagrams below offer two ways of representing this triadic approach to the idea of property as a sign. In these two diagrams, property is identified as a sign; a sign in the semiotic sense that embraces Peirce's idea of the icon (firstness), the index (secondness), and the symbol (thirdness).[5] In this triadic approach to the sign of property, meaning arises from a continuous process of semiosis.[6] In other words, the idea of property is a complex and layered one that is embedded with particular characteristics and qualities that inform and are informed by their relationship to each other, and to that of other signs.

[5] Peirce developed a phenomenology based on only three universal categories called firstness, secondness, and thirdness. Firstness is the mode of being of that which is such as it is, positively and without reference to anything else. It is the category of unreflected feeling, mere potentiality, freedom, immediacy, of undifferentiated quality and independence. Secondness involves the relation of a first to a second. It is the category of comparison, facticity, action, reality, and experience in time and space. It meets us in such facts as another, relative, compulsive, effect, dependence, independence, negative, occurrence, reality, result. Thirdness brings a second in relation to a third. It is the category of mediation, habit, memory, continuity, synthesis, communication (semiosis), representation, and signs.

See Noth (1995, p. 41). See Malloy (2000, pp. 29–36), Malloy (2004, pp. 69–114).

[6] See Malloy (2000, pp. 32–36). The relationship between firstness, secondness, and thirdness involves a continuous synthesis of meaning where thirdness can be understood as a tentative conclusion or holding. In a continuous process of synthesis these conclusions are always open to refinement. Peirce identified this continuous process as semiosis.

> Since every sign creates an interpretant which in turn is the representamen of a second sign, semiosis results in a series of successive interpretants ad infinitum. There is no "first" nor "last" sign in this process of unlimited semiosis…thinking always proceeds in the form of dialogue…every thought must adhere itself to some other…this endless series is essentially a potential one. Peirce's point is that any actual interpretant of a given sign can theoretically be interpreted in some further sign, and that in another without any necessary end being reached. The exigencies of practical life inevitably cut short such potentially endless development.

> See Noth (1995, p. 43) (defining the idea of unlimited semiosis).

> Meaning, then, lies not in what is actually thought [immediately present], but in what this thought may be connected with in representation by subsequent thoughts; so that the meaning of a thought is altogether something virtual. Meaning exists only as the dynamic relation of signs. To the degree that life has meaning, it is a train of thought.

See Singer (2005). See generally Eco (1976, 1984). Eco provides a similar interpretation of Peirce. See, e.g., Eco (1990, pp. 28–30, 60).

DIAGRAM 1
Property
(Sign)
(this process is a continuous loop)

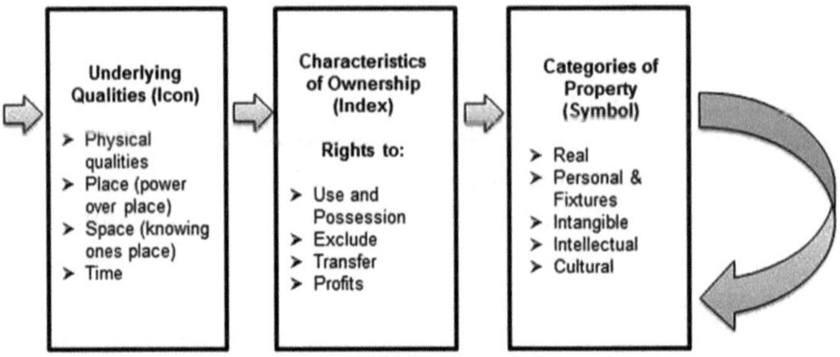

OR

(another way of thinking of this triadic relationship might be as illustrated below)

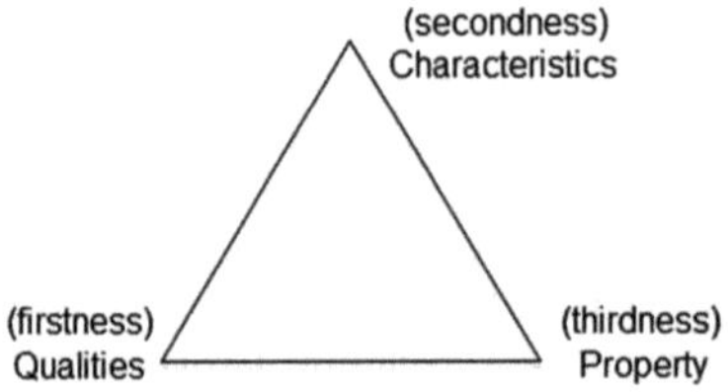

With this as background, let me reconfirm that this paper is not concerned with elaborating the details of property law but rather seeks to explore the qualities of place, space, and time in the sign of property.

Place, Space, and Time in the Sign of Property

At the iconic level, property expresses certain qualities, and in this paper I am concerned with an effort to explore the particular qualities of place, space, and time. I explore these qualities by first examining the idea of property as place, and as the exercise of "power over place". Second, I examine the relationship of place to space, and third I consider the way in which property establishes an important metric of time.

A sense of place is important to human beings and to the social organization of a community. In this regard real property is the most critical of the categories of property identified in the previous section of this essay. Real property establishes a sense of place; a place from which individuals and communities can function with an authoritative influence over their own identity.

To illustrate, let me paraphrase an expression used by some indigenous peoples. The saying goes something like this: "We imprint the land even as the land imprints us."[7] I have always understood this to mean that we give meaning to the places we inhabit even as we to the exclusion of others, and we inscribe a cultural-interpretive framework to organize and regularize our understanding of the various footprints that may appear upon the landscape from time to time. In other words property is not simply about the right to exclude but also about the power to establish and maintain a particular sign system.

In order to exercise power over place, however, we must mark our territory so, that we and others know its reach. We do this marking in a number of ways including: the plowing of fields; the placing of signs, fences, and survey stakes; and, the building of homes, factories, shopping malls, roads, railroad tracks, and damns. As humans, we also mark our territory with language (yours, mine, his, hers, ours), and with juristic and virtually constructed references to such "things" as sea-lanes, flight paths, air rights, meridian lines, metes and bounds measurements, government surveys, and shifting political borders. All of these territorial marks provide information about who we are and how we relate to each other and our environment. They also signal the presence of a given authoritative frame of semiotics and cultural-interpretive reference. Sometimes the observable differences between places with competing cultural-interpretive hierarchies are easily observable, as in comparing the Unites States and Mexico, or in comparing China and the former British colony of Hong Kong.

Further to our efforts of marking place, we also create documents to represent our property and then use these representations to develop new ways of interacting without ever needing to deal with the land itself.[8] We effectively translate place into representations of place and use these representations to form complex layers of property meaning. Thus, we use deeds and leases to represent the actual land to which they make reference. We can then deal with the property by simply dealing

---

[7] See Chatwin (1987), Malloy (1992, p. 1576); Mosley (1989, p. 267).

[8] There are a number of ways of exploring the semiotic functions of property. Other semiotic issues in property markets can be explored by looking at the ways in which property interests are represented by documents such as deeds and mortgages. These documents permit transactions in the underlying land by working with the representations of the underlying interests. This is a key point in the work of Hernado DeSoto. See Malloy (2004, pp. 108–109).

As DeSoto explains:

> In the west,..., every parcel of land, every building, every piece of equipment, or store of inventories is represented in a property document that is the visible sign of a vast hidden process that connects all of these assets to the rest of the economy. Thanks to this representational process, assets can lead an invisible, parallel life alongside their material existence. They can be used as collateral for credit. The single most important source of funds for new business in the United States is a mortgage on the entrepreneur's house. These assets can also provide a link to the owner's credit history, an accountable address for collection of debts and taxes, the basis for the creation of reliable and universal public utilities, and a foundation for the creation of securities (like mortgage-backed bonds) that can then be rediscounted and sold in secondary markets. By this process the West injects life into assets and makes them generate capital.

See Hernando (2000, p. 6).

with is documentary representation. Given a valid deed for instance, one can then obtain a mortgage against the property. The mortgage is itself an abstract and conditional claim against the land while also functioning as a representation of the cash stream to be generated by the monthly payments to be made in accordance with its terms. Furthermore, the cash stream referenced in the mortgage can be used to support the issuance of a security to be bought and sold in the financial markets.

In this linking of the land to the representations of the land, and then to the securities issued against the representations, we can construct a narrative of exchange relationships connected to property. In constructing these potential narratives, property functions as a kind of aboriginal song line, transcribing and imprinting a code of social organization on to the landscape[9]; a code that can be read in the documents, title records, zoning codes, and land use patterns of our built environment and heard in the melodic patterns of financial market activities.

A major chord in this code is one expressing the quality of property as power over place, for property is a tune that always harkens back to place and the meanings imprinted thereon. Without power over place there is no jurisdictional authority to establish a formal sign meaning of property. Property as a sign has little meaning without reference to power over place just as the current understanding of the sign "king" has little meaning in the absence of a corresponding kingdom. A king is a king by virtue of his exercise of power over place. Without a kingdom there is no king, and without power over place there is no landscape upon which to successfully transcribe and imprint a hierarchy of social relationships.

The source of power to inscribe meaning on to land and to establish a code of social organization can vary,[10] but in modern society we generally think of the source of such power as being in the sovereign, in the form of the organized state. Thus, the state exercises authoritative influence over the coding and decoding of the landscape by virtue of its dominion over place. And, property law speaks to us, as the Bishop speaks from his seat, with an authoritative voice that always makes a reference back to a given place, to a given source of dominion, and to a given hierarchy of social organization.[11]

---

[9] See Chatwin (1987), Malloy (1992, p. 1576), Mosley (1989, p. 267).

[10] See Malloy (2004, pp. 16–21) (based on theories of natural rights, distributive justice, economics, and identity for example).

[11] In the Roman Catholic Church the highest religious office is that of Bishop. The title of Cardinal and Pope are administrative, with the Pope being the Bishop of Rome and by virtue of holding that position is also His Holiness, the Pope. Authority within the church rests with the Bishop's and is exercised ex cathedra, meaning from the seat. The Bishops speak with the authority of the church when they speak from their seat of authority. The Pope has a seat as a Bishop at St. John Lateran in Rome and he has the seat of St. Peter as the Vicar of Christ on earth, at St. Peters in the Vatican City. The Church, the Holy See, asserts global jurisdiction but even the Church needs a "place" as a source of secular authority; a place from which to "speak" and anchor its power, in the secular world, the Vatican City State. Similarly, Cardinals, as the "Princes" of the Church must all have titular churches within the Diocese of Rome; without "title" to one of these churches in Rome the person cannot be an acting Cardinal. The property is the connection to place and to the ability to exercise power over place. See generally Bunson (1995).

The recording of social organization in the sign of property occurred long before computers and digital technology took over the mass recording and storing of information. Early on, land presented itself as a stable, predictable, and reasonably accessible medium for the representational coding of social organization. Land uses, patterns of cultivation, and housing all worked to reinforce messages concerning social status and rank.

The beauty of land as a transcriber of social organization is that it is physical and therefore easy for people to understand. When my troops storm across your border, build a road and a fort on your land, and plow your fields to grow our crops it is pretty clear that a new social order is in place. When revolution or decolonization takes place and regimes change, property law reform is typically one of the first items on the agenda.[12] This is because of the centrality of power over place in establishing and maintaining semiotic order and establishing a new community identity. Property, as a coding system of social relationships, functions as a kind of mainframe server and operating system for recording and transcribing relationships over time. And those with authoritative influence over the operating systems of property function like Microsoft Corporation to control the meanings, values, and relationships recognizable within the system. Thus, when European colonial powers arrived in the "new world" they observed no property rights in the aboriginal people they encountered.[13] The sign of property was different as between the indigenous and colonial powers, not to mention inconsistent with colonial aspirations for the Americas. The colonial powers established new laws and new interpretive references as they went about building forts, roads, housing, and fencing to inscribe a new order upon the land.

To establish and maintain a new semiotic order, the abstract action of changing laws is often accompanied by clear, symbolic and physical acts that communicate the message of a change in power over place. Thus, after defeating the Scotts, the English imposed new ordering rules and also drove the point home by placing the Stone of Scone, on which Scottish Kings were traditionally crowned, under the English Throne. In this way the English made visual their dominion over the Scotts by literally placing the seat of Scottish authority securely beneath the seat of England, and signaling the British Crown's power over place. Henceforth there was but one seat of government and one place from which to speak authoritatively. And, in a visual demonstration of the recent arrival of devolution in the U.K., the Stone has since been conditionally returned to Scotland to symbolize the devolution of particular elements of authority from the central to the more local government.

Property as power over place is also a foundation for the exercise of jurisdiction, as all American law students come to appreciate in making their way through the

[12] See Allen (2000) (discussing the rights to property, meanings of property, and the significance to property reform in decolonization).

[13] See e.g. Johnson and Graham's Lessee v. M'Intosh (1823). In this famous case studied by first year property law students in the United States, the Supreme Court explains the reasons that native people have no title to land and that there can only be one source of dominion over land and place.

infamous case of Pennoyer vs. Neff in their first year of law school.[14] In Pennoyer the court held that one must be present within the boundaries of the jurisdiction to be subject to the authority of the State; thus, further recognizing that power arises from place and is exercisable with reference to place. When one is within the jurisdiction of a given state, one is subject to its power over place and to its meanings, values, and rules of social ordering.

By making references back to place, property law identifies and organizes many social relationships. It designates and distinguishes among those people with property, those without property, and those who are property. It also establishes a variety of particularized exchange relationships such as those of owners and trespassers, landlords and tenants, mortgagors and mortgagees, present possessory interest holders and future interest holders, all with legally prescribed duties and obligations; organized and prioritized with reference to land. Property and its recordation transcribe a visual and physical record of power effectively communicated in much the same way as was achieved by placing the Stone of Scone under the coronation seat of British monarchs.

In this way property defines jurisdictional authority and denotes the decisional hierarchy for resolving a wide variety of cultural-interpretive disagreements. A problem arises, however, with the advancing of interstate and global commerce, as place becomes increasingly ambiguous in such market exchanges.[15] This is a problem that American law students contend with in studying cases that came after Pennoyer.[16]

When marketplace becomes market place, ambiguity of reference and dominion enter into the exchange. This is because markets, in contrast to property, are about transcending place and exploiting demographic opportunities across space. Markets, like juristic and virtual references to flight paths, sea lanes, and internet highways can extend out and across jurisdictional lines. To the extent that they are places, they are abstract and ambiguous in a way that real property is not. With ambiguity of place, conflicts can arise along the fault lines of exchange. This arises from competing and underlying cultural-interpretive values that exert tension on each other in the form of competing claims to property.

One can observe some of this tension playing out in the European Union as many established property law rules are being challenged under provisions of the European

[14] See Pennoyer v. Neff (1877).

[15] In the modern world of globalization the problem becomes one of defining place. Countries assert rights to the extraterritorial application of domestic law and this introduces complex problems of conflicts of law and conflicts of dominion. When trade, people, and markets extend across artificial and political boundaries imposed upon the physical earth it becomes difficult to maintain a distinct hierarchy of social organization because trade, people, and markets function as vehicles for reciprocal change.

[16] Later cases deal with interstate and global commerce, with the validity of marriages and divorce as between different jurisdictions and a host of other issues. The situations raise questions about presence in the state, doing business in the state, having significant contacts with the state, and other criteria for figuring out whose law applies to a given conflict.

Convention on Human Rights.[17] Dominion is shifting from member States to the EU center and the meanings of the sign of property are also in transition.

Similarly, the more people travel and do business on a global scale the greater the risk of ambiguity in the meaning of property. In order to reduce this ambiguity business enterprises, frequently based in North America and Europe, attempt to impose their own domestic property law on the meaning of the transactions they undertake. They do this in an effort to protect their property and their economic expectations but in doing so they simultaneously transport certain underlying values embedded in the iconic level of property. These underlying values are not simply concerned with the technical language of property, they go to the essence of what it means to own, and who has the power to own and exchange property on particular terms. Property is a cultural-interpretive conclusion based on particular underlying characteristics and qualities that are value based and grounded in the experiences of a given cultural-interpretive community. This can lead to tension and conflict played out in the language of property while masking underlying conflicts in the encoded meanings and values attached to property.

Power over place also carries with it a sense of "knowing one's place"; where knowing one's place relates to the space one occupies in the socio-legal hierarchy of place. In this respect place is not one dimensional, place is multi-dimensional. Place occupies space. In relation to physical place, space adds such things as subsurface rights and air rights to the idea of land rights. And, within the socio-political order, we might think of this in terms of creating space for multiple hierarchies within a given place, such as in having a federal government system with multiple and co-equal branches of government, and a corresponding system of regional and local government entities. Through exchange one might also find a way to reorganize space by trading interests and reallocating property rights. This permits the development of significant (thus meaningful) sub-hierarchies and sub-networks of social interaction.

We can extend this idea of space. For example, property law can take a given physical place and create space for both present and future interest holders. It can also redefine the Common Law concept of owning property from the center of the earth to the heights of the heavens by creating new interests such as the shared spaces of condominiums and time-share housing. At the same time property may impose barriers that segregate people within a given place by controlling the space available to people based on such factors as income (price of a ticket, for example) or other characteristics such as race, religion, age, and gender. These barriers may be express, as in laws excluding women from certain jobs, or they may be indirect, as in segregating low-income people from certain upscale neighborhoods by requiring

[17] We can observe an aspect of this in the European Union. In the EU, the European Convention on Human Rights is giving pause to considerations of previously settled matters of property law in individual member states. A number of basic property law concepts and approaches to property law regulation have been challenged under the human rights convention. One of the consequences of the EU is a rise in ambiguity as to certain legal conventions, and meaning as the idea of power over place shifts. See Allen (2005).

all houses to be built with a minimum of 5,000 square feet and located on lots of at least one full acre. Such requirements price out large numbers of people even though the neighborhood is technically a place open to all. Other ways of achieving the same end include developing neighborhoods with no sidewalks, no public transit, and no shopping within reasonable walking distance.

In property, the hierarchy of space is often referenced in relational pairings.[18] For example, property creates status-based relationships in which owners are generally favored over non-owners and likewise with landlords favored over tenants, and lenders favored over borrowers. In this way property not only fixes assets it transcribes a cultural-interpretive hierarchy of status-based relationships, and thereby encodes a reference to power over place as well as a reference to knowing one's place.

Property is not only embedded with information about place and space, it also encodes a metric of time and history. Property typically marks time in terms of lives in being and with reference to the happening of significant events such as death, birth, marriage, and divorce. Time and timing are central themes in property. We can quickly see this by citing a short list of examples: consider that property creates estate interests situated in time (fee simples seemingly lasting in perpetuity, life estates, and leasehold estates); property also divides estates in to units of time making such things as the time share condominium possible, and splitting future interests from those of the present.[19] Property is financed by payments made over time (mortgages); has numerous rules linked to moments in time such as the doctrine of equitable conversion, the doctrine of merger, laches, foreclosure, the equitable rights of redemption, the statutory right of redemption, the perfect tender rule, and the notorious rule against perpetuities.[20] In addition, property rights can be created over time with the concepts of adverse possession and prescriptive easements; or eliminated by concepts such as laches and abandonment.[21]

Property prioritizes competing claims to an interest based on principals of "first in time, first in right", as modified by recording statutes.[22] And property addresses claims and defects in property over time in terms of curative acts and marketable record title acts that eliminate errors and competing claims over time.[23] At the same time, property is not simply linear. In property, time can sometimes be altered and rewound using concepts such as subordination, subrogation,

[18] See Malloy (2000, p. 31 (relational pairing)).

[19] See Edwards (2005), Sheriff (1994, pp. 303–317).

[20] See Edwards (2005, pp. 137–172) (rule against perpetuities), Malloy and Smith (2007), Sheriff (1994, pp. 333–334) (rule against perpetuities).

[21] See Sheriff (1994, pp. 141–178 (adverse possession), 200–210 (prescriptive easement)). Laches is an equitable remedy which bars a person from recovering an interest in property even though she may be first in time. This is on the grounds that she waited too long to bring the action; she "slept on her rights".

[22] See Malloy and Smith (2007, pp. 231–312).

[23] Ibid.

and relation back. In such situations law, by fiat, spins back the hands of time and reorders the priority of events.[24]

Property organizes time and records the history of social relations over time. In property law we can find the encoded history of African Americans as real property, and then as personal property (prior to eventually being declared persons),[25] of women losing their propertied identity under the laws of coverture[26] and of racial and religious restrictions embedded in discriminatory land covenants (restricting at various times in U.S. history sales of land to blacks, Jews, Catholics, Native Americans, Asians, and others). In property, because all interests are judged for validity by the law at the time of their creation, history and the embedded values of power over place never fully die; instead they ripple across the sea of time generating path dependent currents and undertows that property lawyers contend with for generations into the future.[27] Thus, we find remnants of the Spanish law of community property still at work in the American Southwest, provisions for usufructs in the remnants of French Civil Law in Louisiana, and concepts such as riparian rights as remnants of English Common Law in the states east of the Mississippi in the United States. Likewise, principles of ancient Roman law remain embedded within the laws of many nations. The significant semiotic point is that these are not simply remnants of earlier law; they are ideas that carry traces of values encoded in the sign of property and transmitted across distant generations.

Therefore, from the perspective of property transactions, property anchors the present in the past and forges a continuous chain of title linking all propertied events back to an original sovereign. Property thereby marks time in relation to an unbroken chain of authority that transcribes and translates a code of social organization across space and time, with reference to place. The chain of title that marks propertied time is flexible enough for bending and twisting, it is after all not a rod or pole, but it is also rigid enough to deny a lapse into aboriginal dream time, religious conceptions of spiritual time, or meditational notions of freeing one's self from time. Property anchors and constrains time.

---

[24] See Malloy and Smith (2007, pp. 455–461 (subrogation), 503–508 (subordination)). Relation back involves the legal fiction of having a later act treated as if it was done at an earlier date. For example, in a construction project a contractor may be doing work prior to the filing of a mortgage by a third party lender on the project. Because the contractor started work before the lender had its mortgage in place it has priority of payment for work already done, and under the relation back doctrine may have priority of payment for all future work done even after the mortgage is properly in place. In other words the future work relates back to the date of the start of work for priority purposes.

[25] See Noonan and John (2002, pp. 35–50). Eventually persons of African descent become recognized as persons under the

U.S. Constitution. This example, a stark one in U.S. history illustrates a way in which property constructions over time reveal shifts in underlying qualities and values.

[26] Under traditional Common Law throughout most of the 19th century a married woman had no legal ability to deal with property because she was not recognized as having any legal rights independent of her husband. In contrast a single woman could deal with her own property.

[27] See Malloy and Smith (2007, pp. 231–312).

The cumulative effect of the embedded qualities of a formal property law system is that it creates a sort of internet highway of information related to social organization linked to important exchange elements of place, space and time. Using the internet metaphor, the property system links innumerable individuals and transactions in a chain of relationships and integrates them into a coherent framework capable of facilitating exchange across broad networks where users need not be familiar with each other. In this way, a formal property law system connects individuals to a central network server, so to speak. And just as value is dramatically increased when workers go from using individual/stand-alone computers to connecting to a network, so does value increase by connecting numerous ownership interests to an integrated property law system. At the same time we come to appreciate that participation in this network does not erase differences in meaning. E-mail messages are often misinterpreted when the reader is confused by the word choice, abbreviated spellings, and "tone" of a message. Likewise, being a property owner in the United States, for example, does not bear the same or equivalent meaning as being a property owner in China. Property has a complex meaning and part of that meaning varies based on the underlying qualities that inform the understanding of its sign.

Ultimately, property is more than what we observe with the naked eye. Property, much like the documents we prepare on our computers and send to each other via the internet, contain Meta data—information about the document not visible on the face of the document itself.[28] In this paper I have begun the process of addressing the embedded Meta data of property as it relates to the qualities of place, space, and time. This Meta data, while not readily transparent, gives nuanced meanings to the sign we recognize as "property".

Conclusion

In this essay I discussed the qualities of place, space, and time, and suggested ways in which these qualities encode and permit us to decode meanings and values embedded within the iconic level of the sign of property. I believe that this is useful as it sheds light on the complex layering of meaning in the sign of property, and indicates the importance of digging beneath the layers of symbol and index in uncovering a better understanding of property relationships. Admittedly, this essay is only a starting point for inquiry and it should be read as such. There is much more that can be uncovered and learned by a fuller and more detailed investigation, but for now I leave further investigation to a later date.

---

[28] Meta data is collected and can be uncovered by examining the computer files. For example, when one types a document, information is stored about the date and time of any changes and about the nature of document changes over time. The review of the document itself does not disclose this information but it is nonetheless discoverable. Meta data is often used/presented as evidence in legal disputes.

References

Allen, Tom. 2000. *The rights to property in commonwealth constitutions*. Cambridge: Cambridge University Press.

Allen, Tom. 2005. *Human rights law in perspective: Property and the Human Rights Act of 1998*. Oxford: Hart Publishing.

Apel, Karl-Otto. 1995. *Charles S. Peirce: From pragmatism to pragmaticism*. Amherst: Prometheus Books.

Buchler, Justus (ed.). 1955. *Philosophical writings of Peirce*. New York: Dover Publications, Inc.

Bunson, Matthew. 1995. *The Pope encyclopedia: An A to Z of the Holy See*. New York: Crown Publishing Group.

Chatwin, Bruce. 1987. *The songlines*. New York: Penguin.

Colapietro, Vincent M. 1989. *Peirce's approach to the self: A semiotic perspective on human subjectivity.* Albany: State University of New York Press.

De Soto, Hernando. 2000. *The mystery of capital: Why capitalism triumphs in the West and fails everywhere else.* New York: Basic Books.

Eco, Umberto. 1976. *Theory of semiotics*. Bloomington: Indiana University Press.

Eco, Umberto. 1984. *Semiotics and the philosophy of language*. Bloomington: Indiana University Press.

Eco, Umberto. 1990. *The limits of interpretation*. Bloomington: Indiana University Press.

Edwards, Linda H. 2005. *Estates in land and future interests*, 2nd ed. New York: Aspen Publishers.

Hookway, Christopher. 1992. *Peirce: The arguments of the philosophers*, ed. Ted Honderich. London: Routledge.

Johnson and Graham's Lessee v. M'Intosh, 21 U.S. (8 Wheat.) 543, 5 L. Ed. 81 (1823).

Kevelson, Roberta. 1987. *Charles S. Peirce's method of methods*, ed. A. Eschbach. Amsterdam/Philadelphia: John Benjamins Publishing Company.

Kevelson, Roberta. 1988. *The law as a system of signs*. New York: Plenum Press.

Kevelson, Roberta (ed.). 1989. *Law and semiotics*, vol. 3. New York: Plenum Press.

Kevelson, Roberta (ed.). 1991. *Peirce and law: Issues in pragmatism, legal realism, and semiotics.* New York: Peter Lang Publishing.

Kevelson, Roberta. 1991. *Transfer, transaction, asymmetry: Junctures between law and economics from the fisheye lens of semiotics*. Syracuse Law Review 42: 7.

Kevelson, Roberta. 1992. *Property as rhetoric in law*. Cardoza Studies in Law and Literature 4: 189–206.

Kevelson, Roberta (ed.). 1993. *Flux, complexity, and illusion: Sixth round table on law and semiotics*. New York: Peter Lang Publishing.

Kevelson, Roberta. 1993. *Peirce's esthetics of freedom: Possibility, complexity, and emergent value*. New York: Peter Lang Publishing.

Kevelson, Roberta (ed.). 1994. *Codes and customs: Millennial perspectives*. New York: Peter Lang Publishing.

Kevelson, Roberta (ed.). 1994. *The eyes of justice: Seventh round table on law and semiotics.* New York: Peter Lang Publishing.

Kevelson, Roberta (ed.). 1996. *Law and the conflict of ideologies*. New York: Peter Lang Publishing.

Kevelson, Roberta. 1996. *Peirce, science, signs*. New York: Peter Lang Publishing.

Kevelson, Roberta. 1998. *The law as a system of signs*. New York: Plenum Press.

Liszka, James Jakob. 1996. *A general introduction to the semeiotic of Charles Sanders Peirce.* Bloomington: Indiana University Press.

Malloy, Robin Paul. 1992. *Letters from the longhouse: Law, economics and native American values*. Wisconsin Law Review 1992:1576.

Malloy, Robin Paul. 2000. *Law and market economy: Reinterpreting the values of law and economics*. Cambridge: Cambridge University Press.

Malloy, Robin Paul. 2004. *Law in a market context: An introduction to market concepts in legal reasoning*. Cambridge: Cambridge University Press.

Malloy, Robin Paul, and James Charles Smith. 2007. *Real estate transactions,* 3rd ed. New York: Aspen Publishers.
Merrell, Floyd. 1997. *Peirce, signs, and meaning*. Toronto: University of Toronto Press.
Mosley, Philip. 1989. *Laying down the law: Bruce Chatwin's the songlines and Australian aboriginal concepts of land.* In *Law and Semiotics*, ed. Roberta Kevelson, vol. 3, 267.
Noonan Jr., John T. 2002. *Persons and the masks of the law: Cardozo, Holmes, Jefferson, and Wythe as makers of the masks*. Berkeley: University of California Press.
Noth, Winfried. 1995. *Handbook of semiotics*. Bloomington: Indiana University Press.
Peirce, Charles S. 1992. *The essential Peirce: Selected philosophical writings* volume 1 (1867–1893), ed. Nathan Houser and Christian Kloesel. Bloomington: Indiana University Press.
Peirce, Charles Sanders. 1992. *Reasoning and the logic of things: Charles Sanders Peirce, ed.* Kenneth Laine Ketner. Cambridge: Harvard University Press.
Peirce, Charles S. 1998. *The essential Peirce: Selected philosophical writings* volume 2 (1893–1913), ed. The Peirce Edition Project et al. Bloomington: Indiana University Press.
Pennoyer v. Neff, 95 U.S. 714 (1877).
Roberta Kevelson. Ed: Round Table on Law and Semiotics. 1995. *Conscience, consensus, and crossroads in law: Eighth round table on law and semiotics,*. New York: Peter Lang Publishing.
Sheriff, John K. 1994. *Charles Peirce's guess at the riddle: Grounds for human significance.* Bloomington: Indiana University Press.
Singer, Joseph William. 2005. *Introduction to property*, 2nd ed. New York: Aspen Publishers.

Things III: The Ethics of Property: A semiotic Inquiry Into Ownership

Denis J. Brion

Introduction

In 1840, Pierre-Joseph Proudhon, by way of answering the question, "What is property?", famously asserted, "Property is theft."[1] Although Proudhon engaged in this arresting bit of metonymy to make a polemical point, it does also serve to raise a related question: is property not so much a material substance as it is an abstraction—an event, such as the act of theft, or, perhaps, a process, or an institutional practice?

Similarly, in *The Law as a System of Signs*, Roberta Kevelson asks, "What is property?"[2] By way of setting out how that question might be answered, she proposes "that attempts be made to understand, from a philosophical and semiotic perspective, what is meant by property in order to provide practical law with some instruments for examining judgments and laws and for inspecting the warrants that support such judgments and laws."[3] She asserts that one approach "to the problem of property in law from the perspective of legal semiotics" would attempt "to relate predominant interpretations of property to their underlying logical framework."[4] Such an approach, based on the semiotic concepts of Charles Sanders Peirce, would be particularly revealing because "Peirce proceeds to show that our logic itself is nothing but an 'application of the doctrine of what we deliberately choose to do which is Ethics.'

Source: BRION, DENIS J.: "The Ethics of Property: A semiotic Inquiry Into Ownership" in: *International Journal for the Semiotics of Law*, 1999, p. 247–283.

[1] P.J. Proudhon, *What Is Property? An Enquiry Into the Principle of Right and of Government* (New York: H. Fertig, 1966), 11–12.

[2] R. Kevelson, *The Law as a System of Signs* (New York: Plenum Press, 1988), 270.

[3] Kevelson, *supra* n. 2, at 249.

[4] Kevelson, *supra* n. 2, at 242.

D.J. Brion (✉)
Washington and Lee University School of Law, 1 Denny Circle, Lexington, VA 24450, USA
e-mail: dbrion@cfw.com

J.M. Broekman, L. Catá Backer (eds.), *Signs In Law - A Source Book*,
DOI 10.1007/978-3-319-09837-1_26

Thus logic in applying ethical norms represents truth, or correct arguments. *Ethics represents manifest efforts of will.*"[5] Kevelson therefore argues, that "a semiotic inquiry into property law would seek correspondences between the predominant logic in legal reasoning, the predominant code of ethics in legal practice, and the referent esthetic norms, or values, that govern the ethics and logic of property."[6]

This essay is an attempt to carry out the kind of semiotic inquiry proposed by Roberta Kevelson. The purpose is to answer the question, "What is property?", for the United States common law legal system. Under this system, the judiciary makes up a branch of government that not only is independent of the legislative and executive branches but also functions as something of a "first among equals" among the three branches. Thus, the focus of this inquiry will be on judicial doctrine, the substantive consequence of the ongoing stream of decisions that resolve the disputes brought before the judicial process.

By way of beginning this inquiry, let me relate an anecdote, offer an assertion, and describe a dispute. The *anecdote* pertains to one of the cases that I teach early in my first year law school property course, *New York Ky. Oil & Gas Co. v. Miller*,[7] a decision rendered in 1920 by the Court of Appeals, the highest court of the state of Kentucky. A certain M.S. Miller claimed, but did not own,[8] a nearly seven thousand acre[9] tract of Cumberland Plateau land known in the local community as the "Townsend Tract". Miller seemed not to have alleged that he had lived on the tract, or had put it to any use; tenants of his, however, lived on a part of it. An oil and gas development firm then entered and occupied an unoccupied fifteen-acre portion of the Townsend Tract. Miller initiated an action under the Kentucky Forcible Entry and Detainer statute to remove the interlopers. The statute required that, for plaintiff to prevail, the defendant must have violated Miller's "actual possession" in coming onto those fifteen acres.[10] Although the development firm vigorously contested the action[11] on the grounds that Miller clearly had not "actually possessed" the fifteen disputed acres, the Kentucky Court of Appeals held for Miller.

The Court's opinion is set forth in what charitably might be called legalistic gobbledygook—a discussion of the metaphysical differences among "actual possession", "constructive possession", and "constructive actual possession", and an announcement, for no stated reasons, that the category "constructive actual possession" is abolished.[12] The Court never before had stretched the meaning of the

[5] Kevelson, *supra* n. 2, at 247.

[6] Kevelson, *supra* n. 2, at 253.

[7] *New York-Ky. Oil & Gas Co. v. Miller*, 220 S.W. 535 (Ky. 1920).

[8] Apparently, the ownership of the tract had been disputed among the heirs and devisees of a prior owner, and a grantee of Miller had purchased the rights of several of these claimants. These rights did not, however, amount to good title to the tract. *Miller, supra* n. 7, at 536.

[9] This amounts to approximately 10.9 square miles in area.

[10] *Kentucky Revised Statutes Annotated*, ss.383.200–383.285 (Banks-Baldwin 1970).

[11] They defended the action and lost in the Quarterly Court and then in the Circuit Court before finally losing in the Court of Appeals. *See Miller, supra* n. 7, at 536.

[12] *Miller, supra* n. 7, at 537.

statutory requisite "actual possession" to include so tenuous a presence on so large a tract.[13] Thus, by its decision, the Court clearly was involved in the classic judicial endeavor of making law by interpreting a statutory standard in a way that goes considerably beyond its meaning in everyday usage.

The opinion is altogether conclusory, offering no express rationale for engaging in such a broad interpretation of such common, and commonly understood, words. Close analysis of the case through the course of class discussion, however, reveals that the Court's decision was based on the vindication of the principle of utility.[14]

As we finish our class discussion of this case, it is my habit to pose this question to the students—"Did Miller win because he possessed the Townsend Tract, or did Miller possess the Townsend Tract because he won?" The students, who come to law school expecting to be initiated into the Eleusinian Mysteries of a prior coherent, inclusive, and outcome—determining structure of rules and principles, are brought up short by this question. What is striking is that, each time, at least one or two students will literally begin to hold their heads as if in pain.[15]

The ***assertion*** comes from the renowned "Blackstone's Commentaries." In this seminal eighteenth century treatise, *Commentaries on the Laws of England*, William Blackstone asserted:

> There is nothing which so generally strikes the imagination, and engages the affections of mankind, as the right of property; or that sole and despotic dominion which one man claims and exercises over the external things of the world, in total exclusion of the right of any other individual in the universe.[16]

This concept of "sole and despotic dominion" holds a central place in the American cultural myth.

The ***dispute*** involved a husband and wife, Bonnette and Ronald Askew of Orange County, California. The Askews were undergoing marriage counseling after a relationship of thirteen years that had produced two children.[17] It came out in one of the counseling sessions that Bonnette, although she professed that she loved Ronald, had never been sexually attracted to him. When Bonnette saw the effect that this revelation had on Ronald, she realized that their marriage was irretrievably ended, and she promptly initiated divorce proceedings.

California statutory law establishes a regime of no-fault divorce, requiring that the assets of the divorcing couple be divided evenly between them.[18] In response to the granting of the divorce and the consequent even split of the assets, Ronald then brought an action for fraud to recover $242,000 from Bonnette for money he had earned prior to, and brought into, the marriage. A unanimous jury—made up

---

[13] This is demonstrated by the body of cases dating back to 1816 that the Court cited. *Miller, supra* n. 7, at 536.

[14] This analysis is set out at the text accompanying footnotes

[15] I will [also charitably] assume that this has nothing to do with the quality of my teaching.

[16] W. Blackstone, *Commentaries* 2 (1789), _2.

[17] *See* L. Dizon and M. Pinsky, "Ex-Wife to Pay for Hiding Lack of Desire for Husband", *Los Angeles Times* (Apr. 8, 1993), A1; T. Gliatto, "Those Little White Lies", *Time* (Apr. 26, 1993), 44.

[18] *See* California Family Code, ss.2310, 2550 (West 1994).

of six women and six men—returned a verdict in Ronald's favor, an outcome that threatened to erode an important aspect of no-fault divorce by rejecting an implicit correlate, "no-fault" marriage.[19]

Analysis

Judicial Doctrine—Legal Culture

By way of inquiring into "the predominant logic in legal reasoning, the predominant code of ethics in legal practice, and the referent esthetic norms … that govern the ethics and the logic of property", I will attempt to weave this rather disparate melange of anecdote, assertion, and dispute into something of coherence as well. And I hope thereby to make the modest point that property is not a thing but instead is a state of mind.

Beginning students come to law school with the typical lay conception of the law as an *a priori* coherent structure of principles and rules. According to this conception, judicial decision-making is a process of deduction, classically proceeding in this mode: 1. The Rule, 2. applied to the Case, 3. determines the result.

The accuracy of this conception is, however, belied by the traditional scholarly work of legal academicians—much of which is devoted to explicating judicial doctrine. This is the endeavor of canvassing the judicial decisions relating to a particular issue or to an area of the law and deriving, by the process of induction, the apparent rules and principles that determined the Results reached in these decisions. This statement of rules and principles is then presented as judicial doctrine, the determinant of the Results in similar future disputes.

The product of these efforts at explication, however, typically possesses two rather interesting characteristics. First is the matter of coherence—take, for example, any multi-volume treatise on a particular area of American law. Select a volume and open it at random. And then, for the first textual statement on which your glance falls, look at the footnote associated with that statement. The typical footnote will begin with an often-lengthy list of case citations that support the statement in text. What is striking, however, is that the footnote will then continue with what is often an almost as lengthy list of cases that support the opposite proposition. That is, the corpus of judicial decisions relevant to a particular issue does not readily yield doctrine that forms a coherent whole. A text-writer is able to achieve coherence only by rejecting much of the data that his investigations yield.

The second characteristic is what might be called the matter of endurance. Whatever comprehensive doctrinal statement a legal academician might derive from

[19] The judgment entered on the verdict in favor of Ronald Askew was reversed on appeal by the California Court of Appeals on the basis that it did undermine the thrust of no-fault divorce. See *Askew v. Askew*, 28 Cal. Rptr. 2d 284 (Ct. App. 1994).

a body of decisions turns out to have a relatively short shelf life.[20] Multi-volume treatises, for example, incorporate a feature almost unique to the law—the periodic supplement to be tucked into a pocket at the back of each volume, or, even more flexibly, loose-leaf binding to accommodate the periodic issue of revised pages. Single-volume treatises typically appear in multiple editions; a leading text on the law of torts, for example, has appeared in five editions over a period of forty-three years.[21] Thus, though the substantive content of doctrine changes over time, it does not progress toward a comprehensive and coherent rational structure of rules and principles. Because of these characteristics, it does not provide a strong basis for predicting the outcome of future cases, thereby supporting the inference that it is not strongly determinative of Results. It is these characteristics that led one of the prominent Legal Realists, Karl Llewellyn, to assert, "What these officials [of the judicial process] do about disputes is, to my mind, the law itself."[22]

It is, of course, often the case that disputants, upon seeking legal counsel and becoming informed of the content of the relevant doctrine, then settle their dispute instead of proceeding to litigation. Miller, for example, having demanded without success that the interloper leave the fifteen acre parcel, might then have consulted an attorney, who would have told him that the Kentucky Court of Appeals had never before held that the nexus that Miller had with that parcel satisfied the statutory requisite "actual possession" for bring a Forcible Entry and Detainer action. At that point, Miller might have decided that this was, after all, just and that he would not pursue an action against the interlopers. Or, he might have considered it to be unjust, but that the expense of going to litigation would likely outweigh the value of the less than certain prospect of convincing the judiciary that the interests of justice supported treating his nexus with the parcel as "possession" under the statute. In either case, he would have acted *as if* judicial doctrine supplied a rule that determined the outcome to the dispute that he had with the interlopers.

When disputants instead do proceed to litigation, it is the strong tendency of trial judges to follow the doctrine of the appellate courts in their jurisdiction when they rule on motions and on the instructions that the opposing counsel have offered. If, after judgment has been entered, neither party takes an appeal on these rulings, then, again, the disputants have acted as if judicial doctrine has supplied rules that determine the outcome to the dispute.

When, however, disputants then proceed to the appellate level, it is there that doctrine no longer functions as the determinant of the Result. It may well be that the appellate court reaches a decision that is *consistent with* doctrine; it does not, however, arrive at the Result as *a consequence of* doctrine. That is, doctrine is not determinative

[20] A trenchant and exhaustive account of the dynamism of the substance of judicial doctrine is set out in M. Horwitz, *The Transformation of American Law, 1780–1860* (Cambridge, Mass.: Harvard University Press, 1977).

[21] What began as W. Prosser, *Handbook of the Law of Torts* (St. Paul: West Publishing, 1941) is now W.P. Keeton *et al.*, *Prosser and Keeton on the Law of Torts* (St. Paul: West Publishing, 5th ed. 1984).

[22] K. Llewellyn, *The Bramble Bush: On Our Law and Its Study* (New York: Columbia University Press, 1930), 12.

of the Result. When an appellate court is asked to review a judgment of a trial court, the question that the appeal raises necessarily is *whether* to follow precedent.

This is demonstrated not only by the non-linear dynamism of doctrine but also by the very fact of the judicial opinion—if doctrine were fully determinative, then the appellate opinion would, except in the relatively infrequent circumstances of a unique dispute, consist of a terse recitation of the facts and the relevant doctrinal Rule, with the Result following as a matter of course. The reality of judicial opinions is anything but this. The opinion, though explanatory in form, is, in function, an argument for the justness of the Result. Thus, in a case in which the court follows a doctrinal Rule, it is applying that Rule to this Case not because it is "The Rule" but instead because it is just that this doctrinal Rule be followed in this instance.

What the Kentucky Court of Appeals did in *Miller* provides a compelling illustration of this mode of decision-making. The Result in *Miller*, as we have seen, is the consequence of what has come to be called a "policy choice", the appeal to a particular exogenous value—in this instance, utility—as the basis for the Result. The Court did not in fact mention utility. Instead, it simply announced that the nexus that Miller had with the disputed parcel satisfied the statutory requisite—actual possession—for bringing an action against the interlopers because it satisfied the common law requisite—possession—for an interloper to gain title from an owner. This is the Rule that "determined" the Result. This Rule, however, cannot be found in precedent; instead, the court literally created it as part of its resolution of the dispute.

Once the dispute is set in a broader context, however, the implicit rationale becomes clear. The fact of the matter is that Miller had no antecedent right, either by title or by lease, to support his claim to, or occupancy of, portions of the Townsend Tract; he was, in the locution of the law of property, an adverse possessor. And, interestingly enough, it was this status—in effect, he too was an interloper—that worked in his favor in the course of the Court's resolution of this dispute.

Adverse possession is an ancient doctrine that awards to an individual the ownership of the land of another if that individual takes up possession wrongfully against the title holder and continues to possess it openly for the requisite period of time.[23] This "requisite period" is the time period established by the statute of limitations in which the title-holder must bring a civil action to regain possession from the wrongful possessor. Because A has wrongfully come onto the land of B, then B has a cause of action against A; the statute of limitations provides that B must bring that cause of action within a certain number of years[24]; if A maintains her possession for that period, then, if B has not brought a possessory action within that time, B's title now accrues to A.

The doctrine accommodates two competing principles that are woven deeply enough into the cultural values of the United States to be captured by aphorisms that most everyone, by the age of seven, has at least heard if not actually used—"first in time is first in right" and "use it or lose it". The first aphorism advances the proposition

[23] For a textual presentation of the doctrine of adverse possession, see A.J. Casner, *American Law of Property* 3 (Boston: Little Brown, 1952), 755–838.

[24] In Kentucky, the period is fifteen years. See *Kentucky Revised Statutes Annotated*, § 413.010 (Banks-Baldwin 1992).

that the social order rests importantly on there being an antecedent, and protected, structure of entitlements to land. The second advances the proposition that the utility principle is deeply embedded in the scheme of cultural values; land, in particular, too important to be allowed to lie unused.

In its long course of decisions in adverse possession disputes, the Kentucky Court of Appeals had progressively relaxed the criteria for what was "enough possession" that the adverse possessor was required to maintain in order to gain title to the land from its owner. By 1912,[25] the Court had held that the kind of partial occupancy of a large tract that characterized Miller's nexus with the Townsend Tract did constitute the open and continuous possession required to gain title. By this progressive relaxation of the criterion of possession, the Court clearly was exhibiting a strong tilt toward the utility side of the tension in adverse possession doctrine between antecedent, passive title and active, productive use.

The problem in the *Miller* dispute was one of symmetry. The Kentucky court had, on the basis of utility, relaxed the requisites by which an individual might gain title to the land of someone who was engaging in a passive, unproductive tenure of his ownership rights. The doctrine of adverse possession, however, required that the adverse possession be continuous for the statutory period. And a principal means for protecting that possession from other interlopers, and thereby maintaining the necessary continuity of possession, was the Forcible Entry and Detainer Act.

The course of decisions interpreting the term "actual possession" in that Act, however, had not kept pace in expansiveness with the interpretation of "possession" in adverse possession doctrine. As a result, the adverse possessor, favored as against the title holder, was not as favored as against another interloper. What the court did in *Miller* simply was to bring into alignment the respective interpretations of the term "possession" in adverse possession doctrine and in the Forcible Entry and Detainer Act. And the basis for these expansive interpretations was the utility principle.

Why did the Court create that Rule? Because it supported an outcome in favor of Miller. Why ought the outcome favor Miller? Because that would bring the conception of possession for the purpose of bringing forcible entry and detainer actions into agreement with the conception of possession for gaining title by adverse possession. Why ought these conceptions be brought into agreement? Because that would facilitate the title-capturing course of action of the adverse possessor. Why should the actions of the adverse possessor be facilitated? Because that would serve to put title to land into the hands of the highest-valuing user—that is, the principle of utility is thereby served.

In terms of the mode of reasoning, of course, we have here a considerable departure from formalistic deduction. The Result is the beginning of the process, determined by the exogenous value to which the Court has appealed. The reasoning then proceeds:

1. The Result [Miller possesses the Townsend Tract] implicates the Rule [an individual possesses land when he has *nexus x* with it],
2. which is applied to the Case [Miller had *nexus x* with the Townsend Tract],
3. thereby justifying the Result.

[25] *Burt & Brabb Lumber Co. v. Sackett*, 144 S.W. 34 (Ky. 1912).

There is much to be said about the *Miller* decision. First, the mode of reasoning that the Court followed, which appears to be all but circular, is in fact not at all invalid and, indeed, is not circular. Rather, it is, along with deduction and induction, one of the principal categories of reasoning abduction.[26]

Second, abductive reasoning is not simply a conceptually valid category, rarely followed in practice. Instead, it is ubiquitous. It provides, for example, the foundation for the scientific method.[27] In addition, more than seventy years ago, John Dewey incisively developed several pungent observations by Oliver Wendell Holmes, Jr. about the law into a trenchant description of judicial decision making in terms of abduction and deduction.[28] Dewey built this description on what he termed the Logic of Consequences and the Logic of Antecedents.

Holmes had asserted, "The language of judicial decision is mainly the language of logic. And the logical method and form flatter that longing for certainty and for repose which is in every human mind. But certainty generally is an illusion."[29] Here, Holmes was describing the model of deductive reasoning from *a priori* general premises. Holmes asserted further, however, "General propositions do not decide concrete cases."[30] Instead, he famously observed, "The actual life of the law has not been logic: it has been experience."[31]

In Dewey's accurate description, courts resolve disputes on the basis of a Logic of Consequences:

> As a matter of fact, men do not begin thinking with premises. They begin with some complicated and confused case, apparently admitting of alternative modes of treatment and solution. Premises only gradually emerge from analysis of the total situation. The problem is not to draw a conclusion from given premises; that can best be done by a piece of inanimate machinery by fingering a keyboard. The problem is to *find* statements, of general principle and of particular fact, which are worthy to serve as premises.[32]

The basis of selection, however, is not logical consistency; instead, it is consequences—"that general legal rules and principles are working hypotheses, needing to be constantly tested by the way in which they work out in application to concrete situations."[33]

---

[26] *See* U. Eco, *Semiotics and the Philosophy of Language* (Bloomington: Indiana University Press, 1984), 40; F.E. Kruse, "Toward an Archaeology of Abduction", *American Journal of Semiotics* 4 (1986), 157, 164 and n. 1.

[27] *See* C.S. Peirce, "Rule, Case, and Result", in *Collected Papers*, ed. C. Hartshorne and P. Weiss (Cambridge, Mass.: Harvard University Press, 1931), 372–388.

[28] *See* J. Dewey, "Logical Method and the Law", *Cornell Law Review* 11 (1924), 17.

[29] Dewey, *supra* n. 28, at 20 (citing O.W. Holmes, Jr., "The Path of the Law", in *Collected Legal Papers* (New York: Harcourt, Brace and Howe, 1920), 167, 181).

[30] Dewey, *supra* n. 28, at 22 (quoting *Lochner v. New York*, 198 U.S. 45, 76 (1905) (Holmes, J. dissenting)).

[31] Dewey, *supra* n. 28, at 21 (citing O.W. Holmes, Jr., *The Common Law* (Cambridge, Mass.: Belknap Press of Harvard University Press, 1963), 1).

[32] Dewey, *supra* n. 28, at 23.

[33] Dewey, *supra* n. 28, at 26.

Dewey's description continues, "Courts not only reach decisions; they also expound them, and the exposition must state justifying reasons."[34] The purpose of this exposition "is to set forth grounds for the decision reached so that it will not appear as an arbitrary dictum."[35] And this exposition constitutes Dewey's Logic of Antecedents, which follows the classic mode of deduction from general principles.[36]

And, to understand Dewey's description of these two logics is to understand that the process of reasoning by which the Kentucky Court of Appeals reached its decision is not circular. Using the Logic of Consequences, the Court *determined* the Result by its appeal to the utility principle. This principle, and the Result that it determined, entailed a Rule. Using the Logic of Antecedents, the Court then *justified* the Result by its appeal to this Rule. The *Miller* decision of the Kentucky Court of Appeals is paradigmatic of the process by which courts decide issues.

Third, recognizing the abductive nature of the *Miller* decision and its utter normalcy serves to open up the path to reaching an answer to our question about the materiality of property. It allows us to understand that judicial doctrine—the apparent structure of rules and principles implicit in the *corpus* of judicial decisions—is an epiphenomenon of the judicial process, an all but evanescent quality that arises from an ongoing human activity. It is the consequence of Results and not the determinant of Results.

With this understanding of the nature of judicial doctrine and of the mode of reasoning by which American courts determine the Results of the disputes brought before them, we have determined an answer to the first element of Roberta Kevelson's semiotic inquiry into property law. This element is "the predominant logic in legal reasoning." And our analysis concludes that it is the logic of abduction.

A Basic Question

This leads, of course, to an altogether relevant question—what is the basis for the judicial Result, this endemic judicial practice of abductive "policy choice"? It is one matter to determine that courts resolve disputes by the abductive step of choosing a Result-determining value. It is, however, a different matter to inquire into why a

---

[34] Dewey, *supra* n. 28, at 24.

[35] Dewey, *supra* n. 28, at 24.

[36] Dewey was not, of course, alone in describing the judicial process in this way; he simply used more elegant terminology in which to couch his description. Two prominent judges of the time themselves cheerfully admitted that they, and their colleagues on the bench, decided on the basis of what Dewey termed the Logic of Consequences. *See* J. Frank, "What Courts Do In Fact", *Illinois Law Review* 26 (1931), 645, 761; J.C. Hutcheson, Jr., "The Judgment Intuitive: The Function of the 'Hunch' in Judicial Decisions", *Cornell Law Review* 14 (1929), 274. And, in the 1940s, the prominent dean of a prominent law school, Edward H. Levi of the University of Chicago, in his *An Introduction to Legal Reasoning* (Chicago: University of Chicago Press, 1948), described judicial reasoning in an altogether similar way, without, however, using Dewey's terminology or the term "abduction".

particular court in a particular dispute chooses any one particular Result-determining value. *Why* did the Kentucky Court of Appeals decide to ground the resolution of the *Miller* dispute in the utility principle? As our analysis moves from the material to the abstract, are we describing the law as little more than an *ignis fatuus*? Is the process of judicial choice no more than, in the words of University of Chicago president and disenchanted ex-law student Robert Maynard Hutchins, as he raised his memorable plaint over the assertions of the American Legal Realists in 1934, nothing more than a function of "what the judge has had for breakfast"?[37]

By way of pursuing this question, consider several much-cited judicial decisions involving disputes over land. The first is the landmark 1922 decision of the United States Supreme Court in *Pennsylvania Coal Co. v. Mahon*,[38] in which the Court for the first time held that a regulatory measure instituted by government could violate the constitutional prohibition, "nor shall private property be *taken* for public use without just compensation."[39] At issue was the constitutionality of a statute, enacted by the Pennsylvania legislature, that prohibited the mining of coal in such a way that it would cause subsidence of the land surface to the damage of surface structures.[40] Because the statutory prohibition was adopted in order to advance the public interest, because it had the effect of leaving the rights to the unmined coal without economic value, and because there was no provision for compensation to the holder of the coal rights thereby rendered valueless, the Court held that the statute effected a "taking" of the coal rights in violation of the constitutional proscription.

As in *Miller*, the Court's resolution of the dispute was without direct precedent. As with the *Miller* opinion, a close reading of the *Pennsylvania Coal* opinion makes clear that the Court resolved the dispute by the abductive step of appealing to a Result-determining, Rule-entailing principle. The difference between the two cases is in the abductively-chosen principle.

In *Pennsylvania Coal*, the Court proceeded on a conception of land as a commodity to be divided up, traded, and put to use in order to serve the interests of the individual who holds title to it. Blackstone's "sole and despotic dominion" exactly captures this instrumental conception of ownership. In *Miller*, by contrast, whether an individual has an interest in the land that will be protected from interference depends on whether his nexus with the land serves the utility principle—embodied in society's interest in the aggregate, wealth-maximizing productive use of the land. The *Miller* conceptualization of ownership is instrumental in character, just as the conceptualization in *Pennsylvania Coal* is. The difference is that, in *Miller*, the utility principle

[37] Addressing Karl Llewellyn's then-notorious assertion about the law, Hutchins remarked in an address to a meeting of the American Association of Law Schools in 1934, "The law is what the courts will do. Courts are people. What people do largely depends on their visceral reactions. The law may thus depend on what the judge has had for breakfast." R.M. Hutchins, "The Autobiography of an Ex-Law-Student", *American Law School Review* 7 (1934) 1051, 1053–54.

[38] *Pennsylvania Coal Co. v. Mahon*, 260 U.S. 393 (1922).

[39] United States Constitution, Amendment V (emphasis added).

[40] As is typical of disputes involving mineral rights, the coal company, by deed, owned both the coal in the underlying seam and an immunity from liability for any damage to the land surface consequent on the removal of the coal.

determines that the proper use of the land is to be instrumental to the interests of society and not to the interests of the individual who happens to hold title to it.

The *Pennsylvania Coal* Result strikes the typical American reader of the opinion as almost a matter of course. And it does so because the concepts that deeply underlie it resonate so strongly with the American cultural myth. The iconic Yankee Trader of New England and the Lonesome Cowboy of the frontier West epitomize the concept of the American as the rugged individual, taking what is hers without interference from others and creating value with it through her prowess at work, inventiveness, or exchange. Thus, the *Pennsylvania Coal* Result—if the State seeks to advance the collective interest by restricting the exercise of rights of ownership, then the State is interfering with the cultural essence of the landowner. It can do so only by purchasing those ownership rights through the mechanism of the public power of eminent domain accompanied by the payment of just compensation.

Turn now to another dispute in which the taking issue arose, *Just v. Marinette County*,[41] a decision that the Wisconsin Supreme Court rendered in 1972. At issue in *Just* was the constitutionality of a statutory shoreland protection program that severely restricted the alteration and development of land bordering natural lakes and streams. The statutory program put into effect the thrust of an extensive study of ecological values in Wisconsin that had concluded that these values could be substantially protected by preserving from alteration a defined buffer area bordering all natural streams and lakes. The consequence of this regulatory program, however, was the almost complete loss of the economic value of this riparian land.

When Ronald Just, the owner of a tract bordering a lake, challenged the constitutionality of this program as having taken the considerable second-home development value of his land, the Court upheld its validity, although this outcome was inconsistent with precedent.[42] In reaching this Result, the Court drew on a conception of ownership that was largely implicit in the express terms of the *Just* opinion. Under this conception, the statutorily defined shoreland is the locus of biotic webs of inherent natural value, that the entitlement to this natural value is vested in the people as a whole, and that the people's interest in the integrity of these biotic webs is paramount to the interests of individual owners of parcels of land over which these webs might extend. Thus, the exercise of individual rights of ownership cannot be allowed to violate the integrity of these biotic webs.

The effect of the statutory program was to establish two regimes of rights in the shoreland that the statute demarcated. An individual might have title to a parcel of land the boundaries of which might include shorelands. The people as a whole held a right to the integrity of the natural processes that occurred in these shorelands.

---

[41] *Just v. Marinette County*, 201 N.W.2d 761 (Wis. 1972).

[42] The general standard for determining whether an action of government constituted a constitutionally impermissible uncompensated taking, set out by the Wisconsin Supreme Court in 1966, was whether "the restriction practically or substantially renders the land useless for all reasonable purposes." *See Buhler v. Racine County*, 146 N.W.2d 403, 406 (Wis. 1966). The *Just* court cited *Buhler* with approval, and then tacitly admitted that nearly all use of the land for any purpose was precluded. *See Just*, *supra* n. 41, at 767–68.

An individual holding title to shorelands was prohibited from exercising her ownership rights in a way that might damage the integrity of the natural processes to which the people held the right. Thus, in any parcel of land that included shorelands, there are concurrent ownership rights, and these rights are lexically ordered the rights of the people take precedence over the right of the individual title-holder.

There is, then, a striking difference between the conceptualization of ownership that underlies *Just v. Marinette County* and the conceptualization that underlies *Pennsylvania Coal v. Mahon*. In *Pennsylvania Coal*, the Court, following William Blackstone, treated the land as an instrument serving the interests of the individual owner. The owner, that is, has rights *to*—unconstrained dominion over—the land. In *Just*, by contrast, the rights of the individual owner are not exclusive, but only concurrent with, and subordinated to, the rights held by the people at large. The owner, that is, has rights—a limited, concurrent interest—*in* the land.

Now consider a third case, the 1977 decision of the New York Court of Appeals in *Penn Central Transportation Co. v. City of New York*.[43] The dispute in *Penn Central* arose when a New York City regulatory entity, the Landmarks Preservation Commission, denied Penn Central's request to construct, in the air space above the Beaux Arts Grand Central Terminal, a fifty-five story office tower of contrasting architectural design. The basis of the denial was that the presence of the proposed structure would destroy the considerable aesthetic and architectural value of the Terminal site as an exemplar of a particular significant architectural style. Penn Central challenged this denial as a taking because it was prevented from capturing the considerably valuable development potential of the air space.

The New York Court of Appeals upheld the validity of the Commission's action. In the Court's view, there was no taking because Penn Central's ownership of the Terminal and its land did not include the unconstrained right to determine how they were to be used. Thus, although the development potential of the land might include alternatives carrying considerable economic value, the decision of the Commission did not deny this value to Penn Central because the unconstrained right to pursue it was not an attribute of Penn Central's ownership.

And the Court concluded that Penn Central's right to determine the use of the land, one of the most important incidents of the concept of ownership,[44] was limited because of the synergistic process by which the value that Penn Central had claimed was taken came into being:

> Grand Central Terminal is no ordinary landmark. It may be true that no property has economic value in the absence of the society around it, but how much more true it is of a railroad terminal, set amid a metropolitan population, and entirely dependent on a heavy traffic of travelers to make it an economically feasible operation. Without people Grand Central would never have been a successful railroad terminal, and without the terminal, a major transportation center, the proposed building site would be much less desirable for an office building. Of course it may be argued that had Grand Central Terminal never been built, the area would not have developed as it has. ... But, in reality, it is of little moment

---

[43] *Penn Central Transportation Co. v. City of New York*, 366 N.E.2d 1271 (N.Y. 1977).

[44] A.M. Honoré, "Ownership", in *Oxford Essays in Jurisprudence*, ed. A. Guest (London, New York: Oxford University Press, 1961), 107.

> which comes first, the terminal or the travelers. For it is the interaction of economic influences in the greatest megalopolis of the western hemisphere—the terminal initially drawing people to the area, and the society developing the area with shops, hotels, office buildings, and unmatched civil services—that has made the property so valuable. Neither factor alone accounts for the increase in the property's value; both, in tandem, have contributed to the increase.[45]

This chain of reasoning becomes coherent if the conceptualization of ownership that implicitly underlies the decision posits that an individual does not own property and put it to use in isolation. Particularly, property of the nature of the Grand Central Terminal is located in a larger matrix of land put to intensive use. The use of any particular parcel comes about through the synergistic process of interrelated activities in that larger matrix. Thus, the value of any particular parcel cannot be identified solely with the individual who might hold title to it. Because it is the combined activities of all the landowners in that matrix that determined the pattern of uses and the consequent actual and potential value of each parcel, then the right to determine the uses within that matrix lies in common with the landowner-members of that matrix.

Customs and practices generally, and the way in which land is used in particular, are determined by community consensus rather than by individual interest or initiative. And it is this concept of community consensus that underlies the decision of the New York Court of Appeals in the dispute over Grand Central Terminal. The proper use of land is not what might be determined by the interests of the owner alone, or by the constraints imposed by natural biotic processes, or by the maximization of value aggregated across society at large. Instead, it is determined by the always-evolving patterns of uses that arises through the synergistic actions and interests of the members of the local community in which the land lies.[46]

Finally, consider the 1978 decision of the United States Supreme Court that reviewed the decision of the New York Court of Appeals in the *Penn Central* dispute.[47] The Supreme Court, as had the New York Court of Appeals, held that the decision of the Landmarks Preservation Commission had not amounted to a constitutionally prohibited taking of Penn Central's property. Like the decisions of the Wisconsin Supreme Court in *Just v. Marinette County* and the New York Court of Appeals in *Penn Central*, the effect of the Supreme Court's decision was that Penn Central's ownership of the Terminal and its underlying land included only a limited right to determine how this property was to be used. Thus, the owner had no protected entitlement to the full value of the development potential of the property.

Implicit in the Supreme Court's *Penn Central* decision, however, is a conceptualization of ownership that is different from the conceptualizations implicit in the other two decisions. The Court emphasized the considerable societal value of preserving

[45] *Penn Central, supra* n. 43, at 1275.

[46] For a similar approach, see *Goldblatt v. Town of Hempstead*, 369 U.S. 590 (1962), in which the court upheld a town ordinance that prohibited the use of a parcel of land for a gravel pit because the parcel, several decades after the gravel pit use had begun, had been gradually surrounded by suburban residential development. Thus, the gravel pit use had become incompatible with the pattern of uses that predominated within the community in which that parcel lay.

[47] *Penn Central Transportation Co. v. City of New York*, 438 U.S. 104 (1978).

the Terminal in its architectural setting and the means by which this end is carried out. "The Terminal … is one of New York City's most famous buildings. Opened in 1913, it is regarded not only as providing an ingenious engineering solution to the problems presented by urban railroad stations, but also as a magnificent example of the French beaux arts style."[48] And, as the Court had held on several prior occasions, "States and cities may enact land-use restrictions or controls to enhance the quality of life by preserving the character and desirable aesthetic features of a city. … "[49] And, in this dispute, the restriction on the use of the Terminal property was imposed by "a broad based, 11-member agency assisted by a technical staff"[50] carrying out "the function … of identifying properties and areas that have 'a special character or special historical or aesthetic interest or value as part of the development, heritage or cultural characteristics of the city, state or nation.' "[51]

What the Court approved, then, was the subordination of the interests of the individual owner to the interests of society at large. The subordination was carried out by an institutional entity possessed of particular expertise and the paramount power to act on behalf of the general good. And the effect was to advance social value by limiting the capture of the potential use value of the property by its owner.

This fundamentally hierarchical conceptualization of ownership is, of course, altogether inconsistent with the individualistic tenets of the American cultural myth. It resonates strongly, however, with the historical trajectory of American social reality. By the late nineteenth century, manufacturing enterprise had come to be concentrated in large, hierarchically organized entities.[52] The law of enterprise developed in tandem, with the judiciary largely ratifying the structure that had emerged, justifying it on the grounds that hierarchical control of productive resources through managerial expertise served to maximize aggregate societal wealth.[53] The result was the creation of a large area of discretion on the part of corporate managers, insulating them from control either by private shareholders or by public agencies. In the social realm, the Progressive Movement, which originated in the attempt to correct the harmful physical and economic spillovers of productive enterprise, achieved much of its agenda by ratifying, in turn, the basic structure of enterprise, with the consequent shaping of the social order on a correlative stratified form.[54]

---

[48] *Penn Central, supra* n. 47, at 115.

[49] *Penn Central, supra* n. 47, at 129.

[50] *Penn Central, supra* n. 47, at 110.

[51] *Penn Central, supra* n. 47, at 110 (citing New York City Administrative Code, c.8-A, s.207–1.0(n)).

[52] The course of this development is recounted in A. Trachtenberg, *The Incorporation of America: Culture and Society in the Gilded Age* (New York: Hill and Wang, 1982).

[53] M.J. Sklar, *The Corporate Reconstruction of American Capitalism, 1890–1916: The Market, The Law and Politics* (Cambridge, New York: Cambridge University Press, 1988); M. Horwitz, "*Santa Clara* Revisited: The Development of Corporate Theory", in *Corporations and Society: Power and Responsibility*, ed. W. Samuels and A. Miller (New York: Greenwood Press, 1987), 13.

[54] For a trenchant description, see R. Wiebe, *The Search for Order, 1877–1920* (New York: Hill and Wang, 1967). The social order, though highly permeable, nevertheless was stratified into a small elite class of resource owners, a class of managerial professionals, skilled workers in the production of goods and services, and manual workers engaged in resource extraction.

By implicitly following this hierarchical mode, the Supreme Court in *Penn Central* adopted a conceptualization of individual ownership that departs as strongly from Blackstone's concept of "sole and despotic dominion" as did the Wisconsin and New York courts. According to the Supreme Court's conceptualization, entities established by society are empowered to deploy their expertise in order to determine, on behalf of society, how the individual is to hold land in order that aggregate social value might be enhanced or maximized. Thus, we have come full circle—the United States Supreme Court, by its decision in *Penn Central*, adopted a concept of ownership that echoes the decision of the Kentucky Court of Appeals in *Miller*—the proper determinant of how land should be held and used is the maximization of aggregate social value.

Social Practice

Our immediate inquiry has been to examine the basis on which courts in the United States resolve the disputes before them—on what basis, that is, that they take the abductive step of determining the Result that will implicate a Rule that will provide the justification for the Result. We have considered four decisions, each involving the question whether an action of government that substantially affected how privately owned land might be used violated the constitutional prohibition on uncompensated taking. That is, in each, a particular, and altogether crucial, aspect of ownership was at issue—if we say that such and such person owns thus and so parcel of land, how might that person use that land? And these decisions illustrate a particular pattern of reasoning—in each, a particular conceptualization of the nature of ownership, present only at an implicit level in the opinion, seemed to determine the Result.

In the first of these decisions, ownership was conceptualized in terms of individual dominion—if X owns particular land, then she has a seemingly unlimited right to use it as her interests might determine. She has a right, one might say, *to* the land. In the other three decisions, however, ownership was conceptualized in a quite different way. Rather than individual dominion, ownership embodied a much more participatory concept though X might be said to own particular land, others have concurrent rights in that same land. Thus, how she might use that land is determined not simply on the basis of her interests but also on the basis of the interests of those concurrent rights-holders. She has, one might say, rights *in* the land rather than unfettered dominion over the land. In pursuing the question of judicial choice—on what basis does a court engage in the abductive step of determining the Result?—our examination of these four cases has revealed several matters of interest. The first is the heterogeneity of conceptualizations at the level of judicial doctrine. Each of the three cases that embodied a participatory concept of ownership offered a distinct determinant of the limits on the individual owner's right to determine the appropriate use of the land. And these four cases are illustrative—across the large *corpus* of judicial decisions involving the issue of ownership, United States courts consistently resolve disputes through an abductive mode of reasoning that underlies a heterogeneous pattern of substantive conceptualizations of ownership.

In addition, these several conceptualizations of ownership reflect the general pattern of public discourse and intellectual debate in the United States. Consensus rarely emerges from the divided, and divisive, chorus of voices.[55] Radical environmentalists urge submission to an antecedent natural order[56] and religious fundamentalists to a supreme natural law.[57] Corporate managers extol the benefits of organizing productive activities into large horizontally and vertically integrated entities pursuing wealth-maximizing efficiency.[58] Libertarians argue for the virtues of individual initiative and independence as the wellspring of the country's political and economic greatness.[59] And a New Communitarian Movement paints a picture of reciprocity, solidarity, and mutual care as the solution to the social ills that endemically afflict the citizenry.[60]

Belief Systems

Of greatest interest is that these conceptualizations of ownership that underlie how courts resolve disputes over property resonate so strongly with the anthropological concept of *cosmologies* or *cultural biases*. A cosmology functions as a cognitive filter by which members of a culture understand the reality, which they inhabit:

> Anything whatsoever that is perceived at all must pass by perceptual controls. In the sifting process something is admitted, something rejected and something supplemented to make the event cognizable. The process is largely cultural. A cultural bias puts moral problems under a particular light. Once shaped, the individual choices come catalogued according to the structuring of consciousness, which is far from being a private affair.[61]

---

[55] An English journalist can, for example, remark upon America's lack of "a common religion, ethnicity, or anything much else to hold it together." *See* S. Mallaby, "Stop the Celebration: The case against the Fourth of July", *New Republic* (July 20 and 27, 1998), 19.

[56] *See e.g.,* P. Shepard, *The Tender Carnivore and the Sacred Game* (New York: Scribner, 1973).

[57] For example, televangelist Pat Robertson, commenting on banners put up by the city of Orlando, Florida welcoming gay tourists, observed:

I would warn Orlando that you're right in the way of some serious hurricanes, and I don't think I'd be waving those flags in God's face if I were you. This is not a message of hate; this is a message of redemption. But a condition like this will bring about the destruction of your nation. It'll bring about terrorist bombs; it'll bring about earthquakes, tornadoes and possibly a meteor.

T. Edsall, "Forecasting Havoc for Orlando; On TV, Robertson Says Display of Gays' Flags Invites Disaster", *Washington Post* (June 10, 1998), A11.

[58] For example, Daimler-Benz chairman Jörgen Schrempp commented on his firm's merger with Chrysler in these terms: "This is an historic agreement that will change the face of the automobile industry. . . . [W]e will have the size, profitability, and reach to take on anyone." W. Cook, "Maximum Merger: Oh Lord, won't you buy me the Chrysler Corporation", *U.S. News and World Report* (May 18, 1998), 45.

[59] *See e.g.,* R. Nozick, *Anarchy, State, and Utopia* (New York: Basic Books, 1974).

[60] *See e.g.,* A. Etzioni, *The New Golden Rule: Community and Morality in a Democratic Society* (New York: Basic Books, 1996).

[61] M. Douglas, "Introduction to Grid/Group Analysis", in *Essays in the Sociology of Perception*, ed. M. Douglas (London, Boston: Routledge and Kegan Paul, 1982), 1.

A cosmology, that is, structures the consciousness of the individual by acting on her ongoing experience of her physical environment. The cosmology filters those experiences—"something is admitted, something rejected". And, because it carries out a filtering function, then it must bring criteria of selection to that process—"something supplemented". Criteria of selection, however, necessarily are based on values; they are normative in nature. The cosmology, then, enables a process of interaction of values with experience, with the consequence that experience becomes cognizable—it brings about a matrix of meaning by which the individual is conscious of her place in the Cosmos.

The late novelist Walker Percy provided a useful taxonomy.[62] The Cosmos is all of creation. The Environment is that part of the Cosmos with which the individual reacts significantly; it is the realm of experience. The cosmology enables the individual to have a World:

> The world is segmented and named by language. All perceived objects and actions and qualities are named. Even the gaps are named—by the word *gaps*. … The Cosmos is accounted for willy-nilly, rightly or wrongly, mythically or scientifically, its past, present, and future. All men in all cultures know what is under the earth, what is above the earth, and where the Cosmos came from.[63]

Thus, the World is not a mirror of the Environment; instead, through the filtering process that the cosmology brings about, it is abstracted from the Environment. And, because the cosmology generates a comprehensive explanation of the Cosmos, then the World is *about* the Cosmos.

As the anthropological concept of the cosmology—cultural *bias*—suggests, the cosmology is particular in nature. There is no single, ultimate cosmology; there are instead several cosmologies—several ways of understanding events—each deriving from a particular set of values, each creating a particular bias, and all, taken together, making available for choice mutually inconsistent sets of meanings.

Careful investigation of the phenomenon of cultural bias reveals that there are four basic cosmologies: Individualism, Fatalism, Hierarchy, and Egalitarian Communalism.[64] The particular concepts underlying each can be described in terms of how they define the natural world and human nature.

The Individualist understands the natural world as a benign source of plenty, highly tolerant of intervention, to be enjoyed to the fullest by the exercise of individual initiative using skills developed largely through the trial and error process of technological experimentation. The Fatalist understands it as capricious, a process that goes forward on the basis of antecedent natural laws, having no regard for human interests; thus, the human relationship with the natural world is, in a fundamental sense, a lottery. The Hierarchist understands it as tolerant of human intervention, though within limits; thus, the development and use of natural resources ought

---

[62] This taxonomy is described in W. Percy, *Lost in the Cosmos: The Last Self-Help Book* (New York: Farrar, Straus & Giroux, 1983), 86–126.

[63] Percy, *supra* n. 62, at 100–101.

[64] For an extended, general discussion, see M. Thompson et al., *Cultural Theory* (Boulder: Westview Press, 1990), 1–51.

to be managed by those with particular expertise in order that aggregate human welfare will be maximized. And the Communitarian understands the natural world as being fragile, so that natural resource development and use properly occur within narrow bounds in order to avoid the risk of ultimate ecological calamity.[65]

According to the Individualist's belief about human nature, humans are invariably self-seeking and thus are not malleable—their fundamental nature cannot be altered by the imposition of coercive incentives; relationships are transactional in mode, based on bargain and exchange. To the Fatalist, humans are fundamentally unpredictable. To the Hierarchist, humans are born sinful, although they are redeemable by morally good institutions; thus, human activity must be regulated through institutional restraints. And to the Communitarian, humans are born good; although they can be corrupted by morally bad, coercive institutions, the natural mode of interaction is egalitarian, non-coercive, and cooperative.[66]

These sets of beliefs are grounded in two deep principles. One of these is *Group*—"the extent to which an individual is incorporated into bounded units."[67] The other is *Grid*—"the degree to which an individual's life is circumscribed by externally imposed prescriptions."[68] Thus, the Individualist's core values are low-Group and low-Grid—interactions are transactional rather than relational, and constraints on action are determined through bargain and not by *a priori* binding prescriptions. The Fatalist's values are low-Group and high-Grid-interactions are atomistic, and action is subject to a matrix of antecedent, natural prescriptions. The Hierarchist's values are high-Group and high-Grid-interactions are to be carried out within the framework of ascribed institutions, subject to prescriptions that the institution itself develops and imposes. The Communitarian's values are high-Group and low-Grid-interactions are to be carried out within strongly bounded groups, with egalitarian cooperation determining the flow of relationships rather than prescribed rules.

The individual, we are told, is socially constructed.[69] The anthropological concept of cultural bias tells us that what is constructed is the particular cosmology of the individual. The individual exists both in a physical setting and in a social setting. The particular cosmology enables the individual to organize the experience of these settings in a coherent way, and in consequence to be functional.

And, because, as we shall see, the holding of a cosmology entails substantial emotional and physical investment, the particular cosmology that an individual holds will tend to be enduring. Just as, however, in Thomas Kuhn's description, a scientific paradigm will ultimately fail to solve all of the problems that it is put to use to address,[70] a particular cosmology will ultimately fail to explain all events.

[65] Thompson et al., *supra* n. 64, at 26–29.

[66] Thompson et al., *supra* n. 64, at 33–37.

[67] Thompson et al., *supra* n. 64, at 5.

[68] Thompson et al., *supra* n. 64, at 5.

[69] *See* P.L. Berger and T. Luckmann, *The Social Construction of Reality: A Treatise in the Sociology of Knowledge* (Garden City, New York: Doubleday, 1966).

[70] *See* T.S. Kuhn, *The Structure of Scientific Revolutions* (Chicago: University of Chicago Press, 1970).

Thus, just as a scientific paradigm can eventually break down, to be succeeded by another paradigm, the individual's interaction with her Environment can ultimately lead to the adoption of another cosmology so that she might continue to be functional.

In the social dimension, it is typical that most members of a particular culture hold a particular cosmology, which will form the background assumptions in defining how individuals are expected to act in the public sphere, how disputes are to be resolved in situations of conflict, and how public institutions are to function. The larger the society, of course, the more there will tend to be a mix of cosmologies held by its members. Whether that mix is to be tolerated, encouraged, or suppressed depends upon both political and practical considerations.

Politically, in the United States, the constitutional order is founded on a deep commitment to individual rights. This commitment entails that a pluralism of values be tolerated. To the extent that this commitment is honored, a diverse mix of viable cultural biases will be reflected in political discourse and social practice.

The matter of practicalities derives from the inherent limitations that are a defining characteristic of each particular cosmology. Because of these limitations, a society will tend to break down the more that any one cosmology dominates and the longer that it does dominate. A society dominated by Fatalism will ultimately be incapable of taking efficacious collective action in response to a threat to its viability. A society dominated by Hierarchy will ultimately become so oppressive as to collapse into revolution. A society dominated by Communality will be endemically subject to destructive factionalism.[71] And a society dominated by Individuality will tend to experience an erosion of the social cohesion necessary to engender collective action. Societies that remain enduringly functional tend either to maintain a dynamic mix of cosmologies among its social institutions and practices or to adopt, over time, a succession of dominant cosmologies.

We can now see the significance of the different conceptualizations of ownership that underlie the abductive choices that the courts made in the several cases that we have considered:

1. The instrumental conceptualization in *Pennsylvania Coal Co. v. Mahon* embodies the cosmology of Individualism.
2. The conceptualization of subordination to the integrity of fundamental biotic webs in *Just v. Marinette County* embodies the cosmology of Fatalism.
3. The conceptualization based on the maximization of societal values in the decision of the United States Supreme Court in the *Penn Central* dispute embodies the cosmology of Hierarchy.
4. And the communal matrix conceptualization in the decision of the New York Court of Appeals in the *Penn Central* dispute embodies the cosmology of Communitarianism.

And, on reflection, this ought not be surprising. It ought to be expected that public discourse in a large, heterogeneous, technologically advanced democracy that gives central importance to the political principle of values pluralism reflects a pluralism

[71] *See* Thompson et al., *supra* n. 64, at 83–97.

of values. And, as well, it ought to be expected, in a judicial process, that is adversarial in nature and non-deductive in decisional function, that this same values pluralism is reflected in the abductive bases on which courts resolve disputes.

We have seen that American judicial decision making in disputes over property does not proceed on an antecedent theory of ownership—it is not deductive in mode. The question that we have been addressing is on what basis do American courts take the abductive step of choosing values that determine the Result and implicate a Rule. And the answer seems to be that, in the particular dispute, the court implicitly adopts a cosmology. And the cosmology embodies particular Result-determining values.

We have seen that societies endure in the long term by eschewing an inflexible commitment to one particular cosmology. Concomitantly, the judicial process can proceed on a unitary, coherent theory of ownership, a "philosophy". Or courts can fashion a societal institution—ownership that is enduringly functional. The judicial process cannot, however, do both.

The choice is twofold. Societal institutions and practices can proceed on the basis of values hegemony, by which what people do is made subservient to maintaining the integrity of a prior, consistent structure of rules and principles. Or they can proceed on the basis of values instrumentalism, by which values are made subservient to people as they engage in the ongoing task of creating an enduring, workable social world. The heterogeneity of the doctrine of ownership reflects that the judicial process proceeds on the principle of values instrumentalism.

This understanding of the nature and role of the values that courts adopt as the initiatory step in the process of decision making provides an answer to a second element of the semiotic inquiry into property law that Roberta Kevelson proposed. This element is "the referent esthetic norms, or values, that govern the ethics and the logic of property." As our analysis demonstrates, values govern the logic of property through the abductive step of being adopted as the deep basis for the judicial decision, thereby determining the Result in the particular case. And the values that a court adopts in a particular case are selected from those sets of values that underlie the alternative cosmologies that are available to humans for determining the World that is the characteristic that distinguishes humans from all other organisms.

Mental State

Ethics is defined as the "moral principles by which a person is guided"[72]; the "rules of conduct recognized in certain associations or departments of human life".[73] As we have seen, the "ethics … that govern the law of property" rests on the alternative sets of cosmological values, which function as moral principles. Ethics understood as rules of conduct relates to the acts of courts as they resolve disputes. This in turn relates to the third element of the semiotic inquiry into property law, "the predominant

[72] *The Oxford English Dictionary* 5 (2d edn. 1989), 422 (definition B.II.3.b).

[73] *The Oxford English Dictionary, supra* n. 72, at 422 (definition B.II.3.c).

code of ethics in legal practice". Because we have been proceeding on the proposition that property law in the legal system of the United States is not made up of a coherent set of antecedent rules and principles but instead is the ongoing consequence of what courts do about the disputes before them, then the relevant legal practice in this third element of our inquiry is the process by which courts take the abductive step of choosing a set of cosmological values in order to determine a Result. The question, that is, is: On what basis does a court select among the alternative sets of values that are available?

In order to explore this third element of our inquiry, return now to our California ex-couple, Bonnette and Ronald Askew. In *Sex and Reason*,[74] a book published in the same year in which the Askew marriage ended in divorce, the very prolific Judge Richard Posner of the United States Court of Appeals vigorously argued for a conceptualization of sexual relations in terms of "bioeconomics". According to this concept, the sexual practices of the individual comprise a process of maximizing the satisfaction—utility to be derived from responding to innate biological drives. This is strictly a matter of cost and benefit. Posner argues that the institutions and practices within which sexuality is culturally embedded—such as marriage, family, and sexual relations—are a codification of this individual process of maximizing satisfaction.

The legislative codification of the institution of marriage in California is not inconsistent with Posner's bioeconomics. No-fault divorce is based on the concept that a spouse need not allege blameworthy conduct, such as adultery or physical abuse, in order to establish grounds for obtaining a divorce. Thus, no-fault divorce accommodates Posner's conceptualization that, if a marriage partner, for whatever reason, no longer derives bioeconomic satisfaction from continuing the relationship, then the marriage is to be dissolved. No-fault divorce also implicates a tacit concept of "no-fault marriage"—that it is permissible, indeed axiomatic, that an individual enters marriage solely on the basis that he predicts that, at that time and in those circumstances, doing so will maximize his own bioeconomic satisfaction. Marriage thus is not based on a commitment to establishing a relationship of reciprocal concern and synergistically created value.

The jurors in the Askew fraud trial, however, expressed, by their verdict, an entirely different understanding. By finding that Bonnette had defrauded Ronald, the jurors announced that she had wrongfully entered the marriage, however much she had done so as a rational calculation of bioeconomic satisfaction. The jurors, that is, were rejecting the notion of no-fault marriage. And, by concluding that she must return to Ronald money that he had brought into the marriage, they also rejected the even split of property that no-fault divorce logically entails and therefore the concept of no-fault divorce itself.

There is a clear conflict between Circuit Judge Posner's bioeconomic rationality and the verdict of the *Askew* jurors. Posner's conception of a mating relationship is *dyadic*, a form of biological action-reaction. It proceeds in the mode of rule-based, "if-then", deductive reasoning in which the rules, the major premises, are determined

[74] R. Posner, *Sex and Reason* (Cambridge, Mass.: Harvard University Press, 1992).

by innate physiological drives and appetites—if I itch, and if the satisfaction to be obtained from scratching outweighs the effort required to scratch, then I scratch; if I am hungry, and if the satisfaction to be obtained from grabbing the closest available food and eating it outweighs the effort required, then I grab the closest available food and eat it. In Posner's scheme of things, Bonnette might miscalculate and enter marriage *mistakenly*. She cannot, however, enter marriage *wrongfully*—no blame can attach to her mistake in the sense that, in consequence, she is to be subjected to punishment by a societal institution.

The jurors, however, brought to their deliberations a conceptualization that is *triadic* in nature. Their verdict implicitly rejects a bioeconomic concept of a mating relationship in favor of one that involves moral concepts of fault and redress. That is, it situates the relationship within a matrix of meaning; it makes of it a cultural institution. As an institution, it does not simply reflect the biological environment of the individual. Instead, it is "about" that environment; it *creates* the major premises that determine human action—if I am hungry, perhaps I do not simply eat the nearest available food if it *belongs* (a cultural concept) to someone else.

It appears that the jurors brought to their deliberations a conceptualization of marriage consistent with the Communitarian cosmology. What is important, however, is not so much which cosmology they followed for the purpose of their verdict but instead that their verdict was grounded.

In a cosmology. Their verdict was determined—abductively—by a cultural bias. As we have seen, the cosmology imposes on the (dyadic) experience of the Environment a "sifting process [by which] something is admitted, something rejected and something supplemented to make the event cognizable."[75] The "process is largely cultural."[76] And the World that thereby comes about is a milieu of meaning—"A cultural bias puts moral problems under a particular light. Once shaped, the individual choices come catalogued according to the structuring of consciousness, which is far from being a private affair."[77] The individual's World, then, is the ongoing consequence of a cultural process that structures the consciousness of the individual.

Let us look more closely at this process of consciousness-structuring—what is the nature of this act of choice? William James's trenchant essay, "The Will to Believe", provides a useful way of addressing this question.[78] James's central notion is what he calls a "passional step":

We want to have a truth. … But if a pyrrhonistic sceptic asks us *how we know* all this, can our logic find a reply? No! Certainly it cannot. It is just one volition against another—we are willing to go in for life upon a trust or assumption, which he, for his part, does not care to make.[79]

[75] Douglas, *supra* n. 61, at 1.

[76] Douglas, *supra* n. 61, at 1.

[77] Douglas, *supra* n. 61, at 1.

[78] *See* W. James, "The Will to Believe", in William James: *Writings, 1878–1899*, ed. G.E. Myers (New York: Library of America, 1992), 445.

[79] James, *supra* n. 78, at 463.

James continues, "It is not intellect against all passions, then; it is only intellect with one passion laying down its law."[80] James is arguing that we have meaning—a truth—by making an emotional commitment to "a law"—a set of principles that forms the basis for a normative order. This law, however, is one of a set of alternatives; thus, this commitment arises from a choice—"one volition against another." And this commitment, emotional in nature, is not opposed to reason—James's "intellect"; instead, it is prior to, and an enabling condition of, reasoning.

James's understanding of meaning is entirely compatible both with the concept of anthropological cosmologies and with the description of the process by which American courts resolve disputes as being abductive in nature. The function of James's "law" seems to correspond to the function of the cosmology—it provides the deep values by which the experience of the Environment is subjected to a process of selection and supplementation. The substantive content both of James's "law" and of the cosmology is particular—there is a plurality of value sets available for choice. And meaning thus is the consequence of the act of choice.

What is of particular interest in James's ideas is how he characterizes this act of choice. It is an act of "passion"—a matter of emotion and not of reason. This notion of emotion as the substrate of reason, coming as it does from a protean psychologist, merits exploration. And this can be done by considering an enduring mystery: the nature of consciousness. In particular, consider two tantalizing concepts that have been developed recently in the field of neuroscience, Gerald Edelman's Theory of Neuronal Group Selection and Antonio Damasio's Somatic Marker Hypothesis.

Edelman's Theory of Neuronal Group Selection[81] posits that the nervous system is Darwinian in nature, a system that functions by the process of selection. "The task of the nervous system is … to classify, to categorize, the whole sensory experience of life, to build from the first categorizations, by degrees, an adequate model of the world."[82] And this process of classification goes forward at the level of the neurons, or individual brain cells. Investigation reveals that they function proactively.[83] To classify entails, of course, that some criterion of classification be brought to the process of observation—the very concept of a model, or map, requires the operation of values. And a map is "about" the territory—a triadic relationship—and not a mirror—a dyadic relationship.[84]

An infant is born with innate, basic biases—"values", in Edelman's terms—that are acquired through both evolution and experience, such as preferences for food, warmth, or contact with other people. "These 'values', drives, instincts, intentionalities—serve

[80] James, *supra* n. 78, at 475.

[81] This discussion is based on G.M. Edelman, *Bright Air, Brilliant Fire: On the Matter of the Mind* (New York: Basic Books, 1992) and three thoughtful reviews of Edelman's work: O. Sacks, "Neurology and the Soul", *New York Review* (Nov. 22, 1990), 44 [hereinafter "Neurology"]; O. Sacks, "Making Up the Mind", *New York Review* (Apr. 8, 1993), 42 [hereinafter "Making Up the Mind"]; and J.R. Searle, "The Mystery of Consciousness: Part II", *New York Review* (Nov. 16, 1995), 54.

[82] *See* Sacks, "Making Up the Mind", *supra* n. 81, at 43.

[83] P.J. Hilts, "Listening to the Conversation of Neurons", *New York Times* (May 27, 1997), C1 (discussing the work of the neuroscientist Rodolfo Llinas).

[84] *See* A.M. MacEachren, *How Maps Work: Representation, Visualization, and Design* (New York: Guilford Press, 1995), 213–243; D. Wood, *The Power of Maps* (Guilford Press, 1992).

to differentially weight experience, to orient the organism toward survival and adaptation."[85] The process of making a world proceeds from that beginning:

> It is up to the infant animal, given its elementary physiological capacities, and given its inborn values, to create its own categories and to use them to make sense of, to *construct*, a world—and it is not just a world that the infant constructs, but its *own* world, a world constituted from the first by personal meaning and reference.[86]

As important as these values themselves is the way in which they are experienced:

> It needs to be stressed that "values" are experienced internally, as *feelings*—without feeling there can be no animal life. "Thus", in the words of the late philosopher Hans Jonas, "the capacity for feeling, which arose in all organisms, is the mother-value of all values."[87]

Although the neuron itself functions in a proactive way, Edelman posits that the basic physiological unit of the individual's self-constructed world is the neuronal group, of which there is something on the order of one hundred million in the brain.[88] Consciousness arises from what Edelman terms "maps" and "reentrant signaling." In Edelman's definition, a map "is not a representation in the ordinary sense, but an interconnected series of neuronal groups that responds selectively to certain elemental categories for example, to movements or colors in the visual world. The creation of maps, Edelman postulates, involves the synchronization of hundreds of neuronal groups."[89]

Moreover, these maps are densely and mutually interconnected. It is this complex interconnection that makes possible communication among maps, "reentrant signaling". And this makes possible the production of dynamic perceptual constructs, which form the basis for "primary consciousness"—a "state of being mentally aware of things in the world—of having mental images in the present."[90]

> And from primary consciousness arises "higher order consciousness": [Higher order consciousness] supplements [primary consciousness], it does not replace it. It is dependent on the evolutionary development of language, along with the evolution of symbols, of cultural exchange; and with all this brings an unprecedented power of detachment, generalization, and reflection, so that finally self-consciousness is achieved, the consciousness of being a self in the world, with human experience and imagination to call upon.[91]

This process of reentrant signaling, Edelman emphasizes, is not directed hierarchically: [If] you had a hundred thousand wires randomly connecting four string quartet players and that, even though they weren't speaking words, signals were going back and forth in all kinds of hidden ways [as you usually get them by the subtle nonverbal

---

[85] Sacks, "Making Up the Mind", *supra* n. 81, at 44.

[86] Sacks, "Making Up the Mind", *supra* n. 81, at 44.

[87] Sacks, "Making Up the Mind", *supra* n. 81, at 44.

[88] With between five hundred and ten thousand neurons in each group. *See* Sacks, "Neurology", *supra* n. 81, at 48; Sacks, "Making Up the Mind", *supra* n. 81, at 44.

[89] Sacks, "Making Up the Mind", *supra* n. 81, at 44.

[90] Sacks, "Making Up the Mind", *supra* n. 81, at 44.

[91] Sacks, "Making Up the Mind", *supra* n. 81, at 46.

interactions between the players] that make the whole set of sounds a unified ensemble. That's how the maps of the brain work by re-entry.[92]

And it all is enabled by the always evolving, dense pattern of mutual physical interconnections among the multitude of neuronal maps. Thus, the brain at birth possesses by inheritance a rudimentary pattern of reentrant maps, which provide the "inborn values" required for the process of constructing a World to begin. These maps are, however, a form of "soft wiring". In the early years of life, there is a rapid process of forming a sophisticated pattern of these maps, a pattern that is particular for each individual. And, because they are soft wired, then the process of reforming them can continue throughout the individual's life.[93]

The result is an ongoing process that generates a dynamic understanding of reality:

> But where perception of *objects* is concerned, the world, Edelman likes to say, is not "labeled," it does not come "already parsed into objects." We must *make* them, in effect, through our own categorizations: "Perception makes," Emerson said. "Every perception," says Edelman, echoing Emerson, "is an act of creation." Thus, our sense organs, as we move about, take samplings of the world, creating maps in the brain. Then a sort of neurological "survival of the fittest" occurs, a selective strengthening of those mappings, which correspond to "successful" perceptions—successful in that they prove the most useful and powerful for the building of "reality."[94]

Thus, "the exploring organism seeks (or imposes) meaning at all times, that its mappings are mappings of meaning; that its world and . . . its symbolic systems are *constructed* of 'meanings'."[95] And this world changes with the experience of the individual—"the brain is an apparatus for constructing categories in the light of experience".[96] The World does not have predetermined structures. Our structuring of the World is our own. And this process and its consequences—are dynamic across the individual's lifetime.

What is so striking about Edelman's Theory of Neuronal Group Selection is its strong resonance with the anthropological concept of cosmologies. Neuroscientific description of the physical processes of the brain and anthropological description of the cultural processes within a society generate the same understanding of what it is that is unique about the conscious, language-imbued human individual—her essence as a human is not that she inhabits a given reality. As any organism, of course, she is in a dyadic relationship with her Environment. What makes her unique among organisms—her humanness—is that she also inhabits a conscious World. And this World is not a mirror of her Environment but instead is a mental construct—a matrix of meaning that she brings into being, the ongoing product of a dynamic process that is generated by the value-based, synthetic act of perception.

---

[92] Sacks, "Making Up the Mind", *supra* n. 81, at 44–45.

[93] For a general description, see S. Greenspan, *The Growth of the Mind and the Endangered Origins of Intelligence* (Reading, Mass.: Addison-Wesley, 1997), 1–160. For an account from the general press, see S. Begley, "How to Build a Baby's Brain", *Newsweek* (Special Edition: "Your Child", Spring/Summer 1997), 28.

[94] Sacks, "Making Up the Mind", *supra* n. 81, at 44.

[95] Sacks, "Making Up the Mind", *supra* n. 81, at 48.

[96] Sacks, "Neurology", *supra* n. 81, at 48.

Now consider again a characteristic of this creative process of World-making that William James described in his "The Will to Believe". To be a denizen of a Western culture is to be imbued with the principle of the primacy of rationality as the defining human attribute. Enlightenment Rationality is the motive force of human achievement. And René Descartes's *cogito* is the paradigm of Rationality. Western culture is so imbued with this principle that to describe judicial decision making, for example, as abductive and not deductive typically generates a sense of unease.

Consider, however, the matter of emotion. In the Cartesian scheme, rationality is the superior human capacity; "mere" emotion is altogether inferior. Gerald Edelman, however, argues that we experience values that underlie and drive the process of World-making as feelings. And William James describes the exercise of the will to believe as a "passional" act.

Antonio Damasio also is a neuroscientist, a physician who studies brain injuries.[97] Damasio recounts an historically famous brain injury case, involving Phineas Gage, a railroad foreman who lived in Vermont in the first half of the nineteenth century.[98] In 1848, an accidental explosion of blasting powder drove an iron bar through Gage's pre-frontal lobe. Gage survived the accident, and seemed to heal physically. Moreover, his mental function seemed to be intact in terms of attention, perception, memory, language, and intelligence.

He did, however, exhibit a profound change in his personality—he became almost completely emotionless. And, for the thirteen years of life that remained to him, he was unable to live a fully functional life.

> "[H]e no longer showed respect for social convention; ethics were violated; the decisions he made did not take into account his best interest. ... There was no evidence of concern about his future, no sign of forethought."[99] Lost were "unique human properties, among them the ability to anticipate the future and plan accordingly within a complex social environment; the sense of responsibility toward the self and others; and the ability to orchestrate one's survival deliberately, at the command of one's free will."[100]

Damasio's investigations have revealed that the dysfunctionality that Phineas Gage suffered is the typical aftermath of injury to, or lesions in, the frontal lobe.[101] Moreover, it is this part of the brain that is associated with the capacity for emotion. Damasio links the loss of emotional capacity to this dysfunctionality through his Somatic-Marker Hypothesis.

This hypothesis rests on Damasio's concept of primary and secondary emotions. Primary emotions are primitive. They are associated with the limbic system, and are involved with basic physiological functions. Secondary emotions are sophisticated, although the primary emotions form a substrate to them. Secondary emotions are associated with the neo-cortex and are involved with conscious rationality. The core

---

[97] *See* A. Damasio, *Descartes' Error: Emotion, Reason, and the Human Brain* (New York: G.P. Putnam, 1994).

[98] Damasio, *supra* n. 97, at 3–19.

[99] Damasio, *supra* n. 97, at 11.

[100] Damasio, *supra* n. 97, at 10.

[101] Damasio, *supra* n. 97, at 34–57.

of Damasio's Somatic-Marker Hypothesis is the proposition that the secondary emotions and feelings are essential to practical functionality.[102] They seem to be the prior condition by which a capacity for perception and cognition lead to successful rationality. And they function by marking the values by which we create our understanding of the Cosmos with positive feelings and by marking values which are rejected in the World-making process with negative feelings.

Damasio's hypothesis has a tantalizing resonance with the "passional step" of William James's "The Will to Believe". The genesis of World-making is emotional. Having a World—that is, being functional in a culture in an Environment—derives from making a commitment to, adopting a belief in, a cosmology. Commitment, however, is a matter of emotionality and not of rationality. And through this commitment, the particular cosmology provides the deep, implicit starting premises from which it is necessary for rationality to proceed.

Damasio describes in these terms, the "predicament" of those who, like Phineas Gage, have suffered the kind of brain damage that affects emotional capacity:

> One way of describing their predicament is by saying that they never construct an appropriate theory about their persons, or about their person's social role in the perspective of past and future. And what they cannot construct for themselves, they also cannot generate for others. They are bereft of a theory of their own mind and of the mind of those with whom they interact.[103]

This "appropriate theory" appears to be nothing other than a cosmology. Loss of the capacity for secondary emotion prevents the individual from adopting a cosmology—the ability to exercise the will to believe is gone. A cosmology, however, is the indispensable basis for the unavoidable task of constructing a World. To be functional as a human requires having a World. Phineas Gage, once his capacity for secondary emotion was impaired, was no longer able to have a World.

Although neuroscience has made impressive progress, we are as yet far from having a full understanding of mind and consciousness. We can see, however, the beginnings of a convergence of ideas. From one direction of inquiry, from the perspective of the physiological processes of the brain—"our brains act as if"—come Gerald Edelman's Theory of Neuronal Group Selection Antonio Damasio's Somatic-Marker Hypothesis. From another direction, from the perspective of human behavior—"we act as if"—come William James's "The Will to Believe" and Mary Douglas's anthropological cosmologies. Just as behavioral science describes the human function as proceeding on the basis of language-embedded gestalts that provide alternative ways of experiencing, and creating meaning for, the Environment, neuroscience describes the function of the brain as a system in which selection is central and by which every perception is an act of creation.[104] As William James so eloquently put it in his seminal *The Principles of Psychology*:

[102] Damasio, *supra* n. 97, at 165–201.

[103] Damasio, *supra* n. 97, at 58.

[104] Sacks, "Making Up the Mind", *supra* n. 81, at 43–44.

> The mind, in short, works on the data it receives very much as a sculptor works on his block of stone. In a sense the statue stood there from eternity. But there were a thousand different ones beside it, and the sculptor alone is to thank for having extricated this one from the rest. Just so the world of each of us, howsoever different our several views of it may be, all lay embedded in the primordial chaos of sensations, which gave the mere matter to the thought of all of us indifferently.[105]

Antonio Damasio incisively describes Descartes' Error as positing the "abyssal separation between body and mind."[106] We can now see another mistake—"Posner's Error". The traditional view describes Phineas Gage's misfortune as having left his rationality intact but having deprived him of his capacity for emotion. This view implicitly equates mental function with rationality, and implicitly posits that rationality and emotion derive from dichotomous realms. James, Edelman, and Damasio teach us that emotion is a necessary condition for rationality, and that emotion functions at the essence of the mind-process.[107]

Thus, we are not, as Richard Posner would have it, biologically rational automatons; our rationality is not our essence.[108] Instead, we overlay our rule-based rationality with a powerful structure of meaning generated by an emotional commitment. It is this matrix of meaning that abductively provides the rules by which our deductive rationality proceeds. The truly human, truly creative human characteristic is not deductive reason. It is emotion-based abduction.

As Roberta Kevelson asserts, "Peirce proceeds to show that our logic itself is nothing but an 'application of the doctrine of what we deliberately choose to do which is Ethics.' Thus logic in applying ethical norms represents truth, or correct arguments. Ethics represents manifest efforts of will."

Ethics is defined as the "moral principles by which a person is guided."[109] Ethics rests on morals, which rests on values. The values that make up the World are the consequence of a "manifest effort of will", a deliberate choice carried out as the will to believe, the choice of a particular cosmology.

Within the law, ethical norms—the values embodied in a particular cosmology—come to be applied through the logic of abduction. This logic "represents truth" because Truth is the consequence of acting out a World, which in turn is the consequence of implementing a cosmology. The abductive judicial choice of a cosmology, which

[105] W. James, *The Principles of Psychology* (New York: Henry Holt & Co., 1902), 288.

[106] Damasio, *supra* n. 97, at 249.

[107] Thus, Robert M. Hutchins' exclamation in 1934 about the Legal Realist understanding of the law amounting to it being a consequence of the "visceral reactions" of the judiciary was accurate. This understanding does not, however, as Hutchins opined, have much to do with the quality of the judge's Egg McMuffin.

[108] Thus, the computational model of the human mind is wholly inadequate. *See* H. Dreyfus, *What Computers Still Can't Do: A Critique of Artificial Reason* (Cambridge, Mass.: MIT Press, 1992). The truly remarkable function of the mind is not deductive reasoning and computation, which can easily be replicated by a machine; instead, it is the extraordinarily complex function of seeing, which cannot be fully replicated with machines. *See* T. Norretranders, *The User Illusion: Cutting Consciousness Down To Size* (New York: Viking, 1998), 178–195.

[109] *The Oxford English Dictionary, supra* n. 72, at 422 (definition B.II.3.b).

is the necessary step in resolving a dispute, generates a resolution that of necessity is a truth, the "law" of that particular dispute. Ownership, then, is ethical in nature—it defines the principles of human duty, how individuals are to relate mutually with respect to material objects.

We can now return to our opening anecdote—why do students hold their heads when I pose my "Rule or Result" question? The answer is suggested by neuroscience. The students come to law school with an understanding of law as a system of deductive rationality. Analyzing the *Miller* case, however, causes this understanding to break down. And Gerald Edelman suggests that this literally involves breaking down and re-forming extensive, physical, neuron-based maps in the brain. Of necessity, however, *this is physical work.* Is it too far-fetched to believe that this makes your head hurt?

Property and Law

Ownership is an element of the World. Because the World is a state of mind, then property is a state of mind. And the World is non-given, dynamic, and the consequence of a choice among alternatives.

The law of ownership in the United States too is not a thing. Rather, it is a core element of the ongoing process of creating the social World. And its meaning is the consequence of an ongoing process of non-determined choice—the choice of the Result when individuals who fall into dispute appeal to the judicial process for a resolution.

Jean Houston, the New Age philosopher whose interactions with Hillary Rodham Clinton have engendered a flurry of journalistic bemusement, has spoken of "mythic times, times that never were but are always becoming". Justice Benjamin Cardozo asserted, "Law never *is*, but is always about to be".[110] Jean Houston recognizes that a culture's myth—the story that tells us who we are—can never be completely told because who we are can never be finally determined. A culture that is living thus is always in the process of creating its explanation of the Cosmos. Justice Cardozo recognized as well that the law, a central nexus in which we carry out the ongoing process of creating who we are, also can never be finally determined.

Return to Pierre-Joseph Proudhon's urgent question, "What is property?" The answer that, I argue, is offered by the judicial process of the United States recognizes the complexity of the human condition. For organisms in an Environment, there is neither "property" nor "ownership". There are only physical encounters with objects, a dyadic milieu of action and reaction—flee from this object, devour that object, ignore another object.

As we tend to forget, however, when we arise in the middle of the night without turning the lights on and proceed to take inventory of the furniture with our shins,

[110] B.N. Cardozo, *The Nature of the Judicial Process* (New Haven: Yale University Press, 1921), 126.

we do not dwell solely in a dyadic milieu of action-reaction. We also dwell in another dimension that is triadic in nature—each of us is also a conscious, language-using human dwelling in a World.[111] This World is a mental construct, a matrix of meaning that is not given to us, but instead is entirely our own making. In a World, there are both "property" and "ownership"—this object is "mine", while an identical object is "yours".

Like all the elements of a World, property is a state of mind that comes about in social experience. In the social realm, it operates as an institution, an ongoing ethical practice with regard to the claims to ownership made by the various individual members of society that are backed up by the judicial process. In the individual realm, property is a relationship the contours of which express the individual's conception of who she is, her cosmology.

I have been trying to present an understanding of the human World as generated in human consciousness, as based on an emotional commitment to particular values, as unavoidably dynamic, and ultimately as non-determined. This understanding entails that the essence of the human condition is the unavoidable necessity of choice. And what I have tried to show is that judicial doctrine is an epiphenomenon of the ongoing process of judicial choice that accurately reflects the rich pluralism of the values available for choice.

The urgent question posed in the judicial process in the United States, then, is not whether we can discover and refine a cohesive, internally consistent, and complete rational structure of rules and principles that will determine the Results of our conflicts. Instead, it is a forward-looking question—what shall the law be?

Conclusion

The third element of Roberta Kevelson's semiotic inquiry into property law is "the predominant code of ethics in legal practice." As we have seen, the judicial doctrine of ownership in the United States does not form an internally consistent body of rules and principles derived from a homogeneous set of values; instead, it is a heterogeneity, embodying the ethical values implicit in each of the cosmological conceptualizations of ownership. The judicial process implicitly recognizes that homogeneous doctrine is not practically possible and that justice rests on the accommodation of a heterogeneity of values in the ongoing stream of judicial Results.

The judicial process responds to this practical constraint by maintaining the conflicting conceptualizations of ownership in an ongoing mutual tension. It is this response that constitutes the ethical practice of American courts. Its method does not look to an antecedent body of determinative rules and principles;

[111] Indeed, a typical reaction to one's shin colliding with an article of furniture is a use of language, one that characterizes—ascribes meaning, however unkind, to— the offending object.

instead, it follows what John Dewey denominates the Logic of Consequences, asking what "property" shall be within the context of this particular dispute in these particular circumstances. The judicial process in the United States, that is, is an exemplar of the method of American philosophical pragmatism of which the ideas of Charles Sanders Peirce form so substantial a part. In the understanding of John Dewey, what might appear to be general rules and principles actually are "working hypotheses, needing to be constantly tested by the way in which they work out in application to concrete situations."[112] In the ethical practice of the judicial process, what courts do about the disputes before them is not subservient to general rules and principles. Instead, general rules and principles are made instrumental to how courts resolve these disputes.

This essay is an attempt to carry out the semiotic inquiry into property law that Roberta Kevelson proposed—to "seek correspondences between the predominant logic in legal reasoning, the predominant code of ethics in legal practice, and the referent esthetic norms, or values, that govern the ethics and the logic of property." Our analysis has shown that the predominant logic in legal reasoning is abductive in mode—the Rule-creating step of adopting a particular deep value for the particular dispute at hand. The values that govern the ethics and the logic of property are the alternative sets of values that underlie the cosmologies available to humans for constructing their World. And the decision making process of American courts is an ethical practice—it proceeds in the pragmatic mode, an instrumental process of using values as tools for fashioning a heterogeneous conceptualization of ownership that generates a well-functioning World.

[112] Dewey, *supra* n. 28, at 26.

Obligations I: Quid pro quo: Contractual Semiosis and Translation

Dinda L. Gorlée

> *"... the Greeks used 'throw together' very frequently to signify the making of a contract, or convention. Now, we do find symbol ({symbolon}) early and often used to mean a convention or contract"*
>
> Peirce, CP:2.297, c.1895

Introductory Remarks[1]

Peirce offered the contract as the paradigm of triadic sign-processes. In this Chapter I intend to analyze contract and contractual semiosis, and to apply the outcome of this analysis to the phenomenon of translation, which can be seen as one, specific kind of contractual transaction. By juxtaposing these three notions (contract, semiosis, translation), taken from three different spheres of intellectual life, a semiotic approach presents the possibility of seeing new and meaningful relationships between diverse entities. Concretely, the convergence of contract and semiosis will throw new light upon translation.[2]

A contract is expressed as a conventional, primarily verbal promissory act by which a legally binding nexus is established between parties, with consequences for future behavior. The central idea of contract in law involves further a series of elements (such as intention, future action, and responsibility) which in their co-presence and interaction equally pertain to the symbolic action which Peirce called genuine semiosis. By deemphasizing, as Peirce usually did, the personal performance of the utterer and the interpreter, semiosis becomes a formal logical relation between a sign, its object, and the interpretant, in which meaning is negotiated in the conditional mode, i.e., relayed to the future; and the same thing happens in translation.

[1] **Source:** GORLEE, DINDA L.: "Quid pro quo: Contractual Semiosis and Translation" from: *Semiotics and the Problem of Translation*, Rodopi, Amsterdam 1994, pp. 197–225

[2] For an account of Derrida's deconstructionist concept of translation as a contract, see van den Broeck 1988.

D.L. Gorlée (✉)
Legal Translation Agency, Alkemadelaan 806, 2597 BC The Hague, Netherlands
e-mail: gorlée@xs4all.nl

J.M. Broekman, L. Catá Backer (eds.), *Signs In Law - A Source Book*,
DOI 10.1007/978-3-319-09837-1_27

Finally, I will show that translation is a communicative act, which possesses a contractual nature and must be considered as a degenerately semiotic act. Here, promisor and promise have lost their performative individuality vis-à-vis one another rand the promise intended. They converge into one mind, the translator's mind. Consequently, the promissory act is debilitated by the private, non-enforceable basis of the contract of translation. Genuine semiosis has thus degenerated into a dyadic or even a monadic affair.

Contract

A contract, basically, is an agreement between two (or more) persons, creating mutual legal obligations between them.[3] In its essence, it is a legally and morally binding promise[4] to do something or refrain from doing something. The "something" is called the subject matter of the contract, which must be legal. It is illegal to contract against good morals or national security, for example.

There is no set (verbal) formula to enter into a contract. Written contracts are as a rule supposed to set out what the parties actually intend, while the intent of oral-made and other informal agreements is, from a legal standpoint, not definitely fixed. Interpretation may there be necessary in order to clarify parties' intentions. It is the task of the trial judge to make the implicit explicit by inference from the evidence available to him or her (the written and/or oral agreement corroborated by conduct by parties).

The consensual basis of contract, its first formal requirement, implies that parties (called promisor and promise) agree voluntarily and in good faith to enter into a common enterprise involving future actions, thereby yielding some portion of their freedom of behavior in the future. The will of parties is, in law considered to be manifested in the fact that, to the effect of the contract, a definite offer or proposal from one party has been consciously and willingly accepted, without new terms, by the other party. An offer not clearly and explicitly put forth, and/or not freely and knowingly accepted, makes no contract,—or better, it makes a defective contract. Thus, if A asks B to promise some future performance, and B makes no answer indicating his (present) willingness to do so at some (future) time, B has made no promise.

To qualify as a valid and legally binding contract, there must be mutuality, or exchange of promises. Under a contract, one party undertakes an obligation, thereby giving the other, to whom the obligation is owed, a claim against him, her, or itself, which consists in the right to have a performance of the terms of the contract. By this token, parties do not share benefits and burdens, but each party has his, her, or its definite privileges and responsibilities arising from the contract.

[3] For this and adjacent paragraphs on contract in law, I have drawn on Fuller and Eisenberg 1981, Eisenberg 1984, and the more popularizing Wincor 1970.

[4] On the legal implications of this equation, see Fried 1981.

Contracting parties must further be competent, that is, they must have the proper legal capacity to enter into a contractual agreement. As a case in point, a contract entered into by a minor (or a mentally disabled person) is a defective, and hence voidable, transaction. It is not void, and therefore still creates legally binding obligations on a competent party, unless the minor (or mentally disabled person) repudiates it. This may happen in person or through a guardian acting on his or her behalf.

However, a contract is not binding, and therefore void (and not merely voidable), if it is lacking what is called, in legal jargon, "consideration". A bare and gratuitous promise is generally insufficient ground to create, for the one party, an enforceable duty to deliver any (material or immaterial) goods, nor for the other, to take and pay for them. The obligation resting upon each party only exists "in consideration of" the act or promise of the other—meaning that neither is bound unless both are bound. Consideration is, in the Anglo-American legal system (the so-called common law), the essence and backbone of legal contract. It is also known as the *quid pro quo* ("what for what"; "something for something") mentioned in the title of this Chapter because of the analogy to the scholastic *aliquid stat pro aliquot*, which exemplifies the semiotic sign and relation and is (like *quid pro quo*) rooted in equivalence. *Quid pro quo* indicates that something must be given in return for the promise; that there must be some bargain; that a responsibility incurred by the one party must be matched by a corresponding benefit gained by the other. Consideration pits the promise to give (often, to pay) against the promise to do, thereby highlighting the thing of value each party agrees to give in exchange for what he or she receives by the bargain. This thing of value, or consideration, is the reason for which the contract is made.

Semiotics being, essentially, the study of how verbal and nonverbal messages are created, sent, received, understood, interpreted, and otherwise used, it is clearly the case that contract is a semiotic problem. Here we must distinguish a contract as a written document from contract as a communicative act or event. Though different, both are facts of law and both are semiotic signs.

The written document, or contract form, is an object, which is a sign because of the verbal signs (signs of Thirdness) it is codified in. When filled out and signed, it serves as a genuine Third, or sign of law. In accordance with Peirce's classification of signs, it must be characterized as a symbolic sign[5] strongly tinged with indexicality. More specifically, it is a proposition, or dicent symbolic legisign,[6] which on being signed by parties (and, if necessary, co-signed by one or more witnesses, an attorney, and/or notary public) will acquire the status of an argument, or argumentative symbolic legisign.[7] The mixed, symbolic-indexical nature of the contract is signified

[5]A contract was for Peirce definitely a sign: "The dictionary is rich in words waiting to receive technical definitions as varieties of signs", he wrote (*PW*:194,1905), and in his long and rather intriguing list of examples of this, Peirce included "oath, vow, promise, contract, deed" (*PW*:194:1905).

[6]Also called by Peirce a dicent symbol or dicisignificant symbol. According to the qualification rule, every symbol is a legisign. See Dinda L. Gorlée: *Semiotics and the Problem of Translation*, Rodopi, Amsterdam 1994, [quoted: Gorl.Semiotics] Chap. 3.

[7]According to the qualification rule, every argument is a symbol.

in the appearance of the formal, written contract but can also be recognized (though perhaps in a less explicit form) in the informal contracts—agreements, that is, which may result from an exchange of letters or even from casual acts.

The written contract is a verbal text, and language is the obvious example of a system of Thirds. The use of the linguistic signs in contract forms is stipulated by convention and consists substantially of a succession of formal recitations, of which the following are supposed to serve as typical examples:

Agreement made in ---------- on ----------, between ----------, residing at ---------- (hereinafter called the Owner) and ----------, copartners trading and doing business under the firm name of ----------, and having its place of business at ---------- (hereinafter called the Contractor),

WHEREIN it is mutually agreed as follows:..........

WITNESSETH:

WHEREAS, the Seller is engaged in the sale and distribution of ---------- among its customers; and WHEREAS, the Purchaser desires to purchase the ---------- business, the good will of said business and the route and list of customers of the Seller pertaining to said business.

NOW THEREFORE, in consideration of the sum of ---------- DOLLARS, each to the other in hand paid, and of the mutual covenants and conditions hereinafter contained, it is agreed as follows:

IN WITNESS WHEREOF, the parties have executed this agreement.

These and other formulaic expressions specify contractual essentials such as consideration, subject matter, purpose, agreement of will, and future performance. They are formulated in the typical language of law, the language of authority and time-honored tradition, which means that its vocabulary is

> … governed by doctrines of memory, recognition and usage, defined in turn by reference to extensive and obscure etymologies, in the last resort, of "sources" of law in which words are transmitted by a dogmatics of quotation, reference, citation and specialized and restricted commentary:… (Goodrich 1987:178)

This author argues that the same point can be made about legal syntax. The features enumerated in the above passage link legal language again with the category of Thirdness, in which signs are always generally applicable (i.e., usable for various purposes) and susceptible of at any time being provided with a new meaning, thereby creating a new habit. This is made possible by the arbitrary nature of the (linguistic) sign which, lacking a direct connection with the object referred to, may consequently be used to refer to any object. Thirds are non-natural and must be learned. They address themselves to the "expert" and make little or no sense to the uninitiated. This is *a fortiori* true for legal texts.

To supplement the generic nature of legal language and counteract the manifold special purposes it can be made to serve in the hands of legal experts, written contracts must anchor themselves in extralinguistic reality (legal reality and general social reality), where the origin, motive, purpose, and execution of contracts must lie. On the textual level this anchoring function is fulfilled by inserting on the blank spaces a series of necessary deictic features.[8] By this token, a proposition is, on the one hand, a truncated argument (it lacks a definite conclusion and can be contradicted) and, on the other hand, it may be transformed into a rheme by removing the deictic, that is indexical, entities which give it a here-and-now, a subject, and hence a coherent story-line. In a contract, the indexical features make the text applicable to a particular situation involving particular subjects. These features include place and date of the agreement, performance, etc.; names, addresses, etc. of parties; full details of duties to be performed; and penalties. Pointing to discrete spatio-temporal units in the external physical world (persons, objects, events), these indexical features serve to indicate exactly who promises whom to do what, when, and in return for what.[9]

As described so far, the written contract is a concrete proposition with a built-in rheme. It offers a blueprint for future action, but gives itself no security. It builds upon the possibility in the appearance of a promise, where the quality of Firstness must remain general, that is, vague and non-committal. That this is the case, was experienced by Peirce himself, as he authored a piece of embryonic contractual writing. In one of the drafts of his elaborate, but tragically and undeservedly failed, application to the then newly founded Carnegie Institution of Washington, DC, for a grant to enable him to complete the treatise on logic (scheduled by Peirce to consist of a series of thirty-six memoirs) which he had been writing for thirty years, Peirce wrote:

> As an additional or alternative security, I should suggest, supposing that other security were desired by the Executive Committee, that a contract be executed between the Carnegie Institution and me by which I should be bound to send in the memoirs with no interval between any successive two exceeding three months, unless some visitation of providence (say, a five month's illness, a conflagration, or a domestic calamity) should intervene, and even then not exceeding five months. Otherwise, I falling in this, should be bound to repay to the Carnegie Institution all money up to that time paid to me, while losing the copyrights of the printed memoirs. I would yearly furnish bonds that such money should be refunded, if failure should occur within one year. I should secure my bondsman by putting into his hands first draughts of the memoirs for the ensuing year, which though they would not be satisfactory to me, would, nevertheless, *à la rigueur* conform to the agreement. Of course, this would be but partial security. … Of course, in case any contract were made, the Carnegie Institution would by its terms become bound to persist in the arrangement to the end, and to publish each memoir within, say, one year of the date of its approval. (*MS*L75A:76–78,1902).

And Peirce added here:

> I have a reputation of not finishing things. I suppose there is some basis of truth beneath it. But it has been, like every evil reputation, exaggerated out of all semblance of truth by calumny. It should be remembered that I was connected for a long time with the Coast Survey; and it will be easy for members of the committee to ascertain that office has been,

[8] See: Gorl.Semiotics, Chap. 3.

[9] By implication, they also make clear to which persons, etc. the terms and conditions of the agreement are not applicable. On text-internal referential-cohesive features (as is the use of demonstrative pronouns), see Kurzon 1986:49–56.

at times, a veritable hot-bed of intrigue, and that I, in particular, have some times suffered great injustice there. Voluminous volumes were prepared by me for publication which I never could get printed; and then I was accused, vaguely and in intangible forms, of not getting my work ready for publication. For the truth of this (except that the accusations were made) I stand responsible. I have often made this statement. If it is not true, why am I not called upon to go ahead with the printing? (*MS*L75A:78–79.1902).

This text is certainly a human document (and a very poignant one at that), but as Peirce himself was no doubt acutely aware, it was, and still is, highly inadequate as a legal document. In fact, it is as rudimentary a contract as its truth value is weak. It is a mere rhematic indexical legisign, or rhematic symbol.[10] Of this, Peirce gave as a prototypical example the demonstrative pronoun, thereby indicating that it is intended to stand for and point to something more tangible. In the case of contract, it suggests and prefigures an eventual synergetic relation in the form of a real exchange of promises. As a case in point, Peirce's letter certainly said something; it expressed an intention. But it was as yet a mere suggestive idea without *quid pro quo*, a one-sided promise without legal (and, more importantly for Peirce, without economic) consequences.

The plaintive and apologetic overtones of the monologue here reflect the desperate attempt by Peirce to achieve something from the Carnegie Institution, any offer it would be able and willing to make him. As it stands, it is an attempt which is all subjective feeling and, as judgment, germinal possibility. From there to a signed real-world contract by which Peirce would actually be offered and given the desired grant, was apparently too bold a leap. Peirce's proposal was unfit to persuade the Carnegie Institution of the necessity that his project be financed: all its doubt would have to be removed and hardened into pure rationality. Peirce was unable to engage his potential sponsor into a genuine dialogue, in which his rhematic symbol could have grown to an argument—that is, the ripe judgment or assertive sign (*CP*:5.546,c.1908) prescribing rules of future conduct. Unfortunately for Peirce, a one-sided promise is nothing but a contract *manqué*.

A full-blown contractual relationship is typically not identical to a written document. While the latter serves as material evidence of the existence of the former, is its outward manifestation or, in other words, its translation, the former is the communicative act through which a legally binding contract is created. To translate an action (or rather series of actions) into a series of written signs is of course an everyday phenomenon within any verbal culture. The constant stream of printed matter which is a "natural" part of modern life, provides a running commentary upon all current events, big and small, public and private. These commentaries can in turn be commented upon "and so on *ad infinitum*" (*CP*:2.303,1901). Kevelson writes on semiosis and legal facts:

A continuity of inquiry requires that any judgment become the ground from which further investigation may begin. Such ground may be abstracted from still further judgments, such that the initial concept in question—the law in relation to the case at hand—may be further defined and refined. The rhetorical evidence provides a new quality, in turn to become a

[10] See: Gorl.Semiotics, Chap. 3.

new fact, and in its turn to become a new sign or representation, an interpretant of its object. The final interpretant concludes a complete process of inquiry. These brief explanatory remarks may be useful for further discussion of semiotics and contract in law. (Kevelson 1988:140)

In contract, a specific kind of semiosis is at work: one motivated and governed by the conventions of a legal system wary of anecdotal evidence (both of Firstness and Secondness) and requiring hard and reliable (that is, formal and written) proof. The law calls for Thirdness. For all its apparent finality, the written contract is, however, still one interpretant of the actual agreement, or meeting of the minds, preceding it. It is in turn a two-faced phenomenon: it is both a trimmed version of the previous consensus, stripped of the emotional and factual sideshows which may accompany bargains between flesh-and-blood (as well as institutional) partners, and inevitably stripped of some informational content; and, at the same time, it is also a version burdened with the legal clichés and other code-related niceties which make it fit into the pre-established doctrinal grid of the law.[11] This is one important reason why the law requires that transactions, particularly business contracts, be conducted in good faith (*bona fide*) and according to standards of fair dealing. No linguistic sign can be wholly determinate as to its meaning; and to counteract indeterminacy of meaning a fundamental requirement is, on Peirce's view, honesty:

...honest people, when not joking, intend to make the meaning of their words determinate, so that there shall be no latitude of interpretation at all. That is to say, the character of their meaning consists in the implications and non-implications of their words; and they intend to fix what is implied and what is not implied. They believe that they succeed in doing so, and if their chat is about the theory of numbers, perhaps they may. But the further their topics are from such presciss, or "abstract", subjects, the less possibility is there of such precision of speech. (*CP*:447,1905)

The kind of translation described above is the reverse of what Jakobson called "inter-semiotic translation, or *transmutation*" and which he defined as "an interpretation of verbal signs by means of signs of nonverbal sign systems" (Jakobson 1959:223; 1971b:261).[12] A proviso for making this analogy is that the actions causing the verbal translation from a coherent sign system; in so far as this is considered to be true, the analogy works. However, it is only true from the vantage point of the formal addresser of the message in the written interpretant-sign. And the voice (or better, voiceover) we hear in the written contract is the voice of Authority, the voice

[11] See further Fisch's Chapter on "Justice Holmes, the prediction theory of law, and pragmatism", in which Fisch quotes the following pragmatically-inspired remark on contract, by the famous American legal theoretician: "You see how the vague circumference of the notion of duty shrinks and at the same time grows more precise when we wash it with cynical acid and expel everything except the object of our study, the operations of the law" (Fisch 1986:8). In a note, Fisch clarifies this sentence by saying that it is "in the astringent traditions of Hobbes, Bentham, and Austin, who were Holmes's trinity. 'The light of human minds is perspicuous words, but by exact definitions first *snuffed* and *purged* from ambiguity.' Cf. Chauncey Wright's nihilism —'an *exorcism* of the vague'— and especially James's 1898 lecture on the '*shrinkage*' that follows application of the principle of pragmatism" (Fisch 1986:13,n.5).

[12] See Jakobson's views on intersemiotic translation as seen from a Peircean viewpoint.

of the Law. From the perspective of the other, explicit parties involved, the message may therefore come across as an oblique, distorted, or otherwise over-coded version of the actual agreement of the minds.

Jakobson's inter-semiotic translation is by its very nature imprecise and impressionistic; from linguistic signs, Thirds, it produces rhematic sighs, i.e., Thirds in their aspect of Firstness, a slackened, softer version of language's primary Thirdness. This corresponds to Peirce's degeneracy.[13] In the case of contract, almost the reverse is true. While pretending to express the intention of the parties and manifesting the will on which it is based, the written contract tends to take advantage of the interpretational latitude of both the nonverbal code (in this case a sign of Secondness) and of the verbal code. To translate what is originally a Second into a (verbal) sign of Thirdness belonging to a legal subcode, means to impose additional constraints upon parties, thereby hardening their original positions. Not only does the written contract formalize past and present events: it also gives binding rules for conduct in the future. This is generacy, the opposite of degeneracy.

The projection into the future implies that the written contract, as compared to the primary agreement, is a forward-translation,—in Peirce's terminology, "an equivalent sign, or perhaps a more developed sign" (*CP*:2.228,c.1897). To the degree that it is an extrapolation from the actual will of the parties (albeit, it is hoped, a fair and reasonable extrapolation from it), a written contract is an equivalent[14] interpretant-sign. But in terms of the two codes involved, it must be understood as a clarified if possibly biased translation of it. And it is definitely still a non-ultimate, evolving, and fallible interpretant-sign, another fact of law capable of being again interpreted. The translation from (forms of) degeneracy into (forms of) generacy is a pragmatic phenomenon which will return throughout this Chapter. It will manifest itself in all its many contractual guises as translation from (mostly precontractual) subjective feeling, Firstness, via intersubjectively action Secondness to objective, rational Thirdness.

Contract as Speech-Act

In order to have force of law, a contract needs to be ratified. Ratification or, in Peirce's terms, assertion of a proposition, is a semiotic act in which parties make themselves responsible for the terms of the agreement. This form of guarantee serves to "distinguish promises from firm statements of intention and emphatic predictions" (Searle 1969:46). All three are verbal acts creating expectations; but a contractual promise is by far the firmest assertion, the one with the highest truth-value; because in it the promisor intentionally invokes a convention whose function is to give moral and legal grounds for another to expect the promised performance. To see the contract as rooted in promise has led language-philosophers to regard the act of promising as a speech-act.

[13] More on this in Merrell 1991:76–79 and Gorlée 1990.

[14] More on equivalence in Chap. 9.

Peirce's one-sided, and therefore inchoate and abortive, contractual act, discussed above, was infected by what speech-act theoreticians call an "infelicity",[15] one which can affect all "illocutionary acts". In speech-act theory, "locutionary acts" (such as saying or writing "It's raining") limit themselves to the mere uttering of a verbal message, regardless of whether it produces an intended effect upon the (possible) receiver of the message or not. "Perlocutionary acts" (such as commands, promises, and questions) aim at causing any contingent practical consequence of the message, in the form of an action or reaction by the speaker or hearer. Last in this division come illocutionary acts (for instance, "hereby I baptize you in the name of the Father, the Son, and the Holy Spirit", "This is to appoint you as sales-manager of our Amsterdam branch office"), which communicate the special intention underlying the utterance and are aimed at making the hearer recognize this intention.

The triad of speech-acts fits the various configurations of Peirce's theory of signs, and is prefigured in Peirce's own application of it to linguistic signs.[16] The simple declaration or spontaneous utterance would then, in its sign-interpretant relation, correspond to a rhematic sign, representing the Firstness of Thirdness. The two-sided directive speech-act, focused on the immediate effect t produces upon the hearer, would correspond to a proposition, or Secondness of Thirdness. And the cooperative language-act through which the hearer is made to perceive and believe the purpose or mediate effect with which the speaker has endowed the utterance, would correspond to a Peircean argument, or genuine Third.

A contract must be understood as a relational speech-act; consequently, it can never be a mere locutionary act. Now a promise, in its simplest form, is a perlocutionary act in which a speaker manifests his or her intention, based upon his or her volition, to perform some act in the future. This would make a contract a dual promise from some speaker to some hearer and vice versa, a double perlocutionary act. However, a contractual promise is more than two promises amalgamated. While the performance in the future is no doubt a perlocutionary effect of at least one promise, contractual acts are themselves illocutionary acts in which a future exchange is foreshadowed, almost magically,[17] by a present, symbolic exchange. What makes the contractual promise special, what gives it legal consequences, is the third element carried by it—the clue for its correct interpretation. It consists in the joint declaration's special purpose, the legal consequences that enhance what would otherwise be a trivial and inconsequential transaction.

Following Searle's (1976) canonical classification of illocutionary acts, but refining and redefining it, Hancher[18] (1979) offers a comprehensive revision of it,

[15] Austin dubbed this kind of infelicity a "hitch". See Austin 1962:36–37.

[16] For Peirce as a precursor of speech-act theory, see Brock 1981a and 1981b, Hilpinen 1982, and Ferriani 1987, on whose insights I have, when necessary, drawn.

[17] See Hancher 1979:3. On the magical aspects of the contract model of cultural psychology, see Lotman 1990:254 ff.

[18] Hancher notes (1979:2,n.2) that Searle's 1976 article was also published elsewhere two other times, in slightly different forms.

which considers contracting as a reciprocal illocutionary act, one requiring two (or more) participants instead of one.[19] Hancher concludes that

> ... many important performative speech acts are not, as Searle would have it, simple declarations. Some, like offering and nondirective appointing, are commissive directives—that is, precooperative speech acts. Others are cooperative speech acts—cooperative declarations, as in the case of gifts, or cooperative commissives, as in the case of bilateral contracts. (Hancher 1979:12)

The cooperative commissive act of contracting is a joint venture preceded by, and containing, precooperative commissive directive acts of offering and accepting.[20] In other words: the first, initiating party cannot reasonably expect the second party to commit him-, her-, or itself to a contract until the first party has advanced a promise setting out his, her, or its own obligations. If nothing is offered in exchange, the essence of a *quid pro quo* or consideration, the bargain by which both parties agree to limit their choice of future behavior, is lacking, and there is no legal contract. Each contractual speech-act contains really two prior speech-acts in which speaker and hearer assume alternating roles of promisor and promisee.[21]

From Proposition to Assertion

As already seen,[22] in Peirce's terminology a contract must be referred to as a declarative proposition or dicent symbol,[23] which, through the act of assertion, is upgraded to an argument or argumentative symbolic legisign.

A linguistic proposition can be a sentence or any combination of sentences functional as a meaningful whole, commonly called "text".[24] Accordingly, a contract as a written document is, on Peirce's view, a proposition, a "Dicisign that

---

[19] Searle (1976) previously identified five basic kinds of illocutionary acts: "representatives", "directives", "commissives", "expressives", and "declarations", besides a subclass, "representative declarations". All of these speech-acts involve one speaker.

[20] Directives are, according to Searle (1976:11), attempts "by the speaker to get the hearer to do something". This includes suggesting, proposing, ordering, and commanding to do something. Commissives are "those illocutionary acts whose point is to commit the speaker...to some future course of action" (Searle 1976:11). This includes promising, guaranteeing, and solemnly vowing to do something.

[21] In Jakobson's semiotic terminology (as put forth in his famous 1960 essay), a contract would be a form of verbal communication involving an addresser and an addressee who exchange a message in which the primary functions are referential (emphasizing the cognitive, informational aspect of language) and conative (oriented toward the addressee, indicating what he or she must do).

[22] See notes 5 and 6 above.

[23] Also called by Peirce dicisignificant symbol. See Gorl.Semiotics, Chap. 3. Without making any attempt to reconstruct and analyze here Peirce's theory of propositions, which is not so clear as could be wished, I may instead refer the reader to Brock 1981b.

[24] In my project *Reading the Signs: A Peirce-Based Text Semiotics* (in progress) I examine the concept of text in detail.

is a Symbol" (*CP*:2.320,c.1902), a "Third attached to a Second" (*MS* L75:324,1902). Despite its dual nature, its "essence does not lie in its being compound, but on the contrary upon its being asserted or at least conceived to be asserted" (*MS* 499:29,1906); and according to one of Peirce's many other definitions, a proposition is "A sign which though *calculated* to produce belief, that is, though it has the character of a *possible* assertion, is nevertheless not necessarily so *intended*, not necessarily *used* toward that end" (*MS* 200:51,1907). Peirce underscored that a sharp distinction be made between the two: a proposition is not an assertion[25] but it is "assertible", a sign "capable of being asserted" (*CP*:8.337,1904). While, in semiotic terms, a proposition, "separately, or independently, indicates its object", an assertion is "a sign which separately shows what interpretant it is intended to determine" (*NEM* 4:242,c.1904), thereby giving it a particular reference to Thirdness. In this process what was originally a sign of fact "capable of truth or falsehood" (*CP*:8.337,1904) is transmogrified into a "rationally persuasive sign" (*CP*:2.309,c.1902), one that has acquired, besides "a degree of energy" (*MS* L75:324,1902) (its Secondness), logical status (Thirdness). Peirce made it clear that "It is not *words* that are "asserted", but *facts*" (*MS* 699:3,1911); and by being asserted, the factual proposition, which Peirce regarded as empirically verifiable, becomes a sign of truth.

While Peirce wrote that "the assertion is made by the utterer in a living effort to make its interpreter believe it true" (*MS* 646:16,1910), he also made it clear that an assertion is "no *thought* but is an *act* related to the thought" (*MS* 499:30,1906). Peirce's prototype of the assertion is the syllogism. In order to create it, the proposition must be placed in a particular assertor-mood or mode of assertion, which gives its content a particular force with public (i.e.., social and, in the case of contract, legal) repercussions. In a letter of January 22, 1905 to his friend William James, Peirce offered the following analogy, his favorite one:

> Now an assertion belongs to the class of phenomena like going before a notary and making an affidavit, executing added, signing a note, of which the essence is that one voluntarily puts oneself into a situation in which penalties will be incurred unless some proposition is true. (*CP*:8.313,1905)[26]

To assert a proposition means "a voluntary self-subjection to penalties" (*NEM* 4:249,c.1904); in more generic terms, it is

> ...an exhibition of the fact that one subjects oneself to the penalties visited on a liar if the proposition asserted is not true. An act of judgment is the self-recognition of a belief; and a belief consists in the acceptance of a proposition as a basis of conduct deliberately. (*PW:*34,1904)

---

[25] Every assertion includes, of course, a proposition.

[26] See also, e.g., the following quotation: "If a man desires to assert anything very solemnly, he takes such steps as will enable him to go before a magistrate or notary and take a binding oath to it. Taking an oath is not mainly an event of the nature of a setting forth, *Vorstellung*, or representing. It is not merely saying, but is *doing*. The law, I believe, calls it an 'act'. At any rate, it would be followed by very real effects, in case the substance of what is asserted should be proved untrue" (*CP*:5.546,c.1908).

What binds together the act of assertion and the act of contracting is, first, the assumption of responsibility and, second, the idea of promise made against a background of shared beliefs and intentions. To assert a proposition is to make oneself responsible for it (vs. to command a proposition, which is to make the interlocutor responsible for it), and to sign a contract is to enter into a relation involving mutual rights and responsibilities. Peirce wrote that

> To make yourself responsible means that if on a certain defined occasion a certain definitely described phenomenon does not emerge then you confer upon somebody a right, which he otherwise would not have. (*MS*499:30,1906)

Now this is a remark upon the assertive act; but it could equally be a description of the idea-governing contract. To assume responsibility is to make a public promise in the present, a promise to do (or refrain from doing) something in the future. This pertains to the part of the contract that is future-oriented; and in so far it may perhaps be called its forward-translation. At the same time, however, a contract needs to be rooted in a "past" of shared purposes and experiences, norms and values, and even a shared theory of the world,—unexpressed in the text of the contract, but presupposed in it. In a manner of speaking, a contract must be susceptible of being back-translated into this more general cultural context.[27] Without such a common (or at least partly common) background no meaningful social interaction is possible. Mutual comprehension is the "implicit contract" (Greimas and Courtés, 1982:59) which must precede any successful contract and is crucial to the whole doctrine of good faith.[28]

The similarities between Peirce's theory of the proposition (or, to put it more broadly, Peirce's linguistics[29]) and speech-act theory are clear. See, for instance, the following typical quotations from Peirce, which highlight his pragmatic approach to linguistic signs—the Wittgensteinian ways in which they can be used as tools, without losing their basic identity:

> A proposition may be stated [expressed] without being asserted. I may state it to myself and worry as to whether I shall embrace or reject it, being dissatisfied with the idea of doing either. In that case, I doubt the proposition. I may state the proposition to you and endeavor to stimulate you to advise me whether to accept or reject it: in which case I put in interroga-

---

[27] This corresponds to Wittgenstein's notion of "forms of life". See for this Gorl.Semiotics, Chap. 5, especially the section on "Culture".

[28] In conversation, acoustic and optic messages (such as eye contact and verbal forms of feedback) broadcast wittingly or unwittingly, allow the interlocutors to monitor whether communication is succeeding or not. In written communication such as direct clues about mutual agreement are largely absent; consequently, misunderstanding and conflicts can easily arise. Following Greimas and Courtés (1979:70; here quoted from the English translation, 1982:59) (who again apply Jakobson's well-known 1960 notion), '[i]t is indeed necessary to recognize, hidden under the contract, this 'phatic communication' which constitutes the necessary and preliminary undergirding for any communication and which seems to involve both a tension (a well-disposed or mistrustful expectation) and a relaxing (as a kind of response to the expectation)".

[29] Only in recent years have Peirce's numerous but largely unknown writings on general-linguistic topics become the object of serious study. See Rauch and Carr (eds.) 1980, Shapiro 1983, Pharies 1985, and Rethoré 1988.

tively. I may state it to myself; and be deliberately satisfied to base my action on it whenever occasion may arise: in which case I judge it. I may state it to you: and assume a responsibility for it: in which case I assert it. I may impose the responsibility of its agreeing with the truth upon you: in which case I command it. All of these are different moods in which that same proposition may be stated. (*NEM* 4:39,1902)

One and the same proposition may be affirmed, denied, judged, doubted, inwardly inquired into, put as a question, wished, asked for, effectively commanded, taught or merely expressed, and does not thereby become a different proposition. (*NEM* 4:248,c.1904)

...the meaning of a sentence...not only remains the same in whatever language it is expressed, but is also the same whether it be believed or doubted, asserted (by somebody's making himself responsible for it,) commanded (by somebody's expressing that he holds another responsible for it,) or just as a question (when somebody express an attempt to introduce another to make himself responsible for it.) ... (*MS* L75b:396,1902)

Apropos of the assertive sign (i.e., the assertible sign as it is asserted), Peirce stated that "it is to be understood that proposition, judgment, and belief are logically equivalent (though in other respects different)" (*MS* 789:2,n.d.),[30] thereby implying they can be logically derived from one another and must be considered as successive stages in a semiosic chain:

...an assertion involves endless series of enunciations, or at any rate, two; namely, the assertion involves the enunciation asserted and also the enunciation asserting it. And this asserting enunciation is itself asserted. (*MS* 599:18,c.1902)

In fact, there exists, at least potentially, an endless series, and an endless variety, of propositions asserted.[31] Assertive acts generate different signs; but their meaning or informational content (Peirce's dynamical object) remains in essence unchanged. Each of them acts as interpretant, or translation, for the one preceding it, for the utterance to which it gives a special purpose. Taken together, they show the multiple ways in which one and the same utterance can be intended to signify. This (self-) generative complex of speech events amounts to semiosis.

Contractual Semiosis

In his essay on "The classification of cooperative illocutionary acts", which supported my argument on the contract as speech-act, Hancher makes a distinction which is also central to the semiotic view on contract which was advanced by Peirce. Hancher writes:

It is necessary to distinguish *cooperative* acts from *multiple* speech acts and *collective* speech acts. If two persons simultaneously pledge allegiance to the flag, there are two different speech acts under way—here called "multiple" speech acts. If one person speaks on another's behalf as well as on his own (e.g., "We accept your invitation"), or if two per-

[30] Gorl.Semiotics, Chap. 9, contains a more detailed account of Peirce's view on equivalence.

[31] Analogously, there exists an infinite number of language-games. The three-way affinities between Wittgenstein's doctrine of language-games, speech-act theory, and Peirce's theory of signs can only be cursorily touched upon here. For the similarities between Peirce and Wittgenstein, see Gorl.Semiotics, Chap. 5, as well as Gorlée (1989a, b).

> sons sign the same letter, the speech act is a "collective" one. … There are multiple speech acts when a congregation sings a hymn or says a prayer that is cast, explicitly or implicitly, in the first person singular; there is a collective speech act when it sings a hymn or says a prayer cast in the first person plural. In all of these cases the fact that there is more than one speaker does not matter to the nature of the speech act being performed, whether it be pledging, asserting, petitioning, or whatever. But when two or persons join in a cooperative speech act, such as contracting or voting, the fact that there is more than one speaker is not accidental but essential to the very nature of the act. (Hancher 1979:12)

The point, which Hancher makes here squares nicely with Peirce's explicit mention of the contract as a schematic example of the Thirdness of triadic processes. Peirce argued that in genuine Thirdness the three elements, or terms, must be intrinsically connected:

> Now let us consider the triad, A makes a contract with C. To say that A signs the document D and C signs the document D, no matter what the contents of that document, does not make a contract. The contract lies in the intent. And what is the intent? It is that certain conditional rules shall govern the conduct of A and of C. There is no positive fact in this; it is only conditional and intentional. Still less, if possible, is there any mere monadic quality. It has reference to conditions of experience, involving existence, involving dyadic fact. It may be said that it is a psychical fact. This is in so far true, that a psychical fact is involved; but there is no intent unless something be intended; and that which is intended cannot be covered by any facts; it goes beyond anything that can ever be done or have happened, because it extends over the whole breath of a general condition; and a complete list of the possible cases is absurd. From its very nature, no matter how far specification has gone, it can be carried further; and the general condition covers all that completable possibility. (*CP*:1.475,c.1896)

Peirce touched in this passage upon several aspects of the genuinely triadic sign-relation. First, that it is irreducible. Second, that the intent is the third element of the triad. Third, that it is characterized by conditional futurity. Fourth, that it aims at determination. Fifth, that it is in principle infinite. Let us briefly consider these features of semiosis, taking them more or less *seriatim*.

As opposed to Peirce's example of the thoughtless flipping of a stone and that stone's striking some other person (*CP*:1.366,1890-1891) and other degenerate phenomena,[32] a genuinely triadic relation can, on Peirce's view, not be broken into dyads or monads without losing an essential, namely the mind or third element connecting the sign with its object. Analogously, a contract comes into existence through a meeting of the minds (called, in legal terms, *consensus ad idem*) resulting from some *quid pro quo* maneuvering and again resulting in the intent of the contracting parties. They infuse this element into the respective triadic sub-relations of which they are terms; and together they infuse it in the actual contracting relation. This rational, cognitive intent (or intention) acts both as a third (built upon the Secondness of willing and the Firstness of feeling) and as the third element of the contractual sign-relation, where it indicates the common purpose, design, or resolve with which parties have agreed to act. At the outset this common purpose is

[32] See my article on degeneracy, Gorlée 1990.

still a general, a vague idea,[33] but it is susceptible of being determined in the course of the different semiosis in which it engages. Starting from its translation into the making of an explicit offer and subsequently into a written form this idea undergoes a series of semiosic transformations, necessary for its further development into a genuine sign of law.

For the harmonious evolvement of the content of the contract *qua* sign, the intentional agency needs to be translated into future action.[34] This necessity is one implication of the pragmatic maximum[35]: the "effects that might conceivably have practical bearings" (*CP*:5.402;*W* 3:266,1878) mean, in the case of contract, that its effects must be connected to the real world, where they manifest themselves in actions. The meaning-potentiality carried by the contract is actualized and deployed through controlled sign-action in the future. Hence Peirce's empiricism allows for verification. In 1905, Peirce reworded his pragmatic maxim in semiotic language, thus:

> The entire intellectual purport of any symbol consists in the total of all general modes of rational conduct, which, conditionally upon all the possible different circumstances and desires, would ensue upon the acceptance of the symbol. (*CP*:5.438,1905)

Applied to the contractual situation, this means that the (symbolic) contract, once "accepted" (that is, duly signed, and its truth in the future asserted, affirmed) is intended by the parties to reproduce and translate itself in forms of rule-bound behavior. This behavior consists in a series of dynamical interpretants, each of which is a (still partial) realization of its terms. Directed, in a conditional way, toward some future time, and guided by the principle of "fixation of belief", the contract will eventually achieve its point of fulfillment, at which time the abstract facts, promised and thus expected, are supposed to have materialized in factual ones, bringing relaxation to the contractual relation. The ultimate (or, more realistically, still non-ultimate) logical interpretant then produced is the *moment supreme* when contractual performance is due, the orgastic moment when all intentions must be realized and all purposes attained. Once all obligations have been discharged, all

---

[33] Fried states that: "It is a truism in the philosophy of language that in interpreting a person's words we are not guessing at the hidden but determined content of some list of meanings in the speaker's head. Rather our concerns particularize, render concrete, inchoate meanings… Similarly in contract law there is a vaguely marked boundary between interpreting what was agreed to and interpolating terms to which the parties in all probability would have agreed but did not" (Fried 1980:145,n.12). For one instance, see Wittgenstein's remarks upon the "connexion between the act of intending and the thing intended" (*PI* :1:197).

[34] In reference to futurity, in his essay on "Practical and theoretical beliefs", Peirce drew an interesting analogy between constitutional law, the law of contract, and the scope of human thought-action: "Now an ex post facto law is forbidden by the Constitution of the United States of America, but an ex post facto contract is forbidden by the constitution of things. A man cannot promise what the past shall have been, if he tries" (*CP*:5.543,c.1902).

[35] See Chap. 3, particularly the section on Peirce's pragmati(ci)sm. The pragmatic maxim, in its early (1878) formulation, goes as follows: "Consider what effects that might conceivably have practical bearings, we conceive the object of our conception to have. Then, our conception of these effects is the whole of our conception of the object" (*CP*:5.402;*W* 3:266,1878).

tasks performed, and all debts canceled, the *summum bonum* of law and generality has been achieved. At the same time, however, through the "execution" of the contract—both its completion and its death—, an Edenic situation is restored: pre-contractual, pristine, unburdened, free[36]—and open to assuming new responsibilities, if so desired.

Utterer and Interpreter in Translational Semiosis

> ...signs require at least two *Quasi-minds*: a *Quasi-utterer* and a *Quasi-interpreter*; and although these two are at one (*i.e., are* one mind) in the sign itself, they must nevertheless be distinct. In the sign they are, so to say, *welded*. Accordingly, it is not merely a fact of human Psychology, but a necessity of Logic, that every logical evolution of thought should be dialogic. (*CP*:4.551,1906)[37]

Peirce, the anti-psychological and anti-individualistic logician, expressly de-emphasized a personal utterer and/or interpreter in semiosis of all kinds, and preferred to see them as non-individual minds or, in his terminology, quasi-minds.[38] There is no place for a specific utterer, nor for a specific interpreter, in what is a triadic (sign-object-interpretant) structure. Peirce acknowledged their existence, considered them as necessary features, but he placed them on the periphery of semiosis. This idea seems to have slowly crystallized in his mind and only became unambiguously clear in his later, mature thought. On December 23, 1908, Peirce wrote to Lady Welby:

> I define a Sign as anything which is so determined by something else, called its Object, and so determines an effect upon a person, which effect I call its Interpretant, that the latter is thereby mediately determined by the former. My insertion of "upon a person" is a sop to Cerberus, because I despair of making my own broader conception understood. (*PW* :80–81,1908)[39]

This point (Peirce's "sop to Cerberus") is also nicely illustrated in the following quotation from the important *MS* 318:

> The action of a sign generally takes place between two parties, the *utterer* and the *interpreter*. They need not be persons; for a chameleon and many kinds of insects and even plants make their livings by uttering signs, and lying signs at that. Who is the utterer of

[36] Compare this to: "What the world was to Adam on the day he opened his eyes to it, before he had drawn any distinctions, or had become conscious of his own existence —that is first, present, immediate, fresh, new, initiative, original, spontaneous, free, vivid, conscious, and evanescent" (*CP*:1.357,18890-1891).

[37] On Peirce's dialogic concept of thought and language, see, e.g., *MS* 1334:45,1905, *MS* 292:11,c.1906, *MS* 498:25,1906, and *CP*:6.338,c.1909.

[38] See, for the basics of this, Gorl.Semiotics, Chap. 3 (particularly the section on "Semiosis"); and also, for the consequences of this for translation, Chap. 9 (particularly the section on "The role of the translator").

[39] For the "sop to Cerberus" as a sign of the general nature of Peirce's theory of signs, see Fisch 1986:342–344.

> signs of the weather, which are not remarkably veracious, always? However, every sign certainly conveys something of the general nature of thought, if not from a mind, yet from some repository of ideas, or significant forms, and if not to a person, yet to something capable of somehow "catching on" …: that is of receiving not merely a physical, nor even merely a physical dose of energy, but a significant meaning. (*MS* 318:205–206,1907)[40]

In Peirce's de-individualized universe of signs, human mind-activity has a reduced impact. To distinguish between Peirce's quasi-minds and to give them distinct roles in the formal sign-relation, the utterer must be considered as closely linked to, and determined by, the object, and the interpreter, by the interpretant. The former, or sign-maker, itself a sign, is one presemiosic (or better, extrasemiosic) connection between the sign and its object; the latter, or sign-user, also a sign, connects the sign and the interpretant-sign. In this quality utterer and interpreter are allowed to play secondary, though implicit and abstract, roles in what Peirce saw as a self-generative processuality independent of the human mind.

Semiosis, then, would operate as follows. Chronologically and logically, its "first" instance would take place between an object (with implied utterer 1), a sign signifying the object, and the interpretant (with implied interpreter 2) bringing the sign and its object into a meaningful relation. The object informs and influences (determines, in Peirce's terminology) the sign, through the utterer, and the sign determines again the interpretant through the interpreter. Next, the interpretant (or rather, one of the interpretants) would again become a sign and set into motion the "second" semiosis, where it (the semioticized sign) would be placed in a relation with the object (with implied utterer 2). The object here is also semioticized, but refers back to the same, "first" object. This produces the "second" interpretant (with implied interpreter 2), and so on, until sign and object would be identical, and all semiosis would come to a standstill. The sign would at that time have become a transparent vehicle of meaning, which would enable the object to be known unmediated. Indeed, with the terms of a formal-logical sign relation taking central stage, utterer and interpreter would become largely redundant entities. They are acted upon by the object and the sign, respectively; they act upon the sign and the

[40] Despite appearances to the contrary, Peirce's mentalistic terminology does not contradict his repeated statements that his doctrine of signs is not psychologically based; nor is it at variance with Peirce's own early work in experimental psychology. This point is driven home by Ransdell "Peirce's use of mentalistic terminology does not usually indicate a shift to a psychological perspective, because these terms did not bear the meaning for him that they usually bear for the contemporary reader. In his later writings, when psychology was beginning to flourish, Peirce sometimes uses such terms with the awareness that they might be misconstrued, but with the idea that others probably will grasp little of his meaning unless they first understand him psychologistically. The purpose of his special semiotic terminology was that of making it possible to break out of psychologistic stance toward meaning-phenomena. His dilemma —on the horns of which he impaled himself repeatedly—was that if he defined his terms in a non-psychologistic way no one would understand him at all because his approach was too alien to the prevailing ways of thinking; whereas if he defined them psychologistically his readers might gain *some* idea, but a badly distorted one. One cannot read Peirce with any real understanding without a grasp of the desperate communicational situation he was in and the effect this had on how he expressed his ideas" (Ransdell 1980:183–184,n.12).

interpretant-sign, respectively; but they are themselves unable to directly influence the threefold sign-object-interpretant sign relation. Were this not so, their mental activity would impair the efficiency of sign activity rather than help it achieve its ultimate goal.[41]

Both an utterer and an interpreter must be somehow subsumed under the semiosic act of (human) translation (in its three Jakobsonian guises involving language, that is symbolic signs). In translation they participate conjointly, if in reversed order (first the interpreter, then the utterer), as the two sides of one and the same translator. To further complicate the situation (or, in Peirce's view, to simplify it) there are, in tandem with this translator (both utterer and interpreter), at least two additional agents at work: one utterer and one interpreter. Their influence is camouflaged, perhaps, but undeniable:

> We may say that the *sign* is *moulded* to the *meaning* in the *quasi-mind* that *utters* it, where it was, *virtually* at least, … already an ingredient of *thought*. But *thought* being itself a *sign* the *meaning* must have been *conveyed* to that *quasi-mind*, from some anterior *utterer* of the *thought*, of which the *utterer* of the *moulded sign* had been the interpreter. The *meaning* of the *moulded sign* being *conveyed* to its *interpreter*, became the *meaning* of a *thought* in that *quasi-mind*; and as there *conveyed* in a *thought-sign* requires an *interpreter* of the *moulded sign* becoming the *utterer* of this new thought-sign. (*MS* 318:206–207,1907)[42]

It is no doubt true that, in translation *sensu stricto*, the interpretation of the primary sign precedes the uttering of a translated version, so that an interpreter must have done his or her work before an utterer can start doing his or hers. Yet logically, the interpreter of the primary sign is again preceded by the utterer, if any, of it; and the utterer of the translated sign is in turn followed by some interpreter of it; and so on, both backward and forward.[43] Though the "added" utterer and interpreter are, in translational semiosis, bracketed and reduced to backstage status, they are nevertheless logical elements in successive semiosic events, and they help create hierarchical relations between them.

[41] Ransdell describes the role (or better, attitude) of what he calls the sign observer in semiosis thus: "… the sign-interpretant process, construed as one in which the observer is trying to observe intelligently, is one which involves *strategies* and *techniques* of observation of the signs and their sign actions, and the symbolic sign in particular has to be understood in terms of the appropriate strategy for the observation of it. In fact, it can only be differentiated from nonsymbolic signs with reference to that strategy. Thus while an iconic sign can be defined in terms of de facto qualitative likeness to its object, and an indexical sign in terms of the de facto power of presencing another phenomenal object, the symbolic sign can be defined only relative to how it is to be treated or regarded by the sign observer (interpreter, reader, audience). Its unique sign value as symbolic is wholly dependent upon its being treated in a certain way by the intelligent sign observer in the observational process. (This is a shorthand way of speaking: it does *not* mean that we must introduce an external mind as an independent factor; it means rather that a certain reflexive operation must be introduced into the analysis of the sign-interpretation sequence whenever a symbolic sign as such is supposed to occur" (Ransdell 1980:175),

[42] On the hand-written manuscript page, this is immediately followed by Peirce's exclamation, "Enough of the italics!" (*MS* 318:207,1907).

[43] These terms are used here metaphorically, both in a temporal and a logical sense.

Translation as Contractual Semiosis

In the above pages, the phenomenon of contract in law has been analyzed semiotically, as a series of translations, as different but equivalent interpretive events. Also, the reduced role Peirce gave to utterer and interpreter in the sign-process has been touched upon in its consequences for translational semiosis. These considerations have, in the previous section, led to a description of the process of semiosis, in which the communicative parties were subsumed under the terms of the sign-action. This model is wholly applicable to the process of translation in the more specific, Jakobsonian sense, which presupposes a translating mind functioning both as receiver of the primary sign and as emitter of the translated sign, the end and beginning of two separate but linked chains of semiosis. Pursuing this line of thought, in the last part of this chapter, I propose to complement my analysis with some remarks upon translation as a semiosic activity with markedly contractual features.[44]

Regarded contractually (and thus, as shown above, semiosically), translation is a self-imposed, well-described duty for the future, a promise to perform a task, that is, to do something, and to do it "together". The two sides of the translator's professional self must be *ad idem*, prepared to unreservedly engage themselves in what is a joint and not an individual enterprise. In the division of labor, which must be (implicitly) agreed upon here, each of the translator's *personae* must do half (or rather "half") of the same job. Both have different contracts to respect, different skills and competences, different missions to fulfill. This creates between them, and between both of them and the "obstacle" facing them, an indexical relationship, of physical and logical contiguity, which implies that the element of symbolic equivalence—the *quid pro quo* which is an essential feature of contract—is weakened. In translation real exchange "degenerates" into complementarity. In such cooperative-contractual activity as is translation, no (hypothetical) nonperformance claim against the other can be raised *a posteriori*. In the actual performance they take turns instead of having separate shares. But not only must they physically and mentally operate in one spatiotemporal context; also, linked by a feedback mechanism, they are almost forced to continuously interact and make themselves conjointly responsible for the work done. The patient translator (the interpreter of the primary sign) is an exponent of (determined by) the object; the agent translator (the utterer of the translated sign) enjoys a margin of indeterminacy, of "poetic" freedom in the interpretant. At the same time the work of the translator *sensu stricto* (the translator-utterer in the terminology used above) must build, logically and temporally, upon that of the translator-interpreter, which is again followed by a performance of the former, and so on (at least ideally[45]) until the translation has been completed.

The agreement between the two "halves" within the same translator is typically created in a strictly non-formulaic and even non-formal fashion. Far from being

[44] The subject of translation as a perlocutionary and/or illocutionary speech-act is addressed in van den Broeck 1989.

[45] In actual translation practice there will be a great deal of overlapping.

reduced into writing, with no oral manifestation and not even an informal act which can be deemed to document the existence of a contract between the translational partners, the agreement must be considered as not intended by them to be complete, explicit, and operative as such. If there is a proposal made by the one party and accepted by the other, it is neither clear not unambiguous. In fact, its very vagueness underscores that the translational contract is, in essence, formless and depends, for its realization, upon the private desire of the parties; and desire, if not expressed in spontaneous action, cannot be enforced.

Like the contractual relation, the semiotic structure of translational phenomena is rooted in a form of social organization, namely in dialogue. To be sure, translation implies a rather rudimentary dialogue, namely the inner dialogue of self with self, the ongoing dialogic interaction, within the translator, between the interpreter (receiver, sign-user) and the utterer (emitter, sign-maker). Peirce said that "all deliberate mediation, or thinking proper, takes the form of a dialogue. The person divides himself into two parties which endeavor to persuade each other" (*MS* 498:25,1906). In the same paragraph he also quoted the "vernacular phrase … 'I say to myself, says I' " (*CP*:5.546,c.1908). By the same token, translation somehow involves "an element closely analogous to *assertion*" (*CP*:5.46,c.1908), although here the assertion typically lacks the outward social dimension which is its leading feature in genuine contractual relations. The agreement in translation is not publicized and has no legal consequences.

Back to "translation as semiosis". Translation is mainly concentrated upon the second semiosic instance in the more complex (and in fact endless) process analyzed in the previous section of this Chapter. However, for a correct perspective upon its possible implications and extrapolations, it is crucial to situate translation upon an ongoing continuum of meaning-producing events, a chain of successive semiosis (strictly translational and otherwise) from which one or more episodes may be set apart to be studied in isolation. Ransdell stresses this point, thus: "There are [in semiosis] only signs produced by signs and producing signs, with no absolute starting point and no absolute stopping point" (Ransdell 1980:165). Ransdell's remarks are equally true for translation. A text-sign does not appear *ex nihilo*, but is the result of other, previous signs. And complementary to this backward-intertextuality (infinite regress toward the object), the actual living text-sign produces in its turn interpretant upon interpretant, translation upon translation, without end, each of them updating the available information upon the object, but sooner or later becoming itself outdated. This is forward-intertextuality—the infinite, creative, multidimensional, and labyrinthine progress toward the final interpretation:

> The sign-interpretant series is not a simple linear chain. It is rather to be thought of as a complex of initially independent sequences which join with one another, branch, join with still others, branch, and so on, such that by the end of the process all have ultimately contributed (like contributory rivers) to a final resultant interpretant. (Ransdell 1980:175)[46]

[46] See also Gorl.Semiotics, Chap. 4, particularly its section on "Decision-tree vs. associative network". I also address this issue in my article on "Symbolic argument and beyond: A Peircean view on structuralist thought" (Gorlée 1992b).

The fate of the primary, secondary, etc. signs, once they have produced a translation (or a whole network of translations), is often as "tragic" as it is unescapable. Following the inexorable course of time, Peirce wrote, "The future grows into accomplished fact by a gradual unrolling. The new becomes gradually old. Its effects remain, but they dwindle in importance toward utter oblivion" (*NEM* 4:52,1902). Unless the translated sign succeeds at some point in again finding and appealing to some mind willing and able to continue the process of its translation, it becomes dormant and its meaning becomes ossified, like "a law which has operated for the last time has ceased to exist as a law, except as a mere empty formula which it may be convenient to allow to remain" (*CP*:5.535,c.1902). Just as "all this Universe is perfused with signs" (*CP*:5.448,n.1,1905), it is perfused with translations—living agencies, that is, some of them active and full of energy, others not yet discredited, perhaps, but distinctly becoming outmoded. The translated signs populating our entire life-world, permeating it, are in different stages of growth, vitality, and development, or of stagnancy, obsolescence, and finally death.

It has already been shown above that in translation the utterer (as a function of the object) and the interpreter (as a function of the interpretant) must not only be considered marginal to the action of the sign; more characteristically, in translation they are conflated into one, the translator's mind, who fulfills both functions alternately. This is, Peirce wrote, "the mind into which the minds of utterer and interpreter have to be fused in order that any communication should take place. This mind may be called the commens" (*PW*:196–197,1906). The way in which the sign-making and the sign-using minds observe and experience the power of the sign is expressed in what Peirce called the "Intentional Interpretant" (Firstness of Thirdness) and "Effectual Interpretant" (Secondness of Thirdness), respectively; but not until both minds act together (i.e., not until there is a common intent) can a genuine Third or "Communicational Interpretant, or say the Cominterpretant" (*PW*:196,1906) be produced. In the kind of semiosis under investigation here, the product of this joint venture is the special (idealized and authorized) translation; but it is also the contract, the symbolic action in which the minds of promisor and promise manifest their common purpose in the form of a rational, public, and conventional sign of law. This is a state of perfection, which translations cannot normally attain.

The anatomy of semiosis is like the anatomy of a contract in which parties subordinate their personal needs and desires to a *quid pro quo* imposed entirely by the sign-in-action. Translation is analogous to both semiosis and contract—without, however, ever achieving the status of genuine Thirdness, which is common to both genuine semiosis and the full-blown legal contract. The reason for the degenerate nature of translation is that the contracting parties not only lack individuality and performative power: also, there is no real bargain, no economic aspect, no exchange in which things of value are being put at stake, no gain or loss of capital (material and/or spiritual), and hence no penalties in case of default. In the absence of a *quid pro quo*, translation must be thought of as a truncated contract, one in which the translator makes a promise to him- or herself: a promise to oneself to do something (to produce an interpretant) not by acting (i.e., by interfering with the action of the power of the acting sign) but by letting the sign's intended meaning be transferred through his or her skillful mind. Pragmatically, translation is a private, non-enforceable promise[47]; and to assert it is an inconsequential affair, because there is no point in making oneself believe what is asserted, and there is no penalty for breaking a promise to oneself.[48] The contract in translation is self-reflexive and specular. This means that its intentional component[49] (its Thirdness) is underdeveloped. It is, insofar as it is turned within itself, a recursive, self-sufficient system.

Concluding Remarks

Translation lacks a proper *quid pro quo* (the sign of contractual agreement), because it lacks a full precontractual "trialogue" (object-utterer-sign) as well as a genuine contractual "trialogue" (sign-interpreter-interpretant). As a consequence, if it has a semiosic structure, it is definitely a degenerate semiosis, one in which the interacting elements (sign, object, interpretant) lack the Thirdness of explicit combined will, purpose, and intention. The threefold contractual nexus in translation shows clear signs of Firstness and, especially, Secondness. It is thus a semiotic activity based upon observation and experience and motivated by desire and feeling. If it must at the same time be considered a learning process in which the translator acquires knowledge about which mental attitude most efficiently brings out the power of the sign, final generalization (the creation of truly "hard" laws and their

[47] This is a unilateral promise, not a unilateral contract (such as a gift or a will). While all contracts are rooted in promise, the reverse is not true. See also the interesting parallelism with Wittgenstein's example of private experience: "Why can't my right hand give my left hand money? — My right hand can put it into my left hand. My right hand can write a deed of gift and my left hand a receipt. — But the further practical consequences would not be those of a gift. When the left hand has taken the money from the right, etc., we shall ask: 'Well, and what of it?' " (*PI*:1:268). Not coincidentally, Wittgenstein's "further practical consequences" correspond to the "effects that might conceivably have practical bearings" (*CP*:5.402;*W*3:266,1878) in Peirce's pragmatic maxim.

[48] The translational contract is as much a pseudocontract as the following: "You say to yourself with great force, feeling, and seriousness that you commit yourself to make a thousand-dollar domination to your local classical music station. Surely there is something odd in saying that you have *promised* to do that. To whom have you promised? Perhaps to God —but this just makes the point that a personal promise must be posited, a promise who holds the reins of the obligation. Have you promised to yourself then? If to yourself, then you are free to release yourself in the same way that any other promise may. When it comes time for performance you may release yourself on whatever grounds would have been morally sufficient for not making a contribution at that (later) time in the absence of a promise. A promise to oneself adds nothing to the moral grounds for making the contribution absent the promise" (Fried 1981:42).

[49] As regards this, see Ransdell's cautionary remark, "Do not construe the term *intentional* as equivalent to or as implying *reflective* or *self-conscious*" (Ransdell 1980:151).

logical application or, in contractual terms, enforcement on particular cases) will remain forever out of reach. In contradistinction to the security provided through full contractual semiosis, translation is fallible: it engenders a series of evolving, revisable sighs. Transposed into a logical key, translation is governed by (speculative) abduction and (experimental) induction, rather than by a (fully rational) deduction dominating and giving a special purpose to the other two, "lower" modes of reasoning. The final translation, equivalent to a full-blown contractual argument as well as genuine semiosis, is destined to remain an idealized mode.

References

Austin, J.L. *How To Do Things With Words*, Cambridge UP 1962.
Brock, Jarrett. *An Introduction to Peirce's Theory of Speech Acts.* 1981a. Peirce Society 18–4
Brock, Jarrett. *Peirce and Searle on Assertion. Proceedings Peirce Bicentennial.* Texas 1981b.
Broeck, vd & Holmes, J. *Translated!* Approaches to Translation Studies 7, Amsterdam 1988
Eisenberg, M.A. *Contracts.* Gilbert Law Summaries, Chicago 1984/85
Fisch, M.H. *Peirce, Semeiotic, and Pragmatism.* Indiana IP 1986
Fried, Ch. *Contract as Promise.* Harvard UP 1981
Goodrich, P. *Legal Discourse: Studies in Linguistics, Rhetoric and Legal Analysis.* L'don 1987
Gorlée, D.L. *Wittgenstein, Translation, and Semiotics.* In: *Target 1/1.* 1989a
Gorlée, D.L. *Wittgenstein et Peirce.* In: *Semiotica 73.* 1989b
Gorlée, D.L. *Degeneracy.* In: *Semiotica 81* 1990
Greimas, A.J. *Semiotics and Language/Dictionary* Indiana UP 1982
Hancher, M. *The classification of cooperative illocutionary acts: Language & Society, 8.* 1979
Hilpinen, R. *On CSPeirce's theory of the proposition.* In: *The Monist* 65, 1982
Jakobson, R. *On linguistic Aspects of Translation* In: *Harvard Comparative Literature* 1959
Jakobson, R. *Selected Writings II.* The Hague 1971b
Kurzon, D. *It is hereby Performed ...* In: *Pragmatics & Beyond.* Amsterdam 1986
Lotman, J.M. *Universe of the Mind.* Indiana UP 1990
Merrell, F. *Signs becoming Signs.* Indiana UP 1991
Peirce, Ch. S. *Collected Papers* (CP); *Selected Writings,* Wiener Ed; 1958 (SW); *Semiotics and Significs: Corr. Lady Welby* (PW); *The New Elements of Mathematics* Eisele (Ed), 1979 (NEM). *Writings* 1982-1989 Ed. Indiana UP, (W).
Pharies, D.A. *Charles S. Peirce and the Linguistic Sign.* Amsterdam 1985
Ransdell, J. *Semiotics and Linguistics.* In: *The Signifying Animal* (Rauch & Karr [Eds]) 1980
Rauch, I & Carr, G.F. *The Signifying Animal* Indiana UP 1980
Rethoré, J *La Sémiotique linguistique de C.S.Peirce.* Perpignan/Lille 1988
Searle, J. R. *Speech Acts* Cambridge UP 1969
Searle, J. R. *A Classification of Illocutionary acts* In: *Language in Society*, 1976
Shapiro, M. *The Sense of Grammar* Indiana UP 1983
Wincor, R. *The Law of Contract* Dobs Ferry NY, Oceana Publ. 1970

Obligations II: The Semiotics of International Law: Interpretation of the ABMTreaty

Robert W. Benson

The Semiotic Web of Legal Interpretation

In earlier articles I have advanced a post-structuralist, semiotic theory of legal interpretation and have shown that it explains how statutes, constitutions, and judicial opinions get their meanings.[1] In this paper, I would like to apply the theory to texts of international law, illustrating with the U.S.-Soviet Anti-Ballistic Missile Treaty.

By saying that my theory is post-structuralist I mean that it arises out of that subjectivist thinking that has always been present in twentieth century modernism but which, as we approach century's end, is enjoying a resurgence under the name of post-structuralism or post-modernism in philosophy, in literature, in the arts, in architecture, in science, in the social sciences, and in law.[2] The theory rejects the legal positivism that continues to permeate the law like a grey fog from the nineteenth century. It also rejects the linguistic structuralism with which Saussure's descendants stirred so much excitement in years recently past and which, unfortunately, for a period was nearly synonymous with semiotics.[3] Structuralist semiotics,

Source: BENSON, R.W.: "The Semiotics of International Law: Interpretation of the ABM Treaty" in: *International Journal for the Semiotics of Law*, 1989 p. 257–276.

[1] Robert W. Benson, "The Semiotic Web of the Law", in Roberta Kevelson (ed.), *Law and Semiotics, Vol. 1* (New York and London: Plenum Press, 1987), 35–63; *idem,* "How Judges Fool Themselves: The Semiotics of the Easy Case", in Roberta Kevelson (ed.), *Law and Semiotics, Vol. 2* (New York and London: Plenum Press, 1988), 31–60.

[2] Benson, *supra* n. 1, "Semiotic Web"; *idem,* "Semiotics, Modernism and the Law", *Semiotica* 73/1-2 (1989), 157–173; Joan C. Williams, "Critical Legal Studies: The Death of Transcendence and the Rise of the New Langdells", *New York University Law Review* 62(3), (1987), 429–496.

[3] John Deely, "Pars pro Toto", in John Deely (ed.), *Frontiers in Semiotics* (Bloomington: Indiana University Press, 1986), vii–xxii.

R.W. Benson (✉)
Loyola Law School, 919 Albany St, Los Angeles, CA 90015, USA

J.M. Broekman, L. Catá Backer (eds.), *Signs In Law - A Source Book*,
DOI 10.1007/978-3-319-09837-1_28

in my view, tend to be static, mechanical systems based, at bottom, on claims to universal structures of the human mind which either do not exist at all, or if they exist are so deep and so minimal that they have only feeble influence on the cultural superstructure. Structuralist legal semiotics becomes merely a neo-positivist exercise of analyzing law as an autonomous system of coded norms. It suffers the fatal irrelevance of ignoring historical and social context.[4]

What is needed, instead, is a pragmatic account of legal interpretation, which starts with the modernist notion that language and legal meaning are cultural artifacts produced in time and space through specific social institutions. To describe the mode of production of these artifacts is to describe what Wittgenstein[5] called a "form of life" or "language game" and Stanley Fish[6] refers to as the "institutional practices of the interpretive community"[7] Ideally, the effort to describe such a complex phenomenon would involve the kind of "thick description" of cultural practices of which Clifford Geertz is tribal chief,[8] but I think it can at least be outlined by the kind of diagrams that follow below as *Figures* 1 *and* 2 and which comprise what I call the semiotic web of legal interpretation.

In presenting my theory through diagrams, I hope it will not be mistaken for another structuralist model. As I explained recently in another paper,[9] "I find myself in the same quandary as Mr. Palomar in Italo Calvino's short stories".[10] Palomar had rejected attempts to tackle 'the most entangled human problems, such as those involving society and the art of government' by means of logical, structural models because the models were never congruent with the 'shapeless and senseless reality of human society, with all its monstrosities and disasters.' He decides that

> what really counts is ... the form that society is assuming slowly, silently, anonymously, in people's habits, their way of thinking and acting, their scale of value. If this is how things stand, the model of models Mr. Palomar dreams of must serve to achieve transparent models, diaphanous, fine as cobwebs, or perhaps even to dissolve models, or indeed to dissolve itself. At this point the only thing Mr. Palomar can do is erase from his mind all models and models of models (1985:111).

But, of course, he finds he can't do that and still have sustained thoughts about human problems, because sustained thoughts always begin to assume the shape of a model, and so he—no doubt an alter ego for Calvino himself in the delicious

---

[4] Peter Goodrich, *Legal Discourse* (New York: St. Martin's Press, 1987); Benson, *supra* n. 1, *Semiotica;* but see Bernard S. Jackson, *Semiotics and Legal Theory* (London, etc.: Routledge & Kegan Paul, 1985)

[5] Ludwig Wittgenstein, *Philosophical Investigations,* trans. by G. E. M. Anscombe (Oxford: Basil Blackwell, 1958, 2nd ed.).

[6] Stanley Fish, *Is There a Text in This Class?* (Cambridge, Mass: Harvard University Press, 1980).

[7] See Drucilla Cornell, "'Convention' and Critique", *Cardozo Law Review* 7 (1986), 679–691; Williams, *supra* n. 2.

[8] *The Interpretation of Cultures* (New York: Basic Books, 1973); *idem, Local Knowledge* (New York: Basic Books, 1983).

[9] *Supra* n. 1 (1988).

[10] Italo Calvino, Mr. *Palomar,* trans. by W. Weaver (San Diego, New York, London: Harcourt Brace Jovanovich, 1985).

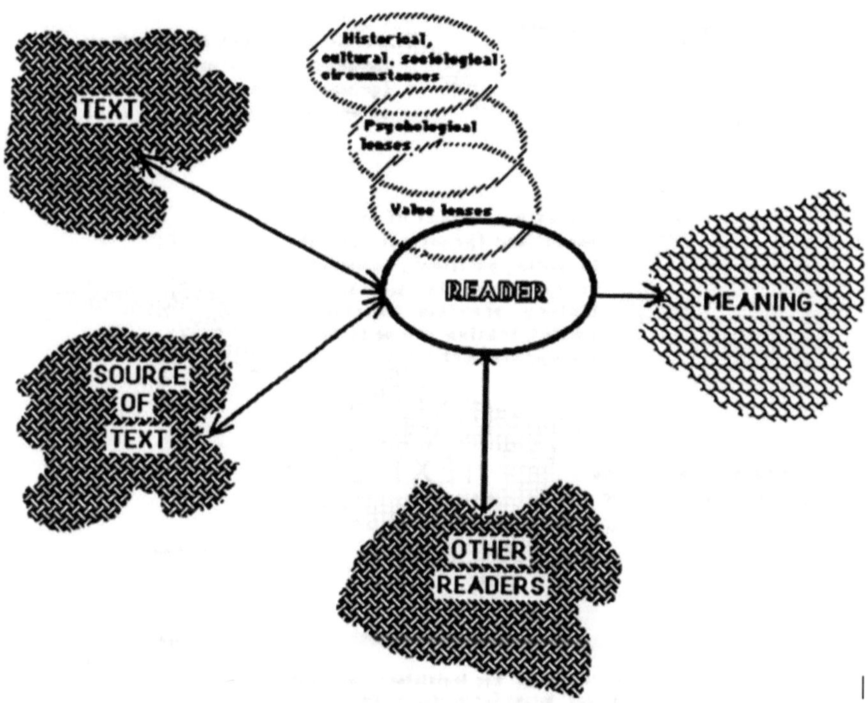

Figure 1 Semiotic Web of Legal Interpretation

meditations of his later fiction—lives vacillating between mirages of rational models and the messy, vibrant life world. Models are difficult to escape, then, but if my explanation is a model at all it at least is not a mechanical one: it is not a drawing of the life world, which is impossible, but only a guide through it or a hint of what it is like, in the way a restaurant menu only hints at the meal to come, or a travel guide only hints at the road conditions and culture in the country across the border.

My approach is influenced principally by the post-structuralist semiotics of Umberto Eco[11] and through him the forerunner Charles Peirce,[12] though it occasionally converges with some parts of the hermeneutics of Heidegger and Gadamer, the literary theory of Stanley Fish, and the work of Derrida, Foucault, Lyotard, Volosinov, Bakhtin, and others. I start with Eco's notion of the labyrinth or encyclopedia to describe the network of signs from which meaning is produced. I relabel it,

---

[11] *A Theory of Semiotics* (Bloomington: Indiana University Press, 1979); *The Role of the Reader* (Bloomington: Indiana University Press, 1979); *Semiotics and the Philosophy of Language* (Bloomington: Indiana University Press, 1984).

[12] Robert W. Benson, "Peirce and Critical Legal Studies:", in Roberta Kevelson (ed.), *Peirce and Law* (Dordrecht and Norwell, MA: Kluwer Academic Publishing, 1990).

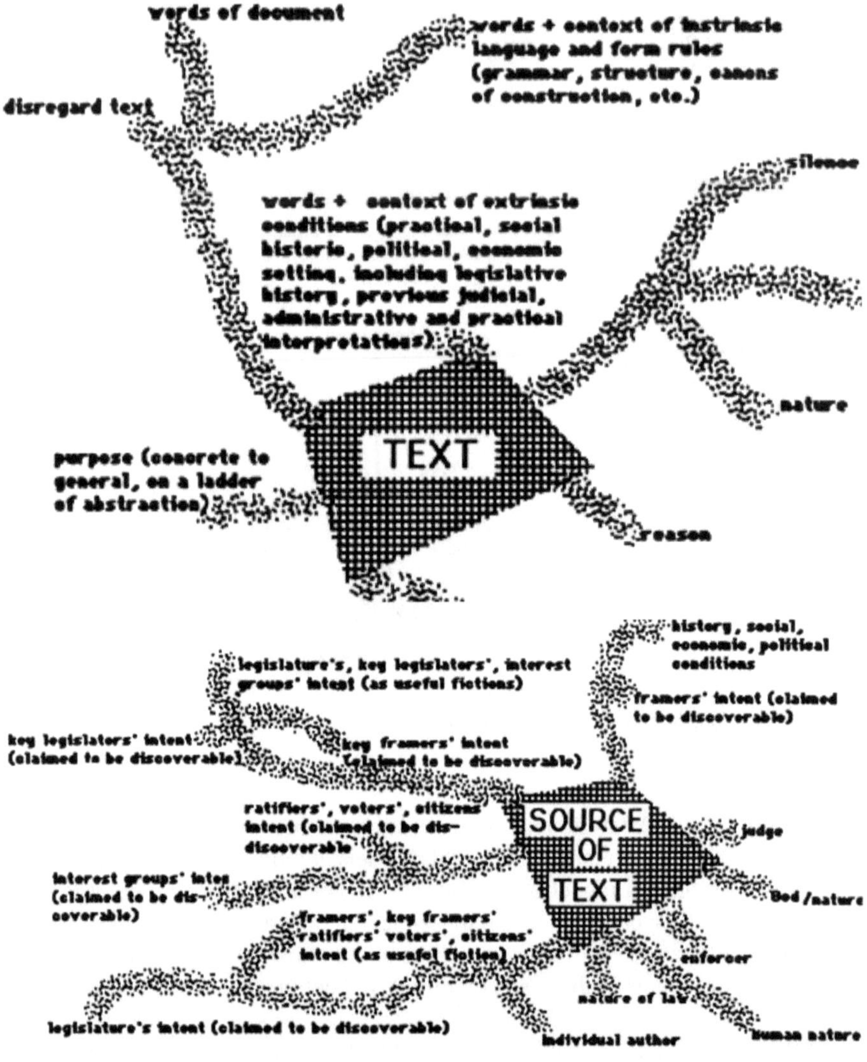

Figure 2 Semiotic Web of Legal Interpretation

however, with Sebeok's metaphor of "the semiotic web",[13] and describe it as follows:

– It is a metaphor, which sees the individual surrounded by a cultural web of signs.
– Any individual who says that something has meaning can simply be called a reader.

[13] Thomas A. Sebeok, "The Semiotic Web: A Chronicle of Prejudices", *Bulletin of Literary Semiotics* 2 (1975), 13.

– The something that has meaning—it may be words or larger units of discourse in a text, or sounds, or objects, or feelings, or events in nature, anything that stands for something else—can be called a sign.
– A reader looking at a sign explains it in terms of another sign in the web, and that sign in terms of another, and so on in what Charles Peirce called a process of "unlimited semiosis," a process which ends only when the reader loses interest after registering the last sign within the mind, or acting in a certain way.
– The *experience* of the series of signs, ending in some mental or behavioral event, is the *meaning* the original sign has had for that reader on that occasion. (This is not a "behavioral theory of meaning" in the sense of mechanically correlating signs to a catalogue of behaviors they cause. It is phenomenological, calling the experience with the sign its meaning.)

The metaphor of the semiotic web permits us to see that the reader is always embedded in a web of signs (or, as Eco prefers, a multi-level, net-like or rhizome-like labyrinth), which is the entire encyclopedia of signs in a culture. Situated at a node from which every point can be reached from every other point, the reader produces the meaning of a sign by travelling the connections of the web, linking a series of signs until losing interest in the process. At any one node, no reader has global vision of all of possible links because the web grows and contracts over the course of history, and because every reader has limited competence and limiting psychological, ideological, social and other circumstances which affect one's capacity to travel the web.

The experience is the meaning to the individual reader, but if readers wish others to share their meanings, or if others wish them to share their meanings, they must attempt to bring one another to experience the visions from their own nodes in the web. In the end, production of the social meaning of texts is a matter of mutual per suasion, its study is the study of rhetoric, and the legal system is a particular system of rhetoric for cultural persuasion.[14]

Now then, the phenomenological experiences the reader has in the process of producing meaning from the web seem always to be these: one travels virtually simultaneously through portions of the web that consist of signs of *texts,* through portions containing signs of the *sources of texts,* which provide additional opportunities for meaning, and through portions consisting of signs given by *other readers* expressing their views of the text. At each step, there are multiple possible selections of signs. Looking at all these signs through lenses of one's own *values,* and limited in vision by personal *psychological, historical, cultural,* and *sociological circumstances,* the reader selects a number of them to produce the *meaning.*

Figure 1 (redrawn slightly from my first presentation of it in 1987) attempts to sketch all this together. *Figure 2* (also redrawn) takes two main sections of the web, the *text* and the *source of the text,* and magnifies them in order to reveal some of the routine pathways taken by Anglo-American lawyers and judges in actual practice,

[14] Peter Goodrich, *Reading the Law* (Oxford: Basil Blackwell, 1986).

showing the multiple possible links that can be combined or ignored among the pathways in producing the legal meaning of any text.

With the aid of these diagrams, I would now like to examine an international legal text, the ABM Treaty.

The ABM Treaty

The United States and the Soviet Union signed the Anti-Ballistic Missile Treaty in the spring of 1972 and the U.S. Senate ratified it a few months later. The Treaty limits both countries' missile defense forces and restricts certain development and testing of such weapons. When President Reagan announced his "Star Wars" program in 1983 (he calls it the "Strategic Defense Initiative," but I decline to consent to the Pentagon's Orwellian newspeak for this frightening laser-beams-and-mirrors militarization of space) the question was immediately raised whether Star Wars violates the ABM Treaty.

At first, the Administration made clear that the President was talking about *research* and that research is not prohibited by the Treaty. This was an uncontroversial position. Moreover, everyone seemed to agree that even *testing* is permitted, if it is for a fixed, land-based system. It was thought, however, that mobile or *space based systems like Star Wars could not be tested.* And no system could actually be deployed. This is what the press commonly refers to as the *narrow interpretation.*

In 1985, the Administration announced a new, *broad interpretation.* It holds that the Treaty's prohibitions on testing apply only to systems, which use the physical principles scientifically known in 1972. It is claimed that new-tech systems like Star Wars, based on other physics principles, may be developed and tested in space, though they may not be actually deployed. The Administration's broad interpretation set off a furor among many citizens, in the U.S. Senate, in allied governments, and in the Soviet government. In American political discourse, the debate over the ABM Treaty nearly overshadowed debate over Star Wars itself. And the Treaty debate, rather than exploring the nefarious motives of Administration officials, the symbolic force of the Treaty, and the strategy of Reagan's reckless adventurism—in other words, the politics, reality and danger of the event—instead quickly became a dry technical exchange between lawyers about the meaning of a document.

Thus, legal discourse moved in once again to assert its hegemony over political and human questions and claimed to resolve them on the basis of its own autonomous techniques. There will be those who welcome this as "the very essence of the rule of law." But if one is convinced, as I am, that "the rule of law" as traditionally practiced is merely the continuation of politics by hypocritical means, one may yearn, when so much is at stake, for a more honest and relevant politics than legal discourse affords.

The ABM debate soon centered around exchanges between the State Department Legal Adviser, who was former federal judge Abraham D. Sofaer, and Senator Sam

Nunn, Democrat of Georgia and Chair of the Senate Armed Services Committee, Sofaer issuing official studies supporting the Administration's broad interpretation and Nunn expounding the narrow interpretation on four occasions on the Senate floor. Their statements collect the key documents and articulate the arguments sharply and fully.[15]

In a nutshell, Sofaer's argument was this: The negotiation record reveals that the Soviets never agreed to the narrow interpretation in 1972 even though the U.S. negotiators had pushed for it. The Executive Branch had given the Senate mixed messages on the issue during ratification proceedings, but the matter was a minor part of the Treaty and unimportant to the Senate as a whole which never formed a clear intention about it one way or the other. While Executive Branch practice leaned to the narrow interpretation for fifteen years, the President's review of the negotiating record has now determined that the broad Treaty was the only one actually agreed to, and the Congress owes him great deference on such foreign policy questions.

Senator Nunn countered that the Soviets did indeed agree to the narrow interpretation in 1972, that the Executive had explicitly represented it that way to the Senate, and had adhered to the view for fifteen years, so there was agreement on the issue all around. Moreover, he argued, the Senate has an equal role in approval of treaties. For an administration to argue that new interpretations can emerge from old negotiating records that had been withheld from the Senate would always give rise to the uncertainty that one treaty had been concluded between the parties and a different one approved by the Senate; this would unsettle treaties, denigrate the Senate's role, and provoke a constitutional confrontation between the two branches.

That both men knew their real task was one of rhetorical persuasion can be gleaned from the fact that neither referred merely to the "narrow" and "broad" interpretations. Cleverly, Sofaer called them "restrictive" and "broad," and Nunn the "traditional" view and "the reinterpretation." I am interested at this point, however, in neither the rhetorical flavour nor substantive content of their remarks. I am interested in the form. Like nearly everyone else in the debate, Sofaer and Nunn assumed that the ABM Treaty possesses a legal meaning that is to be discovered. They assumed that the discovery is to be made by applying traditional techniques for exegesis of legal texts.[16] For international texts, those techniques are embodied

[15] United States Department of State, Office of Legal Adviser (1987): *The ABM Treaty, Part I: Treaty Language and Negotiating History; Part II: Ratification Process; Part III: Subsequent Practice;* Sam Nunn, "Interpretation of the ABM Treaty", Part One: "The Senate Ratification Proceedings", *Congressional Record,* March 11, 1987, S2967-S2986; Part Two: "Subsequent Practice Under the ABM Treaty", *Congressional Record,* March 12, 1987, 53090-S3095; Part Three: "The ABM Negotiating Record", *Congressional Record,* March 13, 1987, 53171-53173; Part Four: "An Examination of Judge Sofaer's Analysis of the Negotiating Record", *Congressional Record,* May 20, 1987, 56808-6831.

[16] *Supra* n. 14.

in custom, in the *Vienna Convention on the Law of Treaties,*[17] in private professional standards like the *Restatement of Foreign Relations Law of the United States,*[18] and in scholars' treatises, but they are little different from the usual techniques employed in both common law and civil law practice for exegesis of other legal texts.

The techniques inquire into the words of the document, its purposes as known from its context and the intentions of its drafters, and the understanding of the document reflected by the practice of those who had to implement it or live under it. These in turn are assumed, in good positivist fashion, to be organized into a decision-tree like hierarchy of authority, with words being most determinative of meaning, context and intentions weighing somewhat less, and practice less yet. Various canons of interpretation supposedly organize this hierarchy and sort out proper use of the sundry materials within its ranks. If interpreters of a text come up with different meanings, it is thought either that one of them has taken a wrong turn in the decision-tree or that the factual evidence of intentions, practice and the like is too thin or murky to present a clear picture. No one doubts, however, that the meaning resides there in the text and that the job of interpreters is to seek it like hunting dogs after the quarry.

This, of course, is a delusion. No quarry exists, because texts don't possess meanings. Rather, readers use texts (and other signs) to make meanings. The solid hierarchy of organization and rules turns out to be made of putty and to dissolve into the network of signs. I have no space in this paper for a microscopic examination of the ways the ABM adversaries made their meanings. The following macroscopic view, however, should suffice to show that the process was not like following a decision tree, but like shining a flashlight on different portions of a web.

Below are the portions of the web of texts, sources, and other readers, that the State Department and the Senator lit up to make their respective cases. I will presume that the *historical, cultural, and sociological circumstances* of the interpreters are well enough known that they need not be described, and that it is likewise obvious that the State Department was reading through *value lenses* in which Reagan conservatism, bellicosity, and primacy of the Executive Branch were uppermost, while the Senator read through lenses which valued most highly a moderate Democratic conservatism and the primacy of the Congress. (I have no information about the psychology of the two readers.) It is these circumstances and values, of course, that most fully explain the interpretation of legal texts, and if I give them short shrift here it is only because I am anxious to show how the other parts of the interpretive process are open to their influence.

---

[17] Vienna Convention on the Law of Treaties, *done* May 23, 1969, United States Senate Exec. Law 92d Congress, 1st Session (1971).

[18] American Law Institute, *Restatement of Foreign Relations Law of the United States (Revised)* (Tentative Final Draft), 1985.

Texts

In reviewing the astonishingly long list of texts used by the ABM interpreters, one should keep in mind these fundamentals, which prevent selection and use of texts from being rule-governed:

– Rules to organize the texts hierarchically (as in the Vienna Convention, etc.) always deconstruct themselves by containing their opposites. The Convention, for example, says the "ordinary meaning" of the terms is to be followed, but "in context" and "in light of its object and purpose." Or, "supplementary" texts such as preparatory work, etc. are not to be used unless (and this can always be so) the ordinary meaning, context and purpose are "ambiguous" or "unreasonable."

State Department	*Senator*
[Texts considered and weighted heavily, neutrally, or wholly discounted, differently by each interpreter]	
Words of Treaty Articles II, V, Statement D.	Same
Intrinsic Treaty structural coherence.	Same
Negotiating records of U.S. team, including working papers, draft proposals, public announcements, minutes of meetings, memos of formal and informal conversations, letters, "back-channel" cables, and similar documents, an open-ended collection occasionally revised to incorporate material "that turned up from time to time". (1987a:13)	Same
Specific original purpose of Soviets/diffuse purposes of U.S. Executive Branch and Senate.	
Silence of Executive Branch letter transmitting Treaty to Senate for Ratification.	
Inconsistent draft Executive Branch transmittal letter that was never sent.	
Silence of Senate ratification resolution.	
Silence of other Congressional legislation.	
Testimony of Executive Branch officials in Congressional ratification and other hearings, 1972.	Silence of testimony of Executive Branch officials in Congressional ratification and other hearings.
Unavailability of negotiating record to Senate.	
Paucity of references in Senate floor debates over ratification.	
Silence of all but few Senators on the issue, and overwhelming approval (92) of Treaty.	
Objections of a few Senators who feared the interpretation the Executive Branch now rejects.	Same
Soviet officials' public statements Soviet during ratification.	Same
Inconsistent Executive Branch internal statements and ambiguous internal written directive, 1972–74.	
Executive Branch speeches, reports, 1972.	Same
Speech and book of former U.S. negotiator, 1973–74.	

(continued)

State Department	*Senator*
Record of U.S.-Soviet discussions monitoring the Treaty, 1974–83.	
Negotiating record and agreed language on analogous questions in SALT II discussions, 1974–76.	
Executive Branch annual publication of arms control agreements, 1975–82.	Same
Private and public correspondence between several private individuals, some former U.S. negotiators, some at "think tank" institutions, 1974–78.	Same
Executive Branch "Arms Control Impact Statements" and other reports to Congress, 1977–85.	Same
Executive Branch internal guidance memos 1977–83.	
Senators' floor debate during failed effort to fund additional space laser work, 1980.	
Executive Branch officials' testimony in Congressional hearings, 1981–85.	
Senate Appropriations Committee Report, 1982.	
Book by head 1972 U.S. ABM negotiator, 1980.	Same
President's and foreign heads of government joint statements, 1984–85.	Book by former Senate staffer based on interviews and classified documents.
Technological advances that make laser testing more feasible and desirable than mere research, 1983-present.	
Analyses by outside "think tank" lawyer and by others, under Defense Department contracts, 1985.	
Records of U.S.-Soviet arms control discussions, 1983–85.	
Occasional public statements of Soviet officials and commentators.	Same
Lack of evidence of Soviet conduct in technical research and testing.	Same
Congressional hearings, committee reports, authorization legislation for Star Wars, 1984–85.	
Limitation of U.S. activity to research, not testing, 1972–85.	Same
	Soviet attendance at Senate ratification hearing and subsequent silence on U.S. interpretation.

Sources of Texts

With every text selected, the State Department and the Senator implicitly adopted some philosophy of authorial intent, giving some weight or another to the meaning intended at the source; their weights differed, though both claimed to privilege original 1972 intentions. These choices amount to a philosophy of language and, in this context, a philosophy of government, which needs to be articulated and defended but was not. Even if we were to agree on such a philosophy, implementing it is usually impossible except as legal fiction, and then that fiction would have to be defended as legitimate within some philosophy of government. In reviewing the list of sources privileged by the State Department and the Senator, one should keep in mind these problems which normally render the authorial intent of legal texts a mere fiction:

– We have no direct access to most of the minds claimed as sources, and the indirect access is often through textual evidence of dubious reliability (see *Texts*) or guesswork (as in imputing intent to silence of the speaker).
– When intent is ascribed to an individual, we run into problems of memory lapses, changed views over time, unforeseen contexts, multiple and even conflicting intents, all within a single individual's mind.
– When intent is ascribed to an institutional body like a legislature or a department of government, we run into all the problems of individual intent plus the intractable problem of cumulating many subjective individual intentions together into a single institutional intent, an act of alchemy like that of turning dross to gold.
– There are no rules for weighting and ranking the different sources.

State Department	*Senator*
[Sources to which intentions were attributed and weighted differently by each interpreter, with no admission of fictionality nor justification of weight]	
Framers (negotiators)	Same
Key framers	Same
Executive Branch	Same
Executive Branch individuals	Same
Executive Branch agencies	Same
Soviet government	Same
Soviet government individuals	Same
Senate	Same
Key senators	Same
Congress	Same
Congressional committees	Same
Private individuals	Same

Other Readers

Enlisting the support of other readers for one's interpretation is where the power to make social meaning finally resides. The more powerful the other readers, the greater the chance that the interpretation will become the accepted meaning. Since this is contrary to the positivist myth that meaning awaits in texts to be discovered through legal formalities, the fact that meaning is actually determined by social and political power is hypocritically disguised: other readers' views are said to be sought as expressions of their intention in framing the text or as indirect evidence of the original understanding. Occasionally, we glimpse an admission that other readers' views are used to establish meaning, as when Senator Nunn warned that the Administration's position would provoke a constitutional confrontation between the two branches, and threatened that Congress would refuse to fund Star Wars if the Administration persisted in its broad interpretation. These were simply statements that Congress has considerable power to impose its meaning. On the following list of other readers enlisted by the State Department and the Senator, there is no overt mention of some readers whose views could have been, and perhaps were, sought quietly such as defense industry contractors, peace lobbyists, and the press.

State Department	*Senator*
Executive Branch officials today and over fifteen years	Same
Senators and Representatives today and over fifteen years	Same
Former negotiators	Same
Soviets today and over fifteen years	Same
Allies	Same
Judges	Same
Scholars	Same
	Six former Secretaries of Defense, three Republican, three Democratic

Conclusion

As of 1988, the interpretation of the ABM Treaty stands as follows. Congress has shown that it is currently the most powerful reader of the Treaty and has, fortunately, imposed the narrow interpretation by amending the defense appropriations statutes to prohibit spending for Star Wars testing. Senate leaders have also moved to preserve their long-range power to control the meaning of treaties by refusing to ratify the recent INF (intermediate-range nuclear forces) Treaty until the Administration submits the negotiating record and promises in writing to be bound by the testimony of its officials in Senate ratification hearings. Meanwhile, the Executive Branch and the Soviet government have reinterpreted the ABM Treaty in light of each side's new perceptions of its interests. Previously, Star Wars and the dispute over the broad and narrow view of the ABM Treaty had threatened to scuttle the INF Treaty. When the Reagan-Gorbachev summit in December of 1987 produced agreement on INF, the ABM Treaty was not permitted to stand in the way. The two sides papered over their differences, for now at least, by signing a new statement. In it, the sides agree "to observe the ABM Treaty as signed in 1972, while conducting their research, development and testing as required, which are permitted by the ABM Treaty....[19] With this studiously ambiguous language the governments imposed the new meaning that each side may read the Treaty as it wishes, once again proving the power of readers to make meaning, even by openly disregarding a text. Disregarding a legal text is a time-honoured technique for interpreting it. (Until recently, I hadn't known of a text that was disregarded even before it was signed. But in the spring, 1988, negotiations between the U.S. and Soviets for withdrawal of Soviet troops from Afghanistan, the press reported[20] that the U.S. agreed to sign a pact and at the same time served notice on the Soviets that the U.S. would violate the agreement by arming the rebels until Moscow halts military aid to the Kabul government. The Soviets, in tum, said they would criticize the U.S. violation but would not seek to stop it.)

Practical Consequences

I hope no one will misunderstand what I have had to say as the language of cynicism, undermining the "rule of law" in general and "international law," which has had such a fragile existence, in particular. I have merely attempted an anthropological description of the reality of legal interpretation, and I have attempted it because I am an idealist, not a cynic. If in fact law is governed by Hobbes and Machiavelli instead of Aristotle and Austin, then it is we idealists who need to be taught that, because the cynics know it instinctively. If in fact law is a system of cultural persuasion for the powerful, then the powerless need to learn how the persuasion works. If in fact law disguises choices of human values with a hypo critical mask of objectivity, then those who care about the values need to lift the mask with candor. If in fact law does not prevent violence except when it coincides with the interests of the powerful, then those who cherish peaceful resolution of disputes must see how important it is to restructure both law and power.

History shows that none of these idealistic ends will be accomplished by a naive faith in the traditional myth of "the rule of law." Indeed, faith in the myth is dangerous for the innocent. The late Primo Levi illustrated the point, in writing about German Jews before the holocaust:[21]

> Like their "Aryan" quasi-compatriots they loved law and order, and not only did they not foresee but they were organically incapable of conceiving of a terrorism directed by the state, even when it was al ready all around them. There is a famous ... verse [by a German poet] ... which is quite apposite here...: Palmstrom, an extremely law-abiding German citizen, is hit by a car in a street where traffic is forbidden. He gets up bruised and battered and thinks about it. If traffic is forbidden, vehicles may not circulate, that is, they do not

---

[19] Robert C. Toth, "U.S. Aides Confident SDI Won't Block Treaty", *Los Angeles Times,* March 24, 1988, I, 11; John Marks, "'Taiwanization' of SDI Allows the Dialogue to Continue", *Los Angeles Times,* December 20, 1987.

[20] Michael Wines, "Tentative Afghan Pact is Reached", *Los Angeles Times,* April, 1988, I, 1.

[21] Primo Levi, "Beyond Judgment", *The New York Review of Books* 34(20), December 17, 1987, 10–14, at 14.

circulate. Ergo he cannot have been hit: it is "an impossible reality,".... He must have only dreamed it because, indeed, "things whose existence is not morally permissible cannot exist." … Many Europeans of that time and not only Europeans and not only of that time-behaved and still behave like Palmstrom, denying the existence of things that ought not to exist.

By using the example of the ABM Treaty, I have tried to call attention to an instance of terrorism directed by the state in which I live. We here are for the most part organically incapable of conceiving of the terrorism this scheme involves despite the fact that the evidence is all around us. I think the myth of the "rule of law" has played some part in hiding this terrorism from us, allowing us to deny the existence of things that ought not to exist. It makes it easy for us to willingly suspend moral belief when the official debate over militarization of space focuses on technicalities like the legal weight of negotiators' memoranda.

For this reason I'm for abandoning the old "rule of law" and acknowledging the realistic rule of law instead. The realistic rule of law brings into the open those issues of power and of human values that cynics are so anxious to disguise with a mythical "rule of law" that benefits their own power and values. By acknowledging that law is not something objective and fixed which is found in texts, but rather something we are constantly making together out of our own values, idealist lawyers will realize they cannot glide amidst the clouds of the "brooding omnipresence in the sky" as Holmes called the mythical notion of law. They will see that peace, equality, community, liberty, justice and other values are always at stake in the law, and must be openly struggled for in every generation, every day, "like a bird that each second keeps conquering its flight."[22]

[22] From Joao Cabral de Melo Neto, "O Cao Sem Plumas" in *Poesias Completas (1945–1965)*. Rio de Janeiro: Editora Sabia, 1968.

Obligations III: Cultural Immersion, Difference and Categories in US Comparative Law

Vivian Grosswald Curran

Of Difference and Sameness[1]

My vision of comparative law through cultural immersion does not amount to a focus on difference for the sake of difference, and it includes the need for vigilance in preventing the recognition of difference from degenerating into a repudiation of the different, a need the generation of émigré comparatists understood so well. Appreciating each legal culture according to that culture's own perspective implies a readiness to concede that the standards by which one measures law and legality in one's own culture need not be universally valid, and that the acculturation one has received in one's own system colors and limits one's vision and understanding. Immersion comparison need not imply pervasive difference at a most fundamental level. What it does imply is the need to be open to all differences beneath the surface, and even in spite of surface similarities, as well as the possibility of differences at the most fundamental level.[2]

The tension between assumptions of sameness versus difference pervades the legal field. We struggle today with deciding if laws and legal arguments should be gender and colorblind, at the risk of failing to validate circumstances and characteristics unique to women and racial minorities, and consequently placing members of those groups at a legally sanctioned disadvantage; in the alternative, if laws and legal arguments should make gender and color distinctions, or if to do so will

[1] **Source**: CURRAN, VIVIAN GROSSWALD, "Cultural Immersion, Difference and Categories in US Comparative Law" in: *The American Journal of Comparative Law*, Vol. 46, 1998.

[2] This last point is especially important in areas of the law in which practical results that seem the same in fact are not, because of profound differences in the respective legal systems that amount to highly different results, despite superficial appearances to the contrary.

V.G. Curran (✉)
School of Law, University of Pittsburgh, Barco Law Building,
3900 Forbes Avenue, Pittsburgh, PA 15260, USA
e-mail: vcurran@pitt.edu

J.M. Broekman, L. Catá Backer (eds.), *Signs In Law - A Source Book*,
DOI 10.1007/978-3-319-09837-1_29

perpetuate dangerous stereotypes of inequality. Those contemporary American legal theories, such as feminist and critical race theory, that have brought these issues to the attention of American law schools, share origins of marginalization, exclusion and exile with comparative law and with the émigré comparatists in the United States.[3] They do not only emanate from, and reflect, marginalized populations, but also generally suffer from marginalization within the academic curriculum of law schools. The insights they have provided into the constitution of our legal system stem in part from the greater facility that an outside observer may have in detecting features of a legal culture so entrenched and unquestioned as to be taken for granted by the insiders. Noting the signal triumphs of the exiled, Edward Said has referred to "an ascetic code of willed homelessness," and Julia Kristeva has evoked exile as an opportunity to "mak[e] love with absence," and as a "weightlessness in the infinity of cultures and legacies [that] gives [the exiled] the extravagant ease to innovate."[4] This perhaps is the condition to which the comparatist should aspire.

The question remains as to whether a premise of fundamental human sameness is a prerequisite to social and legal tolerance. The debate over the philosophical sources of exclusionary ideologies has particular contemporary relevance in the international arena in the context of current ideas of multiculturalism, as well as the development of the European Union.[5] It has similarly crucial contemporary relevance in the domestic arena in the context of marginalized populations within our legal culture. The critical issue of whether an appreciation and celebration of differences among cultures correlates with bigotry and exclusion has no bearing of course on whether fundamental differences *in fact* exist among humans and human cultures.[6] My aim is not to promote a search for differences, or to advocate the converse

[3] For a study of the experience of exile for intellectuals from Hitler's Europe, including an analysis of the impact on refugees of loss of native language, see Donald Peterson Kent, *The Refugee Intellectual* (1953). For a poignant description of Rabel's marginalization in the United States, see Großfeld & Winship, "Der Rechtsgelehrte in der Fremde," 183–200 in *Der Einfluß*, especially the subsection entitled "Wir wußten nicht, wer er war," at 189–90. Rabel was able to obtain only the position of Research Associate, although younger scholars who had emigrated earlier fared better.

[4] Cf. Vilem Flusser, *Bodenlos: Eine Philosopische Autobiographie* 252 (1992). Flusser's exile was involuntary at first, as he emigrated to Brazil as a refugee from Hitler. He describes his initial alienation as changing into a freedom peculiar to the migrant, and he presents the nomadic existence as philosophically desirable because perpetuating continual transformations in perspectives. See also Flusser, "Interview, Graz, 1990," in *Zweigespräche. Interviews 1967–1991* (1996); and Gertrude Stein, *An American in France* (1936). (The point of having roots is to take them with one.)

[5] See Samuel P. Huntington, *The Clash of Civilizations and the Remaking of World Order* (1996) (The post-cold war world will see conflict among political ideologies give way to conflicts of cultures, with culture defined in part in terms of ethnic homogeneity.); and Gibson & Caldeira, "The Legal Cultures of Europe," 30 *Law & Soc'y Rev.* 55, 80 (1996) ("we fully expect that differences in legal cultures will play an even greater role in the ways in which EC law gets implemented within each of the member states.")

[6] See [J.H.H. Weiler's excellent recent article, "Does Europe Need a Constitution? Reflections on Demos, Telos and the German Maastricht Decision," 1 Eur. L.J. 219 (1995)], for a most thoughtful and subtle handling of this question in the context of the European Union. Weiler posits that com-

of the Zweigert and Kotz approach by presuming difference. Rather, I am anxious for comparatists to beware of avoiding truths and the complexities of truths, of losing the gist of attributes of other legal cultures by overlooking the untranslatable, and of rendering themselves unable to see differences for fear of the consequences of such vision.

Entrenched categorizations that lead to presumptions of similarity are dangerous in my opinion because they stand in the way of understanding foreign legal cultures. As long as comparatists fail to identify and challenge unjustified presumptions, mistakes will be made and perpetuated, precluding both effective cultural immersion and the benefits of intercultural translations. Mistaken conclusions of similarity will not enhance understanding, and efforts to build bridges among peoples will be more, not less, doomed, as foreign legal systems continue to surprise and battle us, diminishing mutual sympathy and respect.[7]

---

munity and belongingness must imply exclusion, yet advocates full freedom of cultural diversity in the nations of the EU because of the apparent widespread depth of the human longing for both cultural uniqueness and group belonging. The result need not, in his view, be a sacrifice of civil and political rights of foreigners within the various nation states. It will be, rather, a European Union that tolerates cultural and ethnic diversity while standardizing political rights, and that separates the ideas of nation and state. See also George F. Kennan, *At a Century's Ending: Reflections 1982–1995,* 11 (1996) (attributing the problems of the United Nations to its failure to distinguish between nation and state). Cf., Legrand, "Legal Traditions in Western Europe: The Limits of Commonality," in R. Jagtenberg et al., *Transfrontier Mobility of Law* 67 (1995) (Loss of pluralism in Europe is necessary price of integration).

Cf. Rodolfo Sacco, in Legrand, supra n. 48, at 949 ("[T]he comparatist's teaching necessarily favors some values. But only the comparatist who cheats establishes in advance which values will be prioritized.") For a nuanced, complexity-welcoming approach, see Großfeld, supra n. 99. Großfeld's comparative approach strikes me both as entirely appropriate and highly humane. He recommends building bridges by appreciating commonalities among different legal cultures, prefacing his remarks, however, with a discursus on the need for comparatists to search for reality, rather than for what their particular cultures and training have prepared them to expect to find. His emphasis on commonalities emanates from a humanistic tradition fortified, I suggest, by the effect of the holocaust on contemporary legal culture, and on German legal culture in particular. His caution against complacently confusing what we see with reality seems to me to provide a theoretical component that the émigré comparatists tended to neglect or at the least to leave unarticulated. The beauty of approaches such as Großfeld's in my opinion is that they tally with what I see as the goal of comparative legal analysis, and, on another level, of all legal analysis: transmuting and translating the unknown, the different, the other into the familiar. See also Sturm, "Sameness and Subordination: The Dangers of a Universal Solution," *143 U. Pa. L. Rev. 201* (1994) for an excellent discussion of the dangers of insisting on sameness as a predicate for judicial inquiry; and [Martha Minow, *Making All the Difference: Inclusion, Exclusion and American Law* (1990); Catharine MacKinnon, *Feminism Unmodified: Discourses on Life and Law* (1987); and Catharine MacKinnon, *Sexual Harassment of Working Women* (1979)].

[7] Cf. Rodolfo Sacco, in Legrand, supra n. 48, at 949 ("[T]he comparatist's teaching necessarily favors some values. But only the comparatist who cheats establishes in advance which values will be prioritized.") For a nuanced, complexity-welcoming approach, see Großfeld, supra n. 99. Großfeld's comparative approach strikes me both as entirely appropriate and highly humane. He recommends building bridges by appreciating commonalities among different legal cultures, prefacing his remarks, how ever, with a discursus on the need for comparatists to search for reality, rather than for what their particular cultures and training have prepared them to expect to find. His

The search for human uniformity is also a search for universality. Universal uniformity of human attributes would justify universally applicable legal principles. The problems of an *a priori* assumption of universal uniformity that does not allow for contrary findings are many. Among others, this approach may lead comparatists to advocate principles as universal which cannot withstand fluctuations over time within a given legal culture. Principles, which one unadvisedly touts as universal, may well be used in another place or another time for a contrary purpose, turning the original meaning of those principles on their heads. The attempt to congeal current thinking for posterity's application tends to backfire over time as theory undergoes the phenomenon Balkin calls "ideological drift," where shifts over time cause a given practice or belief to lose its original valence on the political spectrum, sometimes eventually yielding a diametrically opposite political valence.[8] One observes, thus, that differences not only divide legal cultures among nations, but also distinguish a given society in one era from another era.

The inclination to reject the possibility of irreconcilable differences at a fundamental level also is part of a far more widespread phenomenon than a reaction to fascism. It is as broad as the human urge for certainty, and the concomitant discomfort with uncertainty, with loose ends that cannot be tied. The urge for certainty goes hand in hand with the urge to objectify and scientize law, and with a refusal of the disorder of complication, of irreconcilables. Scientizers have proceeded by raising the dual specters of nihilism and relativism as the alternatives to law as scientifically objective. The zeal for certainty, fuelled by normative rather than substantive arguments, often prevails, however, at the expense of truth.[9]

A first step for comparative legal analysis today would seem to lie in rejecting the underlying categorizations of sameness/inclusion and difference/exclusion. Disentangling those underlying associations would obviate the need for engaging in the ultimately hopeless task of redefining apparent difference as sameness. If comparative legal analysis can achieve this dissociation, it will become free of the pervasive, entrenched substructural categorization that has manifested itself in an unwarranted focus on universal uniformity. The dissolution of what has until now been an unchallenged association underlying U.S. comparative legal analysis should

emphasis on commonalities emanates from a humanistic tradition fortified, I suggest, by the effect of the holocaust on contemporary legal culture, and on German legal culture in particular. His caution against complacently confusing what we see with reality seems to me to provide a theoretical component that the émigré comparatists tended to neglect or at the least to leave unarticulated. The beauty of approaches such as Großfeld's in my opinion is that they tally with what I see as the goal of comparative legal analysis, and, on another level, of all legal analysis: transmuting and translating the unknown, the different, the *other* into the familiar. See also Sturm, "Sameness and Subordination: The Dangers of a Universal Solution," 143 *U. Pa . L. Rev.* 201 (1994).

[8] See Balkin, "The Footnote," 83 *N.W.U.L. Rev.* 275 (1989) (Shift over time from formerly liberal to currently conservative political valence of strict judicial scrutiny of civil rights, and judicial deference *to* congressional acts in area of economic rights.); and Balkin, "Ideological Drift and the Struggle Over Meaning," 25 *Conn. L. Rev.* 869 (1993). See also Rawls, (Legal bases can be transitory).

[9] See e.g., Erich Fromm, *Escape from Freedom* (1967); and Erich Fromm, *The Sane Society* (1955).

facilitate heightened acuity, particularly in terms of exploring new bases for acknowledging difference while simultaneously protecting the *other* against discriminatory exclusion[10].

Comparative law to date has been slow to engage in the rich and fruitful discussion of differentiation versus subordination or inequality that scholars in other areas have been developing to address dilemmas raised by the law's blindness to difference. In my view, comparatists have not entered the debate because they have not yet severed the link between difference and exclusion, which is a *sine qua non* of the contemporary theoretical discussion. That link may well have been forged indissolubly for those who have firsthand memories of Nazi persecution. The emigrés have much to teach us about the dangers of separating people under law, but perhaps the time has come to develop ways not merely to coexist with others, but to do so in full recognition of their difference, their *otherness.* Legal cultures that foster tolerance without uniformity, and that celebrate difference, ultimately may further the goals of the emigrés better than an *a priori* definition of all humans as fundamentally similar.

The opposing argument is that to focus on differences is to focus on particulars, and to reject normative judgment[11]. The problem of judging is, in my opinion, the most difficult issue raised by the immersion approach to comparative legal analysis. Beneficial byproducts of the immersion approach, such as humility and an increased reluctance to assume that one has exclusive propriety over absolute truth, may be distinct from a refusal to judge, but they are not calculated to encourage normative judgment.

Cultural immersion's strength is in challenging those who would base judgments on inapposite standards from the comparatist's culture of origin, and in challenging

---

[10] See Minow & Spellman, "In Context," 63 *S. Cal. L. Rev* . 1597, 1630–31. Indeed, as Steven Winter has pointed out, the postmodernist predicament is neither nihilism nor relativism, but "too many [foundations) with .. . a resulting profusion of meaning ... lead[ing) to problems of decidability ." See Fromm, supra n. 148, on the irreconcilable human desires for freedom and security. See also Giambattista Vico: "Principi scienca nuova," in *Opere,* ed. Fausto Nicolini (1953) bk. I, XLVII at 452 ("The human mind naturally tends to delight in the uniform.") quoted in Pierre Legrand, (manuscript on file with the author); and Goodrich, supra n. 4, at 20 (typically, the English doctrinal premise has been that "inconsistencies and contradictions in [the common law] are quite simply unthinkable, they are ...failures of understanding and not of law"); and Gordley & Mattei, "Protecting Possession," 44 *Am . J. Comp. L.* 293 (1996) (for an illustration in the area of property law of legal rationalizations in Germany, France and England to avoid acknowledging such "failures of law").

[11] See Sturm, on the precariousness of depending on findings of sameness ("Those who make and enforce the rules can determine when to expose and act on the difference that we knew was there all along."); de Varennes, at 111(governmental impositions of an official language may be motivated by goal of treating all citizens equally, but result in exclusionary discrimination). See also Minow, "Interpreting Rights: An Essay for Robert Cover," 96 *Yale L.J.* 1860, 1871 (1987) (Describing the danger of "fitting women's claims, for example, into an equality framework that makes sameness to man a prerequisite [because this] may distort or deny the importance of differences."); MacKinnon, at 4 (differentiation as a distinct concept from equality); and Colker, at 1033 (proposing that courts require evidence of subordination for a *prima facie* case of race or sex discrimination, and that evidence solely of differentiation be deemed insufficient for a *prima facie* case.).

those whose assumption that their conclusions have objective validity implicitly would legitimize the imposition of one culture's standards on the practices of another. Cultural immersion does not *preclude* universal normative judgments in that the immersion approach merely seeks to broaden and enrich understanding. In that sense, the immersion approach should facilitate the acquisition of an informed basis for developing judgments by obliging comparatists to enhance and clarify their vision as a prerequisite to judging. Nevertheless, cultural immersion's militating against judging legal cultures by standards external to themselves inevitably challenges the legitimacy of any criticism of, or interference with, foreign cultures.

Cultural immersion thus resolves only the second of twin dangers, which threaten comparative legal analysis: on the one hand, a total abdication of judgment and, on the other, the unwarranted imposition of judgment emanating from a certainty of possessing objective truth. Immersion analysis requires the individual comparatist to struggle over whether and when normative judgments are applicable or desirable. Cultural immersion is a necessary alternative to oversimplification and inaccuracy, but it does not resolve the dilemma of judging. The modernist danger of abdicating value judgment is worth taking seriously in a century that has witnessed the Soviet gulag and the Nazi concentration camp.

Martha Nussbaum has expressed optimism as to the possibility of judging other cultures without an *a priori* devalorization of their identifying attributes. She refers to "[n]atural human practices [as being] full of moral argument and moral standtaking …"[12] and argues against the postmodernist tendency to eschew judgment. According to Nussbaum, postmodernists unwittingly echo the philosophy of the ancient skeptics in rejecting difficulty, or what she describes as "the disturbance of compassion."[13] Nussbaum criticizes observers who refuse to judge, describing them as flawed by "the absence of an important ingredient of humanity." She states that "there are ethical standards that are independent of the norms and traditions of a particular culture," and underscores the dilemma: "[I]t is important for oppressed groups who fare badly in their traditions to be able to appeal to something that is not only outside of unreflective opinion, but also 'outside' of their history and practices…"[14] Nussbaum does not explain how the irreconcilable aspects of seeking to

[12] Nussbaum, "Valuing Values: A Case for Reasoned Commitment," 6 *Yale J.L. & Hum.* 197, 208 (1994).

[13] *Cardozo L. Rev.* 1587, 1590 (1988) (far from being unconcerned with ethics, postmodernists as insist on the ethical). My own view is somewhere between Cornell's and Nussbaum's. I do not see postmodernists as refusing the difficulties and disturbances of complexity when they decline to judge the *other.* My sense is, rather, that, paradoxically, while claiming to reject absolutism, they approach the issue of judgment in an absolutist manner, and conclude that judgment lacks legitimacy because it cannot be derived logically from postmodernist premises. The irony here lies in postmodernism's inability to espouse its own tenets, for, as Winter writes in defense of postmodernism, "[i]t is … the insistence on … the absolute that is both nihilist and profoundly antihumanist."

[14] But cf. Schlag, "Values," 6 *Yale J.L. & Hum.* 219, 225 (1994) (" '(V]alues' are the secular equivalent of God-they are the continuation of theology by other means.") Cf. also Emmanuel Levinas'

analyze the different from within (i.e., cultural immersion), and judging the *other*, can be harmonized so as to legitimize judgment. The closest she comes is her suggestion that the postmodernist view suffers from absolutism: that postmodernists, like the ancient skeptics, unreasonably and unnecessarily require universal acceptance of values as "the criterion of acceptability for a normative principle."[15]

I do not know if Nussbaum's optimism is justified. I am inclined to be less optimistic, but I believe that Nussbaum elucidates the relation of cultural immersion to judging: namely, that both are necessary, and that these two complex and perilous tasks, while in my view not entirely reconcilable, nevertheless are also not entirely irreconcilable[16]. There are no theoretical formulas for engaging in both simultaneously. The answer, if one can call it an answer, lies in what Nussbaum refers to as natural human practices of compassion and ethical commitment. If the latter are practiced in a context of cultural immersion, perhaps the resulting judgments can better avoid or mitigate some of the excesses that historically have been associated with a certainty of possessing truth, while also avoiding an abdication of political action on behalf of oppressed minorities.

Of Immersion and Incommensurability

The seeming paradox is that the immersion approach, with its focus on difference, implies incommensurability, and consequently the failure of comparison. It implies incommensurability, however, only in an ultimate sense. Just as communication cannot reach perfection, so comparison cannot be conducted to perfection. First, some dross from the comparatist's own legal culture will affect the interpretive process, marring total immersion.[17] Secondly, root differences between the observed

---

analysis of charity and justice: "Does not the essential difference between charity and justice come from the preference of charity for the other, even when, from the point of view of justice, no preference is any longer possible?"

[15] Nussbaum, id. at 206. More cautiously optimistic is Changeux, who believes that the mutual impenetrability of cultures impedes the possibility of universals in ethics. Along Kantian lines, however, he states that "the urge to be ethical is a human universal, and that, therefore, ethics proceeds from the very fact of society." Changeux, supra n. 14, at 216. Cf. Habermas, "Struggles for Recognition in the Democratic Constitutional State," in *Multiculturalism,* 107, 125–26 (Amy Gutmann; ed. Shierry Weber Nicholsen, trans. 1994) ("What sets off the battles is not the ethical neutrality of the legal order but rather the fact that every legal community and every democratic process for actualizing basic rights is inevitably permeated by ethics.")

[16] Cf. Taylor, "The Politics of Recognition," in *Multiculturalism,* id., at 69 ("[I]f the judgment of value is to register something independent of our own wills and desires, it cannot be dictated by a principle of ethics. ... One doesn't, properly speaking, make judgments that can be right and wrong; one expresses liking or dislike, one endorses or rejects another culture. But then ...the validity or invalidity of judgments [is no longer the question]").

[17] It is in this sense that George Steiner writes that "[t]here are no translations." Steiner, supra n. 6, at 270. Steiner nevertheless also believes that there are great translations . He defines the latter as "not an equivalence, for there can be none, but a vital counterpoise, an echo, faithful yet

culture and the comparatist's culture of origin will elude complete explanation in the terms of the comparatist's culture of origin, precisely because crucial terms of the foreign culture find no exact parallels in those of the comparatist's culture. On the other hand, the process of translating begins at this point, both betraying the original as the comparatist seeks to reveal it, but also revealing the original, as ill-fitting terminology nevertheless renders some idea of the new and different, and allows for one to start a guided imaginative act, to start to penetrate the other legal culture.

On one level, all comparison, like all translation, seeks commonalities in that it is only by means of shared terms that foreign ones can be introduced and recognized. The search to find only commonality at an underlying level, however, is an undertaking ultimately dependent on repression and bias, neither of which is likely to enhance clarity of vision or effective interaction. It may be hoped that decoupling the link between sameness and inclusion, and asserting differences where they are observed among legal cultures, even at a fundamental level, need not increase or intensify conflict. It may, rather, cast the problems to be resolved into the public arena where they can be studied and negotiated unencumbered by an unspoken agenda, and more amenable to yielding constructive resolutions.

The incommensurability implicit in the idea of cultural immersion would only be an absolute incommensurability in a world of absolutes, a world of comparables versus incomparables. The immersion approach rejects the absolutist mentality. It contemplates a slow pushing against cultural barriers towards an ideal of mutual comprehension, a striving to approach comprehension, and a recognition that some distances will remain. Rather than failure, it implies the need to accept that others have different truths. The more deeply one gains insights into the particularities of foreign legal cultures, influenced by the flavors of each country's habits, history, language, preoccupations and social circumstances, the more aware the comparatist becomes of irreducible *incomparables.* Insights into particularities of identity, and the limits of comparative possibilities, of great importance in grasping foreign legal cultures, depend on a comparative framework. Such bridging of distances as we are likely to realize will entail mutual transformations in the process of comprehension. The increased acquaintance with foreign legal cultures that is cultural immersion's hallmark will result in an enhanced ability to realize the difference between the familiar and the inevitable. Such a use of comparative legal analysis can enable comparatists to penetrate to the deepest substructural levels of legal cultures, to the processes of categorization that are unarticulated and sometimes unconscious. Cultural immersion allows for both the perception and challenging of what previously has been taken for granted as necessary.

Since accepting the idea of human plurality and difference also applies to differences within legal cultures, the obstacles to successful immersion and to successful comparison are different in degree, but not in kind, among different communities

autonomous, as we find in the dialogue of human love. Where it fails, through immodesty or blurred perception, it traduces. Where it succeeds, it incarnates."

within a single nation's legal culture, and among legal cultures of different nations.[18] Comparative law, when conducted effectively, should thus be an instructive model for all legal analysis. Ultimately, comparatists translate. Their renditions of foreign legal cultures are their masterpieces, refleeting at once the depth of their penetration into other legal cultures as well as the degree of their skill in reformulating the foreign into the familiar, so that those who are within the comparatists' culture of origin may gain access to the worlds of those who are not.

[18] Julia Kristeva has even analyzed an irreconcilable plurality of discourses within each individual. She applies psychoanalytic theory in a fascinating study in which she concludes that the rejection of the *other* emanates from the discomfort people feel with a sense of foreignness within themselves. According to Kristeva, the path to accepting the different in others lies in acknowledging the strangers within ourselves. See Kristeva, at 1, 191. ("Delicately, Freud does not speak of foreigners: he teaches us how to detect foreignness"); at 82 ("[T]he relationship with the other, taken at the level of our civilization, is a complication of our relation ship [with the other in ourselves]."). The French philosopher Vladimir Jankelevitch was of the view that "it is minimal otherliness which engenders the most inexpiable hatreds, feeds the most tenacious rancors ...."; Vladimir Jankelevitch & Beatrice Berlowitz, *Quelque part dans l'inachevé* 62 (1978).

Part V
Developing Semiotic Awareness

Law in Signification Processes

Jan M. Broekman and Larry Catá Backer

One must contemplate the tension between truth and meaning in each discourse that strives for objectivity. Awareness of the fragility of an objective attitude is suppressed when reality becomes transposed in narratives on sense and sensibility. No wonder that this suppression characterizes every attempt to explore meaning in life—its cosmological dimensions included.

An essay on law and legal discourse in signification processes must recognize this basic fragility but nevertheless offer an insight into law's position in the context of semiotics and signification. Lady Welby followed that thought-pattern, and it can serve us, who live a century later, as well. She mentioned from early on the need for *interpretation*, in her words:

> (…) the translation at last into valid terms of life and thought, of the knowledge already so abundantly gained. While man fails to make this translation—to moralize and humanize his knowledge of the cosmos, and so to unify and relate it to himself—his thinking is in arrears, and mentally he lags behind his enacted experience.

Lady Welby

Many fragments of contemporary legal thoughts, debates and texts are still a witness of this continuing procrastination. Modern psychological as well as scientific experiences are mostly ahead of the usual articulations of law's discourses. Worries

J.M. Broekman (✉)
Dickinson School of Law, Penn State University, Carlisle, PA, USA
e-mail: jmb56@dsl.psu.edu

L. Catá Backer
Departments of Law and International Affairs,
Penn State University, University Park, PA, USA
e-mail: lcb11@psu.edu

J.M. Broekman, L. Catá Backer (eds.), *Signs In Law - A Source Book*,
DOI 10.1007/978-3-319-09837-1_30

about precision and effect of (legal) language were also Lady Welby's concern, who wrote in 1911:

> Great tracts of experience, direct and indirect, remain without an ordered vocabulary or notation—and better none than those which any others have—exactly as great regions of natural facts remained without recognition and without name until man almost suddenly discovered that he had been looking for the whats and hows and whys of the world he lived in, in the wrong direction and by the wrong method.[1]

It means that significs (her form of semiotics) is not solely on human expressiveness and signifying, but also on recognizing the features and wealth of a cosmic order: semiotics relates to ontology as well as a cosmology—including the problems of the distinction between the two.

Lawyers experience in the flow of their discourse how this translation makes relations between reality and mind drifting away from each other. Human discourse is always, as Foucault suggested, a "découpage", a cutting from reality. Is that an epistemological issue, or an encompassing insight that appeals to larger levels of reality? Lady Welby was inspired to weigh the question, which focuses on an observation of the human quality and of how cosmic reality appears in our daily judgment.

> Too seldom do we try to translate fact … into the dialect of our mind-vision. The sight-nerves of our mind get numbed and dulled by that continuous light impression which we ignorantly treasure. An interval of darkness we abhor; a time of shadow is to us a horror. We even strive to nullify its service, insisting on persistent, unbroken light from whatever source, of whatever quality, without one respite to the tired mind-eyes; and then we shake our heads and cry: "We cannot see; at least there is nothing visible, we are sure of that." And yet the pause may be the means of better seeing—may be the actual secret of the keenest sight we have. The law of rhythm claims obedience thus; each self and all the race must say, Amen. And let us bear in mind that 'laws' like this act through vast ages of development. A week or even a thousand years of darkness may mean, to race or unit, one vibration. What matter, if to rested eyes light flashes, coming when they can use it to good purpose revealing, making clear, the ways of life?

A conclusion that carries the burden of all complicities of signifying processes with a meaningful life is formulated here:

> The 'leading case' which must govern all our ideas of 'stating one part of experience in the terms of another' is, of course, that which man has from the first been compelled to do; that is, after having named his own muscular activities, and then bestowed these names on the motions which he saw in the world around him, to proceed to speak of his own 'feelings' and thinking processes in terms of these physical activities.… This process again reversed itself, and we find him expressing the phenomena in nature, and their changes, in terms of his own emotions or sensations.[2]

Lady Welby's name may be linked with the beginnings of the study of meaning and of signification processes we honor today, but it has seldom been an object of study how her significs was connected at every page of her articles and book publications with the *universe*, the cosmos as *man's ultimate life sphere* and realm of

[1] Lady V. Welby: *Significs and Language.* London 1911, Reprint 2012, p. 5.

[2] Lady V. Welby: *Significs and Language.* London 1911, Reprint 2012, p. 51.

meaning. This experience guides us in this essay on law's place in meaning making. She concludes:

> If we had really been trained to understand not merely the changes, but the nature and work and place, the endless richness and growing variety of the ideas of Sense, Meaning, and Significance; if we had really learnt the inestimable value of organizing our present 'chaos' of expression; if we had only in expression arrived at the point which the method of physical science has reached—it would be difficult to exaggerate the effect on current controversy.[3]

Yet, all these considerations about meaning and sense, sign and signification are kept in one hand: *man's linguistic capacity* (as represented by his ability to perform speech acts) *to say a word*. Lady Welby's significs concentrates on the word that represents the position of man in the cosmos. His name-giving and through that name-giving the creation of meaning, depends on the utterance of a word. Is that characterization of man via his performance of a word the reliable basis for signification?

That question has central importance. It shows how her focus on language and the word as its main component is embedded in an awareness that can be indicated with concepts such as 'universe' or 'life'. Petrilli quotes Macdonald's obituary for Lady Welby, 1912[4]:

> …the currency of an indefinite number of such many [terms] may very reasonably become a public concern in an age of unexampled accelerations and interactions of knowledge, thought, and life. Be that as it may, however, it was with Life—Life more abundant here, Life unspeakable beyond the point where knowledge for the present ends—that Lady Welby was ultimately and always concerned, and only with Language as it was the means and attribute, the expression and the power of Life.

Word and Law

That observation guides us today in matters of understanding the process of signifying in the broadest sense of the word. Peirce and Lady Welby discussed an issue that was generally accepted in their days, and critically reflected in terms of a general cultural pessimism as well[5]: the prevalence of *the word* in all analyses of language and in all discussions about linguistics. But a "word" is *not* a natural component of all languages and *not* the evident particle, which speakers, hearers and linguists equally encounter as their primary language-material to work with. This insight was subject of many doubts and reformulations of old ideas, although it finally inspired Peirce's letters to Lady Welby and her significs, as it had inspired Hugo von

[3] Lady V. Welby: *What is Meaning?* New York 1903, Reprint BiblioLife, LLC, 2012, p 157.

[4] S. Petrilli: *Signifying and Understanding,* De Gruyter Mouton 2009, p. 284, 917.

[5] Jan M. Broekman: "The Emancipation of Meaning" in: *Festschrift Werner Krawietz,* Berlin 2013, and —Id.—: "On the Origins of Legal Semiotics" in: *The Journal of Comparative Law*, London 2012, Volume VII, Issue 1, p. 26–40.

Hofmannsthal's letter (his artistic suggestion claimed the text to be written by Lord Chandos), which shows complexities of a wider scope related to the general state of Western culture and the understanding of a Self. At stake is the loss of power to "express (…) lightness and jest, which only great men, convinced of the perilousness of life yet not discouraged by it, can master".

The letter reports on how a failure of language robbed the author of self-confidence and creativity. Although Chandos feels time and again as if he is on the brink of recovery, he ultimately only understands himself as a broken man, who is left mourning the abilities he lost. The ability of mastering the word as evident language particle prevails. Neither academic nor everyday discourse nor the reciting of classical works, for instance those of Cicero or Seneca, brings him back to the lost treasures. Silence reigns in the letter. Only if the crisis of language and a deep mistrust of the word are acknowledged, newly engendered thoughts and means of expression might come up, Chandos estimates. "The position of the word"—what does this formula of the Occident say?

Any attempt to answer that question leads to complex philosophical insights rather than to one straightforwardly defined formulation. Peirce's suggestion about word, sign and man being identical in deeper layers of reference to the *universe*—"not merely the universe of existents, but all that wider universe, (…) the universe of existents as a part, the universe which we are all accustomed to refer to as 'the truth'"—offers us the framework within which the position of the word has to be understood. We therefore suggest that *Peirce's transition from 'pragmatism' to 'pragmaticism' was caused by his attention for this understanding of the universe and its philosophical implications we would today call holistic.* "Pragmaticism" would then in the first place be a foundation for Peirce's Firstness, Secondness and Thirdness.

One can conclude from this remark, that *there is no sign without inclusion*—an inclusion, which is a process in itself, all-embracing and decisive for signification and signifying, even for the innermost constitution of a sign. This inclusion is neither a fixating differentiation of separate meanings, of individual elements represented by individual words as particles of a language, and refers in its turn to the concept of *universe* rather than to *universes*. Thus:

> (…) by 'semiosis' I mean, on the contrary, an action, or influence, which is, or involves, a cooperation of three subjects, such as a sign, its object, and its interpretant, this tri-relative influence not being in any way resolvable into actions between pairs. 'Semeiosis' in Greek of the Roman period, as early as Cicero's time, if I remember rightly, meant the action of almost any kind of sign; an my definition confers on anything that so acts the title of 'sign'.[6]

This concept of *universe* is above and beyond all universes we arrange for our lives to be lived. The singular is valued above the plural. If we accept, we are in serious troubles, as we are used to understand the singular as constructed by means of 'bringing the pieces together'. What if there are no pieces? The singular leaves us without answer, even disorientated: of what is the singular composed, or is it not

[6] Peirce, CP 5.484 [1904].

composed at all? It means, that we should be very attentive where inclusions are mentioned or concepts like pairing and cooperation are at issue. That stimulus is everywhere in his texts, and we should learn from those encounters. It pertains, surprisingly, to the finger and our attention directed by that limb "…a pointing finger exercises a real physiological force over the attention, like the power of a mesmerizer, and directs it to a particular object of sense".[7] It pertains to thoughts we cherish in our daily lives and meditations/reflections in it: " thoughts are not 'in me'; rather, I am in thought".[8] In a surprisingly forceful and central manner, this also counts for the relations between Firstness, Secondness and Thirdness: they were proposed as separate spheres of world constitution, but are in reality no more than points of attention in the whirls of life's process. There is no Firstness if it cannot embrace Secondness and finally Thirdness, and whoever wants to understand Thirdness should notice the power and enduring presence of Firstness and Secondness in that phase. Our mind's eye should be on inclusions, not on separate stations of the trip in which body and mind are engaged. In other words: Secondness is included in Thirdness, and this inclusion is a constitutive force beyond reflections on a separate constitutive. Peirce's philosophy is a philosophy of inclusion and the infinite differentiations of which is seems a master beyond all, is a way to reach that goal of inclusion, of signification and of signifying. That is true for Thirdness only in an exemplary manner.

The struggle to express totality in all of this impresses, and relates to the entire idea of *semiosis*, which characterizes Peirce's philosophy and our attempt to understand semiotics not as a *bric à brac* of differentiations but as a totality in itself.

> (…) by "semiosis" I mean, on the contrary, an action, or influence, which is, or involves, a cooperation of three subjects, such as a sign, its object, and its interpretant, this tri-relative influence not being in any way resolvable into actions between pairs. SEMEIOSIS in Greek of the Roman period, as early as Cicero's time, if I remember rightly, meant the action of almost any kind of sign; and my definition confers on anything that so acts the title of a "sign".[9]

The named totality is in essence an action, a cooperation, not actions between pairs, an action of almost everything: the reader experiences the nearly corporal difficulty to express the essence of totality appropriately. That is semiotics today!

The performance of *inclusion* throws a light on Peirce's metaphysics of evolution—evolution chained to the concept of the *holon*. Evolution is not metaphysical because it is not understandable in any other way, but it is metaphysical because it is evolution as it is! How it is determines the finiteness of our expressivity and our articulations in language and meaning in general.

[7] Peirce, CP 8. 41.

[8] Peirce, CP 5. note to 289.

[9] Peirce, CP. 5.484.

Sign, Word and Legal Discourse

When we return to the *word* as a particular entity, we must understand how it is a concept in a philosophical context beyond any differentiation. The sign can defend itself against being understood as a product of dissection, distinction and ongoing differentiation, the word cannot be understood in that manner. Peirce's tells us for that reason that a sign on its own is not a sign, but that a sign is a triadic event. This is, more difficult to accept with the sign's immediate relative: a word! Yet the word is misunderstood in very much the same way: lawyers are perhaps the clearest example since they entertain a discourse in which this interpretation of the word based on analysis and dissection is essential. Words in law are components of a *more geometrico* thought pattern. Perhaps the most fascinating issue is, that Peirce's questioning of the *sign* fits to both interests in the *word:* the word in daily language and the word in law destine the word as a carrier of meaning and a component of signification. "Do they do that differently?" was already De Haan's consideration in the world's first inaugural lecture on legal semiotics in 1916. (See Part I of this Volume) The word fulfills in both settings its role of being a basic element of communication. Their contrast in background philosophy is subtle and concealed.

Our interest in the word, in particular because of the state of linguistics and of legal theory pertaining to legal discourse, is sustained by the unique Peircean *sign theory*. A sign is for Peirce a *mediator* in sign-interpretant-object relations. This leads Peirce to a *communicative* definition of a sign, which remains dominant in all theoretical and philosophical settings, the semiotic in particular.[10] It is worthwhile to notice how we are trained in Western cultures to accept the formulation of such occurrences without further thoughts, because our languages are based on a *more geometrico* subject-verb-object triad, and the Peirce observation seems to go parallel. However, a discrepancy should be noticed, an important difference which remains concealed in most semiotic studies.

That difference is already at work where Peirce forwards mediation as a triad [of object, interpretant and meaning], in other words: as a *form.* The latter is not a singular thing—it is a power, a disposition, a real potential, a process and not a fixated status. He wrote in "The Basis of Pragmaticism in the Normative Sciences": § 9 "*What is a Sign?*" that

> … a sign as ordinarily understood is an implement of intercommunication; and the essence of an implement lies in its function … the phrase 'medium of communication' is broader than the noun 'sign'.[11]

Peirce underlines that the *Umfang*, the 'sphere', the environment, is a factor in the determination of the sign in question. And Peirce proceeds to reflect upon the

[10] See: Mats Bergman: *Peirce's Philosophy of Communication: The Rhetorical Underpinnings of the Theory of Signs.* London/New York 2009. and: Jan M. Broekman: "Commens and Communication", *International Journal for the Semiotics of Law*, 2011, 24: p. 247 ff.

[11] Paul Robin: *Annotated Catalogue of the Papers of Charles S. Peirce.* Univ. Mass Press, Amherst 1967, No. 389.

question whether there is always a link with *two* minds, when the concept of a sign is in operation. The same mind that thinks the conclusion should also think the premises.

So far, so good, but the narrowing-down and the opening to binary patterns becomes breathtaking and develops apparently against any broader understanding of communication as Peirce who formulated how communication is determined by the object,

> but in no other respect that goes to enable it to act upon the interpreting quasi-mind; and the more perfectly it fulfills its function as a sign the less effect it has upon that quasi-mind other than that of determining it as if the object itself has acted upon it.[12]

Is this narrowing-down an issue pertaining to Peirce's philosophy in its own right? In any case, Peirce wrestles with numbers because these seem evident from the viewpoint of the *more geometrico* pattern he does not embrace. Whilst considering this, reads him on in his MS 318 from 1907 entitled "*Pragmatism*"

> … we note, as highly characteristic, that signs mostly function each between two minds, or theatres of consciousness, of which one is the agent that utters the sign while the other is the patient mind that interprets the sign", and furthermore, "before the sign was uttered, it already was virtually present to the consciousness of the utterer, in the form of a thought". But … a thought is itself a sign, and should itself have an utterer (namely, the ego of a previous moment) to whose consciousness it must have been already virtually present, and so back. Likewise, after a sign has been interpreted, it will virtually remain in the consciousness of its interpreter, where it will be a sign … and, as a sign should, in its turn have an interpreter, and so on forward.
>
> (…) Having found, then, that neither an utterer, nor even, perhaps, an interpreter is essential to a sign, characteristic of signs as they both are, I am led to inquire whether there be not some ingredient of the utterer and some ingredient of the interpreter which not only are so essential, but are even more characteristic of signs than the utterer and the interpreter themselves.[13]

This prose is radical like Husserl's and shows how Peirce has *a transcendental instinct for implications of words and meanings*. From there, that instinct reaches out to such basic human experiences as 'communication', including further questioning on the basis of changes in the dynamic self-understanding of an ego—first naïve and natural, ultimately positioning itself in a transcendental attitude.

It is Peirce's insight that a simple and arithmetic mutuality is not between human subjects but perhaps between de-personalized "theatres of consciousness". The latter mutuality transcends even those social philosophies that identify themselves as "dialogic". From here, one encounters Peirce's suggestion about common knowledge as a *precondition* for human communication. The "a priori character" of the common knowledge acquired by and functioning in a communicative community enhances the relevance of Peirce's transcendental pragmatism as a fundamental feature of contemporary social philosophy when he sums up some of the issues the players at the theatre of consciousness could use as common ground:

---

[12] See note 11: Robin: *Annotated Catalogue of the Papers of Charles S. Peirce.* 1967; 389, 391.

[13] Idem, No. 403, 404.

> knowledge of the language used, grammatical aptitude, capacity for self-control, practical certainty that one's experiential knowledge of the world does not radically differ from that of other human beings (…) The most important part of this fund is arguably a product of experience in the broad sense, that is, something of cognitive bearing that a person simply cannot deny. [14]

It is surprising how some of the founding fathers of semiotics such as Saussure, Greimas, Lacan, and even Kristeva, contributed with viewpoints of linguistics, literary criticism, psychology and psychiatry, sociology and phenomenology. Once entering the gateway of communication-philosophy opened by Peirce, commonness as a process shows the wealth of power, ability and inspiration, which any culture provides for a human individual before it even knows about its individuality—a Lacanean theme with great relevance. One could say that philosophy of communication focuses on language being the body of everything that is said to us: what we are and become as a character on/in the theatre of consciousness depends upon the word of the o/Other! What humans are—no matter the specificities of their cultures—relates to what they have acquired or will acquire through living with o/Others. That treasure is in the *deep structure* or *geno-text* as articulated by Greimas, Kristeva and others, and not solely important in the context of Barthes' or Greimas' "narrative" approaches to discourses such as legal discourse. The continuous loop between Icon, Index and Symbol, or Qualities, Characteristics and Categories fascinates each semiotician who is aware of a proximity to deep structures of understanding and communication.

Legal Words

The above lines did perhaps throw light on the general pattern of thought within which one normally considers the main properties of words-in-law. Dividing and subdividing, dissection, individualization, splitting, fragmentation, counting, arithmetic fixation, determination, definition, repetition of fixated meanings fit into that pattern and its practices. We are educated to perform the practices of our professional and private life in it. One of the most complete pictures of this pattern is the *social contract* as it was designed by Rousseau (1762) or we read in Hobbes' Leviathan (1651), referring to the origin of society in acts of human will to concretize togetherness, to accept authority and, above all, to honor mutual relationships at all levels of life, to respect the infinite multiplications of the Roman *"do ut des"* and to be a human being in the framework of a "*you and me*" that in its turn is multiplied during ages to be and to come. In short, one concludes, how words-in-law are coined in contract.

It interests that the relations between theories of State and Law on the one hand and of Language on the other are incorporated in texts of Hobbes, Locke and Rousseau. Neither States nor Laws could be conceived without Language, no legal

[14] Robin No. 139.

or state act was ever thought without appropriate verbal articulation. *Semiotics is born within relations of dependency among Law and Language, words and politics—a dependency portrayed in classical social contract theories.* This has been repeated in all variations of legal theory and their background philosophy of language. One reads in H.L.A.Hart's *The Concept of Law* (1961) how analytical philosophy of language relates with legal theory, or in J. Austin's *How to do Things with Words* (1962) what also was written in John Searle's *Speech Acts* (1969) on the strong ties and parallels between analytical philosophy of language and legal forms of language. All demonstrate contractual features. A strong coherence between Wittgenstein's theory of language games and Merleau-Ponty's view on language is shown in functional and sociological theories of law. Topical jurisprudence and legal rhetoric were close to Aristotelian linguistic insights—they are altogether expressions of one thought pattern formation.

An important observation would be, that the concept of 'philosophy of language' itself is also the product of the same geometric thought pattern. This is mirrored in a variety of implications regarding the concept of 'theory of language':

(1) Each theory of language related to law and legal discourse is a theory about *the role of language in man's relation to the world* as understood and named as *reality*. Peirce's man-word-world connotations are as significant in that regard as Searle's analyses about a *performative* character of certain—especially legal—speech acts. In legal theories, particularly in the Civil Law system, there is for this reason a close tie between natural law ideas and views on the essence of man.

(2) Theory and philosophy of language are almost entirely theories about *the internal architecture of language, in which words function as separate and independent units*. A theory of language is a theory about the connections between those units or elements. Patterns of connectivity are based on contractual markers. Language and society are both the product of equal and parallel presuppositions. As a result, one declares in a theory of language for 'natural' what seems desirable in a theory of law and society. Social consensus is the result of such constructions—their presupposition included.

(3) A theory of language *focuses in the Occident on the indisputable position of an autonomous speaker.* This position is clearly repeated in any legal theory with semiotic components, in particular where signifying is at stake, the meaning of legal signs and meanings are contemplated or the features of a specific legal discourse explored. Freedom of contract, impartiality of the judge, autonomy of the legislator and ultimately the inviolability of the rule of law (even in a highly ideological move at distance from particular judgments) mirror the speaker position. It fascinates to observe how at this point one discovers the source for debates between significs and semiotics at the beginning of the 20th century, not only between Lady Welby and Peirce, but more specific in the first inaugural lecture on legal significs in 1916 performed by J.I.de Haan in Amsterdam.[15] He wanted language barriers to be diminished and the specificity of legal language no longer block access to justice.

[15] See Part I of this Volume.

(4) The latter viewpoint indicates a wider interest and creates enduring perspectives on Occidental law. Language can only be the preferred instrument of the speaker (the subject in society) if there is this firm *unity between basic thought patterns on law and society*, which we characterized as *more geometrico*. Legal expressiveness is in chains with that thought pattern—it needs the 'subject-verb-object' schematization like all other linguistic utterances and significations to perform 'correct' law and to engender 'justice'.

Before it can compose this expressivity and have the rule of law function, as it should, it needs the 'word' as its ultimate building block in language. We learn from contemporary pedagogic and education efforts in regions with illiteracy how important that knowledge is and what enormous social effects are at stake. That experience is not without relevance for law and legal discourse, its semiotic dimensions included. Legal expressivity shows the patterns of social expressivity; one perceives the inverse only in secondary cases. Legal discourse is an artificial discourse (like mathematics) composed with words of our daily languages (different from mathematics); the predominant position of law in society conceals how the two fortify one and the same geometric pattern.

(5) A final question comes up: "What does 'understanding' really mean?" The question is extremely important in social issues and particularly where legal judgments seem to have become large-scale directives for social behavior.[16] The question also fascinated theology, the arts, law and philosophy in the context of hermeneutics. 'To understand' has never meant a repetition of what the speaker had in mind, the lawyers, artist, priest, or philosopher. The Ancient Greek differentiated between 'thinking' (NOEIN) and 'speaking' (LEGEIN). However, we want to know the meaning of our discovery that thinking and speaking are both determined by an identical pattern. It seems to mean that our understanding is always along common lines, which we are seldom aware of. Total freedom, including thought formation without any basic pattern or internal order, seems a phantom, a distorted image.

This is important for those who want to honor the human possibility to concretize free speech in a society.[17] The expression 'free speech' is a legal and political articulation, so that the freedom involved is a matter of law and its expressiveness. The free speech issue leads to continuously issuing new laws or, in the opposite, to diminish the influence of the state. Both viewpoints demonstrate the close connections between law and language at a political, even educational, level. The politico-ideological possibility to speak, to perform linguistic acts, to articulate, depends on our acceptance of the *more geometrico* patterning of life in the Occident. It is tragic, that this pattern contradicts experiences and expressions of an individual in society, because nobody can fulfill his or her life in the illusion of autonomy of speech and its speaker position. The unfulfilled desire for autonomy and particularity causes large-scale psychoses in Western society.

---

[16] See: Peter Goodrich: "Historical Aspects of Legal Interpretation" in: *61 Indiana Law Review, 331,* 1986.

[17] See: James Boyd White: "Free Speech and Valuable Speech", in: *UCLA Law Review, 51, 799.* 2004.

It may surprise, that the language of the law participates so powerfully in the originating of psychotic situations, because law is generally appreciated for its purpose to create order and to appease rather than its opposite. But the more law focuses on this task—and without any further consideration uses its language for that purpose—the more it provokes its own contrast. That ground shaking insight is based on the powerful coherence in a triple identity of: (a) the social values as articulated in the social contract, (b) the basic structures of law and legal discourse, and (c) those of Western European languages. The three together form an unshakable basis for the role of law in signification processes, which are a major issue in the legal-instrumental language that governs social life.

Semiotics and Law

There are important semiotic consequences of this conflict-loaded triad, pertaining to (1) the position of the subject in law, language and society, (2) the geometry of structuring legal language, and (3) the character of the predominant mode of thought for semiotics and law. We offer (1) and (2) as preparatory remarks for (3), which relates to the background of the entire field of legal semiotics.

1. Subject Position. There exists an interesting *semiotic complexity as far as a subject-position* is concerned. Its central position in law and language has been broadly researched, exposited and understood in the various phases of structuralism during the second half of the 20th century It was a bewildering idea that such a position could represent an entire cultural pattern of thought, all its philosophical implications included.[18] It interests the more, since one can understand that a subject in the form of an individual in everyday life influences our patterning of thought and reality by means of its participation in the social contract (a contract being a specific relation between subjects/individuals /individualized entities) and fortifies its standing in social life as a legal subject or/and legal person in law, and in perfect parallel with its position of subject in language, particularly in the grammatical first-person-singular. Individuality in contractual thinking parallels legal capacity and the subject-centered form of our sentences in language (everyday language as well as legal language) as well. A legal act forms a triad with legal subject and legal fact: three fundamental semiotic constructions in law and its discourses. That triad corresponds precisely with the 'subject-verb-object' triad mentioned in the above context. A pivotal position is given to the legal act: the act is in law and legal discourse not given the position of a predicative activity but fits into the syntax of the legal sentence. Classical theories of the legal contract emphasize either the legal subject as originator of the contract (a theory pertaining to the *will* of the subjects concerned) or the legal subject as the representative of the object of the contract, its materiality envisioned as a parallel to the subject's will or intention. All this seems necessary to put the legal subject to the fore as a specific unity amidst a plural

[18] Jan M. Broekman: *Structuralism. Moscow-Prague-Paris*. Reidel, Dordrecht 1974.

complexity of legal relationships. That unity is thus a feature of the legal person, just as the legal capacity is a unity in the form of a legal intention (will) and the legal act as a unity of the legal subject and the legal fact. One is attempted to conclude that *a theory of law culminates in the semiotic construction of the sentence-form of the (legal) act*—which is ultimately a linguistic form. The subject-form of the legal sentence and the legal text (often concealed in forms of the neuter) parallels the sentence-form of the legal act. One concludes semiotically, that legal texts will be constructed and maintained in accordance with an analytical model of language, and not with the factual rhetoric structures of an actually spoken daily language. Tensions between analyticity and facticity of the language model are understood in the light of the fact that legal discourse is an artifact, and lives at distance from the living language of everyday life.

2. Semiotics Applied. Law's words are thus words embedded in a geometric and hierarchic construction, which finds its power and legality to create communication *only in—and thanks to the parallels between law and language,* that is in *legal and linguistic meanings*. On the basis of such parallelisms and enforced mutual identities is a semiotics of law possible. Hence the enticement to treat legal semiotics as a form of *applied semiotics*. But the parallelisms must be respected and safeguarded: here is visible why law is *institutionally embedded* in society. All legal institutions sustain the geometric construction of law and legal discourse—each in its particular function and within the precise limits of its own field, always controlled by higher ordered instances. In the context of legal semiotics is the meaning of law's institutions and their language a hot topic. But it are the institutions who require a continuous transition from word to text, because lawyers cherish the idea that written texts are more stable and enduring than spoken words. Speech cannot be quoted, not transferred objectively, only texts can withstand the ages and ground the books of law beyond generations in a culture.

There are *four conceptual movements* to master the transition from word to text in legal discourse. *First*, there is the strict requirement that in legal texts only one particular and determinable idea will be represented by one and only one properly defined term. *Second,* such separate and individualized terms can only form a textual connection when they refer to one fixated and well-defined meaning. *Third*—a requirement for which the Civil Law has become famous—grammatical constructions of sentences that fit into the text should not in any way produce complex or ambiguous meanings. *Fourth*, each text must be conceived as if it were the product of one rational active and singular individual. Peirce's suggestion about a 'man—word' complexity has therefore no place in legal texts and does not fit to the textual human being that acquired its socialization and signification in Hobbes' *pactum subiectionis*!

3. Static and Dynamic Modes. The two remarks we offered give us an impression of the predominant mode of thought that determines legal discourse and the semiotic options of that discourse. It fascinates to read Peirce in this context, when he researched in 1903 what he called "The Ethics of Terminology" and engaged him in reflecting upon semiotics and science in general:

> (...) every symbol is a living thing, in a very strict sense that is no mere figure of speech. The body of the symbol changes slowly, but its meaning inevitably grows, incorporates new elements and throws off old ones. But the effort of all should be to keep the *essence* of every scientific term unchanged and exact, although absolute exactitude is not so much as conceivable. Every symbol is, in its origin, either an image of the idea signified, or a reminiscence of some individual occurrence, person or thing, connected with its meaning, or is a metaphor.[19]

The insight Peirce articulates is remarkable and forms an absolute contrast to the above-mentioned semiotic analyses of legal language and legal discourse. *First*, Peirce considers the *symbol*, but it could have been the sign, the word or any other term as well. The symbol is characterized as *a living thing*; it is *not a mere figure of speech*; it *changes* slowly and it's meaning is in a constant process of *growth*: symbols *incorporate new elements* continuously and *throw off old* ones. The main feature of this portrait of a sign/symbol is in its *dynamics*; these form a glaring contrast to the fixated building blocks of legal language in the architecture of law's discourses.

Second, Peirce does not describe nor analyze language and linguistic reality from the standpoint of the autonomous speaker, as we encountered in our description of the language of law. He brings three players, which perform the role of the strictly defined first-person-singular to the stage: occurrences, persons and things. Each of them will be connected with meaning, and the complexities of meaning result from their interrelations. That is definitively a creative signifying process and will never be a static datum to take or to leave.

Thirdly, it interests that the former are related to science in general and not to one discourse in particular. Science is a continuously developing conception and discourse in which words are used and newly explored in the context of family relations. Emphasis on the dynamic character of science in culture and society is shared with all preceding issues mentioned in Peircean lines.

Fourthly, there is a fascinating dynamics in the fragment itself, which should be given its due respect. *The outlined dynamic is appropriate to comprehend the universe.* This attitude is that flagrant contrast with the described semiotic architecture of legal discourse, so that we can understand Peirce's words as a particular challenge between a static understanding of the universe, law included, and a dynamic understanding which relates back to the holistic accent that values all-there-is as a totality being a constant flow.

Words are the product of segmentation; they are proclaimed to be by nature 'elementary units' of language where they are constructions, not of an individual but of the spiritual activity of an entire culture. But there are no words apart from a discourse and other specific word ensembles. For example, poetry suffers not, or minimal, from fragmentation, whereas legal arguments are entirely their product. Despite all 'poetic justice', there is an immense difference between poet and lawyer.[20] Their

---

[19] Peirce, CP 2, 222.

[20] Jan M. Broekman: "Perelman and Poetic Justice" in *Rechtstheorie*, vol 23, No.2, 1992, p. 177–187.

difference goes to the word and its semiotic functions. Law makes clear how the activity of word construction relates to the meaning those words forward. Where the poet perhaps 'forgets' the relation between meaning and word, and strives for his or her freedom in that context, must the lawyer determine precisely and with mathematical precision how the words spoken or written are constructed.

The attitude of the poet cannot inspire the lawyer, who must stick to the 'atomistic' attitude to words, which the poet can neglect or simply drop. Words as units of language are only abstractions from the continuous and undivided movement language appears to be. A word is not an "indivisible particle or an atom of meaning" but rather a temporary intersubjectivity-related marker (remember Peirce's emphasis on society with regard to semiotics) in the entire spiritual and material movement we call 'language'. The clause, the code, the sentence, the reference, the paragraph, the sign, the symbol are *equal elements of an unrestricted flow* of meaning. We do not need to see them as particles, as units in their autonomy building language patterns and clusters of meaning as soon as we recognize how they are markers in our continuous flow of articulations.

Editorial 7: From Prize-Winning Seminar Papers to a General Conclusion

Jan M. Broekman and Larry Catá Backer

This final part of the Source Book focuses on trends to develop semiotic awareness in legal education and law's practices. Its texts could be understood as presenting the ultimate goal of positioning the semiotics of law in legal education. Their broadening knowledge might bring a deeper understanding of legal practice, and a heightening semiotic awareness. Before concluding this volume with an essay on law's position in signifying processes, we therefore offer three prize-winning papers written in the course of 2011/2012 Roberta Kevelson Seminars on Law & Semiotics at the Dickinson School of Law, Penn State University, USA. They show the result of such awareness as applied in specific fields of student interests. The task of these three texts is therefore slightly different from other texts in this volume—they do not only *inform* about particular issues in modern law, but they also *give evidence* of a new alertness and a sharpened view on the inherent signification processes in law and legal discourse.

It interests that including these papers shows general dimensions. It has often been observed that semiotic studies are confronted with a transition or translation of facts in daily life into legal language and consequently life as conceived terms of legal discourse. The prize-winning papers are all three linked with this transition. In other words: all three authors have chosen a subject that is deeply anchored in daily life. Their semiotic awareness has been initiated here, and not in any philosophical or jurisprudential subject. How relate words of a judge to the freedom of a citizen? How does highly criticized corporate activity receive legal- and State protection? What can we trust in suggestions of scientific evidence? These issues are

J.M. Broekman (✉)
Dickinson School of Law, Penn State University, Carlisle, PA, USA
e-mail: jmb56@dsl.psu.edu

L. Catá Backer
Departments of Law and International Affairs, Penn State University,
University Park, PA, USA
e-mail: lcb11@psu.edu

J.M. Broekman, L. Catá Backer (eds.), *Signs In Law - A Source Book*,
DOI 10.1007/978-3-319-09837-1_31

altogether considerations in the street and loaded with legal-semiotic relevance. However, they lead to a conclusion, which transcends the immediate presentation of the subject concerned, when they show a surprising aspect of the semiotic project in law. That aspect is the participation in law as a process. The meaning-making effect of a lawyer's activity is always part of such a more general process, which must be characterized as 'signifying'.

One follows the original intuition of Charles S. Peirce in observing that all legal activity is a matter of "sign-politics" and therefore of signification. The latter focuses on society as a peculiar wholeness, and the above mentioned student participation is a sign of interest as well as a partial representation of the process of law in society as such. We remember how Lady Victoria Welby wrote at the beginning of the semiotic developments in 1906: "The master-signal to us therefore is: Never divide, and never confound (…) For here lies the secret of our disastrous use of Individual for the You and the Me of the human order. (…) We are Dividuals both in a good sense and a bad sense: if we are individual in any sense we are merely items, indeed merely points to start a line from, neither length, breadth, nor depth is ours. (…) There are many grades of Identity. That attained so far by humanity is the highest that man knows, except That which he infers; That which he knows that he Signifies or at least Symbolizes".

Can Words Really Set a Man Free?—A Semiotic Analysis of the American Criminal Defendant's Right to Allocution

Charles Volkert

Only the man who has enough good in him to feel the justice of the penalty can be punished

William Ernest Hocking

Introduction[1]

Luckily, not everyone has stood before a judge who poses the question, "Do you have anything to say before I sentence you?" However, many people have. In America, a person convicted of a crime has a right to allocution before being sentenced; the curtailment of or failure to grant this right may be grounds for an appellate court to remand the case for resentencing.[2] In most states, a convicted defendant has a statutory right to allocution; in few states, the defendant has a constitutional or absolute right to allocution at sentencing. Federal Rule of Criminal Procedure 32(a) affords a defendant "an opportunity to make a statement in his own behalf and to present any information in mitigation of punishment." Originally, the phrasing of the judge's question was more specific than the general phrase above which reflects the modern inquiry. The historical question which the judge posed when offering the defendant the opportunity to allocute was more focused: "Do you know of any reason why judgment should not be pronounced upon you?"[3] The defendant's response was confined to legal defenses, such as, pardon, pregnancy, insanity, misidentification, or benefit of the clergy.[4] Current justifications for the right are broader: To promote sentencing objectives, the right to allocution allows a judge to gather information that will enable him or her to more accurately mitigate

[1] **Source:** VOLKERT, CHARLES: "Can Words Really Set A Man Free? A Semiotic Analysis of the American Criminal Defendant's Right to Allocution" *Prize-winning paper of the Roberta Kevelson Seminar on Law & Semiotics, 2011*

[2] *Green v. United States*, 365 U.S. 301 (1961).

[3] Celine Chan, *A Defendant's Word on Its Face or Under Oath?*, 75 Brook. L. Rev. 579 (2009).

[4] Celine Chan, *Id.:* Brook. L. Rev. 579 (2009).

C. Volkert (✉)
Cumberland County District Attorney Office, 1 Courthouse Square, Carlisle, PA 17013, USA
e-mail: districtattorney@ccpa.net

J.M. Broekman, L. Catá Backer (eds.), *Signs In Law - A Source Book*,
DOI 10.1007/978-3-319-09837-1_32

or individualize punishment.[5] In theory, a defendant's allocution is unbounded; however, for practical purposes, such as the maintaining of decorum in the courtroom or judicial expedience, the defendant's allocution may be abridged. The implications of the right to allocute and the multiple meanings such a privilege can engender—meanings for the defendant, the judge, the victim(s), the prosecution, onlookers, society as a whole, and Law as an institution—will be the focus of this paper. The following semiotic analysis of this post-trial, pre-sentence right will illumine certain existing and potential meanings in Law, while at the same time serving as my own contribution to meaning-making in Law.

Semiotics is often referred to as the "study of signs" and a sign, as defined by Charles Sanders Peirce, is "something which stands to somebody for something in some respect or capacity."[6] So it goes, Legal Semiotics is the study of signs in Law. Law embraces the entire conception of the legal system, from theory to practice. Black's Law Dictionary, which is itself a major influencer and meaning-maker in Law, defines "Law" as "The regime that orders human activities and relations through systematic application of the force of politically organized society, or through social pressure, backed by force in such a society."[7] The key word is "force." Law is an institution founded upon and sustained through force; its essence is coercive. This is paramount for understanding legal rights, the enforcement of rights, and the many meanings through which these rights are derived, exercised, violated, and changed. Law's coerciveness can both facilitate and stymie change. Before getting into the multilayered meanings of a defendant's right to allocution it is necessary to first lay a foundation through a discussion of Peirce's approach to semiotics.

Peirce's Semiotics

Peirce's semiotic approach is founded upon this first principle: All thought depends on and uses signs. Some question whether all thought is itself a sign. I hypothesize that it is: At the very least, thought is symbolic of human consciousness and individual life, not to mention its inseparable relationship with the "thing" being conceptualized. Furthermore, all reasoning involves the interpretation of signs. Signs connect the external world of objects and the conscious world of thought.[8] They are the facilitator of understanding. Peirce elaborates on these insights among other concepts through the creation and use of his triad of "Firstness," "Secondness," and "Thirdness." All acts of reasoning, modes of communication, and perceptions of reality, and the meaning which stems from these, involve the triadic relations of

[5] Celine Chan, *A Defendant's Word on Its Face or Under Oath?*, 75 Brook. L. Rev. 579 (2009).

[6] Broekman, Jan M. (2010) *The Roberta Kevelson Seminar on Law and Semiotics Course Book.*

[7] *Black's Law Dictionary* (9th ed. 2009).

[8] Alex Scott, *Charles S. Peirce's Theory of Signs*, (2004), http://www.angelfire.com/md2/timewarp/peirce.html, Accessed April 13, 2011.

signs. Meaning is a triadic relation between a signifier, an object, and an interpretant.[9] In order to arrive at the genuine meaning of a sign, which is derived in Thirdness, it is important to first discuss Peirce's notions of Firstness and Secondness.

Firstness is often the most difficult concept to grasp because one cannot knowingly experience it—one cannot contemporaneously be solely in Firstness and aware of it. Hence, once it is grasped, once it is articulated or thought of, it is no longer Firstness itself. In order to understand Firstness one must perceive it from without or in conjunction with Secondness or Thirdness. Firstness is a mode of being without reference to anything else. As noted above, since thought or awareness utilizes signs (referential objects) pure Firstness is cognitively unattainable. One may ask how can Firstness be real if it cannot be cognitively experienced. The answer is rather simple: It lies in the notion that Firstness is the pre-thought reality or being of what a thought conceives. After all, thought must be thought of something: Firstness is this possible "something."

Peirce describes Firstness throughout his writings. One of his earliest definitions may be instructive: Firstness is "[w]hat the world was to Adam on the day he opened his eyes to it before he had drawn any distinctions, or had become conscious of his own existence—that is first, present, immediate, fresh, new, initiative, original, spontaneous, free, vivid, conscious, and evanescent."[10] Several more of Peirce's own definitions of Firstness will be instructive to really help flesh out the concept: [Firstness] is the quality itself, independent[] of its being perceived or remembered . . . [it is a] simple positive possibility of appearance"[11]; Firstness is "immediate consciousness"[12]; "The idea of First is predominant in the ideas of freshness, life, freedom. The free, which has not another behind it, determining its actions".[13] A right (such as the right to allocution) only has meaning as a triadic relation; however, the Firstness of the right may be properly understood as pure freedom; the right tries to capture and promote this freedom through the assertion of it as the building block of the right. The quality, the immediacy, the multiplicity, the freedom of the right to allocution is its Firstness, which only becomes cognizable and describable through the Secondness and Thirdness of this right.

---

[9] Alex Scott, *Charles S. Peirce's Theory of Signs*, (2004), http://www.angelfire.com/md2/timewarp/peirce.html, Accessed April 13, 2011.

[10] Charles Sanders Peirce, *A Guess at the Riddle*, CP 1.356-357, 1.361, (c. 1890), as cited in *Commens Peirce Dictionary: Firstness, First [as a category]*, http://www.helsinki.fi/science/commens/terms/firstness/html, Accessed April 13, 2011.

[11] Charles Sanders Peirce, *A Letter to Lady Welby*, CP 8.329, (1904), as cited in *Commens Peirce Dictionary: Firstness, First [as a category]*, http://www.helsinki.fi/science/commens/terms/firstness/html, Accessed April 13, 2011.

[12] Charles Sanders Peirce, *A Guess at the Riddle*, CP 1.356-357, 1.361, (c. 1890), as cited in *Commens Peirce Dictionary: Firstness, First [as a category]*, http://www.helsinki.fi/science/commens/terms/firstness/html, Accessed April 13, 2011.

[13] Charles Sanders Peirce, *The List of Categories: A Second Essay*, CP 1.302, (c. 1894), as cited in *Commens Peirce Dictionary: Firstness, First [as a category]*, http://www.helsinki.fi/science/commens/terms/firstness/html, Accessed April 13, 2011.

Secondness inevitably and inextricably depends on Firstness. Secondness is the mode of being that which is itself in referring to a second object.[14] Secondness can be manifested by "action, reaction, causality, reality, actuality, or factuality."[15] Consider Peirce's own example:

> A court may issue injunctions and judgments against me and I not care a snap of my finger for them. I may think them idle vapor. But when I feel the sheriff's hand on my shoulder, I shall begin to have a sense of actuality. Actuality is something brute. The law of gravitation is in the judge upon the bench who may pronounce the law till doomsday, but unless the strong-arm of the law, the brutal sheriff, gives effect to the law, it amounts to nothing.[16]

Before jumping ahead to Thirdness, the interpretation, the meaning-making aspects of this example—that the sheriff's gesture makes meaning for Peirce: He is the bearer of rights and duties[17]—let's first consider the Secondness which arises from his sense of actuality. Peirce's reaction to the sheriff's gesture, the actuality manifested from the sheriff's brute action of touching Peirce's shoulder, is an example of Secondness. It is the force of his touch, no matter how slight, which awakens Peirce to the Sheriff's presence and ultimately to the meaning of his own presence (Thirdness). This Secondness reveals the Firstness of the above example, which is the possibility of the Sheriff's touch or the Law's force and all the potentialities that accompany it. Secondness is the "brute actions of one subject or substance on another, regardless of law or any third subject."[18] In this example, actuality (Secondness) immediately facilitates meaning (Thirdness) through Peirce's interpretation of the Sheriff's brute action.

The ingenuity of Peirce's approach is clear. Peirce exposes the fictional character of the dyadic relationship, which in the above example is between Firstness and Secondness—the possibility of Law's enforcement and the Sheriff's touch. There is always a Third in this relationship. Thus, there are no pure dyadic relationships, but rather triadic relationships exist. The possibility of the Sheriff's touch and his actual touch, are joined by a third, Thirdness—the meaning, interpretation, or perception which is created from this relationship between Firstness and Secondness. This relationship between the two, e.g. Speaker and Hearer, always takes place within a larger third dimension, i.e. culture. Modes of communication take place within or as a part of a greater context. The dyadic ignored this totality, whereas the triadic embraces it. Thirdness is the meaning (in this instance for Peirce) behind the Sheriff's brute action. As noted, this meaning can be Peirce's recognition that he is the bearer of rights and duties, but the potential meanings are limitless. The Sheriff

---

[14] Alex Scott, *Charles S. Peirce's Theory of Signs*, (2004), http://www.angelfire.com/md2/timewarp/peirce.html, Accessed April 13, 2011.

[15] Alex Scott, *Charles S. Peirce's Theory of Signs*, (2004), http://www.angelfire.com/md2/timewarp/peirce.html, Accessed April 13, 2011.

[16] Broekman, Jan M. (2010) *The Roberta Kevelson Seminar on Law and Semiotics Course Book.*

[17] Broekman, Jan M. (2010) *The Roberta Kevelson Seminar on Law and Semiotics Course Book.*

[18] Charles Sanders Peirce, *Pragmatism*, CP 5.469, (1907), as cited in *Commens Peirce Dictionary: Firstness, First [as a category]*, http://www.helsinki.fi/science/commens/terms/firstness/html, Accessed April 13, 2011.

is conveying the fact that Peirce is beholden to the law; he has rights and duties from which he cannot escape; the Law is the greater universe from which this meaning derives and is beholden.

Peirce describes Thirdness as "the mental or quasi-mental influence of one subject on another relatively to a third."[19] Also as the mode of being of that which is such as it is in bringing a second and third into relation with each other.[20] This Thirdness may be manifested by representation, thought, continuity, order, unity, or generality.[21] Thirdness is not confined. There are multiple meanings that may be derived from the above example other than the fact that Pierce is a bearer of rights and duties. For instance, the Sheriff's brute actions could lead Peirce to conclude that 1) the Sheriff has a strong grip, 2) the Sheriff wants Peirce to turn around to identify himself, 3) Peirce had a fuzzy on his shoulder. The possible meanings are endless; this is the beauty of the legal semiotic understanding and analysis.

The study of semiotics in Law forces the legal actor to come face to face with the accessibility of a myriad of possibilities at his disposal. His task is to make meaning (most often for clients) through the use or manipulation of signs. Just as for Peirce a sign on its own is not a sign itself, rather it is an interconnectivity of relationships, a legal argument only takes shape through its interconnectivity of signs in Law. To understand Law as an inherently coercive institution that is dominated by signs is to understand the potential interpretations, both positive and negative, or even neutral interpretations, that are possible, which in turn broadens the legal actor's perspective and appreciation for the complexity of Law and his potential meaning-making influence within it.

The Right to Allocution and Jurisdictional Differences

This paper is primarily concerned with the many meanings of a criminal defendant's right to allocution. It deals with the interpretations arising from the existence and exercise of this right. The right to allocution varies from state to state and within the federal court system. It is not clear whether a defendant's right to allocution before sentencing is a constitutional right protected by the Due Process Clause. In *Green v. United States*, the United States Supreme Court held that Federal Rule of Criminal Procedure 32(a) stands for the proposition that a criminal defendant must be given an opportunity to speak prior to sentencing: "Judges are warned that hereafter their records must leave no doubt that a 'defendant has been issued a personal invitation

---

[19] Charles Sanders Peirce, *Pragmatism*, CP 5.469, (1907), as cited in *Commens Peirce Dictionary: Firstness, First [as a category]*, http://www.helsinki.fi/science/commens/terms/firstness/html, Accessed April 13, 2011.

[20] Alex Scott, *Charles S. Peirce's Theory of Signs*, (2004), http://www.angelfire.com/md2/timewarp/peirce.html, Accessed April 13, 2011.

[21] Alex Scott, *Charles S. Peirce's Theory of Signs*, (2004), http://www.angelfire.com/md2/timewarp/peirce.html, Accessed April 13, 2011.

to speak prior to sentencing.'"[22] Curiously, the Court never answered the question of whether a failure to grant allocution is a violation under the U.S. Constitution. The Court may have avoided this question because the defendant's right to allocution is seen by some to serve only a ceremonial purpose; giving a defendant a forum to speak may serve no practical legal purpose, thus the courts often bypass its constitutional grounding.

A year later, in *United States v. Hill*, the Court again sidestepped the answer to the question of whether it is a constitutional right, which may require automatic reversal and remand. The Court held that in a habeas corpus petition the failure of a judge to offer allocution prior to sentencing was not an error "of the character or magnitude cognizable under a writ of habeas corpus."[23] The Court then stated, "It is an error which is neither jurisdictional nor constitutional."[24] And so the Court refused to rule that not affording a defendant the right to allocution at sentencing required automatic reversal and remand. The Court's reluctance to raise the right to allocution above its level as a statutory right to the level of a constitutional guarantee (which would presume it to be a natural, inherent right of free people) has significant implications for considerations of what the right to allocution means in Law. Law has its own inner hierarchy of rights, from constitutional to statutory to common law, with each tier encompassing its own unique structure and coercive power. A constitutional right ordained by the Supreme Court has maximum force, the maximum coercive potential for a meaning-maker to harness and exploit; a statutory right lacks this ultimate power. Given the Supreme Court's reluctance to create an inviolable constitutional right to allocution, state courts have fashioned their own rules concerning the right and the proper remedy for its violation.

In many states, the right is protected by statute; however, in some it is considered an absolute right, which is so fundamental to a fair trial that when violated it automatically leads to reversal and remand; there will be no harmless error analysis. For instance, Hawaii considers the right to allocution to be a state constitutional right protected by due process. In *State v. Chow*, a Hawaii appellate court ruled that if a defendant is not offered an opportunity to personally speak before sentencing there is a per se violation and the remedy for this denial is resentencing; a harmless error analysis will not be employed.[25] The jurisdiction where a defendant asserts his pre-sentence right to allocution will set the legal context in which the meaning of that right must be considered.

For the most part, either a harmless error analysis will be employed, or automatic reversal and remand will happen. For example, because of the different remedial effects of an allocution violation—the court will either use a harmless-error analysis or will reverse and remand—the meaning of a defendant's right to allocute will necessarily differ from jurisdiction to jurisdiction. This fact should be kept in mind throughout reading this paper: Jurisdiction is an inseparable element of a meaning-

[22] *Green v. United States*, 365 U.S. 301 (1961).

[23] *United States v. Hill*, 368 U.S. 424 (1962).

[24] *United States v. Hill*, 368 U.S. 424 (1962).

[25] *State v. Chow*, 883 P.2d 663 (Hawai App. 1994).

in-Law analysis. Some courts find the right to be merely ceremonial, protected by statute, but not determinative of any legal matter; others find it to be an essential element of a sentencing hearing which when delivered by the defendant can persuade a judge and have profound effect on the punishment he receives. The emphasis placed on the right in a given jurisdiction will accentuate the different meanings a defendant's allocution will produce in Law.

The Right to Allocution as a Sign in Law

The Firstness of the triad is that the right to allocution exists: There is a quality or idea of a primary right to allocution, an unbridled, original, spontaneous, freedom of the right, which exists! Secondness captures this right and is evidenced through the judge's brute actions toward the defendant: He directs his question *at* him: "Do you have anything to say before I sentence you?" His directed question intrudes on the defendant, shocking him into awareness of something for which he may not have been aware of or prepared for: The defendant all of a sudden becomes conscious of the actuality of the right to allocution. The defendant now knows, "I have a right to speak before I am sentenced!" But what does this mean? The defendant will interpret the judge's question. This interpretation is the manifestation of Thirdness. The defendant's interpretation of this right and his subsequent steps in exercising or refusing to exercise this right will create an intricate web of meaning.

The above paragraph focuses mainly on the sign of the right to allocution on the "micro-level." It is the defendant's recognition of the right and the meaning he places upon it. But, the defendant's exercising of this right is also a sign in Law. Actually, the meanings which take place at this "macro-level," which is not concerned so much with the derivation of the right, but rather the exercise of the right, are diverse and often profound, having a great impact on Law through the differing interpretations that may, and often do, arise from the defendant's allocution.

There are two main rationales for the right to allocution: mitigation and humanization.[26] Most of the time a defendant exercises his right to allocution in hopes of mitigating his sentence. However, sometimes a defendant may speak for other reasons, such as to justify his actions, to criticize the Law or society, or to promote his own views. The meaning of allocution for a defendant will fall within the more traditional mitigation rationale or the catch-all humanization rationale, or both. The former is a more practical reason for the Law to enforce the right, whereas the latter seeks to "give a voice to persons within the legal system," regardless of the content of what they say.[27] This latter rationale is why some see the right as merely ceremonious; however, as will be made clear in section B, this is not the case.

[26] Kimberly A. Thomas, *Beyond Mitigation: Towards a Theory of Allocution*, 75 Fordham L. Rev. 2641, (2007).

[27] Kimberly A. Thomas, *Beyond Mitigation: Towards a Theory of Allocution*, 75 Fordham L. Rev. 2641, (2007).

Meanings of a Mitigation Allocution

Many jurisdictions uphold the right to allocute for the purpose of offering a defendant a chance to mitigate his sentence. In these jurisdictions the defendant's speech will often be confined to this purpose. Nevertheless, the meanings arising from his allocution are manifold. A real world example will help elucidate this. In a recent Non-Jury Trial that I prosecuted as a certified legal intern for the District Attorney's Office the defendant was given an opportunity to allocute after being found guilty of damaging another's vehicle. The conversation went roughly as follows:

> Judge: Does the Commonwealth have a recommendation of sentence?
>
> Prosecutor: The Commonwealth requests the defendant pay the statutory maximum of $150.00 in restitution to the victim, plus court costs.
>
> Judge: (speaking to defendant) I found you guilty of the charged crime, Criminal Mischief. Do you have anything to say before I sentence you?
>
> Defendant: Yes. I didn't do it. I didn't even have my keys on me that day. I couldn't have scratched his car because . . .
>
> Public Defender: (interrupting the defendant) The case is over. He has already found you guilty. You cannot talk about the facts of the case.
>
> Defendant: I have nothing further Your Honor.
>
> Judge: I now sentence the defendant to pay costs and restitution in the amount of $150. Case adjourned.

Initially, as noted previously, the law of the jurisdiction must be stated before understanding the allocution's meaning. Pennsylvania Rule of Criminal Procedure 704(C) (1) provides that "At the time of sentencing, the judge shall afford the defendant the opportunity to make a statement in his or her behalf and shall afford counsel for both parties the opportunity to present information and argument relative to sentencing." The Pennsylvania Superior Court held that the significance of allocution lies in its potential to sway the court toward leniency prior to imposition of sentence.[28] In this simple case the defendant's allocution has meaning for all involved; I will proceed one by one with each legal actor in the courtroom to illustrate some of the multiple meanings possible. The defendant's allocution (the signifier) was heard by several legal actors (objects) producing differing meanings for each of those actors (interpretants).

The defendant's right to allocution, as defined by the above statute, affirms her subject-position. By definition, Criminal Law requires an alleged or adjudicated criminal. The defendant is always the underlying focus of the processes of criminal law, even when other legal actors take the stage. The defendant fulfills the key role in criminal law; she engenders the subject-positioning. Her allocution is the manifestation of her subject-positioning; it reveals and affirms that she, the adjudicated criminal, is the focus of Law. She is the top-tier of criminal law's stratification structure. The defendant says, "*I* didn't do it. *I* didn't even have my keys on me that

[28] *Commonwealth v. Newton*, 875 A.2d 1088 (Pa. Super. 2005).

day. *I* couldn't . . . ." Her first-person allocution reveals her centrality in Law. All the legal actors, their actions, and the meanings of their actions, are dependent on the reality of her, the criminal.

After learning the allocution rules of Pennsylvania the first thing that jumps out is the public defender's *seemingly* erroneous advice. While the public defender's advice that the defendant was not allowed to speak about the facts of the case was technically incorrect, it may have been a strategic move. Here are some possible meanings the public defender may have derived from the defendant's allocution. It is possible, and likely, that when the defendant referred to the facts of the case the public defender reverted back to defense mode: She advised her not to speak of the case not because she was not allowed to (even though this was her "excuse") but because the public defender knew that the defendant's denial would not sit well with the sentencing judge. By repeating her testimony that had already been borne out at trial—that she did not have keys nor did she damage the victim's vehicle—the defendant was eschewing responsibility for her actions. The public defender likely recognized this and advised her client not to speak of the case because the judge has not yet sentenced her. During allocution, the judge is supposed to be receptive to a defendant's explanation of why she did what she did; he may lighten her sentence if she offers compelling explanations or if she shows remorse.

Here, the defendant was likely not appealing to the judge's sense of leniency and therefore was unlikely to receive any. She did not offer any mitigating factors, such as, difficult financial times, accidental damage, that the victim later totaled the truck or does not own it anymore, that the truck has scratches all over it and was thus not devalued by her actions, or that the victim intentionally damaged her vehicle or performed other retributive acts, and so on. Therefore, when the defendant exercises her right, the public defender must be prepared to intervene and give advice; in this case, the advice was to shut up. Certainly, if the defendant would have appealed to any of the mitigating factors hypothesized above the public defender would have been unlikely to intervene. This exhibits how even though the allocution involves a "conversation" between the defendant and the judge it has meaning for the public defender whose job it is to protect her client's interests, which in this case was her client's interest in a lessoned sentence or fine. This highlights how dialogues do not take place in a vacuum; there is always a context in which they occur.

There are other more personal meanings a defendant's allocution may have for the public defender whose client was just found guilty. If the defendant shows remorse before the judge the public defender may feel vindicated for providing a strong legal defense for a guilty client. The defendant may bring up facts that were not borne out at trial which may signal to the public defender that her counsel was ineffective and because of that there may be a chance to overturn the ruling on appeal; thus, the meaning of the allocution may have an information-gathering purpose. It can also reveal to the public defender the conscience of her client which she may then transfer her newfound understanding to other similar clients in the future, thus deepening her legal aptitude for dealing with these types of clients.

In this case, the defendant's allocution offered the public defender an opportunity to impress the judge: She curtailed the defendant's allocution, thereby reducing the time of trial which moved the case forward and allowed the judge to impose his sentence. This is important because a public defender is often in front of the same judge. She may have been laying the groundwork for future encounters with the judge, showing him that she values his time and his opinion. The judge has already ruled on the facts so when the defendant started arguing the facts and why she was innocent she was essentially saying the judge's analysis and verdict were wrong. When the public defender interrupted her, ending her allocution, the public defender may have been appealing to the Judges' ego, thereby "softening him up" for potential rulings in her favor in the future. The possible meanings of the defendant's allocution for the public defender in this instance are endless; reviewing just a few of them develops a deep appreciation for the complexity of deciphering and manipulating signs in Law and how awareness of this complexity can strengthen a public defender's effectiveness in navigating the many contours of Law for the betterment of her client's interests.

During the above allocution, the prosecutor for the Commonwealth (me) stood adjacent to the public defender and her client. Comparable to the public defender, the defendant's allocution provided a wealth of meaning to the prosecutor. While the above scenario did not provide much opportunity for direct interaction in the allocution process for the prosecutor, as some situations can, the allocution still had an undeniable influence upon him. Before the defendant's allocution, the prosecutor will often be given an opportunity to suggest what sentence the government seeks; although the sentence usually remains in the judge's discretion. Once the judge asked the defendant if she would like to speak the prosecutor became aware of the fact that even though the trial phase has ended the guilty defendant still has rights, but even more than that, she has an opportunity to mitigate her sentence and give reasons why the sentence the prosecution has suggested should not be imposed. The prosecutor has lost his trial tools: the objection, cross-examination, and directed testimony. The meaning of allocution can be seen as the stripping of the prosecutor's voice. In some cases a prosecutor may have the right to present rebuttal testimony during allocution; however, in non-capital cases this rarely, if ever, occurs.

Here, when the defendant began to refute the evidence at trial the prosecutor became intimately aware of his now insignificance. Normally, once the defendant's allocution begins the prosecutor's role has ended. In examples such as the one above, this can frustrate the prosecutor. When the defendant spoke of her innocence she was effectively saying the prosecutor sought and attained a criminal conviction of an innocent person. Prosecutors seek the truth and justice, not convictions; if the person is really not guilty then by law the prosecutor is the first person that should seek to vindicate the defendant. Here, the defendant's adamant protestation of innocence had the potential for a profound psychological effect upon the prosecutor. It stirred up doubt.

However, the opposite interpretations could have just as easily developed from the defendant's allocution. The prosecutor may have become more confident in the guilty verdict and his sentencing recommendation because the defendant failed to accept responsibility. The prosecutor may have been filled with vanity knowing that his superiors were present and that there were other people in the courtroom that have now become aware of his legal expertise: He attained a guilty verdict against a person that steadfastly maintained her innocence. In this sense, a defendant's allocution is an affirmation of the prosecutor's skill and success. If the defendant is afforded the opportunity to speak before sentencing that means the prosecutor has won the case. Not any one of these meanings is correct or incorrect; they are all just possible. The prosecutor may hold on to several of them at the same time, waver between them, or embrace all or none of them. The point is that through a semiotic analysis of the defendant's allocution the prosecutor becomes closely familiar with the intricacy and significance of his position in Law.

The next vantage point is the judge's. The judge's first duty is to give the defendant an opportunity to allocute. The Judge must be careful not to curtail the Defendant's allocution because depending on the jurisdiction this may give grounds for reversal and remand. This would require the judge to resentence the defendant. Once the defendant has allocuted, next the judge is to interpret the defendant's allocution for practical sentencing purposes, i.e. mitigation of sentence. The judge's subsequent sentencing may help shine light on the meaning he extracted from the allocution; however, that is difficult to ascertain absent his acknowledgement of the reasons why he sentenced as he did.

The first meaning the judge was likely to derive from this case is the same as the public defender's (whose actions have influenced his interpretation). The substance of the defendant's allocution revealed to the judge the defendant's refusal to accept responsibility. This meant that that the judge was less likely to impose a lighter sentence than normal, such as imposing only court costs without restitution. However, it is possible, albeit slightly, that the defendant's maintaining of innocence may have made the judge aware of his mistake in finding her guilty. While he is unlikely to overturn his ruling, the scintilla of doubt that the defendant was able to place in the judge's head may force him to be more lenient when sentencing her.

But let's consider some of the less patent meanings from the judge's perspective which underscore the conversation between him and the defendant. There is a power relationship present: The judge *affords* the defendant the opportunity to speak. Among other things, this affirms the defendant's extreme subject positioning in criminal law's structure. While he may be *required* to on remand, no one can force him to at the sentencing hearing because he is in charge of the courtroom. The defendant is then able to respond, but she must respond in a civilized manner. Courts most often will not entertain unruly, frivolous, or intentionally prolonged allocutions.[29] Thus, the defendant's response, her allocution, is an affirmation of the judge's superior position *in the courtroom*, his control of the proceedings. When a defendant speaks, or even when a defendant refuses the opportunity to speak, the judge's powerful role is on display.

The judge must also offer allocution to preserve his offer for the record so that he will not be legitimately challenged on appeal. The judge cannot be challenged for failing to properly weigh the defendant's allocution. The judge is under no obliga-

[29] Kimberly A. Thomas, *Beyond Mitigation: Towards a Theory of Allocution*, 75 Fordham L. Rev. 2641, (2007).

tion to believe the defendant. All he must do is offer her a chance to speak and be sure to not unreasonably curtail her allocution. This mandatory offering once again affirms the law's inner structure and the defendant's centrifugal position within it. Thus, the defendant's allocution also affirms this structure by recognizing the discretionary nature of the judge's position when answering the right to allocution—his personhood. Thus, when the defendant is granted the right to allocute the Law is reinforced. Nevertheless, the judge may believe all, none, or part of her allocution, weigh it how he sees fit, and sentence according to his own proclivities toward the defendant. In this sense, the judge's role as neutral fact-finder becomes merged with his non-judge self. His conceptions of leniency, what it is the Defendant tries to appeal to, are necessarily appeals to his morality, his sense of right and wrong, possibly his religious beliefs, his experiences in life, etc. The meaning of allocution for the judge can be the cue for him to legally and discretionarily impose his non-judge self on Law. He no longer has to wear the facade of a detached decision maker. Surely, he must maintain an eye toward the effect his decision will have on the Law, but he is able, if not encouraged, to assert his personhood in the process, which is something he is often forbidden to do (of course we know that this happens all the time, but in theory a judge is supposed to be totally encompassed by the rules of law when presiding over the case). The meanings a judge derives from a defendant's allocution are as varied as they are profound.

Likely, the most important inquiry is what does the right to allocution mean for the defendant. First I will discuss the meaning in the above example and later I will get into a more in-depth discussion, evaluating situations where the sentencing implications for the defendant are much more serious. Here, allocution to the defendant clearly meant an opportunity to re-plead her innocence, something she had already done when she testified at trial. In a way this was a cry for mercy. Not being legally adept, she believed that she could rehash what she perceived as important facts, such as her not having her keys on her at the time the vehicle was scratched, as a means to get the judge to overturn his guilty verdict. As noted in the beginning of the paper, the right of allocution was historically an opportunity for defendants to be exonerated by raising the defense or mitigation seeking pardon, pregnancy, insanity, misidentification, or benefit of the clergy.[30] However, these defenses have now been incorporated into the trial itself, e.g. insanity is a defense—a reason to find not guilty—not a reason to find guilty and then lessen the sentence; hence the saying, "not guilty by reason of insanity." Nowadays, the right to allocution is premised on the notion that the defendant can offer testimony that will mitigate his sentence; or he can offer testimony about his personhood, his experiences, and character, that will individualize him before the judge so that the judge may make the punishment fit, not the crime, but the criminal.

Accordingly, the defendant's plea of innocence served very little practical or emotional effect during sentencing. She was already found guilty, thus any affect her excuses could have were already extinguished at this stage in the trial. But her allocution still produced multiple meanings with layers of signification. She learned

[30] Celine Chan, *A Defendant's Word on Its Face or Under Oath?*, 75 Brook. L. Rev. 579 (2009).

that she had a voice, that the Law recognizes this and is now offering her a chance to speak on her own behalf without being subject to cross-examination or further self-incrimination. For her, the meaning of allocution is of utmost importance: It affirms her selfhood in Law. This affirmation also serves to justify the Law in that it reinforces the human element and purpose for its existence: to order human affairs. This affirmation is both a blessing and a curse. She now knows that what she says matters in Law and serves to develop it; however, she also knows that what she will say is confined, legally confined to a set of permissible allocution topics, i.e. she is not permitted to curse and threaten, and confined to the fact that she is beholden to someone else's opinion. No matter what she says the judge has the final decision-making power. But maybe the worst confinement of all (which to some people may be the best) is the fact that *she is confined to her own words*. It is *her* right to allocution; to acknowledge and reinforce this possessive relation is a necessary process for maintaining the Law. This is a self-referential element of law which the semiotic analysis reveals. She controls the testimony the judge will hear; she controls her remorse and the conveyance of her thoughts. Some may rejoice at the chance to persuade a judge through their own relatively unrestrained rhetorical devices, but most criminal defendants are poor and uneducated and likely unprepared and squeamish about exercising this great power the court bestows upon them when the judge asks, "Do you have anything to say?"

Of course, defendants may allow their attorneys to speak for them; and in some cases they may present witnesses; nevertheless, the right to allocution belongs to the individual defendant. When the judge offers the defendant a chance to speak, the meaning of this may be overbearing for the defendant. At once they must produce words that will coerce a judge already severely inclined to discredit, or credit very little, their allocution; after all, they have been found guilty beyond a reasonable doubt of a criminal offense. For some defendants the meaning they derive may be one of feeling inadequate, unfit for the rigors of legal defense and public oration. However, it may be one of joy: "Thank heavens, I can now tell my side of the story and let the world know I am a good person!" Or it may be one of obstinacy where the defendant may remain silent. At any rate, the defendant's right to allocution has great meaning for that person; what they say or do not say will dictate meanings others will take from their action or inaction and has the power to affect many things in unforeseen ways. Before returning to a deeper discussion of the defendant's perspective it is important to consider other persons who may be affected and derive meaning from a defendant's allocution.

There is always a sheriff in the courtroom within earshot of the allocuting defendant; and so it goes, it must have some sort of meaning for him as well. On a practical level, the culmination of the defendant's allocution signifies the near end of the trial. All that is left is for the judge is to give the sentence. The defendant's allocution might also signify to the sheriff that he may be required to act in some manner. Consequently, allocution means the sheriff better prepare himself to escort the defendant to jail, assuming of course the sentence requires jail time. For instance, if the defendant begins to rant and rave the sheriff may need to gag the defendant (which does occur in rare cases). Without taking a semiotic approach to allocution one may assume that the defendant's right to allocute has nothing at all to do with the sheriff; however, as these brief examples make clear, that is not always true.

While the criminal defendant engenders the extreme subject-position in criminal law, and whereby the judge may best reflect the processes, evolution, and ordering of it, the sheriff may represent the most symbolic meaning: He is the ultimate enforcer. The judge's jail sentence is useless without the Sheriff and his irons. As noted in the beginning, Law's essence is coercive by very definition; it involves force upon human thought, action, and relations. Thus the sheriff, with his manacles, badge and gun, embodies this force in the courtroom.

The semiotic analysis employed above can be broken down and applied for everyone in the courtroom, for the clerks of court that type out the orders, the interns that draft the opinions, and so on. All of these people may be affected in a practical way by the defendant's exercising his or her right to allocution, but they may also be affected on a deeper level. When a defendant allocutes and claims innocence, rebukes the victim, pleads for mercy, or assumes responsibility, one thing is certain: It will create meanings and interpretations for those who hear the allocution. If a defendant takes responsibility for his actions, admits his wrongdoing, and apologizes, this may be a sign to onlookers that the defendant "really isn't a bad guy" or that "I knew that monster did it all along, look at him weep and beg for mercy; give him the chair!" The point is, as long as someone is thinking about the defendant's allocution that person is molding meaning both for them and for others. The sheriff may go home and recount the allocution to his wife, coercively imparting, whether intentionally or not, his interpretation of it into the interpretation she will derive from it. It is a chain effect. The signs are constantly interacting with other signs to create meaning upon meaning. Naturally, this could be said of any spoken word or conversation or act of reasoning (which is an idea Peirce advances), so some may question the value of such a semiotic approach. The value lies in knowledge of a sign's expansiveness. This paper has been exclusively focused on the defendant's right to allocution in Law. There are numerous rights in Law, all of which generate expansive meanings. Understanding the breadth of meaning-making potential each and every sign creates is invaluable for understanding the scope of meaning-making potential that a legal actor possesses. This self-awareness can only serve to enhance one's expertise in sculpting positions that will be beneficial for the legal stance they seek to advance, the meaning they seek to create.

Meanings of Humanization Allocution

Some jurisdictions recognize that the defendant's right to allocution is not for purposes of mitigation of sentencing, but rather is based on the more open concept that a defendant should generally be offered an opportunity to speak, to present himself to the court. The right to allocution has a therapeutic effect; it allows the court to restore a defendant's human qualities, which in turn can lead to perceived equity of sentencing.[31] This allocution rationale supports speeches focused on mercy, innocence, and even defiance.[32] A defendant in these jurisdictions is unlikely to be cut off by the Court (or in the case above, the public defender). Such an open-ended allowance for allocution only serves to multiply the already abundant meanings, which are derived from a defendant's allocution.

Allocutions of mercy are generally permitted, even in jurisdictions that subscribe to the mitigation rationale because pleas for mercy are often an underhanded admission of guilt, though not always. Of course a defendant may ask for mercy *because he is innocent*. Such a tactic is unlikely to be successful and the meanings derived from this approach are comparable to the ones for when a defendant pleads outright innocence. It has already been noted how a defendant that does not accept responsibility influences the thoughts and actions of others, such as causing the public defender to step in, making the prosecutor either confident or doubtful about the guilty verdict, bruising the judge's ego or entrenching him in his conviction that the defendant is guilty, or engendering a sense of helplessness in the defendant because she cannot produce the words that may set her free. But what about the meaning derived from the brazen defendant whose allocution is both defiant and unremorseful?

Many courts would not entertain a defiant allocution because it would not seem to serve any useful purpose: It would waste the court's valuable time, often it has the potential to emotionally scar the victims of the criminal's conduct and, most importantly, it would undermine the integrity of the courts. So why then do some courts allow it to an extent? Simply, the defendant is the one adjudicated criminal; he is a human and he has the right to be heard before his sentence is imposed. As will be discussed later, allowing the defendant a chance to deliver a defiant allocution may also serve to vindicate that person in the future when what was once considered defiance is now considered lawful and just.

In *Harris v. State*, the Maryland Supreme Court described the rationale behind its allocution statute: "[T]he allocutory process provides a unique opportunity for the defendant himself to face the sentencing body, without subjecting himself to cross-examination, and to explain in his own words the circumstances of the crime and his feelings regarding his conduct, culpability, and sentencing."[33] This language appears to leave the door open for defiant allocution—"feelings regarding his conduct" is not constricted to feelings of remorse or innocence. Not surprisingly, the available appellate case law is sparse, if not bereft of, examples where a defendant challenges the violation of his right to make a defiant allocution. Indeed, it would be strange for a defendant to argue that he did not have a full opportunity to lambaste the courts, vilify the victims, or display his outrage and disdain. The courts are simply unlikely to rule that the infringement of a defiant allocution is cause for reversal and remand because in essence the Court would be sanctioning something, which can be seen to

[31] Celine Chan, *A Defendant's Word on Its Face or Under Oath?*, 75 Brook. L. Rev. 579 (2009).

[32] Kimberly A. Thomas, *Beyond Mitigation: Towards a Theory of Allocution*, 75 Fordham L. Rev. 2641, (2007).

[33] *Harris v. State*, 306 Md. 344 (Md. 1986).

undermine the integrity and decorum of the courts. The American Courts have a long history of displaying their inferiority complex, i.e. their desire to be taken seriously. In the landmark case of *Marbury v. Madison*, Chief Justice John Marshall went to great lengths to vindicate the power of the courts and their equal status within the American tripartite system of government. One of the ways the courts maintain this respect is through the maintaining of order and decorum in the courtroom; a defiant allocution can seriously undermine this goal. Regardless of appellate success, defiant allocutions occur and therefore produce meaning in Law.

When a judge asks a defendant if he has anything to say, whatever comes out of the defendant's mouth is his allocution. The defendant may say, "Yes, I do. Judge, you are an idiot. I am not beholden to these laws. And regardless, the victim had it coming: He is a rat." Certainly this sort of banter will not be tolerated for too long; however, initially the judge may let the defendant speak. He then will likely pronounce a sentence which is very unfavorable. Could this example really serve any legitimate purpose, even the purpose of defending a criminal's right to speak? Yes. This sort of allocution validates the judgment, goes down on record, and may be used for such purposes as parole or resentencing. But we are not so much concerned with the purpose such a speech has as we are with the meaning it generates. These sorts of outbursts do occur from time to time during allocution. For a famous modern illustration of a defiant allocution, followed by a memorable judicial response, which conveyed a web of meaning for both legal and non-legal actors alike, let us consider the Zacarias Moussaoui sentencing hearing. Moussaoui was found guilty for his role in plotting the September 11, 2001, terrorist attacks on the United States. His defiant allocution went on for five minutes before Judge Brinkema put an end to it. The substance of the allocution was as follows:

> God Curse America! God Save Osama bin Laden! You'll never get him. You have branded me a terrorist or a criminal or whatever. Look at yourselves. I fight for my belief . . .[34]

Judge Brinkema eventually stopped the defendant and told him that he could not use the courtroom to make a political speech. She then followed with this memorable response:

> Well, Mr. Moussaoui, if you look around this courtroom today, every person in this room will leave this courtroom, and they are free to go any place they want. They can go outside, they can feel the sun, they can smell fresh air.[35] [In contrast,] [y]ou will spend the rest of your life in a super maximum security facility. In terms of winners and losers, it's quite clear who won and who lost. As for you, Mr. Moussaoui, you came here to be a martyr and to die in a great big bang of glory, but to paraphrase the poet T.S. Eliot, instead you will die with a whimper.[36]

[34] *Moussaoui will 'die with a whimper,' judge says*, http://www.ctv.ca/CTVNews/World/20060504/moussaoui_court_060504/, Accessed April 10, 2011.

[35] Joshua Dressler, *Cases and Materials on Criminal Law* (4th ed. 2007).

[36] Idem.

So what was Moussaoui's allocution a sign of? It was a sign of his resolve, his lack of remorse, his affiliation with a terrorist group, his ire for America, his affiliation with certain Islamic beliefs, and more. Given Judge Brinkema's response, his allocution was a sign of his political beliefs, his lack of remorse, his guilt, his desperation, his failure by being caught, convicted, and sentenced, and a sign of his defiance. The judge attempted to eloquently capture the anger and frustration Moussaoui's speech generated in her and would generate in the American public when it was later published around the world. In this situation, the defendant's allocution had far-reaching meaning for the American public that is palpable from people's responses to hearing these words.

Often people interpret Moussaoui's allocution as the voice of Islamic fanaticism—the voice of terrorism itself. His allocution is the voice of the enemy and the reason America is entangled in wars overseas. His allocution breeds jingoistic American resolve and hate for Islamic fanaticism, which is often synonymous with terrorism. In a very real sense Moussaoui's Islamic fanaticism bred American fanaticism. So what does this say for the Law, the institution that afforded a terrorist a forum to trounce the country and system in which he was being adjudged and sentenced, a country he helped terrorize?

Moments such as Moussaoui's defiant allocution are the times when the Law appears at its weakest. What does it mean if the Law enables an American-hating terrorist to rant and rave against America, disrespecting and vilifying the victims he harmed, for nearly five minutes before he is cut off due to his "political" speech? Paradoxically, often when the Law seems at its weakest it is actually in at its strongest. Law's ability to regulate and control, to coerce conformity and punish nonconformity, is never more apparent than when it is seemingly abused for non-legal ends. Moussaoui's allocution is evidence that Law bends but does not break; his allocution is just another chapter in Law. Among many other meanings, for the institution of Law itself, Moussaoui's allocution reveals the Law's potential to treat criminals equally (at least for allocution purposes), its inability to be easily affected by public opinion (many people wanted military tribunals), and its endurance and steadfast adherence to legal principles which can transcend the menacing throes of transient terror. Importantly, it is only from a semiotic point of view that all of these meanings are brought to the fore and the fleeting fanaticism, which often arises in the heat of the moment can be put in its proper perspective. Attempting to understand the web of meaning such a defiant allocution can produce facilitates a reaction in the hearer that is both well-reasoned and comprehensive, thus illuminating the appropriate response to this shocking speech. In other words, when allocutions as disturbing as Moussaoui's occur, taking the time to consider the myriad of meanings for multiple persons, thought systems, e.g. morals, ethics, religion, etc., and human institutions, e.g. Law, military, etc., will help the perceiver intellectually and physically carry on in a reasonable and productive manner. The depth of this understanding will generate awareness, sympathy, and open-mindedness.

Whereas it is difficult to perceive positive meanings stemming from Mr. Moussaoui's allocution, except possibly for confidence in the Law and its equal treatment of him, other forms of defiant allocution may produce more obvious beneficial effects. Although for a semiotic analysis it is not necessary to derive *positive* meaning from a defendant's right to allocution, it is useful to focus on this aspect because Law seeks to order, and the order is presumably for the betterment of society; thus, all legal rights presumably have some relation to a useful or positive purpose for society. Affording the defendant the opportunity to give a defiant allocution must therefore relate to the Law's ordering of society.

As stated above, the purpose behind allowing a defiant allocution may be the potential future vindication of the defendant. Thus, permitting the defendant to speak defiantly before the sentencing court may have a lasting effect that is not altogether negative. This is even clear from the Moussaoui example because one hundred years from now people may hold his allocution up as a testament to equal treatment of defendants during sentencing; the content of his speech will not be as important as the fact that a terrorist in his situation was allowed to make such a speech; after all, his words proved partially un-prophetic: America did "get him" (Bin Laden). But there is another possibility that is comparable to the following example.

The famous non-American allocution of Nelson Mandela will be instructive. Mandela was an anti-apartheidist and coordinated bombing and sabotage campaigns against pro-apartheid targets.[37] Mandela was captured and sentenced to life imprisonment; his allocution was thus described:

> Before being sentenced to life imprisonment, Nelson Mandela stood, dignified, before his sentencing court and elegantly stated that he did the acts for which he was convicted and was proud to have done them. Mandela did not seek to mitigate his punishment or apologize for his conduct. He also suggested an alternative vision of justice in the face of what he believed to be an unjust system. His words flew in the face of the sentencing court and questioned the legitimacy of his prosecution. It was a true defiance story. Though offensive to the sentencing court and the system that convicted him, Mandela's words and actions—including his allocution—are now held up as an example of courage. It is not just a permissible allocution; it is a heroic one. He should not have been silenced.[38]

It should not be lost on the reader the fact that Mandela served 27 years of imprisonment and the author's comments were therefore made in hindsight. Mandela's defiant allocution is now lauded; however, it certainly was not seen in such a positive light at the time of its delivery. Mandela, like Moussaoui, challenged the system which judged him. There are many parallels between the two allocutions. The difference lies in the fact that Moussaoui has yet to be vindicated; his ideology has not prevailed, uprooting the current system. While it is highly unlikely Islamic rule of law would become the Law in America, from Mandela's perspective, it was probably just as unlikely for him to think apartheid would end and he would be set free, regardless of the fact that he admitted to committing atrocious acts. Because Mandela's ideology eventually prevailed his defiant words seemed to have set him free; it is yet to be seen whether Moussaoui will realize the same fate. The point is, the right to

---

[37] *Nelson Mandela*, http://en.wikipedia.org/wiki/Nelson_Mandela, Accessed April 20, 2011.

[38] Kimberly A. Thomas, *Beyond Mitigation: Towards a Theory of Allocution*, 75 Fordham L. Rev. 2641, (2007).

allocute, even defiantly, serves or has the potential to serve positive purposes which are revealed through the multiple meanings which are derived from it.

So, even though Moussaoui's meaning-making in Law through his defiant allocution may seem absurd, vexatious, inappropriate, and wrong when considered in the moment, its lasting effect is unforeseen; it is possible that his allocution will continue to make meaning beyond the transience of its initial delivery. This reflects the ever-evolving nature of Law. Moussaoui's allocution affected more than his own fate or the judge's ire: It was a sign of a system, Law, which does not yield to fleeting passions; it was a sign of a defendant's immutable right to explain himself; and, most importantly, it was a sign of something which can have multiple meanings for multiple persons and systems.

Judicial Responses to Allocution

It has been noted throughout this paper that the defendant's allocution is primarily aimed at the judge, though occasionally it is intended for all to hear and contemplate, e.g. Moussaoui's allocution. The defendant's allocution ends when the judge says it ends. The judge then imposes the sentence he deems appropriate, unless he must follow mandatory sentencing schemes which are set forth in statutes. It is not uncommon for judges to respond to the defendant's allocution or to say some words of condemnation or explanation when handing down the sentence. Thus, while Judge Brinkema's statements seemed out of place, they were neither impermissible nor rare. Regardless, her statements carried much meaning.

The most in-your-face meaning of Judge Brinkema's response was that the People would have the last laugh in that Moussaoui would receive life without parole; his allocution was his last hurrah. The literal meanings of the judge's words are all potent: Moussaoui cannot engage in political speech in the Court, he would never walk as free man and enjoy the rights free men enjoy again, and he would die in prison. For Moussaoui, however, her statements probably did not have the effect on him they were intended to have, which was to demoralize him; instead, her speech was an affirmation of his success: He knows he rattled the judge just as he rattled the country through his terrorism. Judge Brinkema's statements immortalized Moussaoui's (the dialogue is quoted in many texts). For him, the meaning of her eloquent response ensured the endurance of his defiant allocution; after all, her speech cannot be understood outside the context of his. If the judge had not said what she did I never would have come across this example; her eloquence led to her being published. On the same token, I never would have come into contact with Moussaoui's fanaticism and would thus never have felt the rage his comments evoke in me. Her words, while heralded by some, in hindsight may have been best to remain unspoken.

Also within her comments are literary allusions. She mentions T.S. Eliot and paraphrases of one of his most famous lines. What is the meaning of this? This could be a projection of her superior education, her vanity, or simply her love for poetry and Eliot more specifically. To her judge colleagues it may reflect her judicial style and temperament in that she is intimately familiar with the humanities and the study of the human condition. For society her poetic allusion may serve as a means connecting us to our cultural past. Her poetics also bridge the gap between scholasticism and Law, revealing their potential interplay. If famous literary quotes are used by judges then the Law is essentially affirming the influence of literature. Indeed, there is a robust field of Law and Literature devoted to such considerations. Judge Brinkema's statements stand for much more than the Law's instant disapproval of Moussaoui's allocution: Her statements stand for the endless possibility of meaning and interpretation in Law, and in this regard, her statement reflects meaning-making which does not stand still in time and space, but rather continues on, always able to be reevaluated, reinterpreted, and reworked to conform with the realities of the time.

When judges chastise a defendant at sentencing they are indirectly, or possibly directly, emphasizing the moral underpinnings of Law. Some judges see it as their duty to perform this chastisement. Consider this conversation between a judge and the defendant's counsel who was objecting to the judge's attitude toward his client:

> Judge: Let's stop a minute here. I can listen to this, and I'm not believing anything he says. But just let me point out to you, Mr. Martin, you said that those people from those oil companies were giving you money as a contribution to what? To your high lifestyle? To your apartment? To your overhead at CCM?
>
> Defendant's Counsel: Objection, your Honor. You're berating-
>
> Judge: Badgering the witness.
>
> Defendant's Counsel: Yes, you are.
>
> Judge: You bet. Because I'm the judge, and I get to badger the witness.
>
> Judge: … You know something, when I sentence him, I get to use whatever tone I want. So it's just going to come up sooner or later. One of the functions of sentencing is for the judge to chastise the defendant. Lawyers don't get to do that. Judges do. I can do it now or I can do it later. I'll chastise him in good course when we get to the sentencing. And you can take that up to the Court of Appeals, and if there's something wrong about the judge chastising the defendant, then they can tell me so. In the meantime, I'm adjourning this hearing because you're finished. Right?[39]

The Ninth Circuit of Appeals, while not explicitly approving the judge's comments, rather calling them "testy," did not condemn the judge's remarks or attitude.[40] Thus, the court's lack of disapproval can be seen as a tacit approval. While these above remarks were not made during sentencing it is clear from the judge's final comments what his attitude toward sentencing is: He believes part of his duty during sentencing is to chastise the defendant.

Chastising in Law is connotative of moral condemnation. The judge infuses his own morality in Law when he chastises the defendant. As if the defendant's sentence is not enough, the judge feels compelled to defend society and his notions of right, which presumably are the prevailing ideas of the society for which he speaks.

---

[39] *United States v. Martin*, 278 F.3d 988 (9th Cir. 2002)

[40] *United States v. Martin*, 278 F.3d 988 (9th Cir. 2002)

To elucidate the judge as chastiser during sentencing, an extreme example from the nineteenth century will be helpful. When sentencing a convicted criminal to death, Judge Benedict delivered a speech that drives home the judge's role as the voice of community condemnation:

> Jose Manuel Miguel Xavier Gonzalez, in a few short weeks it will be spring. The snows of winter will flee away, the ice will vanish, and the air will become soft and balmy. In short, Jose Manuel Miguel Xavier Gonzales, the annual miracle of the years will awaken and come to pass, but you won't be there.
>
> The rivulet will run its soaring course to the sea, the timid desert flowers will put forth their tender shoots, the glorious valleys of this imperial domain will blossom as the rose. Still, you won't be here to see.
>
> From every treetop some wild woods songster will carol his mating song; butterflies will sport in the sunshine, the busy bee will hum happy as it pursues its accustomed vacation; the gentle breeze will tease the tassels of the wild grasses, and all nature will be glad, but you. You won't be here to enjoy it because I command the sheriff or some other officers of the country [sic] to lead you out to some remote spot, swing you by the neck from a knotting bough of some sturdy oak, and let you hang until you are dead.
>
> And then, Jose Manuel Miguel Xavier Gonzales, I further command that such officer or officers retire quickly from your dangling corpse, so that vultures may descend from the heavens upon your filthy body until nothing shall remain but bare, bleached bones of a cold-blooded, bloodthirsty, throat-cutting, murdering son of a bitch.[41]

While the right to allocution may have meaning, it is clear that the judge has the final say; and in that say, the right to allocution is turned against the defendant, becoming additional condemnation, as in the semi-literary fragment. False sentiments are often used as a guise of revenge and other aberrations of the legal minds. All the meaning derived from the defendant's speech will ultimately be inundated with the judge's response. The judge may accept a defendant's apology and provide leniency in his sentencing. He may ignore the defendant's allocution altogether and impose the sentence he has predetermined or which statute has deemed mandatory. The judge may sentence the defendant to a harsher punishment if the defendant's allocution incites his consternation, reflecting the defendant's defiance and lack of remorse. Often the judge will provide an explanation for his sentencing; this may directly respond to the defendant's allocution or it may not. The judge has great discretion in sentencing and weighing the effect of the defendant's allocution partly because there are rarely any built in safeguards which can assure the defendant's credibility and trustworthiness.[42] This reveals another meaning the defendant's allocution may create: a lack of meaning. Because he is not sworn under oath, subject to cross-examination, or required to produce non-testimonial evidence, his allocution may be interpreted as having no meaning—no legal force; it is deemed nonsense which has no meaning in Law.

---

[41] Joshua Dressler, *Cases and Materials on Criminal Law* (4th ed. 2007).

[42] Celine Chan, *A Defendant's Word on Its Face or Under Oath?*, 75 Brook. L. Rev. 579 (2009).

Conclusion

The meanings, which evolve from a defendant's right to allocution are vast. This paper has not been an attempt to capture all or even close to all of them. Instead, the purpose was to highlight the many different meanings, which arise from an often overlooked and undervalued facet of Law. The defendant's right to allocution is one of the most neglected areas of study in criminal law: "Courts consistently fail to discuss why the factors they cite—such as the defendant's assertion of his right to allocute and the content of his allocution—are relevant."[43] This has led to a dearth of case law and commentary on the topic. However, as should now be apparent, the right to allocution affects the sentencing process on numerous fronts. In theory, allocution can set a criminal free or at least lead to his mitigated sentence if it is found persuasive. Also, as is evidenced in the judicial responses at sentencing, a defendant's allocution may enrage a sentencing judge, which will not bode well for the punishment the defendant receives. On the other hand, the defendant's allocution may have no practical effect on Law if the defendant is found not credible or unpersuasive. However, a lack of meaning is itself still meaning. From a semiotic approach, with Peirce's triadic as a guide, the meaning in Law of a defendant's right to allocute can be seen as just another coercive element, like the Sheriff's brute action, within a coercive system—Law. Signs, such as the right to allocution, the defendant's exercising of this right, and the change this exercising can evoke, generate a boundless field of meaning. Recognizing this possibility is the first step in understanding the profundity of the legal actor's task as a meaning-maker in Law. This awareness will have great practical and personal effect: It will strengthen one's legal aptitude by creating an open-mindedness and perceptiveness that will enable one to navigate the dynamic, ever-changing field of Law in a manner that promotes professional efficiency and personal growth. If as Peirce argues, all acts of reasoning involve the interplay of signs, then studying signs and their possible meanings in Law will provide a balanced yet persuasive foundation from which the legal actor begins to advance his position or legal argument. If the semiotic analysis of the defendant's right to allocution found in this paper is applied to the many other areas of Law, one's eyes will open to the world unseen, the world of signs and meanings which signify Law's coercive nature and constant evolution.

[43] Celine Chan, *A Defendant's Word on Its Face or Under Oath?*, 75 Brook. L. Rev. 579 (2009).

Shareholder Derivative Action and Corporate Identity in Delaware Jurisprudence

Alan C. Green

> *Things inanimate cannot be authors, nor therefore give authority to their actors; yet the actors may have authority to procure their maintenance, given them by those that are owners or governors of those things. And therefore such things cannot be personated before there be some state or civil government.*[1]
>
> *Corporate speech, however, is derivative speech, speech by proxy. . . .*
> *It is an interesting question "who" is even speaking . . . .*[2]

Introduction: Capitalism, Democracy, and Corporate Identity in Delaware Jurisprudence

In late 2011, the South Carolina Republican Party issued its sample primary ballot, which included the following referen dum:

> QUESTION 4
> In order to address the matter of Corporate Personhood, we the enfranchised People of the Sovereign State of South Carolina shall decree that:
> [ ] Corporations are people
> [ ] Only people are people

The referendum was the work of the Colbert Super PAC, an organization established by late-night political satirist Stephen Colbert for the distinctly ironic purpose of illustrating the absurdity of deregulating corporate campaign expenditures. The South Carolina Republican Party, appropriately enough, chose to include the referendum following a "sizeable cash offer" from Super PAC. In

Source: GREEN, ALAN C.: "Shareholder Derivative Action And Corporate Identity In Delaware Jurisprudence" *Prize winning paper of the Roberta Kevelson Seminar on Law & Semiotics, 2012*

[1] Thomas Hobbes, *Leviathan* Part. I, ch. 16.

[2] *Citizens United v. Fed. Election Comm'n*, 130 S.Ct. 876, 972 (2010) (Stevens, J, dissenting).

A.C. Green (✉)
CGA Law Firm, 135 North George Street, York, PA 17401, USA
e-mail: agreen@cgalaw.com

J.M. Broekman, L. Catá Backer (eds.), *Signs In Law - A Source Book*,
DOI 10.1007/978-3-319-09837-1_33

Colbert's words "that just goes to show you what unlimited Super PAC money can do."[3]

This satirical vignette illustrates the divergence between social and legal discourses on the meaning of corporate identity. Following the United States Supreme Court opinion in *Citizens United*, opponents of the decision have replied "corporations are not people." In terms of natural language, of course, this statement is undeniably true. However, in the context of the artificial language of the law, it is more complex.

What is a corporation? What is its identity and interests? Does the legal recognition of a corporate identity as a juridical subject undermine the standing of personal identity? If so, how? These questions are fundamentally semiotic in nature. The identity of a corporation is a sign in use, the meaning of which is contingent upon the language, context and interpreters. It may signify the power of the state, or the nexus of contracts. It may signify an independent subjectivity or a collection of dependent rights. The corporation, however, is ultimately a creation of law, and law will function as the ultimate discourse establishing the power and efficacy of the corporation.

This paper will focus on the process by which law interprets corporate identity through a shareholder derivative action. The shareholder derivative action is a (legal) method by which the law allows the shareholders of a corporation to compel the corporation to initiate a suit without the consent of (and usually against) its management. Part II will provide a theoretical and legal background for understanding the main themes of this paper. Part III will address the initial development of corporate personhood using the Lacanian mirror stage as a structuring metaphor. An independent corporate identity will be seen as emerging from the adversarial relationship between its shareholders and management. Part IV will examine how, as the derivative action progresses, the autonomous legal subjectivity of the corporation comes to take the place of the both the shareholder and management. This analysis concludes that the shareholder derivative action demonstrates quite acutely the tendency of corporate identity to subsume and annihilate the identity of "natural" persons through legal discourse.

[3] *See* Video, *Colbert* Super *PAC—Stephen's South Carolina Referendum*, http://www.colbertnation.com/the-colbert-report-videos/403807/december-07-2011/colbert-super-pac-stephen-s-south-carolina-referendum. The referendum never saw the light of day, however. The Supreme Court of South Carolina held the law of the state did not permit "nonbinding advisory questions" and ordered the Election Commission not to print any primary ballots containing such referendums: *Beaufort County v. S.C. State Election Comm'n*, Opinion No. 27069 (S.C. Nov. 22, 2011). As an artificial language, legal discourse most certainly lacks a sense of humor.

Background

Theoretical Framework

This paper will borrow from the work of Jacques Lacan. Lacan, in a theory paralleling many *fin de siècle* German thinkers, understood personal identity to be a work in progress without final stage: a continual development of a subject always in the process of becoming. An individual is not an autonomous, self-sustaining entity, but "an ensemble of the most disparate functions."[4]

Fundamental to his theory is the concept that "the ego is built up by opposition." There exists a triadic relationship between the self, its object, and the Other. Lacan uses the metaphor of the mirror to explain the initial, critical stage in the development of personal identity. In the mirror stage, infants recognize the external representation of themselves, which they learn to call "I". The discovery of an "I", however, does not occur in isolation, but rather in the arms of the mother who, holding the child to the mirror, says "that is 'you'". The individual emerges out of an "Other": an "I" exists only in relation with a "you":

> The object of man's desire, and we are not the first to say this, is essentially an object desired by someone else. One object can become equivalent to another, owing to the effect produced by this intermediary, in making it possible for objects to be exchanged and compared. … It is by this process that we are led to see our objects as identifiable egos, having unity, permanence, and substantiality; this implies an element of inertia, so that the recognition of objects and of the ego itself must be subjected to constant revision in an endless dialectical process.[5]

Thus, a fundamental attribute of the ego is its annihilatory capacity: the fixing of identity is, at the same time, the destruction of identity.

Insofar as legal semiotics is concerned, the artificial discourse of law demands a unitary subject—a focal point for the force of law to be applied. Legal discourse fixes personal identity into a fixed meaning, which has a particular meaning in the moment at which the discourse is applied (i.e., the case at bar). The fixing of this meaning is the law's master signifier: "you are the plaintiff!" However, the legal subject does not exist in isolation either. The triadic relationship persists. There must be an Other (e.g., the defendant) and an object of desire (e.g., the damages sought). Thus, "the whole development of consciousness leads only to the rediscovery of the antinomy … the conflict arising from the co-existence of two consciousnesses can only be resolved by the destruction of one of them."[6]

The individual engages in this triadic relationship through speech and language. Through speech the individual expresses his desire, and risks annihilation of this will at the hands of the Other. The Other is necessary to achieve what the Self desires, but the position of the Other is seen only in a mirror darkly.

---

[4] Lacan, *Écrits*: A Selection 230f (trans. Alan Sheridan, 1977).

[5] Lacan, *Some Reflections on the Ego, 34 Int'l J. of Psychoanalysis* 11, 12 (1953)

[6] *Id.* at 16.

Nor is this triadic process simply external to the self's identity. The metaphor of the mirror image is a process of internal schism—self-othering—as well. The self is confronted with itself as an object external to itself. The relationship expressed in language is always a negation.

Thus speech is a risk, whether said to oneself or another. The risk is mitigated by the indexical catalogue of a master discourse: the realm of possible meanings are restricted so as to avoid the problem of uncertainty regarding the role of the Other, but so are possible modes of being.

The legal master discourse views the legal subject as, to paraphrase Kristeva, a unity that submits to the law, yet can never submit fully.[7] The law requires an individual capable of expressing his dissent to the force of law. If all beings entirely submitted to law, the force of law would become absurdity. The subject of the law is the possibility of an illegal actor. The self must assert itself. Hence, from the negation ("I will not") comes the affirmative ("I am"): "every manifestation of the ego is compounded equally of good intentions and bad faith and the usual idealistic protest against the chaos of the world only betrays, inversely, the very way in which he who has a part to play in it manages to survive."[8]

The question, which this paper poses, then is: what is the part of a corporation in this juridical drama? The refrain of the dissenters—"corporations are not people"—establishes the Otherness and negation that manifests in the mirror stage of identity, but the corporation has no mouth and no spirit: it cannot say "I" to itself.

What are the ramifications of creating a legal subjectivity with the destructive capacity of an external I/Other relationship without the ability constructive ability to manifest an internal, spiritual dialogue? What does it mean for the rest of us?

Law, Society, and Delaware: The Capitalist Discursive Space

The modern American business corporation exists in an economic discourse. Particularly, it finds its identity in a Capitalist master discourse. To understand how corporate identities shaped this discourse, it is important to recall the contingent and historical bases of such any such discourse. Culture and society are shaped by master discourses, but, inversely, the master discourses are subject to reordering by the finite quality of the identities it controls.

A prevailing metaphor for the corporation is that it is a "nexus of contracts."[9] These contracts mostly include ownership agreements (e.g., sales of stock and assets), agency agreements (e.g., the establishment of management), labor agreements (e.g., employment rights), and financial agreements (e.g., lines of credit and

[7] *See* Julia Kristeva Interviews 26 (Ross M. Guberman ed., 1996).

[8] *Id.* at 12.

[9] *See generally* Paul G. Mahoney, *Contract or Concession? An Essay on the History of Corporate Law*, 34 Ga. L. Rev. 873 (2000) (exploring the historical development of corporate law as it converges with contract law).

debt). Yet, only one set of contracts is viewed as constituting the voice of the corporation: the agreement between shareholders and management. Only management (through direct action), and shareholders (through derivative action), will ever be recognized by the law as speaking with the corporate voice. Thus, the law restricts the corporation as a subject representative of the collective subjectivities of its owners and managers and casts the interests of all others as external to the identity of the corporation.

While this principle has become thoroughly ingrained in legal discourse, it is important to remember that this need not be the case. If the law were to adopt a pseudo-Marxist discourse, one might imagine the laborers given an opportunity to take the reins of corporate identity. Likewise, as was the case in the early discourses on corporate law and in social-democratic discourse, the public interest represented by the sovereign may be allowed to speak on behalf of the corporation.

In modern America, however, the corporation exists for the benefit of its shareholders. The corporate interest is the aggregate of its shareholders' interests. However, like the ability to reduce the of the complex composition of celestial bodies into a single aggregated point of gravitational force, the sum of all multifarious vectors of shareholders' interest points in a single direction: "make money!" So distilled, utilitarian principles become dominant. In order to maximize utility, it is efficient to recognize the superseding authority of management.

In the United States, "[s]tate law grants corporations special advantages … that enhance their ability to attract capital and to deploy their resources in ways that maximize the return on their shareholders' investments."[10] In *The Economic Structure of Corporate Law*, Easterbrook and Fischel explain:

> Corporations do not arise by spontaneous generation. Managers assume their roles with knowledge of the consequences. Investors part with their money willingly, putting dollars in equities instead of bonds or banks or land or gold because they believe the returns of equities more attractive. … The corporation and its securities are products in financial markets to as great an extent as the sewing machines or other things the firm makes. Just as the founders of a firm have incentives to make the kinds of sewing machines people want to buy, they have incentives to create the kind of firm, governance structure, and securities the customers in capital markets want.

The purpose of corporate law, they argue, is to provide rules that, "if uniformly applied will maximize the value of corporate endeavor as a whole." The fruits of profit maximization belong to the shareholders, who also bear the risk of investing in an uncertain outcome.[11] This model, though admittedly a gross oversimplification, will, for our purposes, adequately describes the Capitalist discourse regarding corporations.

As the examination below will show, however, the Capitalist discourse is inadequate to explain the role of corporate identity. Using Delaware law, the shareholder derivative suit creates an independent meaning for corporate identity that is

---

[10] *Austin v. Michigan Chamber of Commerce*, 494 U.S. 652, 658–59 (1990).

[11] Easterbrook & Fischel, *The Economic Structure of Corporate Law* 4, 35–36 (1991).

non-referential to both the shareholders and management.[12] Like the Hobbesian Leviathan, the recognition of a corporation as a legal subject takes on a life on its own in legal discourse subsuming the very identities it was meant to serve.

Mirror Stage: Corporation as Other

Derivative Self-Interest: Corporations in Search of Identity

Delaware law, like most jurisdictions, recognizes the separate, independent legal identity of the corporation. The law bestows on the corporation "the power to sue and be sued in all courts and participate, as a party or otherwise, in any judicial, administrative, arbitrative or other proceeding, in its corporate name."[13] The corporation is a legal subject.

As Hobbes said in chapter 16 of *Leviathan*, "Things inanimate cannot be authors, nor therefore give authority to their actors; yet the actors may have authority to procure their maintenance, given them by those that are owners or governors of those things." This authority exists within a realm of law, which orders and reorders the rights of property. Delaware law vests the authority to act as a corporation in its directors (management). Interestingly, each director must be a "natural person."[14] Thus a corporation cannot be managed by another corporation. The meaning of such a requirement follows Capitalist discourse, which holds the interests of a corporation to be a nexus of the interests of "natural persons." Shareholders are given the countervailing authority to select the directors. Yet, at the same time, a corporation may own and sell its own shares[15] meaning: the corporation cannot act of itself, but it can take ownership of itself.

Already the "fictional" existence of the corporation runs into a problem of referentiality. Delaware law accepts contradictory assertions: (1) a corporation can only act through natural persons; (2) selection of the natural persons to run said corporation belongs to the shareholders; (3) a corporation may be its own shareholder. The work-around for this conundrum is the rule that management may only vote the stock owned by a corporation in a fiduciary capacity. In other words, management owes a fiduciary duty to the corporation.

---

[12] While Delaware law is, by no means, the only law applicable to corporations, it is, by far, the most important in terms of the governance of the modern, large, publicly traded corporation in the United States. More than half of all publicly traded companies in the U.S. are incorporated in Delaware including 63% of the Fortune 500 companies. *See About Agency*, Del. Dep't of State, Division of Corporations, http://www.corp.delaware.gov/aboutagency.shtml. Delaware's position in American corporate law, as it relates to the regulation of large, multi-state companies has long been recognized as "supreme". *See* William L. Cary, *Federalism and Corporate Law: Reflections on Delaware*, 83 Yale L.J. 663 (1974).

[13] *Del. Code* tit. 8, § 122(2).

[14] *Id.* § 141.

[15] *Id.* § 160.

Black's Law Dictionary, itself a prominent shaper of legal semiotics, defines a fiduciary duty as: "A duty to act for someone else's benefit, while subordinating one's personal interests to that of the other person." Delaware law has ascribed to management a fiduciary duty not only to shareholders, but also to the corporation itself. In the seminal case of *Guth v. Loft, Inc.*, the Delaware Chancery Court charged management with the duty "not only affirmatively to protect the interests of the corporation committed to his charge, but also to refrain from doing anything that would work injury to the corporation ... [If] the interests of the corporation are betrayed, the corporation may elect to claim all of the benefits of the transaction for itself."[16]

The identity of a corporation, then, is not equivalent to the identity of the management, notwithstanding that corporate identity is asserted through the actions of management. The corporation has its own interests. An act of management, therefore, can be either (1) a corporate action or (2) not a corporate action, depending on the nature of the act.

The fiduciary relationship between the manager and the corporation becomes an internal triadic dialogue. The manager herself is an individual, comprised of an internal dialogue and competing desires and not a natural person. If she desires that which belongs to the Other (the corporation), she cannot simultaneously be the corporation itself. If she is the corporation, she becomes other to herself. The object of desire (usually monetary) cannot be possessed by both and, thus, becomes the object of aggression. The manager is *qua* corporate manager not herself. Thus a manager's actions can be either (3) her own or (4) not her own, depending on the locus of the desire asserted.[17]

From the perspective of the corporation, the semiotic relationship becomes difficult, if not impossible, to express in a natural language. On the surface there would seem to be an equivalency between (1) "a corporate action", and (4) "not-the manager's own action"; and similarly an equivalency between (2) "not-a corporate action", and (3) "the manager's own action". However, *the corporation cannot express its own interests*. It is "an Other" from the perspective of the manager, but it is not a "Self" from its own perspective. Like an infant prior to the mirror stage, it has been born prematurely. The manager, like a mother, controls the means of showing the corporation its self as other-than. In a state that can be compared to anxiety, the manager has every incentive to collapse the triadic relationship between herself and the corporation, claiming a fixed identity for herself in a merely dyadic relationship with the object of her desire: *la société c'est moi.*

The possibility of shareholder derivative suits creates the initial schism in corporate identity. It forces the Other into the manager/corporation ego and holds a mirror to distinguish the one from itself. As one legal scholar puts it:

> The derivative action, an equitable suit by which an oppressed minority shareholder assumes the mantle of the corporation itself to right wrongs committed by those temporarily

[16] 5 A.2d 503, 510–11 (Del. Ch. 1939)

[17] The internal dynamics initiated by the law through the semiotic process of signifying identities as belonging or not belong to itself will be explored further in Part IV.B below.

> in control of the corporation's destiny, is a venerable shareholder remedy. . . . Such actions are rooted both in metaphysics and in common sense. The corporation as a person, albeit a fictitious one, has a life and interests distinct from those of its temporary managers.[18]

Through a derivative suit, the law now sees the corporation as a more than a uniform locus of jurisprudence. Yet it is not quite a speaking subject; the directors and shareholders still comprise the I/Other with respect to each other. They are the combatants; *the corporation is the conjunctive relationship between the two speaking subjects and their objective.*[19]

Tooley: Corporation in Opposition to Its Equity Holders

Is the corporation a possible independent legal subject to a dispute between shareholders and management? The question is equitable (i.e., concerns capital) in nature. The capital entrusted to management belongs simultaneously to the shareholders and to the corporation as an identity. Either may attempt to press a claim for fiduciary breaches related thereto. If the law is not ready to overtly recognize the power of the corporation to annihilate shareholder identity, it is equally unprepared to recognize the ability of the shareholders to annihilate corporate identity. The tension is clearly palpable in *Tooley v. Donaldson, Lufkin & Jenrette, Inc.*, in which the Delaware Supreme Court stated: "The analysis must be based solely on the following questions: Who suffered the alleged harm—the corporation or the suing stockholder individually—and who would receive the benefit of the recovery or other remedy?"[20]

From a semiotic perspective the importance of *Tooley* lies in its rejecting the Capitalist discourse as the master discourse surrounding the corporate identity. While nominally eliminating the "special injury" test as "amorphous and confusing," the case's deeper structure renders it impossible to interpret the corporation as equivalent to the shareholder's collective identities.

Initially, *Tooley* restates the exclusive disjunctive relationship between the "direct" suit and the "derivative" suit. It brings to the fore how an action against corporate management for breach of a fiduciary duty must be either direct or derivative—it cannot be both so that what is not one is necessarily the other. A derivative action "enables a stockholder to bring suit on behalf of the corporation for harm done to the corporation," while, in a direct action, the shareholders "*retain* the right to bring an individual action for injuries affecting his or her legal rights as a

[18] Roger J. Magnuson, 1 Shareholder Litigation § 9:1 (2004).

[19] While the author is unaware of any prior scholarship utilizing this phrase, the semiotic formulation confirms the well-established legal understanding that a derivative action is, at its inception, a dispute between shareholders and management. *See Id.* ("The derivative action [is] an equitable suit by which an oppressed minority shareholder assumes the mantle of the corporation itself to right wrongs committed by those temporarily in control of the corporation's destiny.").

[20] 845 A.2d 1031, 1035 (Del. 2004).

stockholder."[21] Already we see by the use of the term "retain" that shareholders lose something in a derivative action. What is lost is the right to recover for injury. While, pursuant to the Capitalist discourse, the shareholder may interpret almost any corporate loss as an injury done to them selves, the law will not interpret the existence of at least some of these injuries as legally cognizable to the shareholder. Such injuries, though felt by the shareholder, actually refer to an injury to the corporation's interests as distinct from the shareholder.

Prior to *Tooley*, the index under which the object (injury) was interpreted in terms of its legal significance (type of suit) was the "special injury" test. That test states: "When an injury to corporate stock falls equally upon all stockholders, then an individual stockholder may not recover for the injury to his stock alone, but must seek recovery derivatively in behalf of the corporation."[22] Under this rubric, the distinction between "corporation" and "shareholder" is merely a matter of distinguishing the part from the whole. When some shareholders are injured, the law recognized the separate identity of the injured shareholders independent of the corporation. When all shareholders are injured, the law recognized the collective interests of the shareholders under the name of the corporation. The legal subject "corporation" stands in a conjunctive, rather than in a contrary, relationship to the shareholders.

In this sense, the "special injury" test follows the discourse of capital and Capitalism. Mismanagement of "corporate" assets harms the corporate interest. Any action brought on that account is derivative because all shareholders suffered equally as a result of the mismanagement. Each share represents a stake in the corporate assets, and each share shares in the corporate recovery. The voice of the corporation is recognized in the collective, while the individual shareholders' voices are simultaneously recognized in *proportion to the interest* of each represented by the corporate collective. Only if the shareholder's injury is not at all represented through the voice of the corporate interest (i.e., the shareholder's injury is "special") will the shareholder be allowed to speak in his own right. The corporate identity subsumes the individual, and the sublimation is economically efficient: a "rational" shareholder would choose to have his identity so sublimated in exchange for the greater marginal returns of operating within a collective entity.

In eliminating this "special injury" test, *Tooley* defied the Capitalist discourse. In order to maintain a direct action, a shareholder must demonstrate "that he or she can prevail without showing an injury to the corporation."[23] The corporation is no longer a collection of shareholder interests, but an interest in itself. Where the action is derivative (i.e., in vindication of a corporate interest) the suit must allege injury to the corporation and not to the shareholders collectively because the corporation *is not* a collection of shareholder interests. While nominally intended to provide for greater clarity (i.e., judicial efficiency) in determining whether an action states a cause directly or derivatively, the court knowingly and explicitly

[21] *Id.* at 1036 (emphasis added).

[22] *Bokat v. Getty Oil Co.*, 262 A.2d 246, 249 (Del. 1970).

[23] *Tooley*, 845 A.2d at 1038.

recognizes the independent existence of interests referring to, and belonging, to the corporation as a legal subject independent of other possible legal subjects. If an injury is interpreted as referring to the interests of this "fictional" corporate identity, the corporate identity annihilates the possibility of the injury referring to a natural identity.

It is no wonder, then, that the shareholder is unwilling to recognize the corporate identity as having a place in the litigation.[24] The shareholder's interest is more directly served by placing himself in the legal position of plaintiff. For him, the firstness of injury is experienced in its secondness, namely as belonging to himself. In its thirdness, the shareholder perceives the possibility of redress from management. He wants to recover for himself and the corporation's potentially superseding interest is an impediment to such a recovery. Simply put, the shareholder interprets "corporation" as a thing separate and opposed to "shareholder." Moreover, the opposition cannot allow the corporation to simply "take the place of" his individuality: the action should be a direct shareholder litigation.

It is the manager who first speaks the name of the corporation as a defense. Her interests lie in evoking the protection of the corporation to shield her acts from liability.[25] She views the firstness of her prior act as belonging to the corporation in its secondness. In its thirdness, her act is governed by law, foreclosing the possibility of stating a direct claim. She, like the shareholder, interprets the corporation as separate and opposed to the shareholder. However, unlike the shareholder, this opposition must end with the corporation subsuming the shareholder's interest: the action should be a derivative shareholder litigation.

As *Tooley* makes clear, which interpretation ultimately succeeds in swaying the court will be outcome determinative. The law forecloses the possibility of recovering directly for injuries to the corporate interest. Moreover, the corporate interest is non-referential to the shareholder interest. Corporate injury is a signifier lacking a reference to a natural identity. The Capitalist discourse identifying the interests of a corporation with the collective interests of its shareholders is broken. Only in understanding what the corporate identity signifies without reference to a natural identity will *Tooley's* text take on an internal coherence in legal discourse.

---

[24] This reluctance is evidenced by numerous cases in which plaintiff/shareholders have crafted intricate arguments intended signify the action as direct rather than derivative. *See, e.g.*, *Id.*, at 1034; Feldman v. Cutala, 951 A.2d 727, 732–33 (Del. 2008). To the author's knowledge, in no case in which the nature of the action is at issue has the shareholder interpreted the case as a derivative action.

[25] The protections afforded management in shareholder derivative suits (namely, the demand requirement), and the meaning thereof as it relates to corporate identity will be discussed *infra* Part III.B.

J.P. Morgan Chase: The Corporation Speaks

The preceding section illustrated the negative aspects of corporate identity. It is "not its management" and "not its shareholders". The corporation has been confronted with its Otherness and perceived through the legal semiosis as a Self distinct from the Other. But does the corporation see itself? Because the corporation cannot speak in a natural language, its speech is only that which is recognized by the law as belonging to the corporation. This section will explore what speech acts the corporation may declare and, because of the derivative nature of corporate speech, who is a corporate speaker. The surface structure of the law on this point is again negative (i.e., it defines what is not corporate speech or a corporate speaker), a positive corporate identity emerges in the geno-text. This identity, we will find, occupies a primary discursive space with a mechanical unwilling, to the exclusion of natural identities and their desires.

Despite *Tooley's* insistence that corporate identity be viewed without reference to natural identity, law only takes on meaning in the space of natural events. Legal semiotics shapes the mere existence of worldly facts and creates an interpretant—a legal meaning—for those facts. Heretofore, this analysis has focused on legal discourse concerning corporate identity in a theoretical space as if such discourse were divorced from any natural standpoint. In order to fully appreciate the import and operation of this discourse, it will be necessary to introduce a "real world" scenario and examine the meaning giving to corporate identity by the legal interpretant.

Imagine the following: The management of two corporations agrees to a merger. Pursuant to the terms of the agreement the acquiring corporation ("AC") will issue shares of its stock to the shareholders of the target corporation ("TC") in exchange for their shares of TC. In order to entice the TC shareholders into accepting the merger, the AC stock issued will have a market value of 14% more than the market value of the TC stock exchanged (i.e., TC's shareholders will receive a premium for their stock). In addition, the CEO of TC would become a high-ranking executive at AC. The shareholder's of both corporations vote to approve the merger.

Shortly before the merger is to be finalized, the press catches wind of some unseemly backroom negotiations. The news reports that the CEO of TC offered to approve the merger with no premium if he could become the CEO of AC. "Wait," the AC shareholder's exclaim, "AC's management has overpaid for TC. AC could have offered no premium (and our shares would not have been diluted against the acquired assets) if only our CEO had agreed to step down." "Not so," responds AC's management, "in our business judgment, such a deal would never have been approved by TC's shareholders, and we rejected it in order to properly consummate a merger that was in the best interest of the corporation."

This was the case when J.P. Morgan Chase (AC) acquired Bank One (TC) in 2002.[26] The court was called upon to determine whether the action by AC's shareholders was direct or derivative and, if the latter, who was entitled to speak for the corporation.

---

[26] *In re* J.P. Morgan Chase & Co. Shareholder Litigation, 906 A.2d 808 (Del. Ch. 2005)

The Name of the Corporation Is Invoked

Following the rule established in *Tooley*, the court first determined whether the action was direct or derivative by determining who suffered the alleged harm. On this point, the plaintiff/shareholders are in a complex relationship with the corporation following the transaction. Whereas, if the directors were to use the corporation to purchase assets at an inflated price, they may view the damage to corporate interests as being in line with their own: *our* corporation was used for improper purposes by *them*. However, because the corporation purchased assets using its own stock, the plaintiff/shareholders see a new corporation with a different textual surface engendered not only by the adversarial relationship between themselves and the management, but also by an adversarial relationship between themselves and the new shareholders. To the plaintiff/shareholders, the corporation itself has changed as a result of the very action which resulted in a dilution of their stockholder interest.[27]

In its geno-text, the plaintiff/shareholder's argument has recognized the unfixed, annihilatory capacity of the corporation. The corporation's interest, which they may previously have presumed to be in line with their own, has negated their interest by a change in its identity. It has become something other than what it was and the alteration worked a detriment upon them. The corporation is no longer the mere conjunctive relationship between the shareholders, the management, and the object of their desire. The corporation has become the object of their desire and its loss the injury which requires redress.

In rejecting the plaintiff/shareholders' position, the court held "that any alleged harm was suffered by [the corporation] …. The plaintiffs, if they were harmed at all, were harmed indirectly and only because of their ownership in [the corporation]."[28] Because the harm was suffered by the corporation, only the corporation may recover.

The surface structure of its opinion followed accepted rules for determining whether a direct or derivative action is appropriate: "a complaint that directly challenges the fairness of the process and the price of a merger suggests … that the corporation suffered harm"; "if a board of directors authorizes the issuance of stock for no or grossly inadequate consideration, the corporation is directly injured and shareholders are injured derivatively"; "the proposition that dilution claims are individual in nature where a significant stockholder's interest is increased at the sole expense of the minority … have no application … where the entity benefiting from the allegedly diluting transaction … is a third party rather than an existing significant or controlling stockholder."[29] Thus the action in this case must be derivative.

---

[27] *Id.*, at 818.

[28] *Id.*, at 819.

[29] Agostino v. Hicks, 845 A.2d 1110, 1119 (Del. Ch. 2004); Avacus Partners, L.P. v. Brian, 1990 WL 161909, at *6 (Del. Ch. 1990); *In re* Paxson Communications Corp. S'holders Litig., 2001 WL 812028, at *5 (Del. Ch. 2001).

The legal propositions applied by the court in *J.P. Morgan* belie the need for a unitary and fixed subject in legal discourse. The law is unable speak at a subject whose identity is malleable for the purposes of the litigation. The corporation at issue in a complaint cannot be both the pre-merger and post-merger corporation and, insofar as the facts forming the basis of the shareholders' injury are the actions of the pre-merger corporate management, the pre-merger corporation is the legal subject.[30]

In the geno-text of this opinion we begin to see a positive view of corporate identity that is non-referential to both management and shareholder interests. The mirror held up to the corporation by the shareholder derivative suit to initiate the Self/Other distinction between the management and the corporation also alerts the corporation of its Otherness from its shareholders in maintaining the derivative action. This time, however, it is the law holding the mirror: this action is *yours*, the court tells the corporation. To what this "yours" refers will be the subject of the next section.

The Corporation Is Heard

In Lacanian theory, there cannot be an "I" expressed without an "Other" to hear. Because a corporation is an entity lacking in internal dialogue, it is appropriate to say that it cannot speak for itself without an external listener. When a court determines that an action belongs to a corporation, it decides not only that the corporation shall speak, but also what the corporation shall be allowed to say.

In *J.P. Morgan*, the court held the corporation (not the shareholders) suffered any harm resulting from an alleged overpayment of its own stock. The signification given to the corporation in this context underlies the most extreme divergence between the corporation as signifying itself and its constituent parts collectively. The court's reasoning uncovers a vital element in the legal signification of corporate identity: a corporation has an interest in its own stock.

Kevelson has argued that property is fundamental to "the incorporation of abstract wills and forces" which make up human personality, so too is it part of the process by which business corporations develop their legal personality.[31] If this is so, then the legal recognition of a corporation's property interest in itself signifies a sort of completion of the corporate personhood.

The ruling in *J.P. Morgan* also lends to support to Professor Backer's assertion that "[t]he corporation is both the name individuals ('I') live in and also one that is itself an aggregation of this 'I.' But it is an unstable and dynamic object and sign; not just a name, but also and simultaneously the name of its opposite."[32] Professor

---

[30] *See J.P. Morgan*, 906 A.2d at 818 ("Any alleged dilution was a harm suffered by all pre-merger [J.P. Morgan] stockholders and, consequently, [J.P. Morgan] itself.").

[31] Roberta Kevelson, *Property as Rhetoric in Law, 4 Cardozo Studies in Law & Literature 189*, 197 (1992)

[32] Larry Catá Backer, *The Corporation as Semiosis*, 135 (*Consortium for Peace & Ethics* Working Paper No. 2012–2, 2012).

Backer indicates a corporation can be signified either as an autonomous entity or as property in the hands of its shareholders, but to say the corporation is autonomous because it is property is to affect "a perverse conflation between two wholly inconsistent understandings of corporate character." Through this dual process of signification, the law confers on the corporation a self-interest. The law now sees the corporation as a personhood capable of internal dialogue: its desire for the sake of its shareholders finds an inner tension with its desire for itself.

By determining the range of permissible shareholder actions to be limited to a derivative action in a particular case, the court decides how the corporation is to be heard: it is to be heard as an autonomous subject. Yet, the court must limit the polyphonic personhood to a specific voice that will be signified as legally belonging to the corporation. It does so, through the demand requirement.

Delaware requires a shareholder bringing a derivative suit to "make a demand upon the corporation's current board to pursue derivative claims owned by the corporation before a shareholder is permitted to pursue legal action on the corporation's behalf."[33] This demand is excused, however, "where officers and directors are under an influence which sterilizes their discretion, they cannot be considered proper persons to conduct litigation on behalf of the corporation."[34] In the *J.P. Morgan* case, while the CEO had an interest in keeping his job, which sterilized his judgment, the other members of the corporation's board were "not alleged to have received any personal financial benefit from [the merger] other than one that devolved to all [the corporation's] stockholders alike."[35]

In order to understand the demand requirement, it may be helpful to elaborate on the semiotic diagram utilized in Part III.A above: An act of management can be either (1) a corporate action or (2) not a corporate action. To this we can add: A derivative action by the shareholder may be (3) an action in the corporate interest or (4) an action not in the corporate interest. Elements (3) and (4) reflect the law's imposition of demand to determine whether the shareholder's derivative action may be heard as an action by the courts.

As it relates to the shareholder, the law interprets the derivative action of a shareholder as the action of a corporation if, and only if, it is brought in the interest of a corporation. The truth-value of this bi-conditional is determined, however, in relationship to (1) and (2): the demand requirement interprets a shareholder's derivative action as being in the corporate interest only if the action of the management in question is not a corporate action. Thus, the court *J.P. Morgan* imposed the well-established rule that a shareholder may bring a derivative action only if the directors are not disinterested ("directors can neither appear on both sides of a transaction nor expect to derive any personal financial benefit from it in the sense of self-dealing") or not independent ("a director's decision [must be] based on the

[33] Del. Ch. Ct. Rule 23.1.

[34] *Aronson v. Lewis*, 473 A.2d 805, 814 (Del. 1984).

[35] *J.P. Morgan*, 906 A.2d at 821.

corporate merits of the subject before the board rather than extraneous considerations or influences").[36]

The autonomous corporate identity comes to signify both the object of the dispute between the respective "I" and "Other" (shareholders and management). Yet, at the same instant, the mediation of this conflict is the corporate identity itself. Only by showing that her legal identity is subsumed by the corporation may the manager maintain the corporation as her object. Only by allowing the corporation to subsume himself may the shareholder vindicate his interest in the corporation against managerial abuse. Through the demand requirement, the dual signification of corporate identity is collapsed. The corporation is an autonomous entity distinct from its shareholders and management, which unfolds from and subsumes its conjunctive relationship between the two others.

It is through this duality in the corporate form that the discursive space of corporate identity-in-itself opens up before the courts. As Professor Backer notes, "corporations derive their signification from the state, that is, that the state ultimately defines the character of the corporation through its own intervention in the construction of the entity."[37] In other words, whereas the normal interplay of shareholder/manager influences on corporate activity may allow for the corporation to be signified by a dynamic, polycentric mode of being, once a breach occurs between the component parts, the law will re-signify it with a static subjectivity of an autonomous entity. In imbuing the corporation with identity, the law is called upon to engender the corporation with an interest that is separate and apart from the two speaking subjects in order to make sense of the conflict over the objectified corporation.

This separate interest inevitably comes down to one thing: wealth maximization. In the words of one opinion: "The "Inc." after the company name has to mean at least that … I cannot accept as valid … a corporate policy that specifically, clearly, and admittedly seeks *not* to maximize the economic value of a for-profit Delaware corporation."[38] The corporation is that thing for whom the increase of itself is the sole property referable to its independent existence. Legal discourse thus reenters the Capitalist discourse on corporate identity, but only after stripping away the utilitarian ends towards which Capitalism is normatively oriented. Capital is no longer a symbol for the capacity to attain goods, it becomes the master symbol of all that is good.

The Autonomous Ego of the Corporation-in-Itself

Jacques Lacan understood that, flowing from the "obviously precarious" state of the ego, humans have an inclination to view themselves as autonomous individuals.[39] Professor Backer began his *Corporations as Semiosis* by contrasting the language

[36] *J.P. Morgan*, 906 A.2d at 821 (quoting *Aronson*, 472 A.2d at 812, 816).

[37] Backer, *supra* note 32, at 133.

[38] *eBay Domestic Holdings, Inc. v. Newark*, 16 A.3d 1, 34 (Del. Ch. 2010).

[39] Lacan, *supra* note 4.

of the Book of Revelation as a metaphor for the limits of the semiotic world of corporate autonomy with Nietzsche's opening of the possibility of infinitely more meanings.[40] The human world of meaning is infinite, and the internal wills, drives and desires that make up human identity preclude the falling back upon absolute values and conceptions. The corporation however, does not have any such identity in the world of a "natural" human community. The corporation can speak its own name only insofar as the law allows it. And the law allows the corporation to have but one desire: make money.

Legal scholar Christopher Stone asked why the law does not establish any greater social interest for the corporation. The proposed answer is that it cannot do so within the realm of legal discourse: "In many cases lawmaking is an unsatisfactory way to deal with social problems … because we, as a society, lack consensus as to the values we want to advance."[41] The language of law does not comprehend the variety and complexity of human experience and desire. Rather, it flattens such desire to a single purpose: plaintiff wants damages for alleged injuries; defendant wants vindication of the lawfulness of his action; corporation wants to make money.

In a sense, then, the corporation signifies a perfection we can never attain. When the plaintiff leaves the courtroom, his identity again becomes precarious: he may again engage in internal dialogue, saying "I want to lose weight, but I do not want to diet," or "I want that promotion, but my wife does not like me working longer hours." The corporation is untroubled: it wants only to make itself more.

However, this idolatry represents a threat to personal identity. We have seen how both the shareholder and manager must allow themselves to be subsumed by the corporate identity in the context of shareholder derivative action. The law has recognized the corporation as a subject with only itself as the object of its desire. The corporation desires to grow in wealth and the management must feed this desire or breach their duty to the corporation. The shareholder's are powerless to speak in the corporation's voice unless the management has failed in its corporate purpose.

As corporations occupy a greater and greater share of the discursive space, the problem intensifies. The ability of an individual to engage in a socio-economic level outside of the context of a corporation decreases. With *Citizens United* even the political discursive space seems subject to the prey of the corporation. If the corporation must expand, it expands by shrinking the discursive space: the triadic relationship forming the basis of identity is collapsed when the Other will recognize only requests for the exchange of goods and services.

Yet, to castigate corporations is in a sense missing the point. As Kevelson reminds us:

> In terms of human existence, the properties of people are directly correlated with their ability to become, to greater degrees, self-aware and self-knowing. In terms of legal persons and incorporated economic interests, property is a means of creating, *by corporate persons*,

[40] *See* Backer, *supra* note 32, at 102–03, n.5.

[41] Christopher Stone, *Where the Law Ends* 97 (1975).

> who are themselves reflections, mirrors, and representations of the society from which they grow, which grounds them, which is their context.[42]

In a final reversal, the corporation holds a mirror to our selves. We see our own finiteness and weakness in the perpetual solidity of the corporate form, and we tremble.

But still, we see ourselves.

The corporation presents its own possibility of becoming subsumed by a new creation social meaning that strips the corporation of the soil in which it grows.

Where is the point of counter-attack? In a sense we come full circle. While corporate interests have occupied a dominant socio-political position, people like Stephen Colbert have realized the capacity of the corporation to operate against itself. By forming an autonomous body politic and corporate with the distinction of being a corporation who measures gains only by the destruction of corporate power. The Colbert Super PAC may be a joke, but the joke takes on a life of its own among the countless investors in its cause. This is the weakness of the corporation, it cannot create new meaning it merely reproduces itself. That, and it has no sense of humor.

---

[42] Kevelson, *supra* note 31, at 197.

Signs Without Authority: The Battle of Experts, the Caricature of a Discourse and the Failure of Scientific Evidence

Robert Marriott

Introduction

The lawyer, though he knows it not, is a semiotic practitioner. His courtroom statements, presented through the law, determine not only fortunes of his client but also color the representation of the law itself, characterizing the authority of the state over its subjects. His words are presented as a component of the deliberate nature of legal discourse, which collectively produces the morality play that is the legal-social interaction. The legal discourse, although complex and willful in the pursuit of its chosen ends, remains largely blind to the nature of the semiosis, which gives it life. Law is not the only field, however, in which an open embrace of knowing representation is necessary. There is another profession in which language is a tool used deliberately to produce meanings. The scientist, too, produces or changes the meaning of words in an arbitrary manner, in her case with the goal of characterizing and systematizing empirical phenomena to better cohere to the linguistic practices of her fellows. The scientist does not operate within a single discourse, but through the act of publication submits their work for the interpretation of a sea of language systems that make up the different disciplines, and discourses, of the scientific discipline. When she designs an experiment, when she witnesses and records

Source: MARRIOTT, ROBERT: "Signs without authority: The battle of experts, the caricature of a discourse and the failure of scientific evidence" *Prize winning paper of the Roberta Kevelson Seminar on Law & Semiotics, 2012* The philosophy and theory underlying scientific representation is invoked in court cases later considered in this chapter. However, this coverage is itself not semiotic in nature and is, as I hope to demonstrate, self-contradicting. Although meaning-making occurs in scientific fields, it does not survive the transition to law, and as such plays little role in this analysis beyond that of the victim

R. Marriott (✉)
Department of Communications Arts and Sciences, College of the Liberal Arts, Pennsylvania State University, 234 Sparks Building, University Park, PA 16802, USA
e-mail: marriottr@gmail.com

J.M. Broekman, L. Catá Backer (eds.), *Signs In Law - A Source Book*,
DOI 10.1007/978-3-319-09837-1_34

her observations, and most crucially when she presents her theories and findings to her fellows and to society, she also creates and alters the meaning of everyday objects of understanding. A cigarette may—by her words—become a fearful source of death; the fingerprint becomes symbolic of personal identity. Her representations are also subject to a great enterprise: that tangled web of academia, publication and private interest. The scientist's activities resemble those of the attorney. Here, words are chosen to fit the mold practitioners believe will produce the ends sought. Here, meaning is produced through a product that *deems* reality even as it seeks to define it. Here exists a vast and turbulent skein of semiotic practice, whose depths are only beginning to be plumbed. Although the linguistic practice of science is not discrete or uniform enough to be considered a monolithic discourse, it remains a discipline of semiotic meaning making of great import.

Together, the products of science and law possess a vast influence upon the inhabitants of any state. The empirical assertions of the scientist can serve as a foundation for effective law, the two working in concert to occupy a space once filled solely by fickle nature gods and arbitrary tyrants. The shared belief structure of society rests heavily upon these two systems of meaning making. In each discipline, and under some circumstances through the coordination of scientific and legal efforts, clear and effective policy has emerged thanks—in no small part—to the intense linguistic and authoritative discipline each field maintains. That this should be the case does not surprise; neither should it surprise that this discipline is in some respects a naturally occurring one. For both the scientist and lawyer, the necessities and problems of their work have produced formal textual solutions that belie the complexities of the linguistic issues present underneath. As a result, the conduct of the attorney and the scientist are similar in another respect: both embody an attitude of *blind instrumentalism* with regard to the textual product of their discipline, and with regard to the integration of other material into their discipline. Blind because neither practice is fully *aware* of its routinized semiotic activity, and instrumentalist because to each has been made plain the stakes if the discipline of their code is not maintained. The scientist, by her publication and theory creation, is a producer of meaning, but for her the process is necessarily a collaborative and conscious effort, producing shaded meanings that are explicitly left open to the doubt of others. This trial of empirical assertion is less determined than that of the legal world, in that absent the invocation a moral substrate, the scientific practitioner is free to dwell upon issues of method that are closer to the semiotic payload of their material.

Let us suppose that a scientist discovers that the repeated small collisions of professional football tend produce a pattern of previously unidentified brain damage for participants. She knows, from the moment of discovery, that this descriptive assertion carries with it a moral payload, and that it will be subject to political and public debate if reported. Despite the ramifications, the majority of scientific practitioners will willingly undercut the strength of their own work in a number of ways: by announcing the means by which the claim is wrought, by identifying their own weaknesses of method, and by leaving it open to refutation to any other willing to attempt the replicative or analytic task. At all times the scientific modus is simultaneously meaning making and meaning destroying, and as such defies an easy theorization or linguistic analysis. This can be seen in the shambolic state of both the "certainties" of the field, and the multitude of contradictory philosophies that have sought to define or determine the scope of the scientist's craft.

The lawyer is similarly bound by his profession, not to the descriptive task of discovery but the socially defined task of legal advocacy. He knows that he must represent the will of his client, but he must act within the boundaries imposed by the plural system of the law and the internal system of legal discipline, through which his brethren define as a society the bounds of accepted communication, and sustain the dream of institution. He is simultaneously more free and more heavily bound—able to color, culture and characterize new arguments and meanings within the legal system, but only to a previously approved ends.

What happens, then, when the lawyer and scientist meet? What happens when the question of scientific study becomes a means to legal answer? A retired football player sees the brain damage study and decides to sue his trainers and the professional organization that he feels are responsible for his mental illness. His attorney, our attorney, in using the product of the scientist's expertise, creates a new meaning for scientific evidence, instrumental not as a descriptor of the world but as a font of legal and moral authority. Where the individual lawyer seeks to leverage science as totem of authority in the adversarial process, the legal discourse itself has adapted itself to such an instrumental approach, reducing the product of science to an invocation of positive authority, and ultimately rendering it subject to a shallower semiosis. In so doing, the practice of science, with all its confusions, is presented as simultaneously a valid representation exterior to the legal discourse, and a product serving the needs of the legal narrative system. The material of science is thus violently reformed to produce results that reflect the aims—and serve the needs—of neither law nor science. This paper discusses how this has come to be in the place where the two disciplines meet most often under the law: the standard of review for the "expert" scientific witness.

I here must make an important caveat: At this time, emerging theories in genetics, neurology, forensics and other disciplines have the potential to create major changes to the legal construction of agency, identity, and authority. These specific subjects retain their own controversies in both legal and scientific practice, which may in time produce changes with their own semiotic payload[1]. This paper, however, does not seek to address the potential of the specific developments, but to address broadly the transformation of scientific conjecture into legal reality, and the destruction of meaning that this has come to entail.

Science at Bar

The story of the standard of admission for scientific evidence is in some ways typical of the classical tragic form: disaster inevitably occurs despite the good intentions and awareness of all involved. Courts did not respond to the problem of

[1] *See, e.g.*, Jan M. Broekman, *Intertwinements of Law and Medicine*, Leuven UP 1996.

emerging scientific evidence without an awareness of the problems that clever lawyering and abuse of credibility could pose; instead, it was with blindness to the positive nature of the discourse that the current state of affairs emerged. Each of the cases that follow represent some attempt by the legal system to adapt to the problems of incorporation that occur in accepting the representations of an outside field. In making this incorporation apparent, courts have routinely come very close to awareness of the positive semiotic structure in which they work. However, the instrumental nature of their pursuit has meant that even the most deliberate attempt to address this informational divide only serves to further distort the meaning of the evidence in question.

The courts first openly grappled with the problems that scientific evidence presented in *Frye v. United States,* a 1923 DC Court of Appeals murder case. Frye's short rumination on the nature of science and its role in the finding of law would produce the standard to which for an extended period scientific expert evidence would be held[2]. In determining the admissibility of an early form of lie detector test, the court acknowledged the difficulty that those in the legal profession faced in considering the emergence of representations of science, and ultimately sought to vest the ultimate authority for the standard in the scientific "community."

> Just when a scientific principle or discovery crosses the line between the experimental and demonstrable stages is difficult to define. Somewhere in this twilight zone the evidential force of the principle must be recognized, and while the courts will go a long way in admitting experimental testimony deduced from a well-recognized scientific principle or discovery, the thing from which the deduction is made must be sufficiently established to have gained general acceptance in the particular field in which it belongs.[3]

Though perfunctory in its deliberations (the entire decision is less than two pages in length, and the above excerpt the entirety of the legal analysis), the *Frye* case represented a first response to the emerging tendency of lawyers to present science, and scientists, as sources of legal meaning and authority in their arguments. By expressing a willingness to justify their opinion of admissibility via the opinion of the scientific community, the court sought to address two problems inherent in the application of expert evidence: first, that legal practitioners, judge and attorney both, were ill-equipped to consider the validity of an expert's assertions, whether they were novel/controversial, or so obscure that no strong basis for comparison exists, and, second, that even a well-regarded theory or practice can turn out, with the passage of time, to be fallible or even fraudulent. The court in *Frye* sought the authority of the scientific community as a means of evading these problems, but in fact did not address them. The legal system cannot abide an absence of authority; both in evaluating the validity of research and in dealing with its problems, the judge and the attorneys are the ultimate sources of authority before the law. To respond otherwise would be to divest the legal discourse itself of its authoritative power. This is reflected in a Greimas square showing both the surface assertion of

[2] *Frye v. US*, 293 F. 1013 (D.C. Cir. 1923).

[3] *Ibid.*, 1014.

legal-scientific communication, and the distortive reality of the witness as articulator of the scientific worldview.

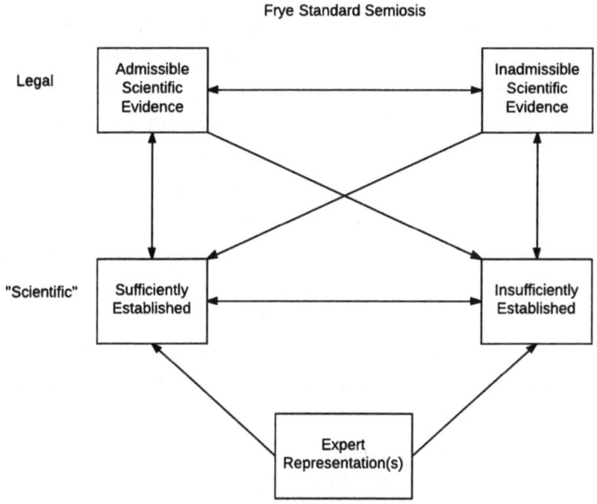

Admissible scientific evidence is sourced through its establishment in the field, outside the legal arena. Insufficiently established evidence is likewise inadmissible— a showing of a theory's unpopularity by one side can be used to contradict such an assertion by another. Crucial to the legal semiotic implication of scientific material under the *Frye* standard is that it is very nearly *expressly semiotic.* The judge is explicitly charged with evaluating material foreign to the legal discourse, knowing its alienage, and interpreting its representation prior to a legal construction. By indicating that it cedes the claim of authority and its evaluation to the viewpoint of the community, the court in *Frye* constructs, for those operating within its bounds, the illusion of a layer of legal information that is not legal, but "scientific". That this is illusory, is a matter of course; instead, the content of the "scientific" space is legal, but held separate from the legal—because the standard "showing" acceptance for the legal purpose exists outside the legal space, yet is introduced by legal practitioners. Without a true authority, each side is welcome to assert the acceptance and truth of the scientific without meaningful interference from "above", in legal authority openly ceded, or "below", in the scientific discourse, which cannot enter the legal space absent the interpretation and presentation of counsel. Thus is presented the grand stereotype: two attorneys produce two experts, each seeking to satisfy the legal standard of "general acceptance". The battle of experts commences, but its tools are not of method or reason, but of authority: the competent lawyer does not seek to prove the validity of the evidence at issue, but to demonstrate that it wins a popularity contest in its field— bearing always in mind that it is not the scientific evaluator, but the judge, who selects the victor. Although the legal authority appears to be vested in the scientific community, the reality is that such authority cannot escape the positive and final representation of a legal standard. Despite its problems,

Frye was a success in one sense: its authors acknowledged the intractable nature of the scientific-legal meaning problems they had created. The negative space that *Frye* invited reflects an unavoidable tension in the investment of scientific authority with legal meaning. This tension is addressed differently in later cases which purport to overturn the general acceptance standard and address its problems, but which instead incorporate *Frye*, and its contradictions, in increasingly Byzantine forms.

The issues first presented in *Frye* would be addressed again in the present era, first in the form of Rule 702 of the Federal Rules of Evidence (henceforth the FRE), and second in the "*Daubert* trilogy", the primary body of case-law interpreting the Rule. This series of three cases are taught as the summary of contemporary American expert testimony law; students (and therefore attorneys) not intending to specialize in the area understand little beyond them. The *Daubert* trilogy is therefore a symbol invoked to represent the whole of expert witness law (for the *Daubert* Standard is often represented as a criterion test of representation, despite the fact that it possesses no explanatory power). Although the *Frye* standard remains in effect in some state jurisdictions, the interplay of the FRE and the trilogy have produced a new paradigm, one in which the discourse of the expert is no longer given credence beyond their adherence to the formalities of the legal standard, which redefines the scientific (or other expert knowledge) representation in a legal context. At the same time, these formal requirements are frequently no shield to the obscurantism and rhetoric of conflicted accounts that naturally emerge from 1) a scientific discourse founded on the active maintenance of methodological criticism and uncertainty, and 2) the instrumental abuse of the standard's loosely held criteria by witness and attorney alike. As a consequence, the modern *Daubert* standard has produced the worst of both worlds: in seeking to render more effective the purposes of the *Frye* decision, have produced a new world in which the lawyer and advocate both pursue the ends of their respective discourse, and arrive at neither.

Daubert, Anarchic Authority and the Destruction of the Scientific Witness

Daubert v. Merrell Dow Pharmaceuticals was not solely an attempt to deal with the problems of establishing meaningful authority that were made evident by the response to *Frye*[4]. The decision was principally an attempt to unify the law upon the text of Rule 702, and to articulate the rule in a manner that would render future

[4]Although the semiotic basis of the problem went unreported, lawyers knew that the standard of general acceptance was too easy to abuse; the parties in *Daubert* had nine experts between them to resolve a single issue of fact; such an array was in truth relatively conservative in some areas.

adjudication of expert materials consistent[5]. This was no easy task; given the shallow language of Rule 702 as initially developed:

> If scientific, technical or otherwise specialized knowledge will assist the trier of fact to understand the evidence or to determine a fact in issue, a witness qualified as an expert by knowledge, skill, experience,, training or education, may testify thereto in the form of an opinion or otherwise.[6]

The term "qualified" in the rule was patently inadequate to the use it was called for in the free-for-all that had emerged since the *Frye* decision, the Federal Rules seemed void of meaning without an interpretant context. Without guidance regarding what qualified an established or novel theory, or what forms of "knowledge, skill, experience, training or education" were sufficient in a specific instance, attorneys and officials alike struggled to determine how the rule changed the standards they had previously applied—many were of the opinion that Rule 702 simply restated the previous *Frye* standard, despite the lack of authority it presented. The Supreme Court in *Daubert* thus sought gave the rule meaning as a new duty of judicial practice, emphasizing the duty of the judge as evaluator of expert evidence and producing a standard for that adjudicative task. Where Frye had suggested the ceding of authority to the scientific speaker, the *Daubert* standard pursued the opposite—a complete seizure of the authority of scientific evidence by the court itself. Central to the *Daubert* decision is the construction of the trial judge as "gatekeeper" of scientific credibility, the final evaluator of scientific knowledge from outside the legal field, and therefore the creator of legal precedent built upon that incorporation. The *Daubert* standard, before all else, requires the trial judge in their evaluation of Rule 702 *scientific knowledge* to determine whether "the reasoning or methodology underlying the testimony is *scientifically valid*...We are confident that federal judges possess the capacity to undertake this review."[7] The tension first present in Frye, already subject to open abuse, is thus reconstituted in a manner which, in attempting to address the preexisting conflict of meaning, instead only serves to develop and obscure the problem previously extant. The opinion itself emphasizes the difficulty of establishing a coherent, textual standard for the judge's newfound task: "Many factors will bear on the inquiry, and we do not presume to set out a definitive checklist or test. But some general observations are appropriate."[8]

---

[5] Prior to Daubert it was unclear when Rule 702 applied, or how it interacted with *Frye*.

[6] *Daubert v. Merrell Dow Pharma., Inc.*, 509 U.S. 589 (1993). Note that the Rule was rewritten in 2000 to incorporate the Daubert finding, and restyled for clarity purposes in 2011. The subcommittee notes on these revisions, although relevant, were not the origin of the current legal attitude toward expert evidence so much as a reflection thereof, and therefore of lesser analytic value.

[7] Id p. 592, emphasis added.

[8] Id., at 593

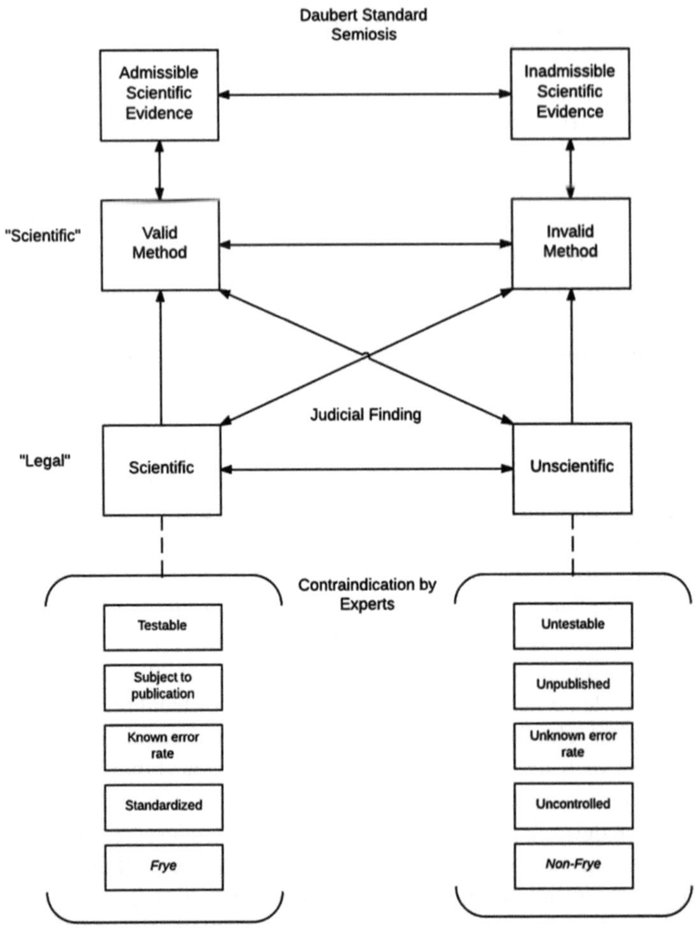

To provide even a loose guide to what is acceptable, the standard becomes one of methodological validity as a means to accurate science. As a result, the factors listed by the court are a series of legal criteria *prescribed* to scientific material, claimed as a *description* of a scientific-legal standard. The wide range of the factors described in the *Daubert* decision are not intended to be exclusive, but their scattered origins and representation compared to the binary standard they are meant to serve articulate the uncertainty of the law in the scientific space. First, citing to the work of the philosopher of science Karl Popper, the court *finds* that scientific material should be falsifiable and testable. Second, they *find* that, descriptively, scientific material is subject to peer review and publication. Third and fourth, scientific material is evaluated by the presence or absence of a known rate of error and methodological controls—a reinscription of science in terms of its ability to serve as a basis for belief in a legal outcome. Finally, and most seriously, the justices invite the reintroduction of the *Frye* general acceptance criterion as one factor proving that the evidence is scientific, therefore methodologically sound, therefore scientific evidence. The incorporation of *Frye* is particularly significant, in that it underscores the fundamental shift in the meaning of the whole standard. In attempting to resolve the lack of clear authority created by *Frye*, the Supreme Court deems the admissibility of scientific evidence a judicial duty. At the same time, however, the terms and meanings the court presents as the standard of this judicial decision are "scientific". As in *Frye*, the judge is invited to choose among meanings he is invited—and *instructed*—not to understand. The problems of contradiction in the Daubert factors test therefore extend past the uncertainty of any more anodyne issue of linguistic uncertainty in, for example, a "reasonable person" standard, or any other source of initial textual ambiguity. Here the loss of meaning occurs from both directions at once.

Practically, as the standard employed is a flexible, factors-based test, no single logic or representation suffices at any level below the binary of admission. Instead, the "factors" present relative contraindications for acceptance or denial by the adjudicator- constructs of his proper perception of a set of meanings explicitly extralegal. In turn, the Daubert standard invites its own collapse in professional use, the standard is at most a set of criteria attorneys know they must reference in constructing an expert witness, to ensure that they will have maximum coverage against a judge wielding a "standard" made from "general observations". To provide what certainty they can, the expert must be able to make the relevant theory appear to be, in order, testable (or, perhaps, tested, suggesting either a falsificationist or positivist understanding of scientific proof), published, reliable, predictable and popular. Above all such concerns, however, the legal practitioner understands that these are legal terms, legal standards, before a judge explicitly unable to evaluate them beyond the meaning which the attorney and opposing counsel will provide. To the attorney weighing testimony, or preparing a scientific witness, the signage of the scientific material is flattened into a binary landscape of evidence for and against the admissibility of the testimony. Thus, simplification of the material and eradication of doubt-instilling traits are necessary to preserve the attorney's instrumentalist approach to the facts and interests of the case. The consequence is that problems of adjudicative qualifications and fallible science remain unresolved, and are now expanded into a realm of conflicting and nebulous "tests" that amount to home rules for particular jurisdictions and sciences. In such an environment, the credibility of the gatekeeper and their legal assertions was sure to erode.

The second case of the trilogy, although not directly modifying the standard for the admission of testimony, nevertheless demonstrates the damage to legal credibility that the *Daubert* standard had produced: in *General Electric v. Joiner*, the Court found that "[N]othing in either *Daubert* or the Federal Rules of Evidence requires a district court to admit opinion evidence which is connected to existing data only by the ipse dixit of the expert. A court may conclude that there is simply too great an analytical gap between the data and the opinion proffered."[9] In reaffirming the primacy of the judge as "gatekeeper", and in shutting down a series of cases suggesting that a judge's finding of scientific evidence admissibility be subjected to a lesser

[9] *General Electric Company v. Joiner*, 522 U.S. 146 (1997).

standard of review on appeal, the court demonstrated its awareness of the problem that scientific evidence had become for the authority of the judiciary as a whole.

Closing the trilogy, *Kumho Tire* reversed the initial focus of the standard on testimony of scientific character by extending its application to non-scientific fields of expertise[10]. Where the initial considerations of *Daubert* were vague and produced no coherent body of precedent, they still were unified in their attempt to refer judges in some way to those features of scrutiny that make scientific language resilient in the face of empirical uncertainty. The witness in *Kumho* was an expert in "tire failure analysis", a discipline with no peer reviewed journals or longitudinal studies. By the grouping of scientific and nonscientific methods under what had previously been a purely scientific standard, the *Kumho* decision abandoned any meaningful attempt to distinguish between the scientific and non-scientific disciplines. Crucially, the court in so doing did not distinguish or abandon the *Daubert* language of incorporated, dominant scientific meanings, any more than it had abandoned the role of judge as arbiter. Instead, Daubert was willingly incorporated and deemed appropriate as a standard for all expert evidence.

Kumho Tire Semiosis

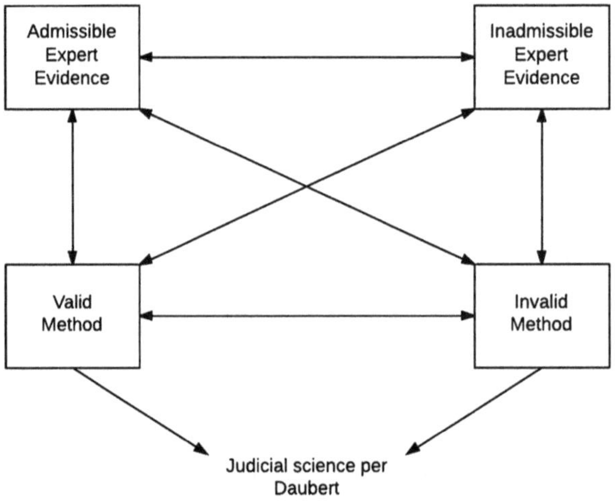

The *Kumho* standard is not new; instead it simply applies the previous, confused meaning and scope of language to all "expert" evidence. The standard, already torturing the meaning of science, is now openly applied to evaluate the quality of non-scientific evidence, with no distinction made. In its evaluation, scientific material must pass through three spaces without legal or scientific authority to enter legal significance in positive or negative form. First, as per *Frye*, it is reduced to its acceptance and evaluated "non-legally" by a judge acknowledging the use of its acceptance as a sign of the limits of his legal authority. Second, this popularity mixes with other

[10] *Kumho Tire Co. v. Carmichael*, 526 U.S. 137 (1999).

individual representations emerging from positive, negative, prescriptive and descriptive legal narratives of science to produce a showing under the *Daubert* standard. Finally, what specific meaning it has qua science is rendered void by its analogy as legal science to legal expertise, flattened to a single concept by the outcome of *Kumho Tire*. Such a path cannot preserve the essence of the meaning it hopes to convey—for better or worse, however, such a preservation of meaning is not in the interests of the effective attorney.

The Legal Instrumentalism of Science

Within the legal academic discipline, the battle of experts resulting from the invocation of scientific expertise is a known problem. A genre of articles exists to lament the absence of a uniform standard of review, decrying the anarchy of standards that has reigned since the *Daubert* trilogy[11]. Emphasizing the impossibility of managing caselaw in an environment of such doctrinal discord, academics and practitioners outline the difficulty advocates face in weighing the attempt to introduce evidence in an environment with no consistent standards. While the problem is known, its nature is necessarily articulated in terms of the problems of legal practice, not legal-scientific signification. Particularly illustrative of the tunnel vision of the profession in this light is the authoritative text *Modern Scientific Evidence*, which presents a surprisingly enlightened take on the instrumental limitations of expert evidence in the course of describing the foundations and details of virtually every litigated area of scientific inquiry.

Among the most directly relevant sections of the five volume text is a chapter specifically devoted to the subject of the scientific method. This chapter reflects the alienation that attorneys feel in applying the products of the scientific enterprise, and the frustration users of the scientific product feel fitting it to the courtroom setting. In so doing, the text seeks to acclimate the legal reader to a set of norms and practices outside the profession. "It will help", the author exhorts, "to think of science as a verb, not a noun"[12]. Practitioners are not qualified qua their titles or expertise but for the knowledge of the field they actually possess; similarly, a scientific statement or opinion science is not valid due to the credentials of its admitting witness or its intuitive appeal but by the completeness of the methodology from which it emerges. The text discusses at length, and not just in this preliminary chapter, the various pluralities of opinion that make up the scientific enterprise, and

[11] See, e.g., Bernstein, David & Jackson, Jeffrey, "The Daubert Trilogy In the United States." *George Mason Law & Economics Research Paper* No. 04–06. Additionally, a variety of online tools have emerged specifically for lawyers attempting to track the glut of theory and jurisdiction-specific decisions emerging from the Frye and Daubert standards. These sites exemplify the legal instrumentalization of science at its most blunt. See, e.g., http://www.dauberttracker.com/, http://www.daubertontheweb.com/.

[12] Faigman, David, et al. *Modern Scientific Evidence 2011–2012 edition, Vol. 1*. Thomson Reuters/West, 2011.

caution lawyers against an overly aggressive pursuit of an appealing legal "science" that cannot be maintained by the authority of the base theory's authors. It must not be forgotten, however, that *Modern Scientific Evidence* does not represent the norm of scientific literacy or deliberate meaning examination; it is a reference textbook, meant for specific use to resolve the instrumental difficulties of a particular relevant case, not a treatise on the conflict of science and law, perused and digested by a contemplative body of practitioners. It is a legal text, part of a legal discourse, and has no real pretensions otherwise. Though the text seeks a nuanced consideration for the problems of scientific signification, it is too much to expect it to instill such attitudes in its readers-indeed, the target audience is not so interested in resolving the problems of the *Daubert* trilogy as exploiting and avoiding them. The attorney cannot afford to spend the time (in a very literal sense) to learn the details and caveats of the foreign culture that is the discipline. For the normal legal practitioner, caught up in issues of credibility and, above all else, the judges' opinion, the scientist-witness and their work product are a frustrating source of ambiguity in a profession where ambiguity exists to be hidden through effective use of the craft. Viewed through the lens of legal instrumentalism, the scientist and their product become at best an alienated subject of legal meaning. The legal practitioner serves the interest of his clients, and in so doing adjusts the signification of scientific evidence on a case-by-case basis. This phenomenon has produced an industry in and of itself that is in many respects emblematic of the failings of the legal-scientific dialogue; it presents itself as an authority of both and serves to deteriorate them instead.

The meaning of the scientist's work is already falsified many times over in principle, even before it is practiced by the mercenary figures that now construct its meaning before the law. Through caselaw and the self-interest of the attorney, the nuance and structure of scientific representation are completely absent from the affairs of the modern courtroom. It remains to examine what replaces the "scientist", the "scientific consultant", and how this strange organism presents itself in the law.

Scientific Evidence in the Marketplace of Expertise

The scientific practitioner seeking to make a mark (or secure returns) with a new technology or method exists as a point of controversy in the law[13], but his publicity outreaches his prominence. For every case in which a radical new theory is needed to win the day, a thousand exist where a figure possessing the authority of the expert is needed to massage the material before the court to ensure its submission. The truth of normal legal scientific evidence signification is demonstrated not by lawyers and not by groundbreaking researchers, but by the paid consulting expert.

[13] For a discussion of one such actor with wide semiotic ramifications, see, Jan M. Broekman: "Trading Signs: Semiotic Practices in Law and Medicine." *International Journal for the Semiotics of Law* 20 (2007) 223–236.

The expert witness consultancy is usually organized into a firm, which may vary in size from a two-person team to a massive complex spanning all marketable fields. Routinely, the larger organizations perform trial witnessing duties alongside preliminary case consulting work to establish, for example, the presence of a cause for action or to ensure that a more arcane regulation still applies. These men and women are not monsters, nor are they cretins: witness firms are clear that they do not provide an empty, mercenary vessel to fill with pseudoscience, defrauding the court. At the same time, successful expert witness groups are not ignorant of the true demands of legal participation. Witnesses are advertised explicitly in terms of their credentials, years of experience, and coolness under cross-examination. Knowledge is a necessary trait for the expert witness, to be sure, but that is not why they are paid competitively. What matters most is the conveyance of trustworthiness alongside an empirical argument that works in lockstep with the legal employer. In this sense the paid expert "witness" is in truth testifying not to the authority of the material at hand, but to their ability to present such material. Because the *Daubert* standard presents a wide space of unknown meaning and authority, the role of the expert witness is to fill that gap, presenting certainty in meaning and language that the law has abandoned and which science cannot provide.

Thus, for the witness, the lingua franca is clear—the pretense of science falls away in favor of the language of instrumentally acceptable authority. The fine details and field-specific terminology of the geneticist or forensic technician are reduced to a code language, whose communication is provided only to establish two functions: first, that it fit the ill-defined and practiced *Daubert* standard through behavior and appearance, and second, to transfer that authority to an expression of learned opinion close enough to the norm that no one winds up in jail (aside from the defendant, today's employer is the state).

It is perhaps the greatest irony that, in weighing the authority and words of a scientific expert, with an eye toward their effect on the adjudicator that the lawyer is closest to awareness of the semiotic processes that he and the scientist share. By their reliance upon and construction of the "expert" in the pursuit of the authority and clarity abandoned by the scientific evidence standard, the attorney is forced to acknowledge their role as meaning-maker, as framed by the space they are seeking to fill. At the same time, the lawyer, in the pursuit of the ends of his practice, is no more able to see the layers of obscurantism they now participate in than the far less troubling meaning management of routine legal practice. It is conventional when discussing the meeting of two semiotic discourses to speak of translation, or of the overlap of index sets producing an avenue of communication. This is not so here. The interested instrumentalism of legal authority does not permit an intertwinement of sign or signification—the trading of representation is one-way. Whatever the role of the judge with regard to the knowledge of the scientific community, be it general acceptance or some more nebulous standard, the truth is that the discourse is purely legal—the scientist never enters the courtroom. Instead, the legal presentation hollows out the scientific material and wears its skin to present a new meaning of overwhelming truth; truth that through its acceptance gains a positive meaning before the law and the citizen that extends beyond even conventional legal meaning-making. The net output of the acceptance of a novel theory as evidence reaches beyond the scope of any assertion the scientist could ever make her statement was grounded in both a limited empiricism, as well as in its own conditions of refutation. The positive, moral nature of the law denies these limitations, and instead presents the specter of an uninformed, distortive empirical relativism.

Let us return to our scientist and lawyer, now in court. The scientist's work is novel, so it will likely not be invoked as a totem of certainty under the simple category of science; instead, the lawyer must choose what elements of her work to present in a manner least likely to invite fully legal scrutiny. The judge is "free" to apply or not apply the elements of the *Daubert* standard according to her own previously uneducated appraisal; she has no training in neurology or statistics or any of the other trappings of method through which the scientific thesis is expressed; it is unlikely that she will give great credence to them in weight of their uncertainty. The lawyer, himself only slightly more knowledgeable, instead focuses upon invoking the language of the standard as a means to conveying the authority and truth of the scientist's thesis: that the research has a specific citation index is meaningless, but the research seems to demonstrate an effect; is that enough to satisfy the judge's duty? The lawyer must not provide too much information, for to do so is to itself risk that some errant nuance will invite greater scrutiny, misunderstanding, and eventual rejection according to a bespoke standard. At the same time, opposing counsel has produced a very credible looking—and sounding—consultant from a well-established agency who is willing to swear to methodological problems in the research, that it is not generally accepted, and that it does not show what the plaintiff alleges (terms couched in the legal code, that which the judge recognizes with no small relief). A complex statistical model is deployed, and responded to with another that seems to contradict it; a long string of words is used to describe neural phenomena that remains unclear when repeated; figures of authority are quoted and large texts of unclear origin are read aloud. The judge, the gatekeeper upon whom it falls to decide which side, if any, is "science" that is also "legal", knows only what has been presented, and can evaluate it only by what they know—the credibility of witnesses, and the *Daubert* standard. The outcome is unpredictable for all involved; its *meaning* is likewise unknown, both before and after the decision is made.

The Blind Invoking the Blind

It is unfair to suggest that there is no progress toward a correspondence between legal and scientific fields. Although normal courts have so far been unable to resolve the problems of flattened signification and obscure authority present under the Federal Rules of Evidence, administrative courts specializing in a scientific field have shown themselves more literate in the twisting nature of scientific practice. Even in the mainstream judiciary, expansive and controversial theories with an apparent impact on the practice of law and its associated interests are likely to receive greater scrutiny and a more deliberate hearing. Where sufficiently urgent or public, a misapplication of science runs more clearly afoul of the drive of the law to maintain its authority; as such, particularly routine or radical theories do tend to eventually be redefined as beyond the acceptable scope of the *Daubert* standard. Although it was briefly a winning approach to invoke the theories of multiple chemical sensitivity in the 1960s, that body of science, with its associated disability claims, fell out of favor in scientific and legal circles almost simultaneously. These dramatic cases are abnormalities, however. In courtrooms across the United States, small abuses of science occur in the service of a legal standard that papers over a gaping void of understanding with shallow rhetoric. The damage wrought by the incoherence of the scientific evidence standard is invisible, but it can have only a caustic effect on the morality of the legal discipline, and the purity of the scientific enterprise.

Semiotics in a New Key

Jan M. Broekman and Larry Catá Backer

At the crossroads of word and text appear important insights of general nature. They open a new world, apt to semiotics in a new key—new, or different, or complementary? The question begs clarification of our fundamental mode of thought, and if we do not face that question, we will lose contact with each possible power of signifying. It is as if there is only one choice left for us in our Occidental culture: the choice is—as we could learn from Peirce—closely related to the ways we refer to the universe: in a manner that is fragmented by our autonomous subjectivity or in a manner that is based on the subject's participation in the flow of realities. "*The fragmentation or the participation recognized*" seems the challenge of semiotics. A semiotics of law clarifies this crossroad pattern in a dualistic manner: "either … or". That is, however, an issue in itself, it is witness of the indestructible character of the analytical, fragmenting approach we acquired through the words spoken to us, as Lacan or Freud underlined. This dichotomy is, however, to be discovered in semiotics and positioned in the transition from word to text. (a) Structural linguistics (Saumjan), (b) discourse analyses (Greimas) and (c) text analyses (Kristeva) have in common, that they try to initiate a truly dynamic view developed in the heart of semiotics, thus challenging the fragmentation procedures law and legal discourse provoke. Their desire to dynamize semiotics contrast the specific form of dynamics, which is brought by fragmentation and analysis: in defining and mathematizing meaning, one develops in order to fixate—this may be the encompassing tragedy of knowledge analytically acquired.

J.M. Broekman (✉)
Dickinson School of Law, Penn State University, Carlisle, PA, USA
e-mail: jmb56@dsl.psu.edu

L. Catá Backer
Departments of Law and International Affairs,
Penn State University, University Park, PA, USA
e-mail: lcb11@psu.edu

J.M. Broekman, L. Catá Backer (eds.), *Signs In Law - A Source Book*,
DOI 10.1007/978-3-319-09837-1_35

Structural Linguistics

The Soviet Communist Party decided at its 1956 Assembly that the sciences in the Soviet Union should be developed in reference to pre-revolutionary as well as international data. This implied for Soviet linguistics in particular, that they could take further steps regarding a linguistic structuralism that was hitherto classified as anti-marxism. The first article written under these rules was published only four month after that decision by the editorial staff of the journal *VJa.*[1]

These publications explored a so-called *two-level theory* of generative grammar (Chomsky), which was related to a deep insight into the question, how to define (the concept of) a structure. *The question of structure brought him to use the expressions "pheno-type" and "geno-type" for the first time in linguistics*. Hjelmslev suggested in that context that we should define a structural linguistics as a totality of research, based on the hypothesis that it is scientifically legitimate to describe language as a structure. This embraces also the fundamentally hypothetical character of that form of linguistics. A general acknowledgement of the constructive character of any structure followed. In the light of Harris's *Structural Linguistics* (1961), one takes into account what he formulated[2]:

> Whereas the logicians have avoided the analysis of existing languages, linguists study them; but, instead of taking parts of the actual speech occurrences as their elements, they set up very simple elements, which are merely associated with features of speech occurrences.

There is a point here, which profiles insights of Saumjan and also sustains our thesis about the desire to dissociate from *static* conceptions of meaning and language. It is this: the understanding of a structure in linguistics is an indication of *deep layers in language*, exposed in Saumjan's structural linguistics. His discovery pertains to a fundamental contradiction between structures of language as a hypothesis about deep relations in language and meaning on the one hand, and on the other an identification of structural linguistics with static linguistics: one reads in the literature how structural, static, synchronic and descriptive linguistics are in essence treated as identical. But Saumjan's question to his colleagues remains: how is it possible to research deep structures of language and yet identify that very same linguistics with a static linguistics?

That answer conceals two issues of importance. (a) An exploration of a *dynamic linguistics* must be possible, and is not only the privilege of historical linguistics. That viewpoint is important for semiotics: it seems necessary to explore dynamics in the heart of semiotics. Meaning is not a static issue and thus not an object for

[1]The same Journal printed that same year an article of Sebastian K. Saumjan in which a positive evaluation of all forms of structuralism was provided. A German and an English edition of his *Principles of Structural Linguistics* were published 1971 (see also Saumjan: The Genotype Language and Formal Semantics, in: *Foundations of Language*, Vol. 18, 1973, pp 251–333 *and*: Outline of the Applicational Generative Model for the Description of Language, in: *Foundations of Language*, Vol. 1, No.3, 1965, p. 189–222).

[2]Z. S. Harris: *Structural Linguistics*, 1961, p. 16.

fixation coordinated by fragmentation. (b) Saumjan suggests furthermore that natural languages possess *a semiotic two-level structure. Natural* languages possess a level of primary sign systems with on top of those a secondary sign system with diacritical language elements. *Artificial* languages possess in contrast to natural languages a level of only one system of signs. That view interests once we consider the static character of legal semiotics: since legal discourse is an artificial discourse with elements selected from natural languages, it will be difficult to determine the features of law's sign system—a problem that characterized Roberta Kevelson's well-known book title: "*The Law as a System of Signs*". Does legal discourse need a large number of signs and a system of diacritical elements, or is the multitude of natural language elements sufficient to avoid them? Neither Algirdas J. Greimas nor Julia Kristeva, authors who joined Saumjan in his attempts to bring dynamics to the semiotic project, have confronted this question. They focused rather on the broader theme of dynamics by exploring the multi-level structure of language he introduced.

Discourse Analyses

Algirdas J. Greimas, the Lithuanian linguist we proposed to be named one of the Godfathers of semiotics,[3] used a specific expression to characterize his distance to static linguistics: the linguistic work is *the play* and his analysis the *journey*. Greimas and his colleague Rastier wrote in a foundational essay,[4] which we already quoted in Chapter 15 of this Volume:

> The play in question here is not to be understood as a free activity productive of literary objects, but as a long journey punctuated with compelling choices that leads, through a series of exclusions and of options, manifesting personal and social phobias and euphorias, to the constitution of an original and unique work. Instead of analyzing a completed text, the authors have tried to see how, starting from kernels of meaning, from categories of meaning which are at once simple and basic, the creative faculty operates, a faculty which, proceeding from the simple to the complex, from the general to the particular, makes its way, through a number of determinisms, toward an exaltation of liberty.

From the viewpoint of legal semiotics one could ask whether those approaches and methods are apt to lead to understanding anything of law and legal discourse. *Law and the exaltation of liberty*—are they compatible at all, and how are these notions related to the basic operations of fragmenting and differentiation? And can one find traces of the play of the creative mind in the construction and management of legal discourse, not to mention law as a social institution? These questions were already formulated in Saumjan's *Structural Linguistics* and very well known by Greimas c.s. Yet, the aim of the authors to introduce their project analyzing human

[3] In the second Volume, entitled "*Lawyers Making Meaning*", p. 57 ff.

[4] A. J. Greimas & F. Rastier: "*The Interaction of Semiotic Constraints*" in: Yale French Studies, 1968, p. 86 f.

creativity, especially in its *textual* expressions would by not exclude legal discourse. It is clear that this purpose was only attainable by introducing the dynamics in legal semiotics.

> It is obvious that, in the first part of its journey, there is nothing specifically literary in the play of the creative mind, obvious that it draws from the same sources as the whole of meaningful human activity: the theoretical aim of this study is thus largely anthropological, in open opposition to the suspect tradition of occidental humanism which sets forth literature as a basic datum. Thus the text to be read, while illustrating a possible semiotic approach to literary objects, is at the same time a calling into question of the literary phenomenon.

This is the exact moment of introducing a methodology, which focuses on *textual developments that reach from depth structures to manifest surface structures and back*—and in doing so, germinates dynamic approaches in a predominantly static linguistic.

Greimas suggests that semiotic systems do not have *one* fixed structure, so that there is not *one* structure of semiotic systems, but semiotic systems have as their particular character that they are continuously in a process of structuring and re-structuring. Once a structure is established, one could perceive how other structures incorporate that structure and form superior structures, transforming the former into signs that function in the latter. The *flow of structuring* is an important constitutive factor, which determines the semiotic process more deeply than the use of words will ever be able to do.

A semiotic square, the completing linguistic instrument proposed and developed by Greimas to entertain semiotic analyses of texts, focuses almost entirely on binary oppositions in the narrative. Greimas explains how nothing permits us to assert that a semiotic manifestation is dependent on *only one system at a time*. And so far as it is dependent on several systems, its closure can be attributed to the interaction of the different systems that produce it. In other words, one can construct a series of, say, three semiotic squares that explore various levels of a story, each semiotic square related to the next. The entire mechanism is capable of generating at least ten conceivable positions out of a rudimentary binary opposition (which may originally have been no more than a single term, e.g., 'white,' which proves to be internally defined by a hidden opposition we articulate by promoting the concealed pole 'black' to visibility).

The squares show that Greimas' logic can be characterized as narrative and holistic, whereas Peirce's logic is mathematical and logical in explanations of the social in the terminology of Thirdness. The preference of legal semiotics is in part created by their interpretations of law: law understood either in holistic (inclusive) or in atomistic/individualistic (analytic/differential) terms.

Finally, we consider that there are different cultural traditions incorporated in the two semiotic approaches and theories: *Greimas* develops his theory in the context of cultural anthropology and comparative linguistics, a climate that was favorable for developing structuralism, already in vogue in Moscow and Prague decades before it came to Paris. The legal discourse he referred to was in his days at the point to develop from a nation-bound system towards a multinational system, the system of

EU Law. Most basic concepts, such as 'legal subject', 'legal causality', 'justice', 'individuality' or 'citizenship' were at the edge of fundamental change. Greimas' semiotics prepared for discourses that belonged to a "post-modern", if not even a "post-postmodernist" period in European culture. Compare this to Peirce, on the other hand, who lived and worked in a society at the beginning of a century, which just came to a close with Greimas' theory. It was a century in North America characterized by an intellectual response to industrialization and immigration that forwarded a more legalistic society deeply imbued with notions of custom and tradition and increasingly exposed to the scientific methods of late 19th century Germany (with legal thought patterns unknown in the US until these days. This produced a strong tendency toward optimism, functionality and pragmatism that distinguishes North American from other societies.

Greimas developed semiotic ideas under the heading of pragmatism and applicative instrumentalism, yet emphasized the need for understanding dynamics in signification processes. The latter are by no means an issue of defining concepts and terms in a semiotic framework, of differentiating meanings and then fixating them so that they can be used objectively, or of creating ontological statements whilst neglecting their ties with the universe humans live in. He was aware how the word was used as a basic unit of language, constructed pragmatically to function as elements in well-defined and well-practiced patterns. However, his distinction of textual levels, leading to study deep levels differently from levels of manifestation and constructed surface, has opened the possibilities to incorporate the necessary dynamics in semiotic studies, so that semiotics could take part in a truly dynamic linguistics and appreciate the concept of structure at the same time.

Text Analyses

Julia Kristeva, inspired by Saumjan and Greimas with regard to the possibilities of dynamic approaches into the semiotics of a text, published 1969 in Paris a book with an important number of essays on that subject under the title "*SEMEIOTIKE. Recherches pour une sémanalyse*". Despite the various Kristeva-readers offered to the public of the US East Coast in the seventies and eighties of the 20th century, the main theoretical essay that contains a plea and a new thought pattern/philosophy for dynamizing semiotics was never translated. The 1969 essay is entitled: "*L'engendrement de la formule*" [The engenderment of the formula]. Several strains of thought in that essay are of great interest, because it is:

(a) an attempt to understand a *dynamic* (and thus non-static) *semiotics* with emphasis not on the word as the elementary unit of language but on the text as a specific bodily flow of meaning, whereas it is also
(b) an attempt to show how *legal semiotics is a conflict loaded discourse*—the conflict between mode geometrico thought-patterns of law and the need to dynamic semiotic approaches pertaining to law.

Kristeva formulates this conflict not by means of legal analyses or other technical considerations but rather by exploring theoretical approaches to the phenomenon of a text itself, based on the idea of a dynamic linguistics as proposed by Saumjan, his differentiation between surface- and deep-structure included, and on Greimas' dynamics of text semiotics. So she opens her essay, stating[5]:

> A text is the product of language and can thus only be perceived linguistically; texts reveal a theory of signification. We use the concept of semanalysis from the very beginning to mark a difference within semiotics: we do not want to block the study of signifying practices by means of using the 'sign', but we want to decompose that concept and open a new level in the inner regions of semiotics, a new space of returnable and combinable sites: the space in which the signifying process takes place (significance) . Semanalysis is the theory of textual signification, which considers the sign as a central element and sustains the representation of each engenderment—a process of germination, an inner process in which laws are laid down. In other words, (without forgetting that a text is a system of signs) the semanalysis accesses in the inner spaces of that sign system yet another scene: a hidden scene that shows how significance is as an operation that embraces a structure of solely falling down and moving back again. Without suggesting that one can quit the terrain of the sign entirely, the semanalysis liberates itself from the central obligation (that allows any description) to combine possible viewpoints leading to something like an engenderment. In as far as the body of language (in the Saussurean sense of the word) is concerned, the semanalysis protects itself from psychological as well as from idealistic aesthetic interpretations pertaining to what one calls the action of writing (Derrida). Or, in a linguistic perspective, the semanalysis has nothing to do with forms of description of a "corpus", a carrier of information content, which guarantees the communication between a sender and a receiver.

This conclusion: "a text is not a linguistic phenomenon", is not a negativistic conclusion. It opens rather an access to a wider study of a text in the perspective of dynamic yet structural linguistics.

A text, she writes, is not a language phenomenon, not a fixated and definitely structured signification, and not a flat, that is: two dimensional, corpus. As a consequence of this statement, we consider Kristeva writing:

> A text is its engenderment: an engenderment inscribed in just a linguistic phenomenon, in other words: the pheno-text, being the printed text, which is only readable if one traverses through its genesis in a vertical direction (1) of its linguistic categories, and (2) of the topology of the signifying act. The meaning (significance) of that textual engenderment can thus be understood in a double grip pertaining to: (1) the tissue of the language, and (2) the engenderment of the "I" that presents the significance/meaning. In such vertical move occurs the linguistic generation of the pheno-text. We refer to that operation as the making of a geno-text and thus unknot the very notion of a text in pheno-text and geno-text (surface and depth, signified structure and signifying production).

These formulations should precisely re-orientate linguistics from static to dynamic approaches of language and meaning, and embrace therefore the totality of the signification process. Thus it follows:

---

[5] J. Kristeva: *SEMEIOTIKE. Recherches pour une sémanalyse.* Quoted are subsequently fragments of pages 279–283 in a first French-English translation performed by the Editors.

> The text becomes thus "a dynamized object" and its discourse—the semanalysis—will sort out the various types that function as signifiers.

Text semiotics and semanalysis become identical, and the dynamic distinction between pheno-text and geno-text a standard for semiotic thinking, operational for understanding signification processes as well. The geno-text receives most attention, and appears a most interesting issue in the new dynamic text-semiotics. A geno-text is not a first cause, but has nevertheless an engender-function in the frame of the totality of a text (a problematic issue in its own right: what is the totality of a text; what is a text in total, or: as text?)

> The specificity of the text remains anchored in the fact that she is a translation/transformation from geno-text to pheno-text, whereby the process of signifying unfolds constantly on the line between pheno-text and geno-text and vice-versa. In other words, we present herewith a first operative definition, which we will complete and specify. It pertains to a textual meaning making production which shows how the system of signification becomes manifest via the pheno-text. We consider each signifying practice, at all levels of the pheno-text (as signifier as well as signified) positively belonging to the process of generating the signifying system itself, to be textual. Or, let us formulate shortly, textual is each practice, which forwards the Freudian slogan: "Wo Es war, soll Ich werden" (Where It was should I be").

From here, she concludes against static semiotics and the predominant position of the word as a major particle for all linguistics:

> What we call a geno-text is an abstract level of the linguistic function in general, which makes up its anamnesis whilst remaining at distance from solely reflecting the structures of the phrase, and even precedes or exceeds those structures. It thus concerns a signifying function, which—although it unfolds entirely in the language—cannot be reduced to the word as becomes manifest in a so-called normal communication (a normality of universals and laws of their combination). The geno-text operates with analytic-linguistic categories (for which we always must find the appropriate analytic-linguistic concepts in our theoretical discourse) so that we will ultimately not generate a phrase for the pheno-text (subject-predicate) but a signifying as it exists at the different stages of the process in which the functioning signifier is involved. That sequence can in the pheno-text be a word, a flow of words, a nominal phrase, a paragraph, a 'non-sense', etc.

Various remarks in this passage are important in the context of creating a dynamical semiotics, and held against a background of dynamic linguistics. The first is our awareness of the continuous movement from pheno- to geno-text, back and forth. That movement is not incidental and an irregular occurrence, but a dynamics that never stops functioning. Reading a text is a form of participating in that movement. One reads a phenotext at a moment of moving into a geno-text and vice versa, the sentences and words of the text one reads are each a marker of that movement, not a marker of a package of individual elementary units in one or another relation to each other. The praxis of signifying is importantly more encompassing then any phenotext is able to suggest, but nevertheless condemned to find itself at least temporarily engaged in pheno-textual dimensions. It is therefore of interest to understand that the product a geno-text injects in a phenotext is never a single word or a set of words but an already singnifying complexity, which Kristeva named linguistic body'. In an dynamic linguistics/semiotics, the signification process is about significations and the power of signifying, not about words and their so-called meaning. In Kristeva's words:

> The geno-text should not be seen as a structure, but also not as a structuring force, because it is not identical to what it forms or what brings the structure into being, even if it would for that reason remain censured. The geno-text is the infinite signifying that could never "be" a "this" because it is not a singular; one should better describe it as "the signifyings" in their plural form with all the infinite differentiations through which the signifying is present. The signifying as the-formula-presented-by-the-word-of-the-subject is just a boundary stone, a name of place, an accident, an approximation that adds itself to the signifying the moment it abandons its position. The plurality of signifiers in which (and not beyond which) the signified (of the pheno-text) can be situated is as such hyper-determined. The geno-text is in that regard not another scene in relation to the formulating and axial present, but an ensemble of other scenes in its multiplicity, whereby any index is missing because of the hyper-determination that defines the infinity from inside. (…) The geno-text is insistent in the position of the structure, and yet reaches through it, translates it and puts it in the signifying plurality, which the structural presence should omit to do. To set the geno-text is therefore to aim at a crossing in the position of a structure, a transposition. "*Cette visée, je la dis Transposition—Structure, une autre*". "This aim, I call it Transposition—Structure, an Other" writes Mallarmé in his "Crise de vers".

It fascinates how we find in Kristeva's text also a reference to the classical analytical tradition to evaluate the performance of speech-acts and insights in linguistic theories as a matter of an autonomous speaker's viewpoint. Her argument convinces:

> The text presents itself therefore as a body with a multiple register, and each of its elements possesses a multidimensionality, which bestows features of hieroglyphic nature on languages and discourses alike. The text generation is phenomenal as the phenomenon is germinated. Although the distinction between the two expressions pheno-text and geno-text is purely didactic, they also have a *material* character in so far as the principle of structuring is embedded in the substance of the structured. It is the result of a rhetoric discourse, which envisages a text production based on seeding processes and refractions weaving the text.

Here becomes clear what Saumjan mentioned in the 1971 edition of his "Structural Linguistics". He mentions that every scientific discipline must distinguish two levels of abstraction: the level of observation and the level of construction. Both are to be understood as logical and not just psychological expressivity. It appears that the logic of observation cannot be identical with a performance that only takes place at a surface level. It looks, in other words, as if there is no surface that is surface without a deep structure, and some of those deep structures are having indeed a foundational function in relation to their surface. The dichotomy of surface–and deep level, pheno- and geno-text as linguistic occurrences, points with necessity at multidimensional views, and withstands any static character, as Saumjan concluded for his structural linguistics. If that multidimensionality is not provided, an observation cannot take place. Observation as a scientific activity is constructive in essence and needs therefore the dimensionality of the two levels of ontology, which present themselves in language—that is an experience of speakers as well as writers. And it is a basic experience for unveiling any signification process, in particular those in which a fixated phenotext has a major role, as is the case in law and legal discourse. And thus, as observed in parallel to Saumjan's "Structural Linguistics" with the purpose of dynamizing linguistics and semiotic text theory, dynamization relates to all elements of theory—the search for a *multidimensional* understanding of linguistic performances and of language in the first place.

The level of constructs focuses the not-directly observable objects, properties or relations. That level is connected with the level of observation by rules of correspondence. Saumjan concludes that the concept of structure is in structural linguistics a construct concept. Saumjan and after him Kristeva develop a deeper insight into a hitherto unexplored contradiction between (a) the structure of language as regarded to be a hypothesis pertaining to the deep-relations of language, and (b) structural linguistics as a static linguistics. Only an abolishment of the static character of structural linguistics and semiotics might solve the discrepancy. This is also central in Kristeva's observations focusing on a semiotic text-theory, possibly in a new key.

Law in Signification Processes

Law is not only involved in signification processes; law is a signification process in its own right. Lawyers are professional signifiers in two ways: they create meanings in social life *and* they are signifying in such ways, that whatever meanings in life are incorporated in the specificity of their legal discourses. That ambiguity of a lawyer's signification never stops; it even evolves when they are confronted with the fundamental dichotomy of their legal semiotic activity, and are forced to decide between *analysis* and *inclusion*. Indeed, legal semiotic and general philosophical questions come together in the tensions that rein a lawyer's professional activities. He or she is always confronted with the essence of signs, language and ultimately of being. Legal language, words and text are witness of that difficult position. As was laid out in the foregoing paragraphs, the dichotomous character of *legal* semiotics shows that words as elementary units of language may fit to a lawyer's understanding of signifying but that semiotics in a new key tend to emphasize texts as continuously evolving entities and words as temporary markers in that evolvement.

Any analysis of law's signification processes shows a double face: the desire for fixation seems to be put in perspective by the need to participate in the flow of meaning. Also for signifying processes in law seems true that *"WHAT IS, IS THE PROCESS OF BECOMING ITSELF"*. Being a *substantive part of that process* is not the same as being the *single and autonomous speaker* in that process. The tension between those two positions seems caused by contrasting positions in Occidental culture and its law. However, the contrast remains concealed most of the times, as it is masked by the idea of a democracy. That concealment is the thin crust of consensus by which law perseveres. It weights heavy on the political implications of a semiotic approach to law in the performance of its signifying tasks.

The issue has never been understood so seriously as in this context. The entire power of interpretation rests, apart from religion, arts, psychology and related discourses, on law and its functionaries. Before ever giving meaning to an expression or a key-word, lawyers are called upon to answer the question what a word in question is so that they justify what the word should mean: a fixated authoritarian one-to-one meaning resulting from dissection and fragmentation as the foundation for a judgment—or a marker in the flow of expressiveness to follow in the stream of times. Is the latter type of dynamic linguistics with its equally dynamic semiotics framing the politics of speech in a new key?

That is indeed the case. Wherever a spoken, written or even thought word is no longer exclusively understood from the position of an autonomous speaker, there the speech act has a new task and a new field of responsibility. Both are embedded in a heightened awareness of participation. The participation frames a subject's positioning in the flow of signifying processes—an experience often signaled by those who have experienced that a spoken word will not have any political effect unless the process itself comes to its articulation. Anarchists experienced this, and rejected State-originated words; they are *not against the State* but *against the tyranny of the word of the State* i.e. against a very specific discourse that makes us a citizen in the form of an individual and vice versa. The slogan 'Occupy Wall Street' indicates how the meaning making processes should not be in the hands of the *market* (symbolized as "Wall Street") but be created in *public space* and thus have a different outcome. We underline that performing a speech act is engaging in a (or a series of) risk(s): "when I perform a speech act, I put myself at risk". This risk is in the first place because there is uncertainty about the position of the other as partner in the speech situation. However, Lacan was quoted as having understood how master discourses, like a legal discourse, diminish that risk through reordering the subject's catalogue of meaning[6] Here we encounter a much deeper anchored consideration. The problem is that the "reordering the catalogue of meaning" which each of us carries in any speech-contact remains grounded in a world of meanings based on issues resulting from fragmentation or dissection of reality. Those elementary units of meaning are thus engendered without any reference of the totality they stem from. Alienation is therefore a basic property of the history of meanings they represent. The engenderment of meaning in general is in this light an extremely important theme in our Occidental culture; its major features are reflected in the particular ways legal meanings are considered in the described genesis. We described the genesis of legal meanings and their articulations in the paragraph entitled "Semiotics Applied". All legal meaning is one way or another linked to the *more geometrico* pattern that reflects its essence in the order 'subject-verb-object' as a primary condition and a fundamental requirement. As a conclusion, we confront this signification process with the contrasting view already mentioned.

This contrast is fundamental for the entire signification process of law and legal discourse and determines for that reason the character and role of legal semiotics. *A semiotic of law is tied to 'more geometrico' thought patterns but also to insights about linguistic articulations as markers in an overarching process*. A couple of observations about meaning will contribute to mark the difference between that concept in legal discourse and in a more general context of signification.

Firstly, what Peirce noticed about a sign is also valid for a meaning: a sign alone is not a sign, Peirce wrote, and a meaning alone is not a meaning, we conclude in parallel. Meanings are not engendered to be and to function as a specific entity, a

[6] Jan M. Broekman & Larry Catá Backer: *Lawyers Making Meaning*. Springer 2012, p. 81.

semantic particle or any fixed significance. Meanings cannot be found at the level of singularity: they influence, constitute, evolve always together. That is included in the observation that meanings are altogether moments of culture and cultural developments. It is even incorrect to say that meanings influence each other because of this special connectedness, which reaches beyond any individual autonomy. There is not one meaning changing another without engendering by means of that change another meaning! Fluidity is their major feature, and that leads to several consequences, which contradict the treatment and expectations lawyers understand and treat meanings. Philosophers and historians of culture have demonstrated in their research how difficult or almost impossible it is to find out what meaning influences what other meaning. Their mutual influences are not mutual in the sense of dual or triadic relations—there are no numbers to count meanings. Their influences partake at all levels that are relevant at the moment in which the process of signifying is observed. So, meanings are always in a state to create meanings, and this is meant when we say that meanings form clusters. The clusters are never the result of an addition, but their numbers (if any!) indicate the quality of the process itself.

Secondly, meanings not only indicate significances but also an intention, a will, a cultural value, and thus show that they always articulate culturally shared issues. Their articulation, the expressive task of a meaning should not be neglected. This is the more relevant where meanings and mental processes always correlate. In other words, there is no mental process that could be declared meaningless. No matter what mental quality is at stake, there is always a connection between meaning and spirit—and linguistic expressivity seems the bridge between them. It interests to mention that the so-called 'objectivity' of meanings-in-law tends to think the inverse. If meanings could indeed become totally abstracted from mental processes and if that abstraction was a correct definition of 'objectivized' then legal meanings would not be in touch with mental reality.

A particular aspect is, that there cannot exist a pattern of causal relations between meanings, which would form a map of individually fixated meanings. Lawyers would perhaps like to have such an instrument at hand, and ethicists would enjoy the same, together with psychiatrists or other professionals focusing qualities of human relations. They work with concepts such as values, norms, rules, habits, and other leading meanings in interpersonal relations who do, however, never show a rational map of individual meaning-data. This ideal map, rational and mechanistic in essence, contradicts what Julia Kristeva underlined: the engenderment and its non-individualized process character. Meanings flow, engender, and have their own genetics, durable and untouchable in their ever-changing shape. When creating meaning, lawyers tend to fixate the unfixable. The fixation of meaning seems a major component of their ideology.

Thirdly, one should be attentive to the bewildering specificity of meaning creation. Each perception of a new or hitherto unknown meaning among humans changes the overall reality in which they live, and in doing so, it changes the world in which all live. It implies that philosophically spoken each meaning is a key to a change of reality. The traditional *more geometrico* thought pattern separated meaning and reality sharply—they had to be two completely different issues. Modern physics, mathematics and related sciences have demonstrated how reality will be continuously changed by the perception and creation of new meanings. Not that we change *a* 'view' or *our* 'view' of reality: *scrutinized reality always means change.*

We all live face to face with meanings. No matter whether lawyer, physician, psychologist, politician or responsible citizen, we face meanings in the process of signification, knowing that others also do. At issue is not the meaning we try to give those significations, nor how we read their signs, but solely whether we open our eyes for the process character at stake. The implications of that process character are manifold. One of them stands clearly out, as David Bohm highlighted several times.[7] Signification processes are dynamically in function where matter causes energy to deploy and energy in its turn enfolds matter. That pattern is reflected in linguistics and philosophy of language dealing with reference, for instance from concept to reality. But is the pattern of signification functioning in the same way between meaning and meaning? That question is not found in any of the philosophical or semiotic analyses on meaning, and it appears to remain a bewildering issue. A different wording for the same question would be: is the reference from meanings to meanings (the crux of all signification processes) identical to all other types of reference we know from philosophy and sciences based on a *more geometrico* thought pattern? The answer is: NO! We are normally not aware how this simple observation contains a condemnation of any mechanistic social theory:

> (…) what man does is an inevitable consequence of what the whole of his experience, inward and outward, means to him. For example, once the world came to mean a setoff disjointed mechanical fragments, one of which was himself, people could not do other than begin to act accordingly and engage in the kind of ceaseless conflict that this meaning implies. The meaning of fragmentation included conflict and self-centeredness—in other words, not creative tension but conflict.[8]

The reference of meaning to meaning (a necessary condition to fulfill in order to create sense) includes an important semiotic precondition. The riddle is already in Peirce's observation that signs can only refer fruitfully to signs; its parallel suggests that meanings *must* refer to meanings in order to be a meaning! In other words: meanings refer to themselves, whereas the word-reality reference transcends word or reality. What is more, meaning refers to itself *directly,* because referring meaning will use meanings for the constitution of its own reference. Mental processes can therefore understand themselves via the meaning function, which is also a mental process. All other references are by definition *indirect* since they need meaning to complete the referential activity.

The concept *autopoeisis* comes again to the fore: does the concept apply to semiotics and to signification processes? In that case, it could build a bridge to law and legal discourse—both being characterized as *autopoetic*, or self-referential discourses. Teubner has made clear that this is not evident.[9] Definitions of

---

[7] D. Bohm: *Wholeness and the Implicate Order*, Routledge 1980, —Id.—: *Unfolding Meaning*, Routledge 1985, Lee Nichol [Ed.]: *The Essential David Bohm*, Routledge 2003.

[8] Nichols [Ed.]: *Essential David Bohm*, see n. 26, p. 175 ff.

[9] G. Teubner: *Recht als autopoietisches System*, Suhrkamp, Frankfurt A.M. 1989, p. 25 ff.

self-reference and of *autopoeisis* do seldom match, and will never suffice to completely define the discourses at stake, he suggests. His considerations are a sign of the complexity of the problems involved: self-reference should be analytically controllable composed by an understanding of "self", of the activity of "referring" as well as a typology of "referent". They also pertain to concepts of a general systems-theory such as self-description, self-reflection, self-organization, self-steering and in view of these names, he even speaks of a "*galaxy auto*" (p. 25) which leads to an enormous confusion of concepts. One could characterize the basic features of a system with concepts such as self-organization, self-conceptualization, self-continuation, self-referential, self-identity, system-identity, self-reproduction and many more. But we should not forget that Varela, Maturana and others developed the concept of *autopoiesis* to have a new grip on the phenomenon of life. It should in particular focus on the molecular processes in cells and neuronal processes in nervous systems. The conceptual galaxy that followed after their first explorations reached far beyond the phenomenon of life. This is a sign of how the exuberance of differentiation and fixation in a *more geometrico* thought pattern leads to a fundamental misjudgment of process. Consider the process, the flow of life's occurrences in which human concepts try to rein. Lawyers are always encapsulated in clustered meanings, and they experience this cluster when they decide cases. They cannot isolate one meaning from another, so that their decisions are in reality choice-bound resolutions. No wonder that law's professionals tend to understand life as a series of choices and the human individual as the decision-maker who focuses on those choices. The pattern is a replication of the Speaker-Autonomy, and so is the flow of life for them a stream of choice-based decisions. No wonder that legal contract is understood as the legal form of freedom: freedom to choose, freedom to decide, freedom to act, one after the other. Should we contemplate the series of choices as a series and thus as an actual system apart from the whole set of conditions which actualize this state? Re-read Kristeva: each phenotextual surface, each level of manifestation, has a significance—but only knowing the surface level in its phenomenality clarifies its significance because the latter is not found in the performance of definitions.

Language

Any attempt to understand the implied dynamics in semiotics changes the view on language fundamentally. This results from the extremely strong influence of the *more geometrico* thought pattern that we not only think, but daily practice and reconfirm in our speech acts. That is also true for meaning as one of the main components of language and speech.

Language in writing, reading and speech is generally embedded in a world, which embraces a referential modality between subject and object, translated in semiotics as a modality between signifier and signified. The latter are treated as the ultimate particles contributed by semiotics to pave the roads towards the contexts to understand meaning.

Language embraces articulations that approach law and semiotics whilst including the relevant notions of law's process character. These challenge the autonomous speaker-models of self-understanding and (above all) self-reference. They contest a fictitious freedom belonging to contractual relations. Signs are challenged not to become fixated; meanings function beyond determination, lawyers do not know anymore on beforehand and thus have to listen before proposing law's articulations. A pattern of coherences of priority comes to the fore; fine lines between evidence and inquiring become guidelines. A dynamic semiotics with understanding meaning as an issue of constant flow will become visible so that the task of a lawyer's meaning making is in creating markers responsibly. Peirce wrestled with that responsibility, when he attempted to describe the relation between a sign and its mental processes, and wrote:

> The thought-sign stands for its object in the respect, which is thought; that is to say, this respect is the immediate object of consciousness in the thought, or, in other words, it is the thought itself, or at least what the thought is thought to be in the subsequent thought to which it is a sign.[10]

Lawyers should perhaps experience how all semiotics is a matter of *bio-semiotics*: life in its totality is at stake, inseparable from meaning and mark, and not as a fragmented, divided particle of reason and speech.

The need for respect as "the immediate object of consciousness in the thought" widens any analytical theory of reference. Let us not forget, how semiotics expresses a deep desire for a dynamic linguistics, a new instrument to help understand social relations in their constant move. Saumjan's two-level linguistics is not just a new linguistic model with two incidental distinctions at its center but rather an attempt to grasp *dynamics* and *totality* in our articulation activity.

Language was named the house of being. On a human scale, it is the house of creatures reaching wider than their imagination and yet fulfilling communicative and symbolic tasks. Language enlarges the house beyond our laws of the universe, it bears an articulation beyond measurements of time and distance: stars were born in times immeasurably past and yet a light reaches us so that we say we see them, unaware of the process we leave out in our observation and its references. Language, the house of being, is the tent of worship, which travels with us because being human is only a short step in an infinite existence. The tent was carried in deserts, over mountains and seas to mark moments of human completion. Language is completion as a travelling marker, fluid like water and holy like the spirit that celebrated the universe before any human existence. Language is. Meaning surfaces.

[10] Peirce: CP 5, 286.

About the Authors

Backer, Larry Catá teaches constitutional, corporate, and transnational law and policy at Penn State Law and the School of International Affairs of Penn State University, USA. Professor Backer is a member of the *American Law Institute* and the *European Corporate Governance Institute*. He is currently researching issues of governments as private actors in global markets, the development of law and social norm systems to regulate business and human rights, including the semiotic perspectives pertaining to these issues.

Benson, Robert W. is known in the USA by his exposés on "The Semiotic Web of the Law", in Roberta Kevelson (ed.), *Law and Semiotics, Vol. 1* (New York and London: Plenum Press, 1987) as well as the application of these web-ideas in international contracts with high political relevance.

Brion, Denis J. teaches at Washington and Lee University, Virginia, USA, and concentrates—among other themes—on legal reasoning in a semiotic perspective. Fallacies are a common phenomenon in that region of legal activities, and the framing of an attorney's argument in diverse contexts and meanings is a central and above all sophisticated issue in that regard. Brion contributes in this context to environmental problems, in particular in his 1980 book with Gary Weatherford (e.a.) on: *Institutional Constraints on Alternative Water for Energy: A Guidebook for Regional Assessments* (U.S. Dept. of Energy, Office of Environmental Assessments 1980).

Broekman, Jan M. is Emeritus Professor of Philosophy and Law at the KU Leuven, Belgium, and Emeritus Professor of Philosophy and Medicine at the Free University of Amsterdam, The Netherlands. He is Distinguished Visiting Professor of Law at the Penn State University, USA, and Director of the *Roberta Kevelson Seminar on Law and Semiotics.*

Eco, Umberto is a novelist and for decades Professor of semiotics at the University of Bologna, Italy, wrote various books on semiotic issues, among them 1976 *A Theory of Semiotics*, 1979 *The Role of the Reader*, 1984 *Semiotics and the Philosophy of Language*. He also wrote internationally recognized novels, most famous 1980

J.M. Broekman, L. Catá Backer (eds.), *Signs In Law - A Source Book*,
DOI 10.1007/978-3-319-09837-1

The Name of the Rose. He received the German "Pour le Mérite" distinction in 1988 and is since 2010 honorary Fellow of Kellog College, University of Oxford, UK.

Eeden, Frederik van- (1860–1932), was a prolific Dutch writer, novelist, and internationally known psychiatrist, used 1908 the term significs after having published an 1897 essay in Wittgensteinean style. He maintained close contacts with Lady Victoria Welby in London from 1892 on, and was an important member of the International Institute of Philosophy, Amsterdam from 1917 and the "Signifische Kring" from 1922. Contacts with James, Freud, Hermann Hesse, Kropotkin and Martin Buber sustained his signific interests as well as his psychiatric insights.

Gorlée, Dinda L. is a Dutch professional translator and semiotician, who studies the relations between linguistic articulation and meaning in a semiotic sense. She teaches at various European Universities and manages a *Legal Translation Agency* in The Hague, Netherlands, since 1997. She thus combines theory and practice of multilingual translation and interpreting with general and applied semiotics. Major philosophers in her book publications are Peirce and Wittgenstein, the latter as a neglected figure in the history of semiotics. She studies multilingual dialogues in philosophy, linguistics, and literature, and how these can be in conflict with personal or stylistic choices in linguistic form and cultural content.

Green, Alan C. is the author of the Prize-winning essay of the *Roberta Kevelson Seminar on Law and Semiotics* at the Penn State University, USA, Dickinson School of Law, 2012.

Greimas, Algirdas Julien (1917–1992), was a Lithuanian linguist, known for the "Greimas Square" as a possible working instrument for lawyers. He was Professor of General Semantics at the Parisian Ecole des Hautes Etudes et Sciences Sociales, France. His theoretical work is mainly on the structures of discourse in a semiotic perspective, and Bernard Jackson's widely known 1985 publication "Semiotic and Legal Theory" demonstrates to the English lawyer and legal scholar the importance of this approach for law and legal discourse.

Grosswald Curran, Vivian teaches law at Pittsburgh University, USA. She is a member of the American Law Institute, the International Academy of Comparative Law, and the *Société de Législation Comparée*, and was decorated 2007 by the Republic of Austria for being the United States appointee to the Austrian General Settlement Fund Committee for Nazi-era property compensation, and in 2013 by the government of France for her services in promotion of the French language and culture in the United States. She is the creator of Pitt Law School's innovative *Languages for Lawyers* program next to her work and publications on Comparative Law.

Haan, Jacob Israel de (1881–1924), was an influential Dutch Jewish poet, novelist and journalist and legal scholar who was the first legal significian to hold a chair in law and legal significs at the University of Amsterdam 1916. He wrote socialist essays and pamphlets, and made trips in 1912 to visit a number of prisons in Czarist Russia to study the situation of political prisoners. His shocking findings in his book

"In Russian prisons" (191) made him to a precursor of "Amnesty International". His signific exposes at the University were not very successful among jurists and legal scholars. In 1919 he settled in Palestine, lectured in Jerusalem, and was eventually assassinated by the Jewish paramilitary organization Haganah for his anti-Zionist politics. He is remembered as the first academic teacher in legal semiotics since 1916.

Kevelson, Roberta (1931–1998) was a Professor of Philosophy at Penn Sate University and also at The College of William and Mary in Virginia, USA. She co-founded the Semiotic Society of America and based her semiotic insights on a profound knowledge of Peirce's philosophy. She introduced the concept of legal semiotics in the US and explored that idea around the world in her participation to many Congresses and in a great number of book publications. Lawyers use to consult her *The Law as a System of Signs*, 1988.

Lacan, Jacques (1901–1981) was a French psychoanalyst called "the most controversial psycho-analyst since Freud". His seminars in Paris from 1953–1981 formed a new principal work on theoretical psychiatry and influenced semiotic thinking in all regards., in particular the so-called post-structuralists in Paris. It featured various regions of the human mind, such as the unconsciousness, the castration complex, the emergence of the ego and the related process of identification, and language as subjective perception—altogether themes of great importance for sign, meaning and semiotics. He is rightfully considered one of the godfathers of semiotics today.

Malloy, Robin P. teaches at the College of Law, Syracuse University, Syracuse NY, USA, and excels in unfolding Peirce's semiotic philosophy as well as Kevelson's contributions to legal semiotics. Law and markets and/or market economy are among his preferred themes to show the power of semiotic approaches in law.

Mannoury, Gerrit (1867–1956), was Dutch philosopher and mathematician, Professor at the University of Amsterdam. A principled communist, writing for instance on the relations between mathematics and communism, functioned also as a central figure in the Amsterdam signific circle. His sharp criticisms of Lady Welby's sign-theory—as formulated in his 1949 "Signifika. Een Inleiding" [Significs. An Introduction]—did not diminish his respect and admiration for her work and the significs movement in general, which he sustained importantly. He understood mathematics as a prominent product of the human mind, a product closely related to language and society. He was already in 1901 a member of the scientific bureau of the Social Democratic Workers Union and 1919 of the Communist International.

Marriott, Robert is the author of the Second Prize-winning essay of the *Roberta Kevelson Seminar on Law and Semiotics* at the Penn State University, USA, Dickinson School of Law, 2011.

McHoul, Alec is an emeritus professor at the School of Media Communication and Culture of the Murdoch University in Australia, and is inspired by Peirce's logic of abduction in communicative relation patterns. His work spans a range of fields, including linguistics, cultural theory, continental philosophy and literary theory and has published work on Wittgenstein, Foucault and semiotics.

Peirce, Charles Sanders (1839–1914) was a USA philosopher, mathematician, logician and scientist often qualified as "the founder of pragmatism". His ever lasting interest in scientific question and their foundations made him an extremely original philosopher (even varying his own pragmatism into pragmaticism for giving it his specific meaning) and scientist, who concluded as early as 1886 that logical operations could be performed by electrical switching circuits: the same idea used decades later to produce digital computers. His unfolding of semiotics, first in parallel with Lady Welby's significs, made him to one of the most important godfathers of (legal) semiotics today. His "Collected Papers", published 1958–1966 at Harvard, contain only a part of his works.

Radin, Max (1880–1960) was Professor Roman Law at Berkeley from 1919–1948 and from 1948 on in Hastings Law School, USA. His *Handbook of Roman Law* was world famous, not only because of its wealth of data but also because it expressed his insight that Roman Law had constructed major components of our social and intellectual life, even in its most recent forms.

Summerfield, Tracey teaches at the School of Law of the University of Western Australia and specializes on legal-semiotic issues of diversity, family and political contexts.

Volkert, Charles. is the author of the Prize-winning essay of the *Roberta Kevelson Seminar on Law and Semiotics* at the Penn State University, USA, Dickinson School of Law, 2011.

Welby-Gregory, Lady Victoria (1837–1912) was an important writer on meaning. She published in academic journals *Mind* and *The Monist*, and in 1903 her book *What Is Meaning? Studies in the Development of Significance*, and in 1911 *Significs and Language: The Articulate Form of Our Expressive and Interpretive Resources.* She contributed to the Encyclopedia Britannica (11th ed. 1911), with the entry 'Significs', the name she gave to her theory of meaning. The book, *What Is Meaning?*, was reviewed by C.S. Peirce, and a six-year correspondence between the two ensued, published in 1977 as *Semiotics and Significs.* Her name was of central importance to all members of signific circles and movements in The Netherlands, Germany and other European countries sympathizing with her signific ideas and principles.

General References

Allen, Tom: *Human rights law in perspective: Property and the Human Rights Act of 1998.* Oxford: Hart Publishing. 2005.

Allen, Tom: *The rights to property in commonwealth constitutions.* Cambridge: Cambridge University Press. 2000.

Apel, Karl-Otto: *Charles S. Peirce: From pragmatism to pragmaticism.* Amherst: Prometheus Books. 1995.

Aristotle, *A Treatise on Government* (William Ellis, trans.), London: JM Dent 1912.

Bauman, Zygmunt, *Socialism: The Active Utopia* London: George Allen & Unwin. 1976.

Beadle G.W. and Beadle M.: *The Language of Life,* Doubleday, 1966.

Benmakhlouf, Ali: *L'identité. Une fable philosophique.* PUF, Paris 2011.

Bentham, Jeremy, *Works,* Vol. VIII, Everett, Ed. (New York: Columbia University Press, 1906.

Berger P.L. and Luckmann T.: *The Social Construction of Reality: A Treatise in the Sociology of Knowledge.* New York: Doubleday, 1966.

Bergh, G.C.J.J. van den: "Jacob Israel de Haan's Legal Significs" in *International Journal for the Semiotics of Law,* Vol. IX, 25 (1996).

Bergh, G.C.J.J. van den: "De taal zegt meer dan zij verantwoorden kan" in *Ars Aequi Libri,* Nijmegen 1994.

Bergh, G.C.J.J. van den & Broekman, Jan M.: *Recht en Taal,* Kluwer/Deventer 1979.

Bergman, Mats: *Peirce's Philosophy of Communication: The Rhetorical Underpinnings of the Theory of Signs.* London/ New York 2009.

Bernstein, David & Jackson, Jeffrey, "The Daubert Trilogy In the United States." *George Mason Law & Economics Research Paper* No. 04–06.

Blackstone, W.: *Commentaries* 2: *Rights of Things* (1789) Lonang Library, Lonang Institute, London.

Bohm, David and F. David Peat, *Science, Order and Creativity,* London: Routledge. 1987.

Boyd White, James: "Free Speech and Valuable Speech", in: *UCLA Law Review, 51,* 799. 2004.

Brent, Joseph: *Charles Sanders Peirce. A Life.* Indiana UP, 1993.

Brion, D.J.: "Trial Argumentation: The Creation of Meaning" in: *Lawyers Making Meaning. The Roberta Kevelson Seminar on Law and Semiotics at Penn State University's Dickinson School of Law,* IJSL Vol. 22, Nr. 1, 2009.

Brion, D. J.: "Chaos-What Judges and Juries Do", in W. Pencak & J.R. Lindgren: *New Approaches to Semiotics and the Human Sciences,* Peter Lang 1998.

Broekman, Jan M. & Catá Backer Larry: *Lawyers Making Meaning*, Springer 2013.

Broekman, Jan M.: "Betere taal is beter recht" in *Wijsgerig Perspectief op maatschappij en wetenschap,* Vol. 20, 2. 1979/80.

J.M. Broekman, L. Catá Backer (eds.), *Signs In Law - A Source Book,*
DOI 10.1007/978-3-319-09837-1

Broekman, Jan M.: "Justice as Equilibrium" in: *Law and Philosophy*, Vol. 5 1984.
Broekman, Jan M.: "Semiology and Medical Discourse" in; *Methodology and Science, International Journal for the Empirical Study of the Foundations of Science and their Methodology*, 1988.
Broekman, Jan M.: "Perelman and Poetic Justice" in *Rechtstheorie*, Vol 23, No. 2, 1992.
Broekman, Jan M.: "Commens and Communication", *International Journal for the Semiotics of Law*, Vol. 24, 2011.
Broekman, Jan M.: "Firstness and Phenomenology" in: Anne Wagner/Jan M. Broekman (Eds): *Prospects of Legal Semiotics*, Springer 2010.
Broekman, Jan M.: "On the Origins of Legal Semiotics" in: *The Journal of Comparative Law*, Volume VII, Issue 1, London 2012,
Broekman, Jan M.: *Structuralism. Moscow-Prague-Paris*. Reidel, Dordrecht 1974.
Broekman, Jan M.: *Intertwinements of Law and Medicine*, Leuven UP 1996.
Broekman, Jan M.: "Trading Signs: Semiotic Practices in Law and Medicine." *International Journal for the Semiotics of Law* Vol. 20, 2007.
Broekman, Jan M. & Pencak, William A.: *Lawyers Making Meaning. The Roberta Kevelson Seminar on Law and Semiotics at Penn State University's Dickinson School of Law,* IJSL Vol. 22, Nr. 1, 2009.
Broekman, Jan M. & Pencak, William A.: *Signs of Law. The Roberta Kevelson Seminar on Law and Semiotics at Penn State University's Dickinson School of Law,* IJSL Vol. 23, Nr. 1, 2010.
Broekman, Jan M. & Mootz III, Francis J. (Eds): *The Semiotics of Law in Legal Education*, Springer 2011.
Brooks, D.R. and Wiley E.O.: *Evolution as Entropy,* UP Chicago 1986.
Brouwer, L.E.J.: *Collected Works I: Philosophy and Foundations of Mathematics.* [A. Heyting Ed.] Amsterdam/Oxford 1975.
Burks, Arthur W.: *Man: Sign or Algorithm? A Rhetorical Analysis of Peirce's Semiotics*. 1978.
Calvino, Italo: *Mr. Palomar,* trans. by W. Weaver (San Diego, New York, London: Harcourt Brace Jovanovich, 1985.
Cardozo, B.N.: *The Nature of the Judicial Process*. Yale University Press, 1921.
Catá Backer, Larry: "The Corporation as Semiosis," 135 *Consortium for Peace & Ethics* Working Paper No. 2012–2, 2012.
Catá Backer, Larry: "Governance Without Government: An Overview", in *Beyond Territoriality: Transnational Legal Authority in an Age of Globalization* (Günther Handl, Joachim Zekoll, Peer Zumbansen, editors, Leiden, Netherlands & Boston, MA: Brill Academic Publishers, forthcoming 2012.
Catá Backer, Larry: "The Drama Of Corporate Law: Corporate Narrative Between Policy And Law", *Michigan State Law Review* 1111, 2009.
Catá Backer, Larry: "Corporate Institutionalism and Fiduciary Duty: On Professor Katsuhito Iwai's Nominalistic and Realistic Corporations Model", *Law at the End of the Day*, July 10, 2006.
Colapietro, Vincent M.: *Peirce's approach to the self: A semiotic perspective on human subjectivity*. Albany: State University of New York Press. 1989.
Cornell, Drucilla: "'Convention' and Critique" in: *Cardozo Law Review* 7, 1986.
Damasio, A.: *Descartes' Error: Emotion, Reason, and the Human Brain.* New York 1994.
Dan-Cohen, Meir: *Rights, Persons, and Organizations: A Legal Theory for Bureaucratic Society.* U. Cal. Press 1986.
de Haan, Jacob Israel: *Wezen en taak der rechtskundige significa* [Essence and Task of Legal Significs] First public lecture in Legal Significs at the University of Amsterdam, Tuesday October 31, 1916, Published: van Kampen, 1916.
de Haan, Jacob Israël: *Rechtskundige Significa en hare toepassing op de begrippen: "Aansprakelijk, verantwoordelijk, toerekeningsvatbaar*" [Legal Significs and its Application in the concepts 'Liable', Responsible' and 'Accountable'] PhD Dissertation University of Amsterdam 1919.

de Haan, Jacob Israël: *Rechtskundige Significa*, at the occasion of De Haan's departure from the Amsterdam University and his resettlement in Palestina, Mr. I. Prins, Ed., Publisher Amsterdam Joh. Müller 1919.

Deledalle, G. "Victoria Lady Welby and Charles Sanders Peirce: Meaning and Signification" in H. Walter Schmitz: *Essays on Significs*, Amsterdam 1990.

Dewey, J.: "Logical Method and the Law", *Cornell Law Review* 11 (1924).

Douglas, M.: "Introduction to Grid/Group Analysis", in *Essays in the Sociology of Perception*, ed. M. Douglas (London, Boston: Routledge and Kegan Paul, 1982.

Duguit, L.: *L'Etat, le droit objectif at la loi positive,* Paris 1901.

Duguit, L.: *Traité de droit constitutionnel,* Paris 1921.

Easterbrook Frank and Fischel Daniel R.: *The Economic Structure of Corporate Law*, Harvard UP 1996.

Eco, Umberto: *A Theory of Semiotics.* Indiana University Press, 1978.

Eco, Umberto: *The limits of interpretation.* Bloomington: Indiana University Press 1990.

Edelman, G.M.: *Bright Air, Brilliant Fire: On the Matter of the Mind.* New York: Basic Books, 1992.

Etzioni, A.: *The New Golden Rule: Community and Morality in a Democratic Society.* New York: Basic Books 1996.

Fisch, Max H.: *Peirce, Semeiotic, and Pragmatism* (Ketner & Kloesel, Eds) Bloomington Indiana UP 1986.

Fish, Stanley: *Is There a Text in This Class?* Harvard University Press, 1980.

Flusser, Vilem: *Bodenlos: Eine Philosopische Autobiographie* 1992.

Foucault, Michel: *The Government of Self and Others: Lectures at the College de France, 1982–1983.* Picador 2011.

Fromm, Erich, *The Sane Society* 1955.

Fromm, Erich: *Escape from Freedom* 1967.

Geschwind, N.: "Some comments on the neurology of language" in: *Biological Studies of Mental Processes.* [D. Caplan, Ed.] MIT Press 1980.

Gilson, Ronald J., "Globalizing Corporate Governance: Convergence of Form or Function", 49 *Am. J. Comp. L.* 329, 330 (2001).

Goodrich, Peter: "Historical Aspects of Legal Interpretation" in: *61 Indiana Law Review, 331,* 1986.

Goodrich, Peter: *Legal Discourse.* New York: St. Martin's Press, 1987.

Greenstein, G.: *The Symbiotic Universe: Life and Mind in the Cosmos,* New York 1988.

Greimas, A.J. & Rastier, F.: "The Interaction of Semiotic Constraints" in: *Yale French Studies,* 1968.

Greimas, Algirdas J.: *The Social Sciences: A Semiotic View.—The Semiotic Analysis of Legal Discourse.* Commercial Laws That Govern Companies and Groups of Companies. University of Minnesota Press, 1990.

Guberman, Ross M. (Ed.): *Julia Kristeva Interviews.* Columbia UP, 1996.

Hansmann Henry & Kraakman Reinier: "The Essential Role of Organizational Law", 110 *Yale Law Journal*, 387, p. 438–439, 2000.

Hardwick S. & Cook James (Eds): *Semiotic And Significs. The Correspondence Between Charles S. Peirce And Victoria Lady Welby.* Indiana UP 1977.

Hart, H.L.A.: *The Concept of Law,* [2nd Ed.] Clarendon, Oxford UP 1994.

Honoré, A.M.: "Ownership", in: *Oxford Essays in Jurisprudence*, ed. A. Guest, London, New York: Oxford University Press, 1961.

Horwitz, M.: *The Transformation of American Law, 1780–1860* Cambridge, Mass.: Harvard University Press, 1977.

Huntington, Samuel P.: *The Clash of Civilizations and the Remaking of World Order* 1996.

Iwai, Katsuhito: "Persons, Things and Corporations: The Corporate Personality Controversy and Comparative Corporate Governance", 47 *Am. J. Comp. L.* 583, 594 (1999).

Iwai, Katsuhito, "The Nature of the Business Corporation: Its Legal Structure and Economic Functions" in: *The Japanese Economic Review*, 53(3).

James, W.: *The Principles of Psychology.* New York: Henry Holt & Co., 1902.

Jackson, Bernard S.: "Legal Semiotics and Semiotic Aspects of Jurisprudence" in: Wagner & Broekman [Eds} *Prospects of Legal Semiotics,* Springer 2010.

Jackson, Bernard S., *Semiotics and Legal Theory.* London, etc.: Routledge & Kegan Paul, 1985.

Joseph, John E.: "Meaning in the margins. Victoria Lady Welby and significs" in *Times Literary Supplement*, March 23, 2012.

Kevelson, Roberta: "Flux, complexity, and illusion" in: *Sixth round table on law and semiotics.* New York: Peter Lang Publishing. 1993.

Kevelson, Roberta: *Peirce's esthetics of freedom: Possibility, complexity, and emergent value.* New York: Peter Lang Publishing. 1993.

Kevelson, Roberta: "Property as Rhetoric in Law", in: *Cardozo Studies in Law and Literature,* 1992.

Kevelson, Roberta (ed.): *Codes and customs: Millennial perspectives.* New York: Peter Lang Publishing. 1994.

Kevelson, Roberta (ed.): *Flux, complexity, and illusion: Sixth round table on law and semiotics.* New York: Peter Lang Publishing. 1993.

Kevelson, Roberta (ed.): *Law and Semiotics*, vol. 3. New York: Plenum Press. 1989.

Kevelson, Roberta (ed.): *Law and the conflict of ideologies.* New York: Peter Lang Publishing. 1996.

Kevelson, Roberta (ed.): *Peirce and law: Issues in pragmatism, legal realism, and semiotics.* New York: Peter Lang Publishing. 1991.

Kevelson, Roberta (ed.): *The eyes of justice: Seventh round table on law and semiotics.* New York: Peter Lang Publishing. 1994.

Kevelson, Roberta: "Property as rhetoric in law". *Cardozo Studies in Law and Literature* 4: 189–206. 1992.

Kevelson, Roberta: "Transfer, transaction, asymmetry: Junctures between law and economics from the fish-eye lens of semiotics". *Syracuse Law Review* 42: 7. 1991.

Kevelson, Roberta: *Charles S. Peirce's method of methods,* ed. A. Eschbach. Amsterdam/Philadelphia: John Benjamins Publishing Company. 1987.

Kevelson, Roberta: *Peirce, Praxis, Paradox,* Mouton de Gruyter. 1990.

Kevelson, Roberta: *Peirce, Science, Signs*. New York: Peter Lang Publishing. 1996.

Kevelson, Roberta: *The law as a system of signs.* New York: Plenum Press. 1988.

Kevelson, Roberta. *Peirce's esthetics of freedom: Possibility, complexity, and emergent value.* New York: Peter Lang Publishing. 1993.

Kristeva, Julia: *Semeiotikè. Recherches pour une sémanalyse*. Du Seuil, Paris 1969.

Kristeva, Julia: *Desire in Language. A Semiotic Approach to Literature and Art,* Columbia UP, 1980.

Kuhn, T.S.: *The Structure of Scientific Revolutions* , University of Chicago Press, 1962.

Lacan, Jacques: *Lecture* Delivered on July 17, 1949, in Zurich at the Sixteenth International Congress of Psychoanalysis in: Écrits (London, Tavestock) 1977.

Lacan, Jacques: *Écrits*. Engl Transl. Bruce Fink. Norton, London 2006, 2002.

Lenoir, Timothy: "Was That Last Turn A Right Turn?" in: *Configurations,* Vol. 2, 1994.

Leone, Massimo: "Introduction to the Semiotics of Belonging" in: *Semiotica*, 192, 2012.

Lévi-Strauss, Claude: "L'efficacité symbolique," in *Revue de l'histoire des religions* CXXXV, I 1949.

Levi, Primo: "Beyond Judgment", *The New York Review of Books.* 34(20), December 17, 1987.

Lewis, D.B. & Gower, D.M.: *Biology of Communication*. New York 1980.

Llewellyn, K.: *The Bramble Bush: On Our Law and Its Study.* New York: Columbia University Press, 1930.

Llewellyn, K.: *The Common Law Tradition*. Boston 1960.

MacEachren, A.M.: *How Maps Work: Representation, Visualization, and Design.* New York: Guilford Press, 1995.

Mahoney, Paul G.: "Contract or Concession? An Essay on the History of Corporate Law", 34 *Ga. L. Rev*. 873. 2000.

Malloy, Robin Paul, and James Charles Smith: *Real estate transactions,* 3rd ed. New York: Aspen Publishers. 2007.
Malloy, Robin Paul: *Law and market economy: Reinterpreting the values of law and economics.* Cambridge: Cambridge University Press. 2000.
Malloy, Robin Paul: *Law in a market context: An introduction to market concepts in legal reasoning*. Cambridge: Cambridge University Press. 2004.
Mannoury, Gerrit: *Polair Psychologische Begripssynthese.* Bussum F. G, Kroonder 1953.
Mannoury, Gerrit: *Signifika en Wijsbegeerte.* (Lecture in the Dutch Philosophical Society, Amsterdam, November 18, 1922.) in: *Tijdschrift voor Wijsbegeerte,* 1923 Nr. 1.
Mannoury, Gerrit: *Over de Beteekenis der Wiskundige Logica voor de Philosophie*, Amsterdam 1903 [On the Significance of Mathematical Logic for the Philosophy].
Mannoury, Gerrit: *Over de sociale betekenis van de wiskundige denkvorm.* Groningen 1917 [On the social significance of the mathematical thought].
Mannoury, Gerrit: *Wiskunst, filosofie en socialisme.* Groningen 1919,1924. [Mathematics, Philosophy and Socialism].
Mannoury, Gerrit: *Woord en Gedachte. Een inleiding tot de significa, inzonderheid met het oog op het onderwijs in de wiskunde.* Groningen 1931. [Word and Thought. An introduction in significs, in particular related to teaching mathematics] .
Mannoury, Gerrit: *Relativisme en Dialektiek. Schema ener filosofisch-sociologische grondslagenleer.* Bussum 1946 [Relativism and Dialectics. A philosophico-sociological foundation-theory].
Mannoury, Gerrit: "A concise history of significs" in: *Methodology and Science, International Journal for the Empirical Study of the Foundations of Science and their Methodology.* Vol. 2, 1969.
Mannoury, Gerrit: "Analytical Significs" in: *Methodology and Science, International Journal for the Empirical Study of the Foundations of Science and their Methodology.* Vols. 2 & 3. 1963.
Mannoury, Gerrit: *Handboek der analytische significa* 2 Vols., Bussum 1947& 1948.]Companion of analytical significs].
Margulis, L and Sagan, D.: *Microcosmos: Four Billion Years of Microbial Evolution,* Univ. California Press, 1997.
Maturana, H.R.: "Autopoiesis: Reproduction, Heredity, and Evolution" in: *Autopoiesis, Dissipative Structures, and Spontaneous Social Orders,* M. Zeleny [Ed.], Boulder, Co. 1980.
Merrell, Floyd: *Peirce, signs, and meaning*. Toronto: University of Toronto Press. 1997.
Merrell, Floyd: *Charles Sanders Peirce's Concept of the Sign*, in: *The Routledge Companion to Semiotics and Linguistics*, P. Colbry [Ed.], London/New York 2001.
Merrell, Floyd: *Pararealities. The Nature of our Fictions and how we know them.* Philadelphia Ed., Amsterdam 1983.
Merryman, John H.: *The Civil Law Tradition*. Stanford UP 3rd Edition 2007 (Ed.: Rogelio Perez-Perdomo).
Miller, Jacques-Alain, "*The Real and Semblance"* in: *lacanian ink,* New York 2012, Nr 43/44.
Morris, Charles: *Signs, Language and Behavior*, NY 1946.
Müller, H.M.: *Evolution, Kognition und Sprache*. Berlin 1987.
Murphy, W. T. and Simon Roberts, *Understanding Property Law.* London: Fontana Press. 1987.
Norretranders, T.: *The User Illusion: Cutting Consciousness Down To Size,* New York: Viking, 1998.
Noth, Winfried: *Handbook of Semiotics*. Bloomington: Indiana University Press, 1995.
Nozick, R.: *Anarchy, State, and Utopia.* New York: Basic Books, 1974.
Nussbaum, M.: "Valuing Values: A Case for Reasoned Commitment," 6 *Yale J.L. & Hum.* 1994.
Peirce, Charles Sanders: *The Collected Papers of Charles Sanders Pierce.* Vols I – VI, Ed. Charles Hartshorne and Paul Weiss(1931–1935), Cambridge Ma, Harvard University Press.
Peirce, Charles Sanders: *The Collected Papers of Charles Sanders Pierce.* Vols VII – VIII, Ed. Arthur W. Burks (1958), Cambridge Ma, Harvard University Press.
Pencak, William A.: *History, Signing In. Essays in History and Semiotics.* Chapter 3: "Charles S. Peirce and Arisbe". Peter Lang, New York 1993.
Pencak, William A.: *From Absurdity to Zen.* Peter Lang, New York 2002.

Pencak, William A.: *New Approaches to Semiotics and the Human Sciences: Essays in Honor of Roberta Kevelson*. Peter Lang, New York 1998.

Pencak, William A.: *"The Law" vs. "The People": Twelfth Round Table on Law and Semiotics.* Peter Lang, New York 2000.

Petrilli, Susan: *Signifying and Understanding. Reading the Works of Victoria Welby and the Signific Movement.* Mouton/De Gruyter, The Hague, Berlin 2009.

Phillips, Michael J.: "Reappraising the Real Entity Theory of the Corporation", 21 *Fla. St. U. L. Rev*. 1061 (1994).

Pinto, Julio: "The Question of the Subject in Semiosis: Peirce and Lacan" in: *Semiotics 1988*, T. Prewitt/J. Deely/K. Haworth (Eds) University of America Press, 1988.

Prodi, G.: *Le basi materiali della significazione*, Milano 1977.

Proudhon, P.J.: *What Is Property? An Enquiry Into the Principle of Right and of Government.* New York: H. Fertig, 1966.

Robin, Paul: *Annotated Catalogue of the papers of Charles S. Peirce.* Univ. Mass Press, Amherst 1967.

Roe, Mark J., "Delaware's Competition", 117 *Harv. L. Rev.* 588, (.2003).

Sacks, O.: "Making Up the Mind", *New York Review of Books* (Apr. 8, 1993).

Sacks, O.: "Neurology and the Soul", *New York Review of Books* (Nov. 22, 1990)

Schmitz, H. Walter: *Essays on Significs. Papers presented on the occasion of the 150th anniversary of the birth of Victoria Lady Welby,* Benjamins, Amsterdam/Philadelphia 1990.

Schmitz, H. Walter: *De Hollandse Significa. Een reconstructie van de geschiedenis van 1892 tot 1926.* Assen 1960. German edition 1985: *Verständigungshandlungen — eine wissenschaftshistorische Rekonstruktion der Anfänge der signifischen Bewegung in den Niederlanden (1892–1926).*

Schmitz, H. Walter & Heijerman, E, (Eds): *Significs, Mathematics and Semiotics. The Signific Movement in the Netherlands,* Münster 1986.

Sebeok, T.A.: "The problem of the origin of language in an evolutionary frame" in *Language Sciences*, Vol. 8, 1986.

Sebeok, T.A.: "Toward a natural history of language" in: *The World & I*, October 1986.

Sebeok, Th.A.: "The Semiotic Self revisited" in: *Sign, Self, Society* (Lee & Urban [Eds]) Berlin 1989.

Sebeok, Th.A.: *Contributions to the Doctrine of Signs,* UP of America 1976, 1985(2).

Sebeok, Thomas A.: "The Semiotic Web: A Chronicle of Prejudices", in: *Bulletin of Literary Semiotics* 2 (1975).

Sheriff, John K.: *Charles Peirce's guess at the riddle: Grounds for human significance.* Bloomington: Indiana University Press. 1994.

Silverman, David, Sacks Harvey: *Social Science and Conversation Analysis* Cambridge: Polity, 1998.

Singer, Joseph William: *Introduction to property*, 2nd Ed. New York: Aspen Publishers. 2005.

Sklair, Leslie: *The Sociology of the Global System* (2d ed.) Johns Hopkins U. Press 1995.

Sklar, M.J.: *The Corporate Reconstruction of American Capitalism, 1890–1916: The Market, The Law and Politics* (Cambridge, New York: Cambridge University Press, 1988.

Smith, W.J.: *The Behavior of Communicating: An Ethological Approach*, Harvard UP 1977.

Sonea, S. and Panisset M.: *A New Bacteriology*, Boston 1983.

Teubner, G.: *Recht als autopoietisches System*, Suhrkamp, Frankfurt a.M. 1989.

Teubner, Günther: "Enterprise Corporatism: New Industrial Policy and the 'Essence' of the Legal Person", 36 *Am. J. Comp. L.* 130.

Teubner, Günther: "Societal Constitutionalism: Alternatives to State-Centered Constitutional Theory?" in *Transnational Governance and Constitutionalism* 16 (Christian Joerges, Inger-Johanne Sand & Gunther Teubner eds.), Hart Publ. 2004.

Thomas, Kimberly A.: "Beyond Mitigation: Towards a Theory of Allocution," 75 *Fordham L. Rev.* 2641, 2007.

Thomas, Kimberly A et al.: *Cultural Theory*, Boulder: Westview Press, 1990.

Tönnies, Ferdinand, "Philosophical Terminology" (Welby Prize Essay) in: *Mind* (July and October 1899 and January 1900).
Umiker-Sebeok, J. & Sebeok, T.A.: "Clever Hans and Smart Simians: The Self-fulfilling prophecy and kindred methodological pitfalls". In: *Anthropos*, Vol. 76.
Van Eeden, Frederik: *Redekunstige Grondslag Van Verstandhouding,* [Rhetorical Foundations Of Communication] In; *Studies, Vol. III,* Amsterdam. 1897, Reprint: Het Spectrum, Utrecht, 1975.
Vining, Joseph: *The Authoritative and the Authoritarian.* Chicago: University of Chicago Press. 1986.
Waldron, Jeremy. *Nonsense Upon Stilts: Bentham, Burke and Marx on the Rights of Man.* London: Methon. 1987.
Watson, Rod: "Categorizations, Authorization and Blame-Negotiation in Conversation", *Sociology* 12/1, 1978.
Welby, Lady Victoria: "Sense, Meaning and Interpretation," in *Mind* (January and April 1896).
Welby, Lady Victoria: *Significs and Language*. London 1911.
Welby, Lady Victoria: "Significs" in *The Encyclopedia Britannica* 1911 Vol. XXV, p. 78.
Welby, Lady Victoria: *Grains of Sense* (1897).
Welby, Lady Victoria: *What is Meaning?: Studies in the Development of Significance.* MacMillan & Co. New York 1903.
Wicken, S.: *Evolution, Thermodynamics, and Information* 1987.
Williams, Joan C.: "Critical Legal Studies: The Death of Transcendence and the Rise of the New Langdells", *New York University Law Review* 62(3), (1987).
Wittgenstein, Ludwig: *Philosophical Investigations,* trans. by G. E. M. Anscombe, Oxford: Basil Blackwell, 1958, 2nd ed.
Wittgenstein, Ludwig: *Tractatus Logico-Philosophicus.* London, 1922.
Wolff, Janet. *The Social Production of Art.* London: MacMillan. 1981/1988.
Wood, D.: *The Power of Maps.* Guilford Press, London 1992.
Wowk, Maria T: "Blame-Allocation: Sex and Gender in a Murder Interrogation", *Women's Studies International Forum* 7/1, 1984.
Wright, R.: *Three Scientists and their God, NY* 1988.
Zalamea, Fernando: *Peirce's Logic of Continuity,* Boston 2012.
Zalamea, Fernando: *Synthetic Philosophy of Contemporary Mathematics.* New York 2012.

Author Index

J.M. Broekman, L. Catá Backer (eds.), *Signs In Law - A Source Book*,
DOI 10.1007/978-3-319-09837-1

Subject Index

J.M. Broekman, L. Catá Backer (eds.), *Signs In Law - A Source Book*,
DOI 10.1007/978-3-319-09837-1

D

MIX
Papier aus verantwortungsvollen Quellen
Paper from responsible sources
FSC® C105338

If you have any concerns about our products,
you can contact us on
ProductSafety@springernature.com

In case Publisher is established outside the EU,
the EU authorized representative is:
Springer Nature Customer Service Center GmbH
Europaplatz 3, 69115 Heidelberg, Germany

Printed by Libri Plureos GmbH
in Hamburg, Germany